NATIONAL PARK
ROADS

NATIONAL PARK ROADS

A LEGACY IN THE AMERICAN LANDSCAPE

TIMOTHY DAVIS

University of Virginia Press
Charlottesville and London

University of Virginia Press
© 2016 National Park Foundation
All rights reserved
Printed in Canada on acid-free paper
First published 2016

9 8 7 6 5 4 3 2 1

Library of Congress Cataloging-in-Publication Data

Davis, Timothy, 1958– author.
    National park roads : a legacy in the American landscape / Timothy Davis.
        pages cm
    Includes bibliographical references and index.
    ISBN 978-0-8139-3776-2 (cloth : alk. paper)
    1. National parks and reserves—United States—Management—History.
2. Roads—United States—Design and construction—History. 3. Automobile
travel—United States—History. I. Title.
E160.D375 2016
363.6'80973—dc23
                                                            2015029742

Publication of this volume has been supported
by the National Park Foundation.

FRONTISPIECE: *Linn Cove Viaduct, Blue Ridge Parkway, completed 1997.*

Park roads determine park history.

SIERRA CLUB DIRECTOR
HAROLD BRADLEY

Contents

Foreword

SIERRA CLUB DIRECTOR Harold Bradley may have been hyperbolizing when he declared that "park roads determine park history," but decisions about when, where, how, and why to build roads have had enormous influence on the national park experience. For the majority of visitors, who rarely stray from the paved path, park roads provide access to key destinations and afford carefully choreographed excursions through landscapes of scenic and historic interest. Those who prefer to explore by nonmotorized means are equally affected by policies aimed at constraining road development, minimizing its visual impact, or proscribing it entirely to allow wilderness values to reign supreme. As historian Tim Davis makes clear, tracing the evolution of park road development affords an ideal means of examining the ways in which park managers and other stakeholders have addressed the challenge expressed one hundred years ago in the National Park Service's founding legislation: balancing preservation and access in America's most cherished landscapes. By placing National Park Service history in the context of broader American and European developments, moreover, he demonstrates that roads have long played an integral role in park creation and underscores the continuity between twentieth-century design practices and precedents established by Frederick Law Olmsted and other notable figures.

As the National Park Service enters its second century of service to the American people, it is important to understand where we came from, learn from our experiences, and rededicate ourselves to the principles expressed by the agency's founders. In addition to affording fascinating reading, the history of national park roads provides invaluable insights for addressing current and future concerns. The remarkable accomplishments of the 1920s–1930s, the recalibration of management policies in the 1960s–1970s, and recent achievements in transit systems, historic preservation, and context-sensitive design provide us with much to build on—not just in terms of transportation but for national park policy in general. As in 1916, we face an era of fiscal uncertainty, overtaxed infrastructure, and rapid social and technological change. Just as our predecessors had to secure support for new initiatives, address changing demographics, and harness the potential of mass mobility, we need to be both creative and conscientious in adapting long-standing ideals to evolving conditions. While early road builders united engineering and aesthetics, we have become increasingly attuned to broader environmental concerns, from climate change to the need for sustainability in design, construction, and management. And while the agency's founders focused on expanding visitation from the carriage trade to the motoring public, we now seek to engage additional audiences, from underrepresented minorities to younger Americans who may prefer electronic diversions to wilderness excursions. New media and associated technologies can enhance appreciation of our national parks, but they will never replace the experience of actually being there. There is little need to increase the amount of roads in existing parks, and we are continually exploring means of reducing the environmental impacts of park transportation, but we remain committed to the ideal that the special places that provoke awe, admiration, and awareness of what it means to be citizens of this great nation remain accessible to the public in ways that allow them to provide similar inspiration for future generations.

JONATHAN B. JARVIS
Director, National Park Service

Acknowledgments

THIS BOOK IS AN OUTGROWTH of an ambitious survey of national park roads and parkways conducted by the Historic American Engineering Record (HAER) between 1988 and 2001. This study produced thousands of large-format photographs, hundreds of measured and interpretive drawings, and detailed histories of individual park road systems. The project was conceived by former HAER Chief Eric DeLony and NPS Chief Historical Architect Randall J. Biallas and funded by the Federal Highway Administration's Federal Lands Highway Office. Former Federal Lands Program Administrator Tom Edick enthusiastically supported the effort, and his successors have followed suit.

My introduction to the topic came in the form of a summer job writing the history of Washington, D.C.'s Rock Creek and Potomac Parkway. After a few summers of parkway research, I became the program's senior historian, supervising teams documenting national park roads in classic western destinations such as Yellowstone and Yosemite, less-celebrated sites such as Hawaii Volcanoes, Wind Cave, and Scotts Bluff, Civil War battlefields, and additional parkways. Seeing the many ways in which designers sought to integrate park roads with their surroundings impressed me with the consistency of their efforts as they addressed the challenges of demanding terrain and evolving social and technological concerns. While most HAER documentation is relegated to archival

storage (where it is now accessible via the Library of Congress's Built in America website), we believed that national park roads were such compelling examples of the intersection of landscape architecture, engineering, and social history that they deserved greater exposure. Our first effort to increase awareness of the unique qualities and cultural significance of national park roads took the form of a major exhibition, *Lying Lightly on the Land: Building America's National Park Roads and Parkways*, which appeared at the National Building Museum in 1996–97. I was privileged to serve as guest curator for the exhibition and as lead editor for the second public outreach effort, *National Park Roads and Parkways: Drawings from the Historic American Engineering Record* (2004). This large-format portfolio included a brief explanatory text, but the richness and complexity of the park road story warranted a more substantial narrative history.

I conducted additional research and expanded the treatment to address broader themes and issues, many of which were introduced in the National Building Museum exhibit. The final research and writing were completed under the auspices of Biallas's Park Historic Structures and Cultural Landscapes Division, a component of the NPS Cultural Resources, Partnerships, and Science Directorate, Stephanie Toothman, Associate Director. Biallas deserves considerable credit for staying the course through numerous bureaucratic twists and turns. Portions of chapters 1 and 2

appeared in "'Everyone Has Carriage Road on the Brain': Designing for Vehicles in Pre-Automotive Parks," in *Public Nature: Scenery, History, and Park Design*, ed. Ethan Carr, Shaun Eyring, and Richard Guy Wilson (Charlottesville: University of Virginia Press, 2013).

The NPS Facilities Management Division provided crucial support for this publication. Mark H. Hartsoe, Transportation Branch Chief, encouraged the original survey work and subsequent phases, making history and historic preservation integral aspects of NPS road management policy. James Evans, Washington headquarters Transportation Program Manager, deserves special credit as the project's most ardent advocate and guardian angel. Terry Haussler, former Director of Office of Program Development, Federal Lands Highway Program, also embraced the project, as did former National Park Foundation (NPF) Executive Director Neil Mulholland, who offered to facilitate publication through a cooperative agreement between the NPS and NPF. We then worked with University of Virginia Press Acquisition Editor Boyd Zenner to develop plans to publish the book in conjunction with the 2016 NPS Centennial. NPF Corporate Partnerships Senior Manager Amber Hanna served as the foundation's liaison and provided invaluable assistance in acquiring reproduction rights for non-NPS images.

This book would not have been possible without the assistance of a wide range of current and former NPS employees.

Denis Galvin shared valuable insights from his illustrious NPS career, beginning with his role as a surveyor on pivotal 1960s road projects and extending through his leadership of the Denver Service Center and his roles as associate and deputy director of the National Park Service. HAER architects Todd Croteau and Christopher Marston played prominent roles in the original survey and helped to prepare graphics for the book. HAER historian Justine Christiansen gave freely of her time and expertise. Former HAER historian Richard Quin and former National Register historian Linda McClelland eagerly shared their knowledge of the subject. The individual HAER park road histories were an invaluable starting point. Heritage Documentation Programs Manager Rich O'Connor and former NPS Editor David Andrews provided much-appreciated encouragement and advice, as did the National Heritage Area team of Martha Raymond, Heather Scotten, and Katie Durcan. NPS Denver Service Center Transportation Branch Chief Kristie Franzmann and Senior Transportation Engineer Seth Greenwell shared their expertise at key junctures. Other NPS contributors include Glacier National Park landscape architect Jack Gordon and curator Deirdre Shaw; Yellowstone National Park historian Lee Whittlesey, archivist Anne Foster, archaeologist Elaine Hale, photographer Jim Peaco, and museum curator Colleen Curry; Yosemite historical landscape architect Kevin McCardle and current and former Yosemite librarians Barbara Beroza and Linda Eade; Blue Ridge Parkway museum curator Jackie Holt; Great Smoky Mountains National Park librarian/archivist Michael Ada; Shenandoah National Park museum specialist Kandace Muller; and Acadia National Park museum technician Robyn King. Wade Myers and Stacy Mason went above and beyond the call of duty in providing images from the NPS Historic Photograph Collection. The NPS Museum Management Program's Amber Dumler took time from her busy schedule to scan scores of images. Department of the Interior Library Director George Franchois and his staff were unfailingly helpful. Interlibrary Loan Librarian Shyamalika Ghoshal miraculously produced all manner of obscure publications.

I would also like to thank Claudia Rice of the Ansel Adams Publishing Rights Trust, Leslie Squyres of the Center for Creative Photography at Arizona State University, and Ellen Byrne of the Sierra Club William Colby Library for helping to track down and secure permission for Ansel Adams's photograph of a bulldozer clearing a path for Yosemite's Tioga Road. Byrne also helped me locate Marion Patterson, who shared precious memories and permitted the use of her cover photograph for the January 1958 *Sierra Club Bulletin*. Premier Yellowstoniana collectors Jack and Susan Davis graciously allowed us to make use of their renowned holdings. Sherry Hayman, Public Affairs Liaison for the Federal Highway Administration's Eastern Federal Lands Highway Division, provided photographs of recent and ongoing projects.

Zenner and the rest of editorial staff of the University of Virginia Press exercised great skill and patience in bringing this long-term project to fruition. The sharp eyes and fine-tuned instincts of copy editors Susan Murray and Kenny Marotta were particularly valuable. Any remaining literary indiscretions can be laid squarely on the author.

Innumerable friends, colleagues, and family members provided advice and encouragement along the way. I would like to extend special thanks to Erin Elliott and Scott Lambert, who provided invaluable moral and technical support throughout the project. I am also grateful to my daughter for her patience with Dad's preoccupation with "the book," which consumed far too many weekends and evenings. I would like to dedicate this volume to her and to my mother, Esther Jane Smith Davis, who would have loved to see the finished product but passed away a bit too soon, albeit at the estimable age of ninety-four.

Introduction

interests, and engaged citizens have long understood that debates about park road development are deliberations about the nature and purpose of national parks. Casual observers might take park roads for granted, but their crucial role was encapsulated in the Sierra Club leader Harold Bradley's declaration "park roads determine park history."[1]

To many people, roads and parks seem like antithetical concepts. The conjunction of cars and parks appears even more incongruous. Yet roads and parks have been integrally related for centuries and the enjoyment of scenery in motion was historically considered one of the highest forms of landscape appreciation. From the origins of picturesque landscape design in eighteenth-century England and the development of nineteenth-century urban oases such as New York's Central Park to the creation of Yellowstone and Yosemite and the twentieth-century expansion of the National Park System, roads were widely regarded as essential components of park landscapes.

The association between roads and parks reflected the consensus that parks were for people. At least that was the thinking governing the creation of English landscape gardens, nineteenth-century municipal parks, and the American National Park System. The first national parks—Yellowstone and Yosemite—were established in the late nineteenth century to preserve outstanding scenic areas "for public use, resort, and recreation" (as Yosemite's authorization proclaimed). When Congress created the National Park Service (NPS) in 1916, the agency was directed "to conserve the scenery and the natural and historic objects and the wild life therein and to provide for the enjoyment of the same in such manner and by such means as will leave them unimpaired for the enjoyment of future generations."[2]

What does it mean to protect natural and historical resources while at the same time providing for their enjoyment by the American public? How can this be done in a manner that leaves them "unimpaired for the enjoyment of future generations"? Who makes these decisions? What role do roads play in achieving the seemingly paradoxical goal of promoting both preservation and access? When is it necessary to devise new solutions to these questions? More than any other aspect of national park policy, roads have served as focal points in the continuing debate

Millions of visitors tour America's national parks, but few pause to consider when, why, or how the roads they travel on were built. This lack of awareness is understandable and to a large degree intentional. Not only do most visitors take automobile access for granted, but the self-effacing nature of park road design deliberately obscures their role in shaping the national park experience. Not only do park roads determine what most visitors see and how they see it, but decisions about park road development epitomize the central challenge of park stewardship: balancing preservation and access in America's most treasured landscapes. National parks were created not just to protect significant sites but also to extend their benefits to an ever-broadening public. While most accounts of national park history focus on the drive to preserve scenic and historic resources, this volume moves the question of access to center stage. The two concerns are inextricably intertwined. Government officials, design professionals, conservationists, commercial

ABOVE Laurel Creek Road, Great Smoky Mountains National Park, 1996.

OPPOSITE Tundra Curves, Trail Ridge Road, Rocky Mountain National Park, 2000.

PREVIOUS Going-to-the-Sun Road, Glacier National Park, ca. 1933.

National Park Roads

over the appropriate management of America's national parks and monuments.

It is easy to see why roads are such an emotional issue. For some people, roads and vehicles appear to be the primary threat to the national parks. For others, they provide the main means of enjoyment. Roads not only afford access, but they play a dominant role in forming visitors' impressions of national parks. Roads determine which parts of a park most of us will see and strongly influence the ways in which we see it. Roads lead us through the park landscape, defining the order in which we view park scenery, regulating our speed and directing our eyes, presenting trees, rocks, cliffs, lakes, historic buildings, and other features as carefully choreographed sequences of sensory experiences. For many people, what they see from the road *is* the national park experience.

At the same time, road development has significant repercussions. In addition to their impact on surrounding scenery, roads can dramatically increase the number of visitors, transforming popular destinations into congested conurbations. Park roads have psychological, symbolic, and philosophical implications as well. Not only do the sights, sounds, and smells of traffic transform their immediate surroundings, but for some people, simply knowing roads are present compromises parks' ability to function as escapes from modern civilization. Many who view parks as ecological preserves or surrogates for primeval wildernesses maintain that roads—or at least the number of motorized visitors—should be greatly reduced. This might be good for the environment—and would make parks more enjoyable for those willing and able to reach them through more

strenuous means—but excluding the bulk of the population from areas expressly created for their benefit raises legal and philosophical questions. Barring the elderly, the physically challenged, and others with limited mobility would be particularly problematic. Political and economic considerations also come into play. If it became harder for people to enjoy parks, public support for the National Park System might suffer, making it harder to preserve existing resources and protect additional areas. The economic impact on communities that depend on national park tourism presents additional complications.

Evolving engineering standards and concerns about the ability of aging infrastructure to accommodate modern traffic demands affect park road decisions, as does the growing recognition that many national park roads are old enough

to be considered historic resources in their own rights. Changing demographics, evolving transportation methods, and new information technologies raise additional questions. Parks roads have been celebrated as exemplars of the harmonious integration of engineering and landscape architecture and vilified as intrusions in the natural order. But the history of national park road development is more than a saga of aesthetic achievement, technical triumph, or environmental exploitation. It is a complex drama involving such archetypal themes as the tensions between nature and technology, wilderness and civilization, the will of the masses versus the rights of minorities, and present demands versus future responsibilities.

Since 1916, the responsibility for determining where roads should go and how they should be

designed and managed has been the responsibility of the National Park Service, which has been assisted by the Bureau of Public Roads (BPR) and its successor, the Federal Highway Administration (FHWA), since a partnership between the two agencies was formalized in 1926. The National Park Service's Organic Act outlined the principal goals, and additional policy directives, regulatory measures, and design decisions have shaped park road development and continue to inform contemporary practice. Perhaps the most succinct statement of national park road philosophy was provided by Major Hiram Chittenden, who presided over Yellowstone's roads at the turn of the twentieth century. "The true policy of the government in dealing with this problem," he proclaimed, "should therefore be to make the roads

National Park Roads

as limited in extent as will meet actual necessities, but to make such as are found necessary perfect examples of their class."[3] Like the Organic Act's injunction to balance preservation and access, Chittenden's directive was both emphatic and elastic. The basic sentiment was widely appealing, but definitions of what constituted "limited in extent," "actual necessities," and "perfect" have engendered ongoing debate and evolved significantly over the course of time.

For many, the perfect road was one that blended with its surroundings and displayed park scenery to optimal effect. Others insisted that roads should steer clear of signature features, which were better approached on foot. Some maintained that engineering factors were the dominant concern. Standards for the appropriate width, grade, and curvature were hotly debated in response to changing technical considerations and cultural concerns. Business interests evaluated roads in terms of their ability to serve as conduits of commerce. The traveling public generally sought an entertaining drive, minimal delays, and a place to park at the end of the journey. Wilderness advocates proclaimed that the perfect park road was no road at all. National Park Service officials often found themselves mediating between divergent perspectives, both in terms of design specifics and the location and extent of development.

Rather than argue for the primacy of a particular point of view, this volume shows how national park road development responded to professional precedents, practical exigencies, and evolving technological factors, social practices, and cultural concerns. The history of national park road development entails much of interest to academic historians, design professionals, and resource managers, but it is also a rich and compelling narrative, populated by strong personalities, imposing challenges, resounding controversies, and remarkable achievements. The key players included many of the most important figures in conservation history, including precedent setters such as John Muir and Frederick Law Olmsted, NPS directors Stephen Mather, Horace Albright, Conrad Wirth, and George Hartzog, and wilderness advocates such as Aldo Leopold, Bob Marshall, and Ansel Adams. Many debates played out in public, but there were internal disagreements within NPS circles and between the NPS and BPR. Design modifications and policies changes resolved many disputes,

but contrasting perspectives on the appropriate balance between preservation and access produced ongoing tensions. Throughout these debates, the automobile-dependent general public never wavered in its enthusiasm. Despite economic challenges, environmentalist admonitions, aging infrastructure, and an ever-broadening array of entertainment options, contemporary audiences appear to enjoy the park road experience as much as their predecessors did during the heyday of twentieth-century automobile culture, the romantic reign of stagecoach tourism, and the exclusive era of private carriages. While this account affords a broad geographic and chronological survey, it is impossible to do justice to the topic in a single volume. Those seeking additional information about the development of individual park roads are encouraged to consult the Historic American Engineering Record's national park road documentation on the Library of Congress website. My goal in chronicling the evolution of development policies and providing an overview of major achievements is to underscore the role of park roads in shaping national park history, trace their evolution over time, and encourage informed debate about their future.[4]

The second part of this introduction, "The View from the Road," provides a synopsis of

the key characteristics of park roads and the design methods employed to create them. Chapter 1 traces the origins of park road design, underscoring the prominent role roads played in shaping the park experience in America and abroad. Chapter 1 also describes the rise of scenic tourism in America, emphasizing the relationship between transportation technologies and tourist practices. Travelers sought to transfer these habits to Yosemite, Yellowstone, and other western wonderlands when they were set aside as scenic reservations in the second half of the nineteenth century. Many of these early visitors were sorely disappointed, but chapter 2 traces the efforts of private entrepreneurs and the U.S. Army Corps of Engineers to improve public access. By the end of the century, both parks boasted impressive road networks served by extensive stagecoach operations, both of which were celebrated by tourists and professional commentators.

The automobile was greeted with a mixture of enthusiasm and apprehension when it clanked and wheezed its way into national parks at the turn of the twentieth century. Chapter 3 shows how park managers came to embrace the automobile as a means of spreading the benefits of national parks to the increasingly mobile middle class. Addressing the needs of the motoring masses played a crucial role in the establishment of the National Park Service in 1916 and remained a top priority over the ensuing decades. At the same time, NPS leaders such as Stephen Mather and Horace Albright sought to limit the extent of development and minimize its impact on park landscapes. Chapter 4 describes NPS efforts to balance preservation and access by adapting traditional design strategies to the automobile age. It also recounts the formation of the long-standing partnership between the NPS and Bureau of Public Roads that set the stage for what many consider a golden age of park road development extending from the 1920s to the outbreak of World War II. Several of the era's most prominent projects are described in chapter 5, including Glacier National Park's Going-to-the-Sun Road, Rocky Mountain National Park's Trail Ridge Road, Yosemite's Wawona Tunnel, and Shenandoah National Park's Skyline Drive.

Even as showpieces such as Skyline Drive and Going-to-the-Sun Road were being celebrated by popular and professional audiences, an influential minority began to question NPS policies and call for tighter limits on automobile access. Chapter 6 recounts this growing discontent along with the NPS's own efforts to resist road-building pressures. Conflicts over road development figured prominently in debates over the development of Acadia, Mount Rainier, and Great Smoky Mountains National Parks. The NPS demonstrated an increasing tendency to constrain road construction in existing parks and newly created reservations such as Isle Royale, Kings Canyon, and Olympic National Parks. National parkways are the focus of chapter 7. While multi-hundred-mile scenic roads such as Blue Ridge Parkway epitomized the adaptation of traditional park-making philosophies to the motor age and were widely embraced by the general public, they also encountered opposition from the growing ranks of wilderness advocates. The rejection of the proposed Green Mountain Parkway and Chesapeake and Ohio Canal Parkway were among the first major victories for park road opponents.

The challenge of balancing preservation and access became increasingly difficult during the 1950s. The postwar Baby Boom, increases in leisure time and automobile ownership, and improving cross-country highways generated pressure to update and expand facilities. At the same time, groups such as the Wilderness Society and Sierra Club gained adherents and became increasingly adversarial. Tensions mounted when the NPS initiated a ten-year, billion-dollar program to accommodate the growing crowds and update facilities in time for the agency's golden anniversary in 1966. Chapter 8 covers this conflict, which culminated in battles over the modernization of Yosemite National Park's Tioga Road and the entrance to Mount McKinley (now Denali) National Park. Chapter 9 takes the story up through the present, tracing the evolution of more environmentally attuned development policies, the growing interest in alternative transportation, and challenges that arose as park roads gained recognition as historic resources in their own right. A brief epilogue surveys current and future concerns. Just as the proliferation of automobiles and expansion of leisure time redefined the relationships between Americans and nature during the twentieth century, social, economic, and technological changes continue to transform the national park experience. Demographic trends, environmental factors, and digital technologies will profoundly affect the ongoing challenge of balancing preservation and access in America's natural and historic landscapes.

THE VIEW FROM THE ROAD

Park roads are not like ordinary roads. They are intended for leisurely sightseeing rather than rapid and efficient travel. Park roads enable visitors to reach prominent features, but they are designed to afford a memorable journey, not to provide the

ABOVE East Side Highway, Mount Rainier National Park, 1992.

fastest route. Ideally, park roads encourage visitors to slow down and enjoy the park experience rather than rush from one destination to the next.

Every park road provides a unique experience, but designers follow a few basic principles in their efforts to strike an appropriate balance between preservation and access. The fundamental goal is to display a park's signature scenery without compromising it in the process. At the same time, park roads must meet safety standards and address challenges posed by increasingly heavy transportation loads. Park road designers use many different techniques to fulfill these demands while integrating motorways into park landscapes with minimal visual and environmental impact. Some roads achieve these results better than others—and changing social, technological, and environmental factors influence both the end results and the ways in which they are

evaluated—but most roads in America's national parks were developed in accordance with the following precepts.

Park roads are generally more narrow, winding, and hilly than conventional highways. Scenic features such as trees, rocks, rivers, and cliffs lie closer to the pavement. These conditions are not considered desirable on highways designed for ordinary travel, but they help create the visual interest and connection with the surrounding environment that give park roads their unique appeal. When a motorist winds through the towering forests of Sequoia National Park passing inches from thousand-year-old trees, emerges from a narrow tunnel to be greeted with a spectacular view of Yosemite Valley, or climbs a steep mountain pass to gain panoramic vistas of snow-covered peaks or gentle Appalachian highlands, the journey can be as rewarding as the destination. In some cases,

park roads afford such outstanding experiences that they become attractions themselves. Skyline Drive in Shenandoah National Park, Trail Ridge Road in Rocky Mountain National Park, and Going-to-the-Sun Road in Glacier National Park afford such acclaimed experiences that many visitors come largely to enjoy the views from the road. The desire to provide extended scenic drives was a dominant factor in the creation of Blue Ridge Parkway and Natchez Trace Parkway, which preserve broad bands of greenery while enabling visitors to motor for hundreds of miles through natural and man-made landscapes.

Park road designers have long sought to create roads that "lie lightly on the land," minimizing impacts on the surrounding terrain by employing graceful curves that follow the natural contours and reduce the need for unsightly excavations. Viaducts and retaining walls further reduce

ABOVE Glacier Point Road, Yosemite National Park, 2001.

ABOVE, FROM LEFT Four Guards-
men, Generals Highway,
Sequoia National Park, 1993.
Zion–Mount Carmel Highway,
Zion National Park, 1993.
Christine Falls Bridge, Mount
Rainier National Park, 1992.

scarring on steep hillsides. Tunnels afford the
ultimate means of disguising a roadway's presence, providing passage through natural obstacles
with minimal visual disruption. Since they are
expensive to construct, tunnels are reserved for
situations where conventional techniques would
disfigure spectacular settings. Since the 1960s,
park road designers have tried to "lie lightly" in
an ecological sense, as well. New construction
and major alterations require environmental

impact studies to ensure compliance with NPS
policies and federal laws. In some cases, existing roads and bridges have been redesigned or
removed to reduce their ecological impact.

Park road builders also try to minimize visual
impacts by employing materials, designs, and
construction techniques that harmonize artificial
structures with their environment. Locally quarried stones laid in seemingly random patterns help
bridges, culverts, guard walls, and other structures

Park road designers focus on enhancing the motoring experience, but they also encourage visitors to leave their cars and enjoy parks on a more intimate basis through scenic overlooks, wayside exhibits, campgrounds, and trail connections. Entrance stations, restrooms, and other roadside structures are also designed to harmonize with their natural surroundings or cultural settings. Designers frequently use traditional materials and adapt vernacular building patterns to modern ends. Examples range from the Colonial Revival motifs prevalent in eastern historical parks to the traditional fences that line the Blue Ridge Parkway and organic adobe forms found in many southwestern parks. The rugged log-and-boulder look prevalent in many parks combines long-held ideas about rustic design's fitness for park structures with the desire to evoke America's pioneering heritage.

The primary function of park roads is to display the features that caused an area to be declared a national park. At the most obvious level, they enable visitors to drive within walking or viewing distance of sites like the Grand Canyon, Yosemite Valley, Old Faithful Geyser, or the monuments and battlefields of national military parks. On a more subtle level, roads shape motorists' encounters from the moment they enter a park, creating both general impressions and specific views. The distant panoramas, intimate woodland scenes, relaxing meadows, burbling streams, breathtaking cliffs, and spectacular canyons and waterfalls encountered along park roads may be natural features, but the sequences in which they are seen and the angles from which they are viewed are not happy accidents, but carefully choreographed compositions involving large-scale location choices and more fine-tuned manipulation of alignment and framing.

Park road designers highlight striking views with long straightaways or propitiously located curves. Vegetation can be manipulated by cutting windows to display attractive scenery or leaving it in place to hide undesirable views. Designers frequently play hide-and-seek with distinctive features, alternating brief glimpses with obstructed views to build a sense of anticipation as visitors approach their destination. Park road designers literally go to great lengths to heighten variety by winding roads up and down mountainsides, alongside watercourses, through confining forests, and across open areas. Spur roads, scenic overlooks, and trails provide access to features not easily seen from the main roadway.

Motorists don't just look; they move through space. Many park roads are designed to enhance the sensation of moving smoothly and effortlessly through natural environments and cultural settings. Banked turns, gently rolling grades, and sweeping curves engender the feeling of flowing in harmony with the landscape. The Swiss architectural historian Sigfried Giedion extolled the sensation of motoring along newly created parkways. "Riding up and down the long sweeping grades," he exclaimed, "produces an exhilarating dual feeling, one of being connected with the soil and yet of hovering just above it, a feeling which is like nothing else so much as sliding swiftly on skis through untouched snow down the sides of high mountains."[5] Landscape architects employed cinematographic allusions, comparing the unfolding impressions to the interplay of close-ups, pans, and tracking shots. Some park road designers allied their efforts with musical composition, contrasting the pianissimo of shady glens with the fortissimo of bolder scenery culminating in crescendos of soaring cliffs and jagged peaks.

The effort to adapt park roads to their surroundings, to present park scenery to best advantage, and to harmonize man-made structures with local landscapes ensures that every park road affords a unique experience. Despite this individual variation, national park roads are united by a common aesthetic. Rustic in construction and designed to "lie lightly on the land," they offer travelers intimacy with the surrounding landscape, a leisurely pace of travel, and carefully configured visual compositions, affording a constant reminder of the difference between park roads and ordinary highways. Motorists may not be consciously aware of these details, but they know they have entered one of America's most treasured natural and historic landscapes.

blend with their surroundings. Rugged native timbers can make guard rails, entrance stations, and other structures seem like pioneer outposts or part of the forest themselves. Both techniques were often used to conceal modern underpinnings of steel and concrete. The pavement itself can be tinted to mimic local hues. Grading road banks to mimic natural contours and replanting roadsides with native vegetation elides the distinction between natural and man-made landscapes.

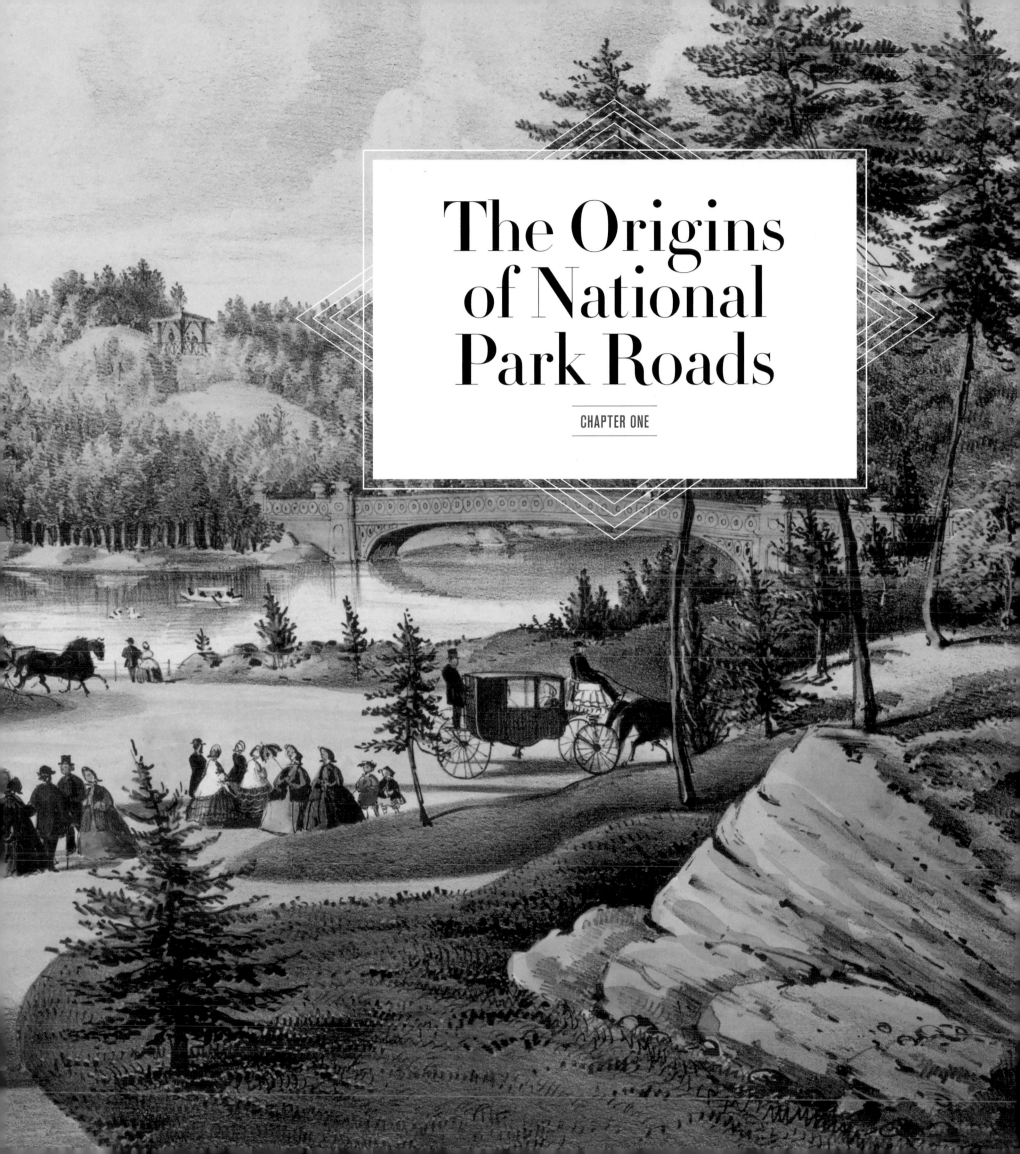

The Origins of National Park Roads

CHAPTER ONE

While this conceit plays into long-standing anti-automobile sentiments and engenders exposés of the park service's ostensibly Faustian bargains with technology, commerce, and popular taste, it belies an imperfect understanding of the history of parks and landscape values, both in America and abroad. In truth, the view from the road emerged as the favored means of experiencing scenery with the development of modern conceptions of landscape appreciation in eighteenth-century Europe. English estates and nineteenth-century municipal parks were explicitly designed for the enjoyment of moving spectators. The history of scenic tourism similarly suggests that travelers not only relished the company of their peers but were also as enamored of the means of locomotion as with the ostensible objects of their peregrinations. While prominent artists and writers elevated the image of solitary pilgrims engaged in solemn contemplation of nature's majesty, the broader population took a more sociable approach to scenic appreciation. For park authorities and the general public alike, the sight of happy throngs enjoying scenic reservations was a cause for celebration, not a source of concern. Underlying this perception was the conviction that parks were cultural institutions for the social, psychological, and physical benefit of the people, not inviolate sanctuaries or ecological preserves where man's presence was a disruption of the natural order. In order for parks to fulfill their intended functions, park officials provided roads and other amenities aimed at encouraging public use. From a historical perspective, the National Park Service's embrace of the automobile was not a rejection of hallowed principles but an extension of long-standing traditions. These precedents extended from general philosophies of park development and landscape appreciation to the goals and methods of road design.

any commentators have taken exception to the automobile's role in shaping the national park experience. Central to these critiques is the implication that the decision to cater to the motoring masses entailed a radical reorientation of management strategies, design practices, and visitor experiences. According to this line of reasoning, vehicular travel and the view from the road supplanted a more refined and authentic relationship with the natural environment. By inundating parks with swarms of motorized philistines, automobiles imperiled the moral, social, and spiritual values of America's national parks, undermining their ability to ameliorate the impact of modern urban life. As technological intrusions and avatars of industrial civilization, roads and automobiles despoiled the hallowed remnants of America's primordial wilderness. These critiques present the NPS's embrace of the automobile as a fall from grace that could only be redressed by restoring a prelapsarian landscape of pedestrian bliss.

ROADS AND PARKS

The antecedents of modern parks were royal forests reserved by European nobles to supply timber, fuel, and habitat for the deer and other game animals they liked to pursue. While these multiple uses might imply a prescient environmental consciousness, the recreational aspect became paramount as hunting evolved into a highly ritualized aristocratic pastime. As protected realms devoted to the thrills of the chase, parks were explicitly intended for the enjoyment of mounted riders, a practice that was celebrated in contemporary tapestries and illuminated manuscripts. Broad swaths, or "rides," were cut through the woods to facilitate passage, allowing the favored few to gallop over hill and dale at speeds unimaginable to pedestrian subjects. As carriage technology improved during the sixteenth century, rides were often improved to accommodate wheeled vehicles. These pragmatic passages served as precedents for the grand allées of monumental formal gardens such as Louis XIV's Versailles, which started out as a royal hunting lodge in the midst of a deer park. London's St. James Park, Hyde Park, Regent's Park, and Kensington Gardens had similar origins, as did the Prater in Vienna and Paris's Bois de Boulogne and Bois de Vincennes. Lesser nobility also surrounded their country houses with parks and gardens. During the seventeenth century, the contemplation of designed landscapes superseded hunting as the primary motive for park development, with carriages replacing horses as the preferred means of locomotion.[1]

Public access to these reservations expanded gradually, with the higher ranks of society gaining admittance first. With the addition of a riding course and carriage circuit, Hyde Park became a rendezvous for London's elite by the early 1600s. Prominent Parisians resorted to carriage drives laid out for their benefit in the Tuileries and Cours la Reine. Many parks were protected by walls and locked gates, the keys to which were distributed to select members of society. Entrance fees and regulations on dress and deportment achieved similar results. Pressure to allow broader access grew as expanding cities engulfed formerly isolated tracts and tolerance for royal privileges waned. After the English Civil War, Cromwell's parliamentarians were in the process of selling off the king's parks when they were deposed by the Restoration. The French Revolution opened Paris's parks to the public, setting the stage for the city's radical transformation in the mid-nineteenth century. Favoring a more measured transition, the ruler of Bavaria commissioned what many consider the first major park expressly intended for public use. Begun in 1789, Munich's Englischer Garten combined its namesake's emphasis on naturalistic landscapes with a beer garden, dance pavilion, and other incentives for public use. Roads and paths provided access to carefully composed woods, meadows, and water features. Another German noble, Hermann Ludwig Heinrich von Pückler-Muskau, gave the public free rein to an expansive park he developed southeast of Berlin from the 1820s through the 1840s. Pückler-Muskau was strongly influenced by English precedents but adopted a simpler and less overtly didactic approach. Broad swaths of turf and trees created the illusion of an exceptionally attractive countryside rather than an overt demonstration of the gardener's art. Carriage drives wound through the property, displaying subtly reconfigured scenery from carefully choreographed perspectives. A complementary network of footpaths afforded access for the less fortunate, but the emphasis Pückler-Muskau placed on the view from the road underscored his priorities.[2]

The rise of the informal or naturalistic style of landscape gardening in eighteenth-century England established precedents that shaped the development of parks and park roads throughout the nineteenth and twentieth centuries. The origins and implications of this transition were diverse and complex, embodying contemporary developments in painting, poetry, agricultural science, civil engineering, politics, and economics. The Enlightenment rejection of a priori constructs in favor of scientific observation and human reasoning fostered the belief that landscapes should be designed to reflect their inherent qualities rather than abstract geometric principles. The emphasis on visual faculties combined with renewed interest in classical precedents elevated the appeal of seventeenth-century painters such as Claude Lorrain and Nicolas Poussin, whose romanticized interpretations of Italian scenery became models for the design and interpretation of English landscapes. Key figures in this transition included William Kent, Lancelot "Capability" Brown, and Humphry Repton. They were aided by advances in engineering and agricultural technology that facilitated large-scale manipulations of topography, vegetation, and hydrology, as well as by the accumulation of wealth made possible by the rise of market economies and industrial processes. Some historians suggest that capitalism itself was responsible for the rise of landscape consciousness by commodifying relationships between citizens and their surroundings and producing a new class of wealthy landowners who sought impressive estates to solidify their social standing. Contemporary writers provided a more optimistic assessment, maintaining that naturalistic landscapes that afforded multiple perspectives and alternative routes embodied democratic principles, in contrast to the autocratic rigidity of baroque gardens

and their manorial offspring. Rousseau's writings helped elevate nature over culture and emotion over reason, while Edmund Burke, William Gilpin, and Uvedale Price elaborated philosophical constructs and visual taxonomies that facilitated the appreciation of natural landscapes and naturalistic designs. Writers extolled the sensation of experiencing landscape as a dynamic succession of unfolding views enjoyed from newly improved lightweight carriages. Burke praised the experience of sweeping briskly along winding park drives as the perfect means of combining aesthetic contemplation with mental and physical relaxation. The essayist Samuel Johnson insisted that his ideal of happiness entailed "being swiftly drawn in a chaise over undulating turf in the company of a beautiful and witty woman."[3]

The typical landscape park of the era was an expansive estate arrayed in the informal style, with a winding circuit drive showcasing artfully improved scenery. The carefully orchestrated sequences were explicitly designed to appeal to the sensibilities of carriage occupants. Humphry Repton, the leading practitioner of the informal style at the turn of the nineteenth century, provided extensive instructions for designing roads that would please the eye and stimulate the imagination, enthusing, "I cannot describe those numberless beauties which may be brought before the eye in succession by the windings of a road." Repton recommended that park roads be laid out to present a diverse array of scenic effects, contrasting prospect and enclosure, light and shade, picturesque woodlands and serene meadows. This could be achieved by carefully studying the characteristics of a site and manipulating the road's alignment in conjunction with the topography and vegetation. Although twentieth-century critics often disparaged the tastes of the motoring masses, implying that earlier travelers were more aesthetically attuned, Repton recognized that his audience was less sophisticated than generally assumed. Contending that most visitors were "heedless travelers" for whom "everything is lost that is not too obviously presented," he emphasized: "Care is requisite in giving the direction of every road or walk, that we may compel the most careless to observe those parts of a design, which have a claim on their admiration." One of his favorite techniques was to configure a road and its surroundings so that the viewer experienced the sensation of "bursting" into the open

to encounter an impressive vista highlighted by some striking visual accent. In Repton's hands, the focal point was usually his patron's manor or an attractive bridge or architectural folly, but subsequent designers employed this device to showcase scenic wonders. Sounding a theme repeated by nineteenth-century park advocates but viewed with growing disfavor by NPS designers and their critics, Repton advised that roads afford views of other parkgoers, whose carriages and colorful attire would add variety and interest to the natural surroundings.[4]

Road development both structured the experience of park landscapes and made it possible for more people to enjoy their benefits. In his 1796 recommendations for the development of the grounds of Blaise Castle, Repton expressed astonishment "that no attempt should have been made to render objects of so much beauty and variety accessible in a carriage." The provision of road access was especially important in hilly terrain, where "the aged and the infirm have been excluded from the beauties of the place by the danger or difficulty of exploring them." Although roads in rugged areas were harder to design and entailed greater manipulation of the surrounding landscape, time would heal the signs of construction and restore the desired naturalistic character.[5]

Pückler-Muskau also provided extensive advice on park roads, which he likened to invisible hands leading visitors along routes designed to afford the most varied and propitious views. Although he maintained that roads should provide easy access "toward every spot which can afford enjoyment," Pückler-Muskau cautioned that they should neither be "too conspicuous" nor "unnecessarily multiplied." In an early articulation of the NPS's "lying lightly on the land" philosophy, he advised that they conform to the nuances of the terrain, "following as far as possible the natural contours of the ground." Winding roads were generally more attractive, but curves should not be inserted gratuitously so as to make the road look like "a serpent wound round a stick." Where natural turning points such as hills, trees, or water features were absent, they could be artificially introduced, taking pains to naturalize their appearance. Since carriage occupants moved at a brisk clip, the roads should be configured to afford prolonged views of important features. Pückler-Muskau maintained that park roads should be smooth, durable, and well-drained, but he cautioned against

National Park Roads

taking improvements too far, emphasizing that it was "unnecessary to make the roads in a park as broad as in a highway." Observing that good park roads were challenging to design and expensive to construct, Pückler-Muskau insisted the effort was essential to the success of the enterprise.[6]

Pückler-Muskau's writings were not readily available, but Repton's ideas, along with those of his successor, the Scottish apostle of rural taste John Claudius Loudon, had an enormous impact on nineteenth-century American designers. Loudon focused more on horticultural matters and practical concerns such as his countryman John McAdam's revolutionary methods for constructing inexpensive and durable gravel roads, but he advised that carriage drives be designed to harmonize with their surroundings while displaying scenery to maximum effect.[7] Loudon's American acolyte Andrew

Jackson Downing borrowed heavily from English influences while adapting his advice to American conditions. Since there were as yet no major public parks in America, Downing focused on the provision of drives for the growing number of large estates.[8] Like Repton and Loudon, he considered pleasure drives essential accessories to scenic appreciation and provided advice on designing them to reveal the variety and extent of an owner's domain while appearing attractive and naturalistic. Provisions for vehicular circulation played a prominent role in Downing's most notable venture into public landscape design, his 1851 proposal for the development of the National Mall. Downing proclaimed that the plan would "afford some of the most beautifully varied carriage-drives in the world." Following his untimely death in 1852, the project was only

partially realized, and most of his recommendations came to naught.[9]

Downing may not have succeeded in creating America's first major public park, but many citizens were enjoying an unexpected alternative. There are several contenders for the title of America's first romantically designed landscaped cemetery, but Mount Auburn, founded in 1831 and located in Cambridge, Massachusetts, was widely hailed as the leading example. Conceived in reaction to overcrowded, unhealthy, and discomfiting urban burial grounds, rural cemeteries, as they were called, united the growing awareness of sanitary concerns with increasingly assuring attitudes about death and the afterlife. Not only was it comforting to envision loved ones slumbering through eternity in artistically landscaped grounds, but the cemeteries' leafy confines afforded soothing settings

Such arrangements, Olmsted claimed, would act "in a more directly remedial way to enable men to better resist the harmful influences of ordinary town life, and recover what they lose from them."

for the bereaved. As in European parks, the combination of attractive scenery and somber monuments was intended to simultaneously comfort and inspire visitors, whether active mourners or excursionists seeking relief from urban conditions. With picturesque plantings and meandering walks and drives, Mount Auburn and contemporaries such as Brooklyn's Green-wood and Philadelphia's Laurel Hill introduced Americans to the pleasures and possibilities of public parks. Highly ranked among these enjoyments was the appeal of escaping congested and poorly maintained streets for the manicured surfaces and graceful curves of exquisitely arrayed carriage drives. The attraction was so great that regulations often limited carriage access to plot-holders. Similar strictures were applied to pedestrians as crowds grew larger, especially on Sundays and holidays.[10]

Downing and allies such as William Cullen Bryant pointed to the popularity of rural cemeteries as evidence of the need for public parks where access was not restricted and visitors were freed from melancholy overtones. The public health benefits of parks as "lungs of the city" were amply noted, but advocates emphasized that parks were social institutions of central significance to the success of the American experiment. American democracy was believed to have been conceived in a largely rural environment by a relatively homogeneous and egalitarian population. The rapid growth of cities, rising income inequality, and waves of immigration spurred by the Irish potato famine and revolutions in central Europe appeared to threaten these hallowed foundations. According to the reformer's logic, large parks with a mixture of naturalistic and pastoral scenery would not only allow the upper- and middle-class native-born population to gain sustenance from the virtuous rural surroundings from which they came but would improve the lot of immigrants and the urban poor by exposing them to morally and spiritually uplifting environments. Given contemporary anxieties about the cultural refinement of Americans in general, exposure to the beauties of nature augmented by the landscape gardener's art would exert a beneficent influence on all levels of society. Like museums or art galleries, Downing declared, parks would "soften and humanize the rude, educate and enlighten the ignorant, and give continual enjoyment to the educated." By appealing to all classes and bringing them together in safe and attractive surroundings,

parks would ease social tensions and strengthen the communal bonds that formed the foundation of American democracy. With former royal parks being thrown open to the public throughout Europe, Downing and others insisted on the need for Americans to provide even better opportunities, conceived from the start as public parks for the benefit and enjoyment of a diverse populace. Idealistic—if naïve and paternalistic—motives aside, park promoters noted that attractively designed pleasure grounds had improved property values and stimulated commerce in European cities and would undoubtedly do the same at home.[11]

Frederick Law Olmsted and his partner, Calvert Vaux, played a leading role in transforming nascent ideas about public parks from dream to reality. Born in 1822, Olmsted enjoyed a comfortable upbringing as the son of a Hartford merchant, imbibing the wisdom of Repton, Gilpin, Price, and Ruskin and gaining further appreciation for rural scenery on extended carriage tours of New England's highway and byways. He studied scientific farming, surveying, and a bit of engineering and eventually secured a position managing a farm on Staten Island. A facile writer with finely tuned moral and aesthetic sensibilities, he garnered acclaim for a series of books and articles on the relationships between people and the environments they created, from English farming practices to the impact of slavery on southern landscapes and culture. Vaux was an English architect who came to America in order to work with Downing, enjoying a brief but successful partnership before his mentor's untimely demise. Olmsted and Vaux joined forces to submit a proposal for the design of New York's Central Park. Their winning 1858 design, known as the Greensward Plan, combined an array of formal and informal features, natural and reconfigured landscapes, and rustic structures and classical embellishments with an elaborate circulation system providing separate networks for pedestrians, equestrians, carriages, and commercial traffic. The park contained broad lawns for leisurely contemplation, densely wooded rambles for more adventurous exploration, bustling promenades for social interaction, a wealth of water features, and winding drives affording circuits of varying length and character. The widely acclaimed design, together with extensive writings and the immensely popular public spaces they devised for Brooklyn, Buffalo, and other major cities, placed Olmsted and Vaux in the forefront of efforts to articulate the form, function, and underlying social values of the American public park.[12]

Like Downing, they believed that exposure to verdant groves and pastoral scenery would elevate the minds and morals of visitors while affording relief from the pressures of modern life and the ugly, artificial, and unwholesome environment of rapidly growing cities. Since parks were supposed to soothe overstimulated urbanites, Olmsted and Vaux maintained that designers should eschew complex visual arrangements and provide broad, grassy expanses to relax the eye and mind, surrounded by trees to afford shade and screen out urban influences. Such arrangements, Olmsted claimed, would act "in a more directly remedial way to enable men to better resist the harmful influences of ordinary town life, and recover what they lose from them." Although admirers of nineteenth-century metropolitan parks tend to focus on aesthetic concerns and prioritize the pastoral tranquility exemplified by Prospect Park's Long Meadow, Olmsted insisted that the opportunities parks provided for "gregarious recreation" among a diverse and democratic citizenry were as important as the relief their scenery afforded from urban landscapes. Olmsted extolled the social benefits parks afforded as places where large groups of friends and strangers commingled in healthful, informal, and scenically appealing settings. As a measure of Prospect Park's success, he noted that a hundred thousand visitors could congregate, "all classes largely represented, with a common purpose, not at all intellectual, competitive with none, disposing to jealousy and spiritual or intellectual pride toward none, each individual adding by his mere presence to the pleasure of all others, all helping to the greater happiness of each." In order for parks to perform their dual function as asylums from urban ills and instruments of social cohesion, designers had to balance the presentation of attractive scenery with provisions for its enjoyment.[13]

Roads played a preeminent role in this process. While roads were intended to provide access to a park's chief attractions, in many cases they *were* the chief attractions. The association between parks and pleasure driving was so strong that nineteenth-century writers often referred to large public reservations as "driving parks." The absence of such amenities was considered an indication that American cities lacked sophistication and civic pride. "As a metropolis of wealth and fashion," the popular writer Nathanial Parker Willis lamented, "New York has one great deficiency—that of a *driving* park." The appeal of park roads was demonstrated not just by the calls for their creation or the lengths park designers and guidebook writers went to describe them, but by the extent to which descriptions of roads and their users dominated popular accounts.[14] Publications such as *Harper's New Monthly Magazine* and the *Atlantic Monthly* extolled Central Park's appeal for carriage users, who were depicted enjoying the newly laid out drives even as the broader scenic features remained under construction. More than eighty thousand carriages passed through Central Park in June 1860, when the park had barely opened and major landscaping work was still under way. Two-thirds of 1863 visitors arrived by carriage, with close to ten thousand vehicles entering on a single day. Boasting of this achievement, Central Park's commissioners observed that if these carriages were lined up in a row, the procession would extend from one end of Manhattan to the other and back again.[15] By 1873 as many as eighty-five thousand carriage occupants enjoyed the park on a busy day. More than five million visitors entered in carriages or sleighs over the course of the year.[16] John Bachmann's 1863 chromolithographed view highlighted the carriage drives, portraying the park as a symphony of vehicles in motion.[17] Currier and Ives produced several popular prints celebrating Central Park's vibrant mix of carriages and crowds. Olmsted himself touted the correlation between parks and carriage driving. "Twelve years ago there was almost no pleasure-driving in New York," he observed in 1870. With the completion of Central Park's drives, he boasted, "there are now, at least, ten thousand horses kept for pleasure-driving." With similar

enthusiasm he noted that Prospect Park dramatically increased carriage ownership and pleasure driving in Brooklyn.[18]

The mid-nineteenth-century mania for carriage driving had multiple sources. On the technological front, improvements in carriage manufacturing produced lighter, faster, and more comfortable vehicles, while McAdam's paving technique made it easier for public authorities to provide the roads to accommodate them. On the social front, the burgeoning ranks of metropolitan bourgeoisie found the proliferation of carriage styles and accoutrements to be an ideal means of displaying their affluence and taste. Park driving also provided opportunities for flirtation and courtship, attractions that were not lost on the purveyors of popular culture. Even for those who could not afford to participate, the colorful display afforded considerable amusement. *Harper's* described the thronged carriage roads of Central Park as "a brilliant and inspiriting spectacle, as seen upon sunny afternoons, when alive with the whirl of a thousand gay and gorgeous carriages, bearing the elite and fashion of the city on their daily airings."[19]

Another indication of the carriage roads' prominence was that park proposals routinely described prospective developments from the perspective of drivers enjoying the primary circuits. Olmsted and Vaux's reports for cities such as New York, Brooklyn, Boston, and Montreal elaborated the proposed drives in considerable detail. Once the parks were completed, guidebook writers took a similar approach, escorting visitors on literary excursions along popular drives. In addition to describing general configurations, Olmsted and Vaux extolled the joys of viewing scenery in motion, suggested strategies to enhance the sensation, and emphasized the role of roads in fulfilling the social and psychological functions of the American public park.[20]

Olmsted maintained that people enjoyed carriage drives not just for the social pleasures and physical enjoyment they provided but because "the eye is gratified at the picture that constantly changes with the movement of the observer."[21] Underscoring his emphasis on the dynamic experience of scenery, he advised that roads be designed "less with a purpose of bringing the visitor to points of view at which he will enjoy set scenes or landscapes than to provide for a constant mild enjoyment of simply pleasing rural scenery while in easy movement."[22] Rather than emphasize discrete views and treat the intervening roads as utilitarian corridors, Olmsted insisted that the entire road network be conceived as a unified work of art in which scenic highlights were presented as "successive incidents of a sustained landscape poem, to each of which the mind is gradually and sweetly led up, and from which it is gradually and sweetly led away, so that they become part of a consistent experience."[23] He maintained that the results were not just more aesthetically pleasing but that the soothing sensation of flowing effortlessly through constantly changing scenery was the most effective means of counteracting the stresses of modern urban life. Since Olmsted considered this therapeutic function to be the primary purpose of public parks, the provision of attractive and compelling roads was one of the park maker's highest priorities.

Olmsted emphasized that park road design required judicious planning, solid engineering, and sophisticated aesthetic sensibilities. At the most basic level, roads needed to be located where they made the most sense, both for circulation and to display scenery to best advantage. The layout should respond to the park's landscape features, whether natural or man-made, and afford a wide range of visual and sensory experiences. Roads should never cut arbitrarily across the terrain or meander excessively for no apparent reason. While they should be constructed to high technical standards, park roads should also harmonize with the surrounding landscape and be as unobtrusive as possible. "Although the drive can hardly be expected in itself to add to the beauty of the scenery," Olmsted observed, "it must always be more or less in view as part of it, and it should therefore be artistically designed so as to interfere as little as possible with the views, and to present at all points agreeable and harmonious lines to the eye."[24]

Olmsted maintained that curvilinear alignments were preferable on practical, aesthetic, and psychological grounds. Long straightaways required expensive and unsightly grading. They also presented extended views of the road ahead instead of breaking it up with well-placed curves. Even worse, straight roads encouraged drivers to travel faster than was desirable or safe. These effects ran counter to the goal of affording relief from the city's artificial geometries and the rushed pace of modern urban life. The preferred solution was to avoid the straight lines and mathematical arcs favored by engineers and lay out roads in serpentine curves of constantly varied radius. Olmsted maintained that fluidly winding alignments acted in a directly remedial way to soothe the overstressed nerves of harried urbanites. Gracefully curving roadways would "suggest and imply leisure, contemplativeness and happy tranquility." Sharp turns, steep grades, blind corners, and rough or muddy pavements were to be avoided so that visitors could enjoy the scenery without worrying about the road ahead. In Central Park and elsewhere, Olmsted and Vaux went to great lengths to provide separate circulation systems for pleasure carriages, equestrians, pedestrians, and ordinary city traffic, further enhancing the safety and appeal of park driving.[25]

Easy grades, long curves, widely separated intersections, and smooth, well-drained road surfaces afforded dramatic contrast to the crowded, dirty, and chaotic streets of nineteenth-century cities. Major roads were generally paved with cobbles, granite blocks, or other materials that could withstand the pounding of heavy teams and wagons but produced an unpleasant ride in the light carriages favored by recreational drivers. Park roads had elaborate drainage systems, sturdy foundations, and smoother and more pliant surfaces that were expensive to construct and maintain but more pleasurable for man and beast. Since parks were considered civic showpieces and benefited from commensurately high budgets, bridge designers were able to go to greater artistic lengths and employ new technologies such as cast iron and reinforced concrete. Official reports and popular imagery celebrated the beauty and diversity of these structures, which ranged from rustic designs in wood and stone to traditional masonry and more modern materials—sometimes all in the same park. This eclecticism accorded with the contemporary enthusiasm for picturesque variety and exemplified the harmonious integration of engineering and aesthetics.

When the two motivations conflicted, Olmsted left no doubt that aesthetics should prevail. In most cases, he maintained, the two were integrally related. Since the goal of park road design was to produce attractively landscaped drives, rigid adherence to engineering standards and short-term savings in construction costs were counterproductive. Approaching road development as "mere engineering" and running roughshod over the terrain to produce straight alignments and steady grades generated unsightly cuts flanked by raw and unstable banks. These scars required extensive remediation, which conventional road builders rarely provided. Nature might eventually lend a helping hand, reseeding vegetation and reestablishing attractive contours, but such crude tactics left a host of practical problems in their wake, from excessive erosion to bare, treeless expanses that were hot in summer and windblown in winter.[26]

The preferred alternative was to develop park roads *"with reference to economy in the ultimate development of resources of poetic charm of scenery."* Olmsted contended that this approach was ultimately more cost-effective, though it required greater sophistication to execute. Careful study could reduce costly and problematic excavations by following the lay of the land. In addition to avoiding "unnecessary violence to nature," minor deviations in grade and alignment interjected pleasing variety and allowed road designers to retain or highlight picturesque features and distinctive views. Where cutting and filling were unavoidable, roadsides could be sculpted to naturalistic profiles, rehabilitated with topsoil, and replanted with appropriate vegetation. The underlying goal was to ensure the resulting roadway blended seamlessly with its surroundings so it seemed to spring organically from natural

BELOW Boston's Riverway, postcard, ca. 1910.

OPPOSITE *The Grand Drive at Central Park*, from *Appletons' Journal*, 1869.

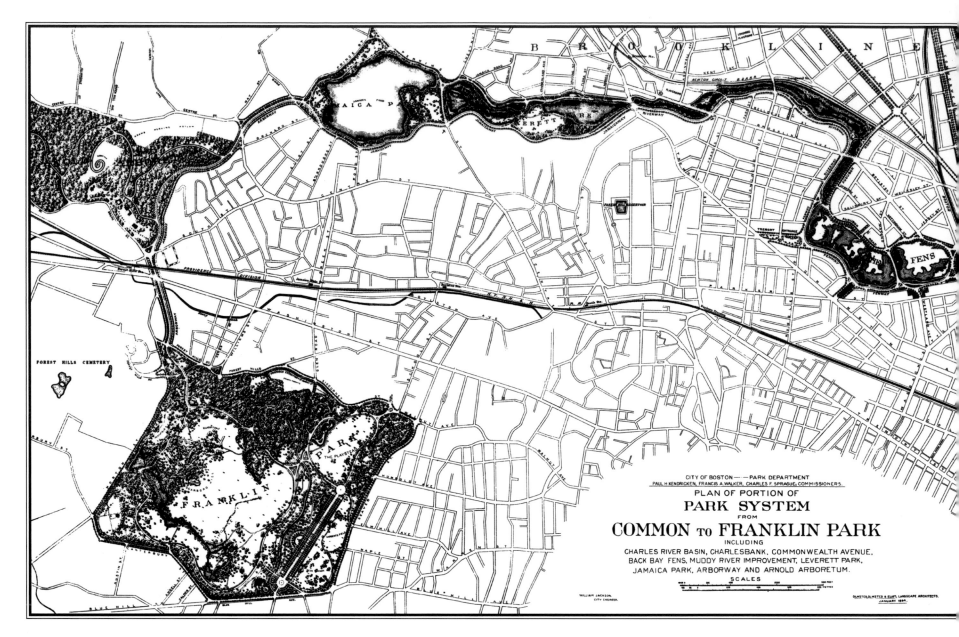

PLAN OF PORTION OF
PARK SYSTEM
FROM
COMMON TO FRANKLIN PARK
INCLUDING
CHARLES RIVER BASIN, CHARLESBANK, COMMONWEALTH AVENUE,
BACK BAY FENS, MUDDY RIVER IMPROVEMENT, LEVERETT PARK,
JAMAICA PARK, ARBORWAY AND ARNOLD ARBORETUM.
SCALES

WILLIAM JACKSON
CITY ENGINEER.

OLMSTED, OLMSTED & ELIOT, LANDSCAPE ARCHITECTS.
JANUARY 1894.

processes rather than stand out as a heavy-handed imposition of technological prowess. Since designers could augment or highlight existing attractions while downplaying deficiencies, an artistically designed park road was not only less destructive than utilitarian engineering but more appealing than unadulterated nature. Olmsted did not invent these strategies, inheriting and adapting them from predecessors such as Repton, Downing, Gilpin, and Price, but his celebrated designs and compelling writings established an American tradition of park road development that remained a dominant influence well into the twentieth century.[27]

Olmsted and Vaux also built on European precedents to develop landscaped roadways that provided access to parks and linked multiple parks to form far-reaching park systems. By surrounding the main drive with parkland and restricting traffic to pleasure vehicles, these "park-ways" freed recreational drivers from the dangers and disruptions of ordinary city streets. Stylistically, parkways could resemble conventional formal avenues or elongated parks. Most were developed as integral components of broader park systems. Their status as park reservations rather than public streets made it possible to prohibit commercial traffic and limit access to select intersections.[28]

Olmsted and Vaux first used the term "parkway" in their 1860s proposals for Brooklyn's Prospect Park. To distinguish the two major approach roads from ordinary streets, Olmsted and Vaux emphasized that they were "designed with express reference to the pleasure with which they may be used for walking, riding, and the driving of carriages; for rest, recreation, refreshment, and social intercourse." Designated Eastern and Ocean Parkway, they were 260 feet wide with a central pleasure drive flanked by park strips containing rows of trees and parallel pedestrian walkways. Service roads on either side accommodated local traffic and utilitarian vehicles.[29] Olmsted and Vaux also called for an informal carriage drive winding through Brooklyn, Queens, and Upper Manhattan to Central Park. "Such an arrangement," they claimed, "would enable a carriage to be driven on the half of a summer's day, through the most interesting parts both of the cities of Brooklyn and New York, through their most attractive and characteristic suburbs, and through their great parks."[30] The Brooklyn proposals generated considerable attention, but funding problems delayed completion. The two parkways were constructed,

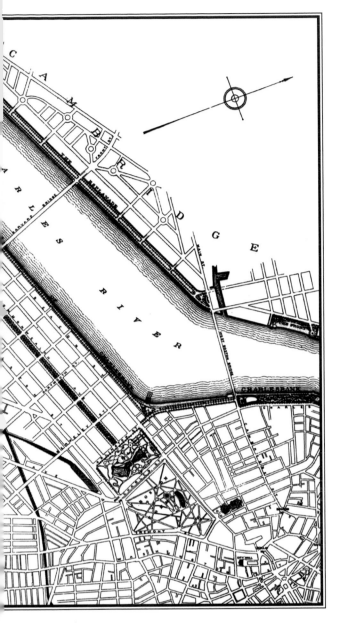

LEFT Olmsted, Olmsted, and Eliot, Landscape Architects, *Plan of Portion of Boston Park System*, 1894.

Rather than emphasize discrete views and treat the intervening roads as utilitarian corridors, Olmsted insisted that the entire road network be conceived as a unified work of art.

but the more roundabout route dropped out of the program. Formal parkways played a prominent role in the partners' plans for Buffalo. Several broad parkways linked widely placed parks, providing relaxing drives and serving as amenities for the neighborhoods along their routes.[31]

After breaking with Vaux in 1872, Olmsted developed park and parkway plans for Boston and other municipalities, bringing his stepson John C. Olmsted and son Frederick Law Olmsted Jr. into business with him. The Boston developments represented the next major step in the evolution of parkway design. When Olmsted designed what is now commonly known as the Emerald Necklace along Boston's Muddy River, he reproduced the pastoral effects of his larger reservations, creating a linear park with a carriage drive as its unifying feature. The streamside location limited the

number of cross streets, while the broader width and informal landscape treatment provided a greater sense of separation from the surrounding city.[32] Naturalistic parkways quickly became popular, but formal parkways remained in favor, especially in more densely developed areas. Charles Eliot's 1893 proposal for the Boston metropolitan region employed a mixture of formal and informal parkways, as did the Senate Park Commission's 1901 plan for Washington, D.C. By the turn of the twentieth century, virtually every major American city either possessed an elaborate system of parks and parkways or was in the process of developing one. The popularity of park systems testified to the continued belief that exposure to naturalistic surroundings afforded essential relief from the stresses of modern urban life, while the proliferation of park roads and parkways underscored the association between parks and pleasure driving. Lofty rhetoric aside, the bustling drives thronged with gay carriages may have exerted more popular appeal than the contemplation of scenic compositions.[33]

AMERICAN SCENERY AND THE RISE OF TOURISM

Another, less widely recognized influence on national park road development was the relationship between the rise of scenic tourism and evolving transportation improvements. Few Americans expressed interest in scenic tourism

during the colonial era or early decades of the new republic. Given the primitive state of the nation's transportation network, the term "pleasure travel" would have struck most observers as an oxymoron. Nature was not seen as an aesthetic or recreational resource but as a commodity to be exploited or obstacle to overcome. These perceptions began to change around the turn of the nineteenth century, when European intellectual currents combined with attempts to forge a uniquely American national identity to foster more positive perceptions of the natural environment. The growing economy also created a middle class with the means and inclination to enjoy leisure travel, while advances in transportation technology both improved comfort and expanded the range of potential tourist destinations.[34]

Toward the end of the eighteenth century, scientists and men of letters began to color their accounts of American nature with sentiments that reflected the appreciation for wild and rugged scenery inspired by British aestheticians such as William Gilpin and Edmund Burke. By developing elaborate theoretical precepts about scenery's impact on the human mind, Burke, Gilpin, and their followers created frameworks for appreciating nature in aesthetic and emotional terms. The pursuit of such experiences—and the landscapes that engendered them—played an important role in the development of scenic tourism, first in England and Europe, and then in the United States. Burke was best known for differentiating between the beautiful and the sublime. Beautiful landscapes were smooth, delicate, harmoniously proportioned, and pleasing in a calm, relaxing manner. Well-tended fields, rolling lawns, and gracefully balanced compositions exemplified the concept, which was rooted in aesthetic discourse dating back to Plato and Aristotle. Part of the pleasure in experiencing the beautiful stemmed from the intellectual act of discerning it and relating it to classical precepts. The sublime transcended such rational engagement, impacting the senses directly and engendering awe, terror, excitement, and delight. The catalyst for these extreme emotions was the sort of scenery that had previously been considered unappealing, worthless, or even dangerous: mountains, chasms, cataracts, and other scenes that made the viewer feel small, insignificant, and imperiled. With its emphasis on emotional impact, the sublime was the embodiment of Romantic ideals.[35]

Occupying a middle ground between the serenity of the beautiful and the shock of the sublime, the picturesque was characterized by irregular forms and lively variations in light, line, and texture. As defined by Gilpin in his 1768 essay "On Prints," picturesque landscapes recalled the paintings of seventeenth-century masters such as Claude Lorrain, with dark foregrounds and flanking vegetation framing golden-hued middle-distance scenes backed by layers of hills and vegetation receding into the distance. While Great Britain was not overly endowed with manifestations of the sublime, picturesque landscapes could be found in the Lake District and other regions that were becoming accessible through improvements in transportation. Gilpin's accounts of his travels through these areas provided inspiration and instruction for those who wanted to follow in his footsteps. The penchant for picturesque tourism became even stronger with the publication of Uvedale Price's *Essays on the Picturesque* in 1794, which elaborated on the visual qualities of the genre and provided additional guidance for aspiring aesthetes.[36]

Armed with Gilpin, Price, and a rapidly growing array of guidebooks by lesser writers, well-heeled tourists literally took to the hills, exploring the British countryside in pursuit of landscapes exhibiting the desired characteristics. The ability to identify appropriate scenes and extemporize on their attributes was considered a mark of sophistication and social attainment. Well-bred ladies and gentlemen—and those who aspired to be taken for well-bred ladies and gentlemen—traveled from one sanctioned scene to another, rhapsodizing on the sights they encountered and committing their observations to paper in sketches, poetry, and prose. A tourist-oriented infrastructure soon developed, with improved roads, inns, and other accommodations. The popularity of picturesque tourism attracted growing crowds, many of whom were less concerned with scenic contemplation than with the associated social interactions. The fad was sufficiently widespread by the end of the eighteenth century to generate satirical commentary from those who decried the popularization of the practice and the pretensions of its acolytes.

A similar progression occurred in America, with the articulation of landscape values by a literary and artistic elite, leading to upper-class acceptance, the development of a tourist-related infrastructure, and increasingly broad-based participation. A few well-educated Americans such as Thomas Jefferson, the naturalist William Bartram, and Yale University president Timothy Dwight began to employ the new modes of landscape appreciation around the turn of the nineteenth century, along with an occasional painter or engraver. The scenic tourism phenomenon did not really take off until the 1820s, when writers and artists began to celebrate eastern landscapes and improvements in transportation combined with the growth of a moneyed class made leisure travel physically possible, financially viable, and socially desirable.[37]

Painters and poets led the way. In 1804, Alexander Wilson recounted his journey to Niagara Falls in an epic poem published to considerable acclaim. Commencing with an exhortation for the "sons of the city" to join him in roaming America's hinterlands in search of "scenes sublime," Wilson lamented the lack of poetic attention to America's vast and varied landscape, a shortcoming he attempted to rectify with more than two thousand lines of verse. The language of the sublime suffused his accounts of towering mountains, foaming torrents, and thundering cataracts. None was more magnificent than Niagara, whose "wild tumults" and "awful grandeur" elicited a "flood of rapture" and "holy awe." Wilson's enthusiasm for sublime scenery was tempered with pragmatism. Much of the poem, including its title, "The Foresters," was devoted to those whose lonely exertions subdued the American wilderness.[38]

The poetic embrace of nature reached greater heights with the 1817 publication of William Cullen Bryant's "Thanatopsis." The poem's paean to the uplifting effects of nature's beauty epitomized evolving attitudes. Along with subsequent offerings such as "Green River" and "A Forest Hymn," the poem established Bryant as the leading apostle of nature's beneficent impact on humans in general and Americans in particular. Poems, travel

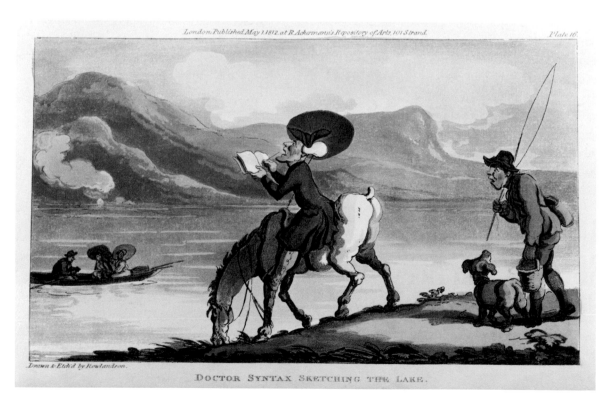

ABOVE Thomas Rowlandson, *Doctor Syntax Sketching the Lake,* 1809.

ABOVE Alvan Fisher, *Niagara: The American Falls,* ca. 1821.

accounts, and fictional vignettes proliferated in the popular periodicals that played an increasingly important role in shaping middle-class American tastes. Notable authors such as James Fenimore Cooper, Washington Irving, and Nathanial Hawthorne fueled the enthusiasm for American scenery by locating their stories in impressive natural settings such as the Hudson River Valley, Catskills, and White Mountains, bolstering these places' appeal by instilling a sense of romance and human interest, which critics contended were absent from America's primeval landscape.[39]

Painters both contributed to and capitalized on this interest. Although a few artists ventured forth around the turn of the century, landscape painting rose to prominence in the 1820s with the flourishing of what came to be known as

the Hudson River School. Thomas Cole, who emigrated from England in 1818, was the central figure in this movement. Cole spent several years exploring and sketching, producing little of note until he traveled up the Hudson River to New York's Catskill Mountains. Cole created a series of paintings that attracted considerable attention when they were displayed in 1825. Flushed with success and backed by prominent patrons, Cole made numerous return trips, producing paintings that, like Gilpin's writings, both taught people how to appreciate natural scenery and helped establish a vibrant culture of scenic tourism. Cole's popularity prompted other painters such as Asher Durand, Thomas Doughty, and Sanford Gifford to turn their attention to the region. Soon galleries, drawing rooms, and popular publications

abounded with paintings and engravings of the Hudson River, Catskills, and related scenes. Cole ventured farther afield, creating iconic images of Massachusetts's Mount Holyoke, New Hampshire's Mount Chocorua, and Maine's Mount Desert Island. Others followed, ranging throughout the Northeast before turning their attention to the Rockies and Sierras. By the mid-nineteenth century, commentators insisted that the American landscape was not just a source of aesthetic contemplation but an emblem of national identity. Poets, painters, politicians, and popular writers maintained that America's scenic grandeur confirmed the claim that the nation was divinely blessed and that the landscape's unsullied status afforded unmitigated access to the creator's glory. Given the popular belief that

while roaming the deck of a packet boat was a revelation. Rather than capture fleeting glimpses out a stagecoach window, tourists could enjoy sweeping views of passing scenery as it unfolded at the leisurely rate of 4 mph. For first-time travelers, the canal boat experience could be as entertaining as the scenery itself. An Erie Canal guidebook observed, "Of the sources of gratification to the tourist, during the canal passage, that of novelty is perhaps the greatest."[42] Theodore Dwight proclaimed, "The opportunity for looking around on every side is much better enjoyed in a Canal boat than in a stage coach, or even a private carriage." Meandering roads might afford more diverse views, but Dwight contended that canal boats produced more attractive prospects, since "a smooth sheet of water, with level and often grassy banks, is a more pleasant sight than a long stretch of muddy or sandy highway." Dwight added that the canal trip was "always free from the inconveniences of dust, which frequently render the roads in this part of the country extremely uncomfortable."[43]

Canal travel had its drawbacks. Ease of construction and economy of operation determined its location, so the alignment lacked the picturesque variety of park drives. Canal scenery was not always engaging, and some attractions required side trips by foot, horseback, or stage. The plodding pace was another complaint. Gazing at slowly passing scenery grew wearisome over the multiday excursion, especially in the western sections where the landscape was more monotonous. Although it made Niagara accessible to multitudes who would never have contemplated the trip, the Erie Canal's heyday as a tourist conveyance was relatively brief. Railroads began operating along the Hudson River Valley in the 1830s and reached Buffalo in 1842. Embracing the new technology, most tourists opted for speed and convenience over leisurely contemplation.[44]

Steamboats combined the ease and viewing opportunities of canal travel with the ability to move through the landscape at unprecedented speeds. Commentators extolled the novelty of the experience, which some writers cast as more compelling than the scenery itself. Davison's *The Fashionable Tour in 1825* exemplified the tendency to relegate landscapes to second place, observing: "Besides the novelty of a steam-boat passage, the Hudson river presents to the tourist a variety of natural scenery which it will be difficult to find

America was "nature's nation" and that nature was scripture written in stones and brooks, viewing natural landscapes in person, in paintings, or in the prints that adorned middle-class parlors was held to be both a religious act and a patriotic duty.[40]

The extent to which these lofty sentiments permeated American society is open to debate, but by the second quarter of the nineteenth century, scenic tourism had become an increasingly popular recreational pursuit, social activity, and commercial enterprise. The cultural incentives articulated by writers and artists combined with improvements in transportation and increases in wealth and leisure to unleash a tide of vacationers, who swept up the Hudson River and westward to Niagara or north toward New Hampshire's White Mountains in search of picturesque scenery, social stimulation, and relief from cities that were becoming increasingly crowded and unhealthy. Guidebooks and illustrated tomes such as N. P. Willis's *American Scenery* and Gideon Davison's *The Fashionable Tour* provided inspiration along with information on where to go, what to see, and how to see it.[41]

The poetic and painterly celebration of American nature played a vital role in motivating tourists and teaching them how to respond to natural scenery, but the explosion of picturesque

tourism was equally indebted to the revolution in transportation that transformed American lives and landscapes during the nineteenth century. The development of canals, steamboats, and railroads changed both what people could see and the way they saw it. The artistic discovery of Hudson River scenery coincided with region's increased accessibility by steamboat. Cole and other painters readily availed themselves of the new technology to gain access to scenic wonders. Likewise, the completion of the Erie Canal in 1825 dramatically eased the trip to Niagara Falls while calling attention to additional features along the way. Steamboats opened up the beauties of Lake George and Lake Champlain, with Montreal and Quebec City enticing travelers farther north. Early tourists were forced to endure grueling stage rides to reach New Hampshire's Lake Region and White Mountains, but the extension of railroad lines made these areas increasingly accessible.

Travel writers extolled the improvements in transportation. The savings in time and expense were highlighted, but writers ascribed additional benefits to new means of locomotion. For those accustomed to jolting down rutted, dusty, or muddy roads in the cramped confines of an uncomfortable stagecoach, the experience of gliding effortlessly along a smooth canal elsewhere in a journey of the same extent."[45] Even when steamboats became more commonplace, writers enthused about the exhilarating rate of travel, transferring language of the sublime from the surrounding crags to the machines that brought them into view. In his 1843 travelogue, tellingly titled *A Gallop among American Scenery*, Augustus Silliman extolled the "racehorse swiftness" with which the boats ascended the Hudson. Enraptured by the "Steam Spirit . . . dragging us onward with frantic swiftness," Silliman narrated a fast-paced journey from the bustling docks of New York City through the Hudson River Valley and on to the beauties of Lake George. Demonstrating that hasty sightseeing predated the automobile age, Silliman punctuated his remarks on scenery with exclamations such as "now again we rush onward in our swift career."[46]

The steamboat and, to a somewhat lesser degree, canal boat transformed not just the speed at which tourists traveled but the manner in which they experienced landscapes, broadening the appreciation for scenery in motion previously restricted to elite carriage occupants. "Nature seems in merry motion hurrying by," a typical account proclaimed, "and as she moves along displays a thousand varied charms in rapid succession, each one more enchanting than the rest." Travelers emphasized the manner in which objects appeared, passed alongside, and disappeared from view. In this respect, steamboats resembled the moving panoramas that constituted one of the era's most popular entertainments. Embraced by sophisticates and general audiences alike, panoramas were elongated landscape paintings rendered on rolls of canvas that often extended for hundreds of yards. Godfrey Frankenstein's 1853 depiction of Niagara Falls measured 1,000 feet, and John Banvard's Mississippi River panorama stretched a full 3 miles. Panoramas were sometimes arranged around the perimeter of rooms, in which

BELOW Currier & Ives, *American Steamboats on the Hudson*, 1874.

OPPOSITE George Harvey, *Pittsford on the Erie Canal*, 1837.

CATSKILL MOUNTAIN-HOUSE
A Celebrated Summer Hotel about 12 miles S.W. of the Village of Catskill Greene C.N. York.
Stands on a rock near 3000 feet above the level of the Hudson River.

Printed by J.Harris Jr.   *Drawn Engraved & Publd by J.R. Smith, Philada. June 21, 1830.*

ABOVE John Rubens Smith, *Catskill Mountain House*, 1830.

OPPOSITE Mount Washington Cog Railway souvenir spoon, late nineteenth century.

Describing an 1840s Hudson River excursion, N. P. Willis observed: "I commenced dividing my attention in my usual quiet way between the varied panorama of rock and valley flying backward in our progress, and the as varied multitude about me."[47]

Willis's remark underscored the transformation of tourism from rarified adventure to fashionable pursuit. The relative ease and affordability of steamboat travel changed the size and composition of the traveling public. As early as 1828, the satirist James Kirk Paulding observed, "The wonderful facilities for locomotion furnished by modern ingenuity have increased the number of travellers to such a degree, that they now constitute a large portion of the human family." According to Paulding, scenic tourism had become "the most exquisite mode of killing time and spending money ever yet devised by lazy ingenuity."[48] Not only were the standard itineraries increasingly crowded, but the broadening ranks of tourists expressed little interest in traditional modes of landscape appreciation. Erudition aside, the new technology was ill-suited to extended contemplation. The scenery passed by too quickly for travelers to engage in complex analysis. The more sophisticated might seek out classic compositions upon arriving at their destinations, but less cerebral tourists could enjoy the simpler pleasures of social intercourse and constantly changing scenery without recourse to Gilpin, Burke, and their American acolytes.

Sightseeing remained the stated goal of most excursions, but travel to scenic regions afforded myriad attractions. Resorts such as Ballston Spa and Saratoga Springs in New York were famed for the medicinal qualities of their waters. Their pavilions and bathhouses were surrounded by increasingly elaborate hotels housing hundreds of guests. Many visitors were motivated by the desire to escape sweltering cities and socialize with their peers. Grand hotels afforded opportunities to enjoy the same amusements they participated in at home, with rooms for billiards and dancing, along with spacious verandas and manicured walks for promenading. Carriages were available for hire, either with or without drivers, further encouraging visitors to transplant their urban rituals. Courting was one of the principal activities, at least among the younger set. Carriage excursions along country lanes provided the same opportunities for loosely supervised outings that park driving afforded in urban areas. Popular writers highlighted this

case they were called cycloramas, but the most common strategy was to unfurl them across a stage so audiences experienced the sensation of viewing a landscape in motion—exactly as if they were enjoying the view from a steamboat. Travel writers made explicit comparisons. Silliman launched one of his vignettes with the exclamation, "Lo! as we slide along, what moving panorama presents itself!"

correlation, utilizing a White Mountain stage ride as a setting for romance and employing a summer coaching excursion to rekindle a romance initiated on Fairmount Park's pleasure drives.[49]

Entrepreneurs capitalized on the desire for driving opportunities by constructing carriage roads to picturesque locations. Refreshment shacks and even full-service hotels were often developed in tandem. The most famous of these was the Catskill Mountain House. This establishment was one of the most popular destinations on the Hudson River and provided an ideal base for travelers intent on viewing the scenery made famous by Thomas Cole and other painters. The 1824 structure acquired an impressive Greek Revival portico in 1832, eventually expanding to accommodate as many as five hundred tourists, who enjoyed extravagant meals and appointments that impressed both foreign and domestic commentators. Visitors could take a twice-daily stage that climbed 1,400 feet from the steamboat landing along a rugged, winding course that observers characterized as both titillating and terrifying. Few roads in America afforded such stunning views or dramatic encounters with the visceral emotions of the sublime. John Rubens Smith's 1830 print portrayed a stagecoach teetering precariously close to the edge on an implausibly steep ascent. Davison's *The Fashionable Tour* warned travelers that the road's upper portion "often passes on the brink of some deep ravine, or at the foot of some frowning precipice, inspiring at times, an unwelcome degree of terror."[50]

Mount Holyoke, rising above the Connecticut River in western Massachusetts, was another destination rendered accessible by commercially constructed carriage drives. The road was completed in 1821 and soon attracted thousands of travelers a year. Other toll roads lured visitors to lesser Massachusetts summits such as Mount Tom and Mount Wachusett. Visitors to Vermont's Mount Mansfield could avail themselves of a carriage road leading to a three-hundred-room hotel. More modest accommodations beckoned visitors to Mount Equinox, where coaches plied another tourist-oriented private roadway. Considerable fanfare greeted the construction of roads up New Hampshire's Mount Moosilauke and Mount Kearsarge in the 1870s.[51]

While stagecoach travel lacked the novelty of canal or steamboat passage, it remained the primary means of accessing many regions. The association between White Mountain tourism and stagecoach travel was particularly strong. Silliman vividly evoked the sights, sounds, and sensations of a stagecoach jaunt through northern New Hampshire. Given his penchant for speed, he was especially impressed by the rate at which the horses pulled heavily loaded coaches along primitive roads. "We speed over hill, over dale, over mountain, over valley," he enthused, "ascending and descending the mountains in full run."[52] In good weather, tourists vied for the top seats to enjoy the passing scenery. The extension of railroad service made scenic regions more accessible, but travelers generally switched to stagecoaches for the final leg of the journey or to access more remote and rugged scenery. Some writers highlighted the contrast and extolled the experience of coaching through compelling landscapes. "To how many wearied travellers the delightful experience of a stage-ride has come with swift relief, after the noise and clatter of a long railway journey!" exclaimed one guidebook. "Who that has ever taken it can ever forget the delicious coolness of the mountain breezes, the exhilarating motion, the full enjoyment of an ever-shifting panorama of lofty peaks that each turn in the road is constantly bringing into view?"[53]

No road in the East garnered more attention or inspired more striking visual imagery than the Mount Washington Carriage Road. The legendary innkeeper and guide Ethan Allen Crawford had constructed a rough bridle path to the summit of New England's highest peak in 1819. This remained a popular, if arduous and time-consuming excursion throughout the nineteenth century. Recognizing that most visitors were unwilling to subject themselves to the rigors of horseback ascents, in 1853 the State of New Hampshire chartered the Mount Washington Carriage Road Company to construct an easier route to the summit. The agreement specified that the road was to be 16 feet wide, macadamized, and equipped with protective stone walls in dangerous places. Engineers surveyed a winding alignment that looped for 8 miles up the eastern slope of the mountain, climbing 4,600 feet at a relatively gentle 7.5 percent grade, with a few steep sections rising to 16 percent. Construction began in 1855. The road was completed and opened for travel in August 1861. Stagecoaches carried day tourists and visitors willing to spend the night in two small and spartan hotels. The road's winding course

"Nature seems in merry motion hurrying by, and as she moves along displays a thousand varied charms in rapid succession, each one more enchanting than the rest."

A TYPICAL ACCOUNT OF STEAMBOAT TRAVEL

National Park Roads

afforded constantly varying views that became increasingly thrilling as tourists climbed higher, skirting the massive ravines that cut into the mountain's flanks. Guidebook writers described the changing scenery and praised the road as an engineering marvel that bore "eloquent witness to the enterprise, courage and persistence of its projector and builders." The period's preeminent compilation of scenic views, William Cullen Bryant's *Picturesque America*, devoted one of its limited steel engravings to the celebrated ascent, dramatically increasing its steepness to suffuse the scene with sublime grandeur.[54] The road was also a popular subject for stereopticon views that exploited the three-dimensional qualities of the medium to emphasize the serpentine curves and dizzying depths.

The Mount Washington Carriage Road captured the public's fancy and markedly increased traffic to the summit, but it was soon eclipsed by an even bolder and more technically impressive means of ascent. Chartered in 1858 and completed ten years later, the Mount Washington Cog Railway brought passengers to the summit by means of a steam locomotive that turned a wheel outfitted with sturdy teeth designed to grasp a specially configured track. This was the first passenger railway of its type in the world and created an international sensation. President Ulysses S. Grant brought his family to inaugurate the service and contemporary sources hailed it as one of America's most remarkable engineering achievements. Soon hundreds of passengers per day were chugging up and down the mountain, drawn as much by the novelty of the experience as the lure of the surrounding scenery. As a union of the natural and technological sublime, the Mount Washington Cog Railway had few equals. Written accounts detailed both aspects, while visual representations emphasized the technological side, celebrating spectacular engineering features such as "Jacob's Ladder," a steeply inclined trestle that was one of the highlights of the trip. The construction of a railroad through neighboring Crawford Notch in 1875 drew similar acclaim, both for the technical feat of conquering what had long been considered an impenetrable mountain pass and for the stunning visual impressions created by towering trestles carrying passengers between vertiginous cliffs. Both the Cog Railway and the Crawford Notch railroad were memorialized in a wide range of tourist-oriented merchandise from postcards and stereopticon views to Dresden china plates and other souvenirs.[55]

The attention showered on the Mount Washington Carriage Road and Cog Railway exemplified the manner in which nineteenth-century Americans celebrated natural scenery and the means of accessing it. This broader perspective has been obscured by the tendency of historians to focus on prominent writers and artists. Elite interpreters preferred to portray American scenery as a primeval wilderness or idealized pastoral landscape unencumbered by the tourist culture that was transforming it. Popular imagery, on the other hand, celebrated the tourist experience and lavished attention on the means of transportation. While Hudson River School painters depicted depopulated scenes or paid homage to Native Americans and solitary pioneers, popular lithographers such as Currier and Ives enlivened the river with bustling steamboats and devoted entire prints to well-known vessels. Emerson, Thoreau, and their chroniclers might lament the machine's intrusion in the New World garden, but popular illustrators celebrated the contrast between nature and technology, producing striking scenes of bridges spanning mighty chasms and railroads conquering forbidding terrain. Less sublime spectacles were commemorated in photographs, stereopticon views, woodcuts, engravings, and color lithographs. More often than not, such scenes featured tourists themselves, enjoying the scenery, the modes of transportation, and the social pleasures of the tourist experience. It should come as no surprise that when the locus of attention moved westward, travelers sought to transplant these experiences to the scenic wonderlands of the American West.

The attention showered on the Mount Washington Carriage Road and Cog Railway exemplified the manner in which nineteenth-century Americans celebrated natural scenery and the means of accessing it.

OPPOSITE *The Mount Washington Road,* from William Cullen Bryant, *Picturesque America* (1872).

Touring America's Wonderlands

CHAPTER TWO

During the second half of the nineteenth century, the United States did something no nation had ever attempted, setting aside vast tracts of land, far distant from major population centers, as public reserves for the protection and enjoyment of natural beauty. The creation of these first national parks was an extension of the ideas about the social, moral, and economic value of natural scenery that prompted the rise of urban parks and scenic tourism. Similar aesthetic principles, social concerns, and pragmatic factors shaped the ways in which the first national parks were developed and experienced. The earliest areas to be set aside reflected the ongoing allure of sublime scenery and natural curiosities, as epitomized by Yosemite's towering cliffs and Yellowstone's thermal features. By the turn of the century, Sequoia and General Grant National Parks protected towering trees and additional expanses of Sierra scenery. Mount Rainier brought the national park idea to the Pacific Northwest, to be followed soon after the turn of the century by the establishment of Oregon's Crater Lake National Park.

As with the development of eastern tourism, artists and writers helped shape public opinion, appealing to national pride, the reverence for nature and appreciation of scenic beauty, and the desire for distinctive experiences and social exclusivity, which many felt were disappearing from overly popularized eastern resorts. As in the East, broader social developments and advances in transportation played important roles. The Gold Rush brought a growing population to California. Railroad construction stimulated interest in Denver and other Front Range cities, both as mercantile centers and destinations for easterners attracted by the healthful climate and scenic splendors. The alpine majesties of the Rocky Mountains were celebrated by a new generation of artists such as Albert Bierstadt, whose *Rocky Mountains, Lander's Peak* created a sensation when it was exhibited in 1864. Depictions of Yellowstone's wonders by artists such as Thomas Moran and William H. Jackson aroused public interest and provided support for the drive to create the world's first national park. The rise of photography and proliferation of affordable reproductions introduced an expanding audience to the allure of western scenery. Together with traveler's accounts and promotional efforts by railroads and civic boosters, these images bolstered the perception that American nature put Old World landscapes to shame, fueling the feeling that the United States was a uniquely favored nation. As scenic tourism spread from northeastern resorts to the virgin land of the American West, it resonated even more strongly as an expression of cultural unity and national pride. In the contentious period before, during, and after the Civil War, western nature afforded a culturally and geographically neutral symbol of America's manifest destiny.[1]

The completion of the first transcontinental railroad in 1869 prompted a dramatic increase in western tourism, though the cost of the journey was beyond the means of most Americans. The development of regional spurs and northern and southern transcontinental lines brought additional attractions within reach of the traveling public. As in the East, commercial motivations were entwined with elevated appeals to aesthetics, patriotism, and the public interest. Railroads viewed the tourist trade as a highly profitable enterprise and played influential roles in national park development, bankrolling writers and artists, underwriting promotional efforts, and exerting political pressure to advance legislation. Railroads often had stakes in the provision of lodging and local transportation, either directly or through shadow companies headed by nominally independent operators.

PREVIOUS Thomas Hill, *View of Yosemite Valley*, 1865.

As soon as these parks were created—and, in some cases, even before—visitors clamored for improvements to make their wonders accessible. Praise for magnificent scenery was tempered by complaints about the obstacles posed by harrowing trails and rough or nonexistent wagon roads. Exasperated visitors expressed outrage at the primitive conditions. Since these reservations had been set aside "for public use, resort and recreation," as Yosemite's enabling legislation decreed, the lack of access elicited accusations that park authorities were not fulfilling their duties. While early travelers did not expect to find elegant hotels and refined carriage roads, they sought relatively civilized accommodations and expected to reach key destinations by stagecoach rather than on foot or horseback.

Progress came slowly, hampered by meager funding, challenging conditions, and primitive technology. Since the National Park Service did not exist as a distinct agency until 1916, the first national park roads were constructed by private entrepreneurs and the U.S. Army Corps of Engineers. Some road builders tried to incorporate aesthetic concerns, but tight budgets and the difficulties of construction in remote mountainous terrain necessitated a pragmatic focus. Crude and dangerous pack trails slowly gave way to primitive dirt roads. Construction crews labored with picks, shovels, and horse-drawn equipment to carve rudimentary roadbeds out of steep mountainsides. Black powder was used to blast away the worst obstacles, but road builders followed the dictates of the terrain, zigzagging up treacherous slopes with dramatic switchbacks and hazardous hairpin turns. Dirt or gravel surfaces produced choking clouds of dust under the pounding of hooves and heavy stagecoaches and degenerated into mud wallows during periods of heavy rain.

Despite trying conditions, slim resources, and primitive equipment, park road builders accomplished impressive feats. In Yellowstone, the Army Corps of Engineers constructed several entrance roads and completed a circuit linking the park's major features. Between 1883 and 1905, the engineers built or improved approximately 300 miles of roadway along with several major bridges, contending with narrow canyons, precipitous mountain passes, troublesome swamps, and treacherous thermal formations. In Yosemite, which was initially administered by the State of California, private toll road companies provided the first vehicular access. During the 1870s, rival

concerns from outlying communities constructed stage roads that replaced the hazardous trails leading to the valley floor. At Mount Rainier, the Army Corps of Engineers built the Nisqually Road between 1901 and 1910, upgrading an existing private toll route and extending it to the alluring meadows of Paradise Valley. The Corps also constructed some of the first roads at Crater Lake National Park and eventually assumed control of road building in Yosemite Valley. Not only did these roads provide access to America's western wonderlands, but they established precedents for the development, use, and public perception of national parks that influenced National Park Service policies throughout the twentieth century and continue to resonate today.

YOSEMITE

The majestic valley we know as Yosemite was first glimpsed by European Americans in 1833, when a party of mountain men came upon the virtually impassable north rim. Focused on tangible rewards rather than scenic diversions, the group pressed on, and their encounter was more or less forgotten. It was not until 1851, when a company of militia entered the valley in search of purportedly hostile Indians, that reports of a hidden canyon ringed by spectacular cliffs and waterfalls began to circulate. Subsequent expeditions eliminated the Indian threat and produced additional accounts of the region's scenic splendors.[2]

Intrigued by these reports, a San Francisco–based promoter named James Hutchings set out to gather information for a publication touting California's scenic attractions. In July 1855 Hutchings and several associates, including the artist Thomas Ayres, became the first group to enter the valley with the express intention of enjoying—and exploiting—Yosemite's scenery. The party went by steamboat from San Francisco to Stockton, traveled by stage to Mariposa, and followed a trail pointed out by Native American guides. Hutchings's account exemplified the manner in which the conventions of picturesque tourism were transferred to America's western wonders. Hutchings claimed that when the party first glimpsed the valley, they became "almost speechless with wondering admiration at its wild and sublime grandeur." The party spent several

days reconnoitering while Ayres produced renderings of Yosemite's towering cliffs and mighty cataracts. Hutchings's rhapsodic account was reprinted in newspapers across the county. He also extolled the valley's grandeur in *Hutchings' California Magazine* and produced a guidebook, *Scenes of Wonder and Curiosity in California*. Hutchings's writing, engravings based on Ayres's drawings, and Charles Weed's photographs bolstered Yosemite's reputation and established an itinerary of iconic views. Hutchings lectured widely about the valley's attractions and took an active role in the tourism industry, organizing excursions and operating a succession of hotels and related enterprises, where, at one point, he employed a young Scottish immigrant named John Muir. Ironically, or perhaps fittingly, Hutchings died in a carriage accident on the way into the valley in October 1902.[3]

Hutchings's accounts attracted eastern visitors, who helped spread the word of Yosemite's wonders. In 1859 the journalist Horace Greeley lauded the valley's attractions in his widely read *New York Tribune*. A year later, the effusive accounts of Thomas Starr King, a popular writer on eastern scenery, appeared in the *Boston Evening Transcript*. In addition to employing the traditional rhetoric of the sublime and picturesque, both King and Greeley appealed to national pride. Not only did Yosemite's cliffs and cataracts dwarf European counterparts, but the immense age of the giant sequoias countered criticisms that America lacked the associations with antiquity that ostensibly infused Old World landscapes with superior merit. Illustrated periodicals, stereoscopic slides, and dramatic canvases by painters such as Thomas Hill and Albert Bierstadt helped establish Yosemite's status as a national icon rivaling and perhaps even surpassing Niagara Falls.

Despite its remote location, Yosemite quickly gained fame as a tourist destination, at least for the favored few who could afford such excursions. By the early 1860s, a trip to the valley and nearby groves of giant sequoias was de rigueur for wealthy San Franciscans and the steadily increasing stream of eastern tourists who ventured west by steamship, sail, rail, and stagecoach. Yosemite's growing fame made an impression on many people, including Israel Ward Raymond, a representative of the Central American Steamship Transit Company. In February 1864 Raymond wrote to California senator John Conness suggesting that Yosemite Valley and the Mariposa Big Tree Grove be set aside a public reservation. The value of this proposal to Raymond's employers was readily apparent, but the idea exerted broader appeal as a means of preventing the proliferation of tawdry developments that had sullied Niagara Falls, America's first great natural attraction. The transformation of Niagara from an isolated outpost of scenic grandeur to a teeming resort overrun with commercial enterprises demonstrated the dangers of unrestrained development. The desire to prevent Yosemite's scenic treasures from suffering a similar fate was shared by a wide range of individuals including idealistic reformers and aesthetes, travelers seeking sanctuary from the crowds that had begun to overrun more accessible resorts, and private entrepreneurs, who recognized that protecting the valley from overdevelopment afforded better assurance of long-term profitability than unfettered exploitation.

While the idea seemed radical on both economic and political grounds, the recent creation of Central Park underscored the social, aesthetic, and economic benefits of government intervention to protect, improve, and promote public pleasure grounds. Park advocates cast the measure as a means of ensuring that Yosemite's magnificent scenery would continue to afford inspiration and enjoyment to the American public rather than be sacrificed for the enrichment of private individuals. They also emphasized that the federal government would incur no financial obligation and that the remote location made the land worthless for traditional economic purposes. Conness secured congressional support for a bill transferring Yosemite Valley and the Mariposa Big Tree Grove from the public domain to the State of California with the stipulation that the land be preserved in perpetuity for the purposes of "public use, resort, and recreation." When President Abraham Lincoln signaled his approval in June 1864, proponents compared the decision to the wartime reconstruction of the U.S. Capitol and the completion of Central Park as embodiments of the indomitable ideals of republican government. The Yosemite Act authorized the governor of California to appoint a commission to manage the reservation. The most prominent member was none other than Frederick Law Olmsted, who had moved to California a year earlier to supervise a gold-mining estate not far from Yosemite Valley. Although Olmsted does not appear to have played an active role in the park's establishment, he embraced the challenge of devising a strategy to maximize its potential without compromising its unique attractions. His 1865 report underscored both the direct link between western national park development and eastern precedents and the importance of ensuring an appropriate balance between preservation and access.[4]

While the monumental grandeur of Yosemite's cliffs and waterfalls dominated most accounts of the region's attractions, Olmsted called attention to the serene beauty of the valley floor, comparing the luxuriant meadows to the pastoral charm of eastern parks and traditional English landscapes. According to Olmsted, it was the overall impression created by this "union of the deepest sublimity with the deepest beauty" rather than any singular feature that made Yosemite "the greatest glory of nature." Reiterating his justification for the development of Central Park, Olmsted maintained that exposure to attractive scenery was essential for the health, happiness, and moral refinement of individual citizens and society as a whole. Viewed in this light, park making was not a naïve gesture or attempt to entertain idle travelers at the public's expense but "a political duty of grave importance." Central Park had demonstrated the merits of this argument, but Yosemite afforded an unmatched opportunity to demonstrate the public park's role as a democratic institution of vital importance to American society. Olmsted noted that, in contrast to European parks, with their noble origins and elite pretensions, Congress had decreed that Yosemite "be held, guarded and managed for the free use of the whole body of the people forever." He acknowledged that the cultivated few would be the initial beneficiaries but insisted that the enjoyment of attractive scenery was a universal faculty. Invoking the ideals expressed by Andrew Jackson Downing and William Cullen Bryant, Olmsted asserted that, like universal public education, democratic access to Yosemite's wonders would encourage all Americans to develop intellectual and moral faculties that remained stunted in less egalitarian societies. The park's scenery would also benefit those whose single-minded focus on business extracted a heavy toll on their mental and physical health, with increasingly negative consequences for American society. For those unmoved by psychological arguments or appeals to civic virtue, Olmsted outlined the "pecuniary advantage" of scenic preservation. Tourism was the dominant industry in the mountainous parts of Switzerland, due to extensive public and private investment in a profitable network of hotels, railroads, steamboat lines, and "superb carriage roads." With appropriate development, Yosemite would have a similar influence on the surrounding region. Californians would not be the only ones to benefit, since the tourist trade would expand as other scenic regions were developed. The park's inaccessibility prevented the bulk of the population from enjoying its attractions, but when the proper improvements were in place, Olmsted enthused, "these hundreds will become thousands and in a century the whole number of visitors will be counted by millions."[5]

Olmsted's prescription for realizing this vision formed the fundamental precepts of national park management. "The first point to be kept in mind," he asserted, "is the preservation and maintenance as exactly as is possible of the natural scenery; the restriction, that is to say, within the narrowest limits consistent with the necessary accommodation of visitors, of all artificial constructions and the prevention of all constructions markedly inharmonious with the scenery." The first clause is often presented as evidence that Olmsted prioritized preservation over access. While opinions on what constituted "necessary accommodation" might vary, Olmsted considered the two inseparable. If anything, his Yosemite report emphasized the latter. The fundamental goal was "to give every advantage practicable to the mass of the people to benefit by that which is peculiar to this ground and which has caused Congress to treat it differently from other parts of the public domain." Yosemite's appeal was vested in its spectacular scenery. Without preservation, there would be no scenery to see, but to fulfill Congress's wishes, the scenery had to be seen—and not by an elite few but by "the mass of the people." Preservation was a fundamental prerequisite, but Olmsted maintained that the "first necessity" was to overcome the obstacles posed by Yosemite's primitive transportation network so that its value could be realized by "those whom it is designed to benefit."[6]

Olmsted divided the task into two parts: reducing the time and expense of the journey to the park and constructing a carriage circuit to showcase scenic attractions. Tourists typically traveled by steamboat from San Francisco to Stockton, a distance of 120 miles. A hot and dusty daylong stagecoach ride through the San Joaquin Valley took them to the Sierra foothills, where

Mariposa served as the principal departure point. A day of rugged travel by horseback over rough trails led to a primitive hostelry run by Galen Clark near the site of the present-day Wawona Hotel. After staying overnight and making a short excursion to visit the Mariposa Big Tree Grove, visitors made the steep and hazardous descent to the valley floor.[7]

Olmsted maintained that the arduous journey prevented visitors from experiencing the full benefits of the park. "A man travelling from Stockton to the Yosemite or the Mariposa Grove is commonly three or four days on the road at an expense of from thirty to forty dollars," he lamented, "and arrives in the majority of cases quite overcome with the fatigue and unaccustomed hardships of the journey." The result, Olmsted claimed, was that "few persons, especially few women, are able to enjoy or profit by the scenery and air for days afterward." The expense of securing food and lodging in such a remote location was such that even though virtually everyone making the trip was well-to-do, few could afford to stay long enough to achieve the desired results. "Many leave before they have recovered from their first exhaustion," he observed, "and return home jaded and ill." Improving access would not only enable visitors to experience the park more fully but also make it easier to haul the supplies required by the growing tourist trade. The lowered cost would translate into increased visitation and longer, more beneficial stays.[8]

Olmsted enlisted geologist Clarence King to help devise a more practical and attractive road through the Sierra foothills to Yosemite Valley. The best route, Olmsted suggested, would follow the existing road from Mariposa to Clark's, then leave the old trail to ascend a ridge that Olmsted claimed afforded "the finest views of the South Fork scenery that I have ever seen." Turning right on the main divide, it would skirt the head of Devil's Gulch, providing glimpses of this scenic feature, then wind toward the rim of the valley. Within these general guidelines, Olmsted advised King to survey a course along which "the most interesting views are to be commanded, and where the finest forest trees abound." Since the road was intended for recreational purposes, Olmsted reminded King that "much shorter curves and steeper grades will be advisable than would be the case on a road designed to accommodate heavy teaming." This would reduce the expense of

construction and make it easier to adapt the road to the rugged terrain. He also attended to practical necessities, calling for well-watered campgrounds and advising that "there should be no very long hills of a grade so high that six good horses could not be kept upon a slow trot."[9]

Olmsted's recommendations for the valley road system demonstrated the same attention to aesthetic and pragmatic details he applied to Central Park and other municipal pleasure grounds. The drive should be wide enough to accommodate a single carriage or two riders traveling abreast. It would afford a complete circuit of the Valley, enabling visitors to view the principal scenic features. A one-way traffic system augmented by frequent turnouts would reduce the road's footprint, ease congestion, and allow sightseers to enjoy the scenery at their own pace. The road would generally hug the edges of the valley, but to inject variety and afford the best views of key features it would cross the central meadows at select locations. Not only would this alignment minimize the road's visual impact, but shade from the towering cliffs would afford relief to tourists during the blistering summers while reducing the dust generated by horses and carriages. Several small bridges would be necessary, but Olmsted advised that development should be kept "within the narrowest practicable limits, destroying as it must the natural conditions of the ground and presenting an unpleasant object to the eye in the midst of the scenery."[10]

While Olmsted masterfully translated the aesthetics and ideology of the municipal park movement to the management of large western reservations, his fellow commissioners were not favorably impressed. Concerned that the report might threaten their own agendas, they quietly set it aside. Olmsted returned to New York in October 1865 and rededicated himself to urban park development. Given the economic and political realities of the time, it is unlikely his recommendations would have spurred the State of California to improve access to Yosemite. Despite the park's growing popularity, the tourist trade was too small to justify allocations for road construction, especially when more practical and politically expedient projects beckoned.

Even without significant improvements, the attention garnered by the Yosemite Act attracted additional curiosity seekers. Among the most notable were Speaker of the House Schuyler Colfax, who headed a large party that included

The park's inaccessibility prevented the bulk of the population from enjoying its attractions, but when the proper improvements were in place, Olmsted enthused, "these hundreds will become thousands and in a century the whole number of visitors will be counted by millions."

LEFT *The Descent into Yosemite Valley by Mariposa Trail,* from *Appletons' Journal,* 1873.

Samuel Bowles, publisher of the *Springfield (Mass.) Republican,* and Albert Richardson, a correspondent for the *New York Tribune.* Their accounts heightened public interest.[11] An even bigger boost came with the completion of the transcontinental railroad in 1869. This technical and administrative triumph greatly reduced the time and expense of western vacations, though the excursion remained beyond the means of most Americans. The Central Pacific Railroad completed a regional line from San Francisco to Stockton the same year. The combination of increased publicity and improved access produced a marked increase in Yosemite visitation, which grew from 623 in 1868 to 1,122 in 1869. A year later, the tally rose to 1,735.[12]

By this time, tourists could choose from among three major routes. San Francisco remained the primary departure point. Two days of hot and dusty stagecoach travel from Stockton brought travelers to the outlying communities of Mariposa, Coulterville, or Big Oak Flat, where the stages were exchanged for horses, mules, and pack animals. Tourists taking the Mariposa route followed a 40-mile trail constructed by the brothers Andrew, Milton, and Houston Mann in 1856. Tourists on horseback climbed from Mariposa to Clark's Station, switchbacking up the steep grade. The ascent was so rugged and the trail in such poor condition that numerous stops were required to allow horses and riders to recoup. The next day's plunge into the valley was equally trying, consisting, according to an 1871 visitor, of "tedious zigzags and abrupt, almost precipitous, descents."[13] Nevertheless, most early travelers embraced the Mann Brothers' trail as the preferred route. John Muir recommended it, both for the views it afforded and the associated attraction of the Mariposa Grove of giant sequoias.[14] Visitors usually spent the night at Clark's, taking a side trip to view the grove, which was the most impressive collection of giant trees yet discovered. Continuing on their way, they reached the awe-inspiring outlook known as Inspiration Point, where they marveled over the magnificent view while steeling themselves for the descent to the valley floor. Attesting to the precarious nature of the passage and the ongoing appeal of romantic rhetoric, an 1873 account observed that a traveler on the twisting path would experience "constant ecstasies of wonder and delight as the views open and change before him."[15] The Mann Brothers levied substantial tolls on travelers: two dollars per horse and rider, two dollars per pack mule, and one dollar for pedestrians, but traffic remained so low that they were unable to recoup their investment and soon sold their rights to Mariposa County authorities, who eliminated the tariff and opened the trail to the public. By 1876 a competing route descended from Glacier Point, and an even steeper trail plummeted into the gorge near Vernal and Nevada Falls.[16]

Tourists entering from the other side of the valley had two options. "The Coulterville Free Trail," as it was called, took advantage of an existing mining road and then followed a new path constructed in 1856 explicitly for Yosemite-bound travelers. The Big Oak Flat Trail combined another old mining road with portions of the ancient Mono Indian Trans-Sierra Trail and intervening stretches of new construction. The two trails came together at Crane Flat and then proceeded through rolling meadows and woodlands, passing a hostelry known as Gentry's Station before beginning the harrowing descent to the valley floor.[17] By 1870 road construction reduced the horseback portion of the Coulterville Free Trail to 25 miles and the Big Oak Flat Trail to 18. The final descent continued to constitute a formidable challenge, especially for visitors unaccustomed to the saddle. An 1871 visitor pronounced: "It is impossible to repress fear. Every nerve is tense . . . and even the bravest lean timorously toward the mountain side and away from the cliff, with foot loose in stirrup and eye alert, ready for a spring in case of peril." The dizzying height and steep, narrow path created the impression that "one false step would send horse and rider a mangled mess two thousand feet below." The horseback descent was particularly trying, since proper ladies were expected

to ride sidesaddle. Confronted by the prospect of a plunge into the abyss, many traded dresses for bloomers and rode scandalously astride. The pioneering women's rights activist Elizabeth Cady Stanton refused to ride at all, walking the entire way in spite of her guide's assurances that the trail was safer than it appeared.[18]

The perilous saddle trails into the valley were not the only deterrent. Yosemite visitors complained incessantly about the dust and discomfort of the stagecoach portion of the trip. Olive Logan, whose 1870 visit prompted a magazine article titled "Does It Pay to Visit Yo Semite?," proclaimed that the dust was beyond the comprehension of eastern travelers. Logan advised potential visitors to dismiss any expectations that the trip itself would afford scenic interest. Choking clouds of dust made it impossible to see fence posts 6 feet away or even to make out the driver of the coach. Breathing was difficult and conversation impossible. At Chinese Camp on the Big Oak Flat Road, where the six-horse stages were exchanged for smaller vehicles, the dust torture was compounded by painful jouncing along a collection of ruts and boulders that could only loosely be construed as a road. According to Logan, the teamsters appeared intent on heightening their customers' distress. Either through indifference or by design, they terrified their captives by racing at full speed "around jutting and dangerous precipices, where one inch too near the edge will pitch the stage, crashing through pines, to destruction." Logan cast the transition to horseback as a relief, though the ability to control one's own fate was tempered by the difficulty of the descent. After nightfall on the third day of travel, they arrived at the valley floor, "too paralyzed to stir." Confirming Olmsted's fears, Logan reported that even after a full day of lounging, they were too exhausted to enjoy their surroundings. According to Logan, not even the spectacular scenery afforded compensation for the journey's hardships. For Logan's party, at least, the answer to the titular question was a resounding negative. Logan maintained that

most visitors shared this opinion but were such slaves to convention that they parroted the proclamations of travel promoters and starry-eyed artists. Noting the proximity of an insane asylum to Stockton's principal hotel, Logan ascribed the institution's presence to the mental state of returning tourists.[19]

At least Logan's party spent three days in the valley, the length of stay recommended by guidebook writers and other experts. Combined with travel time, this meant tourists had to devote at least ten days to the excursion. As Olmsted predicted, the time and expense of the trip caused many visitors to cut short the most rewarding part of the experience. Many tourists were apparently untroubled by the brevity of their stay. Olmsted's vision of the Yosemite experience as a languorous idyll of mental relaxation and aesthetic contemplation was already at odds with popular preferences. Most visitors treated the park as addition to the fashionable tourist's itinerary of socially approved attractions, the more quickly dispatched, the better. "Sometimes the East stayed in the valley but a day," the writer Bret Harte observed in 1871. "There came men and women, content to ride in, sup, sleep, breakfast, glance at the falls and cliffs, and then ride straight out again. For them, the valley was done, and they thanked heaven that they had done it. It was not to be visited again; and that epoch of a restless, weary life in search of pleasure was over."[20]

By 1870 several hotels of varying size and quality provided accommodations, both in Yosemite Valley and en route. Regularly scheduled saddle trains led by experienced guides plied the trails, though more adventurous parties could rent horses and proceed on their own. During the height of the season, tour groups traveled in strings of sixty or more, often overwhelming accommodations on the valley floor. J. M. Buckley, who defied precedent by spending a full two weeks in the valley, described a spirited contest between two parties speeding past scenic outlooks in order to beat the crowds on a busy weekend in 1871. Echoing Humphry Repton's observations about carriage parties enlivening

country estates, some accounts cast the travelers' presence as a welcome addition to the natural scenery. William Cullen Bryant's *Picturesque America* presented tourist parties as festive counterpoints to Yosemite's solemn grandeur, asserting that "the picturesque effects of a party of pleasure-seekers *en route*" afforded "a never-failing source of pleasure." Buckley took a similar view, asserting that his party "presented a picturesque appearance as it wound along the narrow bridle path."[21]

Even when couched in aestheticizing rhetoric, celebrations of the tourist presence underscored the perception that the park experience was both a social event and a contribution to cultural cohesion. Both the message and the media through which it was delivered attested to the democratic nature of the American public park. While oil paintings of English elites ensconced in private pleasure grounds epitomized Old World exclusivity, the mass-produced images of tourists that appeared in popular periodicals such as *Harper's* and *Appletons' Journal* embodied the egalitarian ethos of the American park movement. The proliferation of stereographic views, chromolithographs, and other souvenirs depicting tourists in the act of enjoying American scenery testified to visitors' desires to memorialize their activities and the belief that the human presence enhanced

the park experience. "Serious" artists such as Thomas Hill also celebrated park tourism. Hill painted numerous versions of Yosemite landmarks during the last quarter of the nineteenth century. He often included figures, but even his unpopulated scenes often contained subtle evidence of the tourist presence, including the trail leading down from Inspiration Point. Three paintings by the California artist William Hahn portrayed tourist parties en route to Yosemite and enjoying the scenery from Glacier Point. While this 1874 series hewed to the tradition of presenting park visitors as colorful complements to the natural scene, the Glacier Point painting suggested growing concern about the negative impacts of tourist culture. Cast-off wine bottles litter the ground, and a visitor appears to have passed out from imbibing the contents, oblivious to the grandeur beyond. The Romantic convention of contrasting verdant foliage with lifeless tree trunks could be interpreted as an allegory of Yosemite's passage from youthful innocence to decaying husk.

Repeating the pattern that accompanied the popularization of scenic tourism in England and the eastern states, it did not take long for those who fancied themselves true appreciators of Yosemite's beauties to decry the transgressions of the traveling public. As early as 1870, John Muir wrote

disparagingly of the "fashionable hordes" that descended on the park. "They climb sprawlingly to their saddles like overgrown frogs," he scoffed, "ride up the Valley with about as much emotion as the horses they ride upon—are comfortable when they have 'done it all,' and long for the safety and flatness of their proper homes." While the glories of Yosemite were wasted on such unimaginative souls, Muir expressed confidence that their impact on the more majestic portions of the park would be negligible. The vast majority were content to follow the primary routes and "float slowly about the bottom of the Valley as a harmless scum," he observed, "leaving the rocks and falls eloquent as ever."[22]

Muir's prediction was soon put to the test, as competing enterprises vied to provide tourists with the conveniences to which they were accustomed. A relatively crude bridle path enabled visitors to make a complete circuit of the valley by 1868, but for many visitors, riding was considered scarcely preferable to walking as a means of experiencing nature. Proper vacationers, and women in particular, required carriages and smooth roads on which to enjoy them. Commenting on resort life in more developed regions, one British traveler observed, "American ladies never walk, but they go out 'buggy-riding' in dancing shoes and ball dresses." To accommodate this desire, hotel keeper Galen Clark dismantled a small wagon and had it packed to the valley floor on mule-back to carry visitors to popular locations during the 1870 season. Hutchings followed suit so that his patrons could enjoy similar pleasures. A wagon road was constructed along the north side of the valley in 1872. A second road traversed the south side, but the two remained unconnected, leaving Olmsted's vision of a classic park circuit unfulfilled.[23]

Rattling around Yosemite Valley in a carriage was undoubtedly appealing, but in 1874 the park itself finally became accessible to wheeled vehicles. The Yosemite Board of Commissioners had made it clear the state had no interest in constructing a public road to the valley. The increase in traffic and associated complaints failed to sway their minds. Since they considered the provision of access to Yosemite to be the responsibility of the communities or individuals who stood to benefit, the commissioners agreed to grant turnpike franchises to prospective road builders. Given the difficulty of constructing wagon roads down the perilous descent from the valley rim or snaking a roadbed through the canyon carved by the

Merced River, the commission predicted that the project would be time-consuming, expensive, and perhaps even impossible. Despite this assessment, several companies formed to undertake the challenge. Not only would the expected increase in visitation provide investors with a steadily rising stream of income, but communities along the way would reap the harvest of tourist dollars. In 1870, the *Mariposa Gazette* proclaimed, "Everyone has carriage road on the brain," reporting that rival organizations in Coulterville, Mariposa, and Big Oak Flat were engaged in a high-stakes race to be the first to provide stagecoach access to Yosemite. "We say 'Success' to these enterprises," the newspaper declared, "and we eagerly await the day we can proceed all the way to the Yo Semite in a carriage."[24] These sentiments were widely shared, though a few commentators expressed foreboding about the inevitable impact. Employing the heated rhetoric that would characterize ensuing debates about Yosemite access, a correspondent for *Appletons' Journal* lamented that the "sacred precincts will then be desecrated by a daily stage."[25]

The Big Oak Flat operation was first under way. In September 1868, a group of local businessmen organized the "Chinese Camp and Yo Semite Turnpike Company," proposing to construct a road along the approximate route of the existing Big Oak Flat Trail. They estimated the cost at a then-considerable twenty thousand dollars. The State of California granted a fifty-year franchise, with the condition that the road be completed by July 1, 1871. Construction began the following spring. Employing what contemporary accounts characterized as a "great army" of Chinese workers, the road builders reached Crane Flat by the summer of 1870. At the end of the appointed period, they had progressed only as far as Gentry's Station near the northern rim of the valley. The state authorized a six-month extension, but faced with dwindling funds and the difficulties of constructing a road down the harrowing cliffs, the company relinquished its franchise. Even though the roadway was not completed, it enabled tourists to reach the edge of the valley by stagecoach, giving Big Oak Flat a significant advantage over its competitors. This failure to fulfill the terms of the agreement opened the door for rivals to forge ahead with their own efforts to capture the growing tourist trade. Coulterville interests organized a turnpike company in 1870. The route followed an existing

road to a tourist attraction known as Bower Cave, climbed east over Pilot Peak, and intersected with the Big Oak Flat Road at Crane Flat. The *Stockton Weekly Independent* predicted the road would be completed by June, but the company ran short of funds and construction stopped well short of the proposed terminus. When progress on the Big Oak Flat Road ground to a halt the following year, it appeared the commissioners had been right in predicting that constructing a road into Yosemite Valley was neither technically possible nor economically feasible.[26]

In July 1872 a San Francisco surgeon named John McLean applied for the right to resume construction on the Coulterville Road. McLean had personal experience with the rigors of Yosemite travel, having taken his family to the valley on horseback during the summer of 1867. Personifying Olmsted's fear that visitors would be too exhausted to appreciate the scenery, McLean's wife spent their stay recuperating at a hotel. Since the Big Oak Flat interests appeared to be making no effort to resume operation, McLean secured permission to extend the Coulterville Road to the valley floor. The agreement granted McLean's Coulterville and Yosemite Turnpike Company a monopoly on traffic entering from the north rim and stipulated that the road be completed by the end of 1873. McLean invested most of his personal fortune in the enterprise, which most observers assumed would suffer the same fate as its predecessors.[27]

McLean quickly engaged a crew to survey the best approach to the valley floor. While reconnoitering potential routes, they discovered an impressive stand of giant sequoias, which McLean christened the Merced Grove of Big Trees. McLean routed the road through the grove to provide additional incentive for tourists to patronize his approach. The new route departed from the existing road at Hazel Flat, heading south through the Merced Grove and then southeast to Buena Vista Gap, where the first views of the valley were obtained. A bit farther south, the road began a steep descent to the valley floor, dropping steadily for 2 miles at a nearly constant 16 percent grade with virtually no turns to slow descending stages or ease the uphill journey. Upon reaching the Merced River, the road turned east, passed beneath scenic waterfalls known as the Cascades, then paralleled the stream to join the existing valley road system. Crews worked from both ends throughout the summer and fall of 1872, cutting their way down the escarpment with picks, shovels, hand drills, and black powder. Considerable blasting was required, and extensive dry laid stone retaining walls had to be constructed to secure passage down the canyon wall. The roadbed was supposed to meet the 16-foot-wide standard required for stagecoaches to pass abreast, but it became apparent that this was unrealistic given the nature of the terrain and the resources of the road builders. Turnouts were provided so that downhill stages could pull aside

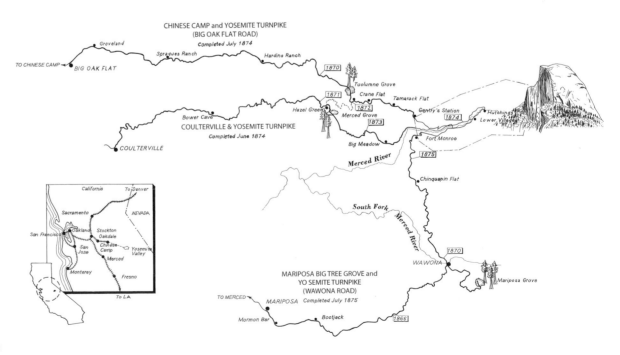

ABOVE Map of Yosemite National Park toll roads.

> "The completion
> of this road made
> access to Yosemite
> easy, speedy and
> comfortable, by
> wheeled vehicles,
> instead of tiresome,
> difficult, and
> dangerous, on
> horseback and
> over trails."

COULTERVILLE ROAD BUILDER
JOHN MCLEAN

BELOW Opening of Mariposa
Road, Yosemite Valley,
Yosemite National Park, 1875.

OPPOSITE Wawona Tunnel
Tree, Yosemite National Park,
postcard, ca. 1910.

and let uphill teams pass. Heavy snows added to the road-builders' burdens. The winter was so severe that the commissioners granted McLean a one-year extension. By August 1873, both the upper section from the previous terminus through Merced Grove and the portion from the valley to the beginning of the steep ascent were completed. The intervening 2-mile stretch was opened to mule travel while crews hurried to widen, stabilize, and grade the roadbed. Barring unforeseen circumstances, the road would be fully open the following season. This would give Coulterville a monopoly on stagecoach travel and dramatically affect traffic on competing routes.[28]

McLean's progress spurred the Big Oak Flat consortium to renew its efforts. In August 1872 the renamed Yosemite Turnpike Road Company asked permission to resume construction. The Board of Commissioners denied the request, citing McLean's exclusive franchise. The Big Oak Flat group was determined to proceed and began lining up political support to overrule the decision. The state legislature would not be in session until early 1874, which would give Coulterville an insurmountable lead in the race to the valley floor. Skirting the letter of the law, the company began to make "trail improvements" to the old bridle path. This ruse fooled no one. The width,

grade, and alignment were clearly intended for wheeled vehicles. A local newspaper sardonically observed that the workmen could not be faulted if a pick or shovel occasionally slipped to widen the way. The subterfuge was abandoned in February 1974, when the legislature ruled that the Yosemite Board of Commissioners had no authority to grant monopoly contracts. The race to the valley was on in earnest, with local and regional papers reporting enthusiastically from the sidelines.[29]

McLean had 150 workers on the job by April 1874. He informed the *Mariposa Gazette* that he was bringing in additional support to ensure the road would be open by the start of the tourist season. Spokesmen for the Big Oak Flat Road insisted they would be ready as well. Not only did the Coulterville group have a significant head start, but the challenge of constructing a road down the 2,000-foot precipice at the end of the Big Oak Flat route was so daunting that the eminent state geologist J. D. Whitney asserted it could not be done. The solution was provided not by professional engineers but by a crew of recently immigrated Italian masons schooled in the Old World art of dry-laid stone construction. They agreed to build the required retaining walls for sixteen thousand dollars. Combined with other expenses, this more than doubled original estimates. The potential rewards were so great that the company quickly agreed. In the space of twenty weeks, the masons constructed a series of impressive retaining walls comprised of meticulously cut stones carefully interlocked to support the weight of heavy stagecoaches. The most difficult section, a harrowing hairpin turn known as the Zigzag, was not just a technical marvel but a visual feast, affording stunning views of Yosemite's imposing cliffs along with stomach-churning glimpses of the dizzying drop to the valley floor. The kaleidoscopic effect of these alternating perspectives viewed from a rapidly descending stage produced a memorable impression for visitors who dared to look. At the top of the cliffs, the location where travelers caught their first glimpse of Yosemite's grandeur became known as "Oh My! Point."[30]

Coulterville's lead proved insurmountable. In mid-June, while the Big Oak Flat forces were eking their way down, McLean claimed the distinction of driving the first wheeled vehicle into Yosemite Valley. A grand celebration followed, highlighted by a procession of fifty carriages from Coulterville to Yosemite Valley, where they were greeted by fireworks, bonfires, and oratorical effusions. The *Mariposa Gazette* detailed the festivities, proclaiming: "The completion of a wagon road into the Valley is a consummation of which Mariposa County can well feel proud." Similarly enthusiastic accounts appeared in the regional and national press. In combination with the extension of the Central Pacific Railroad to Merced, the Coulterville Road enabled tourists to travel from San Francisco to Yosemite in thirty-six hours without piloting an unpredictable four-legged beast down a death-defying trail. Recounting the impact several years later, McLean avowed, "The completion of this road made access to Yosemite easy, speedy and comfortable, by wheeled vehicles, instead of tiresome, difficult, and dangerous, on horseback and over trails." In McLean's estimation, the improvement of access to Yosemite was an achievement in which all citizens of California and the United States should take pride.[31]

The Coulterville monopoly did not last for long. The opening of the Big Oak Flat Road twenty-nine days later engendered festivities that put the previous celebration to shame. Wagons and teams were put in top order and local residents turned out in their finery for a grand parade to the valley floor. Fifty-two vehicles assembled on the appointed morning, forming a line that stretched more than a mile. Leading the procession was a six-horse stage decorated with ribbons and flags in which sat the backers of the Big Oak Flat Road accompanied by a six-piece brass band. Virtually the entire valley population turned out to greet the procession. The boisterous throng made its way from one hotel to the next, engaging in feasting, drinking, and merrymaking. Tuolumne County newspapers touted the superior virtues of both the road and the celebration. Casting the new road as the obvious choice for discriminating travelers, the papers asserted that comparing the Coulterville Road to the Big Oak Flat route was like equating "the sinuous winding of a broken-back eel, to the gentle curves of a majestic boa."[32]

Tourists approaching Yosemite Valley from the south through Mariposa were still forced to endure upward of 20 miles in the saddle over rugged and poorly maintained trails. This situation was particularly galling because the Mariposa route had long been the favored approach. For a time it had seemed that Mariposa would be the first community to complete a road to the valley

California Sequoia Tree "Wawona"   50

floor. Warning that Mariposa would lose its pre-eminence if it failed to construct a wagon road to the valley, Galen Clark had organized a turnpike company in 1869. The first section reached Clark's outpost in July 1870. Financially overextended, Clark was forced to suspend the project, leaving tourists to continue on horseback. The progress on the north rim roads prompted Clark to renew his efforts in 1873. After surveying a route to the valley floor and realizing the immensity of the task, Clark and his partner attempted to sell their franchise to the State of California, insisting that providing access to Yosemite was a public responsibility. The state legislature remained unwilling to accept the burden, so Clark sold out to a

better-funded Mariposa group headed by Henry Washburn, who was already operating the stage line over the completed portion of the route.[33]

The Washburn group secured the support of the Mariposa County Board of Supervisors and began to construct the road from Clark's establishment, which it renamed Wawona, to the valley floor. The bulk of the work was performed by a large force of Chinese laborers, who were divided into two crews to work on both ends simultaneously. By the end of April the upper section reached the edge of the valley. Predictably, the crew working up from the valley floor made significantly slower progress. Both crews labored feverishly on the steep incline to get the road

ready by the start of the summer tourist season. All that remained was one particularly difficult stretch near Lower Inspiration Point. Washburn was so impatient to secure a share of the stage-coach trade that he had his drivers off-load passengers at the end of the completed roadway, where they clambered through the construction site and waited while workmen dismantled the stages, carried the pieces over jumbles of loose rock and gravel, reassembled the coaches, and sent them on their way. Passengers reportedly considered this to be an interesting diversion that contributed to the novelty of the experience. The final section was completed in July 1875. The associated festivities included performances by the Merced and

Yosemite bands, artillery salutes, and elaborate oratory. Echoing earlier pronouncements, the *Mariposa Gazette* enthused, "All vote the road, the procession, and the celebration a success." The 27-mile-long turnpike, which became known as the Wawona Road, featured the steepest and narrowest descent into the valley. It also provided the most impressive views and afforded the additional attraction of side trips to the Mariposa Big Tree Grove and Glacier Point, where tourists could relish the magnificent vista and pose for daring photographs on a protruding rock ledge.[34]

Although the turnpike companies and local merchants assumed the new roadways would produce a dramatic increase in Yosemite travel, broader social and economic developments intervened. The severe economic depression of the mid-1870s suppressed tourism nationwide. The number of Yosemite visitors actually dropped in 1875, the first year all three roads were open. In 1878, fewer tourists traveled to Yosemite than in any year since the completion of the transcontinental railroad. Yosemite travel did not exceed pre-depression levels until 1883, when the economy recovered enough to support the luxury of long-distance tourism. With its multiple attractions, the Wawona Road quickly became the most popular approach, carrying more traffic than the other routes combined. The Wawona Road benefited from its monopoly on tourists approaching from the south, while the Big Oak Flat and Coulterville Roads competed for visitors entering from the north. The Coulterville Road's lower elevation allowed it to open earlier, but once the snow melted, the more scenic Big Oak Flat Road held sway. Washburn's group held a further advantage in that the company controlled both the roadway and the lucrative stagecoach service, whereas ownership was divided on the other two routes. Washburn constructed the elegant Wawona Hotel where Clark's rustic cabin once stood, and acquired additional inns in the valley and en route.[35]

By the 1890s, Yosemite Valley was teeming with tourists. A Thomas Hill painting of Yosemite Village epitomized the simultaneous celebration of tourism, transportation, and natural grandeur. Buggies, stagecoaches, and gaily dressed riders enlivened the foreground, a cluster of hotels filled the middle distance, and Yosemite Falls and the surrounding cliffs afforded an imposing backdrop. While the subdued hues and gauzy outlines of the valley walls reflected painterly conventions for rendering distance and perspective, the contrast between the muted natural landscape and vibrant social scene might have also suggested the priorities of contemporary tourists.

The increase in travel prompted complaints about the propriety of allowing private companies to extract tolls from visitors to a public park. The state eventually forced the turnpike companies to relinquish their rights to the park portions of their improvements. In 1885 the state paid the Coulterville group $10,000 for the road from the park boundary to the valley floor. The Big Oak Flat concern received $3,500 for its section, which according to company claims cost $12,000 to construct. The Wawona group was awarded $8,000 for the park portion of its road, which Washburn claimed was less than half the cost of construction. While the turnpike companies protested that they were being penalized for having taken the initiative to open the valley to the traveling public, the state's action was in many ways beneficial. Tourists were still charged to use the roads leading to the park boundaries, and the companies were no longer responsible for maintaining the steepest and most troublesome portions of their routes.[36]

Despite McLean's assertion that the new roads made access to the valley "easy, speedy and comfortable," the trip to Yosemite remained an arduous and time-consuming affair. Even with the extension of railroad lines to outlying communities during the 1880s and 1890s, visitors endured long, dusty, and uncomfortable stagecoach rides. Travelers on the Big Oak Flat Road trekked 60 miles by stagecoach, whereas tourists on the Wawona Road faced a 72-mile journey. Washburn's Yosemite Stage and Turnpike Company maintained a sizable fleet of coaches, along with hundreds of horses and the barns, stables, blacksmiths, stable hands, and repair shops required to support the enterprise. During the height of the season as many as eleven stages per day made the ten-hour trip to Wawona. Most visitors spent the night at the company's hotel, since another six hours was needed to reach the valley floor. In 1901 Washburn capitalized on tourists' desire to reach Yosemite Valley as quickly as possible by introducing an express service called the "Cannonball Stage." Initially limited to one trip per day, the Cannonball promised to "shoot you through" from the train to the valley in a twelve-hour dash. Two more

horses were added to the standard four-horse teams, and all six were replaced at frequent intervals to cover the distance at top speed. Though it was significantly more expensive, express service proved immensely popular. In addition to cutting a day off the trip in each direction, the exhilarating pace afforded an extra measure of excitement, especially when hurtling pell-mell down the descent to the valley floor. The other stagecoach companies quickly initiated competitive services on their routes. The ability to rush through the park at a gallop was not universally embraced. The author of a 1904 article condemned the express traveler who sped through park "with a rapidity which forbids him the opportunity to take note of flower, tree, rock, or mountain peak." Like the growing crowds that scurried from one Yosemite landmark to another, he lamented, the express tourist's goal was not to commune with the landscape in the manner espoused by John Muir, but merely to count "this marvel of nature as one of the things which he has 'done.'"[37]

For conventional travelers, the stagecoach trip could be both tedious and terrifying. For most of the distance, the scenery was not particularly engaging. Tourists on the Big Oak Flat and Wawona Roads could at least visit the groves of giant sequoias located en route. In order to heighten the attraction of these natural wonders, the turnpike companies carved portals large enough to accommodate stagecoaches. The first of these "tunnel trees" was created in 1878, when the proprietors of the Big Oak Flat Road bored an enormous hole through a hulking specimen known as the "Dead Giant." Three years later, Washburn countered by tunneling the "Wawona Tree," which became one of the main attractions of the Mariposa Big Tree Grove. A second tunnel was cut through the nearby "California Tree." A massive wind-toppled sequoia known as the "Fallen Giant" was flattened on top and outfitted with a ramp so that coaches could climb aboard. These attractions were celebrated in tourist publications, souvenirs, and personal photographs, which became increasingly popular with Kodak's introduction of affordable and convenient cameras in 1888. The Coulterville Road lagged behind its rivals on this front as well. By the time McLean got around to proposing a similar attraction, the superintendent refused to deface yet another ancient specimen "merely to gratify the very questionable taste of tourists who may be ambitious to report that they have gone through a tree while riding on top of a stagecoach." Park officials might deride such diversions, but tunnel trees were considered one of the highlights of a Yosemite vacation. Most travelers rejoiced that, as a correspondent for the popular *Overland Monthly* observed, "All the celebrated features of Yosemite can be enjoyed by a carriage."[38]

The descent into the valley was also widely remarked, both for the views it afforded and the thrills it entailed. All the routes included dizzying descents along steep and narrow roadbeds, with minimal measures to prevent errant vehicles from plunging into the depths. The Wawona and Big Oak Flat routes were punctuated with sharp and hair-raising turns, but the Coulterville Road could be even more terrifying, since even poorly protected curves curtailed the speeds that built up on its long, straight grade. With widths ranging from 8 to 12 feet, the most unnerving experiences occurred when vehicles met head on. Turnouts were provided at propitious locations, but backing up a heavily laden stagecoach was nearly impossible. Since uphill stages needed to maintain momentum, downhill drivers were supposed to give way, pulling tight to the hillside or perching precariously on the outer edge. Light buggies were occasionally suspended off the edge with ropes to allow stagecoaches and freight wagons to proceed. Tourists relished the frisson of danger as long as they felt they were in capable hands. With Yosemite's towering cliffs affording an imposing backdrop for its perilous switchbacks, the Zigzag section of the Big Oak Flat Road provided the most dramatic demonstration of the melding of natural and technological sublimity prized by contemporary audiences. Photographs of stagecoaches clattering around curves next to yawing chasms and foreboding cliffs were popular souvenirs, especially in the stereopticon format that highlighted the dramatic effects of receding planes.[39]

Stagecoach robberies, while not common, afforded another memorable thrill. More than a dozen holdups occurred between 1883 and 1911. The combination of wealthy travelers, minimal security measures, and myriad opportunities to melt into the surrounding wilderness posed a strong temptation to practitioners of this disappearing art. Knowing that the stagecoaches proceeded at widely spaced intervals to avoid each other's dust, bandits set up in secluded locations and robbed multiple parties in succession. Despite their losses,

many tourists apparently considered the experience a highlight of the trip, as it gave them an unbeatable story with which to regale friends back home. According to legend, the highwaymen were often gentlemanly, extending courtesies to lady passengers and declining to take personal jewelry, their main interest being the Wells Fargo boxes containing receipts from the valley hotels. "Holdups" were even staged for the camera, suggesting that Yosemite was seen not just as a scenic wonderland but as a romantic vestige of the Old West.[40]

Less dramatic, but more common, were complaints about the dust that suffocated travelers and blanketed them with thick coats of pulverized earth. In a typical description, Galen Clark decried the dust that "rises in great clouds, enveloping stage coaches and passengers, obscuring vision, penetrating ears, eyes, nose and mouth if not kept closely shut, and covering the whole body with a dusty pall so that as the stages arrive at the Hotel they appear to be loaded with human images carved in brown stone." Hotel employees greeted travelers with feather dusters, both to restore their dignity and protect proprietors' furnishings. The dust also coated roadside vegetation, creating an unpleasant and distinctly unnatural impression. Although the toll roads dramatically improved access to Yosemite, Olmsted's objections were not yet allayed. Tourists continued to complain that the roughness of the roads and rigors of the journey left them too sore and exhausted to enjoy their surroundings, especially with the equally oppressive return trip looming ahead.[41]

The transfer of Yosemite to federal oversight did little to alleviate these concerns. This process occurred in two stages. In 1890 Congress created Sequoia and General Grant National Parks and designated a 1,400-square-mile area surrounding the Yosemite grant as "reserved forest lands." The secretary of the interior clarified this ambiguous designation by changing the name to Yosemite National Park. The original reservation remained under state control until 1905, when the State of California ceded its authority to the federal government. Yosemite Valley and the Mariposa Big Tree Grove were officially incorporated into the surrounding national park the following year. With no personnel to provide oversight, the Department of the Interior sought assistance from the War Department, which allocated a cavalry troop to manage the park's affairs, following precedents established in Yellowstone. This

arrangement afforded access to the U.S. Army Corps of Engineers' expertise in road construction. With minimal budgets and high turnover, the change produced more good intentions than tangible accomplishments. Several small bridges were constructed, replacing utilitarian steel or wooden structures with more attractive stone-faced spans. A further obstacle was that the roads beyond the original grant remained in private hands. Both visitors and park officials called for the acquisition of these roadways and elimination of the onerous charges, but the toll road system outlasted the stagecoach era.[42]

The biggest threat to the turnpike companies was not government action but technological progress. In May 1907 the Yosemite Valley Railroad completed its track from Merced to the park's border at El Portal and began building a wagon road along the Merced River. The Merced River Canyon had long been considered too narrow to permit road construction, but the railroad's forces managed to carve a path to connect with the final section of Coulterville Road near the entrance to the valley. This quickly became the preferred approach to Yosemite. Visitors could travel by train from San Francisco to the park's doorstep and the valley was just a ninety-minute wagon ride away. The low elevation escaped the heavy snows that closed the toll roads during the winter months, allowing year-round access for the first time. As an added attraction, the road threaded a narrow cleft between two giant boulders just after it entered the park, creating a picturesque gateway known as Arch Rock. The Arch Rock Entrance joined the pantheon of iconic images celebrated in souvenirs and personal photographs. Like the tunnel trees, the combination of natural curiosity and human handiwork appealed to contemporary visitors, who were more interested in entertaining spectacles than primeval wilderness. Sightseeing remained the ostensible focus, though picturesque contemplation continued to lose ground to more sociable amusements. While the railroad significantly shortened travel time, the route lacked the scenic grandeur of the other approaches. Chugging along a train track between constrictive canyon walls could not compare to the thrill of rounding Inspiration Point or hurtling down the Zigzag or the Coulterville grade. Many tourists were undoubtedly relieved to dispense with these diversions, though the road between the railroad terminus and the valley was not a marked improvement over its forebears. The narrow roadbed climbed sharply up and down, wound through jarring boulder fields, and produced the same choking dust that plagued its predecessors. Nevertheless, El Portal was firmly established as the principal access to Yosemite, a distinction it would retain through subsequent changes in administration and modes of transportation.[43]

One more road figured prominently in Yosemite's history. Originally constructed to provide access to a remote mining venture, the Great Sierra Wagon Road was revived as a recreational route in the early twentieth century and rechristened as the Tioga Road. The road was constructed by the Great Sierra Consolidated Silver Company in the early 1880s at a cost of sixty thousand dollars. This represented an enormous investment, but the mining company was confident in its prospects. The road left the Big Oak Flat Road near Crocker's Station, crossed the South and North Forks of the Tuolomne River, and then proceeded across the High Sierra past Tuolumne Meadows and Tenaya Lake to the company's minung district. Since the road was intended for hauling heavy freight, grades were relatively low, and it was remarkably well-constructed. Professional engineers directed the enterprise, and Chinese laborers performed most of the work. Considerable blasting was required to secure passage around Tenaya Lake and in other areas where granite protrusions posed formidable obstacles. Extensive stone retaining walls supported the roadbed, including a substantial causeway along the shore of Tenaya Lake. When travelers began taking advantage of the route, the company received permission to charge tolls for public access. The mine itself failed to produce the anticipated riches, and the company ceased operations in 1884. Little effort was put into maintaining the road after that. Most of its length fell within the 1890 national park boundaries, but as with the more popular toll roads, the right-of-way remained in private hands. In 1896 the park's superintendent reported that the road was no longer passable by wagons and suggested restoring it so that recreational travelers could use it to gain access to the beauties of the High Sierras. Subsequent superintendents reiterated the call, but until the ownership issue was settled, there was little the government could do to improve access to what many considered the most appealingly pristine portion of the park. The newly formed Sierra Club was one of the strongest advocates

for the road's improvement, contributing funds and labor to the effort and insisting it should be repaired "without delay, so as to afford one of the most wonderful trans-mountain roads in the world." The realization of this goal would have to await a new form of park administration, along with the imperatives engendered by new modes of transportation.[44]

YELLOWSTONE

Nowhere was the correlation between the park transportation experience and the park itself stronger than in Yellowstone. Not only did Yellowstone's Grand Loop exemplify the adaptation of traditional park road development to the national park setting, but the public identification of the park with its transportation infrastructure was such that stagecoaches and road-related features vied with geysers and bears as icons of the park experience. As primitive tracks and crude lodgings gave way to graded roads and elaborate hotels, the stagecoach tour was celebrated as an attraction in its own right. Writers recounted the journey in elaborate detail, describing the route, regaling readers with the joys and tribulations of stagecoach travel, satirizing the social scene, and calling attention to notable feats of road construction. By the turn of the twentieth century, when the loop was largely complete and the supporting network of hotels and stage lines fully operational, it was hard to say whether the burgeoning crowds were drawn by the park's natural features or the desire to participate in an increasingly celebrated cultural ritual. The idea of national parks as selective resorts where well-constructed roadways enabled travelers to mix scenic diversions with social amusements might not accord with modern sensibilities, but stagecoach-era Yellowstone epitomized the integration of nineteenth-century scenic tourism and municipal park development. As was the case with Yosemite, the park's authorizing legislation explicitly endorsed this agenda. Yellowstone was set aside in March 1872, not as an ecological preserve or an untrammeled wilderness, but as "a public park or pleasuring ground for the benefit and enjoyment of the people." Roads were considered essential to this function. Yellowstone was even larger, more remote, and less developed than Yosemite, with a harsher climate, its own challenging topography,

ABOVE Henry Wellge, *Yellowstone National Park,* bird's-eye view for the Northern Pacific Railroad, 1904.

and a more broadly scattered array of features. At least the federal government expressed a modicum of interest in improving access, though initial outlays and achievements were modest, at best. As with Yosemite, the progression from horse trail to carriage road was slow, halting, and marked by frustrations with trying conditions.[45]

Given the role played by transportation interests in the park's creation, the resort orientation and emphasis on improving access were not surprising. Carefully cultivated myths presented the preservation of Yellowstone's natural wonders as an idealistic achievement, but the Northern Pacific Railroad played a key role in the park's establishment. Tales of a vast region of geysers, hot springs, and other strange features had circulated since the early nineteenth century. Given the area's

inaccessibility, little attention was paid to these reports until after the Civil War, when the nation focused with renewed interest on western lands. In 1870 a party headed by Montana surveyor general Henry D. Washburn and comprised primarily of prominent Montanans set out to explore the region. According to legend, the group's leaders were so impressed with Yellowstone's scenic wonders that they spontaneously proposed setting aside the region to prevent the private exploitation that had led to the despoliation of Niagara Falls and other popular destinations. In reality, one of the party's members, Nathaniel P. Langford, had already made overtures to the financier Jay Cooke, who was raising capital for the Northern Pacific Railroad, which was slated to pass tantalizingly close to Yellowstone's northern border.

The establishment of a unique tourist attraction a short trip from the transcontinental line would dramatically increase ridership while affording opportunities for additional investments in the tourist trade. Langford prepared a vivid description of the "Wonders of the Yellowstone" for *Scribner's Monthly* and promoted the area's attractions in public lectures supported by the Northern Pacific. When Langford took his performance to the nation's capital, he was introduced by Maine congressman James Blaine, who enjoyed a similarly cozy relationship with the railroad. Langford's audience included Ferdinand Hayden, the head of the U.S. Geological Survey. Intrigued by the presentation, Hayden organized an official expedition to determine the nature and extent of Yellowstone's wonders.[46]

Hayden assembled a crew of scientists, topographical engineers, and support personnel. The party included the photographer William H. Jackson and the noted landscape painter Thomas Moran. Moran's participation was underwritten by the Northern Pacific Railroad with the expectation that he would produce appealing images of Yellowstone's attractions. Hayden's group explored Yellowstone in 1871 and 1872, authenticating the area's fabled wonders and producing detailed maps. Hayden suggested that it would be a good idea to prevent private exploitation of this unique region by designating it a public park. Hayden might have come up with the proposition independently, but Cooke's associates pressed him to include the recommendation in his official report. Jackson's photographs and Moran's paintings provided compelling evidence of Yellowstone's attractions. Chromolithographs of Moran's paintings and stereographic reproductions of Jackson's photographs acquainted the broader public with Yellowstone's scenic wonders.[47]

Moved by the visual and scientific evidence along with the railroad's financial clout, Congress declared that approximately 40 square miles of the Yellowstone region would be preserved as a public reservation. Had Wyoming and Montana been states rather than territories, Congress might well have authorized a Yosemite-like arrangement, but on March 1, 1872, Yellowstone became the world's first national park. The railroad ensured that Jackson's photographs and Moran's watercolors were displayed in the Capitol during the deliberations and that Langford's account was presented to every member of Congress before the crucial vote. Despite the evident self-interest, the Northern Pacific's goals meshed with broader conceptions of scenic preservation. Company officials understood that a well-protected and properly developed park would attract more travelers than a haphazardly exploited eyesore. The railroad's intentions were both widely understood and broadly accepted. Without the railroad to provide access, the remote reservation would have little public benefit. The tourist trade would also boost the fledgling economies of Wyoming, Montana, and Idaho. The commingling of public good and private profit would have to wait, however. The economic crisis of 1873 plunged the Northern Pacific into bankruptcy. The company reorganized, but the lingering depression kept the railroad from reaching Livingston, Montana,

until 1883. A spur was soon extended south toward the park.[48]

The 1872 legislation directed that the park was to be administered by the secretary of the interior as "a public park or pleasuring-ground for the benefit and enjoyment of the people." Achieving this goal would require roads and other accommodations. How these would be provided was uncertain, since the federal government's park experience was limited to squares and circles in the nation's capital. *Scribner's* placed its faith in private enterprise, predicting "Yankee enterprise will dot the new Park with hostelries and furrow it with lines of travel." Langford sounded a more decorous note, envisioning a future in which "the march of civil improvements will reclaim this delightful solitude, and garnish it with all the attractions of cultivated taste and refinement." As with Yosemite, an impatient public awaited the provision of access to its promised pleasure ground. Yellowstone's more remote location and considerably greater extent posed even bigger challenges, which federal authorities were not initially eager to embrace.[49]

At the outset, there were two principal means of reaching the park, neither of which was

particularly inviting. Transcontinental travelers could take the Union Pacific to Corinne, Utah, endure a four-day stagecoach ride over crude roads to Virginia City, Montana, and follow an even rougher road 93 miles to the Lower Geyser Basin. Mammoth Hot Springs at the park's northwest corner could be reached by proceeding from Virginia City north to Bozeman and traveling approximately 75 miles on a newly built toll road along the Yellowstone and Gardner Rivers. Although an 1873 guidebook characterized this as "an excellent wagon road," disgruntled tourists disparaged it as "scarcely more than a trail." Travelers seeking comfort over expediency could ascend the Missouri River by steamboat to Fort Benton, Montana, and proceed by stage to Bozeman. The lack of roads within the park forced travelers to explore on horseback. Despite these difficulties, between three hundred and five hundred adventurous tourists visited the park during its first five years of operation. As with Yosemite, the rival routes competed for customers. To counter the lure of Bozeman's toll road, Virginia City residents solicited private contributions for improvements to the west entrance,

BELOW *Yellowstone Lake,* illustration from Edwin Stanley, *Rambles in Wonderland* (1878).

YELLOWSTONE LAKE.

advertising their route as "The National Park Free Wagon Road." The Union Pacific extended a spur line north into Idaho during the late 1870s, enhancing the western approach's appeal by cutting 200 miles off the stage ride to Virginia City. The balance shifted again when the Northern Pacific arrived in Livingston. The Yellowstone spur brought travelers to within a few miles of the park border by 1883.[50]

Improvements within the park proceeded so slowly that both visitors and park officials assailed the government's disregard for the traveling public. Langford's advocacy resulted in his appointment as superintendent. Recognizing that road development was essential not only to accommodate tourists but also to encourage concessionaires to develop the requisite facilities, he spent much of his time pleading for appropriations. Having created the park, Langford asserted, the federal government was obligated to "render it accessible to the people of all lands, who in future time will come in crowds to visit it." Langford's pleas came to naught, and he was replaced by Philetus Norris in 1878. While Norris had no formal training in civil engineering or park administration, he not only made the first real improvements but also provided the blueprint for Yellowstone's road system. Norris proposed to construct a wagon road connecting Mammoth Hot Springs, Tower Fall, the Lower Falls of the Yellowstone, Yellowstone Lake, the geyser basins, and the two main entrances. Like the circuit drives of private estates and municipal parks, the road would form a grand loop showcasing the park's principal attractions. Norris predicted that improving access in this manner would draw "teeming throngs of tourists to the bracing air, the healing bathing-pools, and matchless beauties of the 'wonder-land.'"[51]

Modest appropriations enabled Norris to initiate this ambitious undertaking. He focused first on the segment from Mammoth Hot Springs to the geyser basins. In addition to providing access to the celebrated thermal features, this would connect to the two entrances, creating a through route that would be valuable for practical and recreational purposes. Norris's forces faced numerous difficulties, including the steep ascent from Mammoth Hot Springs and the rugged Gibbon Canyon. The most unique challenge entailed squeezing the road between Swan Lake and an imposing promontory known as Obsidian Cliff. Since picks, shovels, and hand drills could scarcely

scratch the outcrop's volcanic glass, Norris's men built bonfires to heat the rock and then doused it with cold water. The contraction produced by the abrupt temperature change caused the surface to shatter. This innovative solution became part of the lore of the park and was celebrated in keepsake views and recounted by stagecoach drivers and guidebooks. Sixty miles of rough road were completed the first year, providing stagecoach access from Mammoth all the way through to the Lower Geyser Basin. By the end of 1881, Norris's last season as superintendent, a crude road extended around two-thirds of the proposed loop, though the Lower Falls and Grand Canyon could still only be reached by saddle trail.[52]

Crude appears to have been the operative word. The desire to improve access as quickly as possible combined with the inherent difficulty of the terrain resulted in what many characterized as an improved trail rather than a bona fide road. Norris's lack of experience compounded the problem. Rather than take the time to find routes that went around obstacles, he operated on the principle that a straight line was the shortest distance between two points. Grades were often inordinately steep, roadbeds were scraped out of hillsides with little or no reinforcement, and bone-jarring sections of "corduroy"—closely spaced logs placed across the travelway—were employed to excess. The road frequently devolved into an obstacle course of boulders, stumps, and mud wallows. One of Norris's successors, engineer and historian Hiram Chittenden, characterized the work as "ill-conceived and poorly executed" but noted that even a poor road constituted a marked improvement over no road at all. The traveling public was less charitable. Recounting an 1880 visit to Yellowstone, Carrie Adell Strahorn exclaimed, "There are no adjectives in our language that can properly define the public highway that was cut through heavy timber over rolling ground, with stumps left from two to twenty inches above the ground." Given Yellowstone's scenic splendor, she asserted, expending a little more time and effort would have produced "one of the finest drives in the world." Strahorn's party gave up on the idea of proceeding by wagon and completed their tour on horseback. Rufus Hatch, who as president of the Yellowstone Park Improvement Company was developing hotels and stagecoach lines, expressed similar frustration, proclaiming that those "who

make the long journey to the park should not be deprived of visits to the places of interest because of the roads." Widespread dissatisfaction with road conditions was a key factor in the 1883 decision to transfer responsibility for future improvements to the U.S. Army Corps of Engineers.[53]

The first engineering officer assigned to Yellowstone was Lieutenant Daniel C. Kingman, who arrived in the park in August 1883. Kingman was a West Point graduate who eventually became the chief officer of the Army Corps of Engineers. His sense of professionalism led him to pursue a policy that was the exact opposite of Norris's approach. Instead of rushing to expand the scope of the park road system, the engineers focused on constructing the best roads possible, reaching fewer attractions but with better roads. Kingman maintained that inadequate roads not only inconvenienced travelers but also presented the government in a bad light. National park roads, he insisted, should exhibit "the solid, durable and substantial quality that usually characterized the works constructed by the national government." This emphasis on quality over quantity would become one of the primary tenets of national park road development. Kingman also proposed standardized specifications to guide the process. Park roads should be 18 feet wide and surfaced with gravel, with a substantial crown to improve drainage and ditches to accommodate the run-off. Trees should be cleared to a width of 30 feet. Embankments would be supported with dry-laid stone retaining walls. Wet and swampy areas were to be drained whenever possible. When this was not feasible, smooth plank surfaces should replace the expedient but uncomfortable corduroy. Bridges should be solidly constructed of sawn lumber rather than thrown together with rough logs. Kingman brought a portable sawmill into the park to further this end. He also addressed the difficulties imposed by Yellowstone's unique conditions, observing that the park's terrain "presents in varied forms and combinations almost every obstacle that nature ever offered to the construction and maintenance of roads." Along with the normal challenges of steep terrain, rocky ledges, constricted canyons, swampy ground, and multiple stream crossings, the engineers had to contend with the short working season and extensive thermal formations. Nevertheless, Kingman proclaimed, with sufficient funding his forces would succeed in "making a highway into Wonderland that will surpass the famous Appian

Way." Funding limitations prevented Kingman from achieving these goals, but he made considerable progress. His technical specifications constituted the first attempt to develop comprehensive national park road standards.[54]

Kingman first turned his attention to the road between Mammoth Hot Springs and the geyser basins. As the most heavily traveled route in the park and one of the most poorly designed and constructed, it was in dire need of improvement. Over the next three years, Norris's rudimentary road was widened, cleared of rocks and stumps, and relocated to limit grades and reduce the number of stream crossings. Kingman's forces also relocated the north entrance road along the Gardner River, moving it down from its exposed position on the steep hillside. Kingman constructed a new cross-park route known as the Norris Cut-Off, which headed east from Norris Geyser Basin to the Grand Canyon of the Yellowstone. With its lower grades and better construction, this supplanted Norris's rough trail around the lake, though it required visitors to retrace their steps through the geyser basins.[55]

Kingman made his greatest mark by rerouting the road between Mammoth Hot Springs and Swan Lake Flat. The original route through Snow Pass was so steep and tortuous that it caused hardships for horses and passengers alike. Kingman replaced it with a more gradual ascent that followed the West Fork of the Gardner River and reached the Swan Lake plateau by way of a picturesque canyon known as the Golden Gate. To climb out of the canyon, the road had to ascend the steep hillside and cross an imposing cliff. During the summer of 1884, Kingman's forces hacked their way up the canyon wall. Enormous quantities of rock were excavated to make room for the roadbed. Since blasting a passage across the sheer cliff would have been inordinately expensive and would produce an egregious scar, Kingman constructed a 228-foot-long wooden trestle supporting a 16-foot-wide plank roadway. A slim wooden railing was all that separated visitors from the yawning chasm. The rickety-looking structure was completed in 1885. At the lower end of the trestle, workmen encountered a stone pillar split off from the main outcrop. Kingman's pragmatic advice was to send it crashing into the canyon, but the park's assistant superintendent suggested that tourists might enjoy the picturesque feature. A narrow

passageway was carved out of the cliff to provide a "natural gateway" just wide enough for one coach to pass. The stone stub was dubbed the "Pillar of Hercules," while the broader passage was called the "Golden Gate" in reference to the glowing hues of the canyon walls. By eliminating 30 miles of circuitous alignment and improving grades and road surfaces, Kingman's relocation reduced the standard park tour by a full day. The author of an 1886 travel account applauded the effort, proclaiming "so many improvements have been made, particularly during the last year, that whatever may have been the case heretofore, the Park is now traversed by the best roads I have ever seen in a mountain country."[56]

Despite Kingman's success, Yellowstone received minimal appropriations over the next few years. Though hampered by limited funds, the engineers managed to upgrade several troublesome sections and construct a number of bridges, including an 86-foot-long trestle in the Gibbon Canyon and a 115-foot crossing of a tributary of the Yellowstone River. Most of these spans were utilitarian wood or iron structures, reflecting budgetary constraints and the pragmatic orientation of the resident engineers. The Army Corps custodians were more than just technicians, however. In one of his pleas for funding, Kingman's successor, Captain Clinton Sears, echoed Olmsted's articulation of the essential goals of park management. "The National Park is a great national trust," Sears stated, "which

BELOW Golden Gate Viaduct (Kingman version), postcard, ca. 1910.

3551 GOLDEN GATE AND BRIDGE

7625

should be carefully guarded and preserved, while, at the same time, made readily, safely, and cheaply accessible throughout its extent." While Olmsted is widely credited with formulating this policy, the unlikelihood that Sears would have encountered his uncirculated Yosemite report suggests that balancing preserving and access was broadly understood to be the central challenge of park management.[57]

Considerable progress was made in 1891–92, due to a boost in funding and the efforts of Lieutenant Hiram Chittenden, a West Point–trained engineer whose energy and acumen would play a crucial role in Yellowstone's development. During the first summer, he upgraded Norris's crude track between the Upper Geyser Basin and the Grand Canyon so visitors were no longer forced to backtrack. By the end of the following year, tourists could make a circuit from Mammoth through the Geyser basins to Yellowstone Lake and the Grand Canyon and Lower Falls, returning via the Norris Cut-Off. The ultimate goal of incorporating Mount Washburn and Tower Fall remained unrealized, but visitors were finally able to reach most of the park's major attractions with reasonable speed and comfort.[58]

Chittenden was reassigned to Louisville, Kentucky, and another period of intermittent improvements ensued. Side roads were developed to various features, and a rough entrance road was extended south from Yellowstone Lake to the upper reaches of Jackson Hole. Considerable sums were spent spanning a ravine near the Upper Fall with an open-spandrel concrete-arch bridge. Similar structures garnered acclaim in urban settings, but critics complained that the monumental edifice clashed with its sylvan surroundings. An even more inappropriate span was projected to cross the Yellowstone River so that visitors could more easily reach Artist Point, where Thomas Moran purportedly composed his iconic view. The proposed design was provided by a Northern Pacific engineer and looked the part. The iron truss was sturdy and economical, but its utilitarian appearance was incompatible with the aesthetic aims of national park development. For once Congress's stinginess had a salutary effect. Funding shortages prevented the structure from marring the picturesque location.[59]

Protesting the perennial funding woes, Acting Superintendent George Anderson lamented, "There is not an impoverished community occupying a similar area within the limits of the United States that does not yearly devote more money to the single work of road repairs." Reiterating the argument that the federal government was obligated to improve access, his successor, Captain James B. Erwin, asserted: "If Congress intends to ratify and make good its dedication of the park to the people of the United States as a pleasuring ground for its benefit and enjoyment, it should yield to the demands of the people and make additional appropriation for the construction of new roads, which will add to their pleasure and benefit by opening new and wonderful phenomena and scenery." Visitors continued to express their frustrations. After touring the park in 1896, popular travel writer John Stoddard cast the situation as a national disgrace. "Everyone knows how roads in Europe climb the steepest grades in easy curves, and are usually smooth as a marble table, free from obstacles, and carefully walled-in by parapets of stone," he declared. Presenting park road development as a patriotic imperative, Stoddard remonstrated, "Surely, the honor of our Government demands that this unique museum of marvels should be the pride and glory of the nation, with highways equal to any in the world."[60]

Chittenden returned in 1899. Recognizing that Congress paid little heed to minor requests, he proposed an ambitious development program. Chittenden focused his initial attention on the Golden Gate. Kingman's road had been a distinct improvement, but it contained some of the steepest grades in the park, creating a bad impression and accounting for numerous accidents. Along with reducing grades, eliminating dangerous curves, widening the roadbed, and revising the alignment to incorporate a picturesque limestone formation known as the Hoodoos, Chittenden replaced the timber trestle with a more substantial concrete structure. The wooden platform was structurally sound, but its precarious appearance generated what Chittenden diplomatically described as "uneasiness and concern among the traveling public."[61] Rudyard Kipling, who toured the park in 1889, provided a more colorful characterization:

We heard the roar of the river, and the road went round a corner. On one side piled rock and shale, that enjoined silence for fear of a general slide-down; on the other a sheer drop, and a fool of a noisy river below. Then, apparently in the middle of the road, lest any should find driving too easy, a post of rock. Nothing beyond that save the flank of a cliff. Then my stomach departed from me, as it does when you swing, for we left the dirt, which was at least some guarantee of safety, and sailed out round the curve, and up a steep incline, on a plank-road built out from the cliff. The planks were nailed at the outer edge, and did not shift or creak very much—but enough, quite enough. That was the Golden Gate.[62]

Chittenden's viaduct was much more substantial, both from an engineering perspective and, perhaps more importantly, in the eyes of visitors. The massive reinforced-concrete structure consisted of a solid deck supported by concrete arches resting on solid rock. The deck was widened to accommodate the standard 18-foot-wide roadbed, and a sturdy concrete parapet ran the entire length. During the course of construction, questions arose about the fate of the stone column, which had become a celebrated feature of the Yellowstone tour. With the wider roadbed and new grade, the pillar stood squarely in the way of the engineer's plans. Chittenden initially insisted that safety and efficiency should trump "sentimentalism," especially in such a hazardous location, but park photographer F. J. Haynes convinced him that the public would lament the landmark's loss. Preserving the pillar was an engineering achievement in its own right. The 23-ton monolith was jacked up 6 feet to meet the new grade and shifted 6 feet sideways, where it rested on a stout concrete column constructed to ensure its stability. The foundation and other signs of the operation were carefully concealed so that tourists could continue to marvel at the propitious location of this "natural" gateway.[63]

Chittenden constructed two more monumental structures during his final term in the park. Politics and serendipity played a pivotal role in securing the requisite financing. During the summer of 1901, the notoriously stingy chairman of the House Appropriations Committee, Illinois representative Joe Cannon, decided to pay a visit to Yellowstone. Chittenden escorted the congressman around the park, demonstrating the road system's inadequacies and promoting his improvement schemes. The following year, Congress appropriated $250,000, more than doubling the previous allotment. Another $500,000 was authorized over the next two years. Chittenden first set about improving the northern entrance. He wanted to make entering the park a more memorable experience, since the bland expanse

of sagebrush at the reservation's border afforded a poor first impression. When the Northern Pacific constructed a handsome rustic station just outside the boundary, he decided that a monumental stone arch would complement the boulder-clad building while affording an appropriately dignified entrance. Many municipal parks greeted their visitors with imposing entranceways, so the idea of a grandiose gateway was not as outlandish as it might seem. In both cases, the intention was not just to demarcate

boundaries but to emphasize that public parks were important civic institutions, created by benevolent governments for the betterment of society. Chittenden drew up plans for a towering structure framing a portal 30 feet tall and 20 feet wide. Rugged stone walls extended on either side. Constructed of rough-hewn basalt, the arch mirrored the monumental rusticity of the railroad station along with iconic Old Faithful Inn. An inscription across the top of the arch proudly proclaimed: "FOR THE BENEFIT AND ENJOYMENT

8128. Entrance Gateway to Yellowstone National Park.

4022
Golden Gate looking East, Yellowstone Park.

> ## "The work is as attractive as ever falls to the lot of the road engineer, and it is doubtful if another opportunity exists to develop a road system which, if properly done, will reflect so much credit on the government building it."
>
> CHITTENDEN ON THE CHALLENGES OF
> ROAD BUILDING IN YELLOWSTONE

OF THE PEOPLE." President Theodore Roosevelt laid the cornerstone on a widely reported visit in April 1903. The "Roosevelt Arch" was completed later that year and became another iconic element of the Yellowstone experience, appearing on souvenirs ranging from stereoscopic views to silver spoons and porcelain plates.[64]

The third major structure was an elegant arched bridge spanning the Yellowstone River a few hundred yards upstream from the Upper Falls, where his predecessor had proposed an ungainly iron truss. Chittenden insisted the span be designed in "a style and character in keeping with the magnificence of the surroundings." He contemplated a monumental masonry arch, but funding concerns precluded such an expensive approach. Instead, he turned to an innovative new technology patented by Austrian engineer Joseph Melan, which emulated traditional arch construction at considerably lower cost. By encasing iron or steel beams with poured-in-place concrete, the Melan method produced a strong yet slender arch affording the graceful and dignified appearance Chittenden deemed essential. The dramatic site entailed a hazardous and technically challenging construction process. Chittenden found a spot where outcrops narrowed the water-level distance to 47 feet, though the deck stretched to 120 feet. A temporary

pier was constructed in the middle of the river to support false work for the concrete forms, and the steel girders were anchored in place. The concrete had to be poured in one continuous process to achieve maximum strength. This would have been an ambitious undertaking in any circumstance, but the remote location meant that Chittenden's crew had to do all the work by hand. A temporary generating plant was installed for lighting so the crew could work around the clock. Timing the project to coincide with a full moon for additional illumination, 150 men worked in eight-hour shifts to complete the task in seventy-four hours. With a 14.5-foot-wide carriageway flanked by narrow walkways, the bridge fell short of Kingman's standards, but Chittenden maintained that the unique situation merited special treatment. Ornamental balustrades were cast in place on either side. While the design presented a sharp contrast to the rustic aesthetics that came to dominate national park construction, its graceful profile and neoclassical detail were rooted in conventions tracing back through American municipal parks and European landscape gardens to the origins of the picturesque aesthetic in literature and painting. It soon became known as the Chittenden Bridge in honor of its creator.[65]

Although these structures were Chittenden's most conspicuous achievements, his most

significant legacy may have been the articulation of development principles that became fundamental tenets of national park policy. Chittenden's fundamental precept was that since national parks were intended for public enjoyment, the government was obligated to ensure that principal features could be experienced with reasonable convenience. "If the roads are bad, the hotels ill-kept, or the transportation uncomfortable," he contended, "no amount of grandeur of natural scenery can compensate for these defects." At the same time, he insisted that the park "should be preserved in its natural state to the fullest degree possible." Chittenden regarded roads as the "least objectionable of all forms of artificial changes," but he maintained that they should "not be unnecessarily extended." The majority of the park should be reserved for the enjoyment of visitors on foot or horseback. Where roads were deemed necessary, every effort should be made to ensure their quality. "The true policy of the government in dealing with this problem," he declared, "should therefore be to make the roads as limited in extent as will meet actual necessities, but to make such as are found necessary perfect examples of their class." Chittenden's idea of perfection encompassed both practical and aesthetic concerns. Like Olmsted, he insisted that these attributes proceeded hand

in hand. A well-engineered road that marred the landscape or afforded insufficient opportunity for scenic enjoyment failed to fulfill its function just as much as a road that posed undue hardships for the traveling public. As with Olmsted's Yosemite statements and the Organic Act's injunction to balance preservation and access, the question of what constituted "actual necessities" and "limited in extent" would engender impassioned debate.[66]

Chittenden's remarks on the technical and aesthetic challenges of road building focused on Yellowstone, but they were equally applicable to other parks. The terrain was riddled with streams, cliffs, chasms, and other obstacles. The work season was short. The mud was bad and the dust was worse. Conditions changed so much from one place to another that an engineer could "encounter in any single mile of road construction all the varieties of work which he would find in building a turnpike from Portland in Maine to Portland in Oregon." Natural obstacles were compounded by insufficient funding. Despite, or perhaps because of these challenges, Chittenden pronounced: "The work is as attractive as ever falls to the lot of the road engineer, and it is doubtful if another opportunity exists to develop a road system which, if properly done, will reflect so much credit on the government building it." The basic goals, he declared, were to

"secure good gradients and safe locations and to carry the roads where they would best develop the scenery." For engineers who relished the aesthetic aspects of road design, Chittenden enthused, "the opportunities for artistic work in harmony with the surroundings are almost endless." Underscoring the connection between national park road development and historical precedents, he invoked Downing's advice and made repeated references to municipal park practice.[67]

The enhanced budgets and advancing state of Yellowstone's road system allowed Chittenden to pay more attention to aesthetic concerns and visitor's comfort. One of his most basic but widely appreciated improvements was to develop an elaborate dust-control program employing a fleet of sprinkling wagons to soak the park roads every morning and evening. To alleviate the monotonous straightaways encountered on many older sections, he called for new alignments employing sinuous curves in order "to shorten the view ahead and enhance the interest to travelers." In another echo of Olmsted's admonitions, he observed that winding roadways with curves "carefully adjusted to the accidents of the ground" were more aesthetically appealing and minimized the need for expensive and scenery-scarring excavations. Where cuts and fills were unavoidable, they should be supported by attractive stone retaining walls. Precarious passages should be protected with wood rails or rustic stone walls. Grades should be reduced to 8 percent, which was considered the maximum at which stagecoaches could descend safely. Since the purpose of park roads was to enhance the tourist experience and not simply to move traffic from one point to another, the overriding concern was not engineering efficiency, but the desire to make the travel experience "as pleasant and free from monotony as possible." Despite his engineering background, Chittenden maintained that deviations from the official standards were permissible to avoid compromising scenic features. Noting the folly of attempting to widen and straighten the road through the Hoodoos, he suggested stage drivers alter their behavior instead. "It would be better

RIGHT Buggy on
Mount Washburn
Road, Yellowstone
National Park, 1912.

FAR RIGHT Dunraven
Pass, Yellowstone
National Park,
Haynes postcard,
ca. 1912.

ABOVE View of Mount
Washburn Road, from
Northern Pacific Railway,
*Yellowstone National Park:
America's Only Geyserland*
(1914).

RIGHT Corkscrew Bridge at
Sylvan Pass, Yellowstone
National Park, postcard,
ca. 1910.

to require all teams to come to a walk there," he pronounced, "than to remedy the defect by blasting out those picturesque rocks." Chittenden also called for a roadside improvement program to remove dead and downed timber and encourage grass to grow along the roadsides. Along with enhancing appearances, this would attract elk and other animals for the tourists' viewing pleasure. "In these and many other ways," he enthused, "the roads will themselves be made one of the interesting features of this most interesting region."[68]

Chittenden implemented his road-building

philosophy on the final segment of the Belt Line between the Grand Canyon and Tower Fall. This 20-mile stretch encompassed some of the most difficult construction in the park. The relatively level end sections were completed in 1903. An additional two years were required to cross Dunraven Pass and construct a spur to the summit of Mount Washburn, the loftiest peak in the park. The pass topped out at 8,800 feet; Mount Washburn soared to 10,243 feet. The difficulties of working at such elevations and the need for extensive blasting and rockwork delayed progress considerably. The short

working season, hazardous terrain, thin air, and biting wind posed significant hardships. So much blasting was required that Chittenden admitted it sounded as if "artillery was playing upon an enemy." The effort, expense, and aggressive tactics were justified, he declared, because the finished product was "by far the finest road for scenery in the park." Chittenden maintained that the long-awaited link afforded a "marvelous development of scenery which perhaps has no parallel on any other highway in the world." Rising out of the forest, the road wove in and out of deep ravines, then climbed toward Dunraven Pass in graceful curves. The pass itself was relatively mild and sheltered until it reached a rocky spur. From that point on, the views shifted dramatically as it switched from one side of the ridge to the other, affording constantly changing scenery, until it plunged down in a series of tight curves displaying sweeping vistas.[69]

Adventurous parties could take an alternate route passing directly over Mount Washburn. This was by all accounts the most dramatic road in the park. Climbing steeply toward the summit, it curled around imposing buttresses, zigzagged up precipitous slopes, and balanced precariously on a spine of rock Chittenden described as "so broken and wild that it might well appall an engineer who should seek to find a passage through it." A final spiral brought visitors to the windswept summit. Substantial retaining walls were required to create a minimally adequate roadbed. Stone guard walls were constructed in abundance, but some of the most hair-raising stretches were largely unprotected. While the gently curving Dunraven Pass Road lay lightly on the landscape, the Mount Washburn Road was an emphatic declaration of man's triumph over nature. Touting the accomplishment, Chittenden proclaimed: "The road itself is an object of interest here, from the great difficulty of construction and the dangerous situations through which it passes." For Chittenden, the road's visibility was not an aesthetic error or philosophical affront but an expression of progress and testament to the national park ideal. Chronicling the park's development, he enthused, "At last come pick and spade and dynamite, and a roadway is carved up the rocky slopes to this very summit, that man may come here, through all future time, and study the handiwork of nature as it lies outspread before him."[70]

The Mount Washburn Road was not just a means of gaining access to signature scenery. Like Yosemite's Zigzag, it thrilled visitors with a dynamic interplay of sights and sensations that embodied earlier paeans to the sublime. Occupants of the smaller "mountain wagons" that supplanted stagecoaches for the challenging trip were treated to what Chittenden characterized as a "kaleidoscopic effect" as they wound up the mountain. Glimpses of distant scenery alternated with visions of jagged cliffs and dizzying depths as visitors spiraled toward the summit. Anticipation and exhilaration oscillated with fear and foreboding. Arriving at the summit, they encountered a sweeping panorama that revealed the vast extent of the park, with Yellowstone Lake and

other elements of the journey laid out in miniature. The top of the mountain was graded to provide an area where coaches could be turned around, though a small pinnacle representing the original elevation was retained. A stone observatory was constructed to shelter visitors from strong winds and inclement weather. Although Dunraven Pass was officially part of the Grand Loop, its steep grades, lingering snows, and unpredictable weather prompted many visitors to forego the experience. The stagecoach companies hesitated to incorporate it into their itineraries because it was often not passable until mid-July and subjected horses to additional stress. Nevertheless, many visitors insisted on ascending the park's highest peak. While they may not have consciously embraced Chittenden's assertions, the prevalence of souvenir views portraying the road's upper reaches suggested that the juxtaposition of natural beauty and technical triumph exerted widespread appeal.[71]

The East Entrance, or Sylvan Pass Road, was completed in 1905, much to the delight of Burlington Railroad officials and the business community of Cody, Wyoming, whose eponymous founder played a prominent promotional role. The route's most notable engineering feature was the "Corkscrew Bridge," or "Loopover." In order to maintain a reasonable grade on the steep incline,

the road looped over itself in a tight spiral comprised of earthen ramps and a curving timber trestle. This unusual structure became another icon of the Yellowstone tour, appearing in stereo views, postcards, and other souvenirs. A less picturesque but more technically impressive accomplishment entailed spanning the Gardner River with a 410-foot, five-span steel-arch bridge. Towering 70 feet high, this was by far the largest bridge in the park and a distinct departure from the rustic aesthetic. Chittenden also shifted a mile-long section of the north entrance road from the east side of the Gardner River to the west in an unsuccessful attempt to reduce the dangers and disruptions of landslides caused by the canyon's unstable walls.[72]

Chittenden was transferred to Seattle in 1906. Before leaving, he proclaimed that Yellowstone's road system was essentially complete. Additional improvements were necessary, particularly in the realm of road surfacing, but he expressed confidence that subsequent road builders would uphold the principles established by their predecessors. A comprehensive but carefully limited road system constructed to exacting aesthetic and technical standards would not only fulfill the needs of current and future tourists but put an end to ongoing attempts by railroad companies to construct railways in the park. The railroad

No. 143   COACHING PARTY—YELLOWSTONE PARK.   HAYNES-PHOTO.   Printed in Germany.

ABOVE Yellowstone coaching party, postcard, ca. 1910.

Tourists preserved their Yellowstone memories by purchasing keepsakes memorializing not just the park's natural features, but the stagecoach experience and signature elements of the road system itself.

ABOVE, CLOCKWISE FROM LEFT Golden Gate souvenirs: hand mirror, ca. 1910; tray, made in Austria, 1920s; and spoon featuring Roosevelt Arch gateway to Yellowstone, ca. 1903.

OPPOSITE Ludwig Hohlwein, Yellow-stone stagecoach poster, 1910.

interests had been lobbying Congress since the 1880s, insisting their schemes were necessitated by the inadequacies of existing roads. Along with the destructive impact on park scenery, Chittenden believed that rail lines would destroy the park's primitive charm. Claiming that 95 percent of tourists opposed railway development, he predicted that "future generations will commend that wisdom which excluded from this region the innovations of modern travel, and left one place in the world where the horse and the coach can not be displaced by steam or electricity."[73]

The resistance to mechanized transportation underscored the degree to which stagecoach travel was considered an integral component of the Yellowstone experience. The typical visitor journeyed by train to the outskirts of the park and traveled by stagecoach from one major feature to the next, staying at hotels located a day's drive apart. The north entrance was the most popular, but the west entrance saw considerable use. The east entrance was the least heavily trafficked. Visitors arriving from the north were loaded into massive "Tally Ho" stagecoaches, whisked through the monumental arch, and carried up Gardner Canyon to Mammoth Hot Springs.

Arriving in early afternoon, they could explore the area, retreat to their rooms, or linger about the lobby socializing and buying souvenirs. The next morning they boarded smaller four-horse coaches and proceeded toward the park's main attractions at an average pace of 6 mph. Drivers sought to maintain a 200-yard interval in a fruitless effort to minimize the dust clouds, which, a typical account reported, "envelop us so that we are scarcely able to distinguish each other." Thick linen dusters were provided, along with veils for the ladies. Savvy tourists vied for the first coach of the day to limit their exposure to the park's infamous dust menace. Stagecoach drivers described salient features as they wound along, recounting Yellowstone lore and legend to fill the lengthy intervals. The glass road at Obsidian Cliff, the Golden Gate, and other construction exploits were colorfully expounded. After a hot, dusty trek through extensive lodgepole pine forests, they spent the second night at the Lower Geyser Basin. Lodging was initially limited to crude wooden buildings that provoked considerable complaint. The more refined Fountain Hotel opened in 1891, affording many of the niceties of eastern resorts, including heated baths and ballroom dancing. Until Chittenden improved the road to Lake Yellowstone, tourists spent the next day exploring the Upper Geyser Basin and returned for a second night. On the third day they slogged across the monotonous Norris Cut-Off to the Grand Canyon, where they viewed the falls, spent one more night in the park, and returned to Mammoth Hot Springs, covering the return trip in one long, dusty day. Chittenden's improvement eliminated considerable backtracking and made the lake a more prominent component of the tour. The concomitant construction of the elegant Colonial Revival Lake Hotel added another night and day to the itinerary, extending the standard stay from four to five days. Rustic accommodations near the Grand Canyon gave way to a 250-room hotel in 1890, which was replaced by a sprawling 400-room structure in 1910. The opening of Old Faithful Inn in 1904 allowed tourists to spend the night at the Upper Geyser Basin. All three were developed by a subsidiary of the Northern Pacific Railroad and boasted impressive facilities, entertainments, and prices. Most visitors experienced Yellowstone as part of a package tour that included transcontinental rail fare and stagecoach transportation, food, and lodging. The expense of this endeavor, together with the time involved, limited the experience to a primarily wealthy and upper-middle-class clientele. Tourists willing to embrace more spartan conditions could tour the park with one of several companies that housed visitors in tents. The most popular of these, the Wylie Way, was a favorite of teachers, church groups, and others on relatively modest budgets. These tourists were often treated as second-class citizens by the railroads and their affiliates. The minority who toured and camped on their own were viewed even less favorably.[74]

While the tour encompassed a wide range of natural curiosities and impressive scenery, there were long stretches where the road passed through relatively featureless forest. There were also points where the drive could become a bit too stimulating. Guidebooks employed words such as "exciting" and "exhilarating" to describe such passages. Some drivers courted disaster by increasing speed to enhance the thrill. Even on less challenging terrain, horses could bolt, stumble, and cause mishaps ranging from the comical to the tragic. Stagecoach wrecks, while uncommon, occasionally resulted in serious injury or loss of life. As in Yosemite, stagecoach holdups were a rare though highly romanticized event, the possibility of which contributed to perceptions that a visit to Yellowstone was not just a scenic excursion but a journey into America's frontier past. The last holdup in Yellowstone occurred in July 1915, besting Yosemite for the title of last stagecoach robbery in a national park and constituting one of the last crimes of its kind in the United States.[75]

The scope and complexity of the park transportation system impressed tourists and seasoned travel writers alike. The stagecoach companies maintained vast fleets of vehicles along with extensive support facilities, armies of employees, and herds of horses that consumed tremendous quantities of hay, grain, and forage. By 1914, the Yellowstone Park Transportation Company had more than one thousand horses at its disposal. Stoddard expressed wonderment at the magnitude of the operation, while the Arts and Crafts apostles Elbert and Alice Hubbard marveled at its railroad-like efficiency. Even John Muir was impressed, though he lamented that the pace of the standard tour prevented visitors from experiencing the park's full benefits.[76]

By the early 1900s, the roads themselves generated glowing reviews. One guidebook proclaimed that "the drive around the Circuit Road

of the Yellowstone Park has not its equal on earth" and boasted that the circuit afforded "a coaching trip that is talked about all around the world."[77] Marveling at Norris's Obsidian Cliff accomplishment, travel writer William Thayer exclaimed, "Here are cliffs composed of volcanic glass, with a glass road along their base. Nature made the cliffs just as they are, but *man* made the road of materials which nature furnished."[78] The Golden Gate elicited rhapsodic tributes. "A solitary boulder, detached from its companions on the cliff, seems to be stationed at this portal like a sentinel to watch all tourists who come and go," Stoddard effused. "It echoes to the voices of those who enter almost as eager as seekers after gold; and, a week later, sees them return, browned by the sun, invigorated by the air, and joyful in the acquisition of incomparable memories."[79] Most visitors hailed the improved roads, but Chittenden noted that "an occasional crank" lamented their impact. As early as 1894, he reported, skeptics maintained the government should stop improving the roads because further enhancements would attract "a horde of the idle curious whom it would be better to keep away." While they appreciated the improvements that enabled them to enjoy the park, such critics contended that additional development would "convert this grand domain from the wild state in which nature gave it to man, to a crowded summer resort."[80]

Tourists preserved their Yellowstone memories by purchasing keepsakes memorializing not just the park's natural features, but the stagecoach experience and signature elements of the road system itself. The Golden Gate, Roosevelt Arch, Corkscrew Bridge, and Obsidian Cliff were celebrated in souvenirs ranging from playing cards, postcards, and stereo views to hand mirrors and fine china. Images of stagecoaches abounded in guidebooks and other media. One of the most notable renditions was a 1910 print commissioned by the Northern Pacific Railway depicting a heavily loaded Tally-Ho coach drawn by six lively steeds. The Northern Pacific's promotional booklets featured tourist-filled coaches pulling away from the Gardiner station, passing through the Roosevelt Arch, and lining up at the company's hotels. Many items paired stagecoaches with emblems of Yellowstone's natural wonders. The range of stagecoach talismans extended to charm bracelets and silver spoons, where they were often joined by the Roosevelt Arch and Golden Gate. Yellowstone's association with stagecoaches was so strong that automobile opponents suggested the park be reserved as a protected realm for the perpetuation of the fast-disappearing means of travel. When they were finally retired after the 1916 season, a solitary relic at park headquarters was celebrated in postcards and personal photographs.[81]

YELLOWSTONE—PARK

MOUNT RAINIER NATIONAL PARK

In 1899 Congress established Mount Rainier as America's fifth national park, setting aside an 18-square-mile tract centered on the massive snow-capped mountain. As with Yellowstone and Yosemite, support for the park reflected both practical and idealistic concerns. John Muir was an early advocate, as was the British statesman and American park enthusiast James Bryce. The National Geographic Society, Sierra Club, and Appalachian Mountain Club also supported the designation. The Northern Pacific Railroad again played an influential role, lobbying Congress and paying writers and photographers to promote the area's attractions. The railroad's transcontinental line terminated in nearby Tacoma and officials were confident that the same combination of preservation and selective development that benefited

their Yellowstone interests would transform Mount Rainier into a profitable attraction. Commercial organizations in Tacoma and Seattle backed the proposal in the hope of capitalizing on the tourist trade. The motivations were not entirely economic. Many local boosters ascribed to prevailing theories about the social, spiritual, and patriotic value of national parks. Mount Rainier's majestic presence also engendered a strong sense of civic pride in the two cities, which both collaborated and competed in efforts to develop the park.[82]

The first to exploit Mount Rainier's recreational potential was a local entrepreneur named James Longmire, who established a primitive "health resort" at mineral springs within the future park boundaries in 1883. By 1885 he opened a crude trail to his holdings. When his efforts to convince public officials to improve access came to naught, he undertook the task himself. By 1891 he had roughed out a road to "Longmire Springs." As with Norris's efforts, the term "road" was something of a

misnomer, as stumps, boulders, and other obstacles made passage by wheeled vehicles a challenging prospect. Observing that many travelers were more interested in mountain scenery than mineral waters, Longmire opened a horse trail to Paradise Valley, an idyllic subalpine meadow on the southern flank of Mount Rainier that would become the primary park destination. By the mid-1890s a tent camp was located in the vicinity. The increasing interest elicited demands for a more reasonable road to Longmire and on to Paradise. The national park designation produced additional pressure to improve access, though funds to accomplish the task were not immediately forthcoming.[83]

In 1903 Congress made a modest appropriation to survey a road into the park. Despite agitation from Seattle interests, the Longmire entrance was selected. Not only was the route already established, but since it led toward Tacoma, the Northern Pacific wielded its influence. Following the pattern established in Yellowstone, the U.S.

ABOVE Proposed alignment for Nisqually Road, Mount Rainier National Park, 1904.

Army Corps of Engineers was enlisted to provide the necessary expertise. The project was assigned to Eugene Ricksecker. Ricksecker decided the road should follow the existing route as far as Longmire but concluded that the trail to Paradise should be relocated to reduce grades and display scenery to better advantage. The new alignment showcased Narada Falls, Christine Falls, the terminus of the Nisqually Glacier, and a stunning overlook that became known as Ricksecker Point. While Longmire's route climbed straight up the mountain, Ricksecker employed long curves and looping switchbacks to gain elevation. To minimize expensive and unsightly excavations, he instructed his surveyors to "follow the graceful curves of the natural surface of the ground." Echoing Olmsted's prescriptions for municipal parks, Ricksecker contended that conforming the alignment to natural contours was "more pleasing and far less distractive than regular curves laid with mathematical precision." The circuitous alignment would also induce "a keen state of expectancy as to the new pleasures held in store at the next turn." The winding roadway alternately exposed and concealed views of the mountain above and river below while revealing a succession of waterfalls and other picturesque features. The stretch from Longmire Springs to the park border was less spectacular, passing through dense stands of forest that afforded few distinctive views. Ricksecker specified a 16-foot-wide roadway with elaborate drainage features to counter the region's heavy rains. He also called for an unusually broad 60-foot-wide cleared right-of-way, observing that the increased sun exposure would help dry out the road and hasten the melting of winter snows. Occasional trees would be left standing to create a pleasingly natural effect. Several substantial bridges would be required to span rivers and deep ravines. Looking ahead, he called for the eventual development of a circuit road around Mount Rainier, located as high on the mountain as possible to afford the most spectacular views. This Yellowstone-style grand loop would be reached by access roads from all sides of the park, spreading the parks' economic benefits and adding to travelers' convenience.[84]

Construction began in August 1904, but trying conditions, bad weather, and problems with the contractor severely hampered progress. Ricksecker soon discovered that his specifications were overly ambitious. Work slowed to a crawl as he persisted in pursuing his original goals rather

than changing tactics to increase production. The Army Corps of Engineers reassigned Chittenden to the Seattle District in 1906 to try to get the project on track. After reviewing the work, Chittenden contended that Ricksecker's approach was too elaborate for the task at hand. Completing the road as originally envisioned would take far too long and the cost would be astronomical. Chittenden advised that the roadway be narrowed from 16 to 12 feet, to be expanded when resources allowed. This was the exact opposite of the approach he and Kingman had pursued in Yellowstone, but given the primitive state of the park's road system, Norris's emphasis on expedient access trumped the pursuit of perfection.[85]

The road was completed from the park entrance to Longmire Springs by the end of 1907. The upper road reached the Nisqually Glacier the following summer, occasioning remarks on its status as the first and only road in America to afford access to an active glacier. The entire 25 miles from the park entrance to Paradise Valley was officially completed in 1910, though considerable work remained to be done. Although Mount Rainier National Park superintendent Edward Hall heralded the achievement, he noted that the width shrank to a mere 10 feet in places and poor drainage created seas of mud. Hall called for the entire

roadway to be macadamized, widened to 16 feet, and equipped with more substantial retaining walls and parapets. The road included several impressive wooden bridges, including a curved structure over Van Trump Creek. Seeking to provide a regionally appropriate equivalent to Yellowstone's Roosevelt Arch, Hall authorized construction of a rustic gateway comprised of massive cedar logs. The structure was completed in 1911 and immortalized in countless photographs, postcards, and other souvenirs. Hall spoke glowingly of the road's practical value and aesthetic appeal, but the engineering officers who succeeded Chittenden contended that it was already obsolete. The problem, they observed, was that it was designed and constructed as a wagon road, and Mount Rainier had opened its gates to automobiles. This charge was not limited to Mount Rainier. The automobile's arrival introduced new technical, aesthetic, and administrative challenges in all parks. On a broader level, the advent of motor tourism was destined to exert a profound influence on deliberations about the appropriate balance of preservation and access in America's national parks.[86]

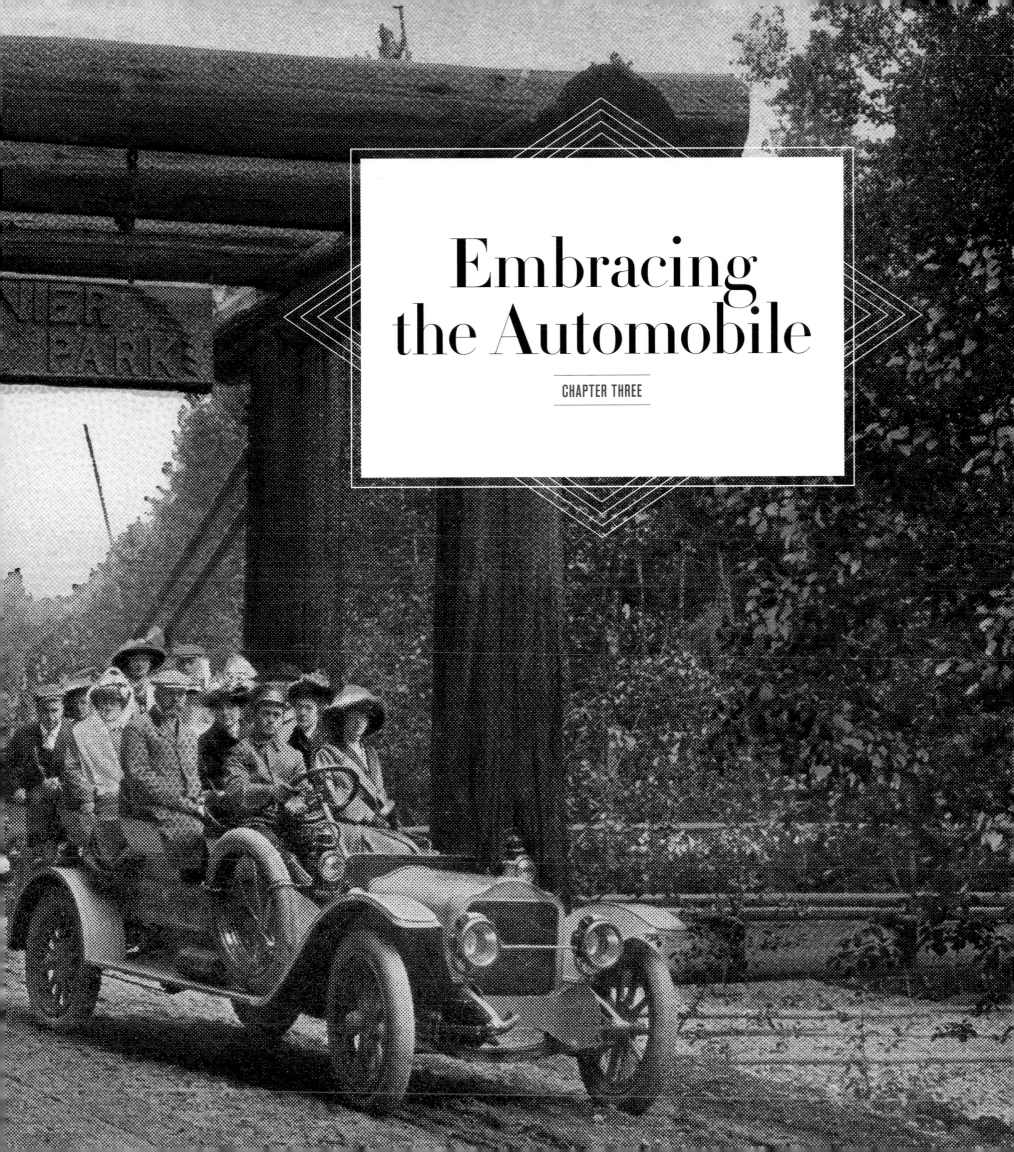

Embracing the Automobile

CHAPTER THREE

ABOVE First auto in Sequoia
National Park, 1910.

PREVIOUS Entrance Arch,
Mount Rainier National
Park, postcard, ca. 1915.

the accessibility of America's national parks, automobiles would allow a broader segment of the population to enjoy their benefits, improving the nation's moral, physical, and spiritual fiber and boosting local economies in the process. On a more pragmatic front, park proponents believed that catering to motorists would broaden support for the national park system. Park managers were not blind to the implications of their decision. They recognized that embracing the automobile increased the challenge of balancing preservation and access. The concomitant creation of the National Park Service was intended to ensure that the management of America's national parks would be guided by committed professionals capable of reconciling potential conflicts through comprehensive planning, sound engineering, and sensitive landscape design.[1]

THE MACHINE ENTERS THE GARDEN

The first automobile to enter a national park set out from the foothill town of Ramona on the morning of June 23, 1900, bound for Yosemite National Park and a rendezvous with history that has been celebrated and reviled ever since. Owned by Los Angeles photographer Oliver Lippincott and driven by a hired mechanic, the Locomobile was a steam-powered vehicle capable of speeds up to 40 mph, though road conditions kept the duo from attaining that remarkable rate of locomotion. Leaving early to avoid conflict with horse-drawn stages, they covered the 44 miles to Wawona in a little over five hours. For stagecoach passengers, this was generally a full day's journey. Despite the early start, they encountered several teams, most of which passed without incident. One freighter lost control of his horses, however, prompting him to exclaim, "What in —— —— do you want to bring such a nuisance up into this country for? You city people, with your contrivances are always making trouble." After a brief stop at Wawona, where the guests greeted them with glee and cadged rides around the hotel's circular drive, they set off for the steep, winding road into Yosemite Valley. "Dashing down the curves," in Lippincott's colorful recollection, they made the daylong trip to the valley floor in three hours. Lippincott recounted that

In the classic account of American attitudes toward technology, *The Machine in the Garden*, the historian Leo Marx highlighted a phenomenon he characterized as "the trope of the interrupted idyll." From train whistles disturbing Hawthorne's Sleepy Hollow reverie to the steamboat's annihilation of Huck Finn's raft and the blighted landscape en route to Gatsby's Long Island, machine-age intrusions signaled the end of Edenic innocence. While Marx's thesis has been challenged by subsequent scholars, his ascription of an intrinsic antipathy between the machine and the garden has long held sway with critics of park road development. Few contemporary observers objected to the automobile's arrival in national parks, however, at least not on philosophical grounds. Park officials expressed reservations, but their primary concern was that the existing roads could not accommodate motorized vehicles. Once this problem was resolved, most agreed, the automobile would exert a positive influence. By dramatically increasing they spent most of their stay "keeping the roads of the valley warm" by providing rides to local residents and curious tourists. The head of the Yosemite Stage and Turnpike Company, Henry Washburn, was particularly intrigued with the machine's potential. At Washburn's urging, the Locomobile's next test was to attempt the steep and tortuous ascent out of the valley and up to Glacier Point. The portly Lippincott proffered his seat to the veteran stage man and followed in a horse-drawn wagon, accompanied by a coterie of onlookers. The climb out of the valley proved more challenging, but after five hours of anxious maneuvering, the group arrived at the Glacier Point Hotel, where they were welcomed with cheers and toasts. The party muscled the vehicle onto the overhanging rock that served as a favored photo opportunity, memorializing the achievement in dramatic images. Lippincott also posed his car in front of Yosemite icons such as Mirror Lake, El Capitan, and the Wawona Tunnel Tree. His most pointed photograph portrayed the automobile atop Mariposa Grove's "Fallen Giant" with a stagecoach relegated to the shadows below. The *San Francisco Chronicle* celebrated the event in its Sunday supplement, reproducing Lippincott's photos and highlighting his assertion that the escapade heralded "a new era in the mode of conveyance into the Yosemite." Asserting that the park remained "inaccessible to the majority of the people," he enthused, "If modern invention can bring it closer to the people the result will be beneficial." Lippincott acknowledged that sentimentalists might bemoan the passage of horse-drawn stages but assured that automobiles posed no threat to park values. "There is only one Yosemite," he declared. "Whatever the new style of conveyance, it cannot detract from the sublimity of the great valley or lessen the majesty of the hills."[2]

Lippincott's adventure had little immediate impact. In 1900 there were only eight thousand automobiles in the entire country. While California laid claim to a disproportionate number, the lack of suitable roads made long-distance travel a daunting proposition. Lippincott shipped his car from Los Angeles to Fresno by train to overcome this difficulty. The next motorists to enter Yosemite—and the first to make the entire trip by automobile—were Frank and Arthur Holmes, who coaxed their Stanley Steamer all the way from San Francisco a month later. Those

two vehicles constituted the only automobile visits to Yosemite in 1900. The valley hosted a grand total of three automobiles the following year, all Locomobiles from the San Francisco area. This party chose to try its luck over the Big Oak Flat Road. Despite deep ruts, choking dust, a cracked frame, and broken drive-chain, the trip was proclaimed a success. Recounting the excursion in an amply illustrated *Overland Monthly* article, one of the motorists proclaimed, "The new century can certainly chronicle a vast undertaking successfully accomplished, when it records an automobile journeying to the Yosemite Valley and back." In what would become a common practice, the Locomobile Company employed photographs of the tourists motoring about Yosemite to advertise their products. The number of motorists attempting the trip increased slightly over the next few years, but the abysmal approach routes combined with steep, narrow, twisting roads into the valley limited the count of those completing the journey to fewer than four per season.[3]

Concerns were voiced about the automobile's impact as early as 1904, when the *Madera Tribune* reported that an effort was under way to ban them as "a menace to the safety of tourists." The paper accused motorists of driving too fast and failing to consider the safety of other visitors. Park residents petitioned the Yosemite Board of Commissioners to prohibit cars from entering the valley. Recognizing the rapidly growing power of the automobile lobby, the commissioners declined to take action. The Automobile Club of Southern California, whose well-connected members promoted the expansion of motoring opportunities throughout the state, was particularly influential. Automobile interests experienced a reversal of fortune in 1906, when the State of California retroceded Yosemite Valley and Mariposa Grove to the federal government. Major Harry Benson, who as commander of the troops protecting the park served as acting superintendent, was both less concerned with local politics and more solicitous of the safety of park visitors. As a cavalry officer, he may not have shared contemporary enthusiasms for the horseless carriage. At the beginning of the 1907 tourist season, Benson announced that automobiles would be prohibited from the park. Rather than express opposition to automobiles in principle, he cast the measure as a matter of public safety, asserting that the existing roads were too narrow and dangerous to accommodate

both motorists and horse-drawn vehicles. Benson blamed inconsiderate motorists for sealing their own fate, asserting that their refusal to follow regulations necessitated the ban. Automobile advocates protested vigorously, lobbying elected officials and decrying the prohibition in local and national publications. Condemning the ban as "an imposition on American citizens' free and restricted rights," the president of the Big Oak Flat toll road company maintained the measure was instituted at the behest of railroad officials and stagecoach companies seeking to monopolize travel. Federal officials denied this charge, insisting that the threat to the broader park-going public outweighed the interests of the growing but still relatively small population of automobile enthusiasts. The chief ranger of Sequoia National Park added a populist dimension to the argument, asserting that the dangers posed by wealthy motorists would prevent "the poorer class of people" from exercising their rights.[4]

In the meantime, the inauguration of service on the Yosemite Valley Railroad from Merced to El Portal produced a different sort of revolution in park travel. The twelve-hour train trip from San Francisco dramatically increased the ease of access and significantly boosted visitation. The railroad's superintendent maintained that despite the seemingly high fare, eliminating the need for overnight lodgings en route significantly lowered overall costs, bringing the park "within easy reach of young and old, weak and strong, rich and poor." He trumpeted the accomplishment as an illustration of the manner in which "modern transportation facilities" allowed national parks to fulfill their destiny as public pleasure grounds. The prohibition on automobiles undoubtedly benefited the company, but given the small number of automobiles and the intimidating road conditions, the impact was probably not as great as opponents maintained.[5]

The Wawona and Big Oak Flat Roads continued to operate, but with steadily declining revenue. The Coulterville and Yosemite Turnpike Company abandoned its struggling franchise, turning the section of the road beyond park borders over to Mariposa County and leaving the park section to its own devices. The cash-strapped turnpike companies cut back on maintenance, exacerbating concerns that the roads were in no condition to accommodate automobiles. The government roads on the valley floor were little

better. Insisting that the dust and discomfort dissuaded potential visitors and reflected poorly on the federal government, Benson pleaded for increased appropriations. While the Army Corps of Engineers had overseen Yosemite's roads since the transfer to federal ownership, he suggested subsequent road work be carried out under the direction of "a competent landscape gardener" to ensure it accorded with park design principles. Neither request was met, but Benson and his successor, W. W. Forsyth, succeeded in macadamizing the main road to Yosemite Village and constructed several small stone-faced concrete bridges. As the toll roads continued to deteriorate, Forsyth repeated Benson's contention that they were too narrow, steep, and poorly maintained to accommodate automobile traffic.[6]

The motorists' prospects began to change in 1912, when Yosemite was selected as the location for the second National Park Conference. The first conference had been held in Yellowstone the preceding year. The goal of these gatherings was to bring together park managers, concessionaires, and other interested parties in the hope of improving conditions within the parks and increasing visitation. At the initial conference, U.S. Geological Service chief geographer Robert Marshall observed that the number of visitors in 1910 amounted to less than one-quarter of 1 percent of the American public. Marshall maintained that the main factor behind this underutilization of scenic resources was the dismal state of park roads and other accommodations. If Congress would authorize funding to improve access and provide appropriate amenities, the American public would reap a tremendous benefit. "A natural park, preserved in all its beauty and at the same time made accessible to the public for all time, is as grand a heritage as it is possible to leave to future generations," he proclaimed, "and too much thought and care can not be given to its development and preservation." Other participants echoed this theme, asserting that bad roads and inadequate facilities were to blame for the public's indifference. Those who did take advantage of these public pleasuring grounds, Marshall noted, came largely from the upper ranks of society and could afford the time and expense of lengthy vacations, along with the exorbitant prices charged by railroad agents and park concessionaires. While the inaugural gathering addressed organizational issues and concessionaire concerns, the 1912 conference focused on the question of admitting automobiles to Yosemite and neighboring Sequoia National Park.[7]

By 1912 there were more than eighty thousand automobiles in California, more than any state in the Union. According to the Automobile Club of Southern California, at least one hundred thousand additional motorists were expected over the course of the year. Major international expositions scheduled to take place in San Francisco and San Diego in 1915 would dwarf these numbers and create overwhelming demand for automobile access. Motoring interests maintained that prohibiting cars from Yosemite was both unfair and unwise. Crater Lake had opened its gates to automobiles the previous year. Mount Rainier had welcomed motorists as far as Longmire Springs since 1907, extending the privilege to the Nisqually Glacier the following year. By 1911, 90 percent of Mount Rainier's visitors arrived by automobile. Glacier began admitting automobiles in 1912. Turning the class argument on its head, the auto club's spokesman pointed out that the high cost of automobile ownership meant that motorists represented the upper strata of society and questioned the logic of policies that prevented "the very best class of tourists" from "enjoying what the Government wisely has set apart and protected for their very use." Yosemite admissions were actually declining, he noted, since those with the time and money for vacations preferred destinations where they could enjoy their newfound pastime. Automotive interests waged a concerted campaign to eliminate the ban, barraging park officials with hundreds of telegrams and sending a contingent to the conference armed with what one advocate characterized as "a magnificent display of pyrotechnics" to bolster their case.[8]

Secretary of the Interior Walter Fisher defused the fireworks by acknowledging that automobiles were "an improved means of transportation which has come to stay" and agreeing that they should be admitted to all parks as soon as possible. Forsyth concurred, characterizing motoring as "the ideal way of traveling" and professing his enthusiasm for the sport. The caveat, both men declared, was that automobiles should be admitted only when they could be operated without endangering other visitors and motorists themselves. Although the government was obligated to make national parks accessible to the American people, it was also responsible for protecting visitors from harm, self-inflicted or otherwise. Instead of wasting their energies preaching to the converted, Fisher admonished, automobile enthusiasts should lobby Congress for appropriations to adapt outmoded roads to modern conditions. Forsyth expressed

National Park Roads

the situation more graphically, proclaiming: "My attitude on the automobile question is that I don't want to have to haul any dead bodies to our hospital and embalm them and ship them out, nor do I want to have any broken bones to set, or anything of that kind."[9]

Despite the consensus that opening Yosemite to automobiles was a desirable proposition, there was considerable disagreement about when, where, and how it should be accomplished. The suitability of various approaches was debated, as was the question of whether automobiles should stop at the rim or continue to the valley floor. The challenge of mixing automotive and equestrian traffic generated lengthy discussion. The Automobile Club of Southern California hired an engineer to evaluate the three main roads into the valley and engaged former California senator Frank Flint to plead its case. Flint contended that the preferred arrangement would be for motorists to enter via Wawona and exit by way of the Big Oak Flat Road. He acknowledged that both roads required substantial

work, including significant realignments to reduce the grades into the valley, which ranged from 14 percent to 20 percent in the steepest stretches. Flint suggested that it would make sense to direct motorists to the Wawona Road until conditions were remedied, stopping traffic at Inspiration Point except for an hour in the morning and an hour in late afternoon, when horses would be barred and adventurous drivers allowed to proceed. Those who did not care to subject themselves or their automobiles to the perilous descent could transfer to the stagecoach, whose operations would be confined to the distance from Glacier Point to the valley hotels. Travelers seeking an even more rustic experience could descend the Glacier Point trail by burro. Flint insisted that automobiles should not proceed beyond the foot of the Wawona Road, declaring that the main part of the valley should be reserved for horse-drawn vehicles to preserve its primitive charm. Fisher expressed doubt that motorists would accept such limitations. Employing an analogy that would become a staple of park road debates, he

cautioned, "There are automobilists who apparently would resent the fact that they were not allowed to run their automobiles into St. Peters up under the central dome, because it could be done, and if they occasionally knocked over an Italian who was engaged in prayer it would be to them a matter of small consequence." The Los Angeles Chamber of Commerce's spokesman was even more incredulous, thundering, "There is not a man here who is going to be satisfied to drive his machine to Glacier Point and then come down the trail with a burro."[10]

Northern California interests were content to allow the Wawona Road to serve as the opening wedge, expressing confidence that the experiment would convince the government to permit automobiles on the more direct Big Oak Flat route. The turnpike company's representatives were not so eager to defer, proclaiming that their route could be readied more quickly and cheaply. They even volunteered to eliminate the chief source of conflict by prohibiting horse-drawn stages. Coulterville Road advocates also signaled

ABOVE Big Oak Flat Road, Yosemite National Park, 1912.

their willingness to switch from horse power to automobiles, asserting that their approach could be most easily adapted to motor traffic. Fisher and Flint challenged both assessments, noting that the auto club engineer's estimate was quadruple the Big Oak Flat Company's figure and that the Coulterville Road was so badly deteriorated it was barely passable by experienced horsemen. Both roads had numerous sharp switchbacks that would have to be widened or eliminated. The Big Oak Flat Road was only 8 feet wide in places, with precipitous drop-offs on one side and steep rock walls on the other. Several attendees contended that both the auto club and the government were being too conservative, pointing out that motorists used equally hazardous roads throughout the state. Others insisted that the safety issue was a red herring since existing transportation methods were at least as dangerous. This point was driven home when a fully loaded stagecoach overturned on the Big Oak Flat Road during the course of the conference. Fisher and Forsyth maintained that

the accident confirmed the government's position that automobiles should not be permitted until its own engineers were satisfied they could operate safely, whether through road improvements, stringent regulations, or a combination of the two. Fisher concluded the conference by calling for further study of engineering factors and regulatory measures. He also encouraged the participants to devote their lobbying prowess to securing funding for road improvements to help realize the goal of opening the park to the motoring public.[11]

While the automobile interests had not achieved complete victory, the battle was nearly won. Most were willing to acknowledge that conditions needed to be improved and to work with federal authorities, toll road owners, and stage line operators to develop a plan to ease the automobile's entrance into the park. Even the Sierra Club endorsed the prospect, in part to further the club's goal of promoting public enjoyment of the park but also to counter accusations that it was plotting behind the scenes to keep motorists

at bay. "We think the automobile adds a great zest to travel," asserted club secretary William Colby, "and we are primarily interested in the increase of travel to these parks." John Muir, who regaled the conferees with an account of his first visit to Yosemite, viewed the automobile's imminent arrival with mixed feelings. "All signs indicate automobile victory," he observed, "and doubtless, under certain precautionary restrictions, these useful, progressive, blunt-nosed mechanical beetles will hereafter be allowed to puff their way in to all the parks and mingle their gas-breath with the breath of the pines and waterfalls." Despite his disparaging comments, Muir had long urged Americans to make greater use of national parks. While walking or riding were the preferred means of travel, he was willing to make allowances for the fact that "most visitors have to be rolled on wheels, with blankets and kitchen arrangements." Since motorists would inevitably follow the routes established by earlier tourists, he maintained that they would have little impact on those who preferred to stray from the beaten path. Not all park lovers were equally optimistic. Speaking at an American Civic Association conference a month later, the former British ambassador and longtime park advocate James Bryce warned, "If Adam had known what harm the serpent was going to work, he would have tried to prevent him from finding lodgment in Eden; and if you were to realize what the result of the automobile will be in that wonderful, that incomparable valley, you will keep it out." Underscoring its pro-automobile stance, the Sierra Club omitted this admonition when publishing Bryce's remarks in the club bulletin.[12]

On April 30, 1913, Fisher's successor, Secretary of the Interior Franklin Lane, announced that automobiles would be admitted to Yosemite, albeit with strict conditions. Explaining his decision, Lane proclaimed: "This form of transportation has come to stay and to close the Valley against automobiles would be as absurd as the fight for many years made by old naval men against the adoption of steam in the Navy. Before we know it, they will be dropping into the Yosemite by airship." Lane noted that the automobile was neither as picturesque nor as romantic as stagecoach travel, but he predicted park motoring would generate similarly sentimental associations, dismissing skeptics with a reference to Rudyard Kipling's poem "Romance Is Dead, the Cave Man Said."[13]

Proponents of the competing routes renewed their arguments. Southern California interests maintained the Wawona Road would serve the largest proportion of the state's population and insisted that motorists should not be deprived of the fabled view from Inspiration Point or the storied attractions of Mariposa Grove. Big Oak Flat advocates emphasized the needs of northern California and touted the attractions of the Tuolumne Big Tree Grove. Central California boosters cast the Coulterville Road as equally convenient for motorists from north or south and underscored that it was the only option that did not charge tolls. Construction was already under way on a new alignment that would bypass the infamously steep descent to the valley floor. The USGS's Robert Marshall examined all three routes and ruled in favor of the Coulterville Road on the grounds that it required the fewest improvements and the lower elevation would allow its use when other routes were still blocked with snow. The Wawona and Big Oak Flat Roads required more substantial investments to widen the roadbed, reduce steep grades and sharp turns, and construct guard walls at dangerous locations. Big Oak Flat advocates again suggested that favoritism was being shown toward the Yosemite Valley Railroad, noting that the company would reap a windfall transporting automobiles to El Portal for motorists who wanted to avoid the long drive over onerous approach roads. Those without automobiles would be steered to the motor buses that replaced horse-drawn stages for the trip from El Portal into the valley. While the Wawona Road would remain off-limits to automobile traffic, the Big Oak Flat Road could be driven as far as the Crane Flat connection to the Coulterville Road. The steep, zigzagging descent into the valley was deemed too dangerous for motorized vehicles.[14]

Automobile interests rejoiced in their hard-earned victory but chafed at the associated restrictions. Motorists were required to pay a five-dollar entry fee, demonstrate that their brakes were in good order, and abide by an extensive list of regulations. Speeds were limited to 5 mph on steep descents, 10 mph in mountainous country, and 15 mph on the flats approaching the entrance to the valley. The times at which vehicles could descend or ascend were closely monitored so motorists would not meet each other where there was no room to pass. The schedule was also designed to minimize encounters between motorists and horse-drawn

traffic. If that should occur, the driver of the automobile was required to wait until the teamster determined it was safe to pass and then take the outer edge of the road. When the Wawona and Big Oak Flat Roads were opened to automobiles in 1914, the list of regulations expanded to sixty-four items, ranging from prohibitions on smoking to instructions that motorists on the precipitous Big Oak Flat Road keep their cars in gear at all times and maintain a 100-yard distance between vehicles. Automobiles were not allowed to move freely through the valley. Motorists had to drive directly to and from the hotels or camps to discharge passengers before returning to an official parking area. Park officials designated a space for parking and constructed a canvas-covered structure capable of housing eighty vehicles. A separate area was set aside for motorists who wanted to camp in proximity to their cars, a relatively new phenomenon that was developing into a full-fledged fad.[15]

The first automobiles were not admitted until late August 1913, when the main tourist season was almost over. Nevertheless, 127 motorists made the trip by the end of October. The following year, 738 private cars carrying 2,814 people were admitted. An additional 400 tourists availed themselves of the automobile stages. This represented an increase of slightly more than 1,000 visitors over the previous year. In 1915, the first year all three roads were open for the full season, the predictions that motor tourism would significantly boost visitation were fulfilled. Of the 31,692 total visitors, 20,814 arrived in 2,270 private automobiles. The dramatic increase was influenced in part by the expositions in San Diego and San Francisco and the curtailment of European travel due to World War I, but the swift transformation portended the future of Yosemite and national parks in general.[16]

The 1915 tourist season was seminal in other respects. Not only did the California expositions generate the first wave of transcontinental automobile traffic, but Yellowstone, the last major park to prohibit motorists, opened its gates to the mechanized masses. As with Yosemite, the decision was preceded by extensive lobbying and undertaken with trepidation on the part of park officials concerned about visitor safety. Automobiles had been expressly excluded since May 1902, when Yellowstone superintendent Major John Pitcher issued a precautionary ban. Rumors of clandestine excursions had begun to

ABOVE, TOP First automobile to enter Yellowstone National Park, 1902.

ABOVE, BOTTOM Tourist with Ford Model T, Yellowstone National Park, 1924.

OPPOSITE First motorists readmitted to Yosemite National Park brandishing "no automobiles" sign, 1913.

circulate and Pitcher was determined to keep potential Lippincotts at bay. Like Fisher and Forsyth, Pitcher acknowledged that automobiles were destined to become the preferred means of park transportation. He even contemplated acquiring one for his own use, but road conditions and the desire to avoid conflicts with horse-drawn traffic compelled him to defer. Pitcher was able to indulge his curiosity a month later, when a local resident named Henry Minton stormed past the surprised troops guarding the Gardiner gate in his 1897 Winton. Minton's historic joyride was short-lived. The little car lost power as the grade steepened, allowing the cavalrymen to subdue their quarry and escort it to the superintendent's office. After an extended lecture on the dangers of park motoring, Pitcher imposed an impromptu penalty, insisting on a ride around the headquarters area in the rejuvenated machine, which was then escorted out of the park by a detachment of soldiers. Henceforth, the officers maintained a watchful eye for motorized marauders. A party arriving from the south was forced to dismantle their machine and transport it across the park in a wagon to avoid defiling the hallowed ground. Even the illustrious Buffalo Bill Cody was rebuked. Cody joined entrepreneurs from his eponymous outpost in petitioning to operate motor stages along the east entrance road to the Lake Hotel. Pitcher's successor, S. B. M. Young, echoed his California colleagues, asserting that Yellowstone's roads were too dangerous for joint use by automobiles and horse-drawn vehicles and maintaining that the commitment to promoting public access gave priority to the more popular conveyance.[17]

The most ardent opponents were Yellowstone's stage companies. By 1911 these operations were transporting approximately twenty thousand tourists per season. Not only were they loath to lose this income, but their investment in horses, equipment, and support facilities was substantial. Since motorists would pass through the park more quickly than stagecoach passengers and spend less on food and lodging, the hotel and lunch station operators also opposed their admission. Many would undoubtedly bring their own provisions and camp out, further destabilizing the traditional tourism model. And, while most early motorists were as well-to-do as those who patronized the railroad, stage, and hotel system, the proliferation of automobiles would inevitably increase the ranks of travelers unwilling or unable to pay for the

expensive service afforded by the park's hotels. Predictably, public safety rather than self-interest was cited as the principal concern. Yellowstone Park Transportation Company president Harry Child protested that admitting automobiles would be "most hazardous to life and subversive to the interests of all concerned, including the automobilists themselves." Emphasizing his experience as both a stage-line operator and a motoring enthusiast, Child insisted it was a foregone conclusion that "a considerable number of the 20,000 visitors would be either killed or injured were the stages to meet automobiles on the mountain roads." Those who survived would suffer as well, since "the pleasure of every one of the 20,000 would be totally destroyed by fear." The results would be the same if the park roads were put into immediate use, doubled in width, or outfitted with guard rails to separate the traffic. Horses and automobiles simply could not coexist, Child claimed, especially the high-spirited animals that pulled Yellowstone's stages, most of which spent nine months running wild and could not be compared to urban horses accustomed to motor traffic. By compromising the safety and enjoyment of all but a tiny minority of wealthy visitors, moreover, the admission of automobiles would make a mockery of the claim that the park was intended "for the benefit and enjoyment of the people."[18]

Park officials remained apprehensive of the automobile's impact. Recognizing that motoring was destined to become a mass phenomenon, Young's successor, Colonel Lloyd Brett, suggested that the primary instigation for their admission came from commercial interests hoping to provide tawdry amusements catering to the plebian tastes of motorists. "If they are permitted to have their way," Brett warned, it would "turn this Park into a place of entertainment that will make Coney Island look like a dime museum." Employing a different strain of argument that would prove to be at least half-correct, Great Northern Railway president Louis Hill asserted that admitting automobiles was an "absurd" proposition because it would enable people to tour the principal sights in one day—and no one would undertake a transcontinental journey for such fleeting amusement.[19]

Agitation by automobile clubs and commercial interests prompted Congress to call for a study of the best means of facilitating the transition. In 1912 Captain C. H. Knight of the Army Corps of Engineers evaluated measures to alleviate

BELOW Yellowstone Park Transportation Company auto stage sticker, ca. 1920.

OPPOSITE Yellowstone Park Transportation Company auto stages crossing Chittenden Bridge, postcard, ca. 1924.

potential conflicts. Knight was sympathetic to the concerns of the transportation companies, who submitted briefs calling for the construction a parallel road network for automobile traffic. F. J. Haynes, president of the Monida and Yellowstone Stage Company, advocated a gasoline-powered light-rail system, which he claimed would bring tourists to the major attractions at a lower price and with greater safety than either automobiles or stagecoaches. By eliminating 75 percent of the traffic, he claimed, the light-rail network would enable the sprinkling of private automobiles to operate with impunity. The government had long opposed efforts to extend railways into the park, so Knight paid scant attention to this option. He did, however, evaluate the possibility of construct-ing a separate roadway for automobile traffic. While this was theoretically feasible, Knight advised that it would be difficult to accomplish and inordinately expensive, since the existing roads occupied the most logical alignments. Predicting that the introduction of automobiles would render horse-drawn stagecoaches obsolete, he insisted there was no point in investing in a redundant road system. He also pointed out that Yellowstone's road system was already operating at twice the capacity for which it was designed. After years of heavy use and meager appropriations, moreover, the roads were in execrable condition, with deteriorated surfaces, outdated bridges, and crumbling retaining walls. Rather than under-take two costly construction programs, Knight suggested improving the existing roadways and instituting regulations aimed at minimizing interactions between the two modes of travel. Knight estimated it would take at least five seasons to complete the necessary improvements, which would give the stage companies sufficient time to shift their operations to gasoline power.[20]

Congress was neither forthcoming with appropriations nor willing to withstand the wrath of automobile advocates, who ranged from local businessmen and elected officials to motorist clubs and other automotive interests. The admis-sion of automobiles to Yosemite had allowed the American Automobile Association (AAA) to focus on eliminating the last barrier to park motoring. The AAA's western manager, A. L. Westgard, reportedly expressed his displeasure by repeatedly driving up to the park's gates and shaking his fist at the uniformed guards. More effective pressure was applied by politicians from the surrounding

17054. CHITTENDEN BRIDGE AND AUTO STAGES, YELLOWSTONE PARK.   HAYNES-PHOTO

states, who recognized that automobile tourism would boost the local economy. Cody interests were particularly vigorous since transcontinental motor traffic would favor the east entrance. The Burlington Railroad exerted considerable pres-sure, believing that most eastern motorists would transport their automobiles to its Cody station to avoid the grueling cross-country trip.[21]

The prospect of motorists en route to the 1915 Panama-Pacific Exposition being denied entrance to Yellowstone did not sit well with motoring organizations or federal officials. Early that year, Secretary of the Interior Lane appointed a committee consisting of Brett, Marshall, and AAA president A. K. Batchelder to resolve the issue. After a quick tour, the committee ruled in favor of admitting automobiles subject to the same sort of regulations applied to Yosemite. Along with brake checks, draconian speed limits, and injunctions to exhibit extreme deference to equine traffic, motorists were required to proceed around the Grand Loop in the counterclockwise direction favored by stagecoach operators, adher-ing to elaborate schedules designed to eliminate interaction. Lane announced the decision in April, but the ban remained in place through July to provide time for road improvements and allow traditional tourists to enjoy the park in peace. Motorists began assembling two days before the ban was to be lifted. Buffalo Bill himself manned the lead car of the Cody contingent. Fifty

automobiles of various makes and sizes entered the park on August 1. Heralding the dawn of a new era in park visitation, five of the first seven vehicles were low-priced Fords. The first auto-mobile to cross Yellowstone's threshold legally was a modest Model T, so loaded with camping provisions that the driver could barely be seen. Characterizing this event as the inauguration of a "new and greater Yellowstone," NPS publicist Robert Sterling Yard rhapsodized, "Those who laughed and those who groaned at sight of it, and there were both, were no seers; for that minute Yellowstone entered upon her destiny."[22]

As predicted, the admission of automobiles spelled the end of the stagecoach era. After a sea-son and a half of uneasy coexistence, horse-drawn vehicles were officially banned and the trans-portation companies consolidated into a single entity. The Yellowstone Park Transportation Company purchased one hundred ten-passenger touring cars and sixteen seven-passenger vehicles from the White Motor Company. Painted bright yellow, these "auto stages" assumed the duty of ferrying visitors around the park. Given the primitive state of long-distance roads, the railway and auto-stage combination remained popular for many years. Postcards and pamphlets juxtapos-ing the gleaming buses with familiar park icons supplanted earlier celebrations of stagecoach travel. While the general public embraced the new-found speed and convenience, some aficionados lamented the passing of the horse-drawn stage. Not only was stagecoach travel a storied aspect of the Yellowstone experience, but given its passing from the American scene, some suggested that preserving the traditional stagecoach tour as a romantic vestige of bygone days should be an explicit goal of park management. Hiram Chittenden echoed both sentiments in the 1918 revision of his Yellowstone book. On the one hand, he applauded the practical advantages of automobile travel and predicted that the motorization of Yellowstone would significantly reduce the amount of development in the park. Shorter travel times and the consolidation of transportation companies would make it possible to eliminate most of the camps and intermediary lunch stations along with at least one major hotel. Not having to pasture a thousand horses all summer would further reduce the impact on park scenery and natural resources. More importantly, from Chittenden's perspective, by making transportation safer, swifter, and more comfortable, automobiles would promote the underlying goal of increasing public enjoyment of Yellowstone's splendors. On a more philosophical level, Chittenden's background as an engineer and historian encouraged him to view change as natural and inevitable. The admission of automobiles was simply the latest stage in Yellowstone's transformation from trackless wilderness to public park. Chittenden considered this a laudable achievement, but he acknowledged a twinge of regret for the passing of "the old Yellowstone." Embracing the automobile was clearly the right decision, but he expressed sympathy with those he claimed no longer cared to visit the park because "the change saddens them and they prefer to see this region as it exists in memory rather than in its modern reality."[23]

GROWING up TOGETHER

As the official NPS publicist, Robert Sterling Yard had no patience for such sentimentality. "It is much easier now to see the Yellowstone than in the much-vaunted stage-coach times," he proclaimed, dismissing lamentations over their removal as a romantic affectation. The automobile made visiting Yellowstone cheaper, easier, and more enjoyable, fulfilling the hallowed goal of making the park truly available "for the benefit and enjoyment of the people." Instead of "six and a half days of slow, dusty travel, starting early and arriving late, with a few minutes or hours at each 'sight' for the soiled and exhausted traveller to gape in ignorant wonder, watch in hand," Yard enthused, automobile tourists traveled "swiftly and comfortably in entire leisure," choosing where to sleep, what to see, and how long to stay. If pressed for time, motorists could peruse the principal attractions in a day or two, but Yard insisted that the freedom afforded by the automobile had the opposite effect, extending visitors' stay in the park and bringing them closer to nature. Unlike the railroad and stagecoach system, which rushed people through so quickly they barely had time to gawk at a few scenic highlights, Yard asserted, "automobiles brought people who came really to see the Yellowstone, who stayed weeks at public camps to see it, or who brought outfits and camped out among its spectacles." Thanks to the growing popularity of the automobile, he proclaimed, Yellowstone was no longer an elite retreat but a destination for middle-class Americans seeking healthy and relaxing vacations in the great outdoors. "With the new order of travel began a new conception of Yellowstone's public usefulness," he declared. "It ceased to be a museum of wonders and began to be a summer pleasure-ground."[24]

Yard's interpretation of the automobile's impact exemplified the perspective of the newly formed National Park Service and, in particular, the vision of its charismatic first director, Stephen Mather. Prior to 1916, each national park was administered as an independent unit. While the Department of the Interior presided over the parks and many national monuments, other monuments were under jurisdiction of the War Department and the U.S. Forest Service, which was housed within the Department of Agriculture. Forest Service officials were generally unsupportive of the Interior Department's park activities, both because they felt they could do a better job of managing natural areas and because new parks were often carved out of existing national forests. In several major parks, the Interior Department was nominally in charge, but day-to-day oversight was provided by U.S. Army officers. The civilian superintendents of other parks were often political appointees with little or no professional training. Not only did this create conditions that were uneven, at best, but there was no centralized presence in Washington to direct policy, plead for appropriations, protect parks from threats to their integrity, or even provide information about where parks were and what they had to offer the American public. By 1910 a coalition of interests began pressing for the creation of an official agency to coordinate the management of national parks and promote their interests to elected officials and the public at large. Although the establishment of the National Park Service reflected the confluence of broad currents in conservation history, the advent of the automobile played an important role by underscoring the need for an agency capable of addressing rapidly changing demands. It is no exaggeration to say that the National Park Service and the automobile grew up together. While later critics have questioned the results of this association, a broad spectrum of park advocates, design professionals, elected officials, and the visiting public considered it an ideal union.[25]

The movement to create a national parks bureau was spearheaded by the American Civic Association, whose president, J. Horace McFarland, was a leading advocate of physical and social improvement in all realms of American life, with influential connections in the nation's capital. The American Society of Landscape Architects strongly supported the cause, as did the General Federation of Women's Clubs, the Sierra Club, and many smaller organizations. The railroads wielded their influence in favor of the proposition, confident that most visitors would rely on trains for long-distance travel. Automobile interests endorsed the proposed bureau as the best hope of improving road conditions within parks and stimulating cross-country travel in general. One of the leading sponsors of the bill to create a national park bureau, California congressman John E. Raker, was an ardent supporter of both causes. Paradoxically, Raker was also a major proponent of the Hetch Hetchy reservoir project, which, by flooding one of Yosemite's most beautiful valleys to create a water supply for San Francisco, incited a national outcry over the need for protecting national parks from competing interests. Underscoring the belief that improved access would build public support, reservoir opponents contended that Hetch Hetchy could have been saved if park officials had done a better job of making its attractions better known by building a road to the isolated valley.[26]

McFarland secured high-level support for the idea of a congressionally authorized bureau to oversee the national parks. President

William Howard Taft and Interior Secretary Fisher endorsed the concept at the American Civic Association's conference in 1911. The conferences convened by Fisher in 1911 and 1912 built support while demonstrating both the range of issues a national park agency would address and the advantages of undertaking them in a coordinated and professional manner. The most commonly sounded theme was that national parks were dramatically underutilized and would remain so without a concerted effort to enhance their stature with the American public. The primary reason Americans evinced little interest in visiting their parks, it was widely agreed, was that conditions were inadequate to accommodate current users, much less attract new ones employing modern means of transportation. Railroad executives complained that legions of potential tourists were deterred by the dust and discomfort associated with park travel, while motorists decried the fact that outmoded roadways prevented their admittance to some parks and full enjoyment of others. Fisher expressed sympathy for the motorists' frustrations but remonstrated that the department did not have any engineers to devise plans to improve them, much less the means to carry out major construction. Proponents pointed out that virtually every major American city possessed a well-staffed park department, whereas the federal government had not a single employee devoted exclusively to park affairs. Everyone agreed the situation was unlikely to change without a more substantial presence in Washington, along with a professional staff to ensure improvements were carried out wisely and efficiently. Landscape architects and engineers were needed to provide the necessary expertise, along with a director possessing strong executive abilities and the stature accorded to the head of an official government agency. Frederick Law Olmsted Jr., who had followed in his father's footsteps to become one of the nation's leading park authorities, strongly supported the proposal, calling for a board of expert overseers to guide the bureau's activities along with a clear statement of purpose to ensure that parks were managed in accordance with the aims for which they were created. President Taft focused squarely on the need to improve access in his American Civic Association address. "If we are going to have national parks, we ought to make them available to the people," he declared. "And we ought to build the roads, expensive as they may be, in order that those parks may become what they are intended to be when

Congress creates them." In a message to Congress calling for the creation of a national park bureau, he proclaimed, "Every consideration of patriotism and the love of nature and of beauty and of art requires us to expend money enough to bring all these natural wonders within easy reach of our people."[27]

Despite Taft's endorsement, initial efforts to create a national parks bureau met with little success. The Hetch Hetchy controversy increased public awareness of the need for stronger measures, but attempts to secure congressional approval continued to falter. In 1913 Lane began to assemble a small staff focused on park affairs. He persuaded Adolph Miller, an economics professor at the University of California, to serve as his special assistant for national park matters. Miller brought with him an ambitious law student named Horace Albright, who came strongly recommended by Sierra Club secretary William Colby. Albright would play a prominent role in park affairs for a half century, as would his mentor Colby. Miller also enlisted a young San Francisco landscape architect, Mark Daniels, to provide technical expertise the department sorely lacked, assigning him the title of general superintendent and landscape engineer of the national parks. Working out of his own design office in San Francisco and hampered by uneasy relationships with park superintendents resistant to sharing their authority and limited funding, Daniels conducted a quick study of pressing needs. Once again, the access issue held center stage. Applauding the replacement of Yosemite's "uncomfortable and slow" horse-drawn coaches with automobile service, Daniels called for significant improvements to the road from El Portal to the valley. With improved access and enhanced accommodations, he predicted, visitation might rise from the current peak of six thousand on a busy weekend to ten or even fifteen thousand. He also emphasized the need to improve the road to Mount Rainier's Paradise Valley and move forward with plans to construct a loop around the mountain. Both Glacier and Rocky Mountain National Parks were in dire need of road development, while Mesa Verde's approach road required substantial realignment.[28]

Daniels commented more broadly on the challenges facing a potential park bureau. Insisting that inadequate access was the primary reason for disappointing levels of visitation, he observed that tourists tended to follow "the line of least resistance." Not only did they gravitate toward well-established

destinations, but they sought the easiest routes and most comfortable accommodations. America's national parks were lacking on both fronts, which was why most travelers who could afford to take extended vacations headed for Europe, where their demands were met by well-developed tourist infrastructure. Along with depriving Americans of the opportunity to get to know and love their country, the millions of dollars a year lost to foreign travel would be better spent bolstering American businesses. The economic argument for national park development had been emphasized by McFarland and other advocates who realized that Congress would not be swayed by idealistic appeals alone. The See America First movement, which was comprised of railroad interests and other tourism promoters, had been advocating along these lines for several years, playing a significant role in the authorization of Glacier and Rocky Mountain National Parks and voicing support for the establishment of a national park organization. The fact that neither of these parks—or even the more established ones such as Yellowstone and Yosemite—were attracting significant patronage while possessing natural splendors that rivaled or exceeded European counterparts, underscored the need for improved facilities, better management, and more aggressive promotion. Contending that the yearly exodus to Europe demonstrated that "the finest scenery without accommodations will not receive so large a travel as an inferior character of scenery which has a better type of accommodation," Daniels insisted that it was imperative "to develop the roads, trails, and other accommodations in the parks to a point where the traveler will not be subjected to serious discomfort." Daniels pointed out that even this modest goal would require much larger expenditures, improved organizational capabilities, and a concerted public relations effort to promote parks to Congress and the public at large.[29]

Although Daniels's assessments were accurate, it soon became clear that he was not the man for the job. His relative inexperience, prickly personality, and insistence on maintaining his private practice resulted in a parting of the ways in December 1914. His replacement, U.S. Geological Survey chief geographer Robert Marshall, was better-versed in park matters due to his previous assistance to the Department of the Interior. Assigned the more manageable title of superintendent of national parks and provided with a small Washington-based

ABOVE First NPS director Stephen Mather (*right*) and second NPS director Horace Albright, with Mather's Packard touring car, 1924.

staff, he continued the process of gathering information and planning improvements. While Marshall made progress, his brusque manner was not suited to the Washington environment. Marshall's combative demeanor was on display during 1916 hearings over the park agency bill, where he challenged the committee to provide adequate appropriations or fire him if they did not think he was capable of putting the funds to proper use. Marshall also suggested the government take over park concessions and use the proceeds to fund improvements, a proposition guaranteed to displease business interests. Marshall's contentious personality combined with cost overruns and other administrative lapses resulted in his return to the Geological Survey in December 1916.[30]

Fortunately, the ideal man for the position of National Park Service director was already effectively on the job. In 1914 Interior Secretary Lane had received a letter from a wealthy businessman decrying the conditions he encountered on a visit to Yosemite and chiding the department for its lax management of park affairs. The author, Stephen Mather, was another University of California graduate and a former journalist who had made a fortune promoting the borax industry and was looking for new outlets for his prodigious energies. An avid outdoorsman and active Sierra Club member, Mather relished the club's high-country outings, during which he encountered John Muir, who shared his enthusiasm for promoting America's national parks and concern about the threats posed by logging, dam building, and other commercial activities.

Mather had traveled extensively in Europe, where he was impressed by the degree to which countries such as Switzerland made their scenic attractions both accessible and profitable. Coincidentally, Lane was looking for a new assistant to take charge of park affairs, since Adolph Miller had been called to work for the Treasury Department. Recognizing that Mather's public relations skills and infectious enthusiasm were just what the nascent bureau needed, Lane replied, "Dear Steve: If you don't like the way the national parks are being run, why don't you come down to Washington and run them yourself?" Mather insisted he had no interest in becoming a Washington bureaucrat. When Lane made it clear that what was needed was an enthusiastic booster who could sell the public on the attractions of the parks and convince Congress to put them into proper condition, Mather agreed to take Miller's place until the bureau was approved and the organization gotten under way.[31]

With Daniels and Marshall focusing on technical matters, Mather threw himself into the task of securing support for what was now being cast as a National Park "Service," on the theory that "bureau" connoted a higher degree of authority than Congress was willing to confer. Arriving in Washington in January 1915, Mather quickly organized a third national park conference. This provided him with a crash course in current concerns while affording an opportunity to meet superintendents, technical experts, concessionaires, and others interested in park affairs. By scheduling the conference to take place in Berkeley in conjunction with San Francisco's Panama-Pacific International Exposition and making the best of his local contacts, he was able to generate additional publicity and reach out to a wide range of park boosters.[32]

The American Automobile Association (AAA) was given a prominent place on the conference program. While it is easy to ascribe narrow self-interest to the organization, motoring was widely considered both a beneficial form of outdoor recreation and an ideal means of encouraging Americans to escape the city and enjoy the natural scenery and rural landscapes celebrated by generations of cultural commentators. With their national sweep and widespread industry connections, moreover, the major motor clubs wielded considerable political power. Mather understood that automobile enthusiasts were at least as influential as conservation organizations and civic groups, both in regard to the broader park movement and the establishment of individual parks. He was particularly appreciative of the efforts of AAA president Batchelder, praising him as "one of the most dependable and energetic co-workers in this movement to advance the interests of the national parks and make them known to and appreciated by the American people."[33]

A few months after the Berkeley conference, Mather treated a select group of supporters to a luxurious camping trip in Sequoia National Park. Comprised of influential journalists, leading conservationists, powerful businessmen, and carefully targeted politicians, the party enjoyed fine meals and magnificent views while being plied with paeans to the virtues of the national parks and the need for an agency devoted to their protection and

improvement. By accident or design, they took the worst road into the park. After getting out to push on numerous occasions and employing mule teams to conquer the steepest parts, the participants were duly impressed with the need for concerted action. Mather tapped his media contacts to support the cause and persuaded *New York Herald* editor Robert Sterling Yard, an old friend from his journalism days, to join the campaign. Since there was no money to pay someone of Yard's stature, Mather covered most of Yard's salary out of his own pocket. Along with ebullient contributions to various publications, Yard produced a collection of profusely illustrated pamphlets showcasing the attractions of each park, which were bound together under the title *National Parks Portfolio*. A lavishly produced edition was distributed to chambers of commerce, professional societies, conservation organizations, newspaper and magazine editors, and anyone else Mather and Yard thought might aid the cause. Echoing the tactics employed to secure approval for Yellowstone, copies were presented to members of Congress when the park service legislation came up for review. The Department of the Interior had no funds for a publicity campaign of this scope, so Mather paid five thousand dollars to prepare the plates and—in another reprise of the Yellowstone strategy—convinced railroad executives it would be in their best interests to underwrite the balance. A more affordable edition was offered through the U.S. Government Printing Office, playing an indispensable role in efforts to inform and attract the public. Major publications such as the *Saturday Evening Post* extolled the attractions of America's national parks and expressed support for the creation of a national park service. The *National Geographic*, whose president, Gilbert Grosvenor, participated in Mather's expedition, featured the parks in a 1916 issue promoting domestic tourism. Newspapers across the country lent their support, while the railroads and other travel interests worked their influence behind the scenes. The American Civic Association continued to press the case, as did the Sierra Club and the American Society of Landscape Architects. The AAA was particularly enthusiastic, urging its members to support the parks bill on the grounds that they constituted "the class of people who will unquestionably benefit in the greatest degree." The long campaign to create a unified park agency finally bore fruit in August 1916, when Congress passed a bill authorizing the establishment of the National Park Service, albeit

with tight budgetary restrictions and assurances that the Department of Agriculture would retain control of the monuments under its jurisdiction.[34]

Mather understood that the agency's establishment was merely a first step toward realizing the potential of America's national parks. Despite the massive publicity campaign and boost to domestic travel due to the war in Europe, Americans were still not going to the parks in appreciable numbers. A significant increase in visitation was needed to convince Congress of the need to expand the system and protect existing parks from the incursions of business interests, who insisted that wartime shortages mandated access for grazing, mining, and logging. Along with touting the traditional benefits of uplifting contact with nature, Mather catered to the business ethic and Progressive ethos of the day, remonstrating that poorly attended parks were underutilized resources that, like other assets, would perform better with wise investment and efficient management. "Our national parks are practically lying fallow," he declared, "and only await proper development to bring them into their own." Secretary Lane echoed Mather's appeal, asserting, "Parks without people are a burden, not a benefit." In order to transform parks from liabilities into assets, the government had to ensure visitors that they could enjoy the parks in reasonable comfort and safety. Another national park conference was organized to emphasize the need for increased appropriations to get this process under way. Held in Washington in January 1917 to maximize its impact on key decision makers, the event marshaled an array of prominent speakers proclaiming the need for Congress to increase funding so that Americans could realize the recreational, educational, economic, and patriotic benefits of the nation's unsurpassed scenic resources. Along with reciting statistics about the millions of dollars lost to foreign tourism, speaker after speaker emphasized that the primary problem with American scenery was that outdated and inadequate transportation facilities prevented it from being seen.[35]

An entire afternoon was devoted to the subject of motor travel to the parks. Presided over by the new AAA president, H. M. Rove, the session was kicked off by a typically effusive Robert Sterling Yard paean to the automobile's beneficent impact. Characterizing the motorcar as "one of the most important elements in national parks considerations to-day" and "an increasing accelerator in their future patronage," Yard proclaimed that improving park roads would benefit communities from coast to coast by encouraging "an enormous passage of automobiles back and forth from the eastern seaboard to the Pacific slope." Underscoring the session's intent, he pronounced that the newly formed service was eager to proceed "just as fast as the men 'on the hill' who make the appropriations for us will let us go." The need to improve park roads was emphasized by additional speakers, including Cortland Field Bishop, a wealthy traveler who compared conditions in Switzerland with those encountered in the American West. Bishop pointed out that European roads safely traversed "far steeper and more dangerous territory than anything in this country" and proclaimed it inexcusable that America lagged so far behind. All that was needed, he declared, was technical expertise and willingness to commit the necessary funds. A Southern Pacific railroad official echoed the call for increased appropriations while underscoring his confidence in the newly formed agency and its leader. "The automobile will be a favorite method of transportation to all of these parks," he proclaimed, "if Mr. Mather and the gentlemen who are working with him have their way."[36]

No one took a more positive view of the automobile's role than Stephen Mather. An inveterate motorist who relished the opportunity to roar from park to park in a Packard touring car affixed with the license plate NPS 1, Mather saw the automobile as the key to unlocking the unrealized potential of America's national parks. Not only did he characterize cars as the "open sesame" that would make the national park experience a mass— or at least middle-class—phenomenon, but he believed that motorists would provide the political support needed to protect and expand the system.[37]

Mather was so impatient to fulfill this destiny that within months of his appointment he undertook the task of acquiring the old Tioga Road through the high country of Yosemite. The company that constructed the road had let it fall into disrepair, but occasional travelers braved the deteriorating conditions. Muir and his Sierra Club confederates had repeatedly urged the federal government to buy the road and improve it to provide better access to Yosemite's back-country. For several years the club repaired the road itself so members could use it for outings. The Department of the Interior sued for ownership on grounds of abandonment, but the company's heirs insisted the road had been so well constructed that it still met standards for mountain byways. Park officials provided affidavits attesting to its advanced state of disrepair, but the government's attorney advised against pursuing the case. By 1914 the Sierra Club, the Inyo Good Roads Club, and the Auto Club of Southern California were united in urging the road's acquisition. The upcoming international exhibitions provided additional incentive, as the road would afford an attractive option for motorists heading west over the newly designated Lincoln Highway. Taking matters into his own hands, Mather negotiated a purchase price of $15,500, paying half himself and prevailing on associates to contribute the rest. In typical Mather fashion, he extracted these commitments over a well-appointed luncheon at San Francisco's elite Bohemian Club. In another sign of the Sierra Club's eagerness to afford automobile access to the Tioga region, club secretary Colby served as the nominal purchaser before the deed was transferred to the federal government. The State of California acquired the portion of the road leading from the park to the town of Lee Vining. Repairs to the park portion got under way in mid-June, and within six weeks the road was declared open for travel.[38]

This was an optimistic assessment, but Mather decided to cap off his "Mountain Party" with a run over the Tioga Road to showcase the new acquisition. After crossing the Sierras on horseback, the group rendezvoused with local boosters and auto enthusiasts, who chauffeured them up the steep, winding ascent through Lee Vining Canyon. Portions of the road were barely wide enough to accommodate a single automobile, clinging to the side of the canyon with no guard walls to afford even illusory protection from the 2,000-foot drop. Sharing an open Studebaker with railroad executive E. O. McCormick and writer Emerson Hough, Albright perched with one foot on the running board, ready to leap for safety at a moment's notice. McCormick fumed while Hough sat speechless, transfixed by terror. To everyone's surprise, they reached the summit of Tioga Pass without incident. Mather and Colby cut a ribbon formally opening the route. Wrapped in an American flag, Mather christened the road by breaking a bottle of Pacific Ocean water on what became known as "The $15,000 Rock." The group proceeded to Tuolumne Meadows, where additional speeches were made and the Sierra Club provided dinner and libations. The festivities were memorialized in a poster-sized cartoon celebrating the propitious union of auto enthusiasts, conservationists, economic boosterism, and patriotic zeal.[39]

Considerable work remained to be done. The engineer in charge of the project acknowledged that the rush to put the route into service meant that "it could hardly be dignified by the name road when it was thrown open for travel." While the hasty repairs engendered occasional complaints,

BEGINNING of the TRAIL
HIGHROAD TO PROSPERITY IN NATIONAL PARKS

National Park Roads

four hundred automobiles made the trip before the road closed for winter. The overriding impression relayed by visitors, according to the engineer's report, was that "the beauty and grandeur of the scenery compensated for the small hardships endured." On a more sobering note, he estimated that transforming the antiquated wagon road into the first-class automobile route Mather envisioned would require a minimum of $150,000. This was well beyond the means of the nascent National Park Service, but $30,000 was spent on the road's improvement over the next few years.[40]

Mather soon embarked on an even more ambitious project, supporting efforts by the AAA and western auto enthusiasts to promote a National Park-to-Park Highway that would afford a circuit of the major reservations over improved, or at least well-marked, state and local roadways. A Spokane-based group was also in the process of delineating a park-to-park route under the rubric National Parks Highway. Another organization, the Yellowstone Trail Association, promoted a route from Minneapolis to Yellowstone, eventually extending it to the Pacific Coast with side trips to Glacier and Mount Rainier. In the absence of an official system of interstate highways, many colorfully named long-distance routes were being designated at this time, with the coast-to-coast Lincoln Highway gaining the greatest acclaim. They were promoted by motoring enthusiasts seeking to simplify long-distance travel and by automobile and tourism interests eager to profit from increased traffic. Like earlier park promoters, Mather embraced the idea of combining private profit with public service. Bestowing official blessings on the National Park-to-Park Highway, whose progress he tracked in the agency's annual reports, Mather asserted that the grand circuit was destined to become "the greatest scenic highway in the world." A grand inaugural tour was conducted during the fall of 1920, generating effusive media coverage and warm welcomes from communities along the way. With characteristic enthusiasm, Mather proclaimed, "A journey over this highway will be convincing evidence of the surpassing glory and beauty of our choicest national possessions—the national parks."[41]

To further encourage travel, the NPS issued colorful entrance stickers embellished with attractive depictions of bears, mountain lions, bison, and other animals. Each park's sticker displayed a different species, and motorists prided

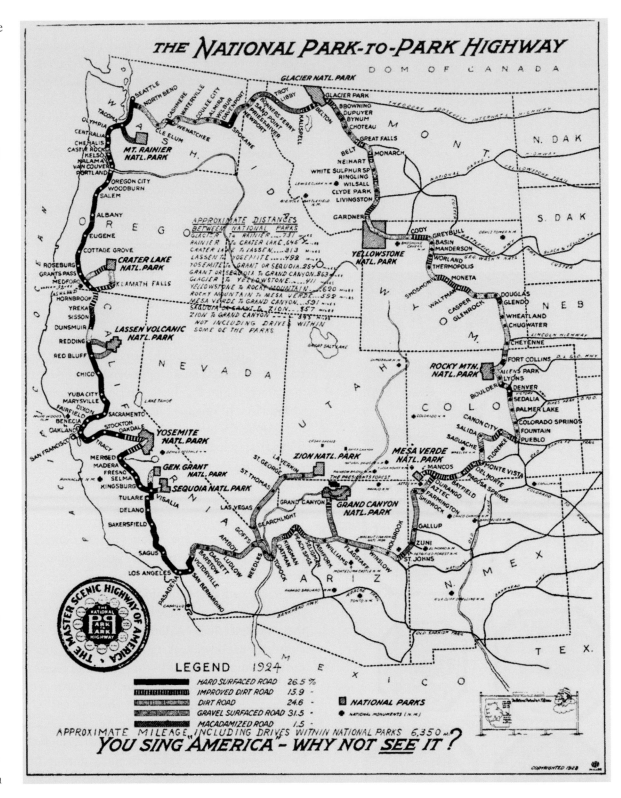

themselves on acquiring as many as possible. From the Park Service's perspective, the stickers provided free advertising along with assurances that park motoring was not beyond the realm of ordinary individuals. The appeal of the window stickers was underscored in the account of a cross-country motor camping excursion undertaken by New Yorker Mary Crehore Bedell and her daughters in 1922. By the time they arrived

ABOVE National Park-to-Park Highway map, 1924.

OPPOSITE Cartoon of Tioga Road dedication ceremony, July 28, 1915.

in Yellowstone, their windshield was bedecked with so many stickers that the park photographer was summoned to take publicity shots. The resulting images attested both to the travelers' pride in their accomplishment and the fact that three women could motor around the park circuit on their own. Within parks, naturalist-led auto caravans helped motorists make the most of their experience. Mather also promoted the construction of impressive entranceways to welcome visitors. Although each gateway was designed to reflect the local setting, the cumulative effect would be to establish another emblem of Park Service–wide identity. Like Yellowstone's monumental arch, the gateways were meant to instill appreciation for the national park experience. Rhapsodizing about the intended effect, Mather extolled "the sense of pride and the thrill of pleasure that are inspired in the American tourist as he passes through imposing pillars or arches that announce to him that he is entering a great playground that belongs to him and to all America."[42]

Despite the undeveloped state of the nation's highway system and even more disappointing roads within the parks, the rapid rise in automobile ownership contributed significantly to the increase in park visitation. When Oliver Lippincott made his pioneering run, there were only eight thousand automobiles in the country, owned mostly by wealthy hobbyists. The number of motor vehicle registrations grew rapidly when more affordable machines began rolling off Henry Ford's assembly lines in 1913. By 1915, there were nearly 2.5 million passenger cars registered nationwide. A million more were added the following year. By 1919 the number of registered vehicles topped 7.5 million. With expanded production, installment-plan purchasing, and the growing availability of used cars, automobile ownership came within reach of an increasingly broad segment of the American public during the 1920s. The ability to take lengthy vacations was not as widespread, restricting the national-park experience to a largely middle-class audience even as the number of cars on the road surpassed 10 million in 1921; by 1926, that number had more than doubled. While the park-going public was not as democratic as NPS officials maintained, the increase in admissions exceeded even Mather's expectations. Between 1914 and 1916, the number of automobiles entering the national parks more than tripled, from 4,455 to 15,536. The attendant

increase in visitation, from 235,193 to 356,097, prompted Mather to proclaim, "No policy of national-park management has yielded more thoroughly gratifying results than that which guided the admission of motor-driven vehicles." By 1919, automobile admissions were just short of 100,000 and total visitation slightly over 750,000. The 1 million mark was reached in 1921. Sixty-five percent of those visitors arrived in automobiles. In 1923 Mather celebrated the quadrupling of park visitation since the agency was established, attributing it largely to the influx of private automobiles. He was particularly proud of the Tioga Road's impact, noting that it experienced a 50 percent growth in traffic in 1923 alone. Three years later, total national park visitation topped 2 million.[43]

Having exhausted superlatives such as "astonishing" and "phenomenal" to characterize the annual increases, Mather emphasized the social benefits of park motoring. "Thronged with thousands of happy vacationists," he exulted, "Yosemite has attained a new record of usefulness in the life of the nation." Echoing the elder Olmsted's ascriptions of the positive impacts of public parks, Mather asserted that motorists "returned refreshed, rejuvenated, better men and women from their visits to the great open breathing spaces." Mather shared Olmsted's optimism about the civic and patriotic potential of public parks, maintaining that the commingling of motorists from across the country engendered a sense of communal citizenship that transcended social and political boundaries. Just as Central Park and its offspring were intended to alleviate social tensions in rapidly changing nineteenth-century cities, national parks would counter the concerns about immigration and political unrest that gripped early-twentieth-century America. "There is no finer opportunity in the Americanization movement," Mather declared, "than to spread the gospel of the parks far and wide." Along with exposing urbanites to the uplifting influence of nature and engendering pride in America's scenic wonders, the sense of ownership gained through visiting lands set aside for public enjoyment would underscore the virtues of American citizenship. It also served the more immediate goal of broadening opposition to the encroachments sought by timber, water, and grazing interests. The rapid growth in visitation strengthened the argument that tourism was more economically beneficial than traditional extractive industries.[44]

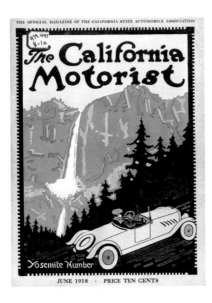 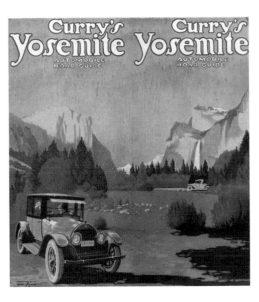  

Mather's sentiments were widely shared by recreation experts, commercial interests, and the motoring public. Most Americans viewed the automobile as a means of escaping modern cares and urban environments, whether in short jaunts through the countryside or extended tours to distant attractions. Acknowledging that "one occasionally meets a modern Thoreau who laments the motorization of our highways and the conquest of the wilderness by the populace," auto-camping advocate John C. Long declared, "For him we must have sympathy and recognize considerable justice in his plaint, but in terms of mass recreation, bringing the millions in contact with the outdoors, credit must be given largely to the automobile." Gateway communities and park concessionaires aggressively targeted the motoring public, producing gaily colored publications touting their services and extolling park attractions.[45]

The automobile's rising popularity transformed the nature of park visits as well as the number of park visitors. As Yard predicted, the enhanced mobility and demographic diversity increased the number of visitors traveling on their own and camping out in the free campgrounds provided by park authorities. The pre-automotive "Sagebrushers" who ventured into parks with their own teams and wagons had constituted a tiny minority of visitors. They were looked down upon by concessionaires, by the "Dudes" who could afford to stay in expensive hotels, and, to some degree, by park managers catering to the primary tourist population. The proliferation of automobiles and the rising popularity of motor camping swelled the ranks of Sagebrushers and transformed management priorities. By 1919

the number of car campers in Yellowstone and Yosemite equaled those staying in all other forms of lodging combined. The balance shifted for good in 1920, with 40,000 car campers counted in Yellowstone and 25,000 in Yosemite. During the early 1920s, auto camping increased at a greater rate than overall visitation. By 1921 more than 5,000 motorists a night were camping in Yosemite Valley at the height of the summer, producing a seasonal total of 40,000. Approximately 75,000 auto campers enjoyed Yellowstone in 1923, with as many as 14,000 pitching their tents on busy nights. Mount Rainier experienced similar increases as car campers carpeted the meadows of Paradise Valley. Many spent weeks or even months in the parks, confirming predictions that the automobile would extend rather than contract the average visit by allowing tourists to avoid expensive hotel bills and tightly scheduled package tours. An entire industry sprang up to cater to car campers, selling a wide range of supplies, including tents and beds that attached to automobiles and books full of instruction and inspiration. Some visitors constructed or purchased innovative homes-on-wheels, primitive forerunners of the self-propelled recreational vehicles that would gain widespread popularity a half century later.[46]

NPS officials hailed the car-camping phenomenon as additional confirmation of their wisdom in embracing the automobile. Maintaining that stagecoach-era tourists had treated parks as "stupendous natural spectacles, to be seen (or we might say *done*) in a short time, as one might view an art exhibit or a pageant," Mather proclaimed that with auto camping "people turned to the national parks as places to *live* during their

vacations and to 'get next to Nature.'" According to Mather, those who opted for "roughing it deluxe" in the free public campgrounds experienced "the greatest joy of a visit" to the national parks. Albright also extolled the phenomenon, rhapsodizing, "It is a thrilling sight to visit any of the camps in the national parks on a midsummer evening and see from five hundred to a thousand city folks busy around their little fires, the evening air filled with odors from a hundred coffee pots and a hundred frying pans." Although some critics complained that the derisively labeled "Tin Can Tourists" were insufficiently schooled in traditional modes of nature appreciation and left trails of litter in their wake, Mather hailed their democratizing influence. "What if they do?" he retorted. "They own as much of the parks as anyone else. We can pick up the tin cans. It's a cheap way to make better citizens." Most travel writers echoed official assertions about the campgrounds' ability to engender camaraderie and promote longer and more fulfilling visits. The author of *Family Flivvers to Frisco* strayed from the party line, however, claiming that Albright had let it slip that Yellowstone's one-way circulation rule was needed to keep motorists from proceeding with undue haste. "If we didn't send them on a wide circle through the park, they would not see any of it, except Old Faithful," Albright supposedly confided. "Parties would come in the East Gate, drive directly to Old Faithful; see it spout and then go out the West."[47]

It soon became apparent that the decision to embrace the automobile was succeeding beyond anyone's wildest dreams. It was also evident that the burgeoning crowds were overwhelming facilities

designed for fewer people and earlier modes of transportation. As early as 1918, landscape architect Warren Manning predicted the NPS would soon encounter the "skyscraper and street congestion problems" faced by contemporary city planners. By the following year, Yosemite officials were issuing warnings that there were no places to stay in the valley on busy weekends. At Sequoia, visitors set up camp beside the big trees, constructing elaborate campsites that infringed on the enjoyment of other parkgoers and endangered vulnerable root systems. One party ensconced themselves atop a fallen

trunk. The NPS featured this achievement in its annual report. While such images were initially presented as evidence of the public's enthusiasm for park travel, agency officials soon realized that conditions were getting out of hand. The tent cities springing up in Yosemite and Yellowstone rapidly outgrew the spaces assigned to them. Mount Rainier's Paradise Valley was beginning to look like a used-car lot or a carnival. Even the superintendent at Platt National Park, a lesser reservation in Oklahoma that was later removed from the system, complained that the crowds of overnight visitors

gave the appearance of "a political rally or camp meeting." With superintendents expressing anxiety about public health implications, the development of larger campgrounds with improved sanitary systems became a top priority. Six were established in Yellowstone by 1922, the largest accommodating 1,500 visitors. The ability to enjoy these facilities free of charge was cast as compensation for relatively high automobile admission fees, which had been a source of contention since their inception. NPS officials pointed out that the total cost of visiting the parks remained lower than in the

National Park Roads

days of packaged railroad-and-stagecoach tours and expensive hotels. They also argued that motorists should bear responsibility for the wear and tear they caused on roads designed for horses and wagons. The few hundred thousand dollars per year generated by automobile fees were inadequate to fund basic maintenance, much less major projects to update park roads from the horse-and-buggy era to the automobile age.[48]

Complaints about the inadequacy of park roads became more insistent as motoring evolved from the esoteric pastime of "auto cranks" in search of adventure into practical transportation for families wanting to travel as quickly and safely as possible. In 1915 the travel writer Thomas Murphy cast the need to inch down the Wawona Road with the transmission locked in low gear as a minor inconvenience. Exiting the valley over the Big Oak Flat Road was a more tenuous proposition, but the veteran motorist embraced the challenge. Coming out of the trees, he noted that the route narrowed into a slim causeway clinging precariously to the mountainside. A few large rocks were arrayed along the edge, but their role appeared more psychological than practical. Even this illusion was short-lived. "The boulder balustrade disappears," he observed, "and we find ourselves on a narrow shelf, with infrequent passing places, running along the edge of a cliff that falls almost sheer beneath." The engine gave out on the final pitch, but a road maintenance gang used their horses to tow the stranded motorists over the lip. Murphy's tone suggested such conditions were considered part of the fun rather than cause for alarm. Some writers made light of the difficulties. "The road pitches down an abrupt slope, the trees thin out, and you are conscious of a mighty void," wrote one wag. "It's a hairpin turn around that point—and a couple thousand feet in which to reproach yourself for not having your brakes adjusted before you started the trip." The same author proclaimed the winding approach to Glacier Point to be "as full of crooks as a councilman's conscience."[49]

Other visitors found little humor in the situation. One irate easterner complained that his party was "so gray with dust and so lame and sore from the intolerable bouncing over the dreadful roads that the original pioneers had undoubtedly been more comfortable." Like Olmsted's nineteenth-century tourists, the fatigued travelers spent their first day in Yosemite Valley recovering at a hotel. Unlike Olmsted's unfortunates, the party had the

means to stay several days. Tracing the traditional itinerary by auto stage, they discovered that bus operators rivaled old-time stage drivers in their indifference to travelers' welfare, speeding along the rough roads so fast "the springs clash and the seats throw forth their fares like volcanoes in action." Encountering other vehicles on roads designed for single wagons engendered "shouting and scraping of fenders and terror on the part of passengers." Despite the onerous conditions, the writer implied that the motorization of Yosemite made the park too accessible, at least from a social perspective. Shocked to find women with their hair down and unkempt motorists lounging about, the author blamed the NPS's auto-friendly attitude for increasing the number of "unpleasant loud-mouthed, grammar murdering folk thronging the place."[50]

The upper reaches of Mount Rainier National Park's road system were considered so hazardous that women and teenage boys were prohibited from driving above the Nisqually Glacier, where the narrow roadbed afforded harrowing views of the canyon floor thousands of feet below. Acting Superintendent Joseph Cotter attributed this proscription to the "well known fact that women as a rule cannot look over a precipice without becoming dizzy and losing their nerve." Irate women and their spouses bombarded government officials with demands for equal access. Noting that his wife did all the family's driving, one husband insisted that park officials had to evolve with the times. "The automobile is here to stay and a woman's right to participate in political affairs is here to stay," he pronounced, "and the thing to do is to determine who are and who are not competent and allow the competent of either sex to drive in any of the parks." Several woman drivers complained that the men they were forced to hire damaged their vehicles and endangered their lives. Succumbing to these pressures and mindful of the wartime shortage of adult males, park officials rescinded the prohibition on women and teenagers in 1918.[51]

The combination of primitive roads and heavy traffic created harrowing conditions for drivers of any gender. The problem was accentuated by the impact of rubber tires, which were more destructive than wagon wheels and steel-shod hooves. NPS officials admitted that park roads were outdated and in many cases unsafe but maintained they could do little to remedy the situation without increased appropriations. Pleading for additional funds, superintendents

reported conditions ranging from "tiresome and unpleasant" to "obnoxious and disagreeable," "wretched," and "atrocious." Noting the mounting accident rate on Yosemite's roads, Mather observed, "That there have been no mortalities since the opening of the park to automobile travel is truly remarkable." Mount Rainier's Nisqually Road continued to cause problems due to its narrow width, blind curves, and degraded surface. Requests for funds to straighten out a sharp turn know as "Blow Your Horn Point" underscored another drawback of early auto travel: the constant bleating of horns as motorists approached blind curves and intersections. Even after the elimination of horse-drawn travel, the NPS maintained traffic control systems on the most dangerous sections of heavily trafficked roads. Cars were allowed to proceed one way for a set period and then the flow was reversed. The "control" system persisted into the 1930s, creating backups and delays that frustrated visitors and NPS officials alike. Congestion also became a problem in popular park locales. As early as 1921 Yosemite officials observed that traffic was "rapidly assuming city proportions." Surveying the scene in Yosemite Village, writer Hoffman Birney observed: "Surrounded by the silent majesty of the eternal peaks the valley has all the cathedral hush of a boilershop and the restfulness of 42nd Street and Fifth Avenue. Officers direct traffic at every road intersection. Motor horns blare and squawk and shriek. Foot travelers dodge frantically between the swiftly moving vehicles. Cars are parked solidly for blocks around Camp Curry. There's every kind of motor-propelled contrivance from 1916 Fords to Rolls-Royces and Isottas, and every last one of them seems to be in a tearing hurry to go some place." Crystalizing public opinion in a telling analogy, the popular author Mary Roberts Rinehart proclaimed, "A Government mountain reserve without plenty of roads is as valuable as an automobile without gasoline."[52]

The NPS was caught between an increasingly irate public and a Congress and administration that were loath to boost appropriations. The chorus of complaints raised concerns that if conditions were not improved, the increase in visitation might be slowed, or even reversed, cutting short the agency's efforts to protect and expand the system. NPS officials responded personally to motorists' complaints, urging them to express their dissatisfaction to Congress. Mather was so desperate for road improvement funds that in 1918 he conspired with western senators to prepare a bill allowing the Interior Department to sell off public lands to cover construction costs. Secretary Lane opposed the effort, insisting appropriations be made through regular channels. His successor, Albert Fall, endorsed a more broadly phrased measure aimed at increasing access to all federal lands. The NPS was undoubtedly better off for avoiding these controversial proposals, given the ensuing scandal over Fall's dispensation of oil leases at Teapot Dome.[53] Mather's frustration was exacerbated by the fact that the Federal-Aid Highway Act of 1916 bestowed millions of dollars on state highway departments but made no provisions for park roads. The NPS found it particularly vexing that the Department of Agriculture was allotted $1 million per year for national forest roads. NPS allies such as the American Automobile Association called for a similar stipend for national parks, but the provision was eliminated out of concern that the prospect of spending tax dollars for pleasure roads might jeopardize the entire measure. As a result, motorists could travel to the parks on improved roadways, pass through the gates, and find themselves slogging through mud, bouncing over rocks, and confronting an array of life-threatening hazards in what were supposed to be the nation's premier playgrounds.[54]

Mather made this disparity the centerpiece of his pleas for increased appropriations, insisting that road conditions within the parks should be as good as or better than approach routes. When his 1919 request went unheeded, Mather arranged for members of the House Appropriations Committee to tour several parks to experience the dangers and discomforts encountered by their constituents. This resulted in the first major funding increase for park road development, a disbursement of $250,000 for 1921. The largest portion, $100,000, was intended to jump-start construction of a road across the continental divide in Glacier National Park. This "Transmountain Road" would eliminate the last gap in the National Park-to-Park Highway. Seeking to capitalize on Congress's newfound appreciation for park road improvement, Mather made a bold request. Rather than plead for funds on a yearly basis, he called for an annual commitment of $500,000 for five years. Congressional sympathy proved to be short-lived. Despite an 80 percent increase in automobile admissions over the previous two years, funding was actually reduced in 1922. Although the cuts reflected government-wide austerity measures, NPS officials reminded those holding the purse strings that poorly maintained parks reflected badly on the entire federal government, not just the NPS. Pointing to the complaints raised by the "annually mounting flood of visitors," Acting Director Arno Cammerer warned that a dramatic increase in funding was necessary "to avoid serious criticism of our national park administration and of the Congress." Cammerer reiterated previous charges that neglecting park roads constituted a

breach of faith with the American public. Summarizing complaints from Yosemite's growing multitudes, he proclaimed, "The motorist can not understand why after having set aside the park as a reservation for the benefit and enjoyment of the people, the Government has apparently allowed the road system on which everyone is dependent for full enjoyment of the park to be so neglected."[55]

To press the matter, the NPS put together an even more ambitious proposal for a comprehensive three-year development program estimated to cost just under $750,000. Bolstered by visitation statistics and paeans to the patriotic, economic, and therapeutic value of park travel, the request was approved by the administration but failed to make headway in Congress. Fortuitously, the House Appropriations Committee was engaged in another western fact-finding trip in June 1923. Mather dispatched Albright to give the congressmen a special tour of the Grand Canyon and the surrounding area. The savvy field director introduced them to seemingly every pothole and mud wallow in the region. At one point the party became so thoroughly mired that teams had to be summoned to free them. Committee Chairman Louis Cramton, a strong park supporter, gave Albright a look of knowing approval. When Albright employed the same tactics on a subsequent trip to Yellowstone, Oregon congressman Nicholas Sinnott cast the quest to upgrade park roads as an epic of biblical proportions. Sinnott's citation from the book of Isaiah meshed so perfectly with the Park Service's ambitions that Albright placed a sign on the summit of Mount Washburn bearing the proclamation: "I will make all my mountains a way, and my highways shall be exalted."[56]

By the time formal hearings on the park road bill were held in February 1924, Mather had upped the request to an even $750,000 and secured support from a wide range of allies. Secretary of the Interior Hubert Work endorsed the measure, characterizing the road program as "the most urgent demand of the national parks to-day." Work laid out the case in a statement prepared by Albright and Mather. Motor vehicle admissions had multiplied sixfold since the agency was authorized in 1916, increasing annual visitation from 356,097 to 1,493,712. Yet there were only 12 miles of hard-surfaced roads in the entire system. The inequitable funding provisions of the Federal-Aid Highway Act of 1916 were cast as the primary reason for the public's "well-merited" criticism of

national park roads. The federal government had provided $540 million in highway funds to the states and $52 million to the Forest Service over the past few years, but in the half-century history of national parks, expenditures for road construction amounted to only $3.5 million, most of which was spent by the Army Corps of Engineers before automobiles arrived on the scene. The income from automobile entrance fees routinely exceeded the amount appropriated for road improvements. Since those funds went directly to the U.S. Treasury, national park roads were bringing in more money than Congress provided to maintain them. Likening NPS roads to Cinderella, with the Forest Service and state highway departments as favored siblings, Mather asserted the pending measure was the most important park-related legislation since the agency's authorization.[57]

The bulk of the hearings were devoted to Albright's exhaustive accounts of proposed improvements. This detailed testimony was intended to assure Congress that the funds would be spent wisely and in a sufficiently dispersed manner to spread their economic and political benefits. The initial emphasis would be on upgrading existing roads by reducing grades, easing curves, widening roadbeds, and erecting parapets in dangerous locations. The plans called for reconstructing 391 miles of the 1,060 miles of roadway then existing in the National Park System. Approximately one-third required complete rebuilding, including significant realignments where old routes could not be adapted for automobile traffic. Hard-surfaced paving was not considered necessary in most cases and could wait for future appropriations. Only 28 miles in the entire park system would be surfaced with concrete or asphalt, all in Yosemite Valley. An additional 353 miles would receive improved crushed-stone and gravel surfaces. The rest would remain dirt for the time being. Approximately 360 miles of new road would be constructed, including key projects such as Glacier's Transmountain Road, Rocky Mountain's Trail Ridge Road, a new approach to Grand Canyon, access and tour roads in Hawaii National Park, a road across Lassen Volcanic National Park, and the first section of the long-contemplated loop road around Mount Rainier. Yosemite's Wawona and Big Oak Flat would be substantially rebuilt, as would the main entrance to Mount Rainier. With California nearing completion of a state highway to Yosemite, improving the NPS portion of the El Portal Road

was a top priority. Albright's presentation extended over several days and was accompanied by detailed descriptions of every project, both to demonstrate the NPS's preparedness and underscore the widespread distribution of federal funds.[58]

Mather made sure these facts and figures were bolstered by effusive testimonials from allies such as the AAA and spokesmen from communities destined to benefit from increased travel. The AAA proclaimed that congressional penny-pinching made it impossible for motorists to enjoy parks "without considerable danger to life and limb." Politicians and business leaders railed against the federal government's unwillingness to uphold its commitment to making the parks accessible to the American public. Washington congressman John Miller complained that his constituents had spent $8 million to build a "magnificent highway" to Mount Rainier, while the federal government had constructed "one little roadway" that was inadequate for modern traffic and provided access to a tiny corner of the park. Alaska delegate Dan Sutherland invoked the See American First argument, proclaiming that European scenery paled beside Mount McKinley's magnificence, which remained virtually inaccessible. Newspapers and magazines vigorously supported the bill. The Yosemite-gateway-based *Stockton Record* published a series of favorable editorials and cartoons, which Mather circulated to bolster the cause. Robert Sterling Yard had left the agency to head the National Park Association but provided enthusiastic support in the organization's publications, asserting: "National Park roads are shockingly poor because Congress has never made appropriations sufficient to construct good roads and keep them in condition." The measure swept through both chambers with unanimous assent and was signed by President Coolidge in April 1924, prompting Yard to pronounce, "The sins of omission of many past Congresses were expiated."[59]

Although Yard was engaging in characteristic hyperbole, Mather's contention that the 1924 park road bill represented the most significant milestone since the establishment of the National Park Service was justified. With substantial funding guaranteed, the agency was faced with an even more challenging task: addressing the needs of the motoring masses in a manner that would satisfy the demand for access without compromising the attractions of the parks in the process.

ABOVE, TOP "KET," editorial cartoon promoting NPS road funding legislation, ca. 1924.

ABOVE, BOTTOM Horace Albright (*left*) on summit of Mount Washburn with sign displaying quote suggested by House Appropriations Committee member Nicholas Sinnott (R-OR), ca. 1925.

OPPOSITE Traffic in Yosemite Valley, Yosemite National Park, 1927.

Reconciling the Machine and the Garden

CHAPTER FOUR

the highest levels of technical and artistic expertise, and followed guidelines established in the Park Service's founding legislation and associated policy statements.

The fundamental principle governing NPS activities was laid out in the Organic Act, which authorized the agency's creation in 1916. The key section was contributed by Frederick Law Olmsted Jr. and distilled the park management philosophies espoused by his father and other predecessors into a single, if somewhat circuitous, sentence:

> *The service thus established shall promote and regulate the use of the Federal areas known as national parks, monuments, and reservations hereinafter specified by such means and measures as conform to the fundamental purposes of the said parks, monuments, and reservations, which purpose is to conserve the scenery and the natural and historic objects and the wild life therein and to provide for the enjoyment of the same in such manner and by such means as will leave them unimpaired for the enjoyment of future generations.*[1]

Although subsequent interpreters have highlighted the seeming contradiction between the mandate to keep parks "unimpaired" and the injunction to provide for their enjoyment, the act's contemporaries considered the directive to be far from ambiguous. With the parks under constant threat from commercial interests seeking timber, minerals, water, and grazing rights, "impairment" meant major interventions that sacrificed park scenery for ends far removed from their designated roles as public parks and pleasuring grounds. A well-developed road system served both ends. Properly designed and located roads would allow the American public to enjoy their parks while limiting impacts to areas designed to accommodate their activities. By expanding public access, moreover, they would strengthen resistance to more damaging incursions. Roads, campgrounds, and other visitor facilities would affect their immediate surroundings, but the impact was minimal compared to proposals to transform scenic canyons, primeval woodlands, and bountiful meadows into submerged or denuded industrial landscapes. Not only did this tradeoff appear self-evident to contemporary conservationists, but it was widely accepted that without roads, parks were not really parks, or at least not parks

T

he 1924 park roads act was a watershed in national park history. After fifty years of pleading, Congress finally agreed to support a sustained effort to bring the wonders of the national parks within reach of the American public—or at least the burgeoning population of automobile owners clamoring to enjoy them by means of the newest national pastime. At long last, it was felt, the commitment to providing access would proceed on an equal footing with the drive for preservation. While Stephen Mather and his supporters were ecstatic, they realized they had set themselves an imposing task. Accommodating motorists without compromising park landscapes would be a tremendous challenge. If the NPS moved too slowly or constructed roads that failed to meet the rapidly evolving demands of automobile traffic, the agency's competence would be questioned and the dream of consolidating and expanding the system endangered. If the roads impaired their surroundings or otherwise compromised park values, the commitment to preservation would be questioned by friends and foes alike. Recognizing that the agency's success hinged on the ability to achieve an appropriate balance between preservation and access, NPS officials looked to past precedents, sought out

of significant value to the American public. This perception was not a product of the automobile age, but a fundamental precept of landscape design and park theory dating back centuries. Park supporters understood that the obligation to provide access was not a mandate for unconstrained development. On the contrary, it entailed a responsibility to limit construction to the minimum consistent with public use, along with a commitment ensuring that the results would impinge as little as possible on park scenery.

Mather exemplified the manner in which the first generation of national park leaders embraced both aspects of the Park Service's seemingly contradictory mandate. While he ardently promoted road development and rejoiced that annual visitation shot up from 356,000 to more than 2 million over the NPS's first decade, he insisted on the need to maintain an appropriate balance between preservation and access. This was particularly true in the realm of road construction. Despite his conviction that automobiles afforded the ideal

means of slaking what he termed "the universal thirst for outdoor living," Mather believed the National Park System should afford opportunities to engage in a wide range of recreational activities. "I am firmly against overdevelopment of the parks by too many roads," he declared. "Proposed roads must be carefully studied as to location, and then only those most important to facilitate easy access to the most scenic sections permitted. We must guard against the intrusion of roads into sections that should forever be kept for quiet contemplation and accessible only by horseback or hiking." As early as 1919, he closed the road through Muir Woods National Monument to automobile traffic. "With machines excluded," he contended, "the monument will offer far more advantages as a camping and picnic ground, and visitors will undoubtedly gain more pleasure from their contemplation of the beauty and majesty of the immense Sequoia trees." He also proclaimed that the greater parts of Yellowstone and Yosemite should be reserved for nonmotorized

travel. To allay fears that increased funding would unleash a flurry of construction in previously undeveloped areas, he announced, "It is not our plan to have the parks gridironed with a system of roads." Upgrading existing roads to accommodate automobiles or adding a few carefully designed tour roads in parks that had yet to be developed would increase, not limit, the opportunities for Americans to get to know and love their national parks. "We want to make a good sensible road system so that the people in the parks can have a good chance to enjoy them," Mather declared, "but at the same time we want to keep a large section of each park a wilderness that will only be covered by trails, so the natural wild character will be maintained." In most cases, development would be limited to "one good road" providing access to signature features. The desire for "one good road" and the commitment to avoiding "gridironing" the parks became the standard shorthand for NPS road development policy.[2]

The degree to which Mather's statements reflected the sentiments of NPS staff was reflected in a "Resolution on Overdevelopment" produced by park superintendents at their annual meeting in Yosemite in 1922. The resolution affirmed that a modicum of development was necessary for parks to fulfill their mission. As Rocky Mountain National Park superintendent Roger Toll observed, "If there were no development, no roads or trails, no hotels or camps, a national park would be merely a wilderness, not serving the purpose for wh[ich] it was set aside, not benefitting the general public." At the same time, the resolution cautioned, "over-development of any national park, or any portion of a national park, is undesirable and should be avoided." While there was general agreement that "some portions should be made easily accessible to motorists, by means of good roads," Toll observed that "not all of Nature's treasures are to be seen from the seat of an automobile." Like Mather, the superintendents affirmed that they were "for adequate development, but against over-development." The challenge, Toll noted, was that there was "no sharp line between necessary, proper development and harmful over-development." The superintendents' resolution was essentially an elaboration of the Organic Act culminating in an equally ambiguous injunction, but its explicit warning against overdevelopment suggested that the dramatic increase in visitation had thrown the

THE IMPORTANT JOB OF HARMONIZING PARK CONSTRUCTION WITH PARK ATMOSPHERE IS UP TO DANIEL R. HULL, NATIONAL PARK ARCHITECT AND LANDSCAPE MAN

challenge into stark relief. The imminent influx of unprecedented funding further underscored the need for careful consideration. The key to reconciling the traditional model of parks as public pleasuring grounds with a larger and more mobile public, NPS officials maintained, was to ensure that improvements were rooted in comprehensive planning and sensitive landscape design.[3]

Horace Albright worked with Mather, Robert Sterling Yard, and external advisors to develop a memorandum outlining NPS design and development policies. To endow the statement with more authority, it was issued as a formal directive from Interior Secretary Franklin Lane to Mather in May 1918. The "Lane Letter," as it became known, covered a wide range of concerns. While it was rooted in classic park design precept, it reflected the urgently felt need to attract increased visitation. In addition to declaring that "the parks will be kept accessible by any means practicable," the injunction to ensure they remained "absolutely unimpaired" was accompanied by the qualifier "in essentially their natural state." While this may have been an attempt to clarify Olmsted's terminology, it suggested a more tolerant attitude toward development. To further the goal of transforming national parks from elite retreats for scenic contemplation into playgrounds for ordinary Americans, "every opportunity should be afforded the public, wherever possible, to enjoy the national parks in the manner that best satisfies the individual taste." Not only were automobiles explicitly welcomed, but cooperation with automobile associations, chambers of commerce, highway groups, and tourist bureaus was strongly encouraged. The emphasis on increasing visitation was accompanied by directives aimed at minimizing associated impacts. "In the construction of roads, trails, buildings, and other improvements," the letter advised, "particular attention must be devoted always to the harmonizing of the improvements within the landscape." In order to accomplish this goal, it would be necessary to employ "trained engineers who either possess a knowledge of landscape architecture or have a proper appreciation of the esthetic value of park lands." Although it would be several years before the NPS had the personnel to prepare detailed master plans, the directive stated that all improvements were to be carried out "in accordance with a preconceived plan developed with special reference to the preservation of the landscape." Mather elaborated on these

precepts in light of 1924 legislation, asserting: "Particular attention also will be given to laying out the roads themselves so that they will disturb as little as possible the vegetation, forests, and rocky hillsides through which they are built." To ensure desirable results, landscape architects were instructed to cooperate closely with the engineers, who had been ordered "to exercise the greatest care in the protection of the landscape in all road construction work."[4]

Following the release of Lane's policy letter, Mather set up a Division of Landscape Engineering to provide guidance on park development. The division's head, and for a period its sole employee, was Charles Punchard Jr. Punchard had studied landscape architecture at Harvard and set up a practice in Cleveland, relocating to Colorado in 1913 upon being diagnosed with tuberculosis. In July 1917 he received an appointment to the federal Office of Public Buildings and Grounds, which was responsible for parks in Washington, D.C. Punchard's talent and enthusiasm impressed the Commission of Fine Arts, whose assistant secretary, Arno Cammerer, became Mather's second-in-command when Albright assumed the Yellowstone superintendent's post. Cammerer recommended Punchard for the NPS position, partly in the hope that the western climate would improve his health. During the summer of 1918 Punchard conducted an intensive survey of park conditions with particular attention to the challenges facing Yellowstone and Yosemite. His wide-ranging and insightful recommendations led Mather to proclaim that the new division constituted "one of the most important influences for the betterment of the national parks."[5]

Mather's recognition that the scope of the enterprise required additional staff prompted him to appoint another Harvard-trained landscape architect, Daniel Hull, to serve as Punchard's assistant. Hull assumed the position of senior landscape engineer when Punchard succumbed to his disease in November 1920. At this time, landscape architecture—or landscape engineering, to use the term preferred by Mather to underscore its pragmatic underpinnings—was an all-encompassing field, addressing the entire range of concerns associated with the design and management of the park environment. Like Punchard, Hull provided general recommendations and, in many cases, detailed proposals for the layout of administrative areas and visitor facilities; the siting and appearance of buildings; the location of roads and the design of associated features such as bridges, guard walls, and entrances; the treatment of woodlands, waterways, and other natural features; and the disposition of utilitarian structures such as telephone poles and electrical lines, which had often been installed with no regard to their impact on surrounding scenery. In order to achieve optimal results with limited resources, Hull solicited assistance from architects, engineers, and planners from the private sector and other public agencies. His collaboration with architect Gilbert Stanley Underwood on Yosemite's Ahwahnee Hotel and other park lodgings was particularly notable. Within a few years it became apparent that he was more interested in pursuing private projects than addressing the daunting but unremunerative task of overseeing the NPS's expanding development program. Hull's refusal to put aside personal projects to attend to urgent road development needs in Acadia National Park led to his dismissal in August 1927.[6]

Although Punchard and Hull set important precedents, the most influential landscape architect during the National Park Service's formative years was Thomas Vint, who was hired in 1922 and became the senior landscape engineer upon Hull's departure. Vint had earned an undergraduate degree in landscape architecture from the University of California and worked for various architects and landscape architects in Southern California. He had also studied planning at UCLA and spent a semester at L'École des Beaux Arts. Along with his formal education, Vint had worked as a nurseryman and contractor, supervising construction jobs and taking pick and shovel in hand to assist the workmen. Though he was only twenty-eight when hired, with boyish looks that made him appear even younger, Vint's practical experience and common touch helped him relate to superintendents and field personnel, many of whom had been less than receptive to his Ivy League predecessors. With the increased workload, Vint was able to hire and develop a coterie of assistants who contributed significantly to the road-building program and other initiatives. Key appointments included Ernest Davidson, John Wosky, Merel Sager, Charles Peterson, and Kenneth McCarter. Based in San Francisco, Vint's office was responsible for design and planning throughout the park system. Their activities ranged in scale from the location and

treatment of roads and visitor facilities to water fountains, comfort stations, and signage. The appearance and location of these features were guided by general development plans that inventoried existing facilities, identified specific needs and broad land-use goals, and articulated the measures required to realize them. The desire for this sort of comprehensive planning had played an integral role in the drive to create the National Park Service, but the requisite procedures were not developed, approved, and implemented until the late 1920s and early 1930s, when the scale of the challenges involved combined with the growing capabilities of the Landscape Division to make a formal master planning process both possible and necessary.[7]

Of all the concerns addressed in the master planning process, none was more important than park roads. Not only did the disposition of roads bear heavily on the increasingly important question of which areas would remain free from development, but the manner in which they were located, designed, and constructed would define

ABOVE *Left to right:* NPS landscape architect Thomas Vint, junior landscape architect Charles Peterson, Rocky Mountain National Park superintendent Edmund Rogers, NPS director Horace Albright, and Charles W. Eliot 2d, 1930.

OPPOSITE Daniel Hull, NPS chief landscape engineer, 1920–27, *Stockton Record* cartoon by Ralph Yardley.

the national park experience for the multitudes who chose to experience nature from automobiles. Although most landscape architects were familiar with the park road design principles espoused by Olmsted and his predecessors, the automobile introduced new challenges and possibilities. On the one hand, distance was no longer such a pressing concern, giving designers more latitude in road location, either to avoid scarring sensitive terrain or to seek out scenic highlights. On the other, the technical aspects of motor roads made them harder to harmonize with their surroundings. They required wider lanes, more gradual curves, lower and more consistent grades, and more substantial bridges, subgrades, and pavements. Not only were the roads themselves more visible, but they required more extensive excavations, especially in the rugged terrain found in most national parks. This placed an even greater premium on skillful location to minimize visual impacts. Since automobile tourists tended to make their own

way rather than rely on professional stage drivers, safety features such as guard walls and ample visibility became more important, further complicating the task. The aesthetic challenges were equaled or exceeded by technical and economic concerns. While wagon-road builders could scrape an 8- to 12-foot-wide shelf out of the side of a mountain, rising and falling and turning with the dictates of the terrain, motor roads required double the width and greater consistency in grade and alignment. Even with judicious location, this often entailed extensive and expensive excavations to bench roads into hillsides. A less destructive but even more expensive approach was to employ retaining walls to extend the roadbed out from the natural slope. Advances in blasting techniques and earthmoving equipment allowed NPS road builders to accomplish things of which their predecessors had only dreamed, but the achievement came at considerable cost, both economic and, if proper care was not exercised, aesthetic and

environmental. Even with the best efforts to "lie lightly on the land," motor roads were intrinsically more disruptive than their forebears.

One of the earliest publications on the automobile's impact on park road design was a 1922 article in the professional journal *Landscape Architecture* written by Charles W. Eliot 2d, who was a nephew of the noted nineteenth-century landscape architect Charles Eliot just launching his career in city planning and landscape architecture. According to Eliot, the higher speeds made it impossible to grasp the intricate compositions of traditional landscape parks, which unschooled motorists were unlikely to appreciate anyway. As a result, automobile road designers had to create broader and bolder scenic effects. The automobile also changed the focal point of park road design. Since carriages moved at a slower pace and horses could be generally trusted to proceed in the proper direction, earlier designers could develop lateral views and create comparisons between scenes in different directions. Motor road designers had to focus on the view ahead and ensure that highlights remained in view long enough to be appreciated at rising speeds. Eliot noted the need for greater consistency in grade and alignment as well as the difficulty of minimizing the impact of broader, straighter, more substantially constructed roads. In addition to being more destructive of natural scenery, the associated clamor of shifting gears, blaring horns, and roaring engines disrupted the peace and repose associated with the traditional park experience. Eliot also contended that motorists were in too great a hurry to enjoy the full benefits of the park experience. Epitomizing Leo Marx's assertion that sophisticated observers objected to the machine's presence in the New World garden, he maintained that the automobile's impact on the park experience was "another case where man in his inventions has outstripped his ability to control them." Given Humphry Repton's comments about the inattentiveness of English carriage drivers and the diverse audience for nineteenth-century urban parks, Eliot's comments reflected a mixture of elitism and misty-eyed romanticism. They may also have stemmed from his objections to road-development plans that threatened his family's exclusive retreat on Maine's Mount Desert Island.[8]

Most contemporary landscape architects greeted the automobile with more optimism, or at least equanimity. The primary textbook

BELOW Evolution of road building and design.

on landscape architecture, Henry Hubbard and Theodora Kimball's *An Introduction to Landscape Design*, contained a lengthy passage on park road design. Acknowledging that roads were artificial intrusions in what should ideally be naturalistic compositions, Hubbard and Kimball characterized them as a "necessary evil" mandated by the need to provide access. They expounded the usual strategies for minimizing negative impacts, asserting that roads should "seem to lie upon the surface of the ground without interruption of the natural modeling." Variety in scenery should be sought, even at the expense of additional mileage. Highlights could be accentuated by carefully placed curves, augmented by vista clearing, if necessary. While they agreed that higher speeds required broader openings for adequate viewing, Hubbard and Kimball maintained that lateral views were permissible as long as scenic highlights did not appear on both sides of the road at once. As with carriage drives, the relationships between location, alignment, and vegetation should be carefully orchestrated so that views unfolded in a "pleasing succession" enlivened by compelling contrasts. Hubbard and Kimball agreed that park designers should facilitate the desires of motorists "proceeding at a leisurely rate to enjoy fresh air and the beauties of the park," but they cautioned against allowing automobile-oriented developments to dominate the scenery or impinge on the enjoyment of other visitors.[9]

Frederick Law Olmsted Jr. believed that neither automobiles nor the roads to accommodate them were antithetical to the goals he set forth in the NPS Organic Act, as long as they were judiciously handled. He acknowledged the appeal of motoring through attractive landscapes and insisted that many landscapes could be enjoyed from of an automobile at least as well as by traditional means. For some types of scenery, such as broad vistas encompassing distant landscape features, the dynamic unfolding of ever-changing perspectives was more appealing than stationary views. While he agreed that it was impossible to savor complex compositions in the manner of traditional picturesque tourists, Olmsted contended that motorists would still enjoy "whirling rapidly through such scenes." Updating his father's embrace of the dynamic experience of scenery to modern conditions, he observed, "Many of the elements of a beautiful kind of scenery are recognized as they flash by

and one has a general stimulating sense of passing through pleasant places." Rather than bemoan the automobile's impact, park road designers should play to its strengths. This entailed a "preference for keeping automobile roads in locations where they command big views rather than little views, long views with a broad base on the road rather than short views or views with only a narrow peep at them from the road, and for keeping a large proportion of the intimate small-scale scenery of a scenic region, and in general the most perfect examples of it, free from automobiles." To add interest and variety, he advocated alternating broad, sweeping vistas with more constricted passages where motorists found themselves "flashing at thirty miles an hour through a succession of beautiful intimate sylvan scenes." Like his father, he advised road designers to think in terms of long-term value rather than short-term savings. Despite the higher initial cost in both dollars and scenic impact, it was better to construct roads with broad curves linked by long, steady grades than to employ the frequent switchbacks favored by utilitarian road builders. Although the latter approach was more expedient, closely spaced switchbacks were more unsightly than one or two sweeping curves. Given the rapid evolution of automotive technology, he noted, their tight turns and constrictive dimensions would become rapidly obsolete, requiring another round of expensive and unsightly construction. Olmsted made a strong case for dividing park roadways into two separate lanes, since the narrower pavements could be integrated more easily into the surrounding terrain. He also emphasized the importance of providing opportunities for motorists to pull aside and enjoy scenery at greater leisure, supplying suggestions on how to design such overlooks to afford a sense of seclusion for those who sought temporary escape from their motoring brethren.[10]

The degree to which these writings influenced national park road building is hard to ascertain. Even those who did not study directly under Olmsted and Hubbard would probably have encountered the latter's textbook and been conversant with the primary professional journals. They would certainly have been exposed to the traditional tenets of park road design, both in school and through their experience of metropolitan parks and parkways. On the other hand, there was no doubt that NPS officials were paying close attention to contemporary park

road and scenic highway developments. Mather frequently sought the advice of Major William A. Welch, general manager and chief engineer of the Palisades Interstate Park along the Hudson River in New York and New Jersey. With its scenic motorway, extensive trail network, monumental rustic lodge, and well-patronized recreational areas, the expansive complex was considered a paragon of contemporary park development. Mather and other NPS officials got a firsthand look at the operation when Welch hosted the 1922 National Conference on State Parks. Extended discussions of park management concerns were augmented with tours of two pioneering park road projects, Storm King Highway and the Bronx River Parkway. One of the first major scenic roads designed explicitly for automobile travel, Storm King Highway was constructed between 1916 and 1922. An 18-foot-wide roadbed was cut across the sheer cliffs of Storm King Mountain, providing surpassing views of the Hudson River hundreds of feet below. The road cut was highly visible, garnering criticism from multiple sources, including Welch, who assailed the contractors for ignoring instructions aimed at minimizing its visual impact. Learning from this experience, Welch went to great lengths to preserve landscape values on other sections of the road. Blasting was limited to carefully controlled explosions, and nearby trees and picturesque outcrops were protected with wooden barriers, techniques Welch urged the NPS to adopt. Welch also extolled the virtues of stone guard walls, noting that they were both pleasingly naturalistic and economical, given the abundance of rock excavated from the right-of-way. The engineers and landscape architects of the Bronx River Parkway faced a task that was in many ways similar to that of their NPS counterparts. Their goal was to adapt traditional parkway design to the motor age. By transforming the Bronx River from a degraded eyesore into a multifaceted recreational landscape centered on a sinuous drive winding through carefully composed scenery, the project created the paradigm for modern motorway development. The Bronx Parkway Commission and its successor, the Westchester County Park Commission (WCPC) also exemplified the value of close cooperation between engineers and landscape architects, another lesson that resonated with NPS officials. Several of the commission's employees eventually went to work for the NPS, including Stanley Abbott, who played a leading role in the development of Blue Ridge

Bronx River Parkway   Scarsdale, N. Y.

Parkway. The commission's principal engineer and landscape architect, Jay Downer and Gilmore Clarke, consulted on several NPS projects and furnished specifications for various park road features. The NPS and WCPC also engaged in a brief staff exchange during the winter of 1930–31 to learn from each other's methods.[11]

A third project exemplifying the fruitful union of aesthetics and engineering was Oregon's Columbia River Highway. Begun in 1913 and completed in 1922, the Columbia River Highway was considered by many to be the country's foremost example of scenic highway development. Designed to showcase views of the Columbia River Gorge while also serving as a practical transportation route, the highway wound along the Oregon side of the river, clinging to the precipitous slopes to provide a breathtaking succession of scenic experiences. The Columbia

River Highway's progenitors, good roads advocate Samuel Hill and engineer Samuel Lancaster, zealously promoted the project, both as a model for mountain motorway construction and an incubator of tourist income. The duo gained inspiration from a tour of Swiss roadways. While Lancaster examined the Axenstrasse, from which he borrowed the idea of opening views from tunnels through large, naturalistically shaped windows, or "adets," Hill garnered ample evidence of the economic benefits of scenic road development. Hill promised local officials that when the expensive project was completed, it would enable Oregonians to "cash in, year after year, on our crop of scenic beauty, without depleting it in any way." In order to accommodate the demands of automobile traffic, Lancaster insisted on a maximum grade of 5 percent and endeavored to maintain a minimum curve radius of 200 feet, though the standard was lowered to

100 feet in the most difficult sections. Whenever possible, broad curves linked with flowing spirals took the place of traditional switchbacks, which were not only hard for automobiles to negotiate but more destructive of scenery. The entire alignment was laid out in graceful curves tracing the natural contours of the gorge, with no straight lines except on bridges and viaducts. The pavement was 18 feet wide to easily accommodate two-way traffic. Even more striking, from the motorist's point of view, was that the entire 80-plus miles were paved with a patented asphalt and crushed-rock surface known as "Warrenite." Not only were there fewer than 15 miles of hard-surfaced pavement in the entire National Park System at the time, but NPS roadways in similar terrain were likely to be one-lane wide, wracked with tortuous curves and switchbacks, and saddled with grades of 10 or even 20 percent. Lancaster employed various

means to minimize the need to cut into the steep slopes. Concrete viaducts were used to extend the roadbed out from hillsides and swing it around protruding cliffs. In some cases tunnels provided a more economical and aesthetically pleasing solution. Random-rubble masonry portals helped integrate the tunnels with their surroundings, and substantial windows cut through the cliff face provided fresh air and striking views. Lancaster conducted arduous surveys to locate the most advantageous viewpoints. During the construction process great care was taken to preserve natural slopes and vegetation beyond the immediate path of the highway. By demonstrating that traditional landscape design concerns could be combined with state-of-the-art engineering even in the most challenging conditions, the Columbia River Highway provided an important precedent for national park road design. Although Lancaster never worked directly for the NPS, he let it be known that his services were available. NPS officials praised the engineer's achievements but deflected his offer of assistance.[12]

Instead, NPS officials sought the counsel of federal highway engineers and tried to enhance the agency's own engineering capabilities. The Army Corps of Engineers had been the principal source of road-building expertise for national parks, but the quality of engineering had declined significantly since Chittenden's day. The Corps's senior officials were undeniably accomplished, but engineers shuttled in and out of parks so frequently that they rarely developed a feel for the work. The NPS was also upset that the army regarded park roads as training grounds for novice engineers and even cited this function as justification for their continued presence. By 1917, Yellowstone and Crater Lake were the only parks in which the engineers retained road-building forces. Dissatisfied with their performance and worried that the Corps sought to reassert authority over all park road development, Albright and Mather lobbied for their removal. The last engineers left Yellowstone in 1918 and Crater Lake a year later.[13]

The other major source of federal highway expertise was the Office of Public Roads (OPR), which had been established in 1893 to promote improved road-building methods throughout the country. Highway construction was traditionally a state and local responsibility, so the OPR focused on conducting research and providing technical advice. Since the OPR was empowered to construct roads on federal lands, and both the OPR and the Forest Service were within the Department of Agriculture, OPR engineers assumed oversight of forest road development in 1913. Recognizing the confluence of interests, Adolph Miller asked OPR chief Logan Waller Page if he could spare an engineer to evaluate the road needs of national parks. Eager to expand the agency's influence, Page assigned senior engineer T. Warren Allen to the task. A former New York State highway commissioner, Allen had extensive experience in civil engineering and had served as a district engineer in Cuba and the Philippines.[14]

In December 1913, Allen issued a scathing report on road conditions in Yosemite. Not only were the roads leading into the valley in dire need of improvement, but the newly reconstructed segment between the El Portal entrance and Yosemite Village was badly laid out and poorly built, with no effort to remediate construction scars, so that visitors were confronted with "evidences of a great struggle to build a road." A conspicuous causeway carried it across meadows in an unnecessarily straight alignment. Allen was appalled by this emphasis on utility over aesthetics. "The whole idea seems to have been to make ways for people to get to a certain spot," he remonstrated, "rather than to spread out before the tourist the wonderfully beautiful natural features, that if properly presented would fill the tourist with a desire to loiter, to wander on indefinitely fascinated by recurrent glimpses of nature's wonderwork." Allen provided a series of recommendations, the gist of which was that future work should be based on plans prepared by the OPR.[15]

The park's military superintendant, Major William Littebrant, acknowledged that the results were less than ideal but laid the blame on insufficient appropriations. Even when funds were authorized, they arrived so late in the year that there was barely time to conduct piecemeal improvements. Noting that repeated requests for a landscape architect had been denied because of funding limitations, he maintained that it was Congress, not park administrators, who had failed to do justice to Yosemite's attractions. When Allen argued that it was better to wait for sufficient funding than to resort to unsatisfactory expedients, Littebrant countered that park officials had to answer to the visiting public, which demanded access in the present, not in some hypothetical well-funded future. Although Littebrant

agreed there was much to be gained from some sort of collaboration, he cautioned against surrendering authority to any outside organization, warning that such an agreement would be "fraught with future troubles and regrets."[16]

Despite these protests, Miller arranged for Allen to develop more detailed proposals in conjunction with newly hired landscape architect Mark Daniels. Allen made a return trip the following May, both to initiate formal surveys and to evaluate the Wawona Road's readiness for automobile traffic. Allen declared it fit for one-way travel, though he identified a number of stretches that needed to be widened. To guard against the scenery-scarring excavation that had characterized recent efforts, Allen noted places where attractive features should be spared even though they constricted passage, underscoring that aesthetics rather than engineering consistency should govern such decisions. Pleased with the results of this initial collaboration, Miller arranged for the OPR to assess the road situation in additional parks. In order to handle the increased workload, the OPR set up a Division of National Park and Forest Roads under Allen's leadership. The consistent refrain of the ensuing reports was that national park road building was proceeding in an unprofessional and inefficient manner, with insufficient attention to basic engineering protocols or the maximization of scenic values.[17]

Allen was invited to address these concerns at the 1915 National Park Conference. Expressing the conventional wisdom on the need to improve park roads, he declared, "The full purpose for which the parks were created will not be attained until they are made, as nearly as possible, accessible alike to the poor and to the rich." To realize this goal, Allen insisted, "there must be roads in abundance." While the latter assertion might not have sat well with park officials, Allen went to great lengths to allay fears that OPR engineers were unconcerned with the aesthetic aspects of park road development. If anything, he waxed overly poetic, extolling park road design as "the harmonious blending of the handiwork of man with that of God." Allen assured his audience that constructing attractive roads was not inherently more expensive, though the initial survey process could be complex and time-consuming. Echoing the advice of traditional park road designers, he asserted that the key to success, both in terms of providing maximum

scenic enjoyment and minimizing disruptions to natural beauty, was to respond to the nuances of the site rather than impose standardized solutions. After park officials defined the general route, engineers should carefully inspect the terrain, seeking out attractive views and identifying the most propitious alignment.[18]

Although Allen was clearly lobbying for the role of chief NPS road builder, Mather had other ideas. As part of his vision for the newly formed agency, Mather considered it essential to build up a civil engineering division to work in tandem with NPS landscape architects. The man he chose to lead this effort would become the most controversial figure in NPS road-building history. George Estyn Goodwin was born in Shelburne, New Hampshire, in 1875. Goodwin received bachelor's and master's degrees in civil engineering from the University of Maine while gaining pragmatic experience working for the Grand Trunk Railroad. In 1905 he moved west to work for the U.S. Reclamation Service on irrigation projects, transferring to the Army Corps of Engineers to direct work on a complex navigation canal through the Columbia River Gorge. In 1913 he was assigned to oversee construction of an access road through national forest land to Crater Lake National Park. Mather and Albright encountered him on a trip to the park in 1915. Impressed by Goodwin's handling of this challenging assignment, Mather solicited his advice on the proposed road around the crater rim. Won over by Goodwin's technical mastery and confident demeanor—as well as his ability to construct the road on a tight budget—Mather soon installed him as the NPS chief engineer. Goodwin was based in Portland, Oregon, to be closer to developments in the field. His primary task was to conduct surveys and formulate plans for the development of roads and trails. Individual projects were overseen by subordinate engineers. Goodwin's Civil Engineering Division would collaborate closely with the Landscape Engineering Division. The plan was for engineers to focus on technical concerns while the landscape architects oversaw aesthetic matters including the location of roadways for maximum scenic effect, the protection of roadside vegetation, and the visual appearance of bridges and other engineered features. Goodwin's expertise and ego led him to challenge this arrangement, seeking greater authority on location and design decisions. The Landscape

Division was also responsible for overseeing the design of entrance stations and other architectural elements that contributed to the visitors' impressions of the park road environment.[19]

Goodwin combined a solid understanding of the aesthetic aspects of park road design with the pragmatic orientation of an engineer accustomed to reconciling idealistic goals with economic realities. Echoing Chittenden's assertion that national parks presented problems unequalled anywhere in the United States or abroad, he proclaimed that the overarching goal was to produce roadways that showcased park scenery and provided access to principal attractions "without marring or detracting from the natural beauty of the area through which they are to be constructed." He also noted that the motorist's desire to "penetrate further and further into heretofore inaccessible places" made the task increasingly difficult. The engineer's duty was to balance these conflicting demands while adhering to technical and financial constraints. While recreational roads need not be as commodious as commercial highways, Goodwin maintained that they should be built to the highest standards consistent with the preservation of scenic values. Like Allen and Olmsted, he advised that it was better to hold off until adequate funds were available, but given the NPS's perennial budget woes, he warned that it might not always be possible to pursue the ideal course. In light of pressure to make parks accessible to motorists as quickly as possible, it might be necessary to construct roads to lower standards and improve them when funds became available. Goodwin's willingness to countenance this approach conflicted with Mather's desire for NPS roads to be second to none and played a significant role in his dismissal.[20]

Another source of contention entailed differences of opinion about the aesthetic character of national park roads. Goodwin agreed with the traditional approach to park road design in most regards. Along with the usual admonitions to minimize damage to surrounding landscapes, he emphasized the value of affording varied and compelling views. Commanding prospects should alternate with intimate encounters with streams, waterfalls, and woodlands. Road designers should approach the latter features with a delicate touch; where conflicts arose, it was better to skirt sensitive areas than to "bore ruthlessly" through them. Goodwin placed special emphasis on the production of "spectacularity," by which he meant scenes that elicited the sensations of wonder, awe, and trepidation associated with the traditional concept of the sublime. The most obvious means of accomplishing this was to carry roads along the brink of precipices and lead motorists to majestic views such as Yosemite's Inspiration Point. Goodwin encouraged road builders to go to great lengths to achieve such effects, benching roadbeds into steep hillsides, locating turns at dramatic vista points, and crossing cliffs with tunnels opened on one side to afford dizzying perspectives. While such arrangements might seem unduly hazardous, he insisted they were safer than more moderate alignments, since the obvious danger prompted motorists to exercise greater caution.[21]

Where Goodwin differed from the standard approach to park road design was in his belief that conspicuous feats of road construction complemented nature's grandeur and afforded appealing spectacles in their own right. Although this approach was at odds with the NPS's policy of "lying lightly on the land," the concept of the technological sublime had ample antecedents in elite and popular culture. Many commentators cast the conjunction of spectacular scenery and engineering audacity as an appealing and quintessentially American phenomenon, testifying to the nation's technological prowess and natural splendor. Nineteenth-century popular imagery abounded with scenes of bridges soaring over mighty canyons, steamboats belching smoke up the Hudson River, and railroads overcoming imposing obstacles. The heavily engineered Alpine causeways that inspired Samuel Lancaster and Stephen Mather generated widespread acclaim, as did Norway's precipitous roads. Postcards and other popular imagery presented the conspicuous cut across Storm King Mountain as a triumph of modern engineering rather than an error of epic proportions, while the most celebrated feature of Massachusetts's Mohawk Trail was a dramatic hairpin turn. Out west, an exceptionally circuitous stretch in the Denver Mountain Parks was known as the "Engineer's Lariat," the Broadmoor–Cheyenne Mountain Highway was acclaimed for its 6 miles of switchbacks, and the road up Pikes Peak was as renowned as the mountain itself. Goodwin would be widely condemned for advocating this approach, but the abundance of imagery celebrating such scenes suggests that popular support for the spectacular approach to scenic road development was as palpable as the Park

Service's determination to supplant it with a more self-effacing strategy rooted in the naturalistic principles of landscape architecture.[22]

Like many of his contemporaries, Goodwin believed nature and technology could be showcased simultaneously. As a matter of professional pride, he saw no reason for engineering to play second fiddle to landscape architecture. By exercising discretion in delicate situations and employing bold strokes in more expansive terrain, he felt that

road builders could strike a balance between preservation and access, landscape architecture and engineering, or, on a more abstract level, nature and technology. As always, the difficulty came in deciding where to draw the line, how to define the terms, and who was empowered to make the decisions. During the early 1920s, these challenges were exacerbated by the exponential increase in automobile traffic, rapidly evolving engineering standards, and the embryonic nature of the National Park Service. Not only was the agency underfunded, understaffed, and still working out basic bureaucratic procedures, but the enormity of the task combined with intense political pressure and public demand put a premium on flexibility, collegiality, and tact—qualities few would associate with the acerbic chief engineer.

Goodwin was said to be good-natured, witty, and even charming when not engaged in official business, but when it came to professional matters he had a reputation for being arrogant, dogmatic, and disputatious. Not only was Goodwin supremely confident in his abilities, but he was older and more experienced than most NPS employees. This contributed to an air of self-importance that rankled superiors, colleagues, and subordinates. Characterizing Goodwin as a stereotype of the autocratic government official, one adversary

maintained that convincing the engineer to concede even the smallest point was like "attempting to pry up a boulder with a toothpick." Although Goodwin was a stickler for regulations when they served his needs, he willfully ignored directives that interfered with his agendas. For all his bluster, Goodwin was also surprisingly thin-skinned, interpreting the merest hint of criticism as a personal affront and responding with petulant outbursts that transformed professional disagreements into emotional confrontations. When his refusal to go through proper channels prompted the normally unflappable Cammerer to issue a mild rebuke, Goodwin flew into a rage. Casting Cammerer's admonition as "an unfair attempt to humiliate and belittle me and my work," Goodwin insisted that the quality of his designs and years of distinguished service should exempt him from petty regulations that held up pressing work with unnecessary layers of bureaucratic approval. Cammerer assured Goodwin that he viewed him as "one of the most enthusiastic, hard-working, earnest, and competent engineers" in government service but reiterated the need to follow procedures aimed at balancing technical and aesthetic considerations. He also noted that the Engineering Division's failure to follow protocol created continual problems for the Washington office and colleagues in

the field. Goodwin insisted that he would continue to act according to what he considered the best interests of the service. This prompted Mather to issue a harsh reprimand, accusing the engineer of insubordination and ordering him to comply with all relevant directives.[23]

Goodwin's intractability created problems during the hearings over the 1924 park road bill. Lassen Volcanic National Park was perennially underfunded, so Goodwin arranged to conduct a preliminary survey with funds provided by the State of California, which was eager to promote the region's attractions. Goodwin advised constructing roads from all four corners of the park, which would meet in the middle to provide motorists with multiple options and, not incidentally, stimulate the economies of twice as many communities as the "one good road" favored by Mather. Not only would Goodwin's plan "gridiron" the park, but it would double development costs with a corresponding impact on the combined road budget. Coupled with the need to address concerns in more heavily used parks, Goodwin's proposition had little chance of approval. Albright made this clear, but Goodwin persisted. Seeking to avoid a direct confrontation, Albright told him to prepare estimates for both alternatives and let Mather decide. Albright briefed the director on his return to Washington, who predictably approved the one-good-road approach. In the meantime, Goodwin touted his plan to the Lassen Volcanic Park Association, whose secretary passed it on to California congressman John Raker. When Albright presented the single-road scheme at the hearings, Raker exploded, proclaiming that his constituents had been shortchanged and insisting the bill be modified to include both roads. Since the legislation specified a $7.5 million appropriation, Raker's revision would put the bill in limbo while Congress renegotiated the total. This would delay urgently needed improvements. Given Congress's fickle nature, Goodwin's maneuver put the entire park roads bill in jeopardy. The other alternative was to subtract funding from another park, but the proposal had been crafted to balance political interests and maximize access to the park system as a whole. Albright reminded Raker that California had been treated more generously than most states and observed that other parks had unmet needs as well. After delivering an extended oration on California's longtime support for national parks, Raker withdrew his demand.

314 ENGINEERS LARIAT ON THE ROAD TO LOOKOUT MOUNTAIN

DENVER MOUNTAIN PARKS, COLORADO

87337

ABOVE Engineer's Lariat, Denver Mountain Parks, postcard, ca. 1925.

While the crisis was averted, Mather could not have been pleased that the legislation was nearly derailed by the unauthorized actions of what he delicately termed "an overzealous engineer."[24]

The perennial tension between engineers and landscape architects contributed to the fractious relationship between Goodwin and other NPS officials. Bridge design became a battleground in this conflict of professional cultures. Both sides agreed that engineers should be responsible for structural concerns while landscape architects attended to matters of location and site rehabilitation. In the absence of an official architectural authority, the visual appearance of bridges became a source of contention. Goodwin insisted that engineers should be the arbiters of form as well as function, while Hull maintained that landscape architects had the final say. More was at stake than bureaucratic power and prestige. Goodwin believed that a well-engineered bridge was intrinsically attractive. He also embraced the aesthetic properties of reinforced concrete, insisting that cladding modern concrete designs in rustic veneer would transform elegant expressions of engineering art into ungainly amalgamations of progressive technology and outmoded aesthetics. Always conscious of the bottom line, he also cast stone facing as an unwarranted extravagance. This was a significant concern given the number of new bridges required to upgrade the parks for automobile travel. Goodwin's thinking was in line with contemporary highway construction practice. Unadorned concrete bridges could be found in many scenic locations, including approach roads to national parks. Most were utilitarian spans, but some were impressive demonstrations of the unique characteristics of the medium, garnering praise in engineering and architectural circles. Although Goodwin did not make the comparison, his comments echoed the form-follows-function principles espoused by contemporary advocates of modernist architecture, who condemned applied ornamentation as aesthetically inappropriate and intellectually dishonest. Traditional park road builders did not restrict their palette to rustic designs, either, as evidenced by Yellowstone's Chittenden Bridge and the neoclassical spans of English gardens and nineteenth-century urban parks. The policy of harmonizing structures with the natural landscape was strenuously promoted by NPS leadership, however, and applied in resolutely literal fashion by the Landscape Engineering Division.

Matters reached a head during debates over bridge development at Sequoia and Mount Rainier. Envisioning the opportunity to showcase the Park Service's ability to produce attractive yet economical structures, Goodwin was incredulous that Hull would insist on archaic rustic arches "so plain that they will be passed by the traveler without being noted." His rival countered that the engineer's spans would stand out in stark contrast to the scenery, insinuating that Goodwin was more interested in aggrandizing his reputation than adhering to NPS policy. Goodwin continued to play the economy card, insisting that stoned-faced designs would violate the will of Congress by exceeding authorized appropriations. Advising Mather that Goodwin's schemes would generate widespread criticism, Cammerer reminded the engineer that it was NPS policy to harmonize structures with their environment. Observing that the landscape architects had been granted final authority in such matters, he directed Goodwin to adopt Hull's suggestions. The Washington office would take responsibility for cost overruns. Ironically, when the BPR assumed responsibility for park road engineering, the agency recommended a bare concrete barrel vault for Mount Rainier's Christine Falls Bridge. Hull approved the design, but when Thomas Vint took over, he ruled in favor of rustic stone facing. The resulting structure along with other stoned-faced bridges in Mount Rainier and Sequoia became celebrated examples of NPS rustic design.[25]

Goodwin and Hull appeared to enjoy a better relationship in regard to more general road development. Even at the height of the bridge dispute, Goodwin allowed that "Mr. Hull has in his landscape considerations of road construction been very fair and broad minded and commonsensed." Hull in turn commended Goodwin's alignment for the lower section of Mount Rainier's Carbon River Road. Admitting that he was initially skeptical, since the engineer had failed to take advantage of opportunities to showcase the river, Hull informed Mather that Goodwin had made a wise choice, since the watercourse served as the park boundary and loggers had ravaged the opposite side. By routing the roadway close enough for motorists to hear the rushing stream but retaining a band of trees to conceal the devastation, Goodwin had made the best of an unfortunate situation. The river came into view farther up the road, where the forest was fully

protected. Hull also praised the manner in which Goodwin had employed curves to avoid monotony and accommodate the terrain. He contrasted Goodwin's decision to retain large trees as close as 10 feet from the center line to the county road outside the park, where road builders followed the common practice of clearing a 60-foot swath through the forest. Hull and Goodwin collaborated to preserve a particularly attractive outcrop with a spring flowing underneath and highlight it as a potential picnic area or camping spot. Terming the overall results "more than gratifying from the landscape point of view," Hull applauded the scheme as an exemplary demonstration of the fruits of collaborative enterprise. Enthused by this report, Mather heaped praise on both parties and instructed Goodwin to have the park photographer document the steps taken to preserve landscape values. "I am going to watch the work on the Carbon River with the keenest interest," he proclaimed, "because I want to give it the greatest publicity in magazines and otherwise as to the way we are practicing what we preach."[26]

Mather's strategy for handling Goodwin was to stroke the engineer's ego when he performed according to expectations and try to restrain his own imperious nature when Goodwin's irksome qualities came to the fore. The Carbon River Road elicited a glowing memo praising Goodwin for demonstrating an "ideal national park point of view." The engineer's handling of contention over road development in Sequoia engendered rare praise for his political savvy and tact. Sequoia's road system was conspicuously inadequate, with a circuitous and poorly constructed wagon track providing seasonal access to the two main attractions, Giant Forest and Moro Rock. During the early 1920s, local boosters lobbied to replace the old road with a more direct approach climbing out of the canyon formed by the Middle Fork of the Kaweah River. Goodwin advocated a relatively narrow roadway ascending by means of tightly spaced switchbacks, while local leaders called for a wider roadbed starting farther up the canyon and gaining elevation more gradually with a single extended switchback. The initial cost of this approach significantly exceeded existing appropriations, but it would produce a higher-standard roadway capable of providing year-round access. Although this would seem to accord with Goodwin's sentiments about the desirability of more substantial and permanent solutions, it was

Not only was Mather loath to relinquish control over a critical component of park management, but NPS officials were skeptical that BPR engineers possessed the requisite sensibilities for national park work.

also a case in which financial constraints mandated a more economical approach. In any event, Goodwin considered his own proposal superior on technical and aesthetic grounds. The plan's advocates included influential politicians and civic leaders whom Mather did not want to offend, since their assistance was essential to the long-sought goal of securing national park status for nearby Kings Canyon. Mather thought Goodwin's proposal less than ideal but accepted his financial logic. Goodwin followed Mather's urgings to reach out to key figures and sealed the case by enlisting engineers from the Bureau of Public Roads and California State Highway Department to provide external opinions. Goodwin's willingness to subject his work to outside review by what he termed "the two best qualified agencies" was both effective and ironic, given the terms of his eventual dismissal. The strategy proved successful, as opponents bowed to the ensuing endorsements.[27]

Mather and Albright ran interference between Goodwin and Sequoia superintendent John White, acknowledging that Goodwin was difficult to work with but expressing faith in his professional judgment. A debonair former army colonel, White possessed a strong ego of his own. He maintained that he could do a better job of overseeing road development in the park, but Mather made it clear that the chief engineer held authority in such matters. As the work progressed, Mather praised the sensitivity with which the road's location and construction were carried out. Lamenting that he had seen "so much devastation in connection with road-building in the last two or three years," Mather characterized the Sequoia work as "a revelation in what can be done with care and judgment," hailing it as "an example to others who are building roads through scenic mountain areas."[28]

Mather and Albright sought Goodwin's counsel in response to the Bureau of Public Roads' efforts to take control of NPS road-building activities. While the partnership between these two agencies would eventually be hailed as a paragon of interagency collaboration, the initial courtship was rocky, at best. The BPR may have thought it was rescuing an agency in distress, but NPS leaders viewed the bureau as an overbearing suitor determined to impose its will on the weaker agency. In recognition of the need to adapt America's highways to the automobile age, the Office of Public Roads had been elevated to a full-fledged federal bureau in 1918. The new Bureau of Public

Roads (BPR) was headed by Thomas MacDonald, a former Iowa state highway engineer who was as messianic about the value of good roads as Mather was about the benefits of national parks. Although their personalities were diametrically opposed, both men combined personal magnetism with administrative acumen to transform their agencies from marginal enterprises to major influences on twentieth-century American life. Mather was more charismatic, with his movie-star looks, exuberant personality, and Rotarian bonhomie. MacDonald commanded a different sort of respect. A short, stocky man who favored somber suits and homburg hats, MacDonald embodied contemporary ideals of the apolitical technocrat committed to scientific principles and bureaucratic efficiency. "The Chief," as he was known, employed economic incentives, engineering expertise, and behind-the-scenes arm twisting to build the BPR into a nearly omnipotent enterprise exerting unprecedented influence on American lives and landscapes. While not as effusive as Mather, MacDonald was capable of casting the BPR's mission in equally grandiose terms. The campaign to modernize America's highways, he proclaimed, constituted one the greatest road-building epochs in human history, rivaled only by those of the Roman Empire and Napoleonic France. Echoing the rhetoric of public park promoters, MacDonald emphasized that unlike its Old World predecessors, American highway building was an egalitarian enterprise conducted by and for the citizens of a democratic republic. Instead of enabling centralized rulers to exert their authority, America's diffused road system afforded broad-based access to economic opportunities and the pursuit of happiness.[29]

MacDonald faced the opposite problem from Mather. The BPR was awash in funding. The Federal-Aid Highway Act of 1916 authorized the expenditure of $75 million over a five-year period. Not only was the bureau hard-pressed to spend the money before the appropriations lapsed, but the Federal Highway Act of 1921 increased annual allotments on an accelerating scale rising to $75 million in 1925. The bulk of these funds went to state highway departments to improve utilitarian highways. The BPR was also building roads in national forests as fast as the U.S. Forest Service (USFS) would allow and wanted to expand its domain to encompass the national parks. MacDonald considered it a foregone conclusion that the NPS would accept this largesse along with the state-of-the-art technical advice that accompanied it. The NPS could clearly use assistance in both respects, but the agency's leaders took their time weighing prospective benefits against potential liabilities. Not only was Mather loath to relinquish control over a critical component of park management, but NPS officials were skeptical that BPR engineers possessed the requisite sensibilities for national park work.[30]

Mather and MacDonald expressed mutual admiration in the manner of Washington officials, but the BPR chief was not one to be denied. Employing techniques honed on recalcitrant state highway administrators, MacDonald mixed financial incentives and offers of technical assistance with political pressure and backroom politics in a sustained campaign to bring national park roads into the BPR fold. When the 1921 highway bill was being prepared, he let it be known that the BPR would support efforts to include national park roads, provided bureau engineers were granted authority over design and construction. The NPS could expect to receive as much as five hundred thousand dollars a year for five years, with additional funding all but guaranteed. MacDonald also appealed to Mather's business sensibilities, underscoring the inefficiencies inherent in duplicative road-building organizations and emphasizing the savings the NPS would accrue by eliminating its Engineering Division. Since the NPS would specify where the roads were to go, MacDonald maintained, there was no reason not to take advantage of the BPR's expertise, along with its ability to work the levers of Congress to secure seemingly limitless appropriations. Intrigued by this logic, Mather solicited Albright's opinion and directed Goodwin to estimate the cost per mile of road construction under the present system.[31]

Apparently unaware that his job was on the line, Goodwin issued a typically acerbic response, insisting that it made no sense to waste time on such senseless speculation because widely varying conditions made it impossible to estimate average costs. Albright understood the situation fully. Mindful of Mather's tendency to embrace grand ideas on the spur of the moment, he laid out the case for retaining autonomy. Although the offer appeared alluring, Albright cautioned that the promised savings were not likely to materialize. Not only would the NPS need to maintain its Engineering Division to address other concerns, but the BPR had a reputation for running up the

cost of projects with excessive staffing, redundant studies, and inordinate overhead charges. The BPR also insisted on building roads to standards that were too high for national park development, further driving up costs and devastating surrounding landscapes. Joining forces with the BPR might result in higher appropriations, but it was likely to triple the cost of construction and inflict unacceptable damage on scenic values. According to Albright, the Forest Service was trying to get out of its agreement for these reasons. If Mather was intent on enlisting the BPR's assistance, Albright advised, the NPS should have final approval over road specifications and administrative charges. To prevent the bureau's engineers from riding roughshod over park scenery, the Landscape Engineering Division should exert authority on all matters affecting the appearance and broader impacts of road construction. The Civil Engineering Division should also be retained and the chief engineer given a strong voice in decisions about design standards and construction procedures. The ever-cautious Cammerer echoed Albright's advice. Mather remained intrigued but accepted his lieutenants' advice, deflecting MacDonald's overtures and redoubling efforts to secure passage of an independent park roads bill.[32]

The 1924 legislation's resounding approval demonstrated that park road development had become a compelling enough cause to command congressional support on its own. At the same time, the influx of funds raised questions about the NPS's ability to undertake the additional workload. With the tremendous push for road building throughout the country, moreover, all agencies were having trouble securing qualified engineers. President Coolidge's insistence on keeping a tight rein on federal spending produced additional pressure to streamline governmental operations. These circumstances afforded another opportunity for MacDonald to promote his goal of consolidating federal road building under one entity. Mather soon received inquiries from the Bureau of the Budget questioning the need for an independent road-building organization. Observing that the arrangement was already hard to justify, the chief budget officer questioned the logic of expanding NPS capabilities when the BPR had proven its ability to oversee large-scale road-building programs and employed an abundance of accomplished engineers, many of whom were engaged in similar

work in nearby national forests.[33]

This time Goodwin mounted a vigorous defense. Like Albright, he challenged the presumption that having the BPR take over would produce appreciable savings. For one thing, the new road program would not require a dramatic increase in NPS personnel. NPS engineers located the roads and drew up specifications, but private contractors performed the actual construction. The BPR was so busy with existing commitments that it would have to expand its own payroll to accomplish the same tasks. Goodwin echoed Albright's assertion that the Park Service could construct roads more efficiently and appropriately. In addition to charging excessive overhead, the BPR adhered to rigid standards devised for mainstream highway development. The NPS approach was more flexible and specifically designed to preserve park values. Narrower and more circuitous roads were cheaper to construct and less destructive to park landscapes. Goodwin insisted that the existing system afforded the best means of ensuring that road construction embodied national park ideals. The only way to improve current arrangement, he maintained, would be to confer additional power on the Engineering Division to minimize interference from second-guessing superintendents and other unqualified personnel.[34]

Albright cast additional doubts on the BPR's ability to adopt the requisite landscape sensitivities. The bureau's determination to equip the United States with the best roads in the world was an admirable goal, but it was also a strong argument for keeping them out of the national parks. Antiquated wagon roads had no place in twentieth-century parks, but neither did modern highways. The NPS was willing to accept a fair amount of curvature, variations in grade, and narrow roadways to ensure an appropriate balance between preservation and access. Acknowledging that the NPS could benefit from additional funding and technical expertise, he advised Mather that the agency should consider accepting the offer if MacDonald would guarantee that the BPR would adhere to "standards consistent with the preservation of the landscape." If MacDonald could deliver on his promise to secure sufficient sums, if the NPS retained full authority over the location, specifications, landscape treatment and budget of all projects, and if parks with existing engineering capabilities were allowed to manage their own affairs, then and only then should the NPS allow the BPR to assume a portion of the responsibility for national park road development.[35]

Albright's skepticism was rooted in his observations of the BPR's work on the approach roads to Yellowstone. Not only did construction through surrounding national forests exhibit little concern for landscape values while consuming an inordinate amount of funds, but bureau engineers let contractors shut down the road for long periods, wreaking havoc with visitors' vacation plans. Prioritizing contractors' convenience over the interests of visitors would be a disastrous policy, he noted, creating more complaints than the current poor road conditions. NPS concerns were heightened by a highly publicized incident in May 1924 in which BPR engineers approved the removal of a four-hundred-year-old sugar pine to make way for an access road to California's Calaveras Big Tree Grove. The *Stockton Record* published a heavily illustrated exposé castigating

ABOVE Editorial cartoon criticizing BPR road building, *Stockton Record*, May 1924.

the engineers for refusing to bend the road around the towering specimen, contending that a minor deviation from standardized plans could have prevented the disaster. The BPR's insistence on clear-cutting an 80-foot swath to construct a 21-foot-wide road exacerbated the "needless destruction." Declaring that highway engineers were neither "Nature lovers nor admirers of the beautiful," the paper editorialized: "Such men would build a Pennsylvania Avenue through a virgin forest." After condemning the BPR and state highway engineers for sacrificing California's natural heritage to "the god of speed," the newspaper extolled the scenery-saving policies pursued by the National Park Service on the orders of its conscientious leader, Stephen Mather. It was Mather, in fact, who called attention to the incident, leading a party of local notables to the scene and posing for photographs by the fallen giant. An accompanying cartoon diagrammed the ease with which the destruction could have been avoided and portrayed a weeping figure paying homage to the severed stump. While his back was turned and a banner extending from one shoulder provided the allegorical association "California," the uniformed figure bore an unmistakable resemblance to the NPS director, who had clearly not lost his flair for public relations.[36]

Mather sent copies of the paper to Goodwin, accompanied by instructions to share them with his staff as an "object lesson" in the dangers inherent in the narrow-minded pursuit of engineering efficiency. Although the *Record* made it clear that the BPR was to blame and praised NPS road-building efforts, Goodwin interpreted this gesture as yet another unwarranted attack. Proclaiming that he had "preached and practiced" the preservation of landscape values long before the National Park Service arrived on the scene, he told Mather that he had no intention of passing the material on to his subordinates. Not only was it unnecessary, given his own instructions on the subject, but he refused to subject his staff to unfounded criticism. Professional pride was also at stake. Goodwin fired off a letter to the editor, declaring: "All civil engineers, in spite of some opinions to the contrary, are not despoilers of natural beauty and many of them, including myself, are as keen to preserve natural conditions and objects of beauty as any landscape architect or anyone who criticizes their work." Mather assured Goodwin that he was not impugning the abilities or intentions of NPS engineers but insisted Goodwin follow orders and circulate the clippings. Goodwin reluctantly complied, composing a cover letter that underscored his preexisting commitment to landscape preservation. At the same time, he admonished his subordinates not to criticize BPR engineers for adhering to different standards.[37]

There was no question about the NPS's commitment to scenic preservation, but the determination of appropriate standards for park road construction was yet another source of contention between Goodwin and the Washington office. The motorization of park travel confronted NPS officials with the same dilemma that Yellowstone road builders had faced at the dawn of the national park era. The question was whether to follow the Norris approach of maximizing road mileage by building quickly and cheaply or to adopt Chittenden's policy of sacrificing distance for technical and aesthetic quality. The first strategy would allow the public to get where it wanted to go but would invite complaints that park roads were not up to contemporary standards. The second would produce the first-class roadways Mather desperately wanted but would take longer to complete, frustrating motorists and the communities seeking to profit from them. This was particularly problematic in cases like Glacier's Transmountain Road, Sequoia's Generals Highway, and Mount Rainier's West Side Road, which had powerful constituencies pushing for their completion. Although Goodwin expressed his preference for the latter approach, his pragmatism inclined him to accept the former as a temporary expedient. He contended that as long as the roads were laid out so they could be upgraded when funding improved, the best strategy was to afford access as quickly as possible and leverage the increased visitation for higher appropriations. This would allow the NPS to claim it had accomplished the tasks set forth in the first park road program and base requests for additional funding on increased traffic. Mather was less willing to compromise his vision or be bound by the terms of an agreement everyone could see was already obsolete. Not only would lower-quality roads reflect poorly on the NPS's ability to fulfill its commitments to Congress and the American people, but he believed it was more politically astute to seek additional funds to build high-quality roads from

ABOVE Logan Creek drainage, Glacier National Park; final route of Going-to-the-Sun Road visible in upper left, ca. 1934.

the start rather than to seek additional money to improve ones that had supposedly been paid for. The agency's commitment to the preservation of scenic values also came into play. From a landscape-protection perspective, it made more sense to do the job right the first time and allow construction scars to heal rather than to come back a few years later and start the rehabilitation process all over again. In many locations, additional excavations or abandoned segments would take decades to recover or leave permanent scars. Mather was particularly concerned with reports that Goodwin was constructing substandard roads in Sequoia and Mount Rainier to stretch funds during the lean years before the passage of the park roads bill. Goodwin acknowledged that he had authorized reduced widths in some locations to stay within budget, defiantly proclaiming that he would be happy to construct roads to higher standards if and when Washington provided sufficient funding. While Mather and his lieutenants acknowledged the need to abide by existing strictures, they insisted that new plans should reflect the budgetary increases included in the pending park roads bill.[38]

The tension between Mather's vision of national park roads and what Goodwin maintained the NPS could afford underlay the most publicized conflict between the engineering and landscape

architecture divisions. Long-simmering tensions came to a head during debates over the development of Glacier's Transmountain Road. Goodwin had been intimately involved in Glacier's road projects since he had been assigned to serve as the park's acting superintendent in 1917. Over the course of several summers, he supervised construction on the lower portions of the road past MacDonald Lake and devised a scheme for extending it over the Continental Divide. Worried that Goodwin was more concerned with saving money than maximizing scenic values, Mather sent Hull to inspect the work in October 1923. Hull praised the way Goodwin wound the road around the lakeshore and up McDonald Creek, reassuring Mather that he had given careful consideration to landscape values. Hull was dismayed by the impact of construction near Logan Falls but noted that the end result was a compelling view of an attractive feature that had been accessible only by foot or horseback. Hull cautioned that such tradeoffs underscored the importance of "weighing carefully the value as gained against the damage wrought." Once the passage of time concealed the construction scars, Hull predicted, the engineer's road would "give real pleasure to the traveler." Never one to take praise lying down, Goodwin defended the design and blamed the damage on funding shortages that precluded

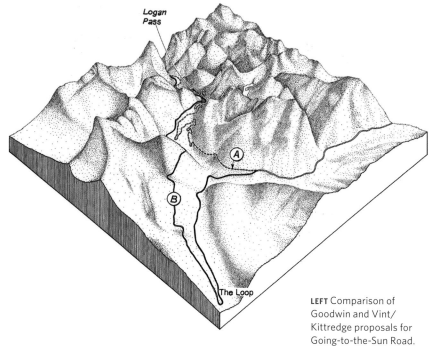

------- **A** **1918 Goodwin Survey**
——— **B** **1924 Kittredge Survey**
(Route Chosen)

the elaborate protective measures employed on big-budget projects like New York's Storm King HIghway. "When $20,000 to $40,000 per mile can be secured for the construction of highways in the national parks," he retorted, "then I am sure that we can fully protect to your satisfaction all natural landscape features."[39]

Mather was not content to wait, especially in regard to the Transmountain Road, which he considered the crown jewel of the NPS road program. In addition to forging the crucial "missing link" in the Park-to-Parkway Highway, the successful completion of such a technically challenging and scenically sensitive project would confirm the agency's ability to balance the competing concerns of preservation and access. Mather's growing reservations about Goodwin's mind-set prompted him to call for a joint inspection of the most challenging part of the route, the ascent from McDonald Creek up and over the Continental Divide by way of Logan Pass. Late in the summer of 1924, Mather, Goodwin, Vint, and Glacier superintendent Charles Kraebel set off on horseback to survey the situation. When they reached a good vantage point, the group dismounted and looked over the lush valley up which Goodwin proposed to run his road. Goodwin had tackled the problem in the most direct manner possible, heading straight up the main drainage and gaining elevation through a series of tight switchbacks. This approach would be easy to lay out and economical to construct, since excavations could be minimized if the initial width was relatively narrow and grades allowed to go as high as 8 percent. From a landscape point of view, Goodwin's plan had serious shortcomings, which Vint was quick to point out. Locating the roadway in such a declivity would limit views from what should be a momentous component of the journey, especially since drivers would be focused on negotiating the hairpin turns. More importantly, the switchbacks would disfigure an attractive and highly visible portion of the mountainside. Vint contended that it would end up "looking like miners had been in there." In short, the proposal called for just the sort of self-assertive engineering that Goodwin embraced and the NPS was trying to transcend.[40]

Vint suggested another possibility: leave the main vista untouched and gain the necessary elevation with a wide detour that gradually ascended the flank of a lesser drainage to the northwest and then looped back in another long easy grade to meet Goodwin's route above the head of the valley. Although the road would be significantly longer and entail difficult construction across rocky headlands known as the "Garden Wall," it would provide surpassing views of the pristine valley and snowcapped peaks beyond. Vint's proposal would require considerable blasting and substantial retaining walls to carry the roadbed across the rugged hillside, but the impact could be minimized through careful location. The scars would not seem as discordant on jagged cliffs battered by avalanches and rockslides as in the verdant valley below. Hesitant to press further, Vint counseled, "Mr. Mather, this job is important enough for you to hire the best engineer and the best landscape architect in the country to look after." Perceiving Vint's comments as a challenge to his competence and authority, Goodwin retorted, "Mr. Mather, there is nobody in the United States that knows as much about road-building in the mountains as I do." Mather stared at the two in stony silence. It was unclear which part of the interchange troubled him the most: Goodwin's unyielding arrogance, the accumulating evidence that his hand-picked engineer lacked the requisite sensibilities, or the manner in which the two men's interactions disappointed his hopes for comity between the landscape and engineering divisions. Most likely, it was a combination of the three. Without disclosing his intent, Mather rode off in a huff.[41]

Most interpreters have subjected Goodwin's proposal to ridicule, portraying the engineer as an incompetent blowhard or, at best, an insensitive technocrat blinded by the parochial logic of his profession. This assessment is not entirely fair. Although Vint's suggestion was superior on

National Park Roads

both aesthetic and technical grounds, it would be considerably more expensive and time-consuming to construct. Goodwin had conducted his original survey in 1918, when expectations about the width, grade, and curvature of mountain roads were lower and NPS budgets severely constrained. Even if he had contemplated a more ambitious and elegant solution, the engineer's sense of fiscal responsibility would have foreclosed the option. Additional funds had been allotted in the new park roads bill, but Vint's proposal would dramatically exceed the increased appropriation. Both Goodwin and Mather were keenly aware of this limitation, but the latter chose to ignore it. Even from an aesthetic standpoint, Goodwin's proposal was not as outlandish as it seems in retrospect. In addition to being more economical, the symphony of switchbacks accorded with popular tastes and Goodwin's sense of professional pride. What Vint, Mather, and subsequent observers viewed as a desecration of landscape values, Goodwin may well have considered an ideal opportunity to showcase the "spectacularity" of highway engineering.

With the increased funding and enhanced scrutiny afforded by the park roads bill, Mather was more intent than ever on demonstrating that the NPS could deliver on its promise to provide access to parks without compromising their attractions in the process. He had deferred to Goodwin's economic logic in the analogous dispute over the location of Generals Highway but would brook no compromises on the agency's signature project. Mather was also losing patience with Goodwin's combative demeanor. Between the engineer's intransigence and his increasingly apparent disconnect with NPS policy, Mather decided it was time to reconsider the BPR's offer. Mather had warmed to the idea earlier in the summer when he chanced upon a BPR road-building project while traveling through the Bridger-Teton National Forest on his way to Yellowstone. Not only had Bill Austin, the engineer in charge, done an impressive job of minimizing the roadway's impact through the steep and winding Hoback Canyon, but he exhibited the enthusiasm and collegiality the director considered crucial for successful collaboration. During the course of their discussions, Austin urged Mather to overcome his hesitations and enlist the BPR's assistance.[42]

Mather considered this prospect on his way down from Logan Pass. The contretemps

afforded an ideal opportunity to give the BPR a chance to demonstrate its ability to adapt to NPS ideals. Although Goodwin would undoubtedly take offense at bringing in an outside engineer to evaluate the two options, he had set the precedent himself during the dispute over Generals Highway. Protocol demanded that Mather contact MacDonald to secure permission for Austin's services, but with his pet project on hold and a twelve-cylinder Packard at the ready, formalities were forgotten. Mather dispatched his driver to fetch the engineer as quickly as possible. Goodwin had moved on to examine other projects, but Vint and Austin spent several days studying the terrain, staying up late at night to discuss not just the Glacier project but the prospect of an ongoing collaboration between the two agencies. Along with confirming that Vint's proposal was aesthetically superior and less technically daunting than it appeared, Austin corroborated other concerns about Goodwin's abilities. Even by engineering standards, Austin confided, the steep grades and frequent switchbacks Goodwin recommended were no longer considered acceptable. They reflected the requirements of an earlier era, when vehicles were slower and road builders had less effective equipment at their disposal. Contemporary engineers preferred fewer, longer switchbacks, as Vint suggested. In addition to being easier for motorists to negotiate at the higher speeds of modern automobiles, one long, looping switchback was easier to integrate into the surrounding landscape than a series of short inclines stacked on top of one another, which, Austin noted, resulted in the "mutilation" of the entire area. Austin could only spare time for a hurried inspection, so he recommended that Mather contact his superiors to arrange for a more detailed survey by one of the BPR's top location engineers.[43]

Kraebel and Austin drove to Yellowstone to share their thoughts with Albright, who, though officially Yellowstone's superintendent, continued to serve as Mather's confidant. Vint headed to Mount Rainier, where he encountered Mather and brought him up to date. Satisfied with the routing decision and eager to move forward, Mather formally requested the BPR's assistance. Sensing the advantage, MacDonald replied that he would happily assign a location engineer, provided the BPR was granted authority to draw up specifications and supervise construction. Mather fired back a telegram telling MacDonald

the deal was off, at which point MacDonald insisted there had been a misunderstanding. The NPS could do the engineering if Mather insisted: he was only concerned that the road conform to BPR standards. MacDonald authorized BPR western regional director L. I. Hewes to provide whatever assistance Mather desired. Seeking to make a good impression, Hewes sent one of his foremost road location experts, senior engineer Frank Kittredge, to Glacier to make a preliminary survey of the revised route. By the time the necessary bureaucratic arrangements were in place, it was already September. Kittredge's crew battled the rugged terrain and wintry conditions to produce an impressive report that confirmed the alternate location's appeal while demonstrating the BPR's ability to embrace NPS landscape sensibilities. Kraebel enthused that the new alignment would produce "just such a road as we have been visualizing and have been promising the public." He acknowledged that the added expense "may seem prodigal" but insisted that "the new location is emphatically worth the increased cost, whatever it may be." While Goodwin was undoubtedly aggrieved, he kept his petulance in check. He not only worked with Mather and Albright to devise a cooperative agreement between the two agencies but facilitated Kittredge's survey and reviewed the results with Kraebel, Hull, and BPR engineers. With the financial constraints removed, Goodwin was willing to acknowledge the superiority of the new alignment. He also harbored expectations of overseeing the project once it was under way.[44]

Goodwin remained embroiled in the debate over technical specifications. While the Bureau of the Budget ruled in favor of the NPS retaining an autonomous road-building organization, the BPR insisted park roads should conform to bureau standards when they served as through roads connecting state highways. This caused considerable consternation until the BPR made it clear that in all but a few cases it would be content with the same standards employed on first-class U.S. Forest Service roads, which called for an 18-foot-wide travel surface flanked by two 2-foot-wide ditches. Once again, Goodwin observed that it was an excellent idea in theory but impossible to accomplish with existing funding. He called for a continuation of the more "elastic" NPS specifications, insisting they were better suited for national park development and more than adequate for existing traffic loads. Following the Glacier incident, however, Mather decreed that the 1924 budget figures would not be considered a limiting factor. National park roads would be designed and built with width, grades, and other considerations on par with BPR forest roads. Funding limitations would also not be accepted as an excuse for skimping on landscape protection, whether in the initial layout, final design, or during the construction process. If project budgets were insufficient, the new policy was to construct first-class roads until the money ran out. Goodwin was instructed not to deviate from these instructions without specific authorization. To encourage uniformity and minimize the possibility of unauthorized changes, Goodwin was provided with blueprints of the BPR's standard cross-sections and instructed to develop NPS equivalents.[45]

Determined to reassert his authority and disdainful of the suggestion that he copy the BPR's guidelines, Goodwin solicited standards from an array of state highway agencies, most of which were geared toward higher speeds and larger traffic volumes. As a result, the standards he proposed in January 1925 exceeded the BPR's at both extremes. In addition to including an option for single-lane construction, which most of his contemporaries considered obsolete, Goodwin proposed that the highest-standard roadways be 2 feet wider than the BPR maximum. Mather's patience wore even thinner. Not only did the BPR drawings provide twice as much technical detail, but constructing park roads to even higher standards would undermine the argument that the NPS should retain its road-building authority because it could proceed more cheaply and with greater sensitivity. Goodwin protested that the maximum dimensions applied only in heavily trafficked locations such as Yosemite Valley and Yellowstone's Gardiner, Montana, gateway, where park roads connected to state highways with even higher standards. Most roads would fall into the second category, which corresponded with the BPR's top level. If that was the case, Mather countered, then it made sense for the NPS to mirror the BPR standards or adopt them outright. In addition to simplifying the contracting process, he noted in language certain to incite Goodwin's ire, the BPR standards were "the result of a number of years of experience." Mather ordered Goodwin to revise his standards to correspond to BPR specifications. Goodwin complied but distanced himself

from the results. An exasperated Mather approved the revised standards in March 1925. To placate Goodwin, he noted that exceptions could be made in special situations such as Yosemite's busy El Portal Road. In another conciliatory gesture, Mather finally acknowledged that Goodwin had been hobbled by estimates that were too low for the type of roads he now proposed to construct.[46]

Mather's doubts about Goodwin's abilities continued to grow, as did his irritation with the engineer's behavior. Concerns about the ongoing friction over Generals Highway prompted Mather to assign the project to Austin, who had been lured away from the BPR. Between Austin's reports and a personal inspection in April 1925, Mather came to the conclusion that Goodwin was not only incapable of adjusting to evolving expectations but deliberately misleading in his reports to Washington. Complaining to Cammerer that Goodwin was "rendering himself more and more impossible," he confided that it was "only a question of time" before all park road engineering responsibilities would be transferred to the BPR.[47]

The dispute over bridge design also boiled over during the spring of 1925, focusing attention on Mount Rainier and providing additional evidence of Goodwin's shortcomings. Despite Hull's praise for Goodwin's work on the Carbon River Road, the NPS had received complaints about its location and quality. Mather was deeply concerned about Goodwin's ability to handle the next phase, which entailed extending the road farther up the mountain and swinging south to connect with the Nisqually Entrance. Mather considered this project to be equal in importance to Glacier's Transmountain Highway, since it would form the first link in the road intended to encircle the mountain, affording expanded access and answering long-standing local demands. Portions of the area to be traversed were as challenging as Logan Pass and Goodwin's preliminary survey raised similar concerns. Mather contacted Hewes, emphasizing the project's significance and asking him to personally review Goodwin's route or assign one of his best engineers. Hewes expressed reservations about passing judgment on the work of the NPS Engineering Division, especially without an official interagency agreement. By the end of June, the arrangement had not been formalized and Goodwin was preparing to conduct a final survey so that construction could begin. When Mather was apprised of the situation, he implored

MacDonald to send Kittredge to the park as soon as possible. At the same time, he ordered Goodwin to hold off until the BPR conducted an independent study. BPR engineers would also review the existing roadway, which had already proven susceptible to flooding.[48]

Goodwin was predictably outraged. Condemning Mather's order as yet another personal and professional assault, he threatened to complain to the secretary and take the dispute public unless his authority was restored. Goodwin concluded his telegram by demanding to know whether he should continue on a planned trip to Wind Cave National Park or return to the office to be "relieved at your very earliest convenience." The engineer was undoubtedly engaging in his usual bluster and had made it clear during earlier disputes that he had no intention of resigning. Mather, however, had had enough. Goodwin arrived at Wind Cave to find a telegram terminating his service. When Mather proudly reported this interchange to Cammerer, who was holding down the fort in Washington, he was quickly reminded that not even the NPS director could dismiss an employee without due process. Cammerer was afraid Mather's impetuous action would create a legal tangle and public relations disaster. After consulting with Interior Department officials, Cammerer advised Mather to cast Goodwin's rhetorical flourish as a letter of resignation and supplied a carefully worded acknowledgment. Goodwin protested that he had merely requested a leave of absence so that he could present his objections to Interior Secretary Work, but he accepted his fate without the promised pyrotechnics. After a brief hiatus, he returned to the Army Corps of Engineers, where he spent the last ten years of his career overseeing flood control, canal, and irrigation work in the Northwest. Hewing to the maxim that revenge is a dish best served cold, Goodwin exacted a measure of retribution in a book on highway location he coauthored with W. W. Cosby, who worked on several NPS projects and served as superintendent of Grand Canyon. Among other thinly veiled allusions, Goodwin warned of the dangers posed by "self-ordained boosters" who wasted taxpayers' money on extravagantly conceived projects and then blamed engineers when financial realities conflicted with unrealistic expectations. Defending his actions while tacitly acknowledging his fatal mistake, Goodwin cautioned that economic considerations were quickly forgotten, "but defects in location are always remembered and stand as monumental errors." Unburdened but unbowed, Goodwin illustrated the virtues of "spectacular location" with an unidentified plan that bore a striking resemblance to his Transmountain Road proposal.[49]

Goodwin was succeeded by his chief assistant, Bert Burrell, who had come to the NPS from the BPR a few months earlier. Burrell took pains to distance himself from his predecessor, emphasizing that he intended to be open-minded and accessible. By this time, it was clear that Mather doubted the wisdom of relying on the agency's small engineering force. Enthused by the results of the Transmountain Road survey, he directed his assistant Arthur Demaray to look into establishing a full-fledged collaboration with the BPR. Demaray consulted with USFS officials, both to find out the details of their arrangement and to ascertain their opinion of its effectiveness. The primary problem with the BPR-USFS agreement, he learned, was that both agencies were on an equal footing. This meant that disputes were settled by the secretary of agriculture, generally to the BPR's benefit. Although the bureau's engineers had gotten better at addressing landscape concerns, USFS officials advised the NPS to maintain final authority in matters of location, design standards, and landscape treatment. As long as the BPR accepted this provision, the agency would benefit by taking advantage of the bureau's technical expertise, organizational structure, and contracting procedures. The BPR's overhead charges might be higher, but the NPS would be relieved of a tremendous administrative burden. Building on Forest Service procedures and the preliminary agreement developed by Vint, Kraebel, Goodwin, and Albright, Demaray proposed an arrangement in which the BPR would conduct location surveys, provide plans and specifications for NPS approval, engage contractors and supervise construction, and then subject the results to NPS review. The NPS chief engineer would address technical details while the chief landscape engineer would review landscape concerns and be empowered to stop construction any time park values were threatened. Park superintendents would be allowed to weigh in on these matters, with any internal disagreements being settled by the director. Between Goodwin's departure and the prospect of dealing with the $2.5 million allotted for the 1926 construction season, Mather decided the time had come to accept the BPR's offer, albeit on terms that left no doubt which agency remained in charge.[50]

Mather made the prospective collaboration a focus of the 1925 National Park Conference. The event was held at Mesa Verde National Park in October, with BPR regional engineer L. I. Hewes providing an overview of the bureau's activities and answering questions from the assembled superintendents. In a typical feat of showmanship, Mather directed participants to proceed to the park in "auto caravans" accompanied by the press and other interested parties. In addition to underscoring the importance of motor tourism, the caravans would allow superintendents to inspect road conditions along the way. Mather prevailed on Hewes, Hull, and Burrell to meet him in Yosemite and drive down together so they could get to know each other better and discuss the upcoming challenges. Mather began the conference by reassuring the audience that enlisting the BPR's expertise did not mean the NPS had wavered in its commitment to park values. He insisted that the BPR was equally committed to roadside aesthetics and had already exhibited impressive results, both in USFS work and general highway construction. When it came to "watching out to see that the whole picture is preserved," Mather declared, there was "no one more earnest" than BPR chief MacDonald. Thanks to the BPR's technical assistance, Mather proclaimed, national park roads would be of even greater value to the American people. He even cast the long struggle for funding as a blessing in disguise, since it prevented the NPS from constructing roads that would have been obsolete by the time they were completed.[51]

Albright and Burrell made it clear that there was no longer any presumption that the original estimates would cover the cost of roads built to BPR standards. Estimates for the Transmountain Road alone more than tripled, from approximately six hundred thousand dollars to well over $2 million. Hewes maintained that the BPR, USFS, and state highway departments had faced similar realizations. Not only had automobile travel increased more rapidly than anyone had envisioned, but motorists demanded roads designed to accommodate higher speeds with increased safety and comfort. The NPS was fortunate, he observed, since design standards could be kept relatively low

Between Goodwin's departure and the prospect of dealing with the $2.5 million allotted for the 1926 construction season, Mather decided the time had come to accept the BPR's offer, albeit on terms that left no doubt which agency remained in charge.

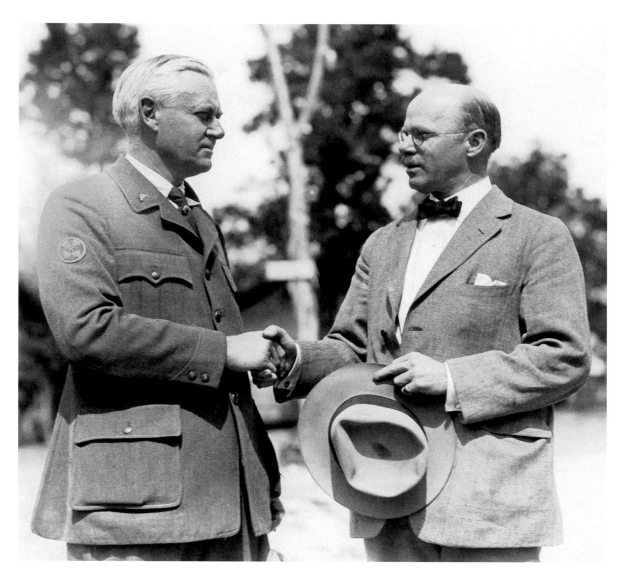

due to the emphasis on scenic preservation and leisurely recreation. While Hewes expressed gratitude for Mather's endorsement, he acknowledged that BPR engineers had much to learn in terms of landscape preservation. Given the contrast in cultures, there would undoubtedly be challenges along the way. "We must be prepared to fight out our differences in good spirits," he admonished, reminding his audience that the ultimate client for both agencies was the touring public, which, he observed, was "an enormous and wealthy and intelligent class of people."[52]

As an aid to planning and budgeting, Hewes suggested the NPS adopt the BPR practice of developing maps outlining proposed road programs and charting their progress. Albright seconded the idea, urging superintendents to produce maps detailing the intended location and class of each road and, equally important, the areas that should remain free of road development. These documents would eventually be incorporated in the master

planning process overseen by Vint's landscape division. Mather and his assistants would prioritize the projects, the BPR would make surveys and prepare estimates, and the maps and data could then be presented to Congress to bolster requests for funding. Between the Park Service's growing popularity, the confidence inspired by the BPR's technical expertise and bureaucratic prestige, and Mather's and MacDonald's political skills, there was widespread agreement that the prospects for significantly increased support were outstanding.[53]

In the meantime, NPS and BPR officials worked out the details of their collaboration. According to the Memorandum of Agreement approved by Mather and MacDonald in January 1926, the BPR would get involved only at the NPS's request, eliminating fears that the bureau would impose its will on park roads. NPS officials determined the need for a road or major reconstruction project. An initial reconnaissance was generally made with park personnel and

representatives of the engineering and landscape divisions. Once the NPS director requested the BPR's assistance, bureau engineers would make a preliminary location survey, prepare plans and specifications, and estimate the cost of the project. The engineers were instructed to cooperate with the park superintendent and chief landscape engineer throughout this process. Once these officials and the NPS director approved the plans, the BPR and superintendent would collaborate to select a contractor and a BPR engineer would be assigned to supervise the construction process. The NPS could choose to pursue the work with its own forces, but this option was reserved for minor projects with few technical challenges. The NPS was responsible for paying contractors and reimbursing the BPR for its expenses. The agreement specifically authorized the NPS to develop procedures aimed at preserving landscape values. It also directed that both agencies make "every effort to harmonize the standards of construction" with those employed on Forest Service roads and the national highway system as well as to "secure the best modern practice in the location, design, and improvement thereof." At the time, both agencies viewed these clauses as expressions of the desire to upgrade park roads from the horse-and-buggy era to the automobile age. The commitment to keeping pace with contemporary highway practice would become a source of contention as standards for road width, grade, and curvature evolved to accommodate increasing speeds and traffic volumes.[54]

The NPS had begun to develop guidelines for the landscape treatment of roads several years earlier. Following the 1923 National Park Conference, Rocky Mountain National Park superintendent Roger Toll prepared a statement of general principles along with a list of more specific considerations. "Roads should be as attractive as possible," he observed, "in order that they may not conflict with the main purpose of the park, which is conservation of natural beauty." Achieving this goal would require the elimination of many standard highway-building practices which, while efficient, detracted from the appearance of roadside landscapes. Borrow pits for road-building gravel would no longer be permitted within sight of the roadway. Nor was it permissible to cast excavated material off the side of the road, a common practice that often devastated downslope vegetation. Excess rocks and gravel would be "end-hauled" rather than "side-cast" and deposited at designated dumpsites or stockpiled to build up the roadbed in other locations. Blasting would be strictly monitored and employ multiple small charges rather than a few large ones, which caused excessive damage beyond the path of the roadway. Whenever possible, road banks should be angled back gently or held in place by retaining walls, which were less desirable because they were expensive and conspicuously artificial even when constructed of native stone. No living timber should be cut within sight of the roadway unless absolutely necessary and all stumps, trunks, limbs, and brush cut down to make way for the road should be burned or disposed of beyond the view of motorists. For years, it had been common practice to leave brush and downed trees by park roadsides, which was both unsightly and an acknowledged fire hazard. John D. Rockefeller Jr. had been so appalled by this practice on his first visit to Yellowstone in 1924 that he financed a multiyear roadside cleanup effort, which included relocating utility poles and wires strung up along the park's roadways in a similar concession to expediency. Clearing away the dead wood and undergrowth allowed grass and flowers to flourish along the roadsides, cultivating what Albright characterized as "a true park atmosphere that did not exist before." Other parks emulated this practice, albeit with congressionally approved funds rather than Rockefeller's largesse.[55]

The NPS issued a press release assuring that the expanded road-building program would not pose a threat to traditional park values. The goal was "to gain the maximum scenic beauty with the least scarring of the countryside" and leave the greater portion of parks free from development. Providing access to key destinations and showcasing the scenery en route would entail cutting trees, excavating roadbeds, and other scenic impacts, but every effort would be made to preserve individual features and general landscape effects. The press release provided a summary of the techniques NPS designers would employ, including protecting roadside landscapes during the construction process, favoring gentle curves over straight lines and hairpin turns, using native stone for features such as bridges and culverts, and exposing motorists to a variety of scenic effects. Mather confided to Hull that he was concerned about the agency's ability to achieve the desired results but welcomed the challenge. "If landscape supervision of road building can be a practical success," he exhorted, "we now have the opportunity of proving it." Despite his effusive pronouncements, Mather worried that the BPR's engineers would resist the prioritization of landscape values, especially where such measures drove up construction costs. NPS landscape architects would have to be firm while understanding that they might have to settle for results that occupied a middle ground "between the idealistic and the practical."[56]

As the NPS-BPR collaboration expanded from Glacier to Yosemite, Mount Rainier, Sequoia, and then virtually every park in the system, Mather's prediction that the arrangement would dramatically improve the quality and quantity of park roads was confirmed. His concerns about the engineers' landscape sensitivity were equally prescient. Tensions arose over numerous points of contention, most of which had been predicted by Albright and Goodwin. NPS officials quickly objected to what they perceived as inordinate overhead charges. Not only did there seem to be too many engineers assigned to projects and excessive visits from higher

officials, but park employees with strapped budgets resented the quantity and quality of equipment employed by the BPR at NPS expense. Another source of friction was the engineers' tendency to develop plans and specifications with minimal NPS input. When landscape architects finally got a chance to make comments, valuable time and money was lost revising plans. In some cases, contracts were advertised or even under way before NPS officials received documents for review. Whether by accident or design, this made it difficult for the NPS to insist on revisions. BPR engineers initially preferred to deal with individual superintendents rather than the Landscape and Civil Engineering Divisions, whose staffs were better equipped to evaluate proposals. Defining the NPS chief engineer's role in the process was another source of tension, especially after Mather enticed Kittredge to assume the position in 1927. Albright maintained that Kittredge's combination of engineering expertise and landscape sensitivity merited a larger role than specified in the original agreement. Vint concurred, but conflicts arose on bureaucratic and philosophical grounds. On many occasions they disagreed strongly about proposed road locations and other design concerns. Although Vint has been portrayed as exhibiting greater concern for the preservation of park landscapes, there were times when Kittredge advocated less intrusive approaches. After the Landscape Engineering and Civil Engineering Divisions were consolidated into a San Francisco–based "Field Headquarters" in 1928, it was decided that both men would review road proposals, with Vint retaining ultimate authority. Albright encouraged Kittredge to inspect roadwork in the parks whenever possible and report to him rather than address BPR officials directly. Hewes and Kittredge maintained a good relationship, but some engineers resented having their projects critiqued by a former subordinate.[57]

The biggest discord arose over damage to roadside scenery during the construction process.

BELOW NPS officials at 1929
Superintendents' Conference,
left to right: chief engineer Frank
Kittredge, associate director
Arno Cammerer, director
Horace Albright, Yellowstone
superintendent Roger Toll,
and chief landscape architect
Thomas Vint.

OPPOSITE Ralph Yardley,
"Homeward Bound,"
cartoon, *Stockton Record,*
October 10, 1925.

Neither the BPR nor its contractors were prepared for the NPS's stringent landscape-protection policies. This became apparent as soon as work began on the Transmountain Road. Not only did the contractors go about business as usual, sending loose rocks cascading down the mountainside and exploding enormous charges that severely damaged their surroundings, but BPR supervisors raised no objections. NPS protests were not limited to scenic concerns. Since the material lost down the hillside could have been used to build up the roadway in other locations, contractors were forced to haul fill from distant borrow pits, delaying progress and increasing costs. The NPS felt that BPR engineers were too cozy with contractors in general, failing to enforce both specifications and deadlines. The resulting cost overruns ate away at budgets that were already strained by the switch to higher standards. From the engineers' perspective, the NPS's overzealous protection measures were responsible for delaying projects and driving up costs. When similar problems occurred at Mount Rainier, Mather complained directly to MacDonald, providing photographs of the destruction to emphasize his points. He also advised Vint to instruct his men to keep closer tabs on BPR projects.[58]

MacDonald was extremely apologetic. His bureaucratic desire to preserve the partnership was bolstered by a genuine commitment to improving the appearance of American highways. As would often prove to be the case, idealistic sentiments expressed by high-level officials did not always translate to the actions of employees in the field. MacDonald explained that project supervisors had been told to follow NPS specifications to the letter, but acknowledged that some were taking longer than others to understand that in national park work, traditional engineering imperatives took a backseat to landscape preservation. The root of the problem, MacDonald maintained, was that engineers were trained to prosecute work as quickly and efficiently as possible. Like Goodwin, many BPR engineers had been building roads for a long time and saw no reason to alter what they considered to be successful practices. MacDonald implied that the NPS was partially responsible, given its oft-stated eagerness to accommodate the motoring public as quickly as possible. MacDonald promised to instruct his staff to exercise greater care but implored Mather to counsel patience. Given the pressure for progress and insistence on minimizing landscape damage, MacDonald maintained that his engineers felt like they were "caught between the devil and the deep blue sea."[59]

As an indication of the engineering community's interest in national park road work, Mather was invited to address the topic at the 1928 meeting of the American Society of Civil Engineers. After recounting the previous half century's trials and tribulations, Mather cast the new arrangement in glowing terms. Praising the NPS-BPR collaboration as "a splendid working agreement," he credited the bureau with helping convince Congress to pass a second road bill providing a previously unthinkable $50 million over the next ten years. As usual, he insisted the parks would not be gridironed and outlined the landscape principles guiding construction. Mather illustrated the benefits of this approach with photographs from the Transmountain Road and touted prospective projects such as the Zion–Mount Carmel Highway and the reconstruction of Yosemite's Big Oak Flat Road. The BPR's H. K. Bishop provided an equally effusive rejoinder. Admitting that the engineers had originally been "a bit inclined to think too much of economy in road construction and too little of scenic effects," Bishop maintained the BPR had "benefitted greatly by its co-operation

with the Park Service." Insisting that the landscape lessons had already taken hold, he proclaimed, "a new appreciation of scenic factors will be evident in the character of the roads built hereafter in the National Parks and National Forests of the West."[60]

From all indications, both sides quickly grew more comfortable with the arrangement. At the 1928 National Park Conference, Albright proclaimed that relations had warmed to the point where "there is something akin to real affection among the Park Service men and the district engineers." Acknowledging that many engineers had been resistant to NPS directives, Hewes enthused that after several seasons in the parks, "Bureau men are becoming landscape conscious to a gratifying extent." Most engineers enjoyed challenges, he noted, and national park work was as challenging as it got. Hewes maintained that being assigned to a park project was considered a badge of honor, since the bureau entrusted the work only to its most accomplished engineers. The park road ethos was so well engrained, Hewes insisted, that BPR engineers had become as proud of their preservation achievements as of their technological prowess. BPR engineer B. J. Finch boasted that NPS officials roundly praised the care being exercised on the new Zion–Mount Carmel Highway project, citing an instance in which the road had been blasted out of solid rock without disturbing a needle on nearby pine trees. Kittredge acknowledged that considerable progress had been made but insisted that additional improvement was needed. He also cautioned against raising engineering specifications any higher. "To construct roads on fast standards would not only tend to limit the appreciation of the scenery being passed through," he counseled, "but the tremendous excavations and embankments would tend to devastate the mountain landscape, and eliminate the very features for which the traveling public has come to the park." Mindful of both agencies' tendency to measure progress by the amount of construction, Kittredge cautioned against getting carried away in "a stampede for road mileage." His closing comments addressed the challenges ahead. "It is vitally important at this time to recognize that we are entering upon a work of tremendous importance," Kittredge exhorted, "a work which will be handed down to our children's children whether poorly or well done. To gain accessibility certain destruction is necessary and the apparent

HOMEWARD BOUND:- - - - - - - - - - - - - - by YARDLEY
NATIONAL PARK SUPERINTENDENTS AND THEIR "BOSS" GETTING BACK TO THE JOB FULL OF PEP 'N EVERYTHING

FROM STOCKTON RECORD — OCT. 10, 1925

necessity relieves the stigma. Beyond this critical point devastation begins, and beyond this point we should not pass."[61] As always, the biggest challenge lay in determining the point where necessity ended and unwarranted destruction began. For most popular and professional audiences, there was widespread agreement that the ensuing decade's work came closer to balancing the tension between preservation and access than that of any period before or since.

The "Golden Age" of Park Road Building

CHAPTER FIVE

T
he period between the two world wars has long been considered the "Golden Age" of national park road development. The designation reflected both the tremendous amount of work accomplished from the mid-1920s to the early 1940s and the degree to which both new and reconstructed roads reconciled the competing concerns of preservation and access. By combining traditional park road design precedents with modern technical expertise, the NPS managed the transition from the horse-and-buggy era to the automobile age in a manner that garnered widespread acclaim. Many of the most celebrated park roads were completed during this period, producing some of the most spectacular scenic drives in the world. Some of these projects were initiated before the NPS-BPR collaboration was formalized but completed under the new alliance. The initial $7.5 million allotment was rapidly depleted, but the second park roads bill and subsequent legislation allowed construction to proceed at a pace that exceeded Stephen Mather's and Horace Albright's expectations. Not only did

Congress display a sustained commitment to improving access to America's national parks and monuments, authorizing the expenditure of $50 million over a ten-year period, but hard times for the country turned out to be good times for park roads. The Great Depression, or, more to the point, programs designed to combat the economic crisis, resulted in even more resources being devoted to park road development. The Works Progress Administration (WPA), Public Works Administration (PWA), and National Industrial Recovery Act (NIRA) funneled millions of dollars into park-related projects, as did special legislation such as the 1934 Hayden-Cartwright Act, which authorized the expenditure of $24 million for road building in national parks, forests, and other federal lands. Another federal initiative, the Recreational Demonstration Area program, helped fund land acquisition for parks and parkways.[1]

The 1933 Emergency Conservation Works program and its offshoot, the Civilian Conservation Corps (CCC), provided an invaluable source of manpower without which the most labor-intensive aspects of park road development would not have been possible. The CCC put thousands of unemployed men to work, organizing them in military-style camps to conduct conservation projects throughout the country. Although private contractors did most of the actual construction, CCC enrollees conducted the less technically challenging but no less important aspects of road development, grading roadside embankments, replanting disturbed areas with native vegetation, and constructing guard rails, picnic shelters, comfort stations, and other amenities. In some cases, CCC crews built more ambitious structures, such as Great Smoky Mountains' Elkmont Bridge. Most CCC enrollees had little relevant experience, but the program also hired skilled workers called "local experienced men," or LEMs, who had plied related trades and were familiar with local building methods and materials. The National Industrial Recovery Administration required private contractors to hire local labor whenever possible, further enhancing the appeal of park road building among segments of the population that had little interest in scenic tourism per se. Here again, NPS road development followed established patterns, as road construction had long served as a means of providing relief during economic downturns, both in the United States and abroad. Politicians were eager to provide for their constituents even when they remained skeptical of broader park agendas. Projects such as Skyline Drive and Blue Ridge Parkway were initiated under the NIRA or similar programs and did not achieve national park status until well after roadwork commenced. Although the economic benefits of motor tourism were more of a long-term prospect at the height of the Depression, job creation had an immediate impact and played a much-appreciated role in stabilizing hard-hit rural communities. In some instances, the desire to provide jobs led the NPS to develop roads that were not previously high on the agency's agenda. This was particularly true in the case of remote national monuments and in state parks, where NPS landscape architects provided technical assistance on issues ranging from general planning to design details.

The results were dramatic. Although estimates varied depending on how costs were calculated, Congress appropriated approximately $120 million for the construction and maintenance of park roads, trails, and parkways between 1916 and 1941, with all but a tiny portion of the funds allocated from 1924 onward.[2] Approximately half came from federal relief programs and the rest from regular NPS appropriations. Between 1933 and 1936 alone, the mileage of improved roads grew by 73 percent. While this sounds like an inordinate increase, belying Mather's promise not to "gridiron" the parks with roads, a significant portion reflected the dramatic expansion of the National Park System.[3]

Roads and automobiles raised park visitation to unprecedented heights, but NPS leaders realized that access was a matter of geography as well as technology. The bulk of the population was in the East, while most national parks were in the West. With the exception of Maine's Acadia National Park, the national park experience was restricted to those who had time and money for cross-country excursions. Even Acadia was far removed from most of the populace. Easterners could avail themselves of the growing number of state and county parks, but there was wide support for the idea that the best way to achieve the twin goals of conservation and recreation was to establish full-fledged national parks within a day's drive of major eastern cities. Given the ever-increasing popularity of automobiles, it was considered a foregone conclusion that these parks would cater to motor tourism. Building on the western National Park-to-Park Highway

concept, Mather envisioned a coordinated system of national and state parks that would allow motorists to undertake extended tours of eastern scenery.

In 1924 Interior Secretary Hubert Work formed a Southern Appalachian National Park Committee to consider areas for national park designation in the Southeast. The committee consisted of the Palisades Interstate Park's William Welch; the U.S. Geological Survey's chief topographer, Glenn Smith; horticulturalist, town planner, and former Appalachian Mountain Club president Harlan Kelsey; National Arts Club president William Gregg; and longtime park supporter Congressman Henry Temple of Pennsylvania, who served as chairman. Prospective sites were to reflect the distinctive characteristics of the southern Appalachians and be at least 500 square miles in extent. The committee stipulated that each park was to serve as a "natural museum, preserving outstanding features of the southern Appalachians as they appeared in early pioneer days." Given the limited amount of remaining wilderness, it was expected that they would contain a mix of primeval pockets and land that had been logged over and reforested, either through natural processes or reclamation. The goal was not to achieve environmental protection in an ecological sense but to protect attractive scenery and preserve

vestiges of landscapes that were thought to have shaped the country's history and national character. Underscoring the belief that preservation meant little without public access, potential park areas were to be accessible by rail and highway. They should also be of sufficient extent that "millions of visitors might enjoy their benefits without confusion or overcrowding." By visiting these areas, Americans would be uplifted by the same beneficial contact with nature that had molded the hardy citizens of yore—even if they experienced these qualities through the modern medium of motor tourism.[4]

The committee received proposals from park boosters in Virginia, North Carolina, Tennessee, West Virginia, Kentucky, Georgia, and Alabama. The two leading contenders were the northernmost section of the Blue Ridge Mountains on the west side of Virginia's Shenandoah Valley and the Great Smoky Mountains straddling the border between North Carolina and Tennessee. The prospects for developing a park in the latter region were complicated by a number of factors, but the question of access loomed large in the committee's calculations. The Great Smoky Mountains were significantly farther from major population centers and providing access to the sprawling region would require multiple roadways and an enormous investment of time and money.

LONG'S PEAK - ELEV. 14,255 FT. - FROM THE TRAIL RIDGE ROAD

Not only was the Virginia alternative within a three-hour drive of the nation's capital and 40 million potential visitors, but a road running along the highest ridge would afford an irresistible attraction for mid-Atlantic motorists. The committee selected the Virginia nomination as the first park to be developed, but it endorsed the Great Smoky Mountains project and a more limited proposal for Kentucky's Mammoth Cave. All three were approved by Congress, and President Coolidge signed the authorizations in May 1926. Land acquisition challenges delayed their official establishment until the mid-1930s, by which time their road systems were already well developed.[5]

The NPS also began developing historic parks in the East, with an emphasis on sites associated with the Revolutionary War and early republic. The historic park initiative reflected the contemporary tendency to present a romanticized version of the nation's past as a source of inspiration for modern Americans. Albright was particularly enamored of history and made his interest felt when he became NPS director in November 1928. His biggest coup was to convince FDR to transform the

NPS from a western-focused scenic tourism agency to a truly national enterprise with the expanded mission of caring for historic sites as well as scenic areas. Hoover had set the stage for reorganizing the executive branch, but his rapidly eroding political capital precluded major changes. Soon after FDR assumed office, Albright accompanied the president on a drive out to Hoover's fishing camp on the Rapidan River, which he had donated for use as a presidential retreat. As they motored back through the Virginia countryside, Albright provided a rolling history lesson while extolling the benefits of consolidating America's foremost historic sites under a single authority. With FDR's approval, Albright worked up a plan under which the NPS would acquire the War Department's battlefields and monuments, along with the national monuments under Forest Service control. To further consolidate the management of the government's scenic and historic properties, the NPS assumed responsibility for parks and parkways in Washington, D.C. Most Civil War battlefields had been outfitted with carriage drives around the turn of the twentieth century, often with

input from the veterans themselves. Washington's parks had been developed by the Army Corps of Engineers with input from noted landscape architects such as Frederick Law Olmsted Jr. When the NPS took charge, the agency sought to minimize changes, recognizing that the injunction to combine preservation and access extended to historic and commemorative landscapes. In cases where existing roads were not considered capable of accommodating contemporary needs, surfaces were improved and alignments updated to more free-flowing configurations. Washington, D.C.'s Rock Creek Park received minor improvements to its turn-of-the-century carriage roads. A long-contemplated parkway between Rock Creek Park and the Mall was completed and parkway development undertaken along the Potomac shoreline. Many national monuments received new or upgraded roads systems as well.[6]

Most attention was focused on the main tour roads of prominent parks such as Glacier, Yosemite, Mount Rainier, and Rocky Mountain in the West, and Shenandoah, Acadia, and Great Smoky Mountains in the East. The BPR's

The Skyway To Clingman's Dome - Great Smoky Mtn's. Nat'l Park

engineering expertise enabled the NPS to undertake a far more ambitious construction program than it could have accomplished on its own, including projects with extreme degrees of technical difficulty involving lengthy tunnels and complex bridges. The results confirmed Mather's prediction that the long battle to secure sufficient funding had been a blessing in disguise, delaying the onset of major road construction projects until higher design standards could be employed.[7] The NPS, in turn, prompted the BPR to pay greater attention to the aesthetic aspects of road construction. BPR engineers embraced the challenge and played a major role in translating the NPS's "lying lightly on the land" philosophy from idea to reality.[8]

The NPS-BPR collaboration produced a distinctive park road aesthetic. NPS landscape architects and BPR engineers drew heavily on carriage-road design precedents but updated these practices to accommodate the demands of automobile traffic and the topographical challenges of national parks. The alignments of park roads were configured to showcase park landscapes in the most attractive and engaging

manner. Turnouts were provided at particularly scenic locations so tourists could stop without endangering themselves or other motorists. Where roadside vegetation obstructed potentially appealing views, trees were cut to create carefully calculated vistas. Variety of scenery was sought to maintain the motorist's interest. Rather than follow a ridgeline for miles, a park road or parkway drive might drop down to a sidehill location for a while or cross back and forth across the crest to provide views in both directions. In forested areas, the distance between the edge of the road and the tree line was often manipulated to produce varying effects, from narrow wooded aisles to broad green corridors or alternating series of smaller and larger "rooms" carved out of the surrounding forest. Selective cutting to create an undulating tree line produced a more natural and informal effect than did the rigidly prescribed "clear zones" flanking ordinary highways. Trees, shrubs, and charismatic rock formations were allowed to remain much closer to the pavement than on conventional roadways, bringing motorists into intimate contact with their surroundings.

ABOVE Skyway to Clingmans Dome, Great Smoky Mountains National Park, postcard, ca. 1935.

OPPOSITE Curve on Trail Ridge Road displaying Long's Peak, Rocky Mountain National Park, postcard, ca. 1935.

Although hazardous hairpin curves were eliminated wherever possible and most curves were eased to accommodate automobile traffic, park roads were more circuitous than conventional highways. Prolonged straightaways were avoided as much as possible. Not only were sinuous curves more attractive, but curvilinear alignments reduced the need for expensive, environmentally disruptive, and visually unappealing excavations. Road widths were narrower than contemporary highways, but wider than the previous NPS standard, with minimal shoulders. Curbs were employed only on the most highly developed parkways and heavily used areas. Grades rarely exceeded 6 percent and curves were banked and widened to improve safety and comfort. The NPS realized it could not afford to equip all park roads with modern reinforced concrete or bituminous "asphalt" paving during the initial improvement campaign but tried to stabilize as much of its road network as possible with oil-treated gravel or macadam surfaces. More substantial road-mixed asphalt pavements were applied in some situations. Whenever possible, local rock was used for the crushed-stone component of park road pavements. Not only did this save on material costs and hauling expenses, but it helped roads blend in with their surroundings. The results of this policy were most striking in the southwestern parks, where the sparse vegetation put a premium on harmonizing road surfaces with desert rock formations.

Where excavations were unavoidable, park road builders did their best to minimize disruptions and rehabilitate areas disturbed during the construction process. Instead of leaving steep, raw banks along newly graded roadways, as was the common practice in contemporary highway construction, the NPS insisted roadside embankments be sloped back gradually and rounded to resemble natural contours. Sodding and planting programs helped stabilize disturbed roadsides and naturalize their appearance. Revegetation policies promoted the use of native species arrayed in naturalistic groupings. Retaining walls or less intrusive stone-reinforced embankments were used to stabilize steeper slopes. Tunnels minimized the visual impact of road construction on particularly steep and prominent mountainsides. Excavating tunnels required specialized equipment and expertise, but it eliminated sidehill cuts and conspicuous retaining walls while reducing risks associated with rockfalls and avalanches. Designers also employed tunnels to direct the motorist's gaze, either through windows providing lateral views or by using exit portals to frame striking scenes.[9]

The desire to protect motorists in dangerous locations led the NPS to develop an array of attractive guard-wall designs, which were eventually codified into standardized plans. Constructed of locally quarried hand-laid stone in most cases, the walls had a rugged appearance and blended with the hues and texture of neighboring outcrops. Considerable variation was possible within the NPS rustic design framework. Different sizes and shapes of rocks were used and laid in patterns ranging from seemingly random to relatively regular, though every effort was made to avoid a formal rectilinear appearance. Both flat-topped and crenelated walls were constructed. Further variation could be achieved by changing the height, width, shape, and spacing of the crenellations. Log guard rails were used in some locations, and a mixed design of stone and timber was used in parts of Yellowstone and elsewhere. Traditional split-rail fences flanked many southern park roads and parkways, though these were intended more for scenic and sentimental purposes than for safety considerations. Although the subtle variations between different styles may not be apparent to casual observers, the sensation of driving along winding roadways flanked by rugged stone or timber barriers has long been one of the classic components of the national park experience.

Park bridge construction followed a similar design ethos. While the BPR's structural systems embraced the latest technology, the architectural

ABOVE Obsidian Cliff "Nature Shrine," Yellowstone National Park, 1934.

ABOVE East Entrance, Glacier National Park, ca. 1932.

designs and surface treatments reflected the NPS's naturalistic design philosophy. Most bridges were faced with rustic stone veneers. Longer spans were occasionally left undecorated, especially if their elevations were unlikely to be seen by the general public. In addition to favoring locally quarried stone and random masonry patterns, NPS guidelines stipulated that care should be taken to ensure that drill marks and other signs of quarrying be turned inward and only the weathered surfaces of rocks exposed to view. Most NPS bridges from this period tended to have simple lines with subtly accented arch rings. Where steel girders were used to support bridge spans, they were often covered with heavy timbers to harmonize with their surroundings and maintain the rustic design aesthetic. Tunnel portals were generally left in their natural state or, where stabilization was necessary, faced with random rubble masonry. Culvert headwalls were also given rustic stone treatments if they were likely to be viewed by the public.

Park entrances similarly embodied the determination to harmonize structures with their natural and cultural surroundings. Considerable variation could be found within the reigning rustic aesthetic as designers sought to evoke local materials and building traditions. Oversized log structures were popular in the western parks. Adobe—or concrete made to mimic adobe—was favored in the Southwest. Vernacular building motifs were adapted for many park structures in the Appalachian parks. While entrance stations were often the most prominent buildings, similar policies shaped the design of a wide range of visitor facilities, from comfort stations and concessions to water fountains and picnic shelters. Reflecting the demands of twentieth-century park travel, Mount Rainier and several other parks were equipped with rustic-style service stations. Since most visitors drove themselves, the stage driver's role as colorful tour guide gave way to signs presenting information provided by NPS professionals. For those seeking additional guidance, some parks organized "auto nature caravans" led by NPS naturalists. These eventually gave way to self-guiding auto tour pamphlets developed by the NPS and its partners.

The intention behind these design strategies was to showcase park scenery, minimize the visual impacts of development, and ensure that improvements harmonized with their surroundings. The narrow, winding roads, enfolding trees, looming chasms, and encroaching vegetation brought motorists into intimate contact with nature while simultaneously discouraging them from driving too fast. By encouraging motorists to slow down and enjoy their surroundings instead of racing to the next destination, NPS and BPR designers enhanced both the safety and the appeal of the park road experience. The visual quality, intimate scale, and rustic character of roads constructed during this period profoundly shaped the way Americans viewed their national parks. The sensation of motoring along sinuous curves, crossing rustic bridges, winding beside rugged guard walls, and encountering carefully choreographed series of superlative views rapidly became an integral component of the national park experience. The increased budgets and enhanced capabilities of the landscape and engineering forces brought park roads closer than ever to attaining Hiram Chittenden's goal of technical and aesthetic perfection.

NPS designers and BPR engineers adapted these basic principles to the exigencies of individual sites. With conditions varying dramatically from park to park, every road entailed unique challenges. Concerns ranged from minute technical and aesthetic details to the larger question of whether a road should be built in a particular location. The broader development strategies were laid out in master plans. Design and construction details followed general guidelines but were finalized through intensive collaboration in the field. Since a comprehensive survey would run to many volumes, a few signature projects have been chosen to illustrate the manner in which the NPS attempted to fulfill its obligation to provide access to America's most treasured landscapes without compromising their attractions in the process.

GOING-TO-THE-SUN ROAD

Glacier National Park's Going-to-the-Sun Road's status as the premier example of "Golden Age" national park road construction rests not just on the pivotal role it played in fostering the NPS-BPR agreement, but in the degree to which it epitomized the challenges and rewards of park road development. Constructing a motorway across the Continental Divide through some of the most rugged terrain in the Northern Rockies would have been an impressive technical achievement under any circumstances, but to do so without marring the beauty of the park's mountainous heartland required a remarkable combination of engineering expertise and landscape sensitivity. While there were frictions between the two viewpoints, both agencies learned from the experience, and the results were widely applauded by a broad spectrum of popular and professional observers. The lessons acquired from this first major collaboration ranged from technical matters and design details to contract supervision and accounting procedures. On a more fundamental level, Going-to-the-Sun Road confirmed the commitment to the quality of design over the quantity of construction, demonstrating to Congress and the American public that the NPS was willing and able to meet the demands of modern motor tourism. By completing the "missing link" in the National Park-to-Park Highway, moreover, Going-to-the-Sun Road stimulated travel not just to Glacier but throughout the National Park System. As Mather predicted, this further enhanced the NPS's stature with the motoring public, business interests, and elected officials. While Going-to-the-Sun Road literally paved the way for future projects, it also epitomized the NPS's commitment to concentrating development along one primary route while reserving most of the park for nonmotorized enjoyment.

The Going-to-the-Sun Road story is one of the epic chapters in national park history, but transportation issues played a prominent role in Glacier National Park long before tempers flared at Logan Pass on that fateful afternoon in 1924. The park owed its existence to the machinations of the Great Northern Railroad, which skirted its southern border. As with Yellowstone, railroad officials promoted the park as a means of increasing tourist traffic and profiting from ancillary businesses. Local residents began catering to outdoorsmen soon after the line passed through the region in 1893, but the Great Northern president, Louis Hill, had a more ambitious vision. Enlisting the support of prominent nature writers such as George Bird Grinnell and Emerson Hough, Hill lobbied for the creation of a national park encompassing a vast swath of spectacular scenery between the Great Northern tracks and the Canadian border. Most of the area was designated a Forest Reserve in 1897. National park status was conferred in 1910. Hill began constructing a network of guest accommodations on the east side of the

park highlighted by the massive Glacier Park Hotel. The cavernous log structure was a worthy competitor to Yellowstone's grand resorts, as was the Swiss-themed Many Glacier Hotel located on a scenic lake deep within the park. An ardent proselytizer for the See America First movement, Hill promoted Glacier as a patriotic alternative to European travel and strongly supported the

legislation authorizing the National Park Service.[10]

While Hill was investing heavily in hotel construction, the development of park roads proceeded at a slower pace. So slow, in fact, that the railroad grew frustrated and took on the task of providing access to its facilities. The lack of progress exemplified the concerns that led to the establishment of the National Park Service. Not only was funding

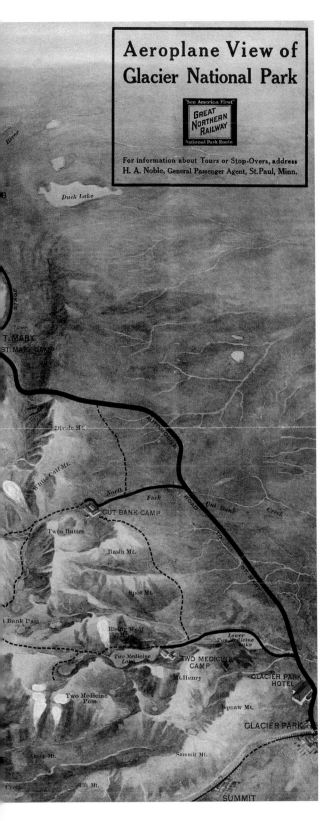

Aeroplane View of Glacier National Park

"See America First"
GREAT NORTHERN RAILWAY
National Park Route

For information about Tours or Stop-Overs, address H. A. Noble, General Passenger Agent, St. Paul, Minn.

severely limited, but with minimal professional staff, the Department of the Interior was forced to rely on borrowed expertise and the mixed abilities of short-term superintendents. As a new park, moreover, Glacier faced different challenges than did Yellowstone or Yosemite, where the NPS focused on upgrading existing roadways. The first tasks were to decide where the park's roads should go and prioritize their construction. While the Glacier Park Company borrowed engineers from the Great Northern Railroad, the Department of the Interior prevailed on U.S. Geological Survey chief topographer Robert Marshall to devise a plan for developing the park. Marshall called for the construction of two hundred miles of "first class" roadways affording access to the park's scenic attractions. Although this ambitious vision would require a considerable investment, Marshall expressed confidence that the results would justify the effort. Lower standard roads could be constructed more quickly and cheaply, but for the park to fulfill its destiny, he advised, "the roads themselves must be one of the attractions."[11]

Since the Great Northern was addressing matters on the east side of the park, Marshall suggested the government focus on the west side. The park's first superintendent, William Logan, had initiated improvements to the primitive wagon road from the railway station at Belton to the foot of Lake McDonald. Marshall advised that the road be extended along the west side of the lake, follow McDonald Creek north, and continue to the Canadian border. This would be augmented by side roads leading to points of interest. The Great Northern's engineer suggested that the road to the company's camp on St. Mary Lake might eventually be extended over the Continental Divide to meet one of these spurs. While these schemes contained the seeds of what would become Going-to-the-Sun Road, neither the government nor the Great Northern had the means to attempt such an ambitious undertaking.[12]

As part of the preliminary collaboration with the Office of Public Roads, T. Warren Allen examined the Glacier situation in 1914. Like Marshall, he acknowledged the value of constructing a road over the Continental Divide but agreed the first priority should be building a road between Belton and the Canadian border. Nevertheless, he scouted potential routes for a transmountain road. Allen advised that Logan Pass afforded the most promising prospect. From there, he suggested, the road could split in two, with one fork heading southeast to St. Mary Lake and the other to the Many Glacier Hotel. Marshall called for an additional road across the north end of the park that would link various scenic features and connect with a north–south route on the east side of the park. Like Marshall's plan, Allen's recommendations would produce a Yellowstone-style grand loop, providing access to a wide array of attractions but girdling the park with roads in the process.[13]

Competing proposals quickly ensued. Glacier's next superintendent, James Galen, agreed that opening up the west side of the park was the top priority but suggested routing the road at a higher elevation to provide better views. He maintained that Swiftcurrent Pass would be a better route for the transmountain road, since its central location eliminated the need for two crossings. The Kalispell Chamber of Commerce put its weight behind yet another option, over Gunsight Pass. Allen and Galen had dismissed this possibility, but local leaders secured the endorsement of Lyman Sperry, a former Oberlin professor regarded as the leading authority on the park's geography. Insisting that motorists should have access to the park's most spectacular scenery, he dismissed the Logan Pass route as "non-scenic" and warned that a road in that location would be "subject to freshets, avalanches of rock and timber and deep snows." Sperry's views received extensive coverage in local newspapers, where they were presented as the product of long experience rather than the result of hasty reconnaissance by federal technocrats. Sperry agreed the road should follow the west side of Lake McDonald and cross McDonald Creek above the head of the lake. A series of switchbacks would take it up the slopes of Mt. Edwards, where the road would loop around the Sperry Glacier basin, passing the Great Northern's Sperry Chalet, Gunsight Lake, and Mt. Jackson before descending along the St. Mary River. While the challenging terrain would require extensive—and expensive—construction, Sperry contended that the superlative scenery was worth the cost, both in construction expense and scenic impact. Any road constructed through the alpine terrain would be highly visible, but Sperry echoed George Goodwin's assertions that visitors would be impressed by conspicuous demonstrations of the road-builder's art. "A national park highway should have not only fine natural scenery," he asserted, "but exhibitions of engineering skill. It should have at least a few tunnels, galleries, terraces, bridges, 'hairpin' turns, and all that sort of thing, to produce the surprises, thrills and joys that tourists seek."[14]

Another faction maintained that any transmountain road was a waste of time and resources, since the goal of linking the two sides of the park could be accomplished by building alongside the Great Northern tracks. This alternative would not be as scenic, but it was the quickest and cheapest means of eliminating the existing detour. The low-level highway would also be open year-round, whereas a transmountain road would only be available for a few months in midsummer. Many surrounding communities supported this option, both to improve local transportation and because they saw it as the most expedient means of generating lucrative tourist traffic. If and when park authorities decided on a route through the high country, they reasoned, there was no guarantee that funding would be forthcoming. When it did come, construction was sure to be slow and costly, further delaying economic benefits. Transmountain road advocates counseled patience, insisting that an excursion through spectacular scenery would draw far more visitors than would a road along a railroad track. This argument resonated with businessmen in regionally important cities such as Kalispell, Missoula, and Columbia Falls, along with motoring clubs and the Montana State Highway Commission, which was undoubtedly eager to avoid the burden of constructing the low-level route, which extended beyond park borders.[15]

Both sides bombarded park officials with letters and petitions. In the meantime, Mather sent Goodwin to Glacier, putting in motion the chain of events that would lead to the NPS-BPR agreement. Goodwin filled in as acting superintendent during the summer of 1917, but his primary mission was to sort out competing claims and devise a plan for moving forward. With the NPS firmly committed to the transmountain road, Goodwin considered the options and ruled in favor of Logan Pass. He returned the following summer to initiate a more detailed survey. Goodwin also shifted the lower portion of the route to the east side of Lake McDonald, influenced in no small part by pressure exerted by the owners of a lodge located on that shore and accessible only by boat. Goodwin's 1918 route followed MacDonald Creek for 8 miles, rose around the base of Mount Cannon, and then climbed toward Logan Pass with the series of switchbacks that would eventually seal his fate. To Goodwin, this represented solid, economical engineering, making the most of Park Service's perennially low appropriations by gaining elevation without extraordinary feats of construction. The same could be said of the

proposed width, which, while wider than some roads he advocated, was barely capable of accommodating two-way traffic. In Goodwin's defense, road standards were evolving rapidly, and it remained uncertain how many motorists would be drawn to the park's remote location.[16]

Due to limited appropriations, construction on the initial segment had proceeded only 8 miles beyond Lake MacDonald by the summer of 1924. Mather's insistence on the road's importance resulted in Glacier receiving nearly half of the initial $1 million allocation resulting from the 1924 park road bill. By this time, it was apparent that Goodwin's plan was not only technically outdated but also at odds with the NPS's commitment to preserving landscape values. The subsequent controversy had an enormous impact on national park history, but the actual design and construction of the transmountain road was a momentous achievement itself.

Mather may have expected his young fraternity brother Bill Austin to take charge, but L. I. Hewes assigned the task to senior highway engineer Frank Kittredge. Widely regarded as one of the agency's top location men, Kittredge was a graduate of the civil engineering program at the University of Washington, where he had studied under Columbia River Highway designer Samuel Lancaster. Before coming to the BPR in 1917, he honed his skills with the Washington State Highway Commission, the Oregon State Highway Commission, and the Alaska Central Railway. The Going-to-the-Sun Road survey would challenge Kittredge's abilities as well as his fortitude. While the route Thomas Vint proposed was elegantly simple in theory, surveying the actual location on the precipitous slopes of the Garden Wall was not just extraordinarily difficult, but exceedingly dangerous. The survey crew had to negotiate sheer cliffs, frequent rockfalls, and increasingly wintery conditions. The bureaucratic hurdles associated with the use of BPR personnel delayed Kittredge's arrival until mid-September. This guaranteed the survey crew would encounter heavy snows and frigid weather, but Kittredge was determined to proceed as far as possible. Due to the harsh conditions and hazardous terrain, labor turnover exceeded 300 percent before Kittredge finally halted operations in early November.[17]

While the main survey crew was preparing base camps, Kittredge took a few of his best men and made a quick reconnaissance. By following

MacDonald Creek and then curving west in a long but relatively gentle ascent to the one major switchback, Kittredge was able to gain a good deal of elevation. The challenging portion began when the road swung back across the nearly vertical slopes below the Garden Wall. In order to carry the roadway across this precipitous terrain, Kittredge called for a combination of sidehill excavations, retaining walls, and "half tunnels," which were passageways cut into the cliffs with the outer side "daylighted" to provide unobstructed views. By sculpting rock cuts to resemble natural conditions, the road's visual impact would be reduced if not entirely eliminated. Short tunnels on either side of the pass provided passage through formations that were so large the half-tunnel approach would have created unacceptable scars. The west side tunnel contained a naturalistically sculpted window, or "adet," reminiscent of Kittredge's mentor's work on the Columbia River Highway. Stone or wood parapets would be constructed on the most exposed sections. Kittredge recommended the road be built with a 16-foot-wide surface and 3-foot shoulders, leaving open the possibility of widening the pavement when funding and travel volume increased. Where Goodwin had employed exceptionally sharp 50-foot-radius curves, Kittredge maintained a 100-foot minimum radius with an even more generous 200-foot radius on blind curves. A number of rustic masonry bridges and culverts would be required to cross permanent streams and temporary freshets.[18]

Kittredge highlighted the route's scenic appeal, both in his written report and the accompanying photographs, which showed the alignment looping in languid curves around spectacular and seemingly impassable cliffs. Following the contours in this manner afforded constantly changing views ranging from yawning chasms and distant peaks to intimate close-ups of rock-strewn gullies and rugged outcrops. In one memorable passage, the road ran so close to a waterfall that travelers would be showered by the spray. Throughout most of the upper section, motorists wound along on a narrow causeway carved out of solid rock, with vertiginous depths on one side and the Continental Divide towering above. In some places, Kittredge noted, "The impression is more that of seeing the country from an aeroplane than from the ground." While the new approach emphasized the integration of natural and man-made features rather than the triumph of technology embraced by Goodwin, Kittredge was equally proud of his achievement, asserting that the finished product would constitute "a great scenic feature in itself." Not only would the road afford "an appropriate and harmonious setting from which to view" the distant grandeur, but westbound motorists would be treated to a magnificent panorama encompassing snowcapped peaks, the undefiled Logan Creek drainage, and, clinging to the rugged mountainside, "much of the 11 miles of road required to reach the valley floor 3,400' below."[19]

Kittredge made numerous recommendations aimed at harmonizing the roadway with its surroundings and minimizing the damage associated with construction. These included the aforementioned tunnels and half tunnels along with subtle variations in alignment to reduce the extent of excavation; rubble masonry or hand-placed stone embankments to stabilize slopes; and ashlar or semi-ashlar masonry guard walls rather than more finished and formal designs. Replacing the usual quick-and-dirty clearing process with a two-stage procedure where trees were left on the roadbed to serve as a buffer until the slopes above were excavated would reduce damage to the landscape below. Downed timber could be employed as padding to protect trees and other features during the construction process. Using only enough dynamite to shatter the rock and

then clearing the residue by hand would eliminate the damage caused when large detonations rained debris on their surroundings. The alignment was calculated with balanced cuts and fills to minimize the unsightly and inefficient practice of casting excavated material to the side and relying on borrow pits to fill depressions. These tactics would drive up the price of construction, but Kittredge insisted the expense was warranted to preserve the mountainside. While these techniques would become standard practice in the ensuing years, Kittredge's recommendations demonstrated that at least some of the BPR's engineers were already attuned to the challenges of scenic road design. Kittredge also foresaw an early point of contention. Since western road builders were unaccustomed to employing such measures, it was essential that landscape preservation procedures be clearly enunciated and estimates prepared accordingly. Otherwise, contractors would skimp on the desired precautions, either out of habit or the desire to stay within budget and keep pace with unrealistic expectations.[20]

Vint endorsed Kittredge's recommendations wholeheartedly, casting the proposal as the best embodiment of national park road ideals to date. According to Vint, the best roads not only provided access to signature scenery but also choreographed the visitor's movements so that a park's landscape character was revealed in a logical and

Throughout most of the upper section, motorists wound along on a narrow causeway carved out of solid rock, with vertiginous depths on one side and the Continental Divide towering above.

BELOW Route location photographs from Frank Kittredge's "Trans-mountain Highway" report, Glacier National Park, February 1925.

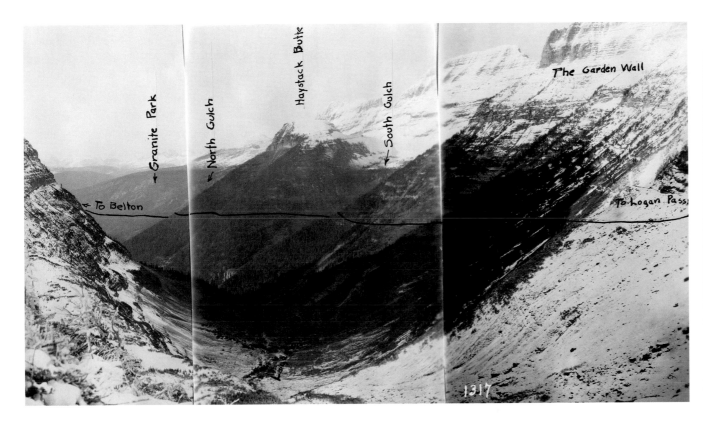

engaging manner. Every effort should be made to minimize the appearance of human intervention. The finished roadside should be free of excavation marks and other signs of construction so that the unpracticed eye would not be able to tell that the surroundings had been disturbed at all. By these standards, Kittredge's proposal was a tour de force. Not only did it harmonize with its surroundings and lead the visitor "on easy curves at a comfortable grade" through every type of scenery Glacier had to offer, but the progression was superbly orchestrated, winding alongside lowland lakes and rushing streams, climbing gradually through changing forests with occasional hints of distant views, and then

bursting out of the trees and across the Garden Wall in a crescendo of soaring cliffs and sweeping vistas. Compared to the staccato effect of certain unnamed alternatives, Vint observed, "it performs its work more silently." Vint's only significant suggestion was to reroute the road on the west side of the park away from St. Mary Lake to avoid impinging on the scenic shoreline.[21]

Prior to the onset of construction the following spring, Vint met with Charles Kraebel, Kittredge, and BPR engineers C. H. Purcell and J. A. Elliott to discuss policies and procedures. Skeptical that other BPR engineers shared Kittredge's commitment to scenic preservation, Vint emphasized the need to "minimize the

effects of the work of the hand of man so that the effects of the work of nature will predominate in the picture." At the same time, NPS officials underscored the importance of producing a high-quality road that would reflect well on the agency's efforts. Even with the new appropriation, Kraebel was concerned that the budget was insufficient to accomplish these goals. Rather than try to cover the entire distance with a substandard road that could be improved later, he insisted that construction start on the underserved west side and proceed at full width. By the time the money ran out, he reasoned, Congress would be sufficiently impressed to provide the required funding.[22]

As might be expected, this initial collaboration did not proceed as smoothly as both sides had envisioned. To begin with, both the BPR and the contractors underestimated the difficulty of the work in general and the impact of NPS landscape preservation concerns in particular. While considerable progress was made the first year, not as much mileage was completed as contracts stipulated. More importantly, the contractors flouted stipulations aimed at protecting the park landscape, casting excavated material off the side of the road so that it destroyed the vegetation below and setting off large explosions in shallow "gopher holes" that wreaked havoc on the surroundings. The NPS had provided detailed instructions on proper blasting procedures along with guidelines specifying that excavated material should be hauled to designated sites. It was bad enough that the contractors flouted these rules, but from the NPS's perspective, the BPR was doing little to enforce them.[23]

Early in 1926, Glacier National Park hired its own resident engineer, Charles Randels. Randels's principal duty was to oversee general park construction, but Kraebel asked him to monitor the contractors' activities. This would have exacerbated tensions in any case, since the BPR bridled at being second-guessed, but Randels had worked for the bureau before coming to the Park Service, and there was lingering animosity between him and the lead engineer, who challenged Randels's competence and complained he was interfering with the process. Hewes passed these concerns on to Arno Cammerer, who ordered Kraebel to keep Randels away from the project. Both Kraebel and Albright protested, insisting the NPS had the right to monitor the project. They recognized that the conflict resulted at least in part from personal issues but insisted it was essential to establish the NPS's authority, not just in terms of the Glacier project but in regard to future collaborations. As Kraebel explained: "Our friends of the Bureau are essentially road builders, dirt movers, rock blasters, [and] surfacing experts. They are only beginning to learn what the Park roads require in the way of landscape protection. . . . We are not safe in giving them too free a hand."[24]

Kittredge met with BPR chief Thomas MacDonald during the fall of 1927 to discuss the NPS's concerns. In addition to scarring the mountainside, the contractors' habit of casting excavated material off the side left insufficient

fill to build up the road bed where necessary. To compensate, the contractors were forced to haul fill from borrow pits and construct more retaining walls than specified, increasing costs, creating additional delays, and making the roadway more noticeable. NPS landscape architect Ernest Davidson, who was assigned to monitor the project, insisted that the contractors use slower, less destructive methods. This did not sit well with the company or the bureau's resident engineer. Davidson also noted departures from prescribed procedure in masonry work, which sometimes failed to blend with natural surroundings or had to be rebuilt for structural reasons. Apparently some of the men decided to exercise their creativity by employing colored rocks to produce decorative patterns that represented the antithesis of NPS ideals. The NPS again faulted the BPR for not enforcing contract stipulations.[25]

The contractors admittedly faced a challenging task. The slopes were so steep that it was often necessary to haul supplies uphill by hand or with horses. In some places, the terrain was so rugged that ladders were required. In many locations a careless misstep could result in serious injury or death. Some areas were so hazardous that workers had to be suspended by ropes, especially during the initial clearing process. To make room for the roadbed across the steepest sections, the lead men used jackhammers to cut narrow ledges for blasting crews, who drilled holes and set charges to expand the excavation to the point where power shovels could be moved in to complete the job. Nearly 500,000 pounds of explosives were expended during the course of the project. In order to save time, workers lived in temporary camps close to the construction. In addition to the cold, wind, and high altitude, workers had to contend with bears. Most were relatively benign black bears, but the occasional grizzly elicited frantic calls for NPS assistance to drive them away. Although turnover was not as high as on the survey crew, the conditions forced the contractors to pay higher than normal wages, further eating away at appropriations. Despite the safety measures, three men died during the course of construction.[26]

When the initial three-year funding cycle came to an end, the road was far from finished. After a few stopgap allocations, construction ground to a halt in 1929. This was primarily the result of austerity measures decreed by President

Hoover, but there were grumblings from other parks that Glacier was consuming an inordinate share of the road-building budget. Pressure to complete the road was reduced somewhat in 1930, when the Montana State Highway Commission completed the Theodore Roosevelt Highway along the low-level route on which local communities and highway interests had insisted to accommodate year-round travel. Construction resumed in 1931, with the focus shifting to the east side. This also entailed heavy rock work, including a 405-foot tunnel. Progress was slow until these obstacles were surmounted, leaving the relatively easy descent to the existing roadway leading to East Glacier.[27]

The Transmountain Highway project attracted considerable attention. Engineering periodicals followed the proceedings, and tourist publications such as *Sunset* magazine heightened the sense of anticipation. The NPS supplied photographs attesting to the difficulty of construction and underscoring the efforts taken to minimize scenic impacts. BPR engineer Jean Ewen combined technical details and broader commentary in an amply illustrated article for the professional journal *Civil Engineering*. Embracing the Park Service's perspective, Ewen insisted that the technical aspects of this feat paled in comparison to its scenic significance. "Our only prayer," he proclaimed, "must be that our work may be truly a component part of this wonder of nature, that we may not have marred that which we, with all our science, knowledge, and experience, could never reproduce." The ultimate measure of success, he maintained, was that despite the enormous technical challenges, "this highway appears merely as a faint scratch on a child's slate against this background of sheer stone."[28]

As the project neared completion, there was widespread agreement that it deserved a more inspiring title than "The Transmountain Road." Various stories surround the "Going-to-the-Sun Highway" designation. Glacier Superintendent J. R. Eakin insisted the name was suggested by Congressman Louis Cramton, who played a major role in securing funding. While Cramton took a personal interest in road-building matters, Eakin's attribution may have reflected the desire to curry favor with one of the NPS's most influential benefactors. Another version attributed the designation to a request from the Blackfeet tribe that the NPS use Native American names for park features. A 1933 Department of the Interior press

Going-to-the Sun Road remains an extraordinarily popular attraction. Its significance as an engineering achievement and contribution to NPS history has been widely recognized. The road was listed on the National Register of Historic Places in 1983, declared a National Historic Civil Engineering Landmark in 1985, and designated a National Historic Landmark in 1997. For many people, driving the road is the main reason for visiting the park. In 1934, the first full season it was officially open, attendance jumped from 76,000 to 116,965. After a drop in visitors during World War II, the numbers rose to 201,000 in 1946 and 485,000 in 1950. Total visitation topped 2 million in 1980 and peaked at more than 2.2 million in 2010, the park's centennial year. Few of these visitors ventured far from the road. Although Mather would be disappointed that Glacier's extensive hiking and horse-riding opportunities remain under-utilized, he would undoubtedly applaud the road's ability to showcase the park's scenery while leaving thousands of acres free from motorized intrusions.[32]

release explained that tribal legend held that a deity named Sour Spirit had come down from the sun to teach the Blackfeet how to hunt. When this task was completed, Sour Spirit returned to the sun, leaving his image on a prominent peak as a reminder. Going-to-the-Sun was purportedly an anglicized contraction of the original name: "The Face of Sour Spirit Who Went Back to the Sun After His Work Was Done." Other sources suggest the legend was a romantic concoction invented by local boosters in the 1880s.[29]

The NPS held a highly publicized dedication ceremony at Logan Pass on July 15, 1933. More than four thousand people attended, including park officials, BPR personnel, tourists, and various dignitaries including Montana's governor and highway commissioner. Albright, McDonald, and Secretary of the Interior Harold Ickes sent messages praising the project as a momentous achievement and paragon of public-spirited collaboration. Politicians from surrounding communities took turns singing the road's praises. The Civilian Conservation Corps and the Blackfeet Tribal Band provided musical entertainment. The highlight of the afternoon was an elaborately choreographed "peace ceremony" between Blackfeet, Flathead, and Kootenai leaders. This

compact was ostensibly necessary because the new roadway eliminated the mountain barrier separating the historically hostile tribes.[30]

Going-to-the-Sun Road was open for travel, but it would be many years before it was fully finished. The preliminary surface was replaced with a more substantial crushed-rock pavement over the next few years. Additional guard walls were constructed, along with improvements to shoulders, ditches, and roadside embankments. The lower portions constructed before the NPS-BPR collaboration were narrow, wracked by tight curves, and relied on outdated wooden bridges. Additional work was necessary to bring these sections up to current standards. The contractors also had trouble coping with tourist traffic, as motorists flocked to Going-to-the-Sun Road despite the hardships of the Great Depression. By the end of 1937, all but a short section west of Logan Pass had a crushed-rock surfacing and minimum roadbed of 22 feet. This last stretch was improved the following year. Like most NPS roads, Going-to-the-Sun did not receive a bituminous concrete, or "asphalt," surface for many years. While the process began before World War II, the road was not completely blacktopped until 1952.[31]

ROCKY MOUNTAIN NATIONAL PARK

Road development in Rocky Mountain National Park followed a somewhat different path. Since the area was an established tourist destination prior to its designation as a national park in 1915, the first roads were constructed by private interests, the State of Colorado, and counties in which the park was located. Not only did these entities have limited capabilities, but the initial cross-park route, Fall River Road, was built at a time of rapid evolution in road development. As a result, it was essentially obsolete by the time it was completed. Its replacement, Trail Ridge Road, benefited from the NPS's landscape sensitivity, the enhanced technical expertise provided by the BPR, and a dramatically improved budgetary climate. With its gentle grades, broad, sweeping curves, and meticulous attention to scenic values, Trail Ridge Road exemplified the benefits of the NPS-BPR partnership. Even with these advantages, the achievement did not come easily. Road development in Rocky Mountain National Park entailed unique challenges, as the extreme weather conditions taxed men and machines alike. With a high point of 12,183 feet and almost a dozen miles located at 11,000 feet or more, Trail Ridge Road remains the highest major roadway in the National Park System. The park's unique history produced political challenges as well, underscoring the difficulties in dealing with roads subject to multiple jurisdictions.[33]

Located north of Denver along Colorado's Front Range, Rocky Mountain National Park encompasses a region of spectacular scenery with extensive areas of alpine tundra and dozens of peaks soaring above 11,000 feet. The highest, Longs Peak, was first climbed in 1868 by Denver newspaperman William Byers and geologist Clarence King. Byers was an ardent booster of the region's attractions who touted the area as a scenic wonderland with convenient rail access to eastern cities. Additional exposure was provided by photographer William Henry Jackson, who produced a series of impressive views in the 1870s. This publicity attracted the attention of an entrepreneurial Irishman, the Fourth Earl of Dunraven, who developed a resort in an idyllic valley known as Estes Park. Dunraven acquired more than 15,000 acres, constructed a capacious inn, and attracted well-heeled visitors from the East Coast and abroad. As evidence of the resort's popularity, he proclaimed, "The marks of carriage wheels are more plentiful than elk signs."[34]

Tourists flocked to Estes Park in increasing numbers during the 1880s and 1890s. Not only was the region gaining fame as "the Switzerland of America," but its proximity to Denver rendered it accessible to easterners traveling westward by train. In 1907 Dunraven sold out to a partnership formed by the pioneering automobile manufacturer F. O. Stanley, who employed his namesake vehicles to ferry visitors to increasingly elaborate accommodations. Stanley joined with other local businessmen to form the Estes Park Protective and Improvement Association. This organization supported improvements to roads leading to Estes Park along with the construction of a scenic loop known as the "High Line Drive," which afforded an excursion along the Fall River, across Deer Ridge at the west edge of the valley, and back to Estes Park along the Big Thompson River. Access was improved in 1904 with the completion of a road through Big Thompson Canyon. This impressive feat required numerous bridges and considerable excavation. The

county put some funds into the project and local businessman contributed the rest, confident the increased traffic would repay their investment.[35]

In 1905 President Theodore Roosevelt extended Wyoming's Medicine Bow Forest Reserve southward into Colorado, encompassing most of the area that would become Rocky Mountain National Park. A movement soon developed to provide additional safeguards through national park designation. The leading force was Enos Mills, a charismatic but cantankerous guide, writer, and innkeeper. Mills promoted national park status through speaking engagements, magazine articles, and an extensive letter-writing campaign. The proposal's chief adversary was H. N. Wheeler,

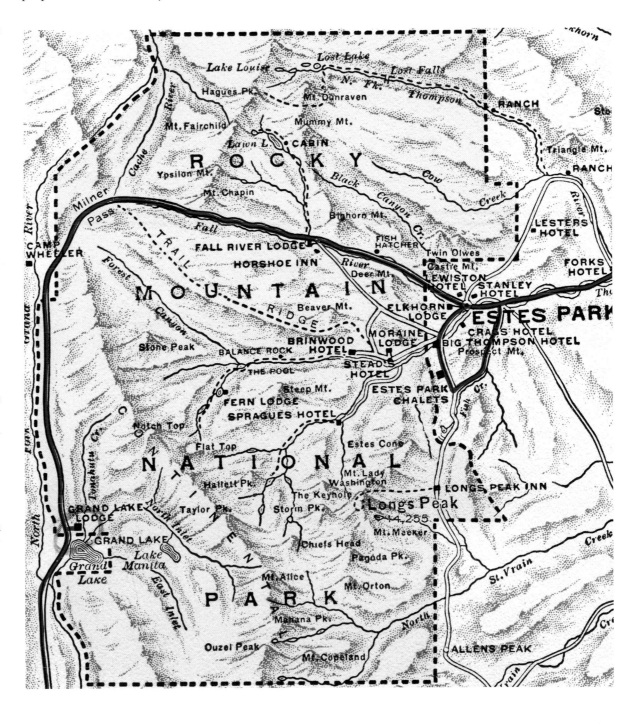

chief forester of the Medicine Bow National Forest, out of whose domain the park would be carved. Not only was the Forest Service unsympathetic to the national park movement in general, but Wheeler wanted to designate the region around Estes Park as a game preserve while leaving most of the area open to logging, grazing, and mining. The improvement association initially supported Wheeler, but Mills convinced its members to back the park proposal. The Denver Chamber of Commerce also promoted the park concept. Supporters emphasized the region's growing popularity with tourists in general and motorists in particular. As many as fifty-six thousand visitors passed through Estes Park in 1914. While most rode in auto stages provided by the various hotels, at least ten thousand arrived in private automobiles. When the park was authorized in January 1915, supporters predicted the number of motorists would more than double within a year.[36]

Even the most enthusiastic boosters acknowledged that the existing road system was in dire need of improvement. The most pressing concern was to complete the proposed Fall River Road, which would allow visitors to travel from Estes Park over the Continental Divide and out the west side of the park. In conjunction with a newly improved road over Berthoud Pass, this would allow motorists to make a grand circuit of Rocky Mountain scenery. Colorado's capital was already gaining fame as a motorist's mecca due to the system of scenic drives being developed in its western foothills. Fall River Road would further enhance Denver's role as the starting point for eastern motorists intent on touring western attractions, most of whom preferred to ship their vehicles by rail rather than endure the rigors of cross-country travel. National Parks Superintendent Mark Daniels endorsed the Fall River Road project but pushed for an even more ambitious undertaking. He called for a 100-mile-plus scenic roadway linking Long's Peak and Pike's Peak by a yet-to-be-determined route along Colorado's Front Range. Denver's motoring organizations and chamber of commerce embraced Daniel's proposal, but the administrative hurdles and exorbitant cost convinced authorities to focus on more achievable goals.[37]

The proposed route climbed sharply over Fall River Pass in a series of tight switchbacks and then descended more gradually down the west side of the mountains. Grand County agreed to construct the western portion, while Larimer County cooperated with the Colorado State Highway Department to tackle the eastern ascent. Construction began in 1913. The initial labor force consisted of convicts from Colorado State Penitentiary. This reduced costs, but the prisoners had little skill and less motivation. Just over a mile was completed the first year. Conventional contractors were brought in to continue the project. As in Glacier, the harsh weather and difficult location resulted in high employee turnover. Contractors repeatedly cited labor shortages and adverse weather in response to complaints of inadequate progress.[38]

By the time the Park Service entered the picture, the road extended about 2 miles into the park and was a source of continual complaint. Not only was the surface barely wide enough to accommodate one-way travel, but the grades were excessively steep. Several switchbacks were so sharp that motorists had to eke their way around by maneuvering back and forth while perched precariously on the side of the mountain. At first there were not even any railings to prevent cars from tumbling down the mountainside. The NPS attempted to remedy the situation by widening the worst turns and constructing masonry retaining walls topped with stone parapets, but concerns about the steep grades and hazardous switchbacks persisted.

The NPS's ability to remedy the situation was severely limited. In addition to the standard obstacle of low appropriations, the road was still under the jurisdiction of the state highway department. As the project dragged on, a dispute arose over the road's location. The NPS and most tourism interests pressed for the original route over Fall River Pass, while state highway engineers pushed for a less-expensive option over the lower and less scenic Chapin Creek Pass. NPS officials contended that in addition to being less attractive, the lower route would be buried in snow until early August, dramatically limiting its utility. This was no accident, NPS sources maintained. The agency and its allies accused state highway officials of colluding with Fort Collins interests in favor of an alternative that would capitalize on the city's proximity to the newly established Lincoln Highway and supplant Estes Park as the primary gateway for Rocky Mountain motorists. Secretary of the Interior Franklin Lane eventually ruled in favor

of the higher route. Even with the road less than half-finished, Rocky Mountain National Park was fulfilling predictions that it would become the most popular destination for eastern motorists. Almost 20,000 automobiles entered the park in 1917, carrying 120,000 visitors. Visitation increased to 170,000 two years later, prompting officials to boast that the park drew more people than Yellowstone, Yosemite, Glacier, and Crater Lake combined.[39]

NPS officials and local boosters pressed for the road's completion, but progress remained slow. The unfinished roadway presented a major frustration for tourists, an embarrassment to the Park Service, and a lingering liability for the state highway department. Tourism promoters brought pressure to bear on state, county, and federal officials. The NPS maintained that its hands were tied and the highway department finally returned to work in earnest. Grand County also committed substantial resources to hasten completion. Fall River Road was finally finished in September 1920. The NPS held a dedication ceremony to celebrate the long-awaited achievement. This drew the ire of state highway officials, who were not invited despite having funded the project and overseen its construction. The *Denver Post* declared Fall River Road to be the "most perfect drive in America," proclaiming that a "glorious vista of real fairyland within a circle of eternal hills [was] opened before the eyes of motorists."[40]

As a pioneering attempt to produce a scenic mountain motorway, Fall River Road demonstrated both the appeal of such amenities and the challenges involved in their construction. The 37-mile roadway was undeniably spectacular, but it was also intimidating. The lengthy section above tree line was relatively level and afforded impressive views along with the novel sensation of motoring across tundra-like terrain. The main source of complaint was the ascent from Estes Park to Fall River Pass. With its narrow track, perilous grades, and tortuous alignment, the road struck fear in the hearts of all but the most intrepid motorists. There were sixteen switchbacks, many with steep drop-offs and hairpin turns, several of which still required backing and turning to negotiate. A ranger was assigned to the most notorious stretch to assist those unable or unwilling to proceed. Some motorists in low-powered cars found the grades too steep to surmount, while those with gravity-feed fuel systems were forced to take the steepest sections in reverse to keep gas in their engines. The unpaved surface washed out frequently and was plagued with dust, potholes, and loose rocks. Muddy conditions rendered it virtually impassable. Because it was located in a deep ravine, the road accumulated enormous quantities of snow that severely limited its usable season. Despite these obstacles, more than 30,000 vehicles traveled the roadway during its first season. Total park visitation surpassed 240,000.[41]

Over the next few years, the NPS labored to keep the road passable, alleviating the worst switchbacks, reconstructing retaining walls, repairing washed-out sections, and upgrading flimsy bridges. Nevertheless, the poor quality of the initial construction combined with harsh conditions and minimal maintenance funding created public relations problems. Conditions were so bad in July 1921 that the *Denver Post* advised motorists to avoid the park. The president of the park transportation company complained that impassable mud wallows, broken axles, and hysterical passengers forced him to suspend services, to the consternation of paying customers and railroad officials, who depended on his buses to carry visitors to and through the park. Snow removal proved even more problematic than expected. The NPS tried to open the road by June 15, but it was often not passable until early July. This caused considerable friction with the railroads and concessionaires, who pressed for a dependable opening date. Snow-clearing crews began work in May and labored a month or more to carve a trough through drifts that routinely measured 20 feet deep and sometimes exceeded 40. Working in freezing cold, high winds, and blowing snow, they battled frostbite, snow blindness, and hypothermia, using dynamite to break up the drifts and shoveling the loose snow out of the way by hand. Snow clearing required 3 to 10 tons of explosives, depending on the severity of the winter. A specially equipped steam shovel was eventually acquired, but the annual ordeal delayed the road's opening and consumed a disproportionate share of the park's budget. Making a virtue out of necessity, promotional material highlighted the road-opening epic and lauded the novel sensation of motoring through towering snowbanks.[42]

As early as 1922, park officials began casting about for a route that would reduce maintenance

411. ROCKY MOUNTAIN NATIONAL PARK, COLORADO.

THE SWITCHBACKS ON THE FALL RIVER ROAD—ESTES PARK TO GRAND LAKE.

15067. Estes Park-Grand Lake Highway, Colorado. Rocky Mountain National Park

costs, improve safety, and extend the tourist season to bring it more in line with other western parks. A further reason for seeking an alternative was that the State of Colorado continued to claim ownership of the Fall River Road, despite agreements that it would be transferred to the NPS upon completion. The NPS was on dubious grounds enforcing rules or expending funds on a roadway it did not own. The legal case centered on the federal

ABOVE, TOP Switchbacks on Fall River Road, Rocky Mountain National Park, postcard, ca. 1922.

ABOVE, BOTTOM Dangerous hairpin turn on Fall River Road, Rocky Mountain National Park, postcard, ca. 1922.

government's right to restrict access to a road constructed with state and local funds, but the conflict reflected broader concerns about federal versus local control of western resources. One particularly vitriolic opponent, *Boulder News-Herald* editor Arthur Parkhurst, remonstrated: "It would be unwise and foolish to let a monopoly-granting, fee-charging Federal Bureau like the National Park Service become the absolute czar of State-built, State-owned roads leading to and through the Rocky Mountain National Park." The most concerted opposition came from transportation companies resistant to paying fees for carrying tourists into the park. Mills was particularly outraged at having to pay to take clients into the park he helped create. Colorado's governor worried that ceding control to the NPS would encourage other federal agencies to lay claim to roads in their jurisdictions. The NPS pointed out that the state had already ceded repair and maintenance responsibilities, but the controversy dragged on for several years. Denver's civic and business leaders pressed for the state to cede jurisdiction, maintaining that poor road conditions turned away millions of dollars in potential tourist revenue. Underscoring

the perception that a park without adequate roads was worthless to the American public, Secretary of the Interior Hubert Work hinted that Rocky Mountain National Park might be abolished if Coloradans did not come to their senses. Federal funding afforded the ultimate leverage. The lack of jurisdiction forced the NPS to reallocate funds authorized in the 1924 road bill to other parks. When the same fate threatened the even larger appropriation outlined in the second bill, Colorado officials relented, authorizing the transfer in February 1929. Albright responded by committing $1.75 million to upgrade the park's road system.[43]

While the dispute was being resolved, NPS and BPR officials developed plans for a new road that would be more enjoyable to drive, easier to maintain, and afford more sustained and impressive views. The proposed alternative swung away from the existing road a little beyond the Fall River entrance station and then curved back along Trail Ridge, which owes its name to the remaining traces of an ancient Native American footpath. Several reverse curves were required for the initial ascent, but they were neither as

frequent nor as severe as the switchbacks on its pioneering predecessor. The constricted location of lower Fall River Road provided few views, but the new location's broader features and rolling terrain afforded expansive vistas, which the road's alignment displayed in cinematic sweeps. The tundra-like topography made it impossible to conceal the roadway, but the graceful arcs flowed with the contours in serpentine compositions reminiscent of eighteenth-century carriage roads. A particular photogenic stretch known as Tundra Curves became one of the park's iconic images, reproduced on postcards, brochures, and other memorabilia. After reaching its maximum elevation shortly before the junction with the old route at Fall River Pass, Trail Ridge Road began a gentle descent to Grand Lake along a mixture of old and new alignments. Like Glacier's Going-to-the-Sun Road, the new design was both more in tune with NPS aims and significantly more expensive to construct. As with Going-to-the-Sun, the Trail Ridge Road project was so challenging that initial funding projections and construction schedules proved wildly optimistic. Both projects spanned the transition period, but the greater part of Trail Ridge Road was constructed under the NPS-BPR agreement.[44]

The park began upgrading a portion of the old "High Drive" to serve as the link to the Fall River entrance road in 1925. The BPR took over engineering duties the following year. Superintendent Roger Toll, Assistant Superintendent Edmund Rogers, and NPS landscape architect Howard Baker accompanied BPR location engineer Steven Wallace on a reconnaissance of possible locations. Wallace followed up with a more formal survey, which he submitted in January 1928. The results met the desired specifications of maximum grade of 5–7 percent (versus 16 percent on portions of Fall River Road), minimum curve radius of 100 feet or 200 feet on blind curves (versus 20 feet on Fall River Road), and a 22-foot-wide roadbed (versus 8–14 feet). The road was also located to minimize snow accumulation, reducing maintenance costs and extending the travel season. While the design met the BPR's technical standards, Wallace paid close attention to scenic concerns. Working closely with park staff and NPS landscape architects, he laid out a roadway that wound in long, graceful curves following the undulations of the topography. Approximately 12 miles were above tree line, affording an unprecedented opportunity

June-25-1926 FALL RIVER ROAD

to motor through alpine conditions with spectacular views stretching in every direction. While the driving experience would be more relaxing than on Going-to-the-Sun Road, the route skirted several dramatic canyons with overlooks into their dizzying depths. Albright was particularly enthusiastic about the project. "It is hard to describe what a sensation this new road is going to make," he marveled. "You will have the whole sweep of the Rockies before you in all directions. It is going to give you the quintessence of the Rockies in one view."[45]

The western portion was also revised. The new road followed a lower line, replacing problematic switchbacks with fewer and more manageable curves. It passed around the northeast side of Poudre Lake, meeting the old road near Milner Pass. From there, the road followed the old route for 2 miles, though the alignment and grade were improved. At a panoramic bend christened "Far View Curve," the road turned northeast toward the Colorado River, descending gradually through forests and meadows. The new route was somewhat longer, but the additional length made it possible to obtain easier grades. As with the Going-to-the-Sun Road, the older sections were eventually upgraded to conform to new design standards.[46]

Due to the importance of the project, senior NPS and BPR officials paid particularly close attention. Hewes and BPR engineer Junius Johnson inspected the proposed route in August 1928. Kittredge examined the line later in the month, proposing several alterations. Vint arrived shortly thereafter to provide the landscape division's perspective. Albright made another inspection before giving his approval. Wallace made several modifications to address NPS concerns. Kittredge, Vint, and NPS landscape architect Merle Sager inspected the final line in 1929, returning often during the course of the project. Both Albright and Hewes made additional visits. Park Superintendent Rogers and landscape architect Baker monitored the construction, issuing numerous recommendations aimed at improving the road's scenic quality and protecting the delicate terrain.[47]

The BPR chose seventy-three-year-old veteran road builder W. A. Colt to begin work on the Estes Park side in September 1929. Colt had extensive experience in mountain road building, including the construction of a noted

FALL RIVER ROAD
1913–1920

GRADE

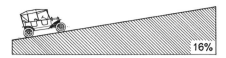

The road climbed to Fall River Pass on steep grades sometimes reaching 16%. Some early automobiles had to climb in reverse due to their weak engines and gravity-fed fuel systems. Surfacing materials washed off quickly.

TURN RADIUS

Motorists had to negotiate sixteen switchbacks with radii as tight as 20'. Some vehicles had to turn back and forth repeatedly to make the curves.

ROAD WIDTH

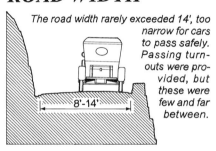

The road width rarely exceeded 14', too narrow for cars to pass safely. Passing turnouts were provided, but these were few and far between.

ELEVATION GAIN

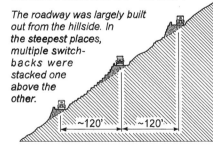

The roadway was largely built out from the hillside. In the steepest places, multiple switchbacks were stacked one above the other.

PULLOUTS

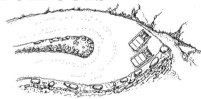

Few pullouts were provided to allow motorists to stop; some were located on switchbacks, making the curves even more difficult.

TRAIL RIDGE ROAD
1926–1932

GRADE

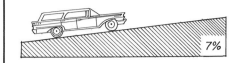

The road was designed with a ruling grade generally less than 5% and never exceeding 7%, less than half as steep as the Fall River Road.

TURN RADIUS

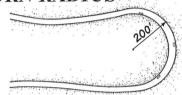

Minimum radii for open curves was 100', and 200' on blind curves. Many curves were designed to sweep across but not dominate, the landscape.

ROAD WIDTH

Unlike the single-track Fall River Road, Trail Ridge Road was designed as a two-lane with a 22' roadbed and 3' ditches in cut sections.

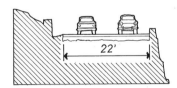

ELEVATION GAIN

The roadway was largely built into the hillside, elevated on rock fill once it reached the tundra. Long continuous curves were used to gain elevation.

PULLOUTS

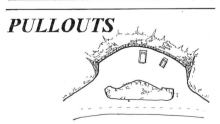

The commodious stone-walled turnouts, often located on major curves, provided ample space for visitors to take in the views.

LEFT Comparison of Fall River and Trail Ridge Roads, Rocky Mountain National Park.

OPPOSITE Snow on Fall River Road, Rocky Mountain National Park, June 1926.

highway over Colorado's Wolf Creek Pass. To reduce time lost in travel while minimizing damage to surrounding landscapes, Colt quartered his workers in wood and tarpaper shacks that were loaded on trucks and moved forward as the work progressed. Local men were hired when possible, but labor shortages forced the contractors to engage workers from Denver, Fort Collins, and other cities. The proportion of local hires increased as the Depression deepened, building community support.[48]

Work on the west side got under way in October 1930. Both contractors used a mix of power and horse-drawn equipment, which was typical at the time. Diesel, gas, and steam shovels performed the bulk of the excavation work. Tractor-pulled graders handled most of the grading, but horse-drawn scrapers, or "fresnos," were considered better for light work and more delicate finishing treatments. When bedrock was encountered, pneumatic drills powered by portable compressors bored holes for explosives. Following NPS policy, most blasts were limited to a couple dozen small charges fired simultaneously. To carve a path through a large outcrop subsequently known as the Rock Cut, however, the NPS authorized a massive detonation consisting of a half ton of explosives loaded in 178 separate holes. Protective mats of heavy timbers protected natural rock surfaces from the blast. While the NPS prided

itself on avoiding such extreme measures, the Rock Cut became one of the most celebrated features of the drive, memorialized on innumerable postcards and souvenir views.[49]

A number of problems were encountered when the crews pushed beyond timberline. The quasi-permafrost underlying the tundra-like surface posed a unique challenge. Conventional excavation processes were ill-suited to dealing with the rubbery material. Instead of blasting and clearing, crews stripped away shallow layers loosened by intervals of natural thawing. The top layer was salvaged and used to rehabilitate construction scars. The work above tree line had to be carried out with extra care to protect the fragile alpine environment. Learning from the Going-to-the-Sun Road conflicts, the BPR enforced detailed regulations aimed at minimizing damage beyond the right-of-way. Temporary walls were constructed at the base of cuts and fills to contain loose material. When errant blasts scattered shards of rock, contractors were required to retrieve the debris. Otherwise, they were under strict orders to stay within boundaries staked out to prevent damage that would take years to heal in the harsh alpine environment. Only rocks matching stone in the surrounding terrain were used in masonry features. Guidelines specified that the lichen side face outward to maintain natural appearances. NPS landscape architects

specified a crenelated design for the abundant guard walls, which became another distinctive feature of the drive.[50]

Both contractors pressed to complete the project as quickly as possible, working multiple shifts and employing more than three hundred men during the height of the season. Since much of the construction took place at high altitudes in open, windswept terrain, workers had to cope with thin air, electrical storms, sleet, snow, and numbing cold. Praising the workers' fortitude, BPR inspector Daniel Harrington observed: "To appreciate the scope of this endeavor one must remember the main ingredient in the accomplishment of the work was brawn, tempered by a tough and willing work ethic." Most significantly, he noted, the entire project was completed without a single fatality. The *Estes Park Trail* also called attention to the workers' contribution, proclaiming: "These men are building an enduring monument to themselves in the name of beauty and of the spectacular."[51]

As work on the east side drew to a close, the *Estes Park Trail* proclaimed Trail Ridge Road to be "Eighth Wonder of the Modern World." The newspaper reported that visitors were already calling it "a trip of more majestic vistas than any other road in the world." Announcing the opening of the eastern segment on July 15, 1932,

GREAT ROCK CUT ON THE TRAIL RIDGE ROAD

the *Trail* quoted Superintendent Rogers's proclamation: "Tomorrow will mark the culmination of almost 3 years of hard work performed under adverse conditions when the internationally famed Trail Ridge road across the Continental Divide will be open to public travel." With the west side still under construction, motorists had to descend Fall River Road and return to Estes Park, but even the abbreviated loop was widely praised for its scenic appeal and driving ease. The western segment opened with little fanfare in August 1933. The old Fall River Road remained in use, allowing visitors the choice of proceeding west or looping back around to Estes Park. As a safety measure, the old road was designated as a one-way uphill drive.[52]

The road was extended another 8 miles west between 1934 and 1936. This left several miles of old road approaching the town of Grand Lake. Civic leaders wanted the road to pass through town in order to capitalize on tourist traffic, but the NPS maintained that park roads should bypass developed areas. Disputes over routing and land acquisition delayed completion of the final segment until 1941. The cost of the initial 28 miles was about $950,000. The subsequent relocation of the Grand Lake segment brought the total to around $1.25 million. Eleven miles of roadway were more than 11,000 feet in elevation, and 4

miles exceeded 12,000 feet. In addition to being the highest road in the National Park System, Trail Ridge Road was the highest continuous paved roadway in the United States, a distinction it holds to this day.[53]

THE ZION–MOUNT CARMEL HIGHWAY TUNNEL

The Zion–Mount Carmel Highway Tunnel was another celebrated achievement of the early years of NPS-BPR collaboration. Due to its remote location in southwest Utah, the area of deep canyons and spectacular rock formation that was set aside as Mukuntuweap National Monument in 1909 and designated Zion National Park in 1919 exemplified assertions that what America lacked was not great scenery but the means to enjoy it. A primitive road from the park's south entrance followed the North Fork of the Virgin River for 4 miles up the scenic Zion Canyon, coming to a dead end where the stream disappeared into a cleft carved into the sandstone cliffs that formed a barrier between the geographically isolated

southern section and a northern plateau closer to major cross-country highways. The situation was analogous to Glacier in that the lack of a cross-park road not only limited Zion's appeal, but complicated efforts to promote a regional version of the park-to-park highway known as the "Southwest Circle Tour." A modern, all-year road across the park would cut the 440-mile-long circuit in half, greatly enhancing its appeal. In combination with a new state highway being extended south from the town of Mount Carmel, it would also provide a more direct route for utilitarian traffic. This pragmatic value enhanced the road's appeal for local residents and Utah's congressional delegation, which lobbied for the necessary funds. While the Going-to-the-Sun project received more attention, constructing a road up Zion's sandstone escarpment was arguably a more impressive achievement on both technical and aesthetic grounds. The challenge of surmounting sheer cliffs and crumbling sandstone was compounded by the commitment to preserving landscape values. The unique conditions forced the NPS to explore alternative means of minimizing the road's visual impact. Retaining walls and sidehill excavations that would meld with the tree-covered, avalanche-scarred slopes of the northern Rockies would stand out in stark relief against the bare sandstone faces of the desert Southwest. Some sort of tunnel was clearly the answer, but it would take skill and ingenuity to determine the appropriate configuration and carry the project through to completion.

Since the road would serve as part of Utah's highway network, the initial investigation was undertaken jointly by BPR district engineer B. J. Finch and Howard Means, chief engineer for the Utah State Highway Commission. In 1923 the two men explored the rugged terrain surrounding Zion Canyon and decided the best route would climb a cleft where the gorge narrowed near a natural sandstone bridge known as the Great Arch of Zion. They contemplated tunneling through the arch but wisely reconsidered. Instead, they recommended using a full or half tunnel to ascend a neighboring cliff. A BPR team spent the fall of 1925 conducting more detailed surveys. Their initial recommendation included an approach road with grades of up to 8 percent and numerous switchbacks leading to a spiral tunnel near the arch, culminating in a tortuous ascent carved into the face of the cliff. This was rejected on technical and aesthetic grounds. Several more options were considered until the NPS settled on a route that employed fewer and broader switchbacks to reach a tunnel entrance shifted a considerable distance from the arch to avoid impinging on the scenic crux of the canyon. The decision to move the entrance lower and farther away mandated an extraordinarily long tunnel. Extending 5,613 feet with a maximum grade of 5 percent, it would be the longest tunnel ever constructed in a national park. The tunnel was designed to poke

through the face of the cliff in six locations to provide fresh air and stunning views.[54]

These openings, or "galleries," played key roles in the construction process, which in many ways resembled a mining operation more than a conventional road project. To expedite the work, it was decided to employ several galleries as entry points and tunnel in opposite directions. Relatively narrow pilot bores were excavated by drilling and blasting, then enlarged by excavating laterally to the full dimension of 22 feet wide by 16 feet high. Experienced miners were brought in to accomplish the task, though the general construction was done by local workers, two of whom died during the course of the project. Mining-style railways and carts were used to remove the excavated material. The unstable sandstone was shored up with timber framing that was later replaced with a concrete lining. The steepness of the canyon wall combined with the desire to minimize scenic damage ruled out the conventional approach of running a pioneer road to the gallery openings, so workers resorted to narrow trails, ladders, and precarious

scaffolding. An inclined tramway was used to transport supplies and remove excavated rock. A longer aerial tramway extended from the canyon floor to the contractor's camp, which was located halfway up the switchback section to minimize the time lost traveling to and from work.[55]

Construction on the road leading up to the lower tunnel portal got under way in September 1927. Heavy equipment bogged down in the sandy soils, and the soft sandstone proved ill-suited for retaining walls, but the road from the valley floor to the tunnel was essentially complete by October 1928. Work on the tunnel itself began in October 1927. The basic excavation took a little over a year. The concrete lining, portals, and pavement were in place by January 1930. The upper or east portal opened onto a ravine formed by Pine Creek. Completed in 1930, the bridge was specifically designed to accommodate automobile traffic, with a curved alignment and superelevated roadway. Local sandstone was used to blend the bridge, guard walls, and other masonry features with the surrounding terrain. The contractors were under

ABOVE Projected Route of Zion–Mount Carmel Highway Tunnel, ca. 1926.

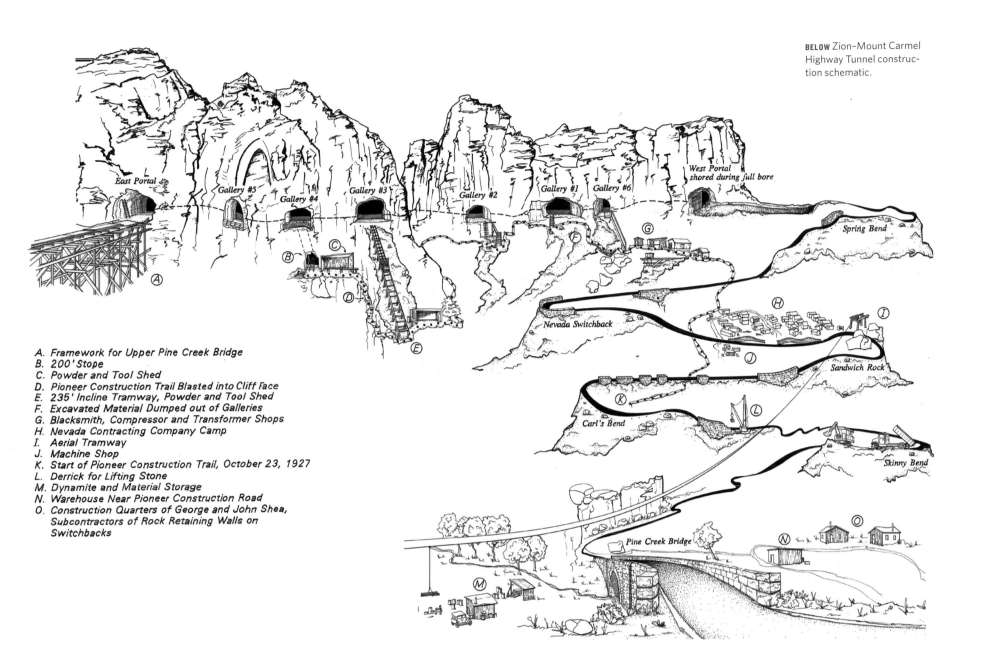

A. Framework for Upper Pine Creek Bridge
B. 200' Stope
C. Powder and Tool Shed
D. Pioneer Construction Trail Blasted into Cliff Face
E. 235' Incline Tramway, Powder and Tool Shed
F. Excavated Material Dumped out of Galleries
G. Blacksmith, Compressor and Transformer Shops
H. Nevada Contracting Company Camp
I. Aerial Tramway
J. Machine Shop
K. Start of Pioneer Construction Trail, October 23, 1927
L. Derrick for Lifting Stone
M. Dynamite and Material Storage
N. Warehouse Near Pioneer Construction Road
O. Construction Quarters of George and John Shea,
   Subcontractors of Rock Retaining Walls on
   Switchbacks

strict orders to prevent debris from defacing the cliffs or the hillside below. The stakes were even higher in Zion's arid environment, where the lack of vegetation meant scars would be visible for decades. When the road was paved, local rock was ground up and used for the aggregate and chip seal, producing a red-tinted surface that harmonized with the surrounding terrain.[56]

The Zion–Mount Carmel Highway was unofficially opened in January 1930. Not to be outdone by his Rocky Mountain counterparts, Zion superintendent Eivind Scoyen issued a press release touting the new road as "perhaps the most spectacular highway in the world." The NPS postponed the official dedication ceremony until the following Fourth of July to maximize its public relations value. Not only would this provide

an ideal opportunity to expound on the patriotic significance of national park road building, but it coincided with the conclusion of a national governors' conference in Salt Lake City. Union Pacific tour buses transported the governors and other dignitaries to the ceremony. More than a thousand onlookers gathered near the lower opening, which had been draped with American flags and red, white, and blue bunting. Albright served as master of ceremonies. Mormon Church president Heber Grant provided an invocation, and a local choir entertained the assemblage with songs of pioneer hardiness and patriotic virtue. Speakers included Utah governor George Dorn and BPR chief MacDonald. Asserting that "well-informed highway engineers have pronounced this the most remarkable road ever

built," Dorn declared that "the road itself will prove another outstanding attraction added to Zion Canyon." While NPS and BPR officials highlighted the Zion tunnel as an example of engineering in the service of landscape preservation, the circuitous approach road attracted attention on other grounds. Marveling at the spectacle of 3.5 miles of road crammed into less than a quarter of a square mile of space, *Ripley's Believe It Or Not* published a cartoon providing additional evidence that Goodwin's "spectacular engineering" continued to exert popular appeal.[57]

GENERALS HIGHWAY, SEQUOIA NATIONAL PARK

Generals Highway was another signature achievement of the "Golden Age" of national park road building. Motorists enjoy an impressive variety of scenic experiences as they pass from the foothills of the southern Sierras into the canyon formed by the Middle Fork of the Kaweah River, climb sharply by means of dramatic switchbacks, and then wind through luxurious pine forests punctuated by groves of giant sequoias. In addition to showcasing diverse natural landscapes, Generals Highway provides a linear lesson in the evolution of NPS road building. The climb out of the canyon affords a striking demonstration of Goodwin's approach to park road development, with twenty-three major switchbacks and more than two hundred additional curves snaking up the mountainside in full view of Moro Rock, the park's primary outlook. Proceeding north, the road widens and flows in broadening curves, reflecting the increasingly high standards promulgated by the BPR from the mid-1920s to late 1930s. Along the way, motorists encounter rustic entrance signs, hand-laid native stone embankments, guard walls and drainage structures, and the classic stone-faced

Lodgepole and Clover Creek Bridges. Few roads integrate nature and technology so successfully, as epitomized by a configuration known as the Four Guardsmen, where lanes divide to pursue separate paths around a quartet of giant sequoias. Even the circuitous ascent from the canyon floor was intended to minimize the need for excessive excavations by hugging the contours as closely as possible. This section has been widened and straightened somewhat since Goodwin's day but affords an enduring illustration of the initial stage of NPS motor road development.

When Sequoia National Park was designated in 1890, a few primitive private roads provided meager access. The Mineral King Toll Road connected the foothill community of Three Rivers with a small mining settlement east of the park. The Colony Mill Road was begun in 1886 by a short-lived utopian community. In 1900 the Army Corps of Engineers extended the Colony Mill Road to the park's premier attraction, a spectacular grove of sequoias called the Giant Forest. The road was completed in 1903, but the narrow wagon track pursued a circuitous course through inhospitable terrain. An apologetic superintendent lamented, "Forty-five miles of travel up hill at a snail-like pace through stifling dust does not appeal to the modern traveler." Another wagon road was constructed partway

up Middle Fork Canyon by the Mount Whitney Power Company to further hydroelectric development. This road ended at a dramatic outcrop known as Hospital Rock. The engineers began constructing a road from Giant Forest down to Hospital Rock, but limited funds hindered progress. Predicting that upgrading the park's road system would attract motorists "by the hundreds," Sequoia's military superintendent emphasized the need for additional appropriations. Presaging Mather's no-gridiron philosophy, he asserted, "It is not necessary to build roads to all the various points of interest. One good road into the park and out again should suffice."[58]

When the NPS assumed responsibility, Mather authorized a survey for an improved road to the Giant Forest. As laid out by NPS engineer William H. Peters in 1919 under Goodwin's direction, the route climbed approximately 3,600 feet from Hospital Rock to the plateau above, snaking up a steep side canyon by means of multiple switchbacks and tight turns with minimum radii of 50 feet and a maximum grade of 8 percent. To reduce costs, minimize excavations, and speed construction, it would be constructed as a narrow, one-way road—with the Old Colony Road serving as a "back door" for exiting traffic. In short, it was just the sort of narrow, steep, tortuous, conspicuous, and economical alignment Goodwin was surveying up Glacier's Logan Creek drainage that same summer.[59]

The Peters/Goodwin route was opposed by local civic leaders, including *Visalia Delta* publisher George Stewart and *Tulare County Times* editor Ben Maddox, both of whom wielded considerable political power and played key roles in the park's authorization. Their continued support was essential to the NPS's ultimate goal of expanding Sequoia's boundaries northward to encompass the Kern and King River Canyons. Sequoia superintendent John White also opposed Peters's route. Maddox, White, and Stewart called for a radically different approach. By extending the power company road farther up the canyon and then cutting back in one long switchback, the requisite elevation could be gained in a gradual ascent culminating east of Moro Rock. Like Vint's Going-to-the-Sun proposal, this approach would produce a higher-standard road with a more subtle visual impact. While more expensive, its location, width, and alignment would be better suited to year-round automobile operation. This

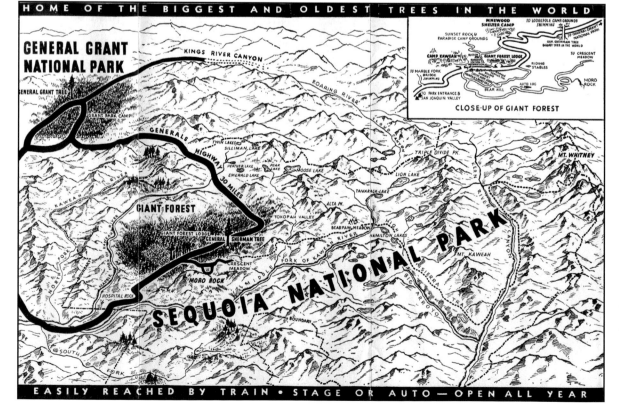

would not only benefit local businessmen but also encourage the park concessionaire to provide more appealing accommodations.[60]

Goodwin was predictably dismissive, insisting that the proposed alternative reflected a conspicuous lack of engineering acumen. At Mather's urging, he invited White, Maddox, and other boosters to join him and engineers from the BPR and California Highway Commission on an inspection of the terrain. While the local experts were content to opine from afar, White accompanied the engineers and agreed that the alternate route was not a viable option, at least with the funds at hand. Citing the engineers' concurrence, Goodwin convinced the others that the best course was to proceed along a modest revision of Peters's survey, upgrade the road when funds became available, and reconsider the alternate route when circumstances warranted. Presciently, he suggested that the underlying agenda of local interests was to press road development farther up the canyon in the hope of extending it to Kings Canyon and beyond.[61]

Construction began in 1921, but the phenomenal growth in motor tourism prompted the NPS to revise plans to accommodate two-way traffic. The switch in standards created several problems. Widening the roadbed increased the amount of excavation along with the need for rockwork to shore up roadside embankments. This drove up costs and made the road more conspicuous. In some of the steepest and most tortuous stretches, the road was essentially carved through solid rock. Great care was taken to limit blasting scars and naturalize excavated surfaces. While Mather applauded the efforts to harmonize the road with its surroundings, the cost overruns caused considerable consternation. The Washington office was particularly incensed that Goodwin exceeded projections based on verbal assurances from House Appropriations Committee chairman Louis Cramton that he would make up the shortfall. Although Mather accepted the underlying rationale, the conflict contributed to Goodwin's downfall.[62]

The initial leg of Generals Highway was dedicated in September 1925. Since this was the first major road project completed by the NPS, Mather assembled a coterie of dignitaries and had the proceedings filmed for publicity purposes. The director pronounced Generals Highway to be "the best road in any National Park yet." White characterized its construction as equal in importance

401 ARCH ROCK, THE GENERAL'S HIGHWAY, SEQUOIA NATIONAL PARK, CALIFORNIA

120184

to the projected acquisition of the untrammeled wilderness to the north. The new road significantly reduced the time and difficulty of the trip to Giant Forest, though the interpark connection was still in relatively primitive condition. A record 23,465 automobiles traversed the road in 1926, the first year it was fully operational. Despite predictions that the narrow, winding road posed an unacceptable threat, no accidents were reported even though guard walls and other safety measures had

ABOVE, TOP Generals Highway, Sequoia National Park, ca. 1925.

ABOVE, BOTTOM Arch Rock, Generals Highway, Sequoia National Park, postcard, ca. 1929.

OPPOSITE Sequoia National Park road map, Sequoia National Park travel brochure, 1936.

not yet been installed. As Goodwin had foreseen, the slow speeds and conspicuous danger induced sufficient caution.[63]

While the NPS opposed road development in the prospective Kings Canyon addition, the agency had arranged with the Forest Service to link Sequoia with General Grant National Park by extending Generals Highway across the intervening national forest. The roadway's name symbolized its role as a link between Sequoia's General Sherman Tree and the General Grant Tree in the eponymous park that was subsumed within Kings Canyon National Park in 1940. Connecting the two parks with a modern auto road would create a compelling circuit from Visalia through the mountains and back down into the San Joaquin Valley toward Fresno. NPS officials and private supporters made comparisons to Rocky Mountain National Park's Fall River tour and the Yosemite–Tioga Road–Tahoe loop. While local boosters eyed potential profits, the NPS hoped the drive would relieve pressure on Yosemite Valley.[64]

The BPR entered the equation in 1926. The engineer's first order of business was to bring the existing road as close to BPR standards as possible. Bill Austin was lured away from the BPR and put in charge in the hope that he could replicate

his Going-to-the-Sun Road accomplishment. It was determined that reconstructing the lower portion of the ascent from Hospital Rock would be too destructive of the surrounding scenery, but the upper section and the lower entrance road were significantly upgraded. Demonstrating that engineers were not averse to whimsy, Austin tunneled the roadway under a tremendous boulder near the park entrance. Mather applauded the maneuver for exemplifying his goal of creating distinctive entrances that provided motorists with unique and memorable experiences. Like Yosemite's Arch Rock and the stone sentinel guarding Yellowstone's Golden Gate, this seemingly serendipitous conjunction of natural and man-made curiosities became one of the park's iconic features. Postcards produced over the ensuing decades documented both the evolution of automotive technology and the gradual improvement of the road. CCC workers reinforced the arrangement during the 1930s, constructing masonry sidewalls along with a staircase to the top of the boulder.[65]

The northward extension of Generals Highway began in 1926. By 1931 construction had progressed to within 7 miles of the park border. This section included the stone-faced Lodgepole and

Clover Creek Bridges, with façades designed by NPS landscape architect John Wosky, one of the original participants in the NPS-WCPC exchange. The new construction and rehabilitated sections of the older route adhered to the 1926 BPR standards calling for an 18-foot-wide surface with 3-foot shoulders, 6 percent maximum grade, and 300-foot minimum curve radius. Hewes insisted that the changes were necessary not only to improve safety, but also to provide a more relaxed driving experience as traffic loads increased. White argued successfully for a relaxation of these strictures to preserve the unique experience of motoring through the Four Guardsmen. The final 7 miles within the park were completed in 1933 with the 20-foot-wide surface specified in the BPR's revised 1932 standards. This width was maintained on the link to General Grant National Park, which was completed in June 1935. Touting the road's construction as "an outstanding history-making episode," the accompanying press release applauded "the attainment of a long-sought goal by park officials—that of connecting the two Big Tree Parks with an easy grade, modern mountain highway; and at a cost of 2 ¼ million dollars an unbroken circle tour of outstanding scenic splendor has been provided through both National Parks."[66]

FROM FAR LEFT Switchback on
Generals Highway, Sequoia
National Park, postcard, ca. 1938.
The Gateway, or Four Guardsmen,
Generals Highway, Sequoia
National Park, postcard, ca. 1936.
Generals Highway Entrance sign,
Sequoia National Park, ca. 1936.

Between the exorbitant cost of the proposed construction and mounting opposition to road construction in undeveloped terrain, the alternative route out of Middle Fork Canyon faded from consideration in the mid-1930s. Incremental improvements were made to improve real and apparent safety, but the original routing was retained. Bituminous paving was added during the late 1930s, creating a more stable surface. Other portions of Generals Highway were upgraded as well. The most conspicuous concession to modernity was the construction of a second roadway through the Four Guardsmen. White had resisted altering the original 12-foot-wide configuration. His successor approved a more efficient arrangement in 1938 incorporating a second narrow roadway to divide traffic around the signature feature. Motorists still wind in close proximity to the towering trunks, retaining the essence of the original attraction.[68]

The CCC conducted considerable work in Sequoia National Park. In addition to improving roadsides, adding safety barriers, and other routine improvements, the CCC enhanced Austin's Tunnel Rock and developed an extensive interpretive feature at Hospital Rock. A parking lot defined by large boulders provided access to rock pathways leading to pictographs and other Native American relics, including bowl-shaped depressions ground into rocks to pulverize acorns. A stone drinking fountain evoked these artifacts, while rustic posts held hoses to fill radiators that boiled over on the steep ascent. Additional watering stations were spaced along the route. The CCC constructed an impressive entrance sign featuring the carved profile of a headdress-wearing Indian intended to represent the park's Cherokee namesake. The rustic landmark became a favorite backdrop for snapshots documenting visits to Sequoia National Park.

The winding ascent from Hospital Rock continued to generate controversy. BPR engineers considered the configuration dangerously outdated and urged the NPS to reconsider the alternate route. The park concessionaire pressed the agency to acquiesce, insisting that the hazardous conditions scared away visitors and compromised efforts to transform Sequoia into a year-round destination. NPS officials expressed mixed opinions. White had become the existing route's most ardent defender. Surprisingly, he embraced the very characteristics that Vint opposed in Goodwin's proposal for Going-to-the-Sun Road. Praising the manner in which the road wound "like a brown ribbon" up the mountainside, White observed, "It is doubted whether in any other park or part of the country the full length of an approach road from the valley to the high mountains will be as plainly seen as will the Middle Fork Road from Moro Rock." While Vint and Mather considered such conspicuousness to be proof that Goodwin had no business constructing park roads, White enthused, "It is not difficult to foresee the day when one of the chief attractions of Giant Forest will be the view of the road and the automobiles climbing up from Hospital Rock." The steep grades, hairpin turns, and infrequent guard walls were undeniably taxing,

but White cast these attributes as assets rather than liabilities. "No matter how good a road we might build up the Middle Fork," he insisted, "it would be a pity to do away with the thrill that people get climbing up the switchback grade and later looking down on it from Moro Rock." Vint, Kittredge, and Albright initially aligned themselves with the BPR but deferred action on the grounds of insufficient funds. As pressure to replace the road increased, White enlisted the Sierra Club's support in opposing the road as an unwarranted intrusion on an area of remarkable natural beauty. Albright eventually changed his stance, adding a historical dimension to the argument. "The time will soon come when a road like the switchback section of the Generals Highway will be extremely unique," he advised his successor Arno Cammerer when Depression-relief funds breathed new life in the BPR's proposal. "People will come to the Park to travel over this road because of its interest." Invoking Goodwin's signature term, he concluded, "It is and always has been a most interesting and spectacular highway." The proliferation of postcards highlighting Generals Highway's circuitous alignment suggests that Albright and White were correct and that Goodwin's much-criticized approach was attuned to popular tastes in scenic road development.[67]

BELOW Shenandoah National Park proposal, 1931.

OPPOSITE President Franklin Delano Roosevelt (*at head of table*) with "CCC Boys," Shenandoah National Park, August 17, 1933; Interior Secretary Harold Ickes is seated third from left.

SKYLINE DRIVE

When the Southern Appalachian National Park Committee recommended the establishment of Shenandoah National Park, its members predicted that the park's "greatest single feature" would be a "skyline drive" following the crest of the Blue Ridge and affording sweeping views of the Shenandoah Valley. On clear days the eastward vista would extend as far as the nation's capital.

If the park was approved and the road developed as planned, the committee enthused, "few scenic drives in the world could surpass it." President Hoover strongly endorsed the concept. According to Albright, the two men investigated the prospect on a horseback ride from Hoover's camp on the Rapidan River in May 1931. When the president paused to take in the sweeping views, he declared, "This mountain top is just made by God the Almighty for a highway" and insisted the NPS provide one. This story should be taken with a grain of salt, as with other attributions of convenient revelations to prominent politicians, but Hoover was undeniably enamored of the project. His enthusiasm was political as well as personal. Along with providing access to stupendous views, the construction would bring economic relief to the region, which was hard hit by droughts and the deepening depression. Between the president's support and the drive's proximity to his rural retreat, local papers took to calling it the "Hoover Highway." This appellation lost its cachet as the economy crumbled. Albright credited a subsequent *National Geographic* article with popularizing the Skyline Drive designation.[69]

In a striking contrast to the usual pattern of national park development, the first order of business was to reduce access rather than to increase it. The area chosen for Shenandoah National Park was by no means an unspoiled wilderness. People had lived within the proposed boundaries for generations, engaging in farming and other activities that dramatically altered the landscape. Most natural woodlands had been logged or decimated by chestnut blight, leaving an unsightly residue of raw clearings and tangled trunks. A network of primitive roads extended throughout the region and several more substantial turnpikes crossed the major gaps. Conservation authorities and economic planners maintained that relocating the mountain dwellers was the best means of rehabilitating both the land and its inhabitants, who were thought to suffer from their isolation. Both their homesteads and the roads providing access to them would be returned to nature so that visitors could enjoy a leisurely drive through ersatz wilderness. Neighboring communities pleaded with the Park Service to retain the country roads that afforded shortcuts through the park, but the desire to provide a recreational drive uninterrupted by dangerous intersections and evidences of human handiwork prevailed. Asserting that

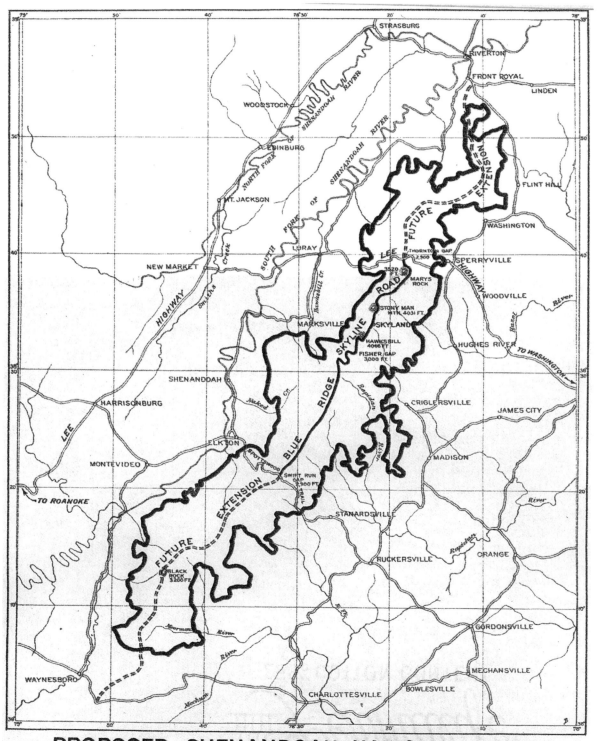

PROPOSED SHENANDOAH NATIONAL PARK

national parks were intended to serve the interests of the nation as a whole, they maintained that parochial demands for utilitarian access conflicted with the greater goal of providing an expanse of unbroken wilderness within driving distance of major population centers. Proclaiming that "the major premise in the establishment of a park is the preservation of its natural state with a minimum of development for public use," Secretary of the Interior Harold Ickes insisted that reopening the roads across the ridge would "violate the principles on which a national park is established."[70]

Shenandoah's enabling legislation gave the responsibility for acquiring land to the Commonwealth of Virginia. The act stipulated that 50 percent of the proposed half-million acres had to be in government hands before the park could be formally established. Subsequent legislation reduced the amount to 160,000 acres, but even this requirement was not met until December 1935. In the meantime, park advocates continued to lobby for the development of Skyline Drive. William Carson, the chairman of the Virginia State Commission on Conservation and Development, was a staunch advocate of both the drive and the broader park project, as was George Freeman Pollock, whose Skyland resort was located along the proposed route. Carson and Virginia governor John Garland Pollard pressed to have the road constructed with federal relief funds. Hoover was sympathetic, but government-wide austerity measures stymied the effort. Virginia authorities pressured the new administration until they succeeded in obtaining NIRA funds to begin construction on the central section extending from Thornton Gap to Swift Run Gap. Preliminary work began in the summer of 1931. Funds for the two end sections were approved the following year.[71]

New Deal programs played a vital role in the development of Skyline Drive. The Recreational Demonstration Area program provided critical support for land acquisition. WPA funds were essential as well. The most visible impact was made by the Emergency Conservation Work program and its offshoot, the CCC. The first CCC camps were established at Skyland and Big Meadows in May 1933. Six additional camps were created before the program shut down in 1942. An estimated twelve thousand CCC enrollees worked at Shenandoah over the years. The men built guard rails, picnic shelters, comfort stations, and other amenities, both along the drive and in associated

recreational areas. CCC crews also rehabilitated landscapes that had been logged, farmed, devastated by the chestnut blight, and disrupted by road construction. These efforts were so successful that many visitors consider the park to be a fortuitously preserved remnant of the traditional southern Appalachian landscape.[72]

Roosevelt took special interest in the CCC work at Shenandoah, both because he genuinely supported the program and because the proximity to Washington provided ideal public relations opportunities. The president first visited the Shenandoah camps in August 1933, accompanied by a delegation of federal and state officials. Roosevelt praised the project, extolled the CCC program, and posed for photographs with the enrollees. Images of the beaming president surrounded by grateful "CCC Boys" appeared in newspapers across the country. Roosevelt returned in 1936 for the park's dedication, using the occasion to emphasize the value of Skyline Drive and similar projects. "In almost every other part of the country there is a similar need for recreational areas," he proclaimed. "For parkways, which will give to men and women of moderate means the opportunity, the invigoration, and

Roosevelt asserted that the access to nature afforded by these recreational motorways would enable ordinary Americans to "forget the rush and the strain of all the other long weeks of the year, and for a short time at least, the days will be good for their bodies and good for their souls."

the luxury of touring and camping amid scenes of great natural beauty." In his nationally broadcast radio address, Roosevelt asserted that the access to nature afforded by these recreational motorways would enable ordinary Americans to "forget the rush and the strain of all the other long weeks of the year, and for a short time at least, the days will be good for their bodies and good for their souls."[73]

The development of Skyline Drive emulated previous road projects, with one important exception. Since the park did not officially exist when work began, the authority normally invested in the superintendent was assigned to NPS engineer James Lassiter. The limited funds were only enough for a narrow corridor, so there were more restrictions on the initial location survey. The decision to route the road along the ridge further narrowed the scope. The landscape responsibilities normally overseen by Thomas Vint were delegated to Charles Peterson, a brash young architect who had worked briefly on western road projects before being placed in charge of a Yorktown-based field office created to address the growing number of eastern parks. NPS landscape architects Roswell Ludgate, Roland Rogers, and Harvey Benson played key roles in the drive's development. The principal BPR engineers were H. K. Bishop and Bill Austin, whom both agencies considered the preferred men for prominent projects. By this time, both engineers were experienced hands at combining the BPR's commitment to high technical standards with the NPS's insistence on preserving landscape values. Albright touted their expertise in a letter extolling the project to Secretary Ickes, expressing confidence that the results "would compare favorably with the outstanding roads in the western parks." Between the 105-mile-long Skyline Drive and two cross-park state highways, Shenandoah would have a higher proportion of roads to natural areas than most western parks, but officials maintained the intensive development was justified by the heavy traffic that would be generated by the park's proximity to densely populated areas.[74]

The location survey for the 34-mile-long Central District began in January 1931. In order to get the project moving and put men to work, plans for the initial contract were prepared under unusually tight deadlines. The hasty approach created problems when Bishop showed the preliminary plans to Gilmore Clarke and Jay Downer, who had come to Washington to consult

on a parkway the BPR was building along the Potomac River. The two veteran designers were appalled by what they saw. Clarke pronounced that the plans appeared to have been drawn up by a conventional highway engineer, and not a very good one at that. Their chief objection was that the proposed alignment was "too mechanically laid down," with no regard for the "artistry in road planning" required in national park work. The prevalence of crude fixed-radius curves lacking the flowing spiral transitions employed in contemporary parkway development, coupled with such basic design flaws as "broken back" alignments where straight lines linked curves in the same direction, prompted Clarke to complain that that "no attention whatever had been given to the refinements of alignment" or other subtleties of park road design. He warned that a road constructed along the proposed lines would be "difficult to drive and extremely ugly and out of character with the type of development which should obtain in our National Parks."[75]

An aggrieved Peterson protested that the maligned characteristics were common attributes of western park construction, where the rugged terrain precluded the sweeping curvature employed on suburban parkways. "If this road is not well laid out," he declared, "then we have no good roads in the western parks." Peterson also questioned the relevance of Clarke's and Downer's expertise, proclaiming, "The Landscape Division of the Park Service has had much more experience on this mountain type of work than all of the other landscape offices which have ever existed in this country." Rivaling Goodwin in his self-righteousness and propensity to deflect blame, Petersen faulted the BPR for not providing adequate topographic sheets, complained about the hectic schedule, and groused that the problem would never have occurred if the NPS was as generously staffed and funded as his critics' Westchester County Park Commission. In another exhibition of Goodwinesque pique, Petersen began sarcastically employing the phrase "landscape refinements" at every opportunity. At the same time, he acknowledged the practical and aesthetic advantages of spiral curvature and admitted that most of the "broken back" curves could be eliminated with further study. While Peterson continued to fulminate, Ludgate and Austin revised the alignment to achieve a more smoothly flowing and landscape-sensitive roadway.[76]

Once the initial contract was let, the design team had more time to fine-tune the alignment. The remainder of the drive reflected the commingling of eastern parkway and western park road approaches. The alignment was more direct and free-flowing than most western park roads, but there were places where the topography dictated sharper curves and grades than parkway designers preferred. Spiral curvature was employed extensively in the final two sections. While this required more complex calculations, the elimination of awkward transitions from straight lines to full curves created a roadway that was both more attractive and easier to drive. The smooth transitions allowed motorists to enjoy a continuous succession of scenic views without worrying about abrupt changes in direction. The scale and focus of the views varied from distant panoramas across the Shenandoah Valley to intimate close-ups of forested hillsides and shady glens. The northern section from Thornton Gap to Front Royal was less rugged, and more time was allotted to produce the desired landscape sensitivity and serpentine curvature. The curves were designed for speeds of 35 mph in the central section but elongated to accommodate 45 mph in the northern section. The graded width was increased from 30 to 34 feet, allowing for a 20-foot-wide pavement flanked by 5-foot-wide unpaved shoulders.[77]

Harlan Kelsey accompanied Austin and NPS officials on an inspection of the proposed northern location in December 1931. Kelsey objected to the BPR's decision to route the road along the east side of a section known as Dickey's Ridge. While the BPR's alignment would be cheaper and easier to construct, Kelsey insisted that the sacrifice of scenic values was unacceptable. The eastern line ran through farmland and orchards, while the western route showcased some of the wildest scenery in the region. Kelsey pointed out that the park boundaries had been expanded at this point for the express purpose of preserving and displaying the compelling scenery. He acknowledged that the rugged terrain would make construction more expensive and require greater care to avoid scarring the mountainside, but predicted that it would be cheaper to acquire rugged and inaccessible woodlands than cultivated fields and orchards. Bishop maintained that the savings would be negligible in comparison to increased construction costs, but when Albright endorsed Kelsey's recommendation, he instructed Austin to revise the location.[78]

As in western park development, great care was taken to minimize the road's visual impact by following natural contours as closely as possible. Retaining walls were used to bench the road out from the hillside rather than cut into it. When blasting was necessary, it was carried out with carefully placed small charges and the disturbed surfaces were sculpted to resemble natural outcrops. Earth cuts were graded at a shallow angle and rounded to resemble natural contours. An extensive planting campaign helped ameliorate construction scars and minimize erosion. Slopes were sodded, seeded with wildflowers, or stabilized with shrubs. Only native species were employed. Mountain laurel was widely utilized. Most of the trees and bushes were either transplanted from the right-of-way or propagated in CCC-operated nurseries. Hundreds of thousands of trees and shrubs were planted during the drive's development.

As in the western parks, the entrance stations, guard walls, picnic shelters, comfort stations, signage, and drinking fountains were designed to harmonize with their surroundings. The rustic style employed in the western parks was adapted to reflect local materials and building traditions. Much of the wood used in the original construction came from dead chestnuts cleared from the roadway or nearby woodlands. Both log guard rails and hand-laid stone guard walls were employed in the original construction, though the NPS eventually insisted log rails be replaced with stronger and more durable stone. While the NPS generally preferred mortared masonry, most Skyline Drive walls were comprised of dry-laid stone with a mortared top course. This approach followed local building patterns and was intended to evoke the region's cultural heritage.

Scenic overlooks were provided more extensively on Skyline Drive than in previous NPS projects. The initial construction included sixty-five parking areas, with a total parking capacity of 1,800 cars. The intention was to afford various means of experiencing the park. The NPS understood that most visitors would be content to enjoy the scenery through car windows. The overlooks were intended to entice motorists to linger at individual vistas and perhaps even step away from their vehicles to experience nature on a more intimate basis. Some were simply widenings in the pavement affording room for cars to pull over safely, but many were larger and more elaborately developed. Some took advantage of natural features; others were constructed on areas of fill supported by retaining walls. Many were separated from the main drive by raised islands to improve safety and reduce the impact of passing vehicles. Some were heavily planted with trees and shrubs, while others were relatively open with a few specimen trees, wildflowers, and grass. Overlooks such as Crescent Rock, Jewell Hollow, and Doyles River provided access to paths leading to scenic vistas, waterfalls, and other natural features. Some afforded access to longer side trails or the Appalachian Trail, which had to be relocated in several instances to make way for the drive. Most Appalachian Trail supporters were sympathetic, considering the two modes of recreation to be compatible or at least tolerating the motorway for the greater good of promoting public enjoyment of the southern highlands. Benton Mackaye, the originator of the Appalachian Trail concept, was highly critical and began to wage a campaign against NPS plans for additional mountaintop roads.[79]

ABOVE Opening day, Jewell Hollow Overlook, Skyline Drive, Shenandoah National Park, October 23, 1932.

The groundbreaking for the first section took place on July 18, 1931. Construction progressed relatively rapidly without the altitude-related problems and long winter shutdowns encountered in western road building. Difficulties were encountered during the construction of a tunnel through a promontory known as Mary's Rock. The crumbling cliff face created safety hazards and delayed progress. According to newspaper accounts, local white laborers objected to the conditions but protested when African American crews were brought in to clear the way. The cliff face around the tunnel entrance fractured in such compelling fashion that NPS decided to leave it in its natural state rather construct a masonry portal. The 610-foot-long tunnel was completed in January 1932. As the first major national park tunnel in the East, it attracted considerable attraction, both as a construction feat and as a demonstration of the agency's commitment to reducing the impact of road construction.[80]

Local politicians and business interests pressed to open portions of the drive as soon as possible. The NPS provisionally opened the section from Thornton Gap to Hawksbill Gap in late October 1932, just in time for fall foliage viewing. The roadway was not yet surfaced, and guard rails were few and far between, but the project generated rave reviews. A *New York Times* correspondent declared it to be the most scenic drive in the Western Hemisphere, rivaled only by the most noted drives in the Alps. The *Washington Evening Star* characterized it as "one of the finest jobs of mountain scenic highway building anywhere in the world." Officials tallied eight thousand vehicles carrying thirty thousand tourists by the end of November, when the drive was closed for the season. Having provided a taste of what the park had to offer, the NPS insisted the road was not ready for public use and emphasized that construction would proceed faster without interruptions from tourist traffic. Albright was elated by the attention, but confided to Kelsey that the enthusiasm generated by the brief experiment demonstrated that, just as in the West, "we have a big problem ahead of us to build roads fast enough to meet the public demand."[81]

The barrage of complaints generated by Albright's decision to prohibit public access until the drive was completed confirmed this sentiment. Local politicians, newspapers, civic groups, and chambers of commerce decried the ruling, accusing the Park Service of prolonging the

region's economic woes by delaying the benefits that were sure to flow from the state's newest attraction. When the NPS continued to resist, Virginia's congressional delegation appealed directly to FDR, who had praised the drive after a personal tour and expressed surprise that it was not open to the general public. With the president applying additional pressure, the NPS agreed to open the central section in September 1934 to accommodate foliage seekers. Warnings were issued about the project's incomplete status, both to promote public safety and ward off criticism of the drive's unfinished condition and the lack of amenities such as comfort stations and picnic areas. The much-anticipated opening day proved to be a bust, as a torrential downpour dissuaded all but the hardiest motorists and caused considerable damage to the unfinished surface and raw embankments. Only three hundred automobiles made it through the deluge. News accounts noted that the "mountain folk" turned out in large numbers to witness the spectacle and hawk flowers and handicrafts to the tourists. Those living within park boundaries were forced to leave the following spring. Most were relocated to communities constructed by the Subsistence Homestead Corporation. Those who could afford cars could use Skyline Drive to watch their former homesteads give way to resurgent woodlands.[82]

Construction on the northern section began during the summer of 1934. The 32-mile stretch was opened in time for foliage viewing in October 1936. Locating the southern section proved more challenging because it contained a considerable amount of rugged terrain. The desire to stick close to the ridgeline increased the difficulty of providing attractive views without running up costs or causing excessive scenic damage. At an exceptionally scenic section encompassing Black Rock Mountain, several alternatives were staked out to evaluate their implications. The general rule was to route the drive in the best location to maximize views. When it was determined that this would cause unacceptable scarring, a tunnel initially appeared to be the logical solution. While this approach could be justified in western parks, where it often provided the only means of negotiating difficult terrain, the idea of encasing motorists in a 1,700-foot-long tunnel was incompatible with the goal of affording a scenic skyline drive. The NPS decided to shift the road to the other side of the ridge, where the views were not as compelling

but it was easier to blend the construction into the mountainside. The roadway was scaled back to the original 30-foot width to reduce excavation. The 31-mile section between Swift Run Gap and Jarman Gap officially opened on August 29, 1939, making it possible for motorists to drive the entire length of Skyline Drive from Front Royal to the beginning of the Blue Ridge Parkway, which would eventually extend all the way to Great Smoky Mountains National Park.[83]

Skyline Drive was created to provide an engaging motoring experience, but it was accompanied by more traditional recreational facilities. These ranged from the venerable Skyland Resort to picnic areas, campgrounds, and overnight cabins. At two of the larger waysides, Elkwallow and Big Meadows, the Virginia Sky-line Company provided gasoline stations, lunchrooms, and stores. Most of these developments were located out of view of the main drive and accessed by spur roads or loops. As with the main roadside features, they were designed in the rustic style and constructed by a combination of private labor and CCC manpower. Picnic grounds contained CCC-built shelters and water fountains made out of boulders and chestnut logs. Comfort stations were sided with chestnut logs or boards and roofed with chestnut shakes or cement shingles with a slate-like appearance. To accommodate the increasing popularity of trailer camping, the Shenandoah campgrounds provided elongated, drive-through parking areas. Big Meadows, the first large facility, opened in 1937.[84]

The NPS soon discovered that balancing preservation and access entailed social considerations the agency was ill-prepared to address. In order to secure support for preserving southern landscapes, the agency found itself in the position of preserving southern mores, which entailed limitations on access afforded to persons of color. While there were no restrictions on entrance to the park or Skyline Drive, the concessionaire operating Big Meadows and other park amenities insisted on maintaining separate facilities, claiming white visitors would not patronize mixed accommodations. Bowing to pressure from business interests and state officials, including the powerful Senator Harry Byrd, the NPS acquiesced to the creation of separate and ostensibly equal facilities throughout the park. Comfort stations were designated for white or "colored" use and most picnic areas and campgrounds were designated white-only. A single

N231:—A CLOSE-UP AND DISTANT VIEW OF THE SKY-LINE DRIVE, VIRGINIA

Photo by Virginia Conservation Commission.   47762

ABOVE Lewis Mountain Negro Area sign, Skyline Drive, Shenandoah National Park, 1941.   **ABOVE** Skyline Drive, Shenandoah National Park, postcard, ca. 1940.

"colored" wayside area was provided at Lewis Mountain, which NPS officials privately acknowledged was less appealing than the premier whites-only developments. A picnic area was opened in 1939 and cabins, a small lodge, and campgrounds eventually followed. The disparity was rationalized with the self-fulfilling logic that African Americans constituted a tiny proportion of the visiting public. The park's first superintendent and locally hired personnel appeared content with arrangement, and NPS director Arno Cammerer was more concerned with mollifying Byrd and other park supporters than enforcing the nondiscrimination policies prevailing in western parks. Even the pugnacious and racially progressive Harold Ickes backed down in response to opposition from Byrd and fellow Virginia senator Carter Glass. Acknowledging that "the history of discrimination for many years cannot be changed at once by an order of the Secretary of the Interior," he took the initial step of declaring that at least one picnic ground would be integrated and insisting that references to segregated facilities be eliminated from official signs and maps. Ickes had always been frustrated by what he perceived as Cammerer's timidity, and the director's dissembling about this issue likely contributed to his forced "resignation" in June 1940. His replacement, Newton Drury, integrated the rest of the park's picnic areas in 1941. The NPS issued a directive desegregating all park facilities in 1945. The concessionaires resisted at first, but the policy

was at least nominally observed by the early 1950s. The NPS can be faulted for not pressing harder to make the national park experience open to all, but Skyline Drive and other southern parks formally eliminated racial barriers well before public institutions were desegregated in the surrounding regions. Lewis Mountain remained the favored destination for African American visitors for decades, serving as a source of multigenerational memories and community pride. The NPS has begun to interpret the site's history as a reminder that the challenge of providing access to America's national parks entails more complex concerns than blending engineering and landscape architecture.[85]

Predictions that Skyline Drive would prove immensely popular were well-founded. Visitation quickly surpassed the combined total of all other parks and monuments. More than a half million visitors made the drive between October 1, 1934, and October 1, 1935, arriving in 149,408 automobiles. A year later, when the park was officially dedicated, the total was 694,098 visitors and 203,525 automobiles. Visitation exceeded 1 million the following year. A 1941 Department of the Interior publication characterized Skyline Drive as "ninety miles of splendidly built highway curving easily along the crest of the range." The author assured prospective visitors that "the motoring mountaineer can find the things a motorist must have" but emphasized that the drive was free from the tawdry developments that defaced conventional scenic

highways. Acknowledging that "out of 940,000 visitors to the park only a small percentage leave the concrete," the piece proclaimed that "those who stop and begin to delve into the wilderness features will find endless opportunities for exploration in mountain places."[86]

YOSEMITE NATIONAL PARK

While initial pleas for the motorization of Yosemite focused on improving the Wawona and Big Oak Flat Roads, the first modern highway into the park followed neither route and the greater part of the road was constructed not by the National Park Service but by the State of California. The idea of a low-level route to Yosemite Valley had long exerted appeal, but constructing a roadway through the narrow, flood-prone canyons was a daunting task. The Yosemite Valley Railroad built a rough stage road from its El Portal terminus to the Coulterville Road in 1907, and the NPS gradually improved its end, but neither section was suited to automobile traffic. More importantly, the only way for motorists to access the road was to pay to have their vehicles transported by train to El Portal. Automobile clubs and other boosters put heavy pressure on the state legislature to close the gap. Not only would

a low-elevation road afford year-round access, but the absence of steep grades and hairpin turns would allow motorists to reach the park more quickly and easily, without the constant gear shifting demanded by mountain roads. California authorities committed to constructing an "All-Year, High-Gear Highway" to Yosemite but were unable to say when the project would get under way given the fierce competition for construction dollars.[87]

In 1919 the Yosemite Valley Highway Association launched a campaign to raise $1 million in private subscriptions from motorists, automobile interests, and tourism businesses. The plan was to sell two hundred thousand certificates at five dollars each. Demonstrating his flair for salesmanship and disregard for bureaucratic strictures, Stephen Mather proclaimed that anyone who purchased a certificate would receive a year's free admission to Yosemite. This novel experiment in private-public partnership landed the NPS in serious trouble. Not only did the Department of the Interior's solicitor contest the arrangement's legality and question the association's accounting

procedures, but more than five thousand motorists redeemed their certificates, costing the agency more than twenty-six thousand dollars in entrance fees. When the association failed to generate anywhere near the needed amount, the idea of a privately funded road was abandoned. Putting a positive spin on the affair, Yosemite superintendent W. B. Lewis observed that the campaign promoted widespread awareness of the need to make the park more accessible to motorists.[88]

The state's efforts proceeded slowly, hampered by austerity measures, competing concerns, and the commitment to constructing a high-standard roadway. By 1922 the highway extended only as far as Briceburg, 17 miles from the park border. In June 1923, the highway commission announced it would begin constructing the final stretch through the Merced River Canyon. Plans called for a 28-foot-wide pavement and maximum grade of 7 percent, which would make it the most modern motorway leading to a national park. Mather pressed California officials to pay attention to scenic concerns and offered the services of NPS landscape

architect Daniel Hull. These overtures met with limited success. For the state's highway engineers, conquering the canyon with a modern motorway was a sufficiently ambitious accomplishment. To save money, the state used convicts from San Quentin and Folsom, placing the crews at opposite ends and having them work toward the middle. This arrangement proved more successful than its Colorado counterpart. The "All-Year Highway" was formally opened in July 1926 with a ceremony attended by California's governor and other civic leaders. Mather was front and center, touting the new roadway's value to the citizens of California and the American public as a whole. An associated celebration commemorated the seventy-fifth anniversary of the Mariposa Battalion's "discovery" of Yosemite Valley. To many observers, the All-Year Highway was an equally momentous achievement. Rejoicing that Yosemite had finally fulfilled its destiny as "the motorist's National Park," the American Automobile Association hailed the highway's completion as the realization of a dream that began when Olivier Lippincott's Locomobile bucked and wheezed its way into the valley. The trade journal *Concrete Highways* proclaimed the park "a motorist's paradise," boasting with considerable justification that "Good roads have made Yosemite." Even the U.S. Geological Survey's Francois Matthes, who had questioned the impact of road development at Mount Rainier, cast the All-Year Highway as "the crowning achievement in man's conquest of the mountain wilderness that guards the Yosemite."[89]

As the state's project neared completion, NPS officials pleaded for funds to upgrade the park portion of the El Portal Road. Congress responded with a $1.5 million appropriation. Preliminary work began in spring 1925 and BPR engineers arrived on the scene that fall. The roadway was widened to 18 feet, graded, and surfaced to accommodate automobile traffic. The 6-mile stretch beginning at the park border received a reinforced concrete pavement, the first application of this technology in a national park. As with the initial NPS-BPR collaborations at Glacier and Mount Rainier, the project produced tensions between the two agencies. While the engineers relished the opportunity to equip Yosemite with a first-class modern roadway, NPS landscape architect Daniel Hull condemned the bureau's efforts as an example of "standardization run riot" and prepared a detailed photographic account of the transgressions. In the narrow-minded pursuit of "a so-called *better* alignment," Hull protested, the BPR had ignored directives to preserve features that contributed to the road's picturesque charm. Hull acknowledged the need to eliminate excessive grades and hazardous curves but pleaded for flexibility, insisting that in most cases minor deviations would have curtailed the damage. "The very charm the tourist seeks may be destroyed by holding too strongly to a standard specification," he admonished, insisting that park roads should not be governed by engineering concerns alone. Driven by what he characterized as a "railroad-grade" mentality, the engineers turned picturesque roadsides into mechanically precise raw cuts, felled or undermined bordering trees, constructed unsightly elevated causeways, and dug deep roadside ditches. To prevent motorists from injuring themselves on these man-made hazards, BPR engineers proposed lining the roadway with concrete curbing, which NPS officials insisted would inject an inappropriately urban appearance. Hull pushed for irregularly spaced boulders, which would elide the distinction between man-made and natural landscapes, especially when pine needles and roadside vegetation filled the interstices. The compromise solution entailed a cut-stone curb surmounted by a rustic stone guard wall.[90]

Mather was deeply disturbed by Hull's report. Not only did it raise questions about the BPR's suitability for park road work, but the NPS had been harshly critical of the state's disregard for landscape values and could ill afford to make similar mistakes of its own. With characteristic optimism he expressed confidence that the differences could be resolved. Thomas Vint was dispatched to instruct the engineers about NPS landscape preservation principles. Vint quickly discerned that the bureau was neither as proficient nor as cooperative as its reputation suggested. Staff turnover was responsible for the most egregious errors and the work had proceeded with minimal consultation. After hashing matters out in his avuncular low-key style, Vint assured Mather that the engineers would be more sympathetic to NPS goals and better informed about the means to achieve them. From the NPS perspective, the experience underscored the need to spell out preservation strategies more clearly, insist on early involvement in the design process, and maintain close watch to ensure orders were followed. The lessons learned during these preliminary collaborations were incorporated in the formal memorandum of agreement and associated guidelines.[91]

With the completion of the All-Year Highway and improved El Portal Road, visitors could motor to Yosemite along 87 miles of modern highway instead of struggling for 93 miles over the primitive Coulterville Road or risking life and limb descending the antiquated toll roads. As expected, the improved access dramatically increased visitation. Between 1924 and 1927, the number of automobiles registered at the El Portal entrance increased by 51 percent, and overall attendance soared from 146,070 to 490,030. The surge overwhelmed entrance arrangements, causing massive backups that angered visitors and embarrassed NPS officials. In 1928 the roadway at Arch Rock was widened to four lanes and the checking stations moved to a more convenient location. The increased visitation played a decisive role in convincing the Yosemite Park and Curry Company to construct the deluxe Ahwahnee Hotel, which Mather considered essential to attract patrons who considered car camping to be too rustic and democratic. Year-round access transformed Yosemite

The trade journal *Concrete Highways* proclaimed the park "a motorist's paradise," boasting with considerable justification that "Good roads have made Yosemite."

BELOW Ralph Yardley, "Without a Gear Shift," cartoon depicting All-Year Highway, *Stockton Record*, July 31, 1926.

OPPOSITE View of Yosemite Valley from Wawona Road's Artist Point, Yosemite National Park, ca. 1932.

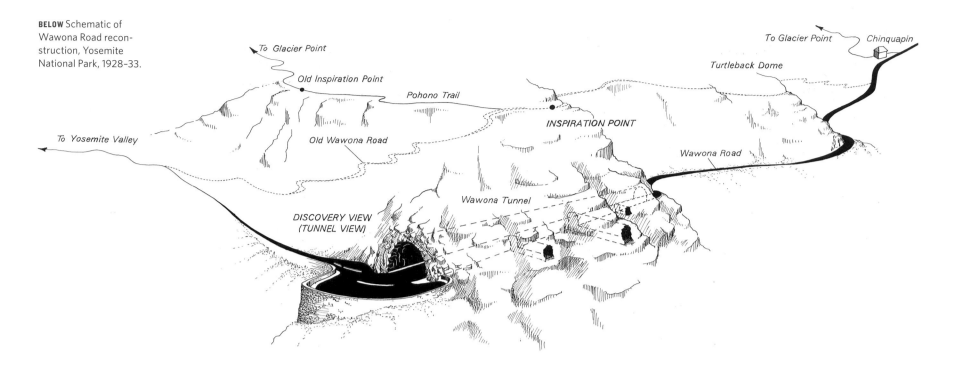

To Glacier Point

Old Inspiration Point

Pohono Trail

To Yosemite Valley

Old Wawona Road

DISCOVERY VIEW
(TUNNEL VIEW)

Wawona Tunnel

INSPIRATION POINT

Wawona Road

To Glacier Point   Chinquapin

Turtleback Dome

into a four-season resort. The NPS worked with the concessionaire to develop activities that would draw visitors during the winter months. A Swiss sports director was engaged to promote skiing, skating, and other entertainments, including a boisterous winter carnival. The All-Year Highway dealt the final blow to the Yosemite Valley Rail Road. By the late 1920s, more than 90 percent of park visitors arrived by private automobile. The National Park Service considered rebuilding the line to maintain an alternate means of transportation, but no funds were available. The last train trip took place in August 1945.[92]

The All-Year Highway dramatically reduced traffic on the traditional entrance roads. While overall admissions nearly doubled between 1926 and 1927, travel on the Wawona Road declined by 50 percent. Traffic on the Big Oak Flat Road was down 30 percent, even though it afforded the most direct route from the San Francisco Bay area. The toll road companies were no longer active, but communities along the routes and boosters from as far away as Los Angeles and San Francisco pressured the NPS to make the old routes more attractive to modern motorists. The NPS initially prioritized the Big Oak Flat Road but maintained that both projects were such mammoth undertakings that they could not be commenced with the first round of appropriations. When the second park roads act made funds available, the agency decided to tackle the Wawona Road first. In addition to placating powerful Los

Angeles–based interests, this would make it easier to reach celebrated sites such as Glacier Point, the Mariposa Big Tree Grove, and Inspiration Point. Constructing a modern roadway down the precipitous grade from Inspiration Point presented considerable challenges, but replacing the final few miles of the Big Oak Flat Road would be an even more daunting task. Not only was the terrain equally forbidding, but NPS officials were worried about impacts on the classic vistas from the southern rim. Big Oak Flat advocates raised an uproar over the change in plans, but NPS leaders insisted that additional studies were needed to find a suitable solution. Wawona Road backers were also more successful in securing commitments from state, local, and USFS authorities to improve the approach road beyond park borders and protect views en route.[93]

NPS and BPR officials discovered that replacing the old stage routes with modern motorways was the most difficult assignment they had faced yet. The challenges of reconciling preservation and access were exacerbated by the historic stature of the routes and the iconic terrain through which they passed. Concerns were raised not just about impacts on natural scenery, but about the ways in which proposed changes would alter the traditional Yosemite experience. The BPR's initial suggestion of rerouting the Wawona Road to join the El Portal Road farther down Merced Canyon was rejected on the grounds that it bypassed both the Wawona Hotel and Inspiration Point. The

hotel's owners swayed the decision by granting a permanent right-of-way across their property, but the Inspiration Point issue was harder to resolve. Albright, Cammerer, and Kittredge argued that the new route should include the historic feature, both because it afforded a spectacular view and because the majestic panorama had served as the traveler's introduction to Yosemite Valley since the park's inception. The signature vista was immortalized in hundreds of paintings and thousands of photographs, postcards, and other souvenirs. The inherent beauty of the scene was magnified by the suddenness with which it burst into view as visitors reached the canyon rim, producing an unforgettable first impression of Yosemite's splendors. Noting the efforts European road builders made to achieve such effects, the Geological Survey's Francois Matthes insisted that Inspiration Point was a major contributor to Yosemite's worldwide acclaim. While NPS officials were keen to retain the historical routing, Matthes maintained that the overall effect was more important than the specific location. As long as the new route produced a similarly dramatic first impression, the loss of the original viewpoint could be overcome. Albright and Kittredge continued to press for the original point's retention but were overruled by Mather. The director was swayed by the BPR's insistence that it was impossible for a road constructed to modern standards to incorporate the historic Inspiration Point without extending so far into the valley that other features would be severely compromised.[94]

The BPR conducted initial surveys for the new route in 1926, but it took three years for NPS officials and bureau engineers to devise a mutually acceptable solution. The BPR's first proposal began significantly south of Inspiration Point and descended steadily at a 6 percent grade, reaching the valley floor in the vicinity of Bridalveil Falls. The engineers sought to address landscape concerns by employing a 1,600-foot tunnel to reduce the visual impact on a band of cliffs comprising the central portion of the route. NPS officials and a newly formed board of independent advisors consisting of Frederick Law Olmsted Jr., Sierra Club leader Duncan McDuffie, and geologist John Buwalda objected that excavations for the lower portion would cause unacceptable scarring and desecrate the area around Bridalveil Falls. They also complained that the upper portion cut directly across an expanse of glacially polished granite known as Turtleback Dome, which was both scenically appealing and scientifically significant. Kittredge explored the idea of using switchbacks at the lower end to gain the necessary elevation without intruding on the falls but rejected the approach as incompatible with NPS landscape preservation principles. The BPR's solution of an underpass below Bridalveil Falls was also dismissed. Olmsted suggested that the road below the tunnel be divided into separate uphill and downhill lanes. In addition to affording more design flexibility and requiring less excavation than a two-lane pavement, this would allow motorists on the higher inside lane to enjoy the scenery without having to peer through oncoming traffic. This option was rejected as impractical, but Kittredge, Vint, landscape architect John Wosky, and Yosemite superintendent C. G. Thomson worked with BPR engineers to refine the design. NPS officials kept the Advisory Board abreast of developments, both to solicit members' opinions and to demonstrate the agency's openness to external counsel. By January 1930 all parties agreed that the best means of reconciling engineering requirements with preservation concerns entailed a much longer tunnel combined with revisions of the upper and lower road segments to minimize impacts on Bridalveil Falls and Turtleback Dome.[95]

Work on the less controversial section between Wawona and the valley rim had begun in 1928. Once again, the contractors were accused of employing excessive amounts of explosives, side-casting material, and inadequately protecting roadside vegetation. This time, BPR engineers supported Superintendent Thomson's decision to suspend construction until the company repaired the damage and agreed to follow regulations. A different contractor was engaged for the more critical task of constructing the road to the valley floor. Work on the tunnel began in January 1931. Excavating the 4,230-foot tunnel was a monumental task. Two hundred and seventy-five tons of dynamite were used to blast through solid granite to create the tunnel bore, which measured 20 feet high and 28 feet wide. More than 100,000 tons of rock were removed. Tracks were laid so that a railroad steam shovel operating on compressed air could scoop up the blasting debris and transfer it to mining carts pulled by battery-powered locomotives. At the height of construction, two hundred men worked in multiple shifts to expedite the process. Faced with the task of disposing of enormous quantities of excavated material without defacing the hillside, NPS officials devised an elegant solution. Rather than spread the unsightly detritus along the roadside or spend an enormous amount of time and money to haul it to a less conspicuous location, the spoils were dumped directly below the lower portal, where, held in place by a mammoth stone retaining wall, they created a parking area affording breathtaking views of Yosemite Valley. Since the tunnel entrance had been carefully positioned to produce the same sort of striking first impression provided by Inspiration Point, the turnout presented motorists with the option of pulling over for more leisurely contemplation of the awe-inspiring view.[96]

The tunnel's other distinctive feature was an elaborate ventilation system designed in collaboration with the U.S. Bureau of Mines. In order to maintain the desired grade and alignment, the tunnel was located too far from the face of the cliff for the open galleries employed at Zion and Glacier. To avoid dangerous accumulations of exhaust fumes, three smaller tunnels were drilled to the canyon wall. The center tunnel contained three large fans to supplement natural air currents when sensors registered excessive concentrations of carbon monoxide. If potentially lethal amounts were detected, sirens sounded and semaphores deployed at both entrances to signal motorists to stop. Similar systems could be found in New York's Holland Tunnel and other urban locations, but this was the first and only time such a high-tech solution was employed in a national park. The elaborate measure was considered necessary to accommodate the heavy traffic loads associated with major holidays. NPS officials were dismayed when the mechanism proved to be so sensitive that auto stage drivers entertained passengers by stopping and revving their engines to engage the fans. Park rangers quickly put a stop to the practice.[97]

The tunnel bore was completed in January 1932. It took slightly more than a year to line it with concrete, lay a reinforced concrete floor, complete the ventilation and lighting systems, and construct the approaches. The entrances were designed to blend with the mountainside. The lower portal remained a rough-hewn opening, both to provide a more natural appearance and to frame the view in a suitably rustic manner. The upper portal was a continuation of the tunnel lining, but the exposed concrete and surrounding rock cuts were artificially darkened to blend with their surroundings. A comprehensive landscape rehabilitation program was implemented to alleviate construction scars. Steep slopes were graded to more stable profiles and native vegetation planted to hold the soil in place and beautify the roadside. Much of this work was done with CCC labor. The tunnel project accounted for just under $600,000 of the $2 million in federal funds spent on the Wawona Road's reconstruction. This was considered an enormous amount for such a relatively short roadway, but NPS officials insisted the technical complexity and scenery-saving results more than justified the expenditure. Albright arranged for members of the House Appropriations Committee to visit Yosemite during the construction to impress them with the magnitude of the undertaking.[98]

As the tunnel project neared completion, NPS officials worked with community leaders to commemorate the occasion. The *Stockton Record*'s editor suggested a historical pageant organized around the popular "Parade of Progress" theme, with the Mariposa Battalion's 1851 "discovery" of Yosemite Valley leading triumphantly to the magnificent modern motorway. The June 1933 ceremony was judged a resounding success. Costumed volunteers and historic vehicles portrayed changes in transportation technology to dramatize Yosemite's evolution from isolated wilderness to popular resort. A delegation of local Indians was followed by soldiers of the Mariposa Battalion, prospectors with burros, and tourists aboard horses, stagecoaches, primitive

automobiles, motor stages, and the latest Detroit models. Galen Clark's original carriage was hauled up the mountain to participate in the procession. Interior Secretary Ickes addressed the crowd by telephone over a public address system provided by the Standard Oil Company. This live transmission was itself considered a technological marvel. President Roosevelt sent a more traditional letter of congratulation. The audience was reported to be in excess of four thousand, dwarfing the crowds that had gathered to welcome the first roads into the valley.[99]

Ickes's statement hit all the right notes, characterizing the new roadway as a "great engineering and landscape achievement" and heaping praise on the National Park Service, the Bureau of Public Roads, and the people of California for making Yosemite more accessible to the American public. At the same time, his paean to progress concluded on a wistful note. Science and technology had undoubtedly made life safer and more comfortable, Ickes acknowledged, but he professed to wonder whether earlier generations were not better off for "never knowing the fumes of gasoline or the dust and dirt of cities." Fortunately, the NPS was doing all it could to enable modern Americans to experience the joys of sleeping under the stars in sylvan surroundings. Lest anyone question his support, Ickes expressed eagerness to experience the new wonder, exclaiming, "I can almost visualize the panorama that will

spread out before me as I emerge from the tunnel directly into Yosemite Valley."[100]

There was no ambiguity in Superintendent Thomson's remarks. Expanding on the pageant of progress theme, he pronounced, "With the early completion of the Wawona Road, a new era dawns in the southern approach to Yosemite." From Thomson's perspective, the new road exemplified the harmonious integration of modern engineering and landscape sensitivity that enabled the NPS to accommodate motorists without compromising core values. Without the BPR's assistance, the agency would never have attempted such a technically challenging approach. In addition to safeguarding "the incalculable values for which the National Park Service is responsible," the BPR's engineering expertise enhanced the visitor's enjoyment of park scenery. Not only did the new outlook surpass the view from Inspiration Point, Thomson asserted, but emerging from the constricted tunnel to encounter the full majesty of Yosemite Valley produced a sensation that was so "explosive in its grandeur" that the experience of lumbering over the canyon rim in a creaky carriage paled in comparison. The tunnel view was an immediate hit with visitors and professional commentators alike. Melding the Romantic sensibilities of nineteenth-century tourists with the marvels of modern motoring, the *Standard Oil Bulletin* described the passage in terms that exemplified traditional conceptions of the sublime. "As

you emerge from a hole in perpendicular granite cliffs," the article intoned, "you are greeted by daylight, last in evidence nearly a mile behind you, and with it the whole Yosemite Valley appears to rush toward you. You catch your breath, awed and delighted—perhaps just a bit frightened—by its magnificence and the abruptness with which it has come." Another observer enthused, "Unlike most artificial approaches to a great natural wonder or scenic spot it not only adds to the accessibility of the Yosemite Valley but contributes much to its enthralling grandeur." Even Albright was forced to admit the new vista was both more compelling than its predecessor and better suited to contemporary tastes. While the Wawona Road never regained its status as the primary approach to Yosemite, the improvements markedly increased traffic. As a year-round high-gear road affording the most direct route from Southern California, it was celebrated in motoring publications and touted by tourism bureaus and automobile clubs. The vista from the tunnel outlook joined the pantheon of iconic views, appearing on postcards and other souvenir items. The most popular rendition framed the panorama through the tunnel portal to encapsulate the motorists' introduction to Yosemite's wonders.[101]

BIG OAK FLAT ROAD

The Wawona Road's imminent completion refocused attention on the Big Oak Flat challenge. NPS officials had been united in opposition to the BPR's original suggestion, which called for a new alignment leaving the El Portal Road well below the existing junction and gradually ascending the canyon wall to meet the old road at the Crane Flat Ranger station. Although this would shorten the overall length, reduce grades to the desired 5–6 percent, and increase the amount of southern exposure so the snow would melt earlier in the spring, Albright, Vint, and Kittredge objected that the scenic costs outweighed any practical gains. In addition to forsaking the historic route with its thrilling outlook on El Capitan, benching a two-lane modern motorway into the canyon wall would create a tremendous scar in full view of Wawona Road travelers. Kittredge was strongly opposed but suggested that the visual impact could be reduced by modifying the BPR's alignment, adopting flexible standards for width and curvature, and employing a cross-section with balanced cut and fill instead of the quicker and cheaper full-width excavation. As an alternative, he and Thomson advised upgrading the historic roadway to accommodate inbound traffic and routing outbound motorists along the Coulterville Road or a less conspicuously located new egress. Restricting the roads to one-way traffic would permit narrower widths and sharper curves, but the old route would still require revision including bypassing or significantly reconfiguring the historic Zigzag. Keeping it in the same general vicinity would retain the most important views and much of the original feel. Albright and Vint initially embraced this solution, seeing it as a means of reducing the road's visual impact while providing a unique driving experience. The State of Nebraska was experimenting with one-way roads in its parks, and Olmsted called for a similar approach at Acadia, but NPS officials believed that most visitors would find motoring along a narrow winding road constructed to otherwise modern standards to be a novel experience, especially in such stupendous surroundings. Albright proclaimed that the proposed arrangement would rival the Wawona Tunnel as a memorable introduction to the national park experience.[102]

Albright asked the BPR to conduct a new survey in 1933. He also instructed Kittredge to report on the double road option and compare the alternatives. Kittredge's recommendation was to upgrade the existing road and construct a 12-foot-wide single-lane uphill road in close proximity. Several switchbacks would be required to gain elevation at the bottom of the slope. A series of short tunnels would reduce unsightly excavations on the upper stretches. By climbing quickly to the canyon rim, this scheme avoided the long scar associated with the BPR's location. By this time, however, Kittredge's colleagues had shifted their emphasis from avoiding injury to the Merced River Canyon to protecting the newly created Tunnel View. The full extent of the BPR's handiwork might have been visible from Old Inspiration Point, but motorists on the new Wawona Road would only catch fleeting glimpses from brief open areas above the tunnel. Thomson and Vint acknowledged the theoretical attraction of Kittredge's suggestion but maintained that neither Big Oak Flat Road boosters nor the general public would accept anything less than a full-blown modern motorway. Above all, they insisted that the tunnel view remain unsullied by modern technological intrusions. Kittredge remonstrated that the historic road was hardly visible and nature would quickly conceal the minor disturbance created by a second one-way road, but to no avail. He continued to press the case after Cammerer, the Yosemite Advisory Board, and the Sierra Club signed off on the proposal, earning a sharp rebuke from the new director. In expressing its approval, the Advisory Board observed, "There has been a vast improvement in the landscape control of conditions under which roads are constructed in the National Parks." Continuing with what Cammerer characterized as "a corking report," the board elaborated: "Their location and mode of construction is no longer based on purely engineering considerations. Park officials are exceedingly sensitive to the importance of preserving the landscape features of the Parks from defacement or destruction." The Sierra Club expressed similar confidence, applauding the care being taken to minimize construction scars and praising the agency's efforts to "make roads in the National Parks peculiarly adapted to Park purposes rather than mere highways from one point to another."[103]

While Kittredge's colleagues did not share his opinion that the Park Service "was buying at the recommendation of the Sierra Club the greatest

BELOW Schematic of Big Oak Flat Road construction, Yosemite National Park, with dotted line showing old route, 1935–40.

To Big Oak Flat

Toulumne Grove

Crane Flat

Rainbow Point

Old Big Oak Flat Road

The "ZIGZAG"

To El Portal

To Yosemite Valley

scar and greatest destruction of natural mountainside yet encountered in Yosemite National Park," Thomson acknowledged that the decision was a reflection of "the fine balance between park loss and public convenience." He worked closely with Vint and Wosky to minimize the former without compromising the latter. Before authorizing the BPR to conduct its final study, the landscape architects outlined a series of preconditions. The road was not to be constructed to the standard BPR width but to the narrower cross-section devised by Kittredge, which minimized the associated excavation. Each 100-yard section would be meticulously studied to ensure landscape values would be preserved or rehabilitated to the fullest extent possible. Tunnels and retaining walls would replace deep side hill cuts. Light open-spandrel bridges with the unadorned concrete substructure favored by Goodwin would span the gullies formed by streams cascading down the hillside. Retaining walls would be constructed of rough-faced stone and exposed concrete, and rock cuts would be stained to harmonize with their surroundings. Pockets would be created in retaining walls and other steep surfaces to hold soil for rehabilitative plantings. To ensure strict adherence to these policies and avoid problems with recalcitrant contractors, the work would be undertaken with direct hires under strict supervision by NPS and BPR officials. Thomson and the NPS landscape architects went over the proposed line with BPR engineers multiple times to fine-tune the alignment and station-by-station treatment. These measures significantly increased costs, but NPS officials insisted that were necessary to reconcile engineering concerns with scenic preservation.[104]

Construction began in January 1935. By fall the route between Crane Flat and the valley floor had been cleared and rough grading was under way. Even by NPS standards, the road required an extensive amount of retaining wall to carry the two-lane width as a balanced cut-and-fill cross-section with minimal disturbance to the hillside. Stone for the retaining walls came largely from material excavated from the right-of-way, both to reduce costs and blend in with surrounding outcrops. In most sections the stones were wrestled into place with hand-operated derricks inched along by mule teams. Reflecting the transitional nature of construction technology, some rockwork was accomplished with a mechanical boom mounted on a caterpillar tractor. The lower

two tunnels received cut-stone portals, but the upper tunnel's entrances were sufficiently solid to leave in their natural state. The two shorter tunnels were constructed by the traditional method of boring a pilot tunnel, drilling outward to the requisite height and width, fracturing the rock with dynamite, and clearing away the debris. A concrete lining ensured stability. The third tunnel was not as long as its neighbor across the canyon, but at 2,083 feet it was nonetheless a considerable undertaking. In what BPR engineers cast as the most ambitious use of the new technology to date, a specially constructed "Jumbo" with six drills mounted on a 5-ton truck chassis bored multiple holes that were loaded with dynamite and exploded simultaneously to clear the full dimension at once. All three tunnels were completed by September 1938. It took another eighteen months to finish the roadbed, pave it with crushed stone, and construct the three bridges. The new road between Crane Flat and the valley floor opened in May 1940. Motorists were permitted to descend the old road until a rockslide destroyed the historic Zigzag in May 1945. Plans to upgrade the upper section of the road from Crane Flat to the park border were put on hold until after World War II due to questions about routing and the state's plans for approach highways.[105]

YELLOWSTONE

Yellowstone possessed the most comprehensive park road system, so no major new roads or large-scale relocations were required. Some sections of the Grand Loop were realigned to better accommodate automobile traffic, but the main emphasis was on widening the road to accommodate two-way travel and equipping it with a durable dust-free surface. Improved machinery and resources made it possible to complete a previously initiated passage showcasing scenic waterfalls and ledges along the Firehole River. Mather praised this section as another illustration of the value of combining landscape sensitivity with engineering expertise. By the late 1930s, however, both the NPS and BPR agreed on the need for a higher-standard bypass for motorists wanting to press on to one of the major park destinations rather than wind slowly through Firehole Canyon's cliffs and cascades. To accommodate the increase in traffic

and growing popularity of travel trailers, the NPS accepted the BPR's recommendation that Yellowstone's roads be constructed to the more expansive standards adopted by the bureau in 1932. Under the new guidelines, the Grand Loop would have a 20-foot-wide surface with 4-foot shoulders. While Mather had assailed Goodwin for suggesting similar standards for main tour roads, some within the NPS and BPR were already suggesting further expansion would be necessary. The last section of the Grand Loop was widened to accommodate two-way traffic in 1938. By 1940, approximately 190 miles of the park's 350-mile road system had some sort of asphalt surface, including two-thirds of the Grand Loop.[106]

The decision to reconstruct Yellowstone's roads to BPR standards had significant implications for some of the Grand Loop's storied attractions. The NPS was forced to decide whether to widen the narrow passage through the Hoodoos known as the Silver Gate or build a bypass. Albright insisted on constructing a bypass so that visitors would have the option of squeaking though the historic cleft or looping around at higher speed. The impact of the bypass was reduced through careful alignment and sculpting rock cuts to mimic natural conditions. Chittenden's Golden Gate Viaduct was too narrow to accommodate the 1926 standards, much less the expanded 1932 dimensions. Insisting that the Golden Gate's historic stature merited special treatment, Kittredge maintained that a regulation-width surface could be constructed with minimal damage to the cliff if the BPR would forego its insistence on standard-width shoulders. Fears of creating a bottleneck where the road narrowed prompted the search for an alternative solution. After deciding that blasting into the bluff would deface the landscape and destabilize the cliff, the NPS and BPR decided to widen the viaduct, cantilevering a 27-foot-wide deck over the old structure and supporting it with steel I-beams. Once again, the stone pillar was relocated to retain the illusion of a natural gateway.[107]

The BPR also insisted on eliminating a narrow curving section above the viaduct, where the road swung around a rocky promontory. Several alternatives were suggested: constructing another viaduct to provide the required clearance; excavating an open cut on the preferred alignment; "daylighting" the cut by blasting away the entire protrusion to avoid a conspicuously artificial gouge and ungainly stub; or boring a tunnel

"BEFORE" FROM JUST BELOW RUSTIC FALLS.

"AFTER" FROM JUST BELOW RUSTIC FALLS

ABOVE Contemporary sketch of proposed solution to problems caused by collapse of tunnel being constructed through bluff above Yellowstone's Golden Gate Viaduct, June 1933.

through the bluff. While the latter approach was being employed with considerable success on other park roads, Kittredge warned that the rock was too unstable to support a tunnel without extensive reinforcing. He preferred the daylighted-cut approach, maintaining that subtle sculpting and natural weathering would conceal the artifice. NPS landscape architects disagreed, asserting that a tunnel was needed to preserve the canyon's natural appearance. BPR engineers provided assurances that the tunnel was technically feasible and excavation began during the winter of 1932–33. Several small slides delayed progress. In late May a catastrophic collapse brought work to a halt. While no one was injured, the disaster was an expensive embarrassment for the BPR. The BPR's district engineer suffered a fatal heart attack on his way to Washington for a reckoning with bureau chief Thomas MacDonald. After reconsidering options, the NPS settled on the daylighting approach as safer and more economical. As Kittredge predicted, naturalistic sculpting and the passage of time rendered the artifice all but invisible. The problem of disposing of the huge amount of excavated material was solved by crushing it to surface the road. The benched section was ideally located to serve as a

scenic pullout affording striking views of Golden Gate Canyon and upgraded viaduct.[108]

A concerted effort was made to modernize the park's bridges, many of which were constructed of wood or cast iron. Most of the new crossings were stone-faced concrete structures, but a towering five-span steel-arch bridge was constructed over the Gardner River in 1939. While this conspicuously modern structure was a departure from NPS practice, it replaced 2,000 feet of circuitous scenery-scarring roadway that entailed steep and dangerous climbs in and out of the gorge. Concerned about the visual impact of such an immense construction, the NPS sought the advice of the noted parkway designer Gilmore Clarke. Clarke endorsed the approach, suggesting the steel be painted gray to blend with surrounding cliffs. Landscaping forces eradicated traces of the old road bed. Several CCC crews were stationed in the park, where they graded and replanted roadsides, constructed guard rails, and conducted other landscape improvement activities, carrying on the work initiated by the Rockefeller-funded roadside cleanup program.[109]

REALIZING MATHER'S VISION

The challenges associated with the preceding projects were encountered in the construction of park roads from Maine to Hawaii, as were the attendant increases in visitation. Despite the economic hardships of the Great Depression, people flocked to the parks in unprecedented numbers, the vast majority traveling by car. At the beginning of the NPS era in 1916, the total number of visitors to national parks and monuments was approximately 356,000. Overall visitation rose from 2 million at the start of the first park road program in 1925 to 3 million in 1928, 5 million in 1933, and 10 million in 1937. The annual count topped 16 million from 1939 to 1941 but dropped precipitously the following year as both travel and road construction were curtailed by America's entry into World War II. The dramatic increase did not stem solely from the Park Service's decision to embrace the automobile. Social trends such as rising wages and increased leisure time contributed significantly, as did the concomitant expansion of the National Park System. Between 1916 and 1941, the system

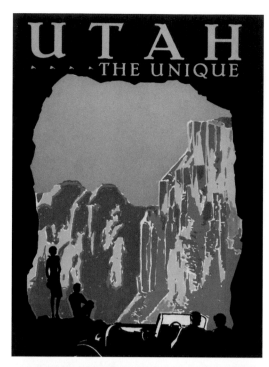

grew from 16 national parks and 21 national monuments totaling approximately 5 million acres to 164 separate sites encompassing more than 21 million acres. The new units included additional parks and monuments, the national military parks and Washington-area reservations added in 1933, and a growing number of national historic parks, national recreation areas, and national parkways. For most observers, however, the primary impetus was from the legions of motor tourists and the roads being built to accommodate them.[110]

The NPS and BPR did their best to encourage this view. Official reports touted the improvements and tallied the results. The BPR's Thomas MacDonald and L. I. Hewes proclaimed that national park work benefited motorists throughout the country by instilling greater appreciation for attractive roadways among engineers and the general public. Hewes relied heavily on national park projects to illustrate his 1942 *American Highway Practice*, which served as the principal manual on the subject for years. A 1934 *Western Construction News* article by BPR engineer Jean Ewen presented the bureau's efforts as an example of democracy at work. "If we consider our national parks as a heritage to all the people," Ewen declared, "we must develop them so that the benefits are available to all, and not merely to a favored few able to spend weeks in travel and exploration with saddle horses and pack trains."[111]

Motoring magazines and industry publications frequently highlighted the work. Standard Oil of California's general-interest magazine covered signature projects and applauded the opportunities afforded by park road development. Publications aimed at the construction trades combined detailed reporting on technical matters with effusive assessments of the social, political, and economic impacts of park road building. Early accounts invoked the See America First theme and praised the NPS's commitment to improving access to "national playgrounds." A 1920 article in dynamite manufacturer DuPont's magazine rejoiced, "Thousands of Americans are discovering for the first time that the United States is really richer in natural scenery of the first order than any other nation." A subsequent article on the Going-to-the-Sun Road cast the project as "a lasting monument to the National Park officials who conceived the route; the engineering forces of the U.S. Bureau of Public Roads who surveyed and mapped it, and to the

contractors, Williams & Douglas, who did the actual work." Mainstream journalists celebrated park road building as well. Local newspapers provided extensive coverage of nearby projects, and national media lauded signature developments while praising the program in general. A typical 1931 *New York Times* overview enthused, "Motorists in the national parks, America's unsurpassed touring ground, will have even more attractions than last year thanks to the activity of Federal highway engineers."[112]

The BPR's most ambitious publicity campaign consisted of a series of educational films on national park road building. These silent shorts combined spectacular scenic imagery with paeans to the achievements of federal highway builders. Footage of cars struggling up steep and narrow roads gave way to men and machines toiling against imposing obstacles and culminated in triumphant scenes of grateful motorists gliding effortlessly along gleaming highways. Films such as *Tunneling to Yosemite* and *New Roads in Mount Rainier* detailed specific projects; others celebrated the saga of park road development in more general terms. *Roads to Wonderland* began with a series of scenic images introduced by a text panel proclaiming, "Mother Nature, jealous of her scenic treasures, hides them behind high mountain walls that defy approach by all but the most daring." The next panel declared, "It is such barriers that the Federal Government, helped by the states and counties, is piercing with automobile roads." Most of these films were produced at the beginning of the interagency agreement, unintentionally documenting the challenges inherit in reconciling NPS and BPR perspectives. While the beauties of nature were dutifully extolled, BPR filmmakers highlighted the more aggressive aspects of park road building, with earth-shaking explosions raining showers of debris and men and machines sending dirt and rocks cascading down pristine mountainsides. In a sequence shot during the construction of Going-to-the-Sun Road, the camera lingered on a crew of workers rolling a giant boulder off the roadside, which careened down the mountainside sowing a path of destruction in its wake. A Wawona Tunnel construction film highlighted the contrast between the machine and the garden and epitomized the presentation of park road building as a triumph of technology over nature. Harshly illuminated shots of churning machinery, pulsating hoses, and billowing dust evoked a modern version of Vulcan's workshop rather than Edenic ideals of peace and repose and were accompanied by text celebrating the engineers' achievements. The BPR's expertise made it possible for "additional thousands" to enjoy Yosemite's natural wonders, which the camera enumerated in admiring detail. The film portrayed the tunnel's signature contribution to the national park experience from the drivers' perspective, presenting the sudden immersion into darkness and the distant circle of light that grew larger and larger until Yosemite's panoramic splendor exploded into view.[113]

The Ford Motor Company collaborated with the NPS to produce a series of films celebrating the increased accessibility of America's national parks. Episodes typically began with motorists entering the parks along smooth new roadways and then followed them along the principal tour routes, detailing the attractions found along the way. The influence of a third partner, the American Museum of Natural History, was evident in the attention paid to flora, fauna, and geology, but the role of improved roads and modern automobiles in making these attractions accessible was the underlying theme. Ford's Yellowstone film began with a typical American family packing their car and pulling out of their suburban driveway. As the scene shifted to attractive landscapes graced by the sweeping curve of a gleaming new road, the narrator intoned, "There's a broad smooth highway that leads from your door to an unforgettable vacation." After passing through the Roosevelt Arch, with the camera panning over the inscription "For the benefit and enjoyment of the people," the narrator reassured, "In spite of the road barriers built by nature, broad safe highways traverse the park and a great national playground is open to all America." Yellowstone's scenic highlights unfolded amid interjections such as, "Back in our car again, refreshed, we continue our travels" and, "It wasn't as easy as this a generation ago. Today you have only to get in your car and go." To emphasize that modern motorways posed no threat to traditional park values, the film praised the Park Service for preserving America's wilderness heritage and underscored the ample opportunities to "get off the beaten track if you want to get entirely away from everything civilized and familiar." For those with neither the time nor inclination for such archaic endeavors, the narrator intoned, "the modern motor car takes you from your front door to this natural treasure house. Gives you a comfortable vacation and brings you

back rested and refreshed with a deeper appreciation of the natural beauty and of the great country in which we live." The parting shot of a streamlined Ford sweeping around a graceful curve epitomized the harmonious reconciliation of the machine and the garden.[114]

Mather did not live long enough to enjoy the fulfillment of his vision, though the process was well under way when he suffered a crippling stroke in November 1928. Albright and Cammerer arrived at the hospital to find him struggling to articulate a word they eventually recognized as "Cascade." After suggesting various possibilities, they realized that even with his life hanging in the balance, Mather was preoccupied with park roads. The director had spent the previous months promoting an agreement aimed at preserving a band of greenery along the state highway crossing the Cascades on the eastern side of Mount Rainier National Park. This would require a unique partnership, since most of the land was national forest, with some portions controlled by commercial interests and others targeted for inclusion in the park. Mather had suggested the project be called "Cascade Parkway." Albright asked if this was the Cascades he had in mind and Mather signaled his

agreement. When his deputies assured him things were proceeding well, the director visibly relaxed. Mather recovered sufficiently to return to the family home in Darien, Connecticut, but recognized that he was no longer capable of overseeing NPS affairs. Albright officially succeeded him at the beginning of 1929. Mather continued to follow his favorite projects, including the Cascades Parkway, but on January 22 he suffered a fatal stroke. All parties agreed the Cascades project should bear the name Mather Memorial Parkway. Expressions of praise and sorrow poured in from around the country. House Appropriations Committee chairman Louis Cramton, who was both a longtime NPS supporter and personal friend, presented a rousing tribute on the floor of Congress, proclaiming, "There will never come an end to the good that he has done." A bronze plaque bearing Mather's likeness was installed at many NPS sites, including Mather Memorial Parkway. Cramton's encomium was cast above a sprig of pine cones, along with the words: "He laid the foundation of the National Park Service, defining and establishing the policies under which its areas shall be developed and conserved unimpaired for future generations."[115]

Trouble in Paradise

CHAPTER SIX

While the majority of Americans applauded the National Park Service's road-building efforts, some private citizens and government officials began to question the agency's policies. Complaints were few during the early years of NPS stewardship, when dramatically deficient roadways fostered alliances between outdoor enthusiasts, automobile clubs, and civic boosters. As the construction program shifted into high gear in the mid-1920s, questions arose about the nature and extent of park road development. Some based their criticism on technical grounds, contending that higher engineering standards eliminated the charms of park motoring. A larger and more influential cohort questioned the impact of road building on the broader park experience. Some sought to protect favored destinations from the motoring masses, but others called for fundamental reconsideration of the relationship between preservation and access. For this group, the NPS's eagerness to accommodate automobile tourism posed a threat not just to the sanctity of individual parks but also to the ability of current and future generations to experience unadulterated nature, which they considered both an American birthright and an antidote to the pressures of modern life. While traditional park advocates believed exposure to attractive scenery afforded sufficient solace, apostles of the new "wilderness ethic" insisted true regeneration could be achieved only through prolonged immersion in extensive tracts of primeval nature. The fundamental requirement for this highest form of nature appreciation was the absence of the very thing the NPS was investing its institutional identity and millions of dollars to produce: roads.[1]

Most calls for broad-based reconsideration of NPS development policies originated from outside the agency. The changing character of the roads themselves was more of an issue within the NPS. George Goodwin and Horace Albright questioned the wisdom of adopting the BPR's higher standards but acceded to Stephen Mather's insistence that national park roads be second to none. Their concern was based on the propensity for roads constructed to higher standards to lie less lightly on the land, but they also questioned the impact of wider, straighter roads on the traditional park experience. Lower-standard roads forced drivers to proceed at a slower pace that fostered a more intimate relationship between motorists and their surroundings, especially in the open touring cars that predominated through the 1920s. By affording greater visibility than cramped stagecoaches and allowing visitors to proceed at their own discretion rather than according to rigid schedules, motor tourism appeared to afford an ideal melding of modern technology and traditional sensibilities. Lower-standard roads also reduced the risk of serious accidents by limiting speeds and inducing caution. With the growing popularity of park motoring, however, it became clear that narrow, winding, one-lane roads were no longer acceptable to the general public. Putting aside their initial skepticism, NPS officials agreed that the BPR's 1924 Forest Road standards afforded a reasonable balance of safety, efficiency, and adaptability to local conditions. They lamented the loss of flexibility engendered by uniform standards, however, and sought exceptions to preserve particularly appealing passages. As more and more of the park road network was upgraded to BPR standards, some NPS officials worried that an important aspect of the national park experience was being sacrificed for the sake of speed and efficiency.

Ironically, the most ardent critic of the drive for higher and more uniform standards was NPS chief engineer Frank Kittredge, who began questioning his erstwhile colleagues' formulaic approach soon after switching employers. Kittredge's opposition to the BPR's plans for the Big Oak Flat Road was based on his belief that a high-standard roadway would not only scar the terrain but would also eliminate one of the park's signature features. The monumental views, dizzying exposure, and fabled zigzag turn had entranced visitors for more than half a century. None of his proposed alternatives came close to meeting BPR standards, but they would allow modern motorists to experience a cherished aspect of Yosemite's history. "There is an opportunity here to do something different from stereotyped highway location and construction," he remonstrated, "something that will conserve, something that will perpetuate the thrill of the old-time road, to do something which will combine adequate service to traffic and protection to the exquisite values of the park." Kittredge also emphasized the historic significance of Yellowstone's Chittenden Bridge, which similarly failed to meet the BPR's standards. Since the structure was on a side trip rather than the main road, it was granted a reprieve until advanced deterioration mandated its removal in the 1960s.[2]

Although Yosemite superintendent C. G. Thomson eventually accepted the BPR's advice, he was saddened by the sacrifice of what he described as "the most pleasant and park-like road in this Park, or in any other." Losing the Wawona Road and its storied Inspiration Point was bad enough, but Thomson maintained that the Big Oak Flat Road possessed "a picturesqueness and intimacy" that no modern road could match. "This meandering dustless road seems to consort with the magnificent forest instead of violating it," he mused, quoting a colleague's observation that the woods were so close to the travelway that "you can fairly feel the trees breathe upon you as you pass along." Characterizing the BPR's routing as "the penalty exacted" by the commitment to public access, he warned that if utilitarian values were allowed to dominate the new road's development, the NPS would be "savagely criticized not only

Even some of the NPS's closest allies worried that the emphasis on increasing the quantity of park users threatened the quality of the park experience.

now but throughout the years by the large and influential (and correct) elements who oppose engineering parks to death."[3]

Thomas Vint was also torn between practical and sentimental concerns. He expressed regret that the NPS was "gradually eliminating all the old time mountain roads" but maintained that Kittredge's idea of retaining the historic route as a one-way road was unrealistic. With the rest of the park's roads updated to modern standards, it would create a bottleneck that would become increasingly untenable as visitation continued to rise. Kittredge continued to insist that a high-speed, high-volume road was not only unnecessary but also inappropriate, since motorists should be encouraged to slow down and enjoy the spectacular views. The contrast between Vint's pragmatic perspective and Kittredge's idealistic stance belies suggestions that the engineer was less attuned to park values than his landscape architect colleagues. The last-minute appeal for Sierra Club intervention was not a calculated act of defiance, he claimed, but the spontaneous reaction of "a man realizing that a most wonderful natural mountainside and one in which he has taken a personal interest and pride for years, is about to be sacrificed." When he accepted the newly created post of western regional director in 1937, Kittredge insisted on the need "to prevent the abandonment of park areas to roads, the loss of park values, and public criticism due to an attempt by some to adopt too 'fast' a standard of construction." Professing the utmost respect for BPR engineers, Kittredge insisted the problem lay in the different missions of the two agencies: "Their job is to build roads and the best of roads. Our job on the other hand is to preserve park areas, to perpetuate the National Park atmosphere while at the same time making certain portions of the park accessible within these limits."[4]

While most drivers praised the new roads, an occasional grizzled veteran expressed nostalgia for the pioneering days of park motoring. Pleading for the retention of a few older, more challenging routes such as Rocky Mountain National Park's Fall River Road, one writer claimed that the improvements had taken the romance out of motoring. Where mountain driving once required skill, daring, and determination, he lamented, "Now we sweep upwards with effortless ease not realizing the great heights we are attaining." Acting Director Arthur Demaray assured him that his sentiments reflected "a rare point of view with which we have much sympathy" and maintained that only major tour roads were being upgraded, leaving opportunities for those who sought more adventurous motoring. Longtime Sequoia superintendent John White responded to a similar letter protesting the upgrading of Yosemite's roads by observing that many NPS veterans shared the writer's regrets "that the old roads or least some of the advantages of the old roads in the national parks are no longer to be had." He noted that sections of the older routes were often retained as administrative roads and could be driven under special permit. Underscoring the significance he attached to such sentiments, White sent copies of the interchange to Vint, Kittredge, and fellow superintendents.[5]

Discerning the differences between engineering standards required a practiced eye, but the broader changes wrought by the Park Service's embrace of the automobile were widely apparent. The dramatic rise in visitation, the expansion of campgrounds and associated facilities, and the changing character of the visitors themselves were impossible to ignore, as were the sounds, smells, and machine-age ambience generated by the now-ubiquitous family automobile. For Mather and others who insisted that expanding access to the national parks was both a public service and a political necessity, this was all to the good, but even some of the NPS's closest allies worried that the emphasis on increasing the quantity of park users

threatened the quality of the park experience. As early as 1916, the American Society of Landscape Architects president James Sturgis Pray warned that courting the general public could result in "too many and too conspicuous and sometimes inappropriate constructions." Pray cast the new agency as the best protection from the "danger of over-exploitation." Like Frederick Law Olmsted Jr. and most early NPS supporters, Pray believed that wise management based on traditional park-making principles would ensure an appropriate balance between preservation and access. The principal focus of this preservation, Pray maintained, was "the primeval character of the scenery." Olmsted elaborated on this goal, asserting that national parks should be managed for "the one dominant purpose of preserving essential esthetic qualities of their scenery unimpaired as a heritage to the infinite numbers of the generations to come."[6]

Five years later, Olmsted articulated a more expansive conception of the fundamental purpose of national parks. The preservation of scenery was still significant, but more important, he claimed, was the immersion in natural surroundings and respite from modern cares. With urbanization and industrialization making life more regimented and threatening the historic bond between Americans and the natural world, large parks afforded essential respite from "the complex mechanisms of civilization." Echoing his father's assertions about Central Park, the junior Olmsted asserted the benefits were both psychological and political. Just as the soothing confines of nineteenth-century urban parks provided a common ground in which diverse populations recognized their commonality, exposing Americans to vast areas reserved for their enjoyment underscored the importance of shared social bonds and promoted tolerance for a wide range of perspectives. The sociability of campground life afforded an analogue to the informal interactions of carriage drives and promenades. Since few Americans were interested in the more strenuous forms of outdoor recreation, Olmsted insisted on the need to make parks more attractive to the general public, even if it meant they would be experienced "under somewhat unfavorable conditions, as a work of art is seen behind glass in a museum, or a wild bird in an aviary." Large areas should be preserved "substantially unimpaired," but signature features should be made "accessible to droves of tourists" through carefully conducted improvements. Given the immense size of Yellowstone, Yosemite, and other major western parks, he insisted, there were ample alternatives for those who sought refuge from the crowded atmosphere of major destinations.[7]

Not everyone was so sure. In November 1921, the same month Olmsted presented these views to the American Civic Association, an article in the *Journal of Forestry* afforded a less optimistic assessment of the future of America's wild lands. The author, Aldo Leopold, was a 1909 graduate of Yale's school of forestry who had gone on to work in several national forests in the Southwest, where he participated in several pioneering studies of recreational activities in national forests. These experiences, along with mounting evidence of the automobile's impact on American society, made a profound impression. Beginning with a series of articles in professional journals and expanding to more general-interest publications, Leopold led the way in articulating the philosophical underpinnings of what would become known as the "wilderness movement."[8]

Leopold believed the primary benefit of America's wild lands accrued not from the contemplation of picturesque scenery or the gregarious enjoyment of pleasant surroundings, but from their ability to allow modern Americans to immerse themselves in large expanses of primeval nature, emulating the pioneer experience credited with creating a robust and virtuous national character. Like many of his contemporaries, Leopold was influenced by the dire predictions of the historian Frederick Jackson Turner about the impact on American culture of the closing of the frontier, as well as by fears about the impact of immigration, urbanization, and the attendant threats of working-class socialism and bourgeois materialism. Bivouacking in unbridled nature would steer the masses away from Bolshevism, save the middle classes from Babbittry, and restore the mental and physical vigor sapped by modern urban life. Leopold acknowledged that the majority of Americans had little inclination to test their mettle in frontier conditions, but he maintained this was all the more reason to preserve places where those who still possessed "the Covered Wagon blood" could engage in the "more virile and primitive forms of outdoor recreation." As relics of frontier America, moreover, wilderness areas would serve an important historical function. Just as Colonial Williamsburg situated the birth of the republic in a tangible educational setting and Henry Ford's Greenfield Village afforded a glimpse of traditional small-town life, wilderness areas would enable younger generations to understand the hardships overcome during what Leopold referred to as "The Romance of the March of Empire," or, in a more colloquial formulation, "Covered Wagon Days." With the elimination of wilderness and the opportunities it provided for historical reflection and character-building recreation, he warned, "dead, too, will be a part of our Americanism."[9]

Despite the centrality of wilderness to the American experience, Leopold remonstrated, there was no concerted effort to preserve the dwindling number of places where Americans could emulate their frontier forebears. The primary cause of this tragic loss, he insisted, was not logging, dam building, or any of the other "impairments" invoked by the NPS and its allies but rather the very force the NPS sought to harness for its own good: motor tourism. Leopold acknowledged that automobiles and improved highways afforded millions with access to nature and could thereby be considered "a benefaction to mankind" but noted that well-intentioned remedies were often toxic when applied to excess. "The Good Roads Movement" he declared, had become "a Good Roads Mania." Throughout America's most scenic regions, politicians and chambers of commerce viewed motor tourism as a means of supplanting struggling agricultural economies. Allied with automobile clubs, fueled by federal dollars, and abetted by the agencies charged with preserving natural resources, these boosters were "thrusting more and ever more roads into every little remaining patch of wilderness." Leopold was too politic to attack the NPS or U.S. Forest Service (USFS) directly. He was also sympathetic with the agencies' plight, observing that they were subject to intense pressure from an automobile-oriented tourism lobby that constituted "a steam roller the like of which has seldom been seen in the history of mankind."[10]

Leopold recognized that both agencies faced complex challenges in balancing competing interests. The conventional USFS approach for ascertaining the best or "highest" use of an area was to identify the solution that achieved "the greatest good for the greatest number." The NPS's Organic Act imposed additional strictures, but similar considerations guided many decisions. Leopold endorsed the concept, professing agreement with the policy of focusing on the mass of visitors who preferred to travel by motor and enjoy other "artificial forms of outdoor life." In an ingenious twist, however, he argued that since the majority's interests were adequately addressed by the recent spate of automobile-oriented recreational development, establishing areas where the minority could seek more authentic natural encounters would increase the sum total of satisfaction and therefore constitute the "highest use" of the few remaining expanses of inviolate wilderness. Comparing the proposition to municipal park management, he observed, "It is just as unwise to devote 100% of the recreational resources of our public parks and forests to motorists, as it would be to devote 100% of our city parks to merry-go-rounds." Leopold maintained that the conflict between competing uses would be minimal since the remaining wilderness areas were so difficult to access that they were unsuited for automobile-oriented development. Not only did Leopold underestimate the ambitions and abilities of federal road builders, but the size of the reservations he proposed almost guaranteed conflict. To qualify as wilderness, Leopold proposed, the designated area should constitute "a continuous stretch of country preserved in its natural state, open to lawful hunting and fishing, big enough to absorb a two weeks' pack trip, and kept devoid of roads, artificial trails, cottages, or other works of man." Leopold's insistence that hunting be permitted underscored his perception that wilderness should function as an arena for the enactment of pioneering activities, as did his assertion that cattle ranching should be condoned as a cherished legacy of "Covered Wagon Days." Personal predilections also came into play, as Leopold was an avid hunter wedded to the daughter of a prominent ranching family.[11]

Since hunting and grazing were prohibited in national parks, Leopold agreed to modify the terms accordingly. The bigger obstacle to preserving wilderness in the NPS domain, he maintained, was that "the Parks are being networked with roads and trails as rapidly as possible." Leopold acknowledged the need to provide automobile access to select destinations but insisted it was only fair to provide opportunities for both constituencies. To illustrate the contrast, he paired a photograph of Mount Rainier's Paradise Valley overrun with car campers—the sort of image the NPS touted as evidence of its success—and a USFS photograph of a lone tent nestled in a tiny clearing described as being accessible solely by foot or canoe. Only the latter, Leopold contended, could provide the "quiet and harmony, peace and renewal so necessary to many." Further underscoring the contrast between the two agencies, Leopold noted that the USFS had taken steps toward establishing roadless areas in New Mexico and on the outskirts of Jackson Hole, where the NPS had designs on extending the southern border of Yellowstone. Although he avoided explicit criticism, Leopold's claim that "the vanguard of American thought on the use of land" had acknowledged the need for designated wilderness areas was bound to offend NPS officials, as was his contention that contrary to the prevailing rhetoric, the economic benefits of motor tourism rarely if ever recouped the expense of road construction. He expressed faith that the NPS would be willing to prohibit road development in selected areas. Given the political clout of motoring interests, however, the agency was unlikely to change its policies without a major public outcry. "Unless the wilderness idea represents the mandate of an organized, fighting and voting body of far-seeing Americans," he exhorted, "the steam roller will win."[12]

A SECTION OF PARADISE VALLEY CAMP GROUND, TATOOSH RANGE IN BACKGROUND, Rainier National Park

Chief Forester William Greeley was eager to cast his agency as superior in regard to wilderness preservation. In a 1927 *Sunset Magazine* article, he portrayed USFS management as the best assurance that vestiges of primitive America would not succumb to "the conquering power of the steam shovel and the gas motor." Greeley appeared to embrace Leopold's philosophy, characterizing the wilderness experience as "the greatest single factor in molding our sturdier national qualities" and asserting that the USFS was committed to protecting the last reserves of virgin nature from the "incessant penetration of roads and motors." Like Leopold, Greeley acknowledged the benefits of road development. He touted the recreational opportunities afforded by the Forest Service and invoked road mileage and visitation statistics on par with NPS achievements. At the same time, the agency was designating a number of roadless wilderness areas ranging in size from 360 to more than 11,000 square miles. Many were areas the NPS sought for national park designation, fueling perceptions that the policy reflected bureaucratic politics rather than a sudden awakening to the beauties of nature. These included the future Kings Canyon, Olympic, and North Cascades National Parks, along with the area south of Yellowstone coveted by Albright and Mather. Insisting that the latter region would remain inviolate under the Forest Service's wilderness designation, he suggested that there was considerable risk in transferring it to an agency that, if history were a guide, would cater to contemporary enthusiasms with a crowd-pleasing plan that "bisects it with roads, plants it with hotels, and sends yellow busses streaking through it with sirens shrieking like souls in torment." What Greeley failed to note was that USFS wilderness designations could be altered or even removed if the land became more valuable for logging or other commercial purposes.[13]

It was bad enough that the NPS's perennial antagonist cast the agency as overly solicitous of automobile interests, but some long-term supporters also questioned NPS development policies. The Harvard professor Henry Hubbard agreed parks should be made "reasonably accessible" but warned that excessive development would "destroy the very values which we attempt to preserve." Hubbard noted that modern construction methods made it too easy to undertake projects "where the scenery made accessible is forever mutilated by the making of the road." Hubbard even questioned whether the

historic injunction "For the Benefit and Enjoyment of All" remained a reasonable goal in the age of mass motorization. "Since indefinitely increasing accessibility often destroys certain essentials of wild scenery," he abjured, "many of us do not believe it is a sound national policy . . . to assume that all the people of the United States have the right to go and see all of the scenery everywhere in whatever way they choose." The noted landscape architect Jens Jensen made no apologies for the elitist connotations of such policies. "It is only the few who get real value out of God's out-of-doors," he proclaimed, "and if it is trampled down and littered up by the many, there will be little left for the few." In Jensen's view, the NPS should focus on the needs of visitors with the means and sophistication to appreciate parks properly rather than cater to the "hordes" who "just go sightseeing without receiving the slightest good out of what they see." Landscape educator P. H. Elwood praised subtle improvements such as Yellowstone's roadside beautification program but condemned Generals Highway as too heavy-handed and characterized Going-to-the-Sun Road as "a necessary evil." He beseeched Vint to employ "every effort possible to keep within control the use of the automobile in the National Parks." If parks continued to be developed at the current rate, he warned, motorists "will over-run them and destroy the essence and spirit prevailing in those great natural wonderlands." Elwood suggested that the NPS cut back on road development and explore the potential of long-distance air-travel augmented by "aerial taxicabs" ferrying visitors around the parks.[14]

The most disturbing defection was none other than former NPS publicist Robert Sterling Yard, whose promotional genius had helped set in motion the forces he opposed with growing fervor. Yard left the NPS in 1919, when a change in federal regulations prevented Mather from supplementing his salary. With Mather's financial backing, he established the National Parks Association to promote NPS interests to Congress and the public at large. The organization proved a valuable ally in battles against conventional threats such as irrigation and lumbering, but Yard began to question NPS policy on multiple levels. His initial objections centered on perceptions that the agency was lowering its standards by approving parks that failed to meet traditional criteria of scenic beauty or scientific interest. Yard contended that many of the new parks were justified

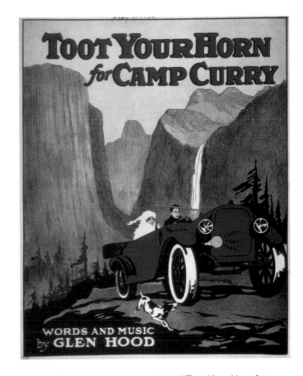

merely by their ability to provide outdoor recreation, and motorized recreation in particular. While Yard had promoted Mather's vision of national parks as "America's playgrounds" and touted automobile tourism as the means through which Yellowstone would fulfill its destiny, by the mid-1920s he was protesting the recreational focus and expressing concerns about the nature and extent of road development. Yard maintained that neither he nor Mather had envisioned the impact motor tourism would have on national park affairs. Past paeans to the automobile's glory as "an accelerator of park travel" aside, he insisted the agency's founders considered motor tourism "too dangerous and expensive a sport ever to affect the destiny of places so distant and difficult of access." Yard contended that the exponential growth in automobile admissions was as surprising to the NPS as it was to the agency's critics. Yard also insisted that the Park Service's role in precipitating the deluge was not as great as boosters like Mather proclaimed. Given the explosion of automobile ownership, he maintained, the "tidal wave" of motor tourism" would have swept across the country regardless of the agency's efforts. The impact on national parks had captured the media's attention, but the motorization of American life affected every aspect of outdoor recreation, from municipal parks and national forests to holiday travel in general. Not only was it inaccurate to credit or blame NPS policies, Yard maintained, but the threat to America's wilderness heritage was not as dire as some critics contended.[15]

The claim that NPS officials were oblivious to the automobile's potential was as specious as it was self-serving, but Yard made a credible argument for the latter proposition. In the first place, he observed, the figures thrown about to tout the NPS's success were misleading. While the numbers seemed striking, the increase was comparable to what the USFS reported and lower than gains experienced in state parks. The numbers were also inflated by the growth of the National Park System, which incorporated popular destinations like the Grand Canyon and Zion. The initial surge of visitation slowed somewhat in the mid-1920s, moreover, leading Yard to conclude that motor tourism was a transient fad that had already run its course. Finally, those parks with the highest increases—Yosemite and Sequoia—received most of their visitors from surrounding regions.

Their soaring attendance was more a reflection of their function as de facto state parks than an indication of the public's insistence on motoring through America's most sacred scenic areas. Many visitors returned multiple times throughout the year, further inflating attendance figures. The same was true of Mount Rainier, which was essentially a recreational extension of Seattle and Tacoma. Yellowstone received its greatest proportion of visitors from Montana and Idaho, while most visitors to Rocky Mountain National Park were residents of Front Range cities who rarely even stopped within the park because they were so intent on completing the grand circuit over the mountains and back around to Denver.[16]

While a closer look at the statistics belied claims that motorists were sweeping across the country to invade the national parks, they pointed to a trend Yard found even more disturbing. Not only did the most popular parks function primarily as regional attractions, but the growing emphasis on recreation threatened to compromise the integrity of the national park experience. Taking additional license with history, he maintained that the idea of national parks as places of popular resort was a recent development. Until Mather and his allies began touting them as "the nation's playgrounds," Yard claimed, visiting the national parks was a serious spiritual, aesthetic, and educational endeavor. Not only did the desire to attract those uninterested in traditional park pursuits result in the proliferation of inappropriate facilities such as golf courses, movie theaters, and dancing pavilions, but local boosters manipulated the "nation's playgrounds" pitch to secure federal funding for areas that should be developed by state or county authorities. Yard was particularly dismissive of efforts to increase the number of national parks in the East. While Great Smoky Mountains met the desired criteria, Yard maintained that Shenandoah set a dangerous precedent by conferring national park status on a recreation-oriented facility lacking distinctive scenery or nationally significant features. Creating a mountaintop roadway for Washington-area motorists, he implied, was not a legitimate argument for national park designation.[17]

Yard was not opposed to park motoring per se. Nor did he seek to eliminate all facilities catering to popular tastes. Like Mather and Albright, he believed that exposing Americans to their natural heritage had profound benefits, no matter how they traveled. He might accuse "the rushing hordes of

the wheel" of missing out on the glories of nature and transforming popular destinations into alpine Coney Islands replete with tawdry amusements, jazz music, and other dubious attractions, but Yard maintained that even those who experienced national parks in "this desultory modern way" received meaningful inspiration. Like John Muir peering down at turn-of-the-century stagecoach crowds, Yard viewed the public embrace of national parks as a positive development posing little threat to more pristine precincts. Yard's confidence reflected his counterintuitive assertion that America's love affair with the automobile was essential to the preservation of wilderness. The motorist's vice, Yard proclaimed, was also his virtue. "Motorists are motorists," he observed. "They stick by the road." With 90 percent of visitors voluntarily consigning themselves to minute areas, there was little danger that those who sought more solitary experiences would be disturbed. The key was to concentrate tourists in a narrow range of areas selected for intensive development. This would take a toll on sites such as Yosemite Valley, but the natural qualities of most celebrated destinations were compromised already. The challenge, once again, came down to the question of balancing preservation and access, or more specifically, determining which areas to consign to the motoring masses and which to consecrate as roadless retreats. The corollary concern, at least for those outside the NPS, was how these critical distinctions would be determined and enforced.[18]

The dramatic increase in visitation attending the opening of Yosemite's All-Year Highway appeared to shake Yard's confidence and engender a more confrontational stance. The concomitant push for a second and decidedly more ambitious road-building budget prompted Yard to openly question NPS policies. In a November 1927 editorial, Yard likened the Park Service's embrace of the automobile to Frankenstein's monster as a misguided experiment that outstripped its master's control. The only way to redress the situation, he maintained, was to rethink basic principles, not throw more money into road building or parse the fine points of pavement widths and landscape design. With the remaining sanctuaries of primeval nature in imminent danger, it no longer mattered how roads were built, but where they were built, or, more to the point, where they were prohibited in perpetuity. Vague assurances that parks would not be gridironed were no longer sufficient. "Strict, well-studied, prompt road limitation alone can save any part of America as God made it," Yard declared. Without such strictures, he warned, "the same agency which makes enjoyment of National Parks possible to multitudes threatens greatly to impair and sometimes to destroy their usefulness for any higher than merely resort ends."[19]

Yard and Leopold capitalized on the 1924 National Conference on Outdoor Recreation to advance their agendas. Authorized by President Calvin Coolidge, the initiative brought together private experts and public authorities to assess recreational needs at the federal, state, and local levels. Coolidge insisted on representation from relevant federal agencies, but the Park Service's participation was perfunctory, at best. Mather made a somewhat disjointed statement at the final gathering in 1926, and Arno Cammerer chaired a panel, but the agency's position was that existing policies afforded sufficient protection. Yard took full advantage of this vacuum, chairing the committee charged with articulating a recreational policy for federal lands. In addition to reiterating his own views, he foregrounded the Forest Service's efforts and gave Leopold a prominent role in the program. Insisting that recreational motoring was so thoroughly entrenched that additional promotional efforts were superfluous, Leopold emphasized the need to provide for those who sought more solitary enjoyment, insisting they should not be forced to "motorize their souls" by administrators capitulating to popular tastes. The Forest Service touted its wilderness policy while acknowledging that areas it claimed to protect could be put to commercial uses if circumstances changed. Nevertheless, the committee concluded that the USFS was best equipped to preserve America's wilderness. The committee called for the formal proclamation of wilderness areas within the national forests and new legislation to define national parks in terms that ensured their preservation "in a condition of unmodified nature."[20]

The National Conference on Outdoor Recreation was a well-intentioned but purely advisory exercise that NPS leaders could confidently ignore, secure in their faith that the agency's policies afforded the best means of maintaining an appropriate balance between preservation and access. Public enthusiasm for park motoring continued to rise, along with political pressure to spread the economic benefits more broadly through new parks and additional construction. As prominent publications such as the the *Nation* and *Saturday Evening Post* called attention to the impacts of park road building and opponents began to protest specific projects along with general policies, however, Albright decided to rebut accusations that the NPS was forsaking preservationist principles in favor of unfettered access. Prevailing on the *Saturday Evening Post* for equal time, Albright presented the Park Service as the premier custodian of America's natural heritage. Entitled "The Everlasting Wilderness" in a pointed allusion to the Forest Service's ephemeral assurances, Albright's response emphasized the similarities between opponents' aims and NPS actions. Acknowledging that the surge in road construction raised valid concerns, he insisted the agency shared the views of a recent letter writer who implored, "Let us not destroy the few remaining bits of wilderness in the national parks by building paved highways through every one of them." Not only was the NPS fully committed to wilderness preservation, but the territory under its care was so vast that expanded funding could never compromise its primeval splendor. At the same time, Albright assured, the NPS had an obligation to make these wonders accessible to the American people. Asserting that the majority of Americans endorsed the NPS approach to balancing preservation and access, Albright noted that the agency was under constant pressure from the two extremes: "Those who want no roads into the parks and who would keep them unbroken wildernesses reached only by trails, and, on the other hand, those who are spokesmen for automobile clubs, chambers of commerce, and other development organizations, whose appetites for road building are never appeased."[21]

Albright maintained that the best indication of the agency's priorities was that 90 percent of the larger parks remained unaffected by road development. The current construction was aimed at upgrading outdated roads to accommodate automobile travel, not increasing total mileage, which would be essentially the same as in stagecoach days. A few new roads were being constructed, but mostly in parks that had yet to receive significant development. Going-to-the-Sun Road was the most conspicuous example, and one whose value few would contest. Even there, the majority of the park was reserved for hikers and horseback riders. When the NPS committed to building a road, moreover, landscape architects oversaw every step of the process, and no expense was spared to minimize negative impacts. Albright expressed his reservations about the new engineering standards, observing that it remained to be seen whether or not the improvement campaign would make park roads "speedier and less safe."[22]

Turning to individual parks, Albright noted that not only did Yellowstone possess approximately 3,000 square miles of backcountry accessible only by trail, but the NPS was hoping to expand the park southward. Characterizing the proposed addition as "a wilderness unparalleled anywhere," he noted that pending legislation prohibited road building. He also insisted that no new road development was planned for Yosemite. The NPS would strongly oppose such action, he asserted, "for the reason that we believe that construction of additional roads would mar exquisite glacially carved cliffs or destroy the natural settings of noble waterfalls." It was true that the NPS was replacing Rocky Mountain National Park's Fall River Road with a new roadway better suited to motor traffic, but the old route would be abandoned, leaving the total mileage essentially unchanged. Already, Albright observed, the NPS had scaled back plans for road development in Mount Rainier. As a result, only 14 square miles of the 352-square-mile park would be accessible to motorists. "The most beautiful park lands," he proclaimed, "are destined to be left in isolation far away from the roads." In closing, Albright applauded the growing concern for wilderness values and affirmed the NPS's commitment to preserving America's primeval splendor for the enjoyment of those "with adventure enough in their souls to look beyond the highways."[23]

Although "The Everlasting Wilderness" was clearly a public relations pitch, the NPS sincerely believed it was pursuing a pro-wilderness policy. Its leaders were both perplexed and aggrieved by assertions to the contrary. The primary differences between Mather's one-good-road policy and Yard's admonition to concentrate visitors along selective corridors centered on the question of who would do the selecting and how the areas would be defined. While Yard and other critics called for comprehensive policies developed through formal consultation, the NPS insisted on autonomy, though it regularly consulted with the Sierra Club and similar organizations about road building and related concerns. The NPS was admittedly more optimistic about the potential for motorists and wilderness enthusiasts to coexist. This was due in part to the lingering tendency to consider park landscapes in aesthetic terms. As long as roads were limited in extent and retained a naturalistic appearance, the NPS maintained, wilderness values were preserved. For purists such as Leopold, wilderness was a broader experiential concept that was compromised by the mere awareness of a road's presence. Albright's assertion that Yellowstone's roadside cleanup program restored the "wilderness appearance" of the park's roads underscored the contrast between the two perspectives. He also maintained that the motorization of Yellowstone had reduced human impact on the park, despite the dramatic increase in visitation. Four hotels had been removed, along with twenty-five permanent camps and scores of barns, stables, and other facilities needed to support the stage companies' two thousand horses, whose destructive grazing was also eliminated.[24]

Many outdoor enthusiasts shared the NPS's view that wilderness values were not compromised by motor roads as long as significant areas remained undeveloped. Struthers Burt, a Jackson Hole dude rancher and outdoor writer, dismissed the contention that motorists were destroying the national parks as an alarmist conceit. Although it was true that Yellowstone's Grand Loop could be as thick with automobiles as Chicago's Lakeshore Drive on a summer afternoon, visitors could enjoy "primeval solitude" by means of a five-minute walk or an extended horseback excursion. Burt had initially opposed the park expansion, but the NPS's ability to balance the needs of motorists and backcountry visitors persuaded him to shift allegiances. With a convert's enthusiasm—and a keen eye to the profits to be made guiding dude ranchers through Yellowstone's backcountry—Burt cast the NPS's limited development policy as the best means of containing the forces calling for automobile access to public lands. Echoing Leopold, Burt acknowledged the benefits of automobile travel while urging readers to support NPS efforts to fend off demands to open up new areas to the motoring masses. "They don't want to build any more roads if they can help it," he assured, but NPS officials were subject to constant pressure from "motor hogs" and "powerful and unscrupulous interests" calling for "a new motor road here or a new motor road there." Unlike Leopold and other skeptics, he expressed faith in the agency's abilities and intentions.

"Support them," he advised fellow sportsmen: "when they want a thing, give it to them, leave them alone; they're the best friends for sanity and character building the country has . . . [with] the preservation and perpetuation forever of our wildernesses as their ambition and goal."[25]

Mather was so pleased with this portrayal that he circulated it throughout the ranks. NPS leaders felt the agency received insufficient credit for the road development it had prevented, often at the risk of alienating politically powerful constituencies. Decisions not to build roads were overshadowed by the attention garnered by prominent projects and the complaints of a well-connected minority. The agency was partially to blame for this situation. While NPS leaders relished the opportunity to showcase projects, they were more circumspect about their efforts to defuse unwanted initiatives. Public pronouncements might have enhanced the agency's stature with wilderness advocates, but the NPS tried to avoid confrontation with politicians and local boosters. Given the agency's financial concerns and desire to expand the system, it was more sagacious to forestall development by suggesting a project might gain approval down the road than dismiss it out of hand as an unconscionable violation of park principles. Demands for unwanted projects were often deflected on the grounds of insufficient funds or the need for additional study. NPS leaders also worked behind the scenes to promote positions the agency was hesitant to advocate publicly. Agency perceptions of the appropriate balance of preservation and access also shifted over time. The biggest controversies occurred when pro-development forces believed the NPS was moving too far into the preservationist camp or when preservationists complained the agency was not going far enough. In many cases both charges were leveled simultaneously.[26]

One of the most surprising proposals emanated from Yard himself. In September 1924, Yard sought Interior Secretary Hubert Work's support for a road along the Continental Divide in Rocky Mountain National Park. Yard insisted that the only thing preventing the park from attaining the stature of Yosemite and Yellowstone was a woefully inadequate road system, "which conceals its majesty from all except a few hundred climbers a year." The park's most attractive features would "remain unknown and in practice unknowable to the vast majority of its visitors" until the NPS remedied the situation. The proposed Trail Ridge Road was a

step in the right direction, but it lacked the grandeur of a drive along the Divide itself. Winding along the top of the continent between rugged cliffs and plunging ravines, with a panorama stretching from snowcapped mountains to rolling plains, Yard's proposal would afford "the most sensational drive in the world." A hotel located as near as possible to Long's Peak would enable motorists to spend the night at altitudes experienced only by hardy mountaineers. "With this extraordinary road penetrating the Rockies' splendid fastness," he enthused, "Rocky Mountain National Park would soon be classified, here and abroad, in the first group of America's great spectacles."[27]

Not only was Yard's suggestion significantly more intrusive than the route ultimately chosen for Trail Ridge Road, but it epitomized the "skyline drive" approach that he and other wilderness advocates would soon oppose. Rocky Mountain National Park superintendent Roger Toll embraced the proposal, however, suggesting that the road be extended past Long's Peak and back down to Estes Park to avoid the congestion associated with dead-end roads. Yard expressed concern that this would encourage motorists to press through without lingering to enjoy the alpine splendors, but he eventually agreed that the improved traffic flow was necessary for the road to fulfill its destiny as "the resort of the real lovers of majestic nature." In a carefully worded response likely crafted by Albright or Cammerer, Work thanked Yard for his suggestion but reminded him that funding was limited and the first priority was improving passage to the other side of the park. When new projects were contemplated, Yard's suggestion would receive due consideration. Cammerer and Demaray advised Mather that the idea was worth considering, but only after more pressing needs were met. In addition to flouting the policy on limiting development to "one good road," the potential costs of "Mr. Yard's Continental Divide Road," as they termed it, were daunting, both in monetary terms and scenic impact. Between Yard's change of heart and Toll's reassignment to Yellowstone, the proposal faded into oblivion, to the relief of NPS officials, and, one suspects, it primary proponent.[28]

In another brush with a former ally, the NPS found itself at odds with William Steel, the founder of Crater Lake National Park, who lobbied long and hard for a road from the crater rim down to the shore of the lake. NPS officials were adamantly opposed but reluctant to publicly rebuke the

"Father of Crater Lake National Park." Having led the drive for the park's authorization in 1902, Steel was intent on making its prime attraction more accessible and made no secret of his disdain for the new custodians' emphasis on scenic preservation. In a widely quoted brief, he maintained that Congress's directive that national parks were for the benefit and enjoyment of the people took precedence over the wishes of "a few men clothed with a little brief authority and possessed of a dainty theory." Albright instructed the superintendent to avoid public statements while wooing local leaders. When the Seattle-based Mountaineers outing and conservation organization expressed frustration at the NPS's silence, Albright explained the agency's predicament and prodded their members to take a public stance. The combination of private persuasion and independent opposition convinced most local papers and civic groups to oppose the plan. Even local chambers of commerce disavowed the proposal, acknowledging for once that too many roads could be as detrimental to business as too few. Concluding that he had overestimated the public's willingness to trade scenery for improved access, Steel reluctantly acknowledged defeat.[29]

The NPS response to pressures for additional roads in Yellowstone was more complex. In some cases, the agency expressed its opposition in no uncertain terms, but in others, political considerations had to be weighed against preservation ideals. With communities in multiple states competing for tourist income, NPS officials were subject to continual pressure from senators, congressmen, governors, civic groups, lodging providers, and transportation interests. Demands ranged from balanced progress in snow-clearing efforts so that no gateway got a jump on the tourist season, to equitable improvements to existing roads, and—most problematically—new entranceways so that additional communities could tap the flow of tourist dollars. Insisting that the southeast corner of the park and the proposed southern addition remain roadless was relatively uncontroversial since major tourist centers in that direction were well served by the south and east entrance roads. When the Chicago, Milwaukee & St. Paul Railway rallied Butte and Bozeman boosters to push for a northwest entrance across the Gallatin and Bighorn Mountains in the early 1920s, Albright convinced Mather and Interior Secretary Work to declare that area off-limits

ABOVE Horace Albright inspecting an area declared off-limits to road development, Yellowstone National Park, 1924.

to road development. Armed with photographs taken on a horseback trip through the remote region, he implored: "I think the Department and the National Park Service would not be faithful to the obligations imposed upon them by the act of Congress dedicating the park, and the act creating the National Park Service, if they permitted civilization, in the form of roads and automobiles, to invade the solitude of the game-filled valleys of the Gallatin range." Idealism aside, he emphasized the absurdity of constructing an enormously expensive and destructive road for the benefit of a single railroad line, especially when the number of visitors traveling by rail was in steep decline.[30]

Defusing a proposed southwest entrance was a more complicated matter. The idea of a direct route from southeastern Idaho to the Grand Loop was originally endorsed by the NPS in a classic demonstration of Mather's belief that motor tourism was the best means of combating more egregious impairments. In one of the first

major crises faced by the NPS, a cabal of western businessmen and politicians sought to impound water in the national parks for irrigation and power generation. Southeastern Idaho interests lobbied for the construction of a reservoir system along the Bechler River in the southwest section of the park. This isolated region of meadows, rivers, and waterfalls lay fallow from both recreational and resource-exploitation perspectives. Since tourists could access it only by horseback, it was rarely visited and then only by the most ardent enthusiasts. Casting their quest as a conflict between hardworking farmers and "a few splendid but overly esthetic people . . . living in luxury in Boston, New York, Philadelphia, and other eastern cities," proponents insisted that if Yellowstone's waters could not be put to practical use, then the region should be removed from the park. The NPS and its allies turned back these efforts but offered to construct a road through the area as a measure of economic compensation. The USFS would build the approach from Ashton, Idaho, through Targhee National Forest to the park border, and the NPS would carry it up the Bechler River and over the Continental Divide to intersect the Grand Loop near the Upper Geyser Basin. Despite their oft-stated opposition to additional road construction in Yellowstone, Mather and Albright endorsed the proposal in 1922. Although Albright praised its potential to relieve crowding and expose visitors to the beauty of the rarely traveled region, subsequent comments suggest he was trying to put the best

face on an unfortunate situation. NPS officials were sympathetic with southeastern Idaho's desire for a share of the Yellowstone trade and conscious of their obligation to reward those who opposed the state's powerful agricultural lobby. Local support was also critical to NPS efforts to gain authorization for a park in the Tetons. In the likely event that reservoir interests renewed their efforts, moreover, the road and associated developments would counter arguments that the region was so remote and inaccessible few visitors would lament its loss. As a final consideration, including the project in

the upcoming roads bill would solidify support from Idaho politicians. Mather played up the latter angle, assuring Idaho senator William Borah that if the measure passed, the southwest entrance would become Yellowstone's premier approach.[31]

While the first road bill was under consideration, irrigation interests again sought to impound water in the park. Proponents claimed to have eliminated the conflict between tourism and reservoir development by lowering the proposed water level. Albright acknowledged that routing the road around a reduced reservoir was technically feasible but insisted the cost would be prohibitive. The reservoir would also inundate proposed camping areas along with the waterfalls that constituted the area's premier attraction. Relying on economic logic rather than idealistic appeals, he argued that the question came down to whether the region would benefit more from tourism or increased irrigation capacity. Albright noted that Yellowstone's visitation was growing by nearly 50 percent per year while farmers produced more crops than they could profitably market. With business leaders from Idaho Falls to Salt Lake City expressing their preference for tourism, dam proponents were again defeated. Mather's logic prevailed, but the NPS remained saddled with an obligation that conflicted with its expressed aims for Yellowstone and the National Park System as a whole.[32]

When the road bill passed, Idaho interests were understandably eager for construction to commence. When it became clear that work would not begin in 1925, the NPS received a barrage of complaints. Local newspapers railed against the agency's duplicity, chambers of commerce issued proclamations, and Idaho's congressional delegation summoned Mather to the secretary's office for a formal chastening. NPS officials insisted they were committed to the project but maintained that extenuating circumstances necessitated a temporary delay. The appropriations bill mandated that funds be spent on eliminating hazards on existing roads before undertaking new projects. Given the unprecedented increase in motor traffic, this would take longer and cost more than anticipated. The shift to BPR standards meant that new plans and estimates would have to be prepared. Seeking to spread the blame, NPS officials observed that it made no sense to proceed until the USFS constructed its portion, which it had not yet committed to build.[33]

ABOVE Map of Yellowstone National Park, with solid lines indicating roads and dashed lines showing trails, from Northern Pacific Railway brochure, 1924.

While the NPS remained publicly committed to the project, agency officials began building a case for its abandonment. Albright was increasingly outspoken about the need to preserve Yellowstone's backcountry. To ward against the inevitable backlash, he sought support on practical and aesthetic grounds. The BPR proved an unexpected ally. A timely visit in July 1925 convinced Thomas MacDonald and L. I. Hewes that bringing Yellowstone's roads up to the bureau's standard was a more ambitious task than previously envisioned. They also noted that constructing a modern roadway along the proposed route would be inordinately expensive. The engineers maintained that it made more sense to improve the existing state highway along the west side of the park. Given the difference between state highways and park road standards, this roundabout route would afford quicker access to Yellowstone's main attractions. When Albright explained the politics of the situation, MacDonald offered to let the BPR take the blame. Once again, NPS leaders could profess sympathy with the project's advocates while insisting the decision was out of their hands.[34]

By this time, there was no question about Albright's leanings. In September 1926 he conducted a horseback tour of the region, bringing along a photographer and several outside allies, including the noted New York landscape architect Harold Caparn. Photographs of pristine meadows and crystalline cataracts underscored the area's scenic beauty. Caparn submitted a brief assailing the proposed roadway as an unwarranted invasion of one of Yellowstone's overlooked treasures. The Bechler River Canyon, he contended, was as compelling as the Grand Canyon of the Yellowstone, but its more intimate attractions were better appreciated afoot or on horseback. Since motorists would pass through too quickly to appreciate its unique appeal, it made sense to maintain these distinctions rather than sacrifice the area's primeval splendor for the sake of "speed-greedy Philistines." Caparn's report and the accompanying photographs afforded additional confirmation of the project's inadvisability, emboldening Albright to declare in his *Saturday Evening Post* article that "the thought of a road in this wild region is abhorrent to everybody who knows and loves that country." Insisting that Yellowstone had more roads than most motorists wanted or needed, he asserted, "It does not seem necessary even to think of any more."[35]

Despite these pronouncements, the NPS was unwilling to court controversy by dismissing it entirely. Officially, the road remained under consideration pending the availability of funds. To overcome this obstacle, Idaho politicians joined with other western delegations to pass a bill authorizing the expenditure of $1.5 million a year to construct access roads to national parks. The primary push for the 1931 legislation came from Montana, which had long pressured the Park Service to create a northeast entrance by collaborating with the USFS to construct a road across the Beartooth Mountains to Red Lodge. Albright protested the program in general and the northeast entrance in particular. Not only would the projects siphon resources from the seemingly endless task of improving the Grand Loop, but they would exacerbate the park's mounting traffic woes. Montana officials would not be denied, and it appeared that the long-delayed Bechler River Road would have to be built, as well. Other regional interests opposed the project, however. West Yellowstone was unwilling to relinquish its role as the primary western gateway. Wyoming interests also saw the road as a threat. Given the struggle to expand Grand Teton National Park, NPS officials were especially solicitous of the state's concerns. Citing the ongoing need to upgrade existing roads, NPS officials again deferred.[36]

When Depression-relief programs made the funding excuse untenable, agency officials finally abandoned all pretense that the road would be constructed. Proponents accused the NPS of reneging on its promises, but assertions that Mather and Albright had promised the road in exchange for support in the irrigation battles were met with disingenuous denials. In retirement, Albright was no longer circumspect about his opposition. Boasting that he had personally scuttled the Big Horn Pass proposal and held off the northeast entrance for seven years, he admitted to favoring road construction over reservoir development but insisted he had always viewed the Bechler proposal as an "invasion of a great wilderness area that should be preserved unspoiled." Echoing Leopold and other wilderness advocates, he conjoined "unnecessary roads" with dams and tunnels as intrusions that should be vigorously opposed.[37]

Balancing competing agendas was even more complicated at Mount Rainier. Not only was the park's road system avowedly incomplete, but NPS leaders were caught between traditional boosters and an increasingly assertive wilderness community. Tensions emerged when changing perceptions of the appropriate balance between preservation and access began to fragment the previously unified coalition of park advocates. NPS leaders had personal ties to both factions, but they were particularly indebted to the booster-dominated Seattle-Tacoma Rainier National Park Committee and its successor, the Rainier National Park Advisory Board, which had lobbied in favor of the agency's authorization and supported subsequent spending increases. Asahel Curtis, the brother of the noted photographer Edward Curtis, was the park's most outspoken advocate. Going against the board's wishes was both politically problematic and personally difficult, especially for Mather, who prized such relationships. Superintendent Owen Tomlinson's concern with improving park facilities also engendered an accommodating attitude toward road boosters and concessionaires. In addition to the usual chambers of commerce, auto clubs, and Rotarians, the board initially enjoyed the support of the Mountaineers and Mazamas, regional outing organizations that sought to improve access for hiking and climbing. The committee's 1912 founding statement expressed the shared goal of encircling Mount Rainier with a complementary system of roads and trails. The park's improvement was also advocated by broader organizations such as the Sierra Club and the American Automobile Association (AAA), which proclaimed, "It is manifest destiny that a motor road shall encircle this stupendous spectacle."[38]

The idea of a "Wonder Road" encircling the Mount Rainier massif had formed the basis of the park's development plan since it was proposed by Hiram Chittenden in 1907. In addition to showcasing scenic features in the manner of traditional park drives and Yellowstone's Grand Loop, the circuit could be combined with multiple access roads to benefit communities on all sides of the park. Selfish motives aside, most road advocates sincerely sought to make Mount Rainier's attractions more accessible to the American public. Mather shared this goal. His desire for others to experience the beauties he had first encountered on a 1905 Sierra Club trip to Mount Rainier coincided with his belief that the motorization of the park was essential to the agency's success. In addition to serving as the primary draw for the northwest quadrant of the Park-to-Park Highway, Mount Rainier's

Constructing a single-lane wagon road through the rugged terrain would have been challenging enough, but building a motor road to BPR standards would not only be enormously expensive but would have a dramatic impact on the park's scenery.

proximity to Seattle and Tacoma afforded an ideal opportunity to demonstrate the expanded role national parks could play in modern American life. In order for this to happen, the park's notoriously deficient main entrance had to be improved and new roads constructed to additional attractions, culminating in the encirclement of Mount Rainier with scenic motorways. The tourism interests that dominated the Advisory Board protested loudly when technical and economic considerations conjoined with preservationist agendas to threaten this vision. Constructing a single-lane wagon road through the rugged terrain would have been challenging enough, but building a motor road to BPR standards would not only be enormously expensive but would have a dramatic impact on the park's scenery. It would also intrude on areas a growing number of people sought to reserve for nonautomotive use. NPS officials had to negotiate these tensions while engaging in internal debates about the best means of adapting traditional park-making concepts to the automobile age.[39]

The first circuit road survey was conducted under the committee's auspices in 1913. Due to the extremely rugged terrain, the cost of this 80-mile "Wonder Road" was estimated at approximately $1 million. This was more than triple the previous investment in all national park roads combined, but boosters insisted it would "pay for itself" by attracting motorists from across the country. At the northwest corner of the park, a road along the Carbon River would provide a more direct link to Seattle. Another entrance would extend from the Nisqually Road across the south end of the park to its eastern border, improving access for transcontinental motorists and inland communities. The Office of Public Road's T. Warren Allen endorsed the ring road concept but advised that portions should be constructed beyond park boundaries, where they would be cheaper to build and open to traffic a greater portion of the year. This suggestion was seconded by USGS topographer Francois Matthes, who was enlisted to review the committee's alignment for a road across the south flank of Mount Rainier. Envisioning the scenic destruction that would attend road construction in the rugged terrain, he characterized the proposal as "a project against which I cannot counsel too strongly."[40]

Matthes raised additional questions about the impact of road building in the fragile alpine environment. In a 1913 statement constituting one of the earliest recorded objections to national

park road development, he warned that "a wagon road, be it ever so well laid really spoils forever the dainty flower-dotted slopes that are the principal charm of these high altitude parks." Not only did roads create "ugly yellow scars in the landscape," but they initiated intractable erosion. Matthes pointed to the sprawling Paradise Park campground as additional evidence of the dangers of ill-conceived road development. Since the road ran straight through the meadows, the celebrated scenery had been overrun by automobile tourists to the detriment of the environment and the park experience. The sensible solution would have been to stop the road at the beginning of the meadow and encourage visitors to proceed on foot, or at least run it along the edge of the trees. The fate of the formerly pristine valley demonstrated that park roads should lead to scenic splendors, not through them. Matthes also noted that Mount Rainier's rugged flanks posed formidable obstacles to road construction. On practical as well as philosophical grounds, the wisest approach would be to improve the Nisqually entrance and construct stub roads to key destinations. Even these should be restricted to lower elevations where forest growth would conceal their presence. Matthes's observations were not only ahead of their time, but in direct conflict with local boosters' desires and the National Park Service's strategy of courting the motoring public.[41]

While Matthes's concerns would be revisited as the impacts of automobile tourism became more widely apparent, the NPS's initial problem was to fend off complaints that it was doing too little to make Mount Rainier accessible to American motorists. Budget limitations forced the NPS to concentrate on the Nisqually entrance, but agency officials reiterated their commitment to the around-the-mountain road. NPS officials agreed with the Advisory Board that first step was to construct a first-class road circling the west side of the mountain from the Nisqually entrance to the proposed Carbon River Road. Since the state was making rapid progress on a highway from Seattle across the Cascades to Yakima that would provide access to the park's northeast quadrant, the West Side Road would satisfy demands for better access from the Puget Sound cities that dominated the Advisory Board. Work on the West Side Road could not begin until the Carbon River Road was completed, however, and progress was slowed by NPS funding shortages and lack of cooperation from the USFS

National Park Roads

and neighboring Pierce County, which had agreed to construct the required road to the park border. Residents of the agricultural region were more concerned with improving utilitarian roadways than building a recreational drive for the benefit of tourists and big-city entrepreneurs. With the state highway nearing an old mining road along the White River in the northeast corner of the park that the NPS planned to upgrade to facilitate development of a new visitor center at Yakima Park, West Side Road proponents feared their project would be sidelined and the locus of tourism shifted to the other side of the park. The Tacoma Chamber of Commerce proclaimed that delaying the West Side Road would be "little less than a calamity." Rainier National Park Company officials insisted the road was needed to relieve congestion, open new areas for public enjoyment, and enable visitors to tour the park without retracing their route. As the first link in the around-the-mountain circuit, moreover, the West Side Road would "give the park a new dignity and a bigger importance in the public mind." Dead-end roads like the White River project might satisfy local demands, but a Yellowstone-style circuit would transform Mount Rainier from a regional attraction into a national destination.[42]

Mather sent Cammerer to reconcile the feuding factions in May 1925. The Advisory Board, chambers of commerce, and Mountaineers drafted a resolution reaffirming that the "ultimate object" remained the construction of a road encircling Mount Rainier. The West Side Road was cast as the immediate priority, followed by the White River entrance and surveys for roads across the north and south ends of the park. The Forest Service and Pierce County agreed to honor their commitments. Cammerer expressed surprise that the Mountaineers had proved so agreeable. The organization had grown increasingly critical of NPS policies, accusing the agency of prioritizing development over preservation. After enjoying "a little smoker and chat" with key members, he assured Mather that the group's leaders sympathized with the agency's need to cultivate broad-based support. Although the Mountaineers endorsed the resolution, they recommended that certain areas be declared off-limits to development. Justifying their decision to more radical members, club leaders drew a distinction between approving the West Side Road and endorsing the broader development

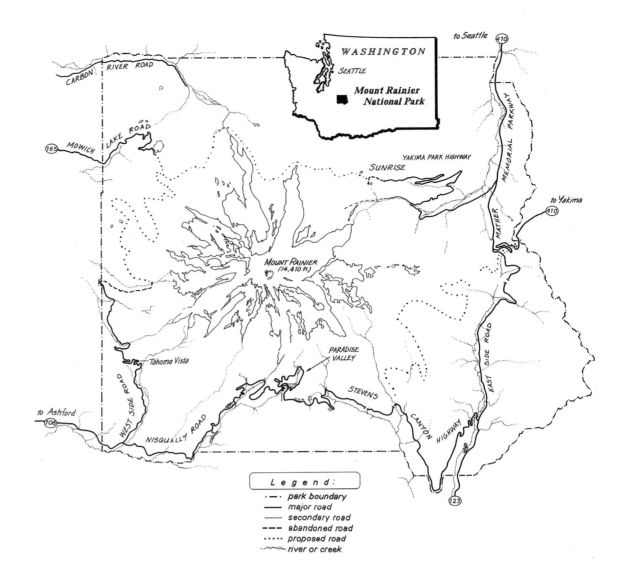

program. Conceding on the West Side Road would make it easier to oppose road construction across the park's northern tier, which contained even more spectacular terrain.[43]

With the construction sequence settled and approach roads nearing completion, pro-road forces pressured the Park Service to fulfill its part of the bargain. The Advisory Board circulated a brochure accusing federal authorities of neglecting their duty. While other parks of comparable size had hundreds of miles of roads showcasing their wonders, Mount Rainier's paltry 24-mile road system restricted visitors to a mere 10 percent of the park. A map entitled "Roads that Are, and Are Not" contrasted the network of state and local highways ringing the park with the abbreviated stubs within. Dotted lines representing the projected West Side and South Side Roads underscored the NPS's empty promises. According to the Advisory Board, state, local, and USFS authorities had invested $7.5 million to surround the park with modern motorways, while only $300,000 had been spent on road construction

within the park since its authorization. The back page contained a form letter for recipients to send their congressmen, invoking the NPS's unfulfilled promises and demanding the agency contribute its share toward making the park's glories accessible to the American public.[44]

Funding was not the only obstacle. As in Yellowstone, perspectives on the appropriate balance between preservation and access began to shift in the mid-1920s, both within the agency and in the broader conservation community. Internally, questions were initially raised in the traditional terms of scenic impact. The BPR's West Side Road survey might have been an improvement over Goodwin's scheme, but when Vint inspected the terrain in August 1925, he warned that any attempt at extending the Carbon River Road south over Ipsut Pass would result in "an extremely visible example of extravagant road construction, destroying one of the landscape views the Park Service was bringing people into the park to see." The BPR agreed to investigate an alternate route that departed from the Carbon River Road beyond the park border and proceeded through somewhat less challenging terrain toward Mowich Lake and Spray Park, scenic showpieces that had long been considered highlights of the western portion of the proposed circuit. To placate West Side Road advocates, the NPS initiated construction on the south end of the project, where conditions were more forgiving. As in other parks, the switch to BPR standards made the work more difficult and expensive, rapidly exhausting the original appropriations. Dissatisfied with the rate of progress, Advisory Board members appealed directly to House Appropriations Committee chairman Louis Cramton, bringing additional pressure to bear on park officials. To demonstrate the NPS's commitment, Albright included a major request for West Side Road funds in the second park roads bill. The proposed road across the north side of the park was quietly omitted, signifying the agency's conclusion that completing the circuit within park boundaries was neither feasible nor desirable. Not only had Vint and Superintendent Owen Tomlinson concluded that constructing a road through the region would be even more destructive to scenic values, but the state highway beyond park borders made it unnecessary to intrude on an area prized for its pristine beauty and sense of isolation. In August 1928 Mather announced that the north side of the park and several other remote regions would be managed as "wilderness areas free from roads, hotels, pay camps, and other commercial developments."[45]

Mather's declaration was embraced by the Mountaineers and generated minimal objection from pro-development forces, but the debate was far from over. NPS officials were again caught between competing agendas when the Rainier National Park Company proposed constructing a scenic loop around the ridge above Paradise Valley. The concessionaire employed the usual arguments about making attractions accessible to the elderly and unfit and even offered to share the cost of construction. Company officials maintained that the patronage generated by the excursion was needed to justify improvements it was implementing at the NPS's behest. The Advisory Board advanced the concessionaire's case, while the Mountaineers were outraged at the prospect of defacing one of the park's premier vistas. NPS opinion was initially mixed. Tomlinson favored the road, sympathizing with

the concessionaire's arguments and noting that Ricksecker's original plan called for construction along similar lines. Vint objected on scenic and practical grounds. Albright initially endorsed the proposal but suggested it be designed as a narrow one-way track to reduce costs and scenic damage. The BPR was authorized to make preliminary surveys in 1927, examining alternatives ranging from a single-width track with 8 percent grades to a two-lane road constructed to prevailing standards. Even the engineers considered the project undesirable since it would be extraordinarily expensive, exposed to dangerous rockslides, and snowbound most of the year. Vint and Mather examined the situation in 1928 and concluded the road would cause unacceptable scenic damage. The Advisory Board again sought Cramton's support. The congressman generally went along with Mather and Albright's recommendations, but in this case he prevailed on them to have the BPR develop more detailed plans. The BPR got as far as staking a final line in 1931, but NPS officials staved off further action by citing funding shortages and the need to focus on major access roads. The company also sought permission for an aerial tramway to provide winter access to Paradise Valley when the Nisqually Road was impassable. Mather embraced the idea of making Mount Rainier a year-round destination with winter sports facilities, but he insisted on the need for careful review. The Mountaineers endorsed the tramway proposal in 1929, enamored by the prospect of improved access for skiing and other activities. Tomlinson supported the concessionaire's position, but Vint and Albright were adamantly opposed. Albright avoided controversy with his usual delaying tactics, but Cammerer officially rejected the proposal in 1934.[46]

Determining the route for the south side road exposed rifts within the NPS along with the ongoing conflict between development and preservation interests. Between 1926 and 1931 the NPS and BPR explored several alternatives for connecting the Nisqually Road with the state highway on the east side of the park. The debate came down to whether the road should be built along a "low line" descending through Stevens Canyon, or an "upper line" crossing the head of the canyon and circling the mountain at a higher elevation. Although the upper line afforded more spectacular views, it would be significantly more expensive to construct. More importantly, it

would have an enormously destructive impact on the fragile terrain and encroach more deeply into areas the Mountaineers, Sierra Club, and NPS landscape architects sought to keep free from automobiles and other artificial intrusions. Tomlinson and Kittredge, who preferred the upper line, countered that both routes entailed significant scarring and maintained that the educational value of providing motorists with close-up views of glaciers and other alpine features justified the intrusion. The Advisory Board strongly supported the upper line on the grounds that it would increase the park's appeal by enabling the general public to enjoy areas known only to ardent mountaineers. Albright made a trip to the park in July 1931 to resolve the issue. After three days of inspecting the terrain with Vint, Kittredge, Tomlinson, BPR engineers, and Rainier National Park Company representatives, he decided that the lower line was more consistent with NPS landscape preservation principles. Although some historians have presented Albright's decision as a broader rejection of the engineering office's influence, Kittredge continued commenting on road plans and conducting studies of sensitive projects throughout Albright's directorship. Many of his recommendations were more preservation-oriented than those of his colleagues, and he became a staunch advocate of wilderness area designation within national parks. His standing in the conservation community resulted in his election to the Sierra Club's board of directors upon his retirement from the NPS.[47]

While Albright's ruling may not have put an end to intra-agency disputes, it represented a significant victory for the Mountaineers, who had grown increasingly assertive in their efforts to limit road construction. Despite the organization's endorsement of the park's general development scheme, dissident members had continued to express their opposition. In one of the attacks that prompted Albright's "Everlasting Wilderness" article, club member George Vanderbilt Caesar condemned "excessive road-building programs within the confines of national parks." The Mount Rainier situation was alluded to in his denunciation of the agency's eagerness to "encircle the wilderness with roads." In a striking demonstration of the NPS's intimate relationship with the park's Advisory Board, Asahel Curtis offered to submit a ghost-written article affirming the agency's commitment to preservation. Tomlinson and Kittredge worked up a draft, the gist of which would be incorporated in Albright's article when it was decided that the rebuttal should come directly from the NPS and address issues beyond Mount Rainier. Their main argument was that only a small fraction of the park was impacted by road construction. With a projected 114 miles of roadway, it might sound like Mount Rainier was being overdeveloped, but according to NPS figures the affected area amounted to less than a third of the park's 325 square miles. Kittredge insisted that "the best areas and plenty of them will always be reserved for those who want the untouched wilderness." According to Tomlinson, one could stop anywhere in the park and "by walking one quarter mile away from the highway find himself in absolutely undisturbed natural surroundings" that were bound to "satisfy the most ardent nature lover."[48]

The Mountaineers, as it turned out, were far from satisfied. Arguing that less than a quarter of the park would remain wilderness if the NPS carried out its plans, the organization called for a drastic reduction in road construction and official designation of the northern section of the park as a wilderness area off-limits to development. While the latter proposal received Mather's endorsement, the agency had to contend with equally ardent efforts by the Advisory Board and local chambers of commerce to compel completion of the West Side Road. Several miles were added to the stub heading north from the Nisqually Road in the early 1930s, affording access to scenic turnouts where visitors could enjoy impressive views of Mount Rainier. The final section of this stub entailed the construction of a monumental timber trestle across the North Fork of the Puyallup River. Flooding, rockslides, and other maintenance issues caused the NPS to abandon the segment and remove the bridge in the 1960s. At the north end, a rough road was extended to Mowich Lake, which NPS officials considered a worthy terminus. In response to renewed agitation in April 1935, NPS landscape architect Ernest Davidson expanded on Vint's critique. Since the South Side Road provided access to similar scenery, Davidson maintained that completing both roadways would be "overdoing the highway development of Mt. Rainier, to the definite detriment of National Park scenic and wilderness values." While Tomlinson had long shared the Advisory Board's preference for

ABOVE Constructing timber trestle over North Fork of Puyallup River on final segment of West Side Road, Mount Rainier National Park, ca. 1934.

ABOVE Bird's-eye view of Yosemite Valley and environs from *The Yosemite Trip Book* (1938).

through-roads over dead-end stubs, Davidson dismissed the argument that declining to connect the two ends would impair visitors' enjoyment of the park. "Instead of simply buzzing along over the connected road and perhaps never stopping the auto," he countered, "it will compel tourists to stop, get out of their autos, and spend some time at the road termini." Citing the high cost of construction and "inevitable destruction and desecration incidental to highway construction," Davidson advised that plans to complete the West Side Road be abandoned "as a matter of preservation of Park values and economy." The Advisory Board made periodic attempts to revive the project, but by the mid-1930s the growing influence of wilderness advocates outweighed boosters' demands for increased access. In July 1935 NPS director Cammerer acknowledged that the West Side Road had been a politically motivated mistake. Three years later Interior Secretary Ickes declared that the completion

of the South Side road would mark the end of road construction in Mount Rainer. Praising the secretary's action, Tomlinson observed that the announcement would be "most helpful in resisting local pressure by groups who demand additional roads." Reaffirming NPS opposition to the proposed tramway and other attempts to expand access beyond existing commitments in 1941, NPS director Newton Drury proclaimed: "Large amounts of money have been expanded at Mount Rainier National Park in developing roads that will make the park reasonably accessible. We believe that to penetrate further the remaining wilderness will violate the main purpose for which the park was set aside for this and future generations to enjoy."[49]

Contemporary deliberations about road development in Yosemite National Park were equally significant, though they have received less historical scrutiny. By modifying and even abandoning well-established plans, the NPS exhibited rarely

acknowledged flexibility along with a firm commitment to working with conservation groups to find mutually agreeable solutions. These negotiations were aided by the long-standing personal relationships between NPS officials and Sierra Club leaders. Both Mather and Albright were native Californians who had participated in club activities before coming to Washington. The club's most outspoken leader, William Colby, mentored Albright in law school and encouraged him to apply for his position, facilitated Mather's Tioga Road purchase, and assisted in the development of the Lane Letter and other key statements. While later critics complained such cozy relationships made the club's leaders too conciliatory, they did not hesitate to express their objections and exerted significant influence on NPS policy. Both sides believed it was better to work out their differences through private collaboration rather than public confrontation. As in Yellowstone and Mount Rainier, moreover, opinions within the NPS were changing as the impacts of increased automobile tourism became more apparent. While Sierra Club sentiments were often one step ahead, NPS officials generally followed suit. Road proposals that once appeared desirable, or at least unavoidable, were questioned, qualified, and in some cases abandoned. Similar patterns applied to road building in other California parks.[50]

Since the turn of the twentieth century, it had been an article of faith that a road out the east end of Yosemite Valley would have to be constructed to reduce crowding and provide better access to the High Sierra region than was afforded by the roundabout route over the tortuous Tioga Road. One or more roads around the rim of the valley were also projected. In addition to dispersing the crowds that had already begun to diminish the valley's appeal, these drives would afford outstanding views and expose visitors to expanses of scenery enjoyed by only the hardiest adventurers. Constructing a road through one of the canyons at the east end of the valley would also benefit communities on the far side of the park and facilitate travel to the Lake Tahoe region. Hiram Chittenden was among the earliest advocates of this plan, which was endorsed by the Office of Public Roads' T. Warren Allen, the USGS's Robert Marshall, Mather, and other NPS officials. John Muir called for a grand circuit leading up Little Yosemite Valley, crossing over to Tuolumne Canyon and then looping back by means of Hetch Hetchy Valley and the Big Oak Flat Road. Such a tour would provide access to expanses of spectacular scenery that would otherwise remain unknown and unappreciated. While the Hetchy Reservoir put an end to such grand speculations, the Sierra Club embraced the idea of constructing additional roads out of the valley, as did the American Society of Landscape Architects, whose representative, Warren Manning, suggested that an old inclined logging railroad near El Portal could be utilized to raise cars to the canyon rim. Manning extolled the advantages of locating campsites in the cool highlands around the valley's rim, but others noted that snow lingered so long at the higher elevations that neither the roads nor the campgrounds would be accessible until the tourist season was well under way.[51]

Leaving the question of rim roads for future discussion, Goodwin's forces made a preliminary survey for a road connecting Yosemite Valley with the Tioga Road near Tenaya Lake. The route passed Vernal and Nevada Falls at the head of the valley, followed the Merced River into Little Yosemite Valley, and then crossed a saddle to Tenaya Creek, following the watercourse to its source. Mather assured that the NPS would take great precautions to protect the sacred scenery at the head of the valley. Sierra Club secretary William Colby heartily endorsed Goodwin's route in 1919, as did fellow founding member Joe LeConte. Colby was enthusiastic about the prospect of improving access to the Sierra High Country and Tuolumne Canyon, a longtime goal of John Muir that was reflected in the club's charter. He raised concerns about certain details, such as the location of a tunnel designed to reduce the road's impact near Vernal Falls, and emphasized the importance of working closely with qualified landscape architects. If these precautions were taken, he proclaimed, it would become "one of the greatest scenic roads in the world."[52]

The Sierra Club's support soon wavered, threatening to create a rift between the NPS and one of its closest allies. At the 1923 NPS Superintendents' Conference, Colby announced that when he initially considered the proposal, he was so focused on the need to relieve congestion and provide access to the High Sierra that he failed to give full weight to the road's scenic implications. Upon further review, he realized that the road would be so conspicuous that it would not only ruin the view from Glacier Point and other points in the valley but also compromise the scenic quality of the canyons through which it passed. Observing that "the fundamental principle in the matter of national parks is to preserve scenery as far as possible," he asserted: "We would be violating most grievously this principle should the road be built up the canyon." Colby's choice of pronouns was significant. Not only was he personally close to NPS officials, but he viewed the Sierra Club as the agency's ally against external critics, not as an adversary itself. If the NPS carried through with the plan, Colby warned, it would sacrifice the agency's hard-earned reputation for an ill-advised scheme that was unlikely to afford more than temporary relief. Underscoring that he was not opposed to the idea in principle, just the chosen routing, he suggested an alternative alignment that followed the existing Pohono Trail, passing behind Glacier Point before swinging around to Nevada Falls.

This would eliminate the most egregious scar in the main valley. Colby also suggested the agency revisit the idea of building roads around the rim of the valley, which would allow for the development of additional campgrounds near the scenery the public expected to see.[53]

Colby's comments created considerable consternation. Despite his professed desire to avoid public criticism, newspapers throughout California reported the objections. The negative publicity was particularly troubling because agency leaders were conflicted about the project themselves. Cammerer made no secret of his distaste, begrudgingly accepting it as "the lesser of two evils" when compared with the prospect of Yosemite Valley being overwhelmed by "a horde of humanity seeking to get rest and recreation and finding neither." The road might offend landscape aesthetes, but the latter would give the park system "a black eye from which it will be hard to recover." Albright implored the sympathetic *Stockton Record* to set the record straight by explaining that the NPS had yet to reach a decision and presenting Colby's comments as part of an open-ended discussion of congestion problems in Yosemite Valley. Other options included an alternative alignment following the Little Yosemite Valley past Merced Lake, a road swinging back around Glacier Point along the lines suggested by Colby, and reconstruction of the Big Oak Flat and Tioga Roads to improve access to the higher country along existing routes. Albright made it clear that the NPS was eager to hear from Colby and his associates, proclaiming that the agency "would not want to be put in the position before the public of having advocated a project in Yosemite Park that was distasteful to the Sierra Club."[54]

Albright was intent on damage control, but the NPS genuinely sought the Sierra Club's approval. Cammerer reached out to Colby, underscoring the personal and professional ties between the two organizations and soliciting the club's advice. He also pointed out that the agency's immediate concern was improving the existing entrances. The contested proposal was simply a means of ensuring that funds for additional study were included in the park roads bill. This soothed Sierra Club leaders, who agreed to let the matter rest until the situation developed further.[55]

The opening of the All-Year Highway focused renewed attention on Yosemite's congestion problems. Nearly a half million people entered the park in 1927, almost twice the previous year's total and quadruple the number of 1924 visitors. More than ten thousand arrived on Memorial Day alone, creating massive traffic jams and swelling the single-day count in the valley to a then-record twenty-five thousand. For the NPS, this was evidence that extraordinary measures were required, including reconsideration of the controversial roadway. The Sierra Club saw things differently. Sierra Club president Walter Huber, a civil engineer and road builder himself, insisted the club pass a resolution condemning the proposed route. Robert Yard entered the fray, inciting the NPS's ire with a *National Parks Bulletin* editorial headlined "Needless Road Project Endangers Yosemite." In keeping with his philosophy of constraining visitors within existing limits, Yard maintained the NPS should consign the main valley to its fate as "the Asbury Park of the altitudes" rather than allow pristine scenery to be "sacrificed on the altar of Gasoline."[56]

In 1928 the NPS established the Yosemite Board of Expert Advisors to provide external counsel on the road controversy and other sensitive matters. Agency officials sought to avoid accusations of acting unilaterally, but they genuinely welcomed such consultations, especially when conducted by longtime associates. In addition to generating valuable advice, independent reports by recognized experts provided political cover for potentially controversial decisions. Frederick Law Olmsted Jr. was persuaded to serve on the initial board, along with current Sierra Club president Duncan McDuffie and John P. Buwalda, chairman of the Geology Department at Caltech. Buwalda was a protégé of the prominent conservationist John C. Merriam, who also contributed to the debate. Merriam agreed that the road would be conspicuous but noted that opinions varied about the visual implications of park roads. Those who believed the NPS's mission was to encourage the public to experience America's natural wonders "might deem a properly constructed road an addition to the attractions of the canyon, because it brought thousands to see its beauty." At this juncture, the route under consideration would be an extension of a proposed relocation of the existing road to Glacier Point, leaving the Wawona Road near old Inspiration Point and running closer to the rim of the valley to afford better views and eliminate steep grades and hazardous turns of the historic alignment. Following Colby's suggestion, it would drop down to Nevada Falls, extend up Little Yosemite Valley, and cross over Tuolumne Pass. While the

primary goal was to relieve congestion in the main valley and improve access to the Tuolumne region, this arrangement would allow for the construction of additional tourist facilities at Merced Lake and other locations if increased crowding made such developments necessary. Both Sierra Club leaders and NPS officials continued to express ambivalence about the prospect. As with the previous proposal, including the project in the second park road program was considered a budgetary maneuver rather than a definitive endorsement.[57]

Due to the politically sensitive nature of the situation, the Department of the Interior assigned its own representative to investigate the project's viability. In the meantime, NPS officials sought to fend off an even more radical proposal for addressing Yosemite Valley's congestion problems. The Yosemite Park and Curry Company was pushing for the construction of a cableway from the valley floor to its hotel on Glacier Point. The company insisted the novel excursion was needed to help the money-losing lodge turn a profit, claiming it would increase patronage and permit year-round operation. It would also benefit the NPS by reducing traffic on the Wawona Road and encouraging the development of additional accommodations on the southern rim. As a further incentive, it would eliminate the need to improve the existing Glacier Point Road, which should be closed to prevent competition with the company's investment. The cableway had the support of the *Los Angeles Times'* Harry Chandler and other prominent businessmen, who lobbied Hoover and Interior Secretary Ray Lyman Wilbur to authorize the project. Noting that such conveniences were common in Europe, Chandler touted the public benefit of replacing the laborious three-hour drive with an effortless seven-minute ascent. Colby suggested an even more ambitious approach: hollowing out a tunnel within the granite walls for a mechanical lift along the lines of Switzerland's Jungfrau railway. Mather was enthused by the idea of attaining the desired results without marring the storied scenery, but the technical and economic considerations were too daunting.[58]

The company prepared a formal application in October 1930, offering to pay for the project itself. Since Yosemite Park and Curry Company president Donald Tressider wanted to maintain good relationships with the NPS and the conservation community, he asked NPS officials to give it a preliminary review. If the agency's experts concluded that

the cableway would do more harm than good, he would table the submission. Both sides were eager to avoid a public dispute that would cast the plan's advocates as rapacious scenery despoilers or make it seem like the Park Service and Sierra Club sought to constrain access to the park.[59]

Albright asked Vint, Superintendent Thomson, and the Advisory Board to present their opinions on the proposal's practical merit and impact on park values. Their first observation was that the cableway was likely to increase congestion rather than reduce it. Not only was its novelty bound to attract additional visitors—and for the sort of nonpark purposes critics condemned—but it would require additional parking areas and support buildings in the most sensitive part of the park. While cableway advocates made much of the supposed savings in automobile fees and gasoline costs, the economies would only be realized by singles and couples. The more common parties of four or more would pay more than if they drove themselves. The cableway's value in ensuring the company's profitability was also questioned. Reducing a full-day's outing to a quick excursion would lower the number of overnight guests, unless the concessionaire was allowed to provide the gratuitous entertainments the NPS was under fire to eliminate. Thomson cast the cableway itself as an inappropriate attraction, proclaiming that "a longitudinal merry-go-round" had no place in a national park. While it might provide a momentary thrill, comparing a high-speed tram to a well-designed park road was like equating "a minstrel show to a grand opera." There was also no guarantee the public would embrace tramways in the same manner as their European brethren, who were accustomed to public transportation and heavily developed tourist sites. According to Thomson, the question came down to whether a road or a cableway was a more appropriate means of providing access to national park scenery. Roads had been considered integral components of park landscapes for centuries and Americans had clearly embraced automobiles as their favored means of locomotion. One could argue that a cableway's support structure had a smaller physical footprint, but in terms of visual impact and cultural expectations, the road clearly came out ahead. "A road is a normal thing," Thomson asserted, "the logical response to a universal demand."[60]

NPS officials and Advisory Board members maintained that the fundamental objection to the cableway was that "artificial conveyances" and "mechanical features" did not belong in national parks. As a conspicuous example of "man's mastery over nature," Vint protested, "its presence does not preserve for future generations the Glacier Point John Muir knew." No amount of careful placement could prevent the steel towers, gondolas, and cables from standing out as technological intrusions in Yosemite's timeless landscape. The assault was aural as well as visual. Condemning the cableway as "a bizarre distraction from the supreme dignity of the spectacle," Thomson protested, "the hum of machinery, combined with the laughter and shouts of the aerial voyageurs, would introduce a disturbing element into that peace which has pervaded that lofty and compact area." He maintained that the tramway would make the ascent so quick and easy that visitors would no longer appreciate the significance of the climb. While roads and automobiles would seemingly be subject to the same objections, such statements underscored the degree to which automotive transport had been naturalized within the NPS realm, both literally and figuratively. Approving the Glacier Point tramway would also set a dangerous precedent. If the project were approved, the NPS would be hard-pressed to deny similar proposals, either elsewhere in the valley or in other national parks. It would also add fuel to arguments that the agency was more interested in coddling concessionaires than preserving park values. When Albright outlined the practical, political, and philosophical objections, Tressider honored his commitment and shelved the application.[61]

With the cableway issue settled, it was time for the NPS to come to terms with the controversial Tenaya Road proposal. The Sierra Club remained opposed to the original routing but suggested an alternative alignment passing between Mirror Lake and Half Dome and heading directly up Tenaya Canyon. The construction problems would be even more challenging, but the scenery was outstanding and Little Yosemite Valley and the upper Merced Canyon would remain inviolate. Mather had looked favorably on this possibility, but NPS officials were increasingly skeptical that the benefits of a road out the east end of the valley would outweigh the cost in scenic values. Revisions to parking and circulation arrangements had significantly reduced traffic congestion and eased the overall sense of crowding. In addition, the surge associated with the All-Year Highway was followed by five years of relatively flat growth, contravening assumptions that exponential increases were inevitable. While visitation was bound to increase, there was growing confidence that modernizing the existing approaches could accommodate growth for the foreseeable future. This view was not shared by the state's tourism industry and communities east of the park, who maintained that the long-promised road would better serve their interests. The Interior Department's special investigator also touted the practical advantages of the plan.[62]

ABOVE Proposed Tenaya Road route, Yosemite National Park, 1932 Kittredge report.

Determined to make a stand, Thomson called on Kittredge to prepare a definitive analysis. This was ostensibly a matter for Vint's attention, but Thomson insisted Kittredge's word carried greater weight with outside parties. Kittredge and his assistant Walter Attwell studied a number of potential routes, presenting their findings in August 1933. Every alternative entailed heavy construction, including extensive blasting, tunnels, massive retaining walls, and snow sheds to protect motorists from avalanches and rockfall. Given the steepness of the terrain, it was impossible to avoid multiple switchbacks, some of which might have to be enclosed in tunnels for safety and scenic preservation. It would be far and away the most expensive road yet attempted, dwarfing the cost of Going-to-the-Sun Road and the Zion tunnel. On the other hand, all the options afforded extraordinary views. The canyons, cliffs, and granite domes extending eastward from Yosemite Valley were not just visually stunning but scientifically significant. Motorists would encounter textbook glacial moraines and drive through "acres of perfect glacier polish," affording unprecedented exposure to the natural forces that shaped the park. Kittredge portrayed the scenic and scientific attractions in a

series of striking of black-and-white photographs. Equally sensational were the implications of road development in such spectacular terrain, which he conveyed through the inked-in alignments that had become a hallmark of NPS location studies. In this case, the enthusiastic comments of Kittredge's Going-to-the-Sun Road report gave way to stark admonitions. The NPS and BPR were certainly capable of constructing a road along one of the proposed routes, Kittredge observed, but "only at a tremendous sacrifice of the natural landscape." Given the inordinate scenic damage, he declared, "The Tenaya Canyon should never be occupied by a highway." Albright, Cammerer, and Demaray quickly concurred, as did Vint and the Sierra Club. Pro-development groups sought to revive the project, but Albright refused to budge, closing the books on a proposal that would have been far more destructive of Yosemite's natural splendor than any road proposed before or since.[63]

This largely forgotten decision set the stage for the debates over reconstruction of the Tioga Road, which were settled amicably in the 1930s but erupted into a major controversy in the postwar era. At the time, however, the NPS and Sierra Club agreed that upgrading the existing

roadway was infinitely preferable to the desecration of Tenaya Canyon or Little Yosemite Valley. After the initial rehabilitation sparked by Mather's acquisition, the Tioga Road had received little more than cursory maintenance and occasional minor upgrades. By the late 1920s, deteriorating conditions and increasing traffic prompted the NPS to consider comprehensive improvements. While Kittredge and the BPR contemplated modest revisions to the road's grade and alignment, Thomson and the landscape architects advocated a more ambitious relocation. Contending that the scenery along the current route was uninspiring and visitors deserved to be treated to the best views possible, Thomson, Vint, and NPS landscape architect John Wosky suggested the middle section be radically revised. Their proposal, dubbed the "High Line," would swing west from the old road on the far side of Tenaya Lake, climbing toward a remote and rugged region known as the Ten Lakes Basin, skirting the rim of Tuolumne Canyon, and passing high on the flanks of several peaks before rejoining the existing road 2 miles west of Tuolumne Meadows. Much of the route lay above 9,000 feet, with several stretches even higher. In addition to affording spectacular views of Yosemite's high country, the High Line would achieve the long-sought goal of providing convenient access to the dramatic scenery of Tuolumne Canyon. Thomson insisted reasonable grades could be secured without undue damage and maintained that the expense, though significantly higher, was justified by the opportunity to expose visitors to unmatched scenic splendor. Albright was enthusiastic, though he had yet to inspect the route in person. By June 1933 Thomson and Vint were eager to proceed, but resistance arose from multiple quarters.[64]

The BPR was predictably opposed. Not only would the High Line cost considerably more, but lingering snows would limit the road's availability to two or three months at the height of summer. In addition to constraining its function as a tour road, the abbreviated season would compromise its role as a trans-Sierra route for utilitarian traffic. The implications extended beyond park borders since the state and Forest Service were unlikely to proceed with plans to modernize the roads on either end if the intervening section was rarely open and designed with the reduced standards mandated by the challenging location. These concerns caused the engineers to raise the

ABOVE Sierra Club board member Walter Huber inspecting proposed Tioga Road High Line route, Yosemite National Park, 1933.

rarely cited provision of the NPS-BPR agreement directing the bureau to ensure that through-routes harmonized with plans for the Federal Aid Highway System. If the NPS insisted on the High Line, BPR engineers maintained, the existing road would still have to be upgraded to serve through traffic and off-season visitors. Kittredge raised similar pragmatic objections but also addressed scenic concerns. While the High Line undoubtedly afforded access to more spectacular scenery, the terrain was so rugged that it could not be constructed without extensive scarring. It would also intrude on an area that was highly prized for its pristine beauty and isolation. Reversing roles from the Mount Rainier Stevens Canyon debate, he remonstrated, "Often the construction of a road through an unusually beautiful or superb area, by its very presence lessens or partially spoils the feeling of beauty or grandeur or sacredness for which the road is built."[65]

The BPR's response was expected, but Kittredge's comments exasperated NPS colleagues, especially since he had not inspected the route and issued his objections after the landscape architects and superintendent had come to agreement. Even Albright was irked, though the target of his irritation shifted when he discovered that neither the Sierra Club nor the Advisory Board had been apprised of the plan. Albright was astounded that Thomson and Vint would consider authorizing a road through the heart of Yosemite's backcountry without consulting club officials. Not only was the decision highly impolitic, but Albright felt personally accountable to Colby and his colleagues, who, he reminded Thomson, had been intimately associated with Yosemite affairs before the NPS had arrived on the scene. Thomson appeared to resent the club's privileged position, suggesting that auto clubs should be consulted to provide a balanced perspective, but he followed Albright's injunction to reach out to club leaders. This soothed the tension, but Albright and Colby recognized that relationships between the club and the NPS were changing. Not only would Albright's imminent retirement sunder the bonds of friendship that united the organizations, but the increasing professionalization of park affairs produced a more formal and potentially adversarial relationship. Albright assured Colby the NPS would continue to seek the club's input, but he noted with unalloyed pride that the agency had developed "a trained body of landscape engineers and architects who are doing a splendid job of protecting national park landscape values."[66]

Albright promised to refrain from making a decision until the club's directors could examine the proposed route. Thomson arranged for Colby, Francis Farquhar, and Duncan McDuffie to inspect the route accompanied by a BPR engineer and NPS landscape architect. Huber and Kittredge made a similar trip shortly thereafter. Buoyed by both groups' enthusiastic responses to the scenic opportunities, Thomson expressed confidence that an endorsement would soon ensue. When the club's board of directors met in December 1933, however, they ruled unanimously in favor of reconstructing the Tioga Road along the general location of the existing route. While the High Line would enable visitors to experience some of the park's most spectacular landscapes with unprecedented ease, the practical and philosophical objections were overwhelming. In addition to the scenic damage, the High Line would intrude on one of the most unspoiled areas of the park. If the existing route was not already established so that both options entailed similar disruptions, then the benefits of providing access to superlative scenery might outweigh the drawbacks, but there was no justification for making additional inroads "into the wild portions of the park." They also echoed the BPR's comments about the route's practical shortcomings. From the club's perspective, it was essential that the Tioga Road be open as long as possible to afford access to the region's scenery, trails, and campsites. The lower location's utilitarian value would also ward against agitation for a direct eastern exit from Yosemite Valley.[67]

Vint was clearly disappointed, but Cammerer and even Thomson appeared relieved by the ruling. Having succeeded Albright as director in August 1933, Cammerer let it be known that the High Line was no longer under consideration, citing the Sierra Club's ruling as the deciding factor. Thomson's account of the deliberations leading to his change of heart constituted such an eloquent expression of the philosophical challenges of park road development that they generated praise from NPS colleagues, Sierra Club leaders, and BPR engineers alike. While he insisted the High Line would not have been as expensive or impractical as claimed, he observed that the decision hinged not on technical concerns but on the propriety of constructing a major road through a pristine wilderness area. It was hard to imagine a better illustration of the tension between preservation and access. No one could deny that the High Line would expose millions of visitors to aspects of Yosemite's beauty they would not otherwise experience, but this benefit had to be weighed against "the terrific impact of a modern highway upon so large an area of unsullied splendor." Not only did roads create lasting scars despite the NPS's best efforts, but they spawned associated developments that further eroded wilderness values. It was not only wilderness enthusiasts who suffered, Thomson maintained, but motorists themselves, who became inured to nature's glories when they were attained too easily. Yet it was also true that the American public had demonstrated its preference for motor travel and park managers needed to deal with realities, not mystical ideals. Given the public demand for automotive access, it was easy to understand the engineer's perspective that it was "the duty and the privilege of the road-builder to bring as much glory into the lives of road users as possible." These were noble sentiments with which the NPS had considerable sympathy, but the agency's dual mandate demanded that the urge to provide access be tempered by the commitment to preservation. In many cases there were no easy answers, and reasonable people could disagree about where the lines should be drawn. Thomson admitted to having gone back and forth over the issue, reaching a decision, regretting it, and reevaluating the situation anew. He was initially swayed by the desire to share the region's beauties with as many visitors as possible, but, in the final analysis, he had come to favor the lower route. The High Line was clearly the most scenic option, but it entailed "violating a virgin area," whereas rebuilding the existing road would confine the impact to a corridor that had served as a transportation route for half a century. The cost of construction also had to be considered, along with the recommendations of NPS staff, the BPR, and the Sierra Club. Noting that all parties expressed mixed opinions about the proposal's benefits and drawbacks, he observed, "Just how much should be done to enhance the autoists' enjoyment of superlative scenic areas, to what extent their enjoyment of a park shall be diminished because time, physical inabilities, or other necessities chain them to a car is a difficult question, and one that will remain debatable through generations."[68]

By this time, the NPS was collaborating with the Sierra Club to combat an even more ambitious incursion into California's scenic backcountry. In 1927 a coalition of local boosters, motoring enthusiasts, and highway interests began agitating for the construction of a scenic road from the southern end of the Sierras through Sequoia National Park to Yosemite. By 1932 they called for extending this "Sierra Way" to Lassen National Park and Mount Shasta. The road would maintain an elevation of 6,000 feet or more for most of its length and be engineered for leisurely cruising at 40 mph. To reduce costs and provide scenic enjoyment, the route traversed federal and state land as much as possible. Existing roads would be incorporated where available, but significant new construction was required. Most of the new mileage would be in national forests. Generals Highway and Yosemite's roads were enfolded, but the plans called for significant relocations and additions in Sequoia and a new connection between state highways and the Big Oak Flat and Tioga Roads in Yosemite. Fears of facilitating this effort figured into Vint and Thomson's resistance to the lower-level route. The proposed additions to Sequoia's road system were even more unpalatable. Along with trying to revive the Middle Fork relocation of Generals Highway and extending it north into Kings Canyon, Sierra Way boosters insisted on a road through the high country in the southern portion of the park. White's objections and a 1931 report from NPS engineer W. P. Webber succeeded in shifting the southern routing to less sensitive terrain, but the overall threat intensified in 1935, when the Forest Service and local boosters sought $15 million in public works money to pursue the project, casting it as a western equivalent to East Coast parkways.[69]

This was another instance in which NPS officials had to walk a fine line between defending preservation principles and offending politically important allies whose support was needed to realize the long-sought goal of wresting the Kings Canyon area from the USFS. Cammerer ordered Kittredge, Thomson, and Sequoia superintendent John White to keep close tabs on the proposal's progress while avoiding statements that might "antagonize needlessly any of our California people." In the meantime, he sent entreaties to the Sierra Club, National Parks Association, Campfire Club of America, Wilderness Society, and American Planning and Civic Association outlining the proposal's ramifications and urging them to make their views known. While the

language of these official appeals was measured, he followed up with more personal pleas characterizing the project as "a needless and destructive invasion of a great wilderness area" and expressing the NPS's determination do everything in its power to prevent the "unjustifiable desecration" of park lands. He also rejected the parkway comparison, noting that these were being developed in gentler terrain, much of which had been subject to logging and other human impacts. Cammerer and Demaray sought Secretary Ickes's permission to go on record against the proposal, but Kittredge and White suggested that it would be more politic for the proposal to be turned back by local opinion rather than by NPS fiat. While some traditional booster elements embraced the proposal, others realized it would be bad for local businesses if tourists could drive the length of the Sierras without passing through their communities. Sportsmen's clubs, dude ranchers, and stock growers also viewed the roadway as a threat, broadening opposition beyond the easily caricatured "nature cranks" and urban elite. Even the BPR and the California Highway Commission were skeptical, not out of concern for wilderness values but because it would be more expensive to construct a north–south road at the proposed elevation than to build in more hospitable terrain and extend lateral routes to select destinations. As the debate wore on, significant elements within the USFS disavowed the proposal. Assistant Regional Forester L. A. Barrett chaired a committee formed by the influential Commonwealth Club of California to address the question of road construction in the state's mountainous regions. Although the question was framed broadly, it was widely viewed as a referendum on the Sierra Way. As the report neared completion, Kittredge expressed confidence that as the product of an independent panel authorized by leading civic institutions, it would serve as a "bulwark of future defense of wilderness against the encroachment of roads in the State of California." Yosemite Superintendent Thomson took an even broader view, predicting that the report would reverse the terms of debate "to emphasize study of the importance of *wilderness*, giving the problem of road construction and routings a properly *secondary* position."[70]

The Park Service's policy of patience and behind-the-scenes maneuvering bore fruit when the Commonwealth Club announced its findings in April 1936. The sixty-page report presented

both sides of the argument but came down firmly in favor of wilderness preservation, concluding that: "California's undeveloped high mountain areas have been reduced dangerously near to a minimum for the welfare of the State, and that no further intrusions by the building of roads should be allowed without convincing proof of public necessity." Kittredge suggested that this afforded an ideal opportunity for the NPS to reassure preservationists by formally establishing wilderness areas. Washington officials were reluctant to make such a definitive statement, asserting that existing measures afforded adequate protection. The automobile clubs and State Chamber of Commerce continued to advocate for the Sierra Way, but the proposal's momentum was dealt a crushing blow. The NPS still had to contend with efforts to construct the segments envisioned for Sequoia and Yosemite, however. White incurred the wrath of road proponents and the everlasting gratitude of wilderness enthusiasts by withstanding pressure to reroute Generals Highway along the Middle Fork and add a second segment to the south. The Forest Service, state highway engineers, and local interests continued to push for a de facto Sierra Way segment along the western edge of Yosemite in an area that was soon to be added to the park. To counter this initiative, the NPS arranged a special ceremony to mark the completion of construction on the upper Big Oak Flat Road and the westernmost section of the Tioga Road. The goal was to emphasize the Park Service's commitment to cooperating with neighboring communities while drawing the line against further encroachments. William Colby was enlisted as speaker based on his stature as senior Sierra Club spokesman and his personal association with the roads in question. Acting Director Arthur Demaray sent a telegram praising the local officials and cooperating agencies while making it clear that once the remaining sections of the Big Oak Flat and Tioga Roads were upgraded, Yosemite's road system would be considered complete.[71]

The NPS also contended with criticism on some of its eastern projects. The first concerted opposition to the construction of roads in primitive settings arose not in the grand western parks but in what would become Acadia National Park. Mount Desert Island's wealthy summer residents prohibited motorists from roaming their elite retreat until 1915, the same year automobiles gained entry to Yellowstone. The prospect of sharing the island's

roads with automotive ingrates prompted the wealthiest summer resident, John D. Rockefeller Jr., to dramatically expand the private carriage-road network he was building to ply his anachronistic pastime in peace. The drives were exquisitely designed, embodying classic principles of park road development, but Rockefeller's neighbors soon complained that he was extending them into areas that should remain the province of hikers enjoying the island's unusually well-developed trail system. When the NPS began acquiring holdings on the island, first as a national monument and then as a national park, the conflict escalated from a private matter to an increasingly acrimonious public dispute. Influential forces were lined up on both sides, which pitted wealthy and well-connected summer residents against local communities and statewide economic and political interests seeking to capitalize on the tourist trade. The NPS was committed to road development but wanted to ensure that it proceeded with minimal impact on the island's attractions and the agency's broader agendas. In this case, it was reluctant to criticize its most generous benefactor, who was spending a considerable portion of his petroleum-based

fortune to enlarge and improve parks throughout the country. This motivation was not lost on contemporary critics, especially when Rockefeller offered to construct the roads at his own expense and donate $150,000 and significant amounts of land. While most opponents spoke in traditional terms of preserving natural beauty and the island's unique "charms," Philadelphia congressman George Wharton Pepper protested that additional roads would destroy the balance between "isolation and accessibility" that constituted Mount Desert's principal appeal. If Rockefeller had his way, he protested, the balance would be upset and "a due portion of Wilderness destroyed." Pepper pursued this line in a 1924 hearing, demarking areas of "wilderness" and "civilization" that should remain separate and inviolate. While it is tempting to credit the congressman with a prescient awareness of wilderness theory, associated comments about visual impacts on the "wilderness of treetops" seen from surrounding summits bespoke his allegiance to traditional modes of landscape appreciation. In any event, his concerns were avowedly more parochial. Pepper was aggrieved that Rockefeller's roads would impinge on the experience of hiking through

the island's rugged interior, which he characterized as "a means of communication as is incidental to our delightful social life."[72]

The dispute became even more contentious with the addition of motor road proposals and grumblings that the NPS was deliberately withholding information to avoid public scrutiny. The agency resolved to clarify the situation by developing a master plan, but Hull's return to private practice in July 1927 delayed this process, providing sophisticated summer residents with an opening to prepare their own master plan. The author, Charles W. Eliot 2d, was not only the grandson of the island's most respected summer resident, Harvard president Charles W. Eliot, but a nephew of the noted landscape architect Charles Eliot. He had studied city planning and landscape architecture at Harvard and been appointed city planner for the National Capital Park and Planning Commission. His 1928 report embodied contemporary planning principles, with an extended survey of existing conditions, identification of key issues, and combination of general goals and specific recommendations. He also summarized the relevant policy directives, highlighting

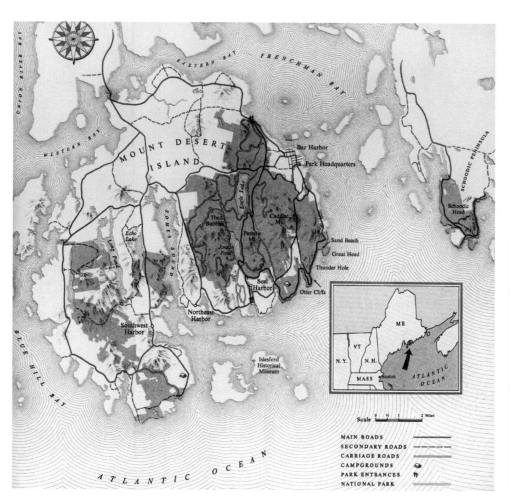

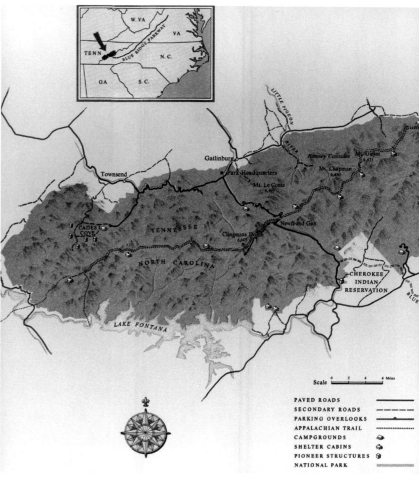

Secretary Work's injunction that "National Parks and Monuments must be maintained untouched by the inroads of modern civilization in order that unspoiled bits of native America may be preserved to be enjoyed by future generations as well as our own." Eliot noted that the conflict pitted "conservatives, who object to all change or development, decrying the construction of roads as desecration of the solitude, wilderness, natural character, and 'scale' of the Island," and those "who wish to make all the unusual scenic features of the Island readily accessible by road and are impressed with the responsibility of the Park management to the great American public." While the diminutive long-settled island had been logged, ravaged by fire, and altered by recreational development since the mid-nineteenth century, Eliot maintained that the rugged terrain and resurgent woodlands afforded many areas "which are apparently wild and untouched or far from what most of us associate with civilization." His primary recommendation was to identify which areas should be placed off-limits to road development as "Conservation or Wilderness Areas" free from modern intrusions. An accompanying map delineated sections

that the island's "eminent scientists or scholars" had deemed worthy of preservation due to their biological, geological, ornithological, or historic significance. Beyond these technical considerations, Eliot maintained that the primary goal was to safeguard those places that fostered an "appreciation of the value and place of beauty, solitude, remoteness, even romanticism."[73]

Although Eliot's report constituted the first, if unofficial, national park master plan and entailed one of the most explicit calls for wilderness preservation to date, it had little impact on either a local or national scale. Not only were the protests of Eliot and other summer residents predicated on traditional aesthetic concerns rather than current wilderness theory, but perceptions that opponents were motivated by selfish desires to prevent the public from overrunning their privileged playground overshadowed more positive interpretations. A renewed round of protests to Rockefeller's 1930 offer to donate $4 million toward development of a motor loop exacerbated this impression. The prospect of losing hundreds of construction jobs to mollify a minority of well-connected aesthetes caused widespread indignation, especially at the height of the Depression. Rockefeller mediated criticism by hiring Olmsted to advise on the project, and the road was relocated around the most contentious area. The construction of a road to the summit of Cadillac Mountain generated less controversy since the island's highest peak had played host to a cog railway and hotel during the nineteenth century. Rockefeller and the NPS agreed to spare the other summits. Opponents' fears that the NPS would succumb to pressure to convert carriage drives to motor roads proved unfounded, but the extensive network of carriage and motor roads clearly exceeded Mather's proscription against "gridironing." Despite their elitist origins, the carriage roads belatedly contributed to the popular enjoyment of the park as bicycling gained in popularity. For contemporary audiences, however, automobiles embodied the democratic ethos. Dedicating the Cadillac Mountain Road in 1932, Maine congressman John Nelson proclaimed, "We open here today a wonderful highway built by the federal government to make available to all men the matchless beauty of this spot."[74]

While Acadia's critics were only modestly successful and represented a waning perspective on the nature and meaning of unspoiled landscapes, protests against road development in Great Smoky Mountains National Park were led by the primary proponents of the new ethic. Their efforts dramatically impacted NPS plans for road construction in the park and profoundly influenced subsequent development strategies. Once again, the NPS found itself mediating between opposing forces. Since the park was not authorized until the late 1920s and development did not begin until the early 1930s, both sides had strengthened their positions. With the economic benefits of motor tourism readily apparent, civic boosters and automobiles interests lobbied hard for the park's creation, exerting as least as much influence as those professing more noble goals. Reflecting the park's location on the North Carolina/Tennessee border, the automobile clubs and chambers of commerce of Asheville and Knoxville led the effort, exhorting politicians and the general public with visions of the riches to be reaped from park patrons. In a typically effusive pronouncement, the *Asheville Citizen* proclaimed the park would "operate as splendidly and as incredibly as a modern combination of Aladdin's Wonderful Lamp, the touch of Midas, the Magic Urn, and the weaving of straw into gold by Rumpelstiltskin." On a

more pragmatic note, the woeful state of regional roads created widespread support for improving the primitive turnpike that bisected the proposed park area at Newfound Gap.[75]

Park advocates counseled patience so that the road would be constructed according to NPS standards, but local interests insisted that construction start as soon as possible. Citing pressing demand and uncertainty over the pace of park development, the Tennessee State Highway Department began construction in 1927. NPS officials pleaded with state engineers to exercise caution. They also requested that the routing be shifted to nearby Indian Gap so the road scar would not compromise the view from Mount LeConte. Exhibiting his awareness of the changing terms of debate, Arno Cammerer insisted on the need to "keep this view entirely free of any construction of any kind which would mar its primeval character." Tellingly, he couched the alteration as a means of avoiding criticism, since the NPS would receive the blame once the park was officially established. The state refused to deviate on the grounds that the Newfound Gap route afforded lower grades and more economical construction. North Carolina was more cooperative, allowing NPS landscape architect Charles Peterson to advise on some aspects of the design and deferring construction on the most problematic section for the agency to complete. Tennessee completed its portion in 1929, and North Carolina was done by 1933. Although the North Carolina side was somewhat better, both would need significant work to meet the aesthetic and technical standards of national park roads.[76]

The NPS and BPR went to great effort to transform the utilitarian highway into a bona fide park road. The first task was to address the damage at the very top of the gap, where the Tennessee Highway Department had made a crude cut through the high ground. This disregard for scenic values epitomized the transgressions of contemporary road builders. To make matters worse, the North Carolina Highway Department established a quarry on its side of gap. Since the landscape was already "ruined," in the words of park superintendent J. R. Eakin, it was decided to create a scenic overlook with a parking lot capable of handling hundreds of cars. The outer side of the quarry was cleared away to open views. Landscaped islands separated the pullout from the main drive. A raised stone terrace was constructed to afford better views and provide an

attractive setting for a memorial plaque dedicating the overlook to the memory of Laura Spellman Rockefeller, whose son, John D. Rockefeller Jr., had donated $5 million from her eponymous foundation to help acquire land for the park. With its sweeping views, rustic features, and location at the apex of the climb, the overlook became one of the focal points of the park. In a striking example of the public's ability to reconcile the ostensible tension between the machine and the garden, the overlook was celebrated in myriad souvenir views. In most renditions, the car-choked parking lot held center stage, with the panoramic vista serving as a backdrop and the highway leading off to either side frequently emphasized.[77]

While the general location was set, NPS landscape architects and BPR engineers realigned much of the roadway to produce lower and more consistent grades, longer and more graceful curves, and less damage to the surrounding landscape. The usual practices were followed, including efforts to maximize scenic opportunities while minimizing views of the road, extensive roadside landscaping, tunnels carved through rocky bluffs, and stone-faced concrete bridges. The most unusual feature was an updated version of Yellowstone's Corkscrew Bridge, which replaced two unsightly switchbacks with an ascending spiral that carried the road around and over itself by means of a graded ramp and rustic stone tunnel. Completed in 1935, the Loopover attracted widespread attention and became one of the park's iconic features, appearing on a wide range of postcards and souvenirs. The reconstruction of Newfound Gap Road was carried on throughout the 1930s. An existing road to the small settlement of Cades Cove, at the south end of the park on the Tennessee side, was also improved. Additional old buildings were brought in to create an interpretive feature on traditional Appalachian culture. Civilian Conservation Corps (CCC) crews made an enormous contribution, grading and replanting roadsides, constructing guard walls and other stonework, and building campgrounds and other features. Approximately twenty camps were established in the park, with enrollees contributing as much as 85 million man-hours of labor per year. According to park official Robert White, this allowed the park's development to proceed "at a much more rapid rate than any other Park ever built by the Federal Government."[78]

The NPS enthused about the accomplishments made possible by the CCC, and park-related

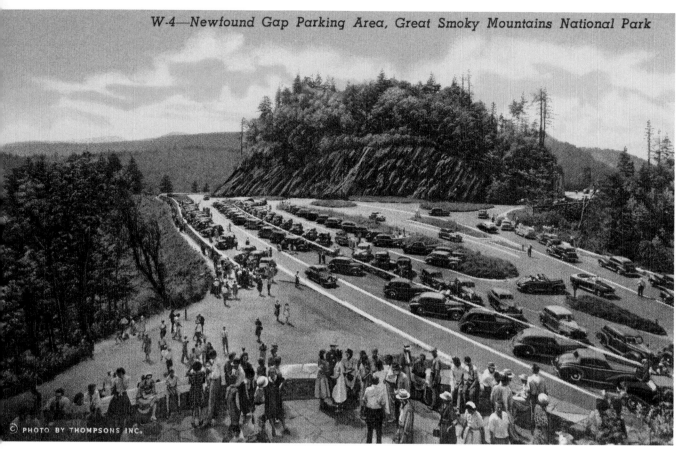

W-4—Newfound Gap Parking Area, Great Smoky Mountains National Park

© PHOTO BY THOMPSONS INC.

projects provided significant boosts to local economies, but the unprecedented scale of New Deal relief programs created growing concern in conservation circles. Rosalie Edge, chairman of the independent Emergency Conservation Committee, laid out the key criticisms in a 1936 publication titled *Roads and More Roads in the National Parks and National Forests.* Maintaining that the road-building boom reflected the prevailing view that public works money should be "buttered evenly over the whole country," Edge observed that the NPS was under enormous pressure to provide outlets for local labor "whether or not their services are needed and the wilderness goes down before these conquerors." She acknowledged that national parks required reasonable access and questioned the judgment of those who were "so naïve as to believe them to be wilderness areas," but she insisted that surviving "primitive areas" remain untouched. Edge also complained that the new roads were built to inappropriately high standards. Not only did the incessant widening and straightening produce gaping scars, but encouraging motorists to drive faster increased the number of serious accidents while decreasing the value of the park experience. Decrying "the hundreds who dash daily over Logan Pass, without so much as a stop," she

suggested that roads be designed to slow motorists down and foster more meaningful engagement with park landscapes. Although Edge condemned the overengineered appearance of high-speed roads, she also cautioned against excessive efforts at landscape beautification, complaining that the parking areas at Logan Pass and Newfound Gap had been laid out "in the manner of suburbs and cemeteries." The latter, she declared, was "a sin against Nature." Edge maintained that the NPS was being forced to undertake projects against its better judgment and needed public support to counter political pressures. This conciliatory tone garnered a warm response from Cammerer, who praised the pamphlet as "distinctly helpful to a sane and helpful development of national parks" and assured Edge that it was his "personal hope" that road building in the parks would not be overdone. While a certain amount of road construction was necessary, he agreed that "there is undoubtedly a saturation point beyond which we should not proceed if we are to conserve intangible but, nevertheless very real wilderness values."[79]

Albright had expressed similar sentiments several years earlier in response to a *Scientific Monthly* article titled "The Problem of Wilderness." The author, twenty-nine-year-old Robert Marshall, was

the son of a prominent New York City attorney and conservationist, who was emerging as the leading exponent of wilderness as Aldo Leopold transitioned to academia. Following in Leopold's footsteps, "Bob" Marshall earned multiple degrees in forestry and went west to work for the USFS in 1925. His eloquent defense of Leopold's theories in a 1928 USFS publication invoked Voltaire, Mills, Paine, and Jefferson to argue that since the American system of government was designed to protect the interests of minorities, the enjoyment of wilderness was a "minority right" regardless of its limited popularity. His 1930 article expanded on this theme, echoing Leopold's assertions about wilderness's influence on national character while elaborating on its aesthetic value with references to Thoreau, Melville, Muir, and the emotional intensity of the sublime. Marshall implied that motorists' demands for access to the remaining pockets of wilderness were not just greedy but un-American. Recognizing that Leopold's original formulation would exclude many desirable areas, he replaced the "two-week trip" requirement with the need to sleep out overnight and depend on one's own resources. Roads remained categorically prohibited. Marshall repeated the call for a nationwide study of wilderness issues and highlighted the need for public activism. "There is just one hope of repulsing the tyrannical ambitions of civilization to conquer every niche on the whole earth," he proclaimed. "That hope is the organization of spirited people who will fight for the freedom of the wilderness."[80]

Albright was so impressed by the article that he ordered copies to circulate within the NPS and sent Marshall a letter praising it as "about the best presentation of the wilderness problem that I have seen." Convinced that he had found a kindred spirit, Albright provided Marshall a copy of his "Everlasting Wilderness" piece and recounted the "very great progress in reserving wilderness areas" that had taken place since. Current plans ensured that approximately 75 percent of every park would remain "in a wilderness condition." Within these areas, the NPS was in the process of setting up "research reserves" with even more stringent protection. Since these areas were intended for the scientific study of primeval conditions, they were located in the most undisturbed portions of parks and precluded not only automobiles but the general public. The NPS was so intent on maintaining the reserves' integrity that in some cases it refused to disclose their locations out of fear that the designation would attract unwanted attention. While not an intentional attempt to outdo wilderness advocates at their own game, the idea of excluding man as well as machine reflected an ecological orientation that conflicted with wilderness advocates' sociological emphasis and desire to further their own recreational interests. Marshall, who had left the USFS to pursue research at Johns Hopkins, replied that he enjoyed the *Saturday Evening Post* article and was "especially encouraged" by the 75 percent figure, returning Albright's sentiments about the desirability of future discussions on wilderness issues.[81]

Albright was not the only senior government official to be impressed by Marshall's eloquence and passion. When Harold Ickes became secretary of the interior in 1933, he wasted little time in declaring his sympathy with wilderness advocates. "If I had my way about national parks," he declared, "I would create one without a road in it. I would have it impenetrable forever to automobiles, a place where man would not try to improve upon God." At the same time, he acknowledged the public's right to reasonable access and was keenly aware of the political significance of the projects under his purview as secretary of the interior and director of the Public Works Administration. In February 1934, Marshall sent Ickes an impassioned plea to use this dual role to ensure that roads funded with public works money did not impinge on the wilderness areas he outlined in an exhaustive U.S. Department of Agriculture report on forest recreation. Although the official document was relatively measured, Marshall exhibited his characteristic flair in a privately printed précis, insisting that the idea of experiencing nature by highways was "as preposterous at it would seem to have moving sidewalks established in picture galleries so that one might enjoy the paintings without stopping." By this time Marshall had secured the position of chief forester within the Department of Interior's Office of Indian Affairs. Sympathetic with his aims and enamored of the young man's charisma and erudition, Ickes made Marshall his de facto advisor on national park roads. NPS officials were predictably distressed, but Ickes made no secret of his skepticism of agency development policies and his disdain for Cammerer's leadership.[82]

Marshall made his presence felt in the debate over the next phase of road development in Great Smoky Mountains National Park. The controversy began under Albright's watch, when the Asheville Chamber of Commerce promoted the idea of a skyline drive, or "Skyway," stretching along the crest of the Smokies from one end of the park to the other. Not only would this afford an extended motoring experience with unsurpassed views, but both end points would be in North Carolina, redressing the perceived imbalance favoring Tennessee. NPS officials privately opposed the concept but realized that the political pressure would be hard to resist, especially with Shenandoah's Skyline Drive garnering accolades for its economic and recreational impact. They were particularly concerned that local boosters would emulate the Shenandoah project by pushing the road through as a public works project before the area fell under NPS control. Albright fended off the initial push with his usual excuse that planning had not proceeded far enough to consider additional roads, but he made it clear that the agency intended to treat the entire eastern half of the park as a wilderness area with minimal motorized access. Superintendent J. R. Eakin seconded this approach, casting the construction of a shorter Skyway extending from Newfound Gap to the west end of the park as a compromise "between those who want roads everywhere and those who want no roads at all." Both Cammerer and Peterson initially opposed the abbreviated version, but acknowledged its political necessity. After reconnoitering potential routes with Peterson and NPS engineer Oliver Taylor, Eakin pronounced that a road could be developed without undue damage if it was located below the crest of the ridge and provided access to only one or two of the open summits, or "balds," that constituted the region's chief attractions. Satisfied that the proposed alignment would afford sufficient protection for landscape values while accommodating public demands for access, Cammerer became a staunch supporter. He and Eakin often enlisted the sympathetic Great Smoky Mountains Hiking Club leader Carlos Campbell to combat critics' claims. The Asheville Chamber of Commerce appeared content with the compromise, but protests soon arose from the opposite quarter.[83]

As word of the compromise plan spread, the NPS received a flurry of complaints, including letters of protest from influential organizations such as the Izaak Walton League, the Society for the Protection of New Hampshire Forests, and the

The NPS enthused about the accomplishments made possible by the CCC, and park-related projects provided significant boosts to local economies, but the unprecedented scale of New Deal relief programs created growing concern in conservation circles.

BELOW The Loopover, Great Smoky Mountains National Park, souvenir plate, ca. 1948.

OPPOSITE Newfound Gap Parking Area, Great Smoky Mountains National Park, postcard, ca. 1946.

Ecological Society of America. Albright responded personally to these missives, refuting the "skyline drive" characterization and underscoring that the entire eastern half of the park would be reserved for nonmotorized use. Emphasizing that he was "a trail person" himself, Albright insisted on the need to share the glories of the park's higher reaches with less hardy souls. In addition to avoiding the high ground except in select locations such as Clingmans Dome, the partial Skyway would be designed by NPS landscape architects, of whom he asserted, "There is no finer, more intelligent and earnest group of nature lovers in the United States," noting that they had repeatedly demonstrated their ability to combine "the practicable and the ideal." Albright's assurances mollified key critics, many of whom admitted to being misinformed about the nature and extent of the proposal. The Izaak Walton League remained opposed, but the Ecological Society explicitly endorsed the project, as did the Smoky Mountains Hiking Club with the exception of one holdout, who proudly characterized himself as an "extremist." The National Parks Association also dropped its criticism, though Yard was suspected of playing a key role in rousing the

opposition. NPS internal correspondence confirmed that agency officials fully embraced the idea of setting everything east of Newfound Gap aside as a wilderness area and were intent on exerting inordinate care to ensure the new road was minimally intrusive. Despite the added cost, extensive retaining walls would be used to carry the road around the rugged contours rather than subduing them with unsightly cuts and fills. NPS landscape architect Roswell Ludgate recommended this approach, "not only because it is common practice in good modern park road construction, but also because it will serve to silence the objections which have been raised against the project."[84]

As the initial section between Newfound Gap and Clingmans Dome neared completion in 1934, it became clear that the earlier dispute was a minor skirmish compared to the all-out war against the road's continuation. Marshall played a leading role in this effort, along with Yard, Appalachian Trail founder Benton Mackaye, and Harvey Broome, the Smoky Mountains Hiking Club's "extremist." Marshall had continued to press Ickes on wilderness issues. In addition to recommending areas for designation, he insisted on the need to bring

the Smokies' road farther down the mountainside so hikers could "enjoy the primitiveness of the mountain crest without the constant distraction of seeing the scar left by the highway, hearing the whir of motor and the honk of horns, and smelling gasoline among the freshness of the spruce forest." Mackaye sounded a similar note at a May 1934 forestry conference in Knoxville. Mackaye compared the Park Service's compromise to Solomon's biblical adjudication, insisting that true appreciators of nature would no more consider sacrificing half the park than a mother would consent to bisecting her baby. Arguing the merits of "flankline" versus "skyline" drives, he insisted that the former were not only less destructive to wilderness values, but also better suited to the needs of motorists and other superficial "frolickers." By skirting the highest ground, dipping into valleys, and crossing ridges at carefully selected locations, flankline drives afforded lazy visitors with more varied and interesting views. According to Mackaye, the primary push for skyline drives came from boosters enamored of the term's cachet. The NPS might have countered that the reverse was also true: most NPS projects including the controversial Skyway

5—Skyway Drive, Great Smoky Mountains National Park

in public and inflaming an already tempestuous situation. Cammerer continued to stew about Marshall's obstructive behavior, not realizing that the full assault was yet to come.[86]

Bringing Yard into the fold as executive secretary, Marshall, Mackaye, Broome, and several other leading conservationists formally inaugurated the Wilderness Society in January 1935. A "Summons to Save the Wilderness," written with Yard's characteristic zeal, declared: "The craze is to build all the highways possible everywhere while billions of dollars may yet be borrowed from the unlucky future. The fashion is to barber and manicure wild America as smartly as the modern girl. Our duty is clear." The society's platform wove together a decade's worth of dissent. The "brutalizing pressure of a spreading metropolitan civilization" made it crucial to prevent remaining wilderness areas from being "sacrificed to the mechanical invasion in its various killing forms." Ickes allowed the Park Service's adversaries to quote from a recent address in which he decried the trend toward overdevelopment. Echoing the call to preserve as much wilderness as possible, Ickes declared his disdain for "people whose idea of enjoying nature is dashing along a hard road at fifty or sixty miles an hour." While he employed the classic qualifier, "I am not in favor of building any more roads in the National Parks than we have to build," Ickes made his sentiments abundantly clear. "I do not happen to favor the scarring of a wonderful mountain side just so that we can say we have a skyline drive," he declared. "It sounds poetical, but it may be an atrocity."[87]

NPS officials insisted that they shared the same sentiments but had to reconcile idealistic goals with practical concerns and political realities. They also pointed out that the agency was obligated to provide means for the public to enjoy the areas under its protection. The NPS was paying greater heed to the concerns of wilderness advocates, but reasonable access had to be provided for those who were unwilling or unable to engage in strenuous recreation. Cammerer also

fit the flankline description, but it was easier to rally opposition with polemics about desecrated mountaintops. Eakin maintained that the number of wilderness enthusiasts was nowhere near the magnitude asserted by Marshall and Mackaye. From Eakin's perspective, it was matter of "limiting the use of the western part of the Park to a few hundred hikers, or permitting it to be seen by hundreds of thousands, perhaps even millions, of motorists." With the more primitive eastern half of the park reserved as a wilderness area, "both the hikers and the motorists should be satisfied."[85]

When Ickes sent Marshall to review NPS road proposals in August 1934, he took advantage of the opportunity to meet with Mackaye and Broome. Rather than fight individual projects, they decided that the best way to influence government decision makers was to found an organization devoted to wilderness preservation nationwide. On his return to Washington, Marshall urged Ickes to prohibit the drive's extension past Clingmans Dome. Expounding on the defilement of wilderness wrought by the roar of machines and scores of irreverent motorists "blaring forth the latest jazz as a substitute for the symphony of the

primitive," he convinced Ickes to put a stop to the Park Service's plans. Ickes announced that no more roads would be built in the park without his approval, effectively killing the Skyway proposal. In mid-September he expanded the edict to include all NPS road projects, including those previously authorized but not yet under construction. Not satisfied with simply usurping the NPS's road-building authority, Marshall repeated his criticisms at an October forestry conference with Cammerer and other NPS officials in attendance, accusing the agency of planning to construct a concrete road along the crest of the Smokies and asserting that the proposed extension "would be the ruination of the finest area still left to the walker and the camper in the Southeast." At the closing session, Cammerer deplored Marshall's "improper and ungracious attack" and emphasized that the NPS had worked closely with the local hiking club to minimize the road's impact. He made similar points in an angry memorandum to Ickes, noting that, among other mischaracterizations, the area Marshall extolled as primeval wilderness had been badly logged and burned. Ickes chastised both men for airing their differences

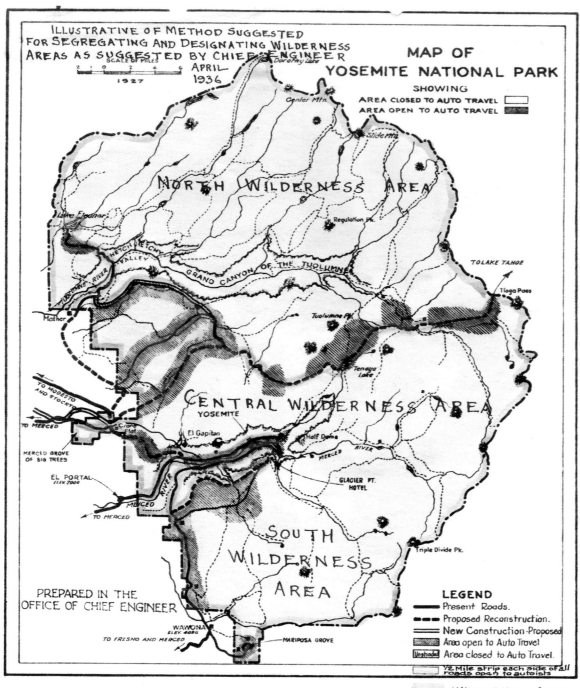

ILLUSTRATIVE OF METHOD SUGGESTED
FOR SEGREGATING AND DESIGNATING WILDERNESS
AREAS AS SUGGESTED BY CHIEF ENGINEER
APRIL 1936

MAP OF
YOSEMITE NATIONAL PARK
SHOWING
AREA CLOSED TO AUTO TRAVEL
AREA OPEN TO AUTO TRAVEL

NORTH WILDERNESS AREA

CENTRAL WILDERNESS AREA

SOUTH WILDERNESS AREA

PREPARED IN THE
OFFICE OF CHIEF ENGINEER

LEGEND
Present Roads.
Proposed Reconstruction.
New Construction-Proposed
Area open to Auto Travel
Area closed to Auto Travel
½ Mile strip each side of all roads open to autoists
WILDERNESS AREA

ABOVE NPS chief engineer Frank Kittredge's suggestion for designating wilderness areas in Yosemite National Park, 1936.

OPPOSITE Undeveloped heartland of Mount Olympus National Monument, 1934.

be remembered that roads may be used as an implement of wilderness conservation."[88]

Cammerer's assertion about the relative numbers of the two constituencies was undoubtedly true, but by the mid-1930s wilderness proponents were exerting a disproportionate influence, especially in regard to areas the NPS had long sought to add to its fold. Some agency officials embraced this trend and urged senior leadership to take a more public stance on wilderness preservation. NPS biologist Lowell Sumner suggested that the agency adopt a formal wilderness policy not just on its own merits but because many potential allies believed that Kings Canyon, the Olympics, and similar areas were safer under existing USFS protection. Kittredge made the same case. Attributing conservationists' resistance to the Kings Canyon proposal to "a wide-spread feeling of discontent because of the road-building orgy which we have gone through," he insisted: "We have to do something to prove to the public that we are not going to continue some of the practices of the past." Kittredge's bluntness elicited Cammerer's ire, but his sentiments were shared by friends and foes alike. White, Thomson, and Mesa Verde superintendent Jesse Nussbaum joined Kittredge in acknowledging that roads and other developments had been taken too far in some instances. In some cases this represented excessive zeal on the part of agency officials, but more often it reflected the understandable failure to envision the exponential increase in automobile tourism. The most problematic situations stemmed from the machinations of local boosters, the pressures of Depression-relief programs, and the BPR's insistence on ever-higher engineering standards. All four men explicitly embraced wilderness-oriented policies and called for even more stringent limitations on road development. Kittredge prepared a map explicitly delineating wilderness areas in Yosemite, but Cammerer insisted such measures were unnecessary given Ickes's ruling that no new roads could be developed without his explicit approval. Vint expressed sympathy with the general concept but questioned its practicality. Even though master plans for Mount Rainier and several other parks identified wilderness zones, he maintained that defining which areas qualified and deciding how they should be managed was such a difficult and contentious process that the best way to proceed was to focus on the other side of the issue. By

maintained that Mather's formula of building public support through motor tourism remained the most effective means of park advocacy, since wilderness enthusiasts were too few in number to overcome development forces. Rather than protest the equitable sharing of park resources, he suggested, wilderness advocates should be grateful that "by building roads into a portion of an area, so that people can enjoy it, we are able to save even larger sections of wilderness for the relatively few who enjoy wilderness." Clearly exasperated at having to reiterate a long-standing precept of park creation, he intoned, "It should ensuring that developed areas were well-designed and limited in extent, the NPS could employ the term more loosely, characterizing all areas without conspicuous construction as "wilderness." This view, which was essentially the same approach Mather and Albright had instituted, would continue to inform NPS policy for decades, creating ongoing tension between the agency and those who advocated stricter definitions and controls.[89]

Although NPS officials resented Marshall's interference and chafed at Ickes's edicts, their pronouncements helped convince skeptical preservationists that the NPS could be trusted not to overdevelop the remaining vestiges of American wilderness. These fears may have been misplaced given the extent to which the NPS had combated proposed incursions and evolved in its own interpretations of the appropriate balance between preservation and access, but perceptions were important, especially when backed by legislative authority. While the agency resisted efforts to impinge on its autonomy, wilderness preservation imperatives loomed large in the creation of several parks established during this period. Grand Teton had set the precedent in 1928. Albright's desire to present the NPS as more preservation-oriented than the USFS in the battle over Yellowstone's extension figured prominently in the decision, though the mountainous topography and local resistance to competing concessions eased the path. Isle Royale, authorized in 1931 though not formally established until 1940, would also be managed on a wilderness basis, though the term was not explicitly invoked in the legislation. Everglades enthusiasts insisted that language guaranteeing the area's wilderness status be included in the 1934 authorization. These relatively small parks reflected unique circumstances. The key victories for wilderness enthusiasts were the designation of Olympic and Kings Canyon as wilderness-oriented parks in 1938 and 1940 respectively. NPS officials from Mather on down had insisted that the sweep of High Sierra surrounding Kings Canyon remain inviolate, and the Forest Service's plans for the Olympics entailed more roads than the NPS would have countenanced with or without Ickes's involvement, but wilderness advocates were divided on which agency would provide better protection. The perception that Ickes shared their disdain for motorists and was adamantly opposed to overdevelopment played a key role in convincing conservationists that both areas would fare better under NPS stewardship.[90]

Despite Ickes's pronouncements and the insertion of wilderness preservation language in the establishing legislation, neither park was completely road-free. Nor did anyone believe that was a realistic option. Kings Canyon more closely approached the goal, with a single entrance road providing access to a modest developed area on the floor of the canyon and the entire high country reserved for nonmotorized recreation. Olympic inherited a stretch of state highway along with several primitive dirt roads leading into the park, including two Forest Service truck trails climbing to modest elevations within driving distance of Seattle and Tacoma. The 1938 master plan envisioned connecting these stubs to produce a modest loop that would allow motorists to glimpse Mount Olympus and the surrounding mountains without intruding on the heart of the park. Funds were not available to undertake the effort until after World War II. Resisting considerable pressure for a more traditional cross-park road and accompanying developments, the NPS opted for upgrading one of the spurs and carrying it farther up Hurricane Ridge to provide a sweeping panorama of the park's interior without compromising its overall wilderness character.[91]

While neither park completely embodied the wilderness ideal, the proportion of roads to undeveloped territory was dramatically lower than in previous reservations of comparable size. NPS officials might argue that this was a logical extension of long-standing policies, but the idea that vehicular access would be dramatically limited represented a significant shift in perceptions about the form and function of public parks. While it is tempting to present the rise of wilderness parks as the realization of the Romantic ideal of national parks as Edenic gardens unsullied by machine-age intrusions, this absolution was accompanied and to a large degree enabled by the apotheosis of automobile-oriented park development in the form of meticulously landscaped parkways stretching for hundreds of miles and designed expressly for the enjoyment of twentieth-century motorists. Wilderness advocates would protest parkway development as well, but by providing unparalleled opportunities for recreational motoring, they reduced pressure to open other areas to automobile incursions.

National Parkways

O n a Saturday afternoon in
April 1935, NBC radio audiences listened to BPR
chief Thomas MacDonald and NPS associate
director Arthur Demaray discussing a new type
of national park designed especially for recre-
ationalist motorists. "The parkway, or elongated
park," Demaray explained, "is a road or highway
on standards suited to heavy continuous travel of
the recreational type, with its roadsides so insu-
lated as to give the motorist over it the impression
of being out in the great open spaces, far from
industrial or other commercial developments."
These roadways would be run through corridors
of parkland at least 800 feet wide so that motorists
could enjoy attractive scenery "with no billboards,
hot-dog stands, gas stations, or other structures
which would be in the nature of eyesores." The
corridors would expand at frequent intervals to
encompass natural features such as lakes, rivers, or
mountainous regions that would be developed as
recreational areas for through travelers and local
residents. Parkways were designed to cater to the

expanding ranks of Americans who preferred to
experience nature from behind the wheel of an
automobile and were disappointed by the commercial clutter despoiling contemporary roadsides.
A corollary benefit that neither man thought to
mention was that by absorbing this population,
parkways would lessen the pressure on areas that
wilderness advocates sought to reserve for more
solitary enjoyment. The combination of wilderness
parks and parkways afforded a new approach to
satisfying the agency's dual mandate, with the
former privileging preservation and the latter
emphasizing access. Several projects of this nature
were already under way. These included the first
section of George Washington Memorial Parkway
along the shores of the Potomac near the nation's
capital and a parkway linking the historic sites
of Colonial National Monument. These initial
forays would provide engaging scenic and historic
drives, but the first full-fledged demonstration of
the new recreational motoring ideal would be the
proposed parkway linking the Shenandoah and
Great Smoky Mountains National Parks. If the
concept proved as popular as the NPS envisioned,
this project might be extended north to Vermont's
Green Mountains or into Maine and south into
Georgia and on to the Everglades. Given the
public's increasing interest in long-distance travel,
additional parkways might stretch westward across
the continent. MacDonald applauded Demaray's
suggestion as "not only a great vision, but a practical reality of the near future." Hailing the achievements of the NPS-BPR partnership, he predicted
the future parkways would be scenic masterpieces
and "a great aid to patriotism, even while promoting a national tourist industry of tremendous size
and far-reaching possibilities."[1]

The NPS did not claim to invent the modern
motor parkway. This distinction is generally
accorded to the Bronx Parkway Commission
and its successor, the Westchester County Park
Commission. While the NPS grappled with
the motorization of rugged western reserves,
these commissions adapted nineteenth-century
parkways to the automobile age. The basic goal
remained the same: to provide attractive pleasure
drives that would serve as the connecting links of
comprehensive park systems while functioning
as multi-use recreational amenities in their own
right. The extended range afforded by automobile
travel led to the development of longer parkways
serving more expansive networks, with beaches,

lakes, mountains, and large wooded reservations as their ultimate destinations. The concomitant increase in speed entailed various adaptations. Roadways had to be wider, sharp turns eased or eliminated, grades reduced and regularized, pavements made more durable, and the number of intersections minimized to facilitate the safe and efficient flow of traffic. Motor parkway designers employed bolder, simpler planting arrangements that could be appreciated more easily at rates that progressed from 20 to 30 to 40 or more mph. Mirroring and to some degree preceding the NPS-BPR partnership, parkway landscape architects worked in close collaboration with highway engineers, whose expertise proved invaluable in addressing a wide range of technical issues including grade-separation design, construction practices, and the complex calculations for the flowing spiral curvature that improved the safety and appearance of parkway alignments.[2]

The first public motor parkway was the Bronx River Parkway, stretching approximately 15 miles from the Bronx River north into Westchester County. The parkway was proposed in 1906 as a traditional metropolitan park project transforming a badly degraded river corridor into an attractive recreational amenity. Since the automobile was still a rarity, only minor consideration was given to the delineation of an associated roadway. By 1918, when the design team began to finalize the development plan, automobile ownership was increasing rapidly and the motor road became a more prominent consideration. When the project was finally dedicated in 1925, America had embraced the automobile and there was widespread agreement that the Bronx River Parkway represented a new paradigm, not just for recreational roadways but for modern motorway design in general. The basic features included the separation of major cross-streets by means of attractively designed overpasses, limitation of access to widely spaced and carefully controlled entrance points, and a broad right-of-way that provided ample freedom to integrate the roadway with the surrounding landscape, maximize scenic potential, and screen out objectionable sights. Given the crowded, dangerous, and unsightly nature of most American roadways, city planners, highway engineers, and the general public quickly recognized that the Bronx River Parkway was not just more attractive than ordinary roadways, but safer and more efficient as well. Instead of being

assaulted by the cacophony of modern consumer culture and confronting the dangers and disruptions of outmoded streets, motorists could proceed without interruption along a gracefully curving roadway through a comprehensively designed and managed landscape.[3]

The Bronx River Parkway's popularity initiated a boom in parkway building throughout the Greater New York region. The Westchester County Park Commission (WCPC) constructed 160 miles of parkways over the next decade: the Saw Mill River and Hutchison River Parkways; the northern extension of the Bronx River Parkway that eventually became known as the Taconic Parkway; and the Cross County Parkway, which provided a link between the three major routes. Robert Moses relied heavily on the WCPC's expertise for his ambitious park and parkway development plans for New York City and Long Island. WCPC parkway designers employed all the hallmarks of classic park road composition. Alignments were carefully chosen so that roadways lay lightly on the land with minimal cuts and fills. Where excavation was unavoidable, side slopes were given gently rounded profiles that simulated natural contours. The roadway curved to preserve attractive landscape features and attractive vegetation. Topsoil, small trees, and shrubs removed from the right-of-way were often recycled to rehabilitate construction scars or enhance the surrounding landscape. Open

meadows alternated with dense woods and carefully crafted compositions of native vegetation. As in national park road development, the goal was to make the parkway blend harmoniously with the natural landscape so that motorists and other users would not be able to tell where one left off and the other began. The underlying aim, according to a contemporary account, was to ensure that "the road should lie comfortably upon the topography, appearing to occupy a miraculously favorable natural location rather than to be cruelly forced through against the 'lay of the land.'"[4]

WCPC parkway design evolved throughout the 1920s and 1930s in response to rising speeds and increasing traffic volumes. Later parkway alignments had longer radius curves accompanied by gradual "spiral" transitions, which replaced the awkward junction of straight lines and radial curves with a smooth adjustment that was both more attractive and easier to negotiate at higher speeds. Superelevation, or "banking," helped motorists maintain control at higher speeds. Grades were generally kept below 6 percent, though 8 percent grades were considered permissible for short distances. In most cases, a single, undivided 40-foot-wide pavement was considered adequate to accommodate two lanes of traffic traveling in either direction. Medians were seen as desirable for both safety and scenic effect, but the added width and associated costs limited their employment. The Bronx River Parkway only provided

grade separations at major intersections, but later parkways generally eliminated all direct crossings. As in NPS road construction, stone facing was used to disguise modern concrete bridges. Recognizing that easily accessible gas stations and roadside rest areas were needed as parkways increased in length, the WCPC provided a limited number in carefully designed locations, giving them rustic treatments in keeping with traditional park and parkway aesthetics. Signs, guard rails, light posts, and other incidental features were similarly designed to harmonize with the overall parkway landscape.

The WCPC design team was headed by engineer Jay Downer and landscape architect Gilmore Clarke. Clarke and Downer became prominent proponents of parkway development, lecturing and consulting widely and publishing articles in engineering, landscape architecture, and planning periodicals. The two men advised the BPR on the development of the parkway-style Mount Vernon Memorial Highway and consulted on the NPS's initial parkway efforts at Colonial National Historical Park. The NPS considered engaging the duo to guide development of Blue Ridge Parkway, but cost concerns and other considerations induced the agency to rely on the traditional NPS-BPR partnership model. The WCPC served as a training ground for several designers who went on to play significant roles in NPS parkway development. Clarke and Downer persuaded the BPR to hire their protégé Wilbur Simonson as lead landscape architect for the Mount Vernon Memorial Highway, which was incorporated

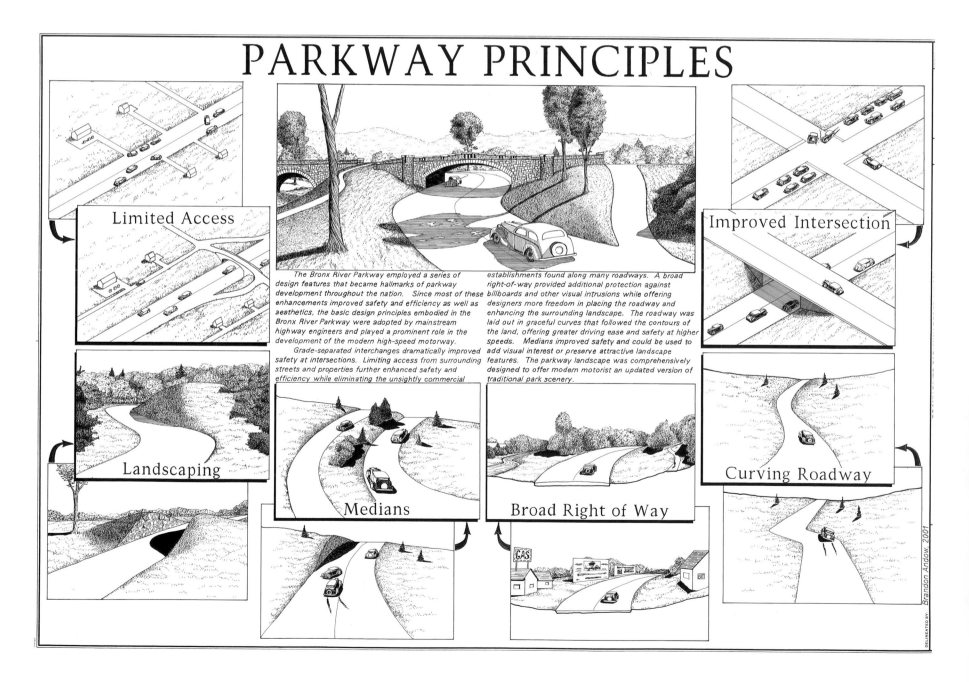

PARKWAY PRINCIPLES

Limited Access

Improved Intersection

The Bronx River Parkway employed a series of design features that became hallmarks of parkway development throughout the nation. Since most of these enhancements improved safety and efficiency as well as aesthetics, the basic design principles embodied in the Bronx River Parkway were adopted by mainstream highway engineers and played a prominent role in the development of the modern high-speed motorway.

Grade-separated interchanges dramatically improved safety at intersections. Limiting access from surrounding streets and properties further enhanced safety and efficiency while eliminating the unsightly commercial establishments found along many roadways. A broad right-of-way provided additional protection against billboards and other visual intrusions while offering designers more freedom in placing the roadway and enhancing the surrounding landscape. The roadway was laid out in graceful curves that followed the contours of the land, offering greater driving ease and safety at higher speeds. Medians improved safety and could be used to add visual interest or preserve attractive landscape features. The parkway landscape was comprehensively designed to offer modern motorist an updated version of traditional park scenery.

Landscaping

Curving Roadway

Medians

Broad Right of Way

DELINEATED BY: Brandon Andow, 2001

into the NPS's George Washington Memorial Parkway. Stanley Abbott, who oversaw the development of Blue Ridge Parkway, was also a WCPC alumnus. Thomas Vint sent two promising subordinates, John Wosky and Kenneth McCarter, to study WCPC design principles.[5]

Although the NPS did not invent the modern motor parkway, it dramatically expanded its scope, both geographically and thematically. The jump from suburban confines to multi-hundred-mile reservations was the most obvious innovation. On a more conceptual level, the NPS expanded the types of landscapes motorists encountered. Previous parkway designers demonstrated little regard for the human history along their paths. Since the Olmstedian tradition viewed parks as naturalistic retreats from human cares, buildings and other signs of habitation and toil gave way to pleasing pastoral compositions to soothe harried urbanites. WCPC designers continued this tradition, providing naturalistic scenery that masked rather than celebrated preexisting buildings and vernacular landscapes. National parkways were intended to preserve and showcase not just natural scenery but also historic sites and more general cultural associations. In the case of George Washington Memorial Parkway, surviving historic sites were few and far between and the association was more honorific than literal. Colonial Parkway was emphatically historical in orientation, serving as the primary circulation system for Virginia's "Sacred Triangle" of Jamestown, Yorktown, and Williamsburg. Blue Ridge and Natchez Trace Parkways celebrated a romanticized vision of rural America with log cabins, gristmills, and vestiges of traditional agriculture serving as cultural touchstones for an increasingly urbanized populace.[6]

This new orientation reflected both NPS's growing involvement in historic preservation and the burgeoning popular interest in American history. The sentimental celebration of the nation's past combined with the rise in automobile ownership engendered a thriving "heritage tourism" industry. Throughout the 1920s, and even under the duress of the Depression, motorists sallied forth in ever-greater numbers in search of historic sites, quaint villages, traditional rural landscapes, and architectural relics consecrated by age or association with famous people and events. Magazine articles and guidebooks commingled heritage tourism with traditional scenic enjoyment. Private entrepreneurs and local history groups

promoted a wide range of attractions ranging from house museums to elaborate tableaux such as Henry Ford's Greenfield Village and John D. Rockefeller's Colonial Williamsburg. State and local jurisdictions acquired historic properties and erected roadside markers to inform and attract motorists. Most of these efforts focused on sites associated with the colonial and early national periods, presenting American history as a romantic saga of frontier fortitude, agrarian ideals, democratic ferment, and patriotic virtue. For the middle- and upper-class Americans of Anglo-Saxon descent who formed the target audience, the popular and professional enshrinement of this ostensibly idyllic past helped assuage cultural anxieties stemming from the rapid pace of modernization and the increasing heterogeneity of American society.[7]

Mount Vernon Memorial Highway was the first parkway to celebrate historical associations. Despite its official name, the memorial highway was designed according to WCPCP parkway design principles, with Clarke and Downer as consultants and Simonson as on-site landscape architect collaborating with BPR engineers. Although senior BPR officials embraced parkway design principles, they encountered the same resistance from rank-and-file engineers that the NPS experienced at the outset of the interagency collaboration. When the BPR was authorized to construct the memorial highway in anticipation of the 1932 celebration of the bicentennial of Washington's birth, MacDonald took advantage of the opportunity to demonstrate the practical as well as aesthetic advantages of parkway design. The existing approach to Mount Vernon along U.S. Route 1 was as outdated, dangerous, and degraded by billboards, gas stations, tourist camps, and "hot dog stands" as any American roadway. Redressing this national disgrace would underscore the virtues of parkway-style design to recalcitrant engineers and stingy politicians alike. The BPR produced pamphlets and articles touting the project as "America's Most Modern Motorway," sponsored tours for engineers from around the United States and abroad, displayed models of key circulation features in the Capitol Rotunda, and produced a movie detailing the roadway's development.[8]

Since the parkway followed the waterfront rather than historical roadways to provide better traffic flow and park amenities, the Washington association was more allusive than authentic. Like the later WCPC parkways, the project's practical

value as a commuter artery was considered at least as significant as its more idealistic attributes. Nevertheless, supporters insisted that motorists would experience a "thrill of Americanism" while driving from the nation's capital to the home of its first president. The primary historical gesture was to include Alexandria's main street in the route. Not only was the city Washington's "home town," but Alexandria merchants had been capitalizing on Mount Vernon–bound tourists for generations and were not willing to forsake the economic benefits just because parkways were supposed to bypass congested commercial centers. To address concerns about conflicting development, the City of Alexandria agreed to one of America's first historic preservation ordinances, restricting construction to "such types of building as will be in keeping with the dignity, purpose and memorial character" of the parkway. Design-wise, the most visible manifestation of the historical connection entailed the use of "colonial-style" broken-pediment signboards with a silhouette of Washington's profile, along with a Colonial Revival concession stand and bus shelters that eschewed the generic rusticity of conventional park structures for timbered allusions to vernacular architecture. Professional publications made token references to historical associations and focused on the parkway's engineering features and landscape design, but popular periodicals embraced all three aspects. When the parkway was completed in 1932, *American Motorist* congratulated the BPR for commemorating George Washington with an achievement "of which he would be proud from a practical, patriotic, and picturesque point of view," proclaiming: "At last there is a highway built for beauty with history for its roadbed and the American ideal for its goal." The memorial highway was subsumed within a broader George Washington Memorial Parkway proposal when the NPS assumed responsibility for Washington-area reservations in 1933.[9]

COLONIAL PARKWAY

Colonial Parkway was the first parkway in which the presentation of historical sites and themes was unquestionably the dominant motivation. Authorized by Congress as an integral component of Colonial National Monument in July 1930, Colonial Parkway would allow motorists to travel between Jamestown, Yorktown, and Williamsburg without recourse to ordinary public roads, which had numerous practical shortcomings and were already succumbing to commercial blight. As the first NPS parkway project, moreover, it provided an opportunity for NPS landscape architects and BPR engineers to unite the expertise gained in western national parks with the design principles pioneered by the Westchester County Park Commission. Although it was overshadowed by later developments, Colonial Parkway played a pivotal role in uniting these two schools of scenic road design and weaving heritage tourism into the traditional mix of scenic appreciation and nature-based recreation. The primary technical difference between parkways and western park roads was that the former traversed more moderate terrain and were intended for slightly higher speeds and heavier traffic volumes. This meant that pavement widths were slightly wider and the curvature more gentle. Balancing modern access concerns with the preservation of historic as well as scenic values raised more complex issues. In some cases, solutions that seemed self-evident to engineers and landscape architects conflicted with the agendas of NPS historians and privately owned historic sites.

During the Mather years, the NPS exhibited little interest in historic sites, focusing on preserving spectacular natural areas and showcasing scenic wonders, flora, and fauna. Mesa Verde and a few other prehistoric ruins were under NPS jurisdiction, but the main responsibility for America's historic and prehistoric resources was split between the War Department, which oversaw an array of forts, memorials, and battlefields; the Department of Agriculture, through its

administration of national monuments on Forest Service land; and the Office of Public Buildings and Parks of the National Capital, whose purview included parks and historic structures in Washington, D.C. Horace Albright's personal enthusiasm for American history combined with his expansionist ambitions and keen reading of contemporary enthusiasms to transform the NPS into the primary custodian of the nation's most cherished cultural landscapes. The first three historical parks authorized under this initiative were the George Washington Birthplace National Monument in Wakefield, Virginia; Colonial National Monument; and Morristown National Historical Park, New Jersey, where Washington and his troops encamped for two trying winters during the Revolutionary War. Albright also appointed a chief historian and established a history division to help inform the preservation and interpretation of historic sites, bringing a new professional perspective into the NPS fold.[10]

The fundamental purpose of Colonial National Monument—reauthorized as Colonial National Historical Park in 1936—was to protect and unify the principal components of Virginia's "Historic Triangle": Jamestown, where English colonists established their first foothold in the New World in 1607; Williamsburg, which served as Virginia's first capital; and Yorktown, where the surrender of British forces in 1781 signaled American victory in the Revolutionary War. The land comprising the long-abandoned Jamestown settlement belonged to the Association for the Preservation of Virginia Antiquities (APVA), which sponsored commemorative activities but made few physical improvements. Congress passed a resolution to memorialize the Yorktown battlefield shortly after the Revolutionary War, but no monument was erected until the battle's centennial in 1881. The idea of establishing a commemorative military park was promoted during the ensuing decades, but most of the battlefield remained in private hands. Having lost its status as Virginia's capital to Richmond in 1780 and settled into its new role as a sleepy country town, Williamsburg retained an exceptional number of relatively unchanged eighteenth-century buildings. In the mid-1920s, the rector of the historic Bruton Parish Church, W. A. R. Goodwin, suggested preserving the central area as an illustration of early American life. John D. Rockefeller Jr. embraced the project, surreptitiously acquiring as many properties as possible and hiring a team of

architects and landscape architects to ensure that the restoration proceeded according to the highest standards of the time. Colonial Williamsburg, as Rockefeller's project became known, exerted a profound influence on the NPS's efforts, both in terms of general approaches to historic preservation and in regard to the location and character of Colonial Parkway.[11]

In 1928 Kenneth Chorley, the director of the restoration project and longtime Rockefeller confidante, approached Albright with the idea of creating a national historical park uniting the three sites. William Carson, the head of Virginia's Conservation and Development Commission, embraced the concept, proclaiming that the proposed park would "present to the Nation and to the world many of the salient facts associated with the birth of the Nation and the Birth of the Nation's liberties." In November 1929 Carson organized a tour of the peninsula for Albright and Congressman Louis Cramton, who was well known for advancing NPS interests as chairman of the House Appropriations Committee. According to Albright, Cramton was the first to propose a parkway as the park's primary circulation feature. Mindful of the commercial clutter that marred contemporary roadsides, he insisted that a visitor should be able to motor between the hallowed sites "without the impression of the early days being driven from his mind by a succession of hot-dog stands and tire signs." Cramton called for the construction of a new roadway "on a strip sufficiently wide to protect it by trees shutting out all conflicting modern development." He maintained that the road itself should harmonize with the historic setting, advising that it should not be "a glaring modern pavement but as much as feasible giving the impression of an old-time road."[12]

With Cramton's backing, the park was quickly approved. The APVA and Colonial Williamsburg retained ownership of their holdings, though Colonial Williamsburg was required to grant a right-of-way to accommodate parkway development. The NPS dispatched engineer Oliver Taylor and landscape architect Charles Peterson to survey the boundaries and propose a general location for the roadway in the fall of 1930. Taylor had developed a reputation as an accomplished road builder while serving as Yosemite's chief engineer. Peterson had worked briefly on western park roads. Despite his limited experience, the ambitious and articulate architect assumed a dominant role in

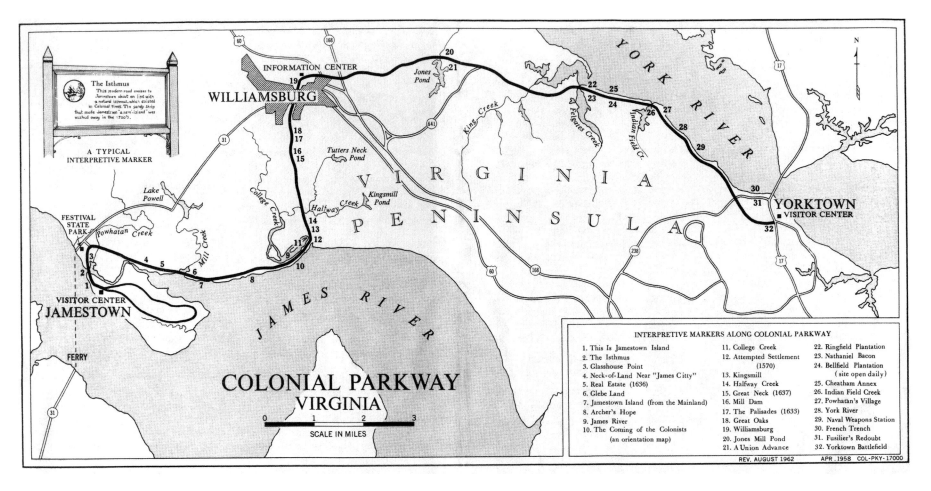

The Isthmus
This modern road crosses to
Jamestown about on line with
a natural isthmus which existed
in Colonial times. The sandy strip
that made Jamestown "a semi-island" was
washed away in the 1700's.

A TYPICAL
INTERPRETIVE MARKER

COLONIAL PARKWAY
VIRGINIA

SCALE IN MILES

INTERPRETIVE MARKERS ALONG COLONIAL PARKWAY

1. This Is Jamestown Island
2. The Isthmus
3. Glasshouse Point
4. Neck-of-Land Near "James Citty"
5. Real Estate (1636)
6. Glebe Land
7. Jamestown Island (from the Mainland)
8. Archer's Hope
9. James River
10. The Coming of the Colonists
   (an orientation map)
11. College Creek
12. Attempted Settlement
   (1570)
13. Kingsmill
14. Halfway Creek
15. Great Neck (1637)
16. Mill Dam
17. The Palisades (1633)
18. Great Oaks
19. Williamsburg
20. Jones Mill Pond
21. A Union Advance
22. Ringfield Plantation
23. Nathaniel Bacon
24. Bellfield Plantation
   (site open daily)
25. Cheatham Annex
26. Indian Field Creek
27. Powhatan's Village
28. York River
29. Naval Weapons Station
30. French Trench
31. Fusilier's Redoubt
32. Yorktown Battlefield

REV. AUGUST 1962   APR. 1958   COL-PKY- 17000

ABOVE Map of Colonial Parkway, 1964.

the project and was soon charged with overseeing all East Coast design activities. Though their primary NPS experience was in the West, both men would undoubtedly have been familiar with WCPC parkway principles from professional articles or personal inspection. While Taylor and Peterson readily adapted their NPS road experience to the more fluid geometries and comprehensive landscape manipulations of contemporary parkway development, reconciling historical and commemorative imperatives with modern motorway design requirements proved more challenging.[13]

The debate hinged on the question of whether the circulation system of a historical park should adopt, or at least emulate, historic roadways, or whether modern traffic demands mandated a more flexible stance. The primary advocate for the former approach was William Robinson Jr., a civil engineer from Atlanta who was appointed the park's first superintendent in June 1931. Robinson insisted that the proper way to convey the area's colonial and Revolutionary heritage was to promote a "visualization of the past" through the preservation of historic structures and the re-creation of

features that had been lost over time. This included not just Williamsburg's colonial buildings, but landscape elements as well. Robinson insisted that the parkway should follow the old road traces that wound throughout the peninsula's fields and forests, maintaining that these historic relics afforded the most effective means of exposing visitors to the nature of colonial travel. Their meandering paths also provided access to numerous historic sites that a modern parkway would inevitably bypass. Acknowledging that there were places where the narrow widths, sharp curves, and steep grades of the historic routes would limit speeds to 25 mph or less, he admonished, "The Parkway is not intended to be a speedway or pleasure boulevard, but rather a convenient way for the visitor to see the historic landmarks that lie along the road and to absorb the Colonial feeling of the landscape." Where circumstances necessitated the construction of new road segments, Robinson called for mediating their modernity with "waved or wobbled" alignments and other historically appropriate imperfections. Robinson also insisted that historical motives take precedence over the NPS's traditional prioritization

of scenic values in the location and landscape development of new roadways. He pointedly condemned the initial section of the parkway, which had been fast-tracked in preparation for the 1931 Yorktown sesquicentennial celebration. Observing that it had been "constructed along the lines of modern highway practices and consistent with the best Park Service traditions," with long, easy curves and gentle grades facilitated by extensive cuts and fills, he protested that "the road structure dominates the landscape with an air of modernity which is foreign to the Colonial character of the Monument."[14]

Peterson, who had designed the section Robinson disparaged, strongly disagreed. Both NPS landscape architects and East Coast parkway designers tailored their roads more sensitively to the natural landscape than did contemporary highway builders, but they were intent on making modern roadways that enabled visitors to drive safely at moderate speeds. Peterson also questioned the accuracy of Robinson's claim that the existing road traces reflected colonial travel routes rather than subsequent meanderings. Even if historical routes could be verified, Peterson maintained

The most innovative manifestation of this effort to reflect the parkway's historic mission was to surface the roadway with a unique concrete pavement designed to emulate the marl and shell roads that predominated in the colonial era.

that such antiquarian diversions would be of little concern to visitors, who would be focused on the park's primary destinations. Peterson insisted that a sensitively designed modern parkway looping gracefully between forests and riverfront was a far more appropriate solution. In addition to meeting NPS standards for scenic beauty and engineering excellence, it would foster an appreciation for the colonial experience by exposing visitors to the natural settings in which events transpired. Where the parkway swept along the York River shoreline, for instance, it would underscore the role tidal waterways played in regional history. Albright sent Frank Kittredge to resolve the disagreement. Although he sympathized with Robinson's intentions, Kittredge voted in favor of "a high standard modern parkway." BPR representatives concurred, and Albright ruled for a continuation of the NPS emphasis on scenic values and state-of-the-art engineering, establishing a policy that would be followed in subsequent parkways and historical parks.[15]

Parkway designers did go to considerable lengths to mediate the modernity of the road's design and construction. As with other park roads and parkways, constant curvature minimized the amount of pavement in the motorist's view, and rustic log guard rails flanked the roadway in hazardous locations. Instead of employing native stone facings, antique-looking brick was laid in traditional Flemish and English bond patterns to echo the architecture of Colonial Williamsburg. The most innovative manifestation of this effort to reflect the parkway's historic mission was to surface the roadway with a unique concrete pavement designed to emulate the marl and shell roads that predominated in the colonial era. In order to achieve the desired effect, concrete was prepared with an unusually large aggregate, then washed with an acidic mixture and swept with stiff wire brushes to partially expose the pebbles. The inspiration for this approach came from contemporary sidewalk treatments at Colonial Williamsburg. Applying the novel approach to an entire parkway in a manner that would withstand the rigors of automobile traffic challenged the ingenuity and patience of the project's contractors and their BPR supervisors. Another unusual aspect of Colonial Parkway was that it was constructed as a 30-foot-wide, three-lane roadway. At the time, some planners and engineers were promoting this approach as an economical solution for roads where traffic burdens were not expected to be high

enough to mandate four full lanes. The third lane would allow impatient motorists to pass slower travelers in either direction. Since the configuration proved dangerously confusing in broader applications, Colonial Parkway's pavement became a historical artifact in its own right.[16]

The NPS implemented its usual extensive grading, planting, and forest improvement program to remediate construction scars and improve the appearance of surrounding woodlands. Deadwood, brush, and diseased trees were removed along with dense growths that might create fire hazards. As with Mount Vernon Memorial Highway, the riverfront location necessitated extensive draining and filling operations that required comprehensive landscape rehabilitation. Cedar, dogwood, pine, tulip, beech, and redbud constituted the bulk of new plantings, along with understory species such as bayberry and sumac. Selective cutting and vista clearing enhanced the motorist's experience by opening up or framing attractive views and creating scenic effects varying from open grassland to canopied forests. Parking pullouts were provided at especially scenic locations. A succession of NPS landscape architects including Edward Zimmer, James Brooks, Ray Wilhelm, and Eugene DeSilets directed these operations, producing highly annotated plans detailing the desired effects. The BPR's H. J. Spelman oversaw the engineering aspects. The prominent Boston-based landscape architect Arthur Shurcliff advised on road location and planting arrangements in the vicinity of Colonial Williamsburg, where he served as consulting landscape architect. Approximately eight hundred men from several Civilian Conservation Corps (CCC) camps provided hand labor, while private contractors operated heavy machinery and performed other specialized tasks.[17]

Disagreements arose about the manner in which Colonial Williamsburg would be integrated into the parkway experience. Peterson originally hoped to route parkway traffic directly through the city, utilizing historic city streets in a manner akin to Mount Vernon Memorial Highway's relationship with Alexandria. Colonial Williamsburg officials rejected this proposal as antithetical to their goal of re-creating the colonial capital's eighteenth-century ambience. Shurcliff proposed an alternative that routed the parkway north of the most historic part of the city, then headed west and approached Jamestown from the north, significantly reducing the amount of scenic river frontage and exposing motorists to such a profusion of modern intrusions that Peterson rejected it as "not compatible with the dignity of Colonial National Monument." Albright and Assistant Director Demaray pressed for an amicable resolution. Along with their general sympathy toward Colonial Williamsburg's preservation efforts, the NPS could not afford to anger Rockefeller, who was contributing to numerous agency initiatives. Gilmore Clarke, Jay Downer, and the noted city planner Harland Bartholomew were called in to consult on the matter.

Though NPS officials initially acquiesced to Shurcliff's proposal, they revisited the issue as parkway construction pressed toward Williamsburg. In 1936, NPS designers and Williamsburg officials began discussing an ambitious alternative that would avoid modern developments and retain the riverfront location without impinging on the historic area. The parkway would approach Williamsburg along a modified version of the original alignment and then pass under the city by means of a tunnel located beyond the historic core. Local leaders opposed this option on the grounds that it would prevent businesses from benefiting from parkway traffic, sparing Rockefeller's project at the expense of actual residents, many of whom would be dislocated during the construction process. The combined influence of Colonial Williamsburg and the NPS ultimately prevailed. The tunnel was largely constructed between 1940 and 1942, but technical difficulties along with shortages of material and labor associated with World War II delayed its opening until 1949. The tunnel's portals and wingwalls were sheathed in "Colonial Style" brick in the same manner as the parkway's other masonry structures. The NPS and Colonial Williamsburg collaborated on an elaborate exit replete with landscaped roundabout and signature "colonial" brickwork. While the Williamsburg tunnel represented a deft solution from a design and engineering perspective, it meant that visitors passed underneath the historic city that the parkway was intended to showcase. This decision afforded additional evidence that NPS parkway development designers privileged technical efficiency, scenic beauty, and associational values over more direct and literal engagement with historical themes. On a more progressive note, it underscored the agency's evolving perspective on the appropriate balance between preservation and

access. By forcing visitors to get out of their cars and walk through Colonial Williamsburg, parkway designers transferred the emerging consensus that new roads should lead to but not through the mostly highly valued areas from natural landscapes to historic settings.[18]

The parkway was completed to the outskirts of Williamsburg by 1937, but the tunnel issues and uncertainties about the routing between Williamsburg and Jamestown delayed construction until the NPS recovered from budget shortfalls associated with World War II. Little progress occurred until 1949, when landscape architect Stanley Abbott was sent from Blue Ridge Parkway to develop a strategy for the parkway's completion. Along with the general desire to bring closure to the long-delayed project, the NPS was under pressure to ready the site in time for the 350th anniversary of Jamestown's founding, which would be observed with a grand celebration in 1957. As with the earlier section along the York River, the James River shoreline required significant amounts of dredging and filling along with the construction of a series of low bridges to carry the parkway through wetlands. These operations significantly altered the local ecology and caused multiple problems as the roadbed settled, but the routing afforded motorists with sweeping views of the river, marshes, and bordering woodlands. The entire parkway was officially opened to traffic on April 27, 1957, just in advance of the planned festivities.[19]

BLUE RIDGE PARKWAY

The Blue Ridge Parkway was in many ways a more conventional parkway project, albeit on an unprecedented scale. As with nineteenth- and early-twentieth-century parkways, it was conceived as a link between two major elements of a park system and designed as an attractively landscaped recreational drive augmented by intermediary developments catering to through-travelers and local residents alike. What made Blue Ridge Parkway unique was that the parks that constituted its end points were nearly 500 miles apart, providing motorists with an opportunity to drive for days through scenic splendors that varied from deep forests and shady glens to upland meadows, rocky ridges, dazzling displays of flowering shrubs, and sweeping panoramas of mountains,

fields, and foothills. Associated developments ranged in size from simple pullouts to tracts of 1,000 acres or more, from picnic areas and scenic lookouts to cabins, campgrounds, large tracts of wilderness, and interpretative displays of traditional Appalachian culture and architecture. The goal was not only to connect the two parks but to make the drive itself "an alluring invitation to the vacationist." Observing that Blue Ridge Parkway would be located within a day's drive of half the United States' population, the NPS characterized it as "a well-chosen laboratory in which to test the soundness of the parkway concept as a means of bringing the national parks and forests closer to the people." Given Colonial Parkway's limited extent and specialized focus, NPS officials cast it as "the first parkway of national scope."[20]

While the NPS embraced the Blue Ridge Parkway as a means of both expanding its East Coast presence and demonstrating the appeal of parkway development, the concept of constructing a roadway though the southern Appalachian highlands between the Shenandoahs and Great Smoky Mountains predated agency involvement. As with many other national park road projects, the parkway reflected a confluence of local desires to reap the benefits of scenic tourism and the NPS mission of preserving and showcasing America's signature landscapes. Local boosters and their political allies took the lead in pressing for the project's inception. The New Deal agenda of relieving unemployment and stimulating the economy played a pivotal role. The parkway's authorization and initial funding came directly through the Public Works Administration (PWA) rather than through traditional NPS channels.

Proposals for a scenic highway along the crest of the Blue Ridge dated back at least to 1906, when Joseph Hyde Pratt of the North Carolina Geological and Economic Survey pressed for construction of a toll road extending from Marion, Virginia, through Blowing Rock, Linville, and Asheville, North Carolina, and on into Georgia. According to Pratt, the single-lane, 350-mile-long, gravel-surfaced roadway was "destined to be one of the greatest scenic roads in America, surpassing anything in the East and rivaling those in Yosemite Valley and the Yellowstone National Park." North Carolina granted a charter for the "Appalachian Highway Company" in 1914. Pratt surveyed a route and even constructed a short segment near Humpback Mountain that was eventually incorporated into Blue Ridge Parkway, but America's entry into World War I put an end to the enterprise. The Park-to-Park Highway movement exerted a more direct influence. While the original concept was limited to the western parks, the authorization of Shenandoah and Great Smoky Mountains National Parks prompted a similar coalition of automobile clubs, tourism interests, and state highway officials to lobby for an analogous effort in the East. In 1930 the Eastern National Park-to-Park Highway Association produced a proposal for highways linking the growing network of national parks, monuments, and historic sites east of the Mississippi. The NPS and BPR advised on efforts to refine the concept over the next few years. Links between Mammoth Cave, Great Smoky Mountain, and Shenandoah National Parks formed the core of the proposal,

along with a loop encompassing Washington, D.C., Colonial National Monument, and various Civil War battlefields, but extensions south to Louisiana's Chalmette Battlefield and up the eastern seaboard to Morristown National Historic Site were also considered. There is no indication that any of these proposals contemplated a ridge-top location or called for anything more than the improved state highways that formed the basis of the western Park-to-Park Highway. Although there proved to be insufficient support to sustain the broader outlines of the Eastern National Park-to-Park Highway concept, North Carolina, Virginia, and Tennessee boosters continued to push for the development of one or more officially sanctioned connections between Shenandoah and Great Smoky Mountains National Parks.[21]

Credit for the proposal that led directly to

the development of Blue Ridge Parkway has been apportioned to various individuals, including Virginia governor John Garland Pollard and Virginia senator Harry Byrd, BPR chief Thomas MacDonald, Maryland senator George Radcliffe, who served as PWA director for the region, and Radcliffe's assistant Theodore Strauss. Byrd credited MacDonald with originating the proposal, but MacDonald denied responsibility. Most sources point to Byrd, suggesting that the senator sought to preempt charges of pork-barrel politics by attributing the proposal to a public servant with a carefully cultivated reputation for apolitical expertise. The most likely scenario was that Byrd suggested the idea to FDR while accompanying the president on a visit to one of Shenandoah National Park CCC camps in August 1933. The development of Skyline Drive had

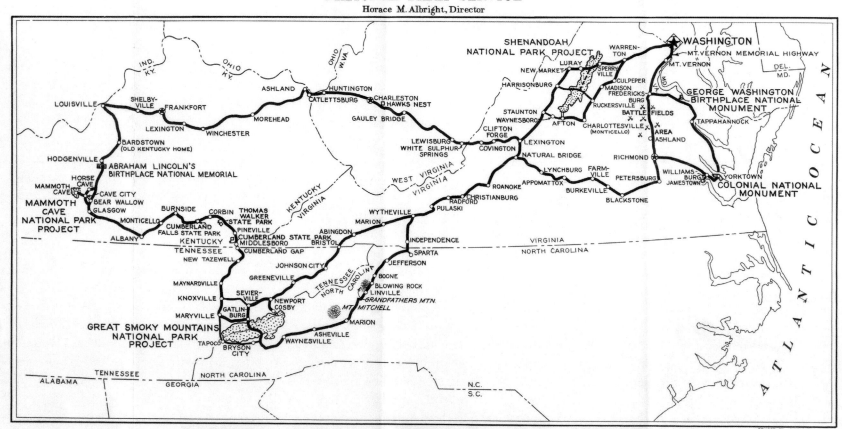

ABOVE Proposal for Eastern National Park-to-Park Highway, 1931.

National Park Roads

garnered considerable acclaim as an illustration of the New Deal's ability to combine conservation, recreational development, and employment relief. Roosevelt's political instincts and personal interest in recreational motoring made him an easy touch for Byrd's suggestion that extending the drive all the way to Great Smoky Mountains National Park would reap myriad rewards. Not only would the project produce highly visible public works benefits through some of the areas of the country that were suffering most, but it would provide a permanent boost to the regional economy while catering to the needs of 60 million motorists, voters, and taxpayers. After securing Roosevelt's endorsement, Byrd worked with Pollard to build support within Virginia and encourage the governors of North Carolina and Tennessee to do the same. In October he convened a meeting that included Arno Cammerer, Macdonald, Radcliffe, Strauss, and political and engineering delegations from the three states and convinced them to push the project forward. A month later Harold Ickes acted in his role as PWA administrator to authorize construction of a "scenic highway connecting the Shenandoah and Smoky Mountains National Parks," allocating $4 million to get the project started. While the NPS assumed responsibility for planning and designing the parkway, it was not initially a component of the National Park System. The authority and funding came through the 1933 National Industrial Recovery Act, which empowered the administration to conduct a wide range of economic relief projects including the construction of "public highways and parkways." Securing authorization in this manner bypassed the lengthy and often contentious negotiations involved in securing congressional approval for a new national park. Although the long-term tourism dividends were undoubtedly important, the immediate payoff entailed jobs for hard-hit communities along the parkway's path. PWA contracts generally required contractors to hire local workers whenever possible. Additional employment was provided through related programs such as the Emergency Relief Administration, Civil Works Administration, and Civilian Conservation Corps. The Blue Ridge Parkway did not become an official national park until Congress passed the authorizing legislation in June 1936.[22]

Ickes's approval was a crucial step, but it left several important matters unsettled. The most pressing concern was determining the route the roadway would take. Skyline Drive would clearly form the northern terminus, and agreement was soon reached that the road would follow the Blue Ridge south to Linville, North Carolina, but controversy erupted over its subsequent path. Both for its own commitment to wilderness preservation and to avoid further controversy, the NPS insisted that the parkway could not pass through the eastern area of Great Smoky Mountains National Park that had been declared off-limits to development. North Carolina interests insisted the roadway should pass close to Asheville, entering Great Smoky Mountains National Park from the southeast. Along with providing the most direct route, the higher elevation would afford more spectacular views, especially where it skirted the flanks of Mount Mitchell, the highest point in the East. This would funnel all of the economic benefits to North Carolina, but supporters pointed out that Tennessee already profited from Gatlinburg's status as the principal entrance to Great Smoky Mountains National Park. As a result, Asheville's formally robust tourism industry had suffered a decline in fortunes that would become even more precipitous if the parkway were routed elsewhere. Tennessee officials objected, insisting their state deserved a portion of the route since they had lobbied for the project's approval. An NPS-BPR delegation reconnoitered both options during the spring of 1934, ruling in favor of the Tennessee terminus. They noted that the Tennessee route's combination of mountain and valley scenery afforded more visual variation, suggesting that motorists might become bored by the extensive stretches of unbroken forest that North Carolina advocates cast as an undeniable advantage. The lower elevation and more gentle terrain would reduce development costs and minimize scenery-scarring construction while allowing for the employment of higher design standards that would enhance its appeal for motorists who were more interested in traveling from park to park than proceeding at a leisurely rate for hundreds of miles. Aware that the political winds were blowing in North Carolina's favor, they raised the possibility of splitting the parkway into two forks so that motorists could chose either gateway.[23]

Ickes then asked Bob Marshall to investigate the competing proposals. While Marshall had no official connection to the project in his role as forester for the department's Indian Service, Ickes made it clear that he valued the outspoken wilderness advocate's opinion on road matters more than official NPS pronouncements. Marshall advised Ickes that either route would provide a satisfactory connection, but he also leaned in favor of the Tennessee alternative, observing that it would be cheaper to construct and less destructive to wilderness values. While North Carolina interests emphasized the appeal of motoring through remote highlands, Marshall made an impassioned plea for "the necessity of keeping the parkway out of the few important primitive areas which are still left in this region." Ickes sympathized with Marshall's sentiments but recognized that this was a situation in which political considerations outweighed preservation concerns. Rejecting Marshall's advice and his own committee's recommendations, Ickes ruled in favor of the North Carolina option in September 1934. While he extolled the route's scenic qualities, his emphasis on the economic impact revealed the underlying motivation. Ickes characterized the decision as a means of spreading the benefits of federal assistance, noting that North Carolina had nothing to compare with Gatlinburg's gateway to Great Smoky Mountains National Park, much less the Tennessee Valley Authority. The North Carolina route was also presented as better suited for eventual extension farther south along the Appalachian chain through South Carolina and on to Georgia.[24]

Although the concept of a scenery-maximizing high-elevation parkway soon came to the fore, the initial authorization not only declined to designate a route but demurred on the basic development approach. Many supporters assumed that the federal government would simply upgrade existing roadways to provide a connection between the two parks along the lines of the western Park-to-Park Highway. This would have been cheaper and more expedient, but it would have given rise to the proliferation of tourist-oriented businesses that were transforming ordinary highways into linear slums. Realizing that a limited-access scenic parkway would solve the problem while affording additional attractions, the NPS engaged Gilmore Clarke and Jay Downer to provide direction. This represented a departure from the usual practice of pairing NPS landscape architects with BPR engineers. NPS officials recognized that Clarke and Downer were the acknowledged experts in the field, whereas the agency's own experience was limited to the relatively minor challenges associated with Colonial Parkway. Since Clarke and Downer's WCPC responsibilities precluded full-time engagement, they persuaded the NPS to hire one of their most promising subordinates as resident landscape architect. Though only twenty-six, Stanley Abbott had impressed his superiors with both his design skills and his ability to communicate with popular and professional audiences. Abbott went to work in January 1934, exploring potential parkway locations on his own and in concert with Downer, Clarke, and Vint. He was joined in April by Hendrick van Gelder, another WCPC veteran known for his expertise in road location, and Edward Abbuehl, a former Cornell instructor who served as Abbott's chief assistant and eventual successor. By this time Abbott was fully in charge of the project, as Clarke and Downer had parted ways after a dispute with Ickes over their consulting fees. The BPR contingent was headed by Stephen Mather's old acquaintance Bill Austin. He was aided by W. I. Lee, who had been involved with western road construction as well as Mount Vernon Memorial Highway, and district engineer Harold Spelman, whose experience included both Mount Vernon Memorial Highway and Colonial Parkway.[25]

Accounts of the parkway's early development cast Abbott as a visionary thinker and master communicator, conceptualizing and articulating the parkway's overarching goals and aesthetic values. Abbuehl was more of a realist, working with van Gelder and other staff members to translate Abbott's vision into what the NPS was soon promoting as the longest road planned as a single unit in American history. Abbuehl was largely responsible for fine-tuning the parkway's location in North Carolina. Van Gelder performed a similar function in Virginia, though North Carolina state highway engineer R. Getty Browning also played a significant role in defining the parkway's route, especially in the region between Asheville and Great Smoky Mountains National Park. Although the BPR did not always appreciate the NPS's insistence on pursuing scenic goals at the expense of technical efficiency, the engineers and landscape architects became more attuned to each other's perspectives as the project progressed. During the postwar construction period, BPR regional engineer William Cron was a forceful advocate for sensitive road location, exhorting his subordinates to "follow the contours" to minimize the roadway's impact on scenic terrain. The American Society of Landscape Architects recognized Cron's contributions by

electing him to honorary membership, a notable gesture given the often contentious relationship between the two professions.[26]

Shenandoah National Park's Skyline Drive may have been the direct inspiration for Blue Ridge Parkway, but Abbott made it clear that new project would bear only a "remote likeness" to what he characterized as its "foster parent."[27] Skyline Drive's ridge-top location provided a unique recreational experience, but both the NPS and the BPR questioned whether motorists would enjoy a roadway that hugged the crest of the Blue Ridge Mountains for 500 miles. As BPR engineer Austin put it, "One could get gorged on scenery, and you can have too much ice cream and too much Beethoven." Vint and Abbott agreed that the parkway should provide a more diversified driving experience, following the ridge line at times, then dropping down along side slopes and into valleys to alternate spectacular vistas with more intimate woodland scenes, glimpses of gurgling streams, and vignettes of traditional agriculture. Adopting a more melodious metaphor than his BPR counterpart, Abbott observed, "One panorama following right on another, thinking of that as *fortissimo*, doesn't make the interesting piece of music that *fortissimo* mixed with a little *pianissimo* provides." Deviating from a strictly ridge-top route would have practical benefits as well, lowering construction costs, reducing unsightly cuts and fills, and making it easier to lay out the roadway with the gentle curves and grades necessitated by motor traffic. Abbott acknowledged that some degree of construction scarring was inevitable, particularly in the more rugged areas, but expressed confidence that judicious alignment, naturalistic grading, and remedial planting would minimize the roadway's visual impact. Seeking to avoid a repeat of the Great Smoky Mountains controversy, he emphasized from the start that "contrary to public opinion, the parkway will not be an all *skyline* location." The road would follow ridgelines on occasion, but for most of its route it would be closer to Benton Mackaye's flankline drive conception.[28]

Another significant deviation from Skyline Drive was that Blue Ridge Parkway was explicitly intended to showcase cultural landscapes as well as natural scenery. Rather than eliminate all signs of human occupation, as in Shenandoah National Park, the NPS sought to celebrate the architecture and culture of the Appalachian Highlands.

Picturesque log cabins were preserved and interpreted, the historic Mabry Mill was restored and made the centerpiece of an exhibition of mountain industry, miles of rail fence were arrayed along the roadside, and farmers were encouraged to carry on traditional agricultural practices through leasing arrangements and scenic easements. Along with adding visual diversity and human interest, these scenes of traditional rural life were meant to instill appreciation for the agrarian values and pioneer fortitude that were cherished as fundamental elements of American history and national identity. The goal, according to Abbott, was to provide "the look of homespun in an East that is chiefly silks and rayons." Automobiles made it relatively easy to venture into the countryside, but the rapid pace of modernization made it increasingly difficult to find reassuring scenes of agrarian bliss. "Only as we save some of the beauty of the countryside and some of the homespun folklore and the rural arts as part of our culture," Abbott insisted, "will this favorite American pastime of touring be the salutary recreation that it might." While later historians have criticized the NPS for moving buildings around, concocting questionable story lines, and selectively editing out discordant elements to present a romanticized image of Appalachian life, parkway designers were explicit in their desire to create a "museum of managed American countryside" that was intended to produce a compelling "pastoral picture" rather than conform to subsequent standards of historical authenticity and cultural sensitivity.[29]

Clarke initially suggested the parkway be developed with the WCPC-standard 200-foot-wide right-of-way. The NPS quickly realized this would provide inadequate protection and that the varying conditions found along the parkway's route required a more flexible approach. Instead of adhering to a rigidly defined width, Abbott proposed that the parkway corridor average 100 acres per mile, with an additional 50 acres per mile protected through scenic easements. This worked out to an average 825-foot right-of-way augmented by 400 feet of scenic easement but allowed the boundaries to shrink where vegetation or topography provided adequate protection and expand in areas where longer sight distances or incompatible development required additional screening. The greater width significantly increased the cost of land acquisition, which was borne by the states rather than the federal government. Virginia initially balked at the change but reluctantly agreed to comply. North

BR 26 The Parkway Through Devil's Garden, Blue Ridge Parkway, North Carolina.

LEFT Blue Ridge Parkway through Devil's Garden, postcard, ca. 1950.

BELOW Blue Ridge Parkway vista at Rocky Knob, postcard, ca. 1950.

LEFT Mabry Mill, Blue Ridge Parkway, ca. 1950.

Carolina was more amenable, approving a 125-acre average. The 100-acre-per-mile standard became official NPS parkway policy in 1936.[30]

The ability to expand and contract the boundaries facilitated the policy of providing a variety of wayside developments along the parkway route. Located at approximately 30-mile intervals, these "bulges," as the landscape architects termed them, provided basic services such as restrooms, food, gas, picnic tables, and various forms of overnight accommodation, along with opportunities to linger and enjoy attractions ranging from solitary cabins and more elaborate displays of Appalachian folklife to lakes, waterfalls, wildflower gardens, and trail networks providing access to thousands of acres of protected woodlands and mountaintops. Approximately half of the twenty planned waysides

would be of the larger, more elaborately developed variety, including Humpback Rocks, Peaks of the Otter, Doughton Park, and Rocky Knob. The NPS maintained that these facilities were as integral to the parkway concept as the motor road itself, underscoring that Blue Ridge Parkway was not just a link between parks but a multipurpose park in its own right. Along with serving the needs of long-distance motorists, many of these developments became local or regional destinations themselves. For through-travelers, they added variety and interest to the trip while providing inducements to step out of the car and experience the southern highlands on more leisurely and intimate terms. Abbott and his colleagues saw no contradiction between this automotive orientation and traditional resource protection and scenic

enjoyment functions. Since recreational motoring had become one of America's favorite pastimes, the NPS felt a responsibility to ensure that the experience was as enjoyable and beneficial as possible. Characterizing the project as the "first direct answer to the requirements of the vacation motorist," Abbott touted it as the ideal "motor vacation land." With hundreds of miles of scenic drives and a wide variety of accommodations and attractions, the parkway was being developed "as a self-sufficient motordom with the expectation that many visitors will spend days or weeks along its route."[31]

The main parkway drive was a 20-foot-wide, two-lane, undivided roadway, with 5-foot unpaved shoulders, a controlling grade of 6 percent, and widening and modest superelevation on curves, which were limited to a 200-foot radius and linked with spiral transitions to provide a relaxing driving experience at the parkway speed limit of 45 mph. After the general location was decided, NPS-BPR design teams spent an enormous amount of time scouting alignments that would afford the most appealing scenic possibilities while conforming to engineering requirements. While it was often possible to nestle the roadway along natural contours with a minimum of excavation, some sections required considerable cutting and filling, resulting in scars that needed extensive rehabilitation and occasionally remain visible to this day. As with general park road construction, retaining walls, viaducts, and tunnels were employed to minimize the roadway's scenic and environmental impact. Although it would have been inordinately expensive to construct grade separation structures at every parkway intersection, all major and most intermediate interchanges were accommodated in this manner. Masonry structures visible from the main drive were generally faced with native stone during the initial development period, though exposed concrete became more common after World War II. Stone guard walls were constructed in hazardous locations, though Abbott and Abbuehl argued that timber barriers would have been more appropriate in areas where stone was not a readily available building material. They also accused their engineering colleagues of insisting on a large amount of unnecessary guard wall, driving up expenses and impinging on the parkway's naturalistic character. The split-rail fences that many consider an emblematic feature of the parkway were generally deployed for aesthetic purposes, though some fulfilled their intended function of defining fields and containing livestock. Many were moved from their original locations to line the parkway, where they played a prominent role in establishing its traditional rural character. Parkway buildings were designed to further this goal. The NPS insisted that gas stations, coffee shops, visitor centers, and lodging facilities reflect the vernacular architecture of the Blue Ridge region. Distinctive signage was developed to establish a unified aesthetic and promote the Park Service's interpretive aims. Routed "gun board" signs, so-named because they were embellished with the image of an old-fashioned rifle, provided information about parkway features along with colorful tales of "characteristic" local residents such as miller Elias Mabry and 102-year-old midwife "Aunt Arlena" Puckett. Although these efforts to emphasize the human history of

the parkway landscape perpetuated regional stereotypes, they represented a significant departure from the NPS's usual focus on scenery and natural resources. Unlike the agency's earliest forays into historic site stewardship, moreover, Blue Ridge Parkway was intended to present the everyday experiences of common people rather than celebrate famous men and notable events.[32]

The construction process got under way in September 1935 with the awarding of a PWA contract for the 12.5-mile segment from the Virginia–North Carolina state line south to Cumberland Knob. Subsequent public works contracts extended the parkway southward. As with Skyline Drive and other national park road projects, private contractors handled most of the heavy construction, while CCC enrollees performed less-skilled tasks such as slope grading, seeding and planting, roadside cleanup, and some gutter and guard rail projects. By the end of 1937, 115 miles, or approximately one-quarter of the parkway, had been cleared, graded, and prepared for paving. The first fully completed portion was a 50-mile stretch near Roanoke, which opened to the public in April 1939. The section between the North Carolina state line and Blowing Rock opened later in the year. More than 290,000 automobiles traveled this part of the parkway during the first nine months of operation. Most of these motorists were residents of the surrounding region out for Sunday drives and other brief excursions. The major investment of New Deal funds and labor enabled work to continue at a relatively rapid pace over the next two years, but, as with other park road projects, the United States' entrance into World War II spelled the end of significant progress. When construction was officially halted in November 1942, 171 miles of the parkway drive were fully paved, another 162 miles were under construction, and another 144 miles remained undeveloped.[33]

The cessation of hostilities did not bring an immediate upswing in construction. The termination of New Deal programs and lean postwar budgets prevented a return to postwar rates of progress. The initial focus was on repairing areas damaged by wartime neglect, which was particularly prevalent on sections that had been partially completed but remained unpaved. Despite the parkway's poor condition, use increased dramatically, putting pressure on the Park Service to accelerate construction. The highest priorities

were the construction of a major bridge over the James River and completion of the stretch between Roanoke and Asheville, which included a 7-mile section between Mount Mitchell and Craggy Gardens and a controversial segment near Roanoke, which the BPR wanted to develop to a higher standard so that it could do double duty as an urban beltway. The NPS protested that this would be an unacceptable infringement on the parkway's character, and the conflict was eventually resolved in the Park Service's favor. By the mid-1950s only about one-third of the parkway was officially completed and open to travel.[34]

The Mission 66 program to upgrade and expand the National Park System provided the financial and administrative impetus to push the long-delayed parkway to the cusp of completion. Construction moved into high gear after the parkway was declared one of the program's priority projects in July 1956. By 1960, the Virginia portion was complete except for the controversial Roanoke section. This gap was finally closed in June 1965. By the summer of 1960, motorists could follow the parkway from the North Carolina state line to Asheville, with the exception of a 7-mile segment around Grandfather Mountain, where the NPS was engaged in prolonged negotiations with an unsympathetic landowner. Mission 66 funding also enabled the NPS to push the parkway through the rugged terrain south of Asheville, where numerous tunnels were employed to minimize scenic impact. By 1963, motorists could drive from Mount Pisgah to Great Smoky Mountains National Park, through the highest and most dramatic portion of the parkway. Progress was delayed in the Asheville area as the NPS and BPR debated the best way to handle the parkway's relationship with the two interstates it would have to cross. When the Asheville section was opened to the public in the fall of 1966, the only thing preventing motorists from driving all the way from Skyline Drive to Great Smoky Mountains National Park was a short stretch of contested hillside on the flank of Grandfather Mountain. Closing this gap would delay the official completion of the parkway for another twenty-one years.[35]

Grandfather Mountain is the highest summit in the Blue Ridge. Its scenic grandeur prompted an unsuccessful campaign to make the peak a national park even before the parkway was approved. In the late 1940s, the owner of the mountain, Hugh Morton, began to develop a

ABOVE Family on Blue Ridge Parkway, 1950s.

private tourist attraction that eventually included a swinging bridge leading to the peak and various other facilities, all accessed by a private toll road. Morton was understandably concerned that the parkway would undercut his lucrative operation. The conflict was exacerbated by the fact that the NPS had decided that the parkway should be routed higher on the mountainside than originally envisioned. Morton mounted a highly effective public relations campaign, comparing the NPS proposal to "taking a switchblade to the Mona Lisa" and misleadingly asserting that it would go right over the top of mountain, though the routing never came within 1,000 vertical feet of the ridgeline and skirted his facilities by almost 2 miles. Morton used his media savvy and political connections to promote a compromise location. The NPS, BPR, and North Carolina state highway engineer R. Getty Browning countered that this alignment would be more ecologically damaging and visually disruptive since a lengthy tunnel on the preferred route would conceal the roadway from view. By 1963, the governor publicly endorsed Morton's alternative. The NPS continued to resist, exploring alternative

routings. Faced with mounting pressure to complete the parkway, the agency finally acquiesced to a variation of the middle route, bringing the impasse to an end in October 1968. The prolonged conflict meant that Mission 66 funding was no longer available, however, and budgeting concerns and technical challenges would delay the parkway's completion for another two decades.[36]

NATCHEZ TRACE PARKWAY

The Natchez Trace Parkway combined the long-distance scenic-drive function of Blue Ridge Parkway with the commemorative and historical imperatives of Colonial Parkway. Although the parkway's 444 miles encompassed thousands of acres of scenic terrain in Mississippi, Tennessee, and Alabama, its primary purpose was to preserve, commemorate, and interpret the historic overland route between Nashville and Natchez. Historians

played an unusually prominent role in the parkway's conception and location, though the design and precise alignment were developed through the usual partnership of NPS landscape architects and BPR engineers. As with Blue Ridge Parkway, the basic configuration was a limited-access two-lane roadway interspersed with scenic pullouts, picnic areas, cultural sites, and natural attractions. The Natchez Trace Parkway was developed with fewer major recreation areas, due in part to the less dramatic nature of the terrain and in part to its greater distance from major metropolitan areas. Unlike Blue Ridge Parkway, where the traditional parkway function of linking major parks was a dominant motive, Natchez Trace Parkway was conceived from the start as an independent entity providing motorists with relaxing and uplifting exposure to nature, history, and pastoral imagery. In this regard it was arguably a more ambitious demonstration of the ability of national parkways to serve as "self-sufficient motordoms" attracting recreational interest on their own merits. Funding shortages delayed completion of the Natchez Trace Parkway even longer than the Blue Ridge

Parkway, causing considerable concern among supporters of the project and contributing to growing skepticism about the viability of the national parkway concept itself.[37]

The original Natchez Trace was a rough path leading from Natchez, Mississippi, through a wilderness of swamps and woodlands to Nashville, Tennessee. Although it was used occasionally by missionaries, traders, and settlers prior to the Revolutionary War, the Trace gained its greatest notoriety after 1785, when it became the primary means by which boatmen returned home after floating their goods down the Mississippi. By the early 1800s, northbound traffic became so heavy that Congress made appropriations to improve the path into a passable, if primitive, road. Fords and ferries were established at major stream crossings, and a number of taverns and inns—or "stands" in the local vernacular—catered to travelers. The western explorer Meriwether Lewis met a violent end at Grinders Stand in 1809, a site that was incorporated in the parkway. The Trace accrued additional historical associations when Andrew Jackson's militia used it during the War of 1812. The Natchez Trace's heyday lasted less than forty years, as the advent of steam travel provided a quicker and easier means of navigation. The Trace had ceased to function as an important regional thoroughfare by the 1830s, and significant portions were abandoned, but many sections continued to serve local traffic, receiving varying degrees of maintenance and improvement into the twentieth century.[38]

In keeping with nationwide patterns of popular history and commemoration, interest in the old Natchez Trace began to grow shortly after the turn of century. A 1905 article in *Everybody's Magazine* celebrated the Trace's history and romantic associations. The Mississippi chapter of the Daughters of the American Revolution (DAR) announced that commemorating the Trace would be one of the club's priorities and proposed to place markers along the route. The first monument was erected with considerable fanfare in Natchez. Twenty more markers were dedicated over the next thirty years, with the Alabama and Tennessee DAR chapters following suit. Other patriotic organizations and civic groups joined the effort, including the United Daughters of the War of 1812, the Nashville Auto Club, and the Natchez-based Pilgrimage Garden Club. Sentimental accounts of the Trace's history and significance appeared in books, magazines, and

newspaper articles. These efforts played a critical role in building enthusiasm for more substantial preservation and commemoration measures.[39]

More pragmatic motives also prompted renewed interest in the Natchez Trace. The South lagged well behind other parts of the country in modern road development. Politicians, farmers, and businessmen recognized that improved roads were vital to the region's prosperity. A modernized version of the Natchez Trace would stimulate growth while bolstering the region's appeal to motor tourists. Some argued that the project was a military necessity, given the lack of decent roadways leading from Washington to New Orleans and beyond to the Mexican border. As early as 1916, Mississippi Good Roads advocates initiated a "Pave the Natchez Trace" movement, publicizing the proposal with speeches, editorials, and windshield stickers. Little was accomplished beyond the placing of a few memorials, but with the New Deal embracing major public works projects as a means of relieving unemployment, Mississippi congressman Jeff Busby recognized that the project's practical value and patriotic appeal stood a good chance of securing funding under the National Industrial Recovery Act. Busby announced his intention to seek congressional funding and urged fellow politicians and opinion makers to support the idea. The DAR continued its efforts, county representative along the proposed route called for action, and the Mississippi state legislature passed a resolution calling on Congress to "Pave the Trace.[40]

In January 1934 the NPS asked the well-known planner John Nolen to study the proposal. Nolen noted that there was tension between pragmatic and preservation agendas, predicting that the former were likely to carry the day, at least during initial debates over the project's approval. As with Blue Ridge Parkway, the public works aspect was crucial, not just to raise local support but because lawmakers rarely criticized relief projects in other members' districts. Busby lined up support in both houses for legislation authorizing fifty thousand dollars for the NPS to conduct a survey and allotting another $25 million toward the project's completion. Interior Secretary Ickes did not think the proposal merited national park status, however, and urged FDR to veto the project. Some NPS officials also questioned the propriety of granting national park status to an area that lacked both scenic splendor and incontestable national significance. Busby and his Alabama and

Tennessee counterparts quelled this opposition by flexing their political muscle and emphasizing the regional importance of the project. The Natchez Trace Parkway bill was passed in May 1934 and signed by the president in June, with the stipulation that funding for the survey come from the NPS's regular appropriation. Although the NPS assumed responsibility for the parkway, the Natchez Trace Association continued to play a supportive role. Under the energetic leadership of prominent Natchez resident Roane Fleming Byrnes, the association pressed on with commemorative activities, celebrated various construction milestones, and politely pressured politicians and government officials to keep the project moving.[41]

The NPS began work on the Natchez Trace Survey in the fall of 1934. In a departure from typical procedure, historians took the lead role, scouring records in Washington, Tennessee, Alabama, and Mississippi to piece together the historical route. Documentary evidence was often slim or contradictory, but by combining archival research with forays into the field, sufficient information was assembled to guide NPS landscape architects and BPR engineers in an extensive reconnaissance of the route in January 1935. Edward Zimmer was assigned as the project's resident landscape architect, undoubtedly because of his experience with Colonial Parkway. His BPR counterpart was Frank Brownell. NPS historians Olaf Hagen and Randle Truett accompanied the team. In addition to locating the historic Trace as well as possible, the group deliberated on the most appropriate course of development. They quickly concluded that the idea of literally "Paving the Trace" was undesirable on both practical and philosophical grounds. Not only would it destroy the historical resource the parkway was intended to memorialize, but the alignment of the meandering footpath was unsuited for modern motorway development. Engineers, landscape architects, and historians agreed that the preferred course was to identify and preserve the historic Trace and then develop the parkway drive along a roughly parallel route with gentle curves and easy grades to accommodate modern motor traffic. Some separation between the two routes was recommended to preserve the historic ambience of the old Trace. Passable sections could be utilized as side roads for more leisurely exploration but kept, in the words of NPS associate director Arthur Demaray, as "a primitive, park-like area, consistence with National Park Service standards." Ickes initially objected to this approach, insisting that if the roadway did not follow the historic Trace as closely as possible, the project lost its main justification. He was eventually persuaded that even though portions could be identified with reasonable precision, the route had changed so many times and so many sections were unclear that large portions would be based on conjecture. From the BPR's perspective, moreover, the parkway was intended to serve as a demonstration of modern motorway development, which could not be accomplished by following century-old alignments. The report underscored the parkway's value as a practical addition to the nation's highway system and suggested that it could also serve as a starting point for additions to the national parkway system.[42]

The survey report acknowledged that the scenery along the route was not "outstanding" in the classic NPS sense, but downplayed the implications on the grounds that "the historic purpose is the one that determines the value of the project rather than its natural scenic value." From that standpoint, the rolling wooded country, open fields, and occasional swampy areas adequately conveyed the "atmosphere of the Old South." In March 1935, a party including Nolen, Vint, NPS chief historian Verne Chatelain, H. J. Spelman, and various subordinates spent a week inspecting the route and endorsing the survey's conclusions. Summarizing his recommendations to Vint, Nolen provided a brief development outline along with a sketch depicting the proposed separation between the historic Trace and the modern parkway drive. The unusually prominent role of history in the parkway's development was further underscored by the fact that Chatelain and his staff were credited, along with NPS landscape engineers and BPR engineers, on the general development plans, while the bulk of the published report was devoted to expounding the Trace's history and explicating historical and archaeological sites. An extensive collection of photographs portrayed current conditions along the Trace and emphasized the variety of historic structures in the region. Malcolm Gardner of the newly established Branch of Historic Sites and Buildings was assigned as the resident NPS official to ensure that historical imperatives continued to shape the project's development. Gardner was involved with several disputes with the engineers and landscape architects based on their desires to enhance the parkway's technical and aesthetic qualities at the expense of historical values. Chief Historian Chatelain reiterated that the parkway should "keep as near

ABOVE Section of Natchez Trace, Mississippi, 1935, from "The Natchez Trace: A Historical Survey," prepared by the Branch of Historic Sites and Buildings, National Park Service, 1935.

the old route as is consistent with the engineering, scenic, and traffic requirement of modern highway construction" and encouraged Gardner to appeal for assistance when decisions could not be worked out to mutual satisfaction.[43]

While the NPS and BPR were in agreement over the general parkway concept, conflicts arose about specific design considerations. Zimmer and Brownell repeatedly clashed over alignment issues. Brownell was a traditional highway engineer wedded to the logic and efficiency of straight lines linked by simple radial curves, whether they bore any relation to the existing topography or not. Given his NPS background and recent exposure to state-of-the-art parkway design principles, Zimmer considered this approach unacceptable on practical and aesthetic grounds. Disagreements over this issue became so frequent and contentious that Zimmer appealed to Vint and NPS assistant chief architect Dudley Bayliss for assurance that alignment decisions would be based "on landscape features alone" and that the NPS, not the BPR, had finally authority in such matters. Nolen was dispatched to resolve the disputes in November

1936. Not surprisingly, he supported Zimmer's contention that every effort should be made to adapt the roadway to the terrain and take advantage of attractive views, even if this resulted in a somewhat longer and more circuitous alignment. Beyond the impact on specific locations, Nolen noted that as the first parkway in the region, it was important to set the proper precedents. The BPR acknowledged that the NPS's preferences held sway in such matters, but the issue continued to resurface. NPS officials also complained that the contractors exercised insufficient care during the right-of-way clearing process, causing unnecessary damage to the surrounding woodlands.[44]

The landscape architects meticulously managed the roadside environment, rounding and replanting excavation scars, varying the distance to the tree line to modulate the sensation of openness and enclosure, and selectively thinning, pruning, and removing roadside vegetation to emphasize attractive views. As with Blue Ridge Parkway, split-rail "worm," or "zig-zag," fences were erected in abundance to enhance the rustic effect, delineate boundaries, and guide both

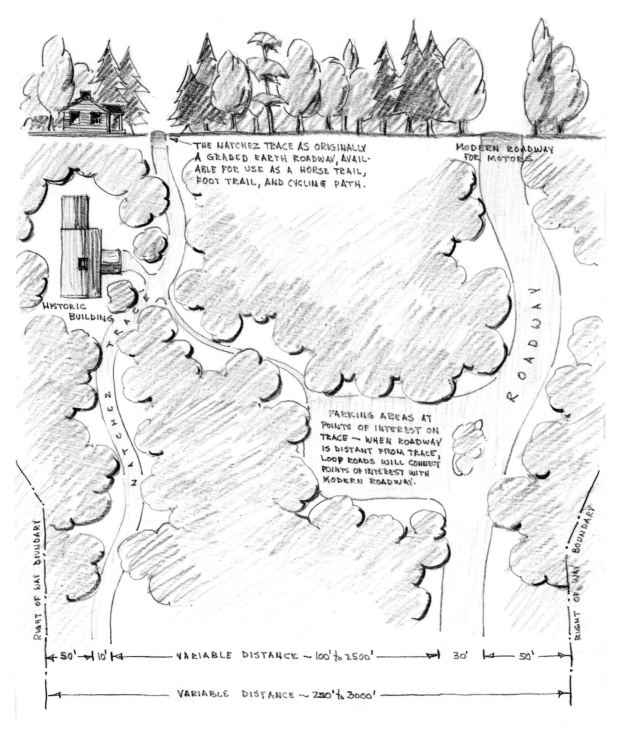

THE NATCHEZ TRACE AS ORIGINALLY A GRADED EARTH ROADWAY, AVAILABLE FOR USE AS A HORSE TRAIL, FOOT TRAIL, AND CYCLING PATH.

MODERN ROADWAY FOR MOTORS

HISTORIC BUILDING

NATCHEZ TRACE

ROADWAY

PARKING AREAS AT POINTS OF INTEREST ON TRACE — WHEN ROADWAY IS DISTANT FROM TRACE, LOOP ROADS WILL CONNECT POINTS OF INTEREST WITH MODERN ROADWAY.

RIGHT OF WAY BOUNDARY

RIGHT OF WAY BOUNDARY

50' | 10' | VARIABLE DISTANCE ~ 100' to 2500' | 30' | 50'

VARIABLE DISTANCE ~ 250' to 3000'

ABOVE John Nolen, suggestion for Natchez Trace Parkway development, 1935.

OPPOSITE Natchez Trace Parkway, 1959.

automotive and pedestrian traffic. Agricultural leases and scenic easements were employed to maintain the rural character with minimal cost to the NPS. Signees agreed to maintain their land in agricultural production and grow traditional southern crops such as cotton, corn, soybeans, and hay. As explained in NPS publicity bulletins, the goal was to prevent the construction of "factories or hot-dog stands or billboards" and ensure that traditional farmlands remained a significant "part of the picture." Learning a lesson from Blue Ridge

Parkway, the NPS constructed underpasses where the roadway bisected fields so that farmers could move machinery and livestock more freely. The Jackson Falls pullout and comfort station was expressly located to showcase a particularly compelling example of the classic family farm. Another pullout was developed around a demonstration of early-twentieth-century tobacco farming, with a small tobacco field, processing area, and drying barn.[45]

Additional pullouts showcased a variety of natural and cultural attractions. Historic sites included Mount Locust, a 1778 dwelling that served as both plantation home and inn; the circa 1818 Gordon House, home of one of the Trace's ferry operators; a monument to Meriwether Lewis at the site of Grinders Stand; and the Old Trace itself, which was preserved and presented to visitors in various forms and locations, ranging from pedestrian-oriented "sunken trace" segments worn deep into the surrounding ground to minor dirt roads passable by automobile. Prehistoric Native American sites such as Bynum Mound and Emerald Mound were also interpreted with signs and displays. Parking areas and educational signage encouraged motorists to stop and learn about the different habitats encountered along the way, from deciduous forests to piney woods, black belt prairies, swamps, and bottomlands. Although the lack of traditionally spectacular landscapes caused some within the NPS to question Natchez Trace Parkway's merits, the subdued scenery was occasionally enlivened by exposed limestone ridges and picturesque bluffs. Special signage consisting of an arrowhead-shaped signboard with an emblem depicting a post rider on the Old Trace was developed during the 1950s to guide visitors and help reinforce the parkway's identity.

The architectural treatment of Natchez Trace Parkway's bridges and visitor facilities represented a departure from the traditional NPS rustic approach, displaying a more stripped-down functionalist aesthetic. Although the more modern appearance stemmed in part from the extensive delays associated with the parkway's completion, the NPS had determined early on that traditional stone-faced bridges would look out of place in a landscape where rocky outcrops were more the exception than the rule. Some of the earliest culverts had masonry-faced headwalls, but even these displayed a more regularized and horizontal orientation than their Blue

Ridge or western park counterparts. Most spans constructed during the early decades of development had bare concrete surfaces that were tinted with carbon black to blend with their surroundings and embellished with rounded abutments, horizontal striations, and slim concrete railings to create a subtly streamlined aesthetic. Their simplicity and horizontality harmonized with the parkway's terrain in the same way that rustic stone-faced bridges mirrored more rugged environments. Later bridges employed concrete box-beam and other more advanced structural systems, producing longer, lighter spans but maintaining the simple, streamlined effect. Several of the parkway's postwar visitor facilities, most notably the Jackson Falls comfort station and Little Mountain Overlook, were unabashedly modernist structures, with bold geometries and dramatic interplays of planes and volumes.

The shift to a more modernist aesthetic was largely a result of the parkway's protracted development process. Construction officially began on September 16, 1937, when Mississippi governor Hugh White scooped up a ceremonial shovelful of earth at the start of a grading, drainage, and bridge project near Madisonville, approximately halfway between Tupelo and Natchez. The ceremony included members of the Choctaw tribe to help generate publicity and emphasize the path's ancient origins. An additional celebration was held six weeks later at Brandon Hall Plantation near Natchez to mark the beginning of work on the parkway's southern section. Local newspapers lauded the project while the Natchez Trace Association and the NPS worked together to expedite the land acquisition process by encouraging landholders to donate property for the right-of-way.[46]

By the outbreak of World War II, 24 miles of the stretch between Jackson and Tupelo had been paved and an additional 71 miles graded. Progress was even slower in Tennessee and Alabama, where popular and political interest in the parkway was not as strong. Only 9 miles were graded in Tennessee and none in Alabama. Land acquisition lagged in these states as well. As with other NPS projects, World War II brought construction activities to a halt, though land acquisition continued sporadically. Wartime shortages of men, materials, and money precluded additional construction, however, and the skeletal parkway forces devoted their minimal resources to maintenance and protection.[47]

Recognizing the need to prepare for post-war growth, Congress passed the Federal-Aid Highway Act of 1944, which provided financial assistance for the development of a national highway system. The act included an authorization of $5 million a year for three years to help fund the construction and maintenance of national parkways. As the war drew to a close, the Natchez Trace Association and the NPS began preparing for the resumption of parkway development. Participants in a fall of 1944 meeting included the governor of Mississippi, NPS director Newton Drury, Vint, regional director Thomas Allen, chief historian Herbert Kahler, and senior Natchez Trace Parkway staff. A week later NPS officials met to review progress and develop a parkway master plan. The 1944 master plan emphasized the parkway's role in preserving and interpreting historical resources. Defining the scope of this mandate elicited considerable debate, with some participants calling for a narrow focus on the history of the Trace, and others viewing the parkway as an opportunity to address a wider range of topics including the story of the Old Southwest in general, Native American history and prehistory, and the region's flora, fauna, and geology. The broader approach prevailed, as NPS officials saw the parkway as a unique opportunity to expose the traveling public to a diverse array of resources including Indian burial mounds, antebellum plantations,

wayside inns, natural curiosities, and, of course, remnants of the old Trace itself.[48]

Despite these plans and public relations efforts by the Natchez Trace Association, minimal progress was made in the 1940s. The outbreak of hostilities in Korea brought further delays. By 1952, only 17 percent of the parkway was completed, highlighted by a 64-mile stretch between Jackson and Kosciusko, Mississippi. Frustration with the pace of development prompted Mississippi representative John Bell Williams to assert that the NPS was treating the Natchez Trace Parkway like an unwanted "stepchild." Williams noted that the Blue Ridge Parkway was 70 percent completed, Colonial Parkway was 40 percent complete, and the Baltimore–Washington Parkway was nearly finished, though it had been started after the Natchez Trace. Inadequate appropriations prompted Natchez Trace Association officials to declare, "We greatly desire it completed in our lifetime." With Cold War tensions rising, the potential military value of a paved roadway linking Tennessee and New Orleans was highlighted, to little avail. Rumors even began to swirl that the federal government was considering abandoning the project and returning the completed portions to the states. In October 1954, NPS director Conrad Wirth acknowledged that the parkway had "been of little public use to date" but underscored the agency's desire to complete the project when

funds became available. By 1956, only 114 of the parkway's projected 450 miles were completed.[49]

The Natchez Trace Parkway was one of the major beneficiaries of Mission 66. A tenfold increase in funding allowed for the construction of approximately 90 new miles of parkway drive and the paving of another 90 miles that had already been graded, along with the completion of a range of visitor facilities, signs and other interpretive features, and support buildings. Many modern bridges were constructed during this period, including a dramatic 5,035-foot span over the Tennessee River. Mission 66 also funded extensive landscape improvement efforts, with more than 34,000 trees and seedlings planted along the parkway, including pine, bald cypress, oak, cottonwood, red cedar, and yellow poplar.[50]

While much was accomplished under Mission 66, much remained to be done. Lagging progress prompted the Natchez Trace Association to promote a "Finish the Trace" campaign in the 1970s, with limited success. Continued funding shortages, land acquisition issues, and planning debates delayed the parkway's completion until May 2005, when a final funding push and the resolution of some routing and design challenges allowed the NPS to finish the final two sections near Jackson and Natchez, Mississippi. Sixty-seven years after the NPS and BPR began the project and a full century after the DAR called for the old Trace's commemoration, the Natchez Trace Parkway was officially declared complete.[51]

GEORGE WASHINGTON MEMORIAL PARKWAY

The development of George Washington Memorial Parkway provided a different set of challenges, both practical and political. As one of several parkways administered by the NPS in and around Washington, D.C., it was shaped not just by traditional park concerns but also by the need to serve practical transportation functions. In this respect, it bore a closer resemblance to New York's multipurpose parkways than to its more prominent NPS siblings. Balancing the demands of recreationalists, commuters, and resource protection advocates became increasingly challenging as traffic volumes rose, activities changed, and environmental

concerns increased in prominence. The parkway's location along the Potomac River in Washington, Maryland, and Virginia created further complications, as the jurisdictions varied in their support for the project. Authorized in 1930 with the goal of extending Mount Vernon Memorial Highway and preserving both banks of the Potomac River from Mount Vernon north to Great Falls, the parkway was developed in fits and starts over four decades. While the northern sections stopped well short of Great Falls and the southern Maryland segment was never initiated, George Washington Memorial Parkway would play a vital role in the national capital region, both as a practical commuter route and as a recreational resource and nature preserve.

George Washington Memorial Parkway resembled other NPS parkways in that it united long-standing local agendas with the belief that parkway development afforded a desirable approach to preserving scenic and historic resources while rendering them accessible to the public. The imposing cataracts of Great Falls had attracted tourists since George Washington's time. Along with the dramatic natural scenery, a canal built around the falls with Washington's backing was considered an engineering marvel, drawing visitors from all over the world. The Patowmack Canal was short-lived, but its successor, the Chesapeake and Ohio (C&O) Canal, provided nineteenth-century excursionists with a relatively easy means of reaching the falls. The construction of electric trolley lines to Great Falls, Virginia, and Glen Echo, Maryland, at the beginning of the twentieth century made the trip even more convenient. Unfortunately the rocky bluffs that contributed to the picturesque character of the Potomac north of Washington engendered quarrying operations that threatened to destroy the gorge's character. The 1901 Senate Park Commission urged Congress to grant the area national park status and provided suggestions for the development of carriage drives along the Maryland side. Little came of these recommendations, but the creation of the National Capital Park and Planning Commission (NCP&PC) in 1926, together with proposals to develop hydroelectric dams at Great Falls, produced concerted action.[52]

In 1928 Michigan congressman Louis Cramton pushed through a bill to stave off the dam project and began marshalling support for the parkway. Mount Vernon Memorial Highway would be incorporated and additional roadways would be constructed in the other quadrants. A

proposed bridge at Great Falls and a ferry at the southern end of the parkway would allow motorists to make a grand tour of the region's natural and historic features. Seeking to capitalize on the patriotic fervor of Washington's bicentennial, the proposal was dubbed George Washington Memorial Parkway. Cramton teamed with Kansas senator Arthur Capper to introduce the legislation, which was signed into law by President Hoover in 1930. The Capper-Cramton Act authorized appropriations of up to $7.5 million for the parkway's development. Maryland and Virginia were required to cover 50 percent of the land acquisition costs. A stipulation that the NCP&PC could not expend any money until Maryland and Virginia contributed their share proved to be a source of continued delays and disappointments.[53]

Parkway proponents cast the project as an opportunity to unite scenic preservation, recreation, transportation, and patriotic inspiration. References to the latter were particular emphatic given the desire to cast the parkway as an undertaking of national significance. NCP&PC planner Charles W. Eliot 2d expounded on the scenic potential and proclaimed, "No area in the United States combines so many historical monuments in so small a district as the Potomac River Valley in the Washington Region." *American Motorist* praised the parkway bill for protecting the beautiful scenery of the Potomac River and elaborated on the region's historic associations. *American Forests* detailed the project's scenic, historic, and recreational attributes and characterized it as "the nation's parkway" and "a monument to the first president." When the NPS assumed responsibility in 1933, Arno Cammerer asserted that the parkway would afford "a 50-mile circuit of the choicest scenery in greater Washington, every foot of it hallowed by memories of the Father of His Country." Privately, he maintained that the project was "not national park caliber" but rather a local amenity for citizens of the nation's capital.[54]

Progress was minimal throughout the 1930s as neither Maryland nor Virginia was eager to commit funds. The only significant development prior to World War II was the construction of a short stretch between Arlington Memorial Bridge and Rosslyn, Virginia, easing congestion across Key Bridge and through Georgetown. Plans were also made to extend the parkway drive north to Spout Run, where a short spur would follow the stream valley and connect with Lee Highway, which served

as one of the primary approaches to Washington.
These practical functions rather than general
park concerns prompted Virginia to contribute
to the project. In order to fit the parkway into the
constricted area with minimal disruption, the
NPS-BPR design team separated the north- and
southbound lanes with a narrow median, placing
the southbound lanes slightly higher on the hillside.
The NCP&PC proposed tunneling under the
bluff where Key Bridge connected to Rosslyn, but
the NPS felt that a tunnel was inconsistent with
the desire to showcase views of the Potomac River.
This section was completed in 1941 by cutting back
the bluff and adding a new arch to the Virginia side
of Key Bridge. America's entry into World War II
brought construction to a halt before design work
for the Spout Run extension was complete.[55]

As with the previous section, the primary
challenge lay in devising a way to fit four lanes
of traffic along the banks of the Potomac River,
which grew increasingly steep and rugged above
Georgetown and Rosslyn. Building on suggestions
by Gilmore Clarke and Frederick Law Olmsted
Jr., the NPS and BPR separated the north- and
southbound lanes with an unusually large median
that varied in width as each roadway pursued an
independent course to minimize disruptions to the
existing terrain. The new section proved an immediate hit with commuters when it opened in 1950,
since it offered unparalleled access to downtown
Washington from the rapidly growing Virginia
suburbs. It also became an iconic example of modern motorway design. Images of the independently
aligned roadways curving gracefully along the
hillside appeared in numerous publications.[56]

The new parkway section was not universally
praised. Local and national conservation organizations protested that roadway development was
incompatible with natural resource protection
in the rugged and constricted terrain between
Washington and Great Falls. No matter how
much care the engineers and landscape architects
exercised, the roadways would seriously compromise the natural resources the parkway was authorized to protect. NPS director Newton Drury
maintained that the parkway had never been conceived as an undeveloped wilderness in the manner
of larger and more remote national parks. It was "a
metropolitan or city park development" intended to
combine recreation, scenic preservation, and transportation. Roadways were vital to its ability to perform these multiple functions. He also pointed out

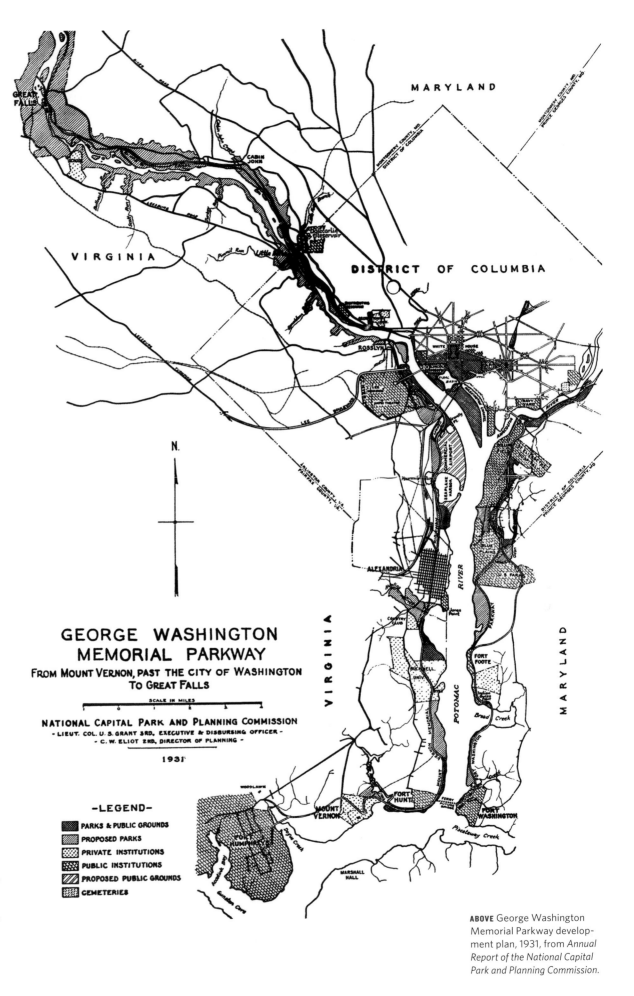

ABOVE George Washington
Memorial Parkway develop-
ment plan, 1931, from *Annual
Report of the National Capital
Park and Planning Commission.*

that George Washington Memorial Parkway was significantly more parklike than other federal parkways under consideration in the Washington area. Unlike the Suitland and Baltimore–Washington Parkways, which were almost wholly devoted to traffic concerns, there would be significant natural areas and "ample provision for nature lovers and the relatively small numbers of people who prefer secluded trails and waterways." Landscape architect Dudley Bayliss advised that there were two types of parkways: rural scenic parkways like Blue Ridge and Natchez Trace, and urban parkways like those found in the nation's capital. "The recreational values of this type of parkway are not to be discounted," he maintained, "but the major considerations are traffic volume and movement." Although the original legislation gave equal or greater weight to resource protection, Bayliss proclaimed that in the case of urban parkways," traffic considerations were "always justification for construction."[57]

Pragmatic transportation concerns clearly drove the next stage in the parkway's development. By the 1950s, the Central Intelligence Agency

(CIA) was looking for a secure facility convenient to downtown Washington. The agency had its eye on a tract of land adjacent to the parkway route in Langley, Virginia, that the BPR had acquired to serve as a testing facility. The BPR agreed to hand the site over in return for the CIA's help in securing an $8.5 million appropriation to extend the parkway to Langley and beyond to intersect with the proposed Capital Beltway. Construction began in 1956. Both the north- and southbound driveways were located along the edge of the Palisades. They were separated by a landscaped median of varying width, with the north- and southbound lanes coming together on soaring modern concrete bridges to cross the deep ravines leading into the Potomac. The roadways were designed to afford striking views across the Potomac gorge, with the southbound drive generally set slightly higher to allow motorists to see over the opposing lanes. Pullouts were provided along the edge of the bluff to allow visitors stop and enjoy the scenery. President Eisenhower officially opened the segment between Spout Run and the CIA interchange in November 1959. Local politicians,

NPS director Conrad Wirth, and other park and transportation officials joined the president in hailing the project as an illustration of interagency cooperation and sensitive roadway design.[58]

Preservationists continued to express their disapproval. When the CIA payment proved insufficient to carry the roadway to the Beltway, opponents packed a congressional hearing on additional funding. Asserting that "the terrible destruction which has accompanied the building of the Memorial Parkway on the Virginia side below Chain Bridge can never be repaired," the Audubon Society proclaimed that the recently completed segment provided "a convincing demonstration that the building of a parkway is not consistent with the preservation of the scenery of the gorge." The Wilderness Society, National Wildlife Society, and Izaak Walton League expressed similar objections. Scott Seegers, a resident of nearby McLean, Virginia, accused parkway builders of conducting a "strip-mining operation" and insisted that the "callous destruction of this inspiring stretch of wilderness" demonstrated that the NPS was more concerned with commuters than conservation.

Wirth defended the compromise, but the chorus of complaints prompted the NPS to locate the next section of the parkway drive farther back from the edge of the bluffs. In addition to leaving the Palisades unscathed, this significantly cut costs by eliminating several expensive bridges. It also afforded space for an extensive recreation area with picnic shelters and trails leading down to the river. This stretch of parkway was completed in 1962, providing a direct link from the Beltway to downtown Washington. The Federal Aviation Administration pushed to extend the parkway to the major international airport being constructed beyond the Beltway, but NPS officials declined for fear of encouraging even more traffic.[59]

The NPS was still intent on continuing the parkway to Great Falls but agreed to scale back to a more modest two-lane drive. Even this proposal encountered stiff resistance from conservationists. County officials also objected, insisting on retaining the area around Great Falls as a local park. In 1958 they voted to oppose additional land acquisition. In view of the continued opposition, the Senate Interior and Insular Affairs Committee put continuation plans on hold. Cost concerns played a significant role in the final decision to terminate the Virginia leg at the Beltway. By 1966 the combined federal, state, and local expenditure on George Washington Memorial Parkway was close to $34 million. The federal government's share well exceeded the amount authorized under the Capper-Cramton Act, and Congress was not inclined to provide additional funds. Given rising land and construction costs, NPS director George Hartzog estimated that completing the parkway as originally envisioned would require at least $19 million in additional appropriations. Congressional opponents also asserted that since the parkway functioned as part of the regional transportation system, it should be financed through existing highway funding procedures rather than by special appropriation.[60]

Highway funds had already been used in the development of the segment on the Maryland side between Washington and the Beltway. Land acquisition for this section received a significant boost from the transfer of the defunct C&O Canal to the NPS in 1938. Roadway development did not get under way until the 1950s, due in part to concerns about impacts on the historic canal. These considerations, along with the steep terrain and constraints imposed by existing development,

convinced the NPS to propose a modest, two-lane undivided roadway ending just beyond the Beltway at Glen Echo. District of Columbia highway officials pushed for a high-volume commuter route, creating numerous delays in the hope of inciting public opinion in favor of a more efficient expressway. The NPS constructed its two-lane parkway as far as the district line in 1965, but the city refused to complete the connection to the district's street system. This standoff was not resolved until 1970, when the missing link was finally paved.[61]

The southern leg from Washington, D.C., to Fort Washington, Maryland, proved the biggest disappointment. A combination of landowner resistance, funding shortages, and general disinterest limited initial land acquisition to a few riverfront properties. Efforts to revive the project during the Kennedy and Johnson administrations failed to overcome congressional skepticism. While northern Virginia's suburbs were booming, there was insufficient development southeast of Washington to justify the parkway on practical grounds and the proposed end point at Fort Washington was not a compelling destination. In 1969, the NPS gave up hope of developing that portion of the parkway. Some additional land was acquired between Great Falls and the Beltway, but it was clear that additional construction was untenable on political and economic grounds. The evolution of George Washington Memorial Parkway exemplified the rise and fall of the parkway ideal. When Mount Vernon Memorial Highway was completed in 1932, proponents could legitimately contend that it represented a successful fusion of park development and state-of-the-art highway engineering. The postwar sections disappointed both constituencies. With the rise of high-speed expressways, the parkway drives appeared increasingly anachronistic. At the same time, both traditional park advocates and more ardent wilderness advocates insisted that any attempt to accommodate automobile access compromised the underlying goal of natural resource protection. George Washington Memorial Parkway was remarkable in that it managed to reconcile these opposing forces to a significant degree. The fate of other parkway initiatives in the Washington area signaled the ascension of the two extremes.[62]

BALTIMORE– WASHINGTON PARKWAY AND SUITLAND PARKWAY

The Baltimore–Washington and Suitland Parkways were even more heavily weighted toward utilitarian access. Early conceptions of Baltimore–Washington Parkway incorporated some traditional park amenities, but the primary motivation was to serve as a safer and more efficient alternative to U.S. Route 1, the main highway between the two cities. Pragmatic concerns dominated when the long-debated project gained approval in 1942 as a wartime defense measure linking Washington and the rapidly expanding U.S. Army base at Fort Mead, Maryland. There was no pretense of higher aspirations when Suitland Parkway was authorized to provide similarly utilitarian access from downtown Washington to Bolling Field and Camp Springs Army Air Base (later Andrews Air Force Base). During the 1950s, Cold War concerns provided critical support, with the parkways being touted as escape routes in the event of a nuclear attack. Pragmatic motivations aside, both roadways were developed according to principles that were far in advance of contemporary highway-building practices, with limited access, free-flowing alignments, substantial rights-of-way, and comparatively high sensitivity to aesthetic concerns. The Baltimore–Washington Parkway, in particular, was heralded as a promising example of the ability to combine a high degree of safety and efficiency with attractive landscape design. It also afforded access to a small park developed in association with the planned community of Greenbelt, Maryland. The NPS's relationship with both projects was initially somewhat tangential. The desire to take advantage of NPS-BPR expertise combined with bureaucratic funding and land acquisition necessities to draw the agency into projects that it recognized from the start had little to do with its fundamental mission.

Early proposals for Baltimore–Washington Parkway envisioned the same sort of multipurpose development that characterized Mount Vernon Memorial Parkway and WCPC precedents. By the late 1920s, the stretch of U.S. Route 1 between Baltimore and Washington was afflicted with the same congested, dangerous and unsightly conditions that plagued most major American roadways. More than one thousand billboards were counted along the 28 miles between the two cities along with innumerable automobile-oriented enterprises. Invoking the Westchester County Park Commission's success in alleviating similar problems, the National Capital Park and Planning Commission (NCP&PC) began discussions with the Maryland State Highway Commission about the possibility of developing a parkway between the two cities. While Maryland officials were primarily concerned with basic transportation issues, the NCP&PC initially viewed the parkway as an integral component of the regional park system. Early proposals placed the parkway along the Anacostia River and its tributaries, taking advantage of low-lying land and marshes that had little commercial value but afforded promising opportunities for park development. Beyond the district boundaries, the parkway would follow meandering stream valleys through several small suburban communities to a height of land near College Park, Maryland, then traverse the boundary of the USDA Experimental Farm before heading farther northeast toward Fort Meade. After passing alongside Fort Meade, the parkway could take various paths through largely undeveloped countryside to Baltimore. NCP&PC director U. S. Grant III proclaimed, "Such a parkway would be a source of delight to a great many people and I believe of economic benefit to the country it would cross, just as the Bronx Parkway has done great things for Westchester County."[63]

In 1932 NCP&PC landscape architect Thomas Jeffers prepared more detailed plans, fine-tuning the route and identifying locations where the parkway could expand to provide recreational facilities including playgrounds, picnic areas, and overnight cabins. Consideration was also given to designating a national forest along a portion of the parkway, but this idea proved impractical. Most of the other more parklike features were eventually eliminated as well. With additional studies calling attention to the shocking rate of accidents along Route 1 and predicting that rapidly rising traffic volumes would increase the danger to life and limb, the emphasis shifted toward pragmatic transportation planning. By the late 1930s, planners were also highlighting the proposed parkway's utility as a strategic connection between Fort Meade, Washington, and Baltimore. They also pointed

out that the roadway would provide access to the USDA's Beltsville research facility along with the experimental New Deal housing project in Greenbelt. Running the parkway through or alongside federal facilities would help justify the expenditure while reducing land acquisition costs. Even the park and recreation aspects of the proposed parkway had practical ramifications. As an extension of the park system of the District of Columbia, the parkway would qualify for the cost-sharing provision of the Capper-Cramton Act, provided the State of Maryland committed to fulfilling its financial obligations.[64]

Despite general agreement on the parkway's desirability, little progress was made on funding and authorization until 1942, when the NCP&PC secured $2 million from National Industrial Recovery Act allocations to initiate the project. Given the parkway's ostensible military justification and the fact that much of the right-of-way between Washington and Fort Meade would be carved out of federal facilities, the U.S. government was authorized to construct that portion of the parkway, while the State of Maryland was given jurisdiction over the northern section. The NCP&PC continued to play the leading role, though it was understood that the NPS would eventually assume responsibility. The BPR cooperated according to its usual arrangement with the NPS. BPR chief Thomas McDonald and division chief H. J. Spelman were directly involved in the planning process, underscoring the parkway's perceived importance.[65]

Questions soon arose about the parkway's location. The BPR contended that not only was the winding alignment ill-suited for modern motorway development, but it also would be prohibitively expensive to drain and fill the low-lying marshlands, whose scenic attractions would be eliminated in the process. The valley route would also require the acquisition and removal of a considerable amount of existing development. The BPR proposed an alternative route along higher ground that would be more direct, cheaper to construct, and more easily integrated into existing development patterns. The NCP&PC protested that the revisions would produce an ugly and utilitarian freeway rather than an attractive multipurpose parkway. The two parties eventually settled on a location that avoided the stream valley but traversed largely undeveloped woodlands that afforded more compelling scenery than the BPR route along with a

broad right-of-way that would allow the roadway to be laid more lightly on the landscape. The two sides were unable to hammer out their disagreements until late 1944, by which time the sense of wartime urgency was waning, along with prospects for the funding required to complete the project.[66]

The right-of-way through federal property was established, but the remaining private property was not fully acquired until 1947. The parkway corridor ranged between 400 and 1,000 feet wide, broadening at interchanges and areas where additional land was readily available. Several miles were cleared and graded, but the initial allotment was quickly expended, bringing progress to a halt. Federal agencies experienced repeated frustration in their efforts to transfer the project to NPS control and secure funding for its completion. Congressional opponents objected to spending federal funds on a road that would principally benefit Maryland and District residents, observing that the project had even less of a claim to national significance than the similarly controversial George Washington Memorial Parkway. Supporters emphasized its role in providing access to federal facilities and pointed out that the parkway would serve as the primary thoroughfare for long-distance traffic traveling up and down the East Coast. Once again, national security arguments carried the day. The legislation transferring the project to the NPS and providing funds for its completion was passed in July 1950, shortly after the outbreak of the Korean War. In addition to facilitating the movement of troops and supplies between Fort Meade and Washington, the parkway was cast as an evacuation route in the event of a nuclear attack on the nation's capital.[67]

The parkway's design underscored the emphasis on high-speed travel over leisurely scenic contemplation. It was constructed with two widely separated roadways for north- and southbound traffic. Each roadway consisted of two concrete-paved twelve-foot-wide travel lanes. Grading extended an additional 32 feet to provide ample shoulders and room for expansion to three lanes if conditions warranted. Long, easy curves with spiral transitions, superelevation, and modest grades that rarely exceeded 3 percent allowed for a design speed of 75 mph, though the posted limit would be 55 mph. Substantial excavation was required to achieve these standards. This was greatly facilitated by the more powerful earthmoving machinery available in the post–World War II era.[68]

The extent of these manipulations was masked through the classic parkway design practices of sculpting rolling, low-angled embankments and stockpiling and reusing topsoil to hasten the recovery process. Although the new technology made it easier to undertake major excavations, the huge graders and earth movers could also be used to remediate road cuts by reestablishing the gently rolling contours of the region's topography. Unlike most NPS parkways, there was no elaborate landscaping plan or extensive planting program. Grass was seeded to stabilize and beautify the immediate roadside, but since the parkway traversed largely undeveloped terrain, the NPS relied on existing vegetation and volunteer growth to provide a park-like setting and screen out incompatible developments. Planting plans were developed for interchanges and other extensively disturbed areas. Preferred species included red maple, river birch, American beech, white ash, red pine, white pine, and various oaks and sumacs. In many places, the north- and southbound lanes were separated by broad, wooded medians that enhanced the sensation of motoring through a natural environment while improving safety by eliminating the glare of oncoming headlights. As with the Natchez Trace and George Washington Memorial Parkways, the bridges reflected the desire to update traditional aesthetics to accord with modernist sensibilities and contemporary budget constraints. Stone facing was used where bridges and overpasses were visible from the parkway drive, as well as on several grade separation structures for local traffic. Dimensioned stonework produced a more formal aesthetic than the random rubble masonry favored for more naturalistic park roads. In some cases, only the abutments and wingwalls were faced in this manner, leaving the spans as pure, unadulterated concrete. Despite these relatively modest beautification efforts, Baltimore–Washington Parkway garnered praise as a demonstration of aesthetically appealing modern motorway design. Compared to the contemporary penchant for bulldozing expressways straight through forests, fields, and neighborhoods, its graceful curves and sylvan surroundings suggested an alternative approach to regional highway development. Within weeks of the October 1954 dedication, more than twenty thousand cars per day were using the parkway. After an initial rush of curiosity seekers, it was clear that the vast majority of travel was practical rather than recreational. The parkway significantly reduced travel time between Washington and Baltimore while dramatically lowering accident rates. As a boon to commuters and interregional motorists, the parkway was an unqualified success. As a recreational amenity or nature preserve, its benefits were less immediately apparent.[69]

Even before the roadway was finished, there was considerable debate about whether the project fit within accepted definitions of a parkway and whether or not the NPS was the appropriate agency to manage it. NPS director Wirth insisted that the Baltimore–Washington and Suitland Parkways were so far from the definition of "true parkways" that retaining the designation and maintaining NPS ownership would have the effect of "deteriorating the real concept of a parkway." Department of the Interior officials agreed, asserting that the two roadways were "distinctly in the nature of highways requiring none of the specialized services inherent in the National Park Service." Since the State of Maryland constructed and managed the parkway's extension from Fort Meade to Baltimore, the NPS contended that it was logical to place the whole roadway under the state's jurisdiction. The Maryland State Roads Commission was not averse to the proposed transfer but raised concerns about the road's suitability as an all-purpose expressway. The state's section had been constructed with wider and thicker pavements and more generous curves to accommodate the heavy loads and extended vehicle lengths associated with commercial truck traffic. Since parkways were restricted to private passenger vehicles, the federal portion had a less substantial pavement and curves that could cause problems for larger vehicles. Upgrading the parkway to freeway standards would be enormously expensive, and Maryland officials argued that the federal government should bear the costs. The public appeared to be divided. Merchants and residents who lived along Route 1 were eager for trucks to be redirected onto the parkway, but many motorists appreciated the enhanced safety and driving ease engendered by their absence.[70]

The NPS made numerous attempts to transfer the parkway to state control, but securing funding to reconstruct the roadway to expressway standards proved a perennial obstacle. Cost estimates rose from $10 million in 1956 to $150 million by the early 1970s, by which time Maryland authorities insisted on three full travel lanes in each direction, extended merging lanes, widened shoulders, additional interchanges, and a host of other upgrades. The parkway was officially added to the interstate highway system in 1969 to increase funding possibilities. By this point, seventy-one

ABOVE Baltimore–Washington Parkway, ca. 1958.

thousand cars per day were using the parkway, creating traffic jams that often extended the length of the roadway. By the end of the 1970s estimates had risen to $200–$300 million, causing even the most ardent expressway enthusiasts to have second thoughts. The construction of a full-fledged interstate highway between the two cities in the mid-1970s relieved pressure and lessened the state's interest in the transfer. In 1981 the Maryland state highway administrator informed the NPS that the state was no longer interested in assuming jurisdiction. Despite subsequent calls to force the state to assume responsibility in the interest of federal budget relief, Baltimore–Washington Parkway appears destined to remain an NPS entity.[71]

Suitland Parkway represented an even greater emphasis on access over preservation, if the latter motivation could be ascribed at all. Extending approximately 9 miles from Washington, D.C., to U.S. Route 4 in Maryland, the roadway was intended to provide express access to air bases located in the countryside east of the city. Several federal office complexes and defense housing projects were also located along the route. As with Baltimore–Washington Parkway, the project was characterized as an extension of the park system of the nation's capital to make it eligible for federal oversight and potential funding, though even less effort was made to include park-related amenities. The NCP&PC had proposed the parkway as early as 1937, but the idea did not gain traction until America's entry into World War II enabled its promoters to cast it as a military necessity. A 1942 presidential decree authorized the secretary of war to acquire land for an airport access road along the proposed route. Planners agreed on the desirability of limited-access parkway-style construction, with a substantial protected right-of-way, grade-separated interchanges, dual roadways separated by a grassy median, attractive landscaping, and bridges and other structures designed to blend in with their surroundings. Two 24-foot-wide roadways would be designed to accommodate speeds of 55 mph. Construction began in September 1943, and the parkway opened in December 1944. Although both roadway alignments were graded, only one was paved, requiring opposing lanes of traffic to share a single 24-foot-wide roadway during the early years of operation. Only the major intersecting roadways received grade-separation structures during this period. In anticipation of future development, the stone-faced concrete arch bridges were constructed with spans wide enough to accommodate the second roadway. After the conclusion of hostilities, the War Department asserted the roadway was no longer vital for defense purposes and asked to be relieved of responsibility. It was transferred to the NPS in 1949, despite widespread sentiment that it was even less deserving of parkway status than Baltimore–Washington Parkway. The NPS tried repeatedly to cede jurisdiction to the D.C. and Maryland highway departments, but neither was willing to accept the financial burden.[72]

ROADS NOT TAKEN: ADDITIONAL NATIONAL PARKWAY PROPOSALS

While the NPS had little interest in assuming responsibility for roadways that functioned primarily as utilitarian traffic ways, it developed an ambitious agenda for the creation of a network of parkways that met more traditional standards of recreation, heritage tourism, and resource preservation. Arthur Demaray followed up his radio broadcast with a more expansive description of parkways under consideration. These included an Appalachian parkway system comprised of the two existing projects, a connection from Skyline Drive to the Potomac River, a Washington–Boston Parkway (of which there were "mountain" and "metropolitan" variations), a Berkshire Hills section through western Massachusetts (also with mountain and metropolitan alternatives), and a Green Mountain Parkway along the backbone of Vermont, with a potential spur through New Hampshire to Maine. The NPS was also considering extending George Washington Memorial Parkway south to Washington's birthplace in Wakefield, Virginia, and developing a parkway along either the Potomac or Monocacy River from Washington through the Civil War battlefield country to Gettysburg. Discussing existing and proposed projects at a 1938 superintendants conference, landscape architect Dudley Bayliss acknowledged that "parkway work was still in its infancy in national park work" but maintained that by combining recreational motoring opportunities with conservation and historic preservation, parkways constituted "a worthy addition to the National Park Family."[73]

GREEN MOUNTAIN PARKWAY

The most controversial parkway project of the prewar era was Vermont's Green Mountain Parkway. It was also one of the earliest proposals to be developed. Congress provided funds to study the proposition in November 1933, around the same time that Interior Secretary Ickes endorsed the Blue Ridge Parkway concept and six months before Natchez Trace Parkway was approved. Like these projects, the proposal reflected the confluence of local boosters' desire to promote their state's attractions, the NPS's commitment to expanding its East Coast presence through automobile-oriented park development, and New Deal imperatives to stimulate the economy and improve the management of natural and human resources. Unlike the Blue Ridge and Natchez Trace Parkways, the Green Mountain Parkway encountered significant opposition and never progressed beyond the planning stage. Although Bob Marshall, Robert Sterling Yard, and other wilderness advocates staunchly opposed the project, the parkway's rejection was rooted in relatively unique local social and political factors.

The idea of building a parkway along the Green Mountains from Massachusetts to the Canadian border was proposed by William Wilgus, a nationally prominent civil engineer who had retired to Vermont. Through his railroad work Wilgus had developed contacts with influential officials who went on to play important roles in Roosevelt's administration. Following the passage of the National Industrial Recovery Act in June 1933, he presented the parkway as an opportunity to take advantage the millions of dollars available for public works projects. Using the same logic as southern parkway advocates, Wilgus maintained that in addition to relieving unemployment, the project would provide long-term benefits to the state's tourist industry. It would also serve the national interest by affording recreational opportunities in line with NPS priorities, becoming the northern terminus of the proposed Appalachian Parkway. NPS officials were initially skeptical, suggesting Wilgus pursue it as a state-park initiative instead. Not only were their hands full with existing work, but they recognized that the project would encounter strong resistance, both from avowed adversaries and more moderate elements concerned with the New England's scenic resources. The parkway's economic benefits generated support from Vermont's governor, chambers of commerce, and the state's largest newspaper, the *Burlington Free Press*. James Taylor, a founder of the Green Mountain Club and the originator of the Long Trail, endorsed the proposal, insisting that the parkway would complement the recently constructed footpath along the spine of Vermont's highest range. Most significantly, National Planning Board chairman Frederic Delano looked favorably on the project, as did his nephew, the newly elected president. In November 1933 Congress provided fifty thousand dollars to examine development options.[74]

Both to augment overtaxed staff and maintain an attitude of impartiality, the NPS engaged John Nolen and New York State College of Forestry landscape architecture professor Laurie Cox to study the proposal in collaboration with NPS landscape architects and BPR engineers. Nolen was forced to drop out due to conflicts with other federal assignments, but the team submitted its report in January 1935. Adapting Wilgus's proposal to NPS parkway policy, Cox called for a minimum right-of-way of 1,000 feet with occasional bulges encompassing attractive lakes, mountains, and stream valleys. A large park of 20,000 to 30,000 acres would be located near the northern terminus. As with Blue Ridge Parkway, the alignment would not follow the ridgeline but pursue a varied alignment, ranging high along mountainsides and dipping down into valleys. The roadway was routed away from the highest peaks to afford better views and preserve their undeveloped character. Campgrounds, boating facilities, and foot and bridle paths would be provided at appropriate locations. Though the Green Mountains lacked the grandeur of western counterparts, Cox argued that the national park system should preserve characteristic scenery throughout the country. He also emphasized the parkway's proximity to major population centers. These virtues would be enhanced by proposed connections to Massachusetts's beaches and across New Hampshire's White Mountains to Maine's rocky coast. The combination of accessibility and scenic variety prompted Cox to proclaim, "Probably no more splendid National Park ideal has yet been contemplated." Vint endorsed Cox's report, characterizing the project as "thoroughly feasible and desirable."[75]

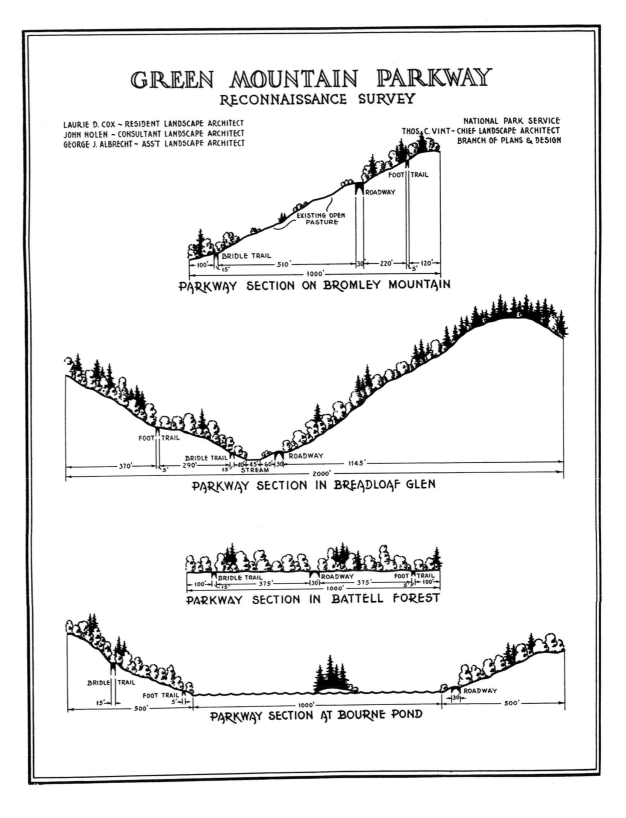

ABOVE Development scheme for proposed Green Mountain Parkway, 1934.

As predicted, the proposal generated heated opposition. The most vocal adversaries were the anti–New Deal *Rutland Herald*, which castigated the project as the epitome of FDR's misguided management, and the Green Mountain Club, which viewed the parkway as a threat to Vermont's undeveloped areas and the club's trail in particular. The *Herald*'s attacks tapped a resonant chord in a state that had not

While parkway advocates celebrated the project's potential to bring the Green Mountains within reach of millions of motorists, opponents cast this attribute as a threat to Vermont's relatively undefiled status. The club's president protested that the "influx of undesirable elements" would "destroy the finest charms of this great natural sanctuary."

elected a Democrat to statewide office since the Civil War, steadfastly voted against FDR, and cultivated a reputation for independence and Yankee thrift. Along with casting the project as an example of wasteful New Deal spending, the *Herald* asserted that the projected economic benefits were illusory. Not only would Vermont have to cover the land acquisition costs, but valuable property would be taken off the tax rolls. The paper also contended that the state would be stuck with maintaining the parkway in perpetuity. This last charge was spurious, since the NPS would assume responsibility, but so were contentions that the parkway would run along the crest of the mountains and that the federal government was bent on acquiring up to 1 million acres—or one-fifth of the state—rather than the projected 50,000 acres. Critics also contended that bisecting the state with a broad swath of federal land would effectively create two Vermonts, to the detriment of the economically challenged eastern portion. Even the predicted boost to the tourism industry was contested on the grounds that motorists would pass through in a day rather than linger and spend more money. The fact that the parkway would cater to out-of-state vacationers rather than address the practical needs of Vermonters was roundly condemned. Given the poor condition of the state's roadways, any federal largesse should be directed toward improvements that would benefit ordinary Vermonters rather than vacationing urbanites. That such decisions were in the hands of federal officials rather than native Vermonters was cited as another example of New Deal overreach.[76]

The *Herald* invoked the parkway's impact on the Long Trail, but this concern was most ardently expressed by the Green Mountain Club (GMC) and its allies. The club mobilized a campaign that quickly commanded national attention. Sympathetic publications and private individuals excoriated the project as a scenic disaster, an infringement on the Long Trail, and a violation of the wilderness values espoused by Aldo Leopold, Bob Marshall, and Benton Mackaye. The Appalachian Mountain Club (AMC) and other organizations protested, as did Robert Sterling Yard and even Frederick Law Olmsted Jr. and Harvard professor Henry Hubbard. Critics repeatedly conflated the proposal with an even more contentious attempt by New Hampshire boosters to secure federal funding for a road along

the top of the state's highest mountain range—an appalling concept to New England nature enthusiasts and NPS officials alike. Either through lack of understanding or calculated intent, the parkway was routinely mischaracterized as a "skyway" or "skyline drive." Even positive articles used this formulation, driving NPS officials to distraction. The agency sought to combat the impression, insisting on the correct terminology and emphasizing that the parkway had been explicitly designed to minimize such conflicts. Only 20 percent of the Long Trail was within a half mile of the route, generally in lower areas where the trail itself followed old roadbeds. Given the rolling terrain and dense nature of New England woodlands, Cox maintained, this was more than enough to block out the sights and sounds of automobiles. The NPS promised to rebuild affected sections in more propitious surroundings. Proponents claimed that the parkway would benefit both the trail and broader conservation goals by preserving thousands of acres from development. Not only was the trail mostly located on private land, but even club members agreed that it had been hastily developed and could use significant improvement in many areas. Both Olmsted and the Massachusetts-based conservationist Harlan Kelsey dropped their objections when they received more details about the proposal. Expressing relief that the NPS rather than the state would oversee that project and that it would be designed as a full-fledged parkway to prevent unwanted tourist developments, the Appalachian Mountain Club pledged to cooperate.[77]

While parkway advocates celebrated the project's potential to bring the Green Mountains within reach of millions of motorists, opponents cast this attribute as a threat to Vermont's relatively undefiled status. The club's president protested that the "influx of undesirable elements" would "destroy the finest charms of this great natural sanctuary." Similarly elitist sentiments surfaced among the small but well-connected cadre of summer residents, who feared the parkway would generate garish tourist attractions. As in Acadia, part-time residents were among the most ardent opponents. Although the GMC leadership strongly opposed the parkway, the general membership was more ambivalent. A 1934 poll revealed that fewer than half of the rank-and-file even cared enough to vote. Among those who did, 42 percent favored the parkway. The margin was even smaller among native Vermonters, giving further credence to suggestions that out-of-staters dominated the preservation aspect of the antiparkway movement.[78]

Interior Secretary Ickes asked Bob Marshall to weigh in, with predictable results. Acknowledging that the proposal would admirably suit the needs of recreational motorists, he maintained that the more important question was whether it would infringe on the rights of hikers and wilderness enthusiasts. Insisting that "sound recreational planning" required the avoidance of wilderness areas, Marshall called for greater separation between the "noisy and nature scarring highway" and "the relatively primitive effect of the Long Trail." Marshall's assessment played well in the secretary's office, but NPS assistant director Arthur Demaray insisted on giving Laurie Cox an opportunity to reply. Noting that Marshall had studied forestry, not planning or landscape architecture, Cox dismissed his remarks as the musings of "a well-meaning amateur." Not only was it evident that Marshall possessed "no real knowledge or appreciation of the practical problems of park location or development," but Cox contended that his opinions reflected "a rather sketchy knowledge of conditions in the Green Mountains." Cox insisted that there was sufficient separation between the roadway and trail, that Vermont's limited second-growth woodlands did not come close to meeting Marshall's own definitions of wilderness, and that the parkway would afford a wide range of recreational opportunities benefiting many thousands more than the five hundred or so who annually hiked the trail. The parkway would also provide permanent protection for a broad corridor of woods, mountains, fields, and forests, along with the trail itself, whose existence depended on the whims of private landowners. Marshall responded with one of his impassioned soliloquies, which Ickes clearly preferred to the Park Service's plodding justifications. Refusing to debate specifics in a manner that lent credence to Cox's underlying assertion, Marshall launched into a tirade against "the prevalent Park Service attitude." If roads and wilderness could coexist as closely as the agency contended, then national parks "might properly be riddled with roads." But the true "lover of wilderness" recognized that such claims were preposterous. Large areas of undisturbed nature were necessary to provide the appropriate effect. "The overwhelming emotional exhilaration of the wilderness can not be gotten from a miniature segment of the whole wilderness," Marshall proclaimed, "any more than the

emotional exhilaration which people have derived from viewing the Mona Lisa could be preserved by cutting up the canvas into little segments one inch square and handing them out as souvenirs." If the parkway could be designed so that it did not infringe on the wilderness experience, there would be no objections, but the Park Service's contention that the two could coexist within a 1,000-foot swath was "wishing away the laws of nature." Marshall maintained that the preferred solution would be to preserve the Green Mountain as a roadless preserve, as New York was undertaking to do with the Adirondacks. Given the proposal's uncertain prospects and high-placed support, Ickes declined to make a public show of vetoing the project, but he forwarded Marshall's memo to NPS officials with the comment, "I can't get rid of the feeling that the objective of the Park Service has been too much that of making it easy for great crowds to visit the parks, whereas we ought more truly to live up to our ideal of preserving for future generations the priceless gems of nature with which we have been so generously endowed."[79]

Despite the impassioned rhetoric of wilderness proponents both within government and without, the parkway's fate was decided by local social and economic concerns. The policy that states were responsible for parkway land acquisition proved to be the proposal's undoing since the project would have to be endorsed by Vermont's famously conservative citizens. Along with circulating false rumors that the parkway would expand to 1 million acres or more, bankrupting state coffers and turning thousands of Vermonters out of their homes, the *Rutland Herald* and its allies conflated the project with an even more controversial proposal to use New Deal programs to resettle farmers from marginal agricultural land, which would be converted from family farmsteads into recreational areas for urban vacationers. When the bill came before the state legislature in March 1935, it failed by a narrow margin. Governor Charles Smith, an ardent supporter, called a special session to reconsider. The second attempt prevailed, with the caveat that the bond measure to pay for land acquisition had to be approved by a statewide public referendum. Following an even more acrimonious campaign, the citizens of Vermont rejected the funding mechanism by a vote of 42,318 to 30,897. While the parkway's defeat was hailed by wilderness advocates as a rejection of NPS road development policies, most observers attributed

the results to fiscal conservatism, anti–New Deal sentiments, and resistance toward outside influences. Historians have substantiated this interpretation through detailed analysis of voting patterns and other indicators. Conservationists may only have played a supporting role in the rejection of Green Mountain Parkway, but they occupied center stage in the next major debate over national parkway development.[80]

CHESAPEAKE AND OHIO CANAL PARKWAY

The subsequent controversy over plans to construct a parkway from Washington to Cumberland, Maryland, along the route of the abandoned Chesapeake and Ohio (C&O) Canal represented an even more direct challenge to NPS road-building practices and park management policies in general. As with the Green Mountain Parkway, the C&O Canal proposal exemplified the agency's faith that properly executed road development afforded the best means of fulfilling the mandate to preserve and present America's scenic and historic landscapes. The defunct canal had been purchased by the federal government in 1938 and turned over to the NPS. The portion nearest Washington was restored by the CCC, allowing canoes and a passenger-carrying canal boat to make their way from Georgetown to Seneca, Maryland, while hikers and bird-watchers enjoyed the parallel towpath. Repairing the entire 186-mile waterway was deemed to be an inordinately expensive proposition, however, especially given the lean budgets of the postwar era. Since there was insufficient support for the idea of declaring the derelict canal a national park, there was no ready mechanism to expand the narrow strip of federally owned land into a broader corridor that would protect the canal and its users from adverse developments. Farmers and other neighboring landowners had informally appropriated portions in the sparsely settled area beyond the Washington suburbs, but the biggest threat to the canal and its environs was posed by the Army Corps of Engineers. Numerous proposals had been presented over the years to dam the Potomac as a means of tapping its hydroelectric potential and providing a recreational reservoir that would inundate the canal and its surroundings. From the NPS perspective, parkway development seemed to be the ideal solution. Parkway designation would preserve a 1,000-foot-wide corridor rich with historic and natural resources, which would be rendered accessible by a sensitively laid out recreational roadway. For much of the parkway's length, single lanes would lie on either side of the canal. Campgrounds and other modest facilities could cater to recreationalists enjoying the parkway by foot, boat, bike, or automobile. The parkway would also have practical value as limited-access motorway leading into Washington from western Maryland, though the NPS emphasized that it would not be designed to the standards of other Washington-area parkways.[81]

The western Maryland congressman J. Glenn Beall secured funding for an NPS-BPR study, which fleshed out the details in a report submitted in August 1950. Twenty-six miles of the historic canal would be preserved, along with a collection of locks, lock houses, and assorted buildings. Other sections were considered too badly deteriorated to restore. These resources were deemed sufficient to convey the canal's historic character, which would be explicated by NPS exhibits, publications, and on-site personnel. As with the rural landscape of the Blue Ridge, the goal was not to preserve the landscape in its entirety but rather to save and interpret select features so visitors could appreciate its history and significance. Protecting a wide swath of Potomac bottomland would serve the dual purpose of illustrating the canal's historic context and providing opportunities for outdoor recreation in a range of natural settings. For those who preferred to experience scenery from behind the wheel of an automobile, the

parkway would afford a panoply of attractions, from sweeping views of the Potomac to rugged gorges where it slipped between the river and natural obstructions to fleeting glimpses of rural landscapes, whitewashed lock houses, and mules towing reconstructed barges. The roadway would pass through the historic Paw Paw Tunnel and utilize a number of restored aqueducts. A parkway headquarters and museum would be built in Cumberland, while gasoline and other services would be offered in carefully designed locations. At Great Falls, the roadways would connect with the northern extension of George Washington Memorial Parkway, providing direct and scenic access to downtown Washington.[82]

While this vision accorded with prewar parkway development policies, the proposal encountered stiff opposition. The principal objections took two forms: local political and socioeconomic concerns and increasingly stringent attitudes toward natural

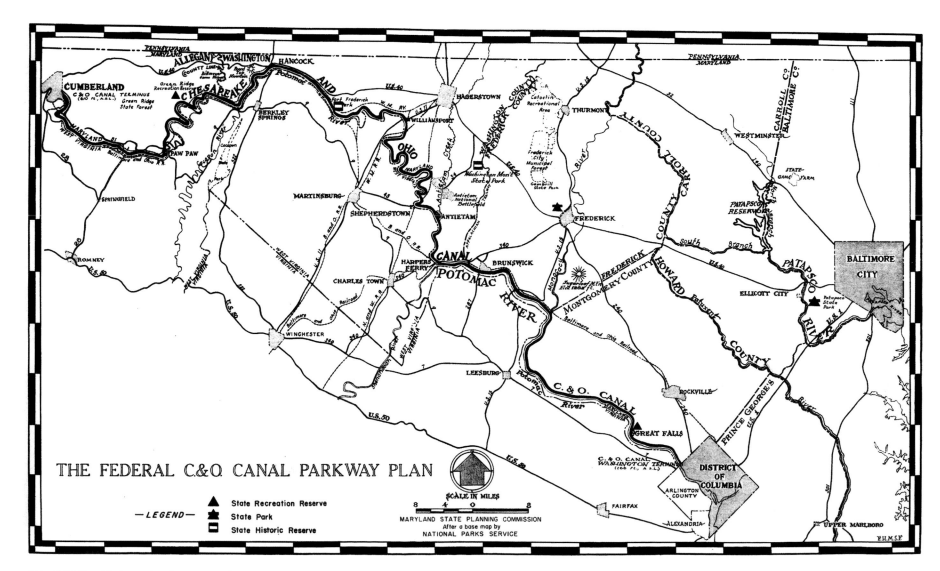

ABOVE C&O Canal Parkway plan, from *Report of Joint Committee on the Chesapeake and Ohio Canal Parkway,* December 1952.

National Park Roads

resource protection. In this case, the latter proved more formidable. Objections from various state agencies provided the first stumbling block, however. Rather than embrace the project as a parallel conservation effort, Maryland's Game and Inland Fish Commission and Department of Forests and Parks cast it as an intrusion on state sovereignty. Along with asserting that the roadway would destroy wildlife habitat, imperil animals, and prevent hunters from gaining access to the Potomac, they opposed ceding Maryland's riverfront to federal control. Echoing Vermont's anti-outsider sentiment but with potentially racist overtones, the Maryland Board of Natural Resources raised fears that the parkway would "unload on the nearby countryside many people from the District of Columbia who would create problems such as we have not been confronted with in the past." Whether this reference pertained to suburban sprawl, the oft-criticized "Coney Island" crowd of vulgar recreationalists, or Washington's predominantly African American population is unclear. The State Planning Commission and State Roads Commission were more ambivalent, observing that a roadway along the Potomac was not a high priority in view of Maryland's other transportation and recreation needs but also recognizing that paying approximately $325,000 for land acquisition to secure $9 million worth of federal investment in parkway development was too good a deal to pass up. The NPS offered numerous concessions, including easements for hunting access, rerouting in contested areas, and assurances that the state's interests would be accommodated as much as possible. Faced with continued resistance, Wirth and National Capital Parks assistant superintendent Harry Thompson lobbied for a modified version of the proposal, which limited roadway construction to the westernmost 60 miles between Hancock and Cumberland. In the section between Hancock and Great Falls, where recreational use was heaviest, the NPS agreed to develop a "walking parkway" with minimal infrastructure improvements. Maryland acquiesced, and Congress approved the abbreviated parkway in March 1953.[83]

News of the parkway's authorization mobilized another—and ultimately formidable—source of opposition. Following the initial acquisition of the historic canal property, the Wilderness Society had expressed concern about its future. Acknowledging that the reservation did not meet conventional definitions in terms of size or primeval quality but asserting that it retained valuable "wilderness characteristics," the society insisted that developing it as a motor parkway with a road running through the center would be a calamity. Conservationists acknowledged the need for recreation areas accessible to the urban masses but insisted that city dwellers should also be provided with opportunities to "enjoy quiet walks away from crowds and automobile traffic."[84] By the early 1950s, this perspective was embraced by a growing coalition of wilderness advocates, bird-watchers, history buffs, outdoor enthusiasts, and ordinary citizens. The National Parks Association and the D.C. Audubon Society joined the Wilderness Society in expressing their opposition. The Izaak Walton League and Daughters of the American Revolution also urged reconsideration of the plan. Irston Barnes, president of the local Audubon chapter, accused the NPS of seeking "to destroy this priceless historic and recreational park by debasing its status to the level of a mere motor highway."[85] Barnes acknowledged that the agency was under pressure to devise a politically and economically feasible means of protecting the canal corridor from dam builders but accused the agency of exhibiting "misplaced zeal" and a "critical lack of imagination" in presenting conventional parkway development as the sole option. Barnes suggested the canal be preserved in its entirety to serve as a combination "living museum" and nature sanctuary. Although approach roads might be provided at select locations, the principal means of access should be by foot, bicycle, canoe, and canal boat. Barnes attacked the NPS for "assuming that the urgent recreational need is for more motoring highways" and insisted that the principle of providing for the enjoyment of the greatest number of people did not apply to rare and endangered resources. "The glory of the canal and the river," he asserted, "lies in its invitation to escape from highway and automobile and to find oneself at peace with nature, and remote from the confusions and frustrations of which highways are the most frantic expression."[86]

The NPS continued to defend the compromise plan. Wirth derided Barnes's proposal as incoherent, impractical, and politically unrealistic. When Frederick Law Olmsted Jr. echoed Barnes's concerns, Wirth ridiculed the notion that "a street wide strip of land that has been used for 75 years as a commercial trafficway be considered wilderness." He maintained that the only hope for saving any portion of the canal from the Army Corps of Engineers' impoundment scheme was to pursue the tried-and-true policy of multipurpose parkway development, combining practical benefits with a broad range of recreational amenities. In January 1954 the *Washington Post* published an editorial decrying the canal's neglected status and endorsing the NPS's proposal as the best means of protecting the river corridor and making its beauties accessible to a broader audience than the "very few" who currently enjoyed its benefits. This opinion, authored by *Washington Post* associate editor Merlo Pusey, had a profound effect, albeit not the one intended.[87]

A few days later the paper printed a response from Supreme Court Justice William O. Douglas. Douglas noted that the parkway proposal had aroused disapproval in many quarters, especially among those "who like to get acquainted with nature first-hand and on their own" and were adamantly opposed to "making a highway out of this sanctuary." Douglas described the canal's attractions with poetic effusion, characterizing it as "a refuge, a place of retreat, a long stretch of quiet and peace at the Capital's back door— a wilderness area where we can commune with God and with nature, a place not yet marred by the roar of wheels and the sound of horns." He challenged Pusey to hike with him along the length of the canal. By the conclusion of the trip, Douglas predicted, even the most die-hard parkway supporter would be transformed by the landscape's subtle beauty and join the campaign to stop the ill-conceived plan. The *Post*'s editors accepted Douglas's invitation while elaborating on their reasons for embracing the NPS proposal. Asserting that they were opposed to any effort to transform the canal corridor into a major traffic artery, they insisted that it was equally misguided to limit enjoyment of its attractions to those who were capable of hiking 15 miles per day. The *Post* pointed to Skyline Drive as an example of a roadway that made natural beauty accessible to many thousands of people without compromising it in the process.[88]

The proposed hike garnered unprecedented publicity along with innumerable requests to participate. A select group of two dozen walkers was organized, including representatives of conservation groups, hiking organizations, and government agencies, along with a coterie of local and national journalists. Wilderness Society president Olaus Murie, vice president Harvey Broome, and executive secretary Howard Zahniser made the

ABOVE *Life* magazine photograph *Walking the C&O Canal; left to right:* Harvey Broome, Supreme Court Justice William Douglas, and Olaus Murie.

trip, as did National Parks Association president Sigurd Olsen and D.C. Audubon Society president Irston Barnes. The NPS sent the region's chief naturalist and a park policeman. Thompson confidently predicted that the excursion would underscore the merits of the parkway proposal. The Potomac Appalachian Trail Club provided logistical support, and the B&O Railroad supplied a specially outfitted observation coach to ferry the hikers to Cumberland. The group set out on March 20, braving rain and snow but spending all but one night in lodgings provided by sportsmen's clubs and other well-wishers. Only Douglas, Broome, Murie, and six other stalwarts completed the entire 184-mile hike, but the ranks swelled as they neared Washington. On March 27 they were met by Secretary of the Interior Douglas McKay and a bevy of NPS officials and then loaded aboard the Park Service's mule-drawn barge for the final approach to the canal's terminus in Georgetown, where they were hailed by a large crowd of sympathizers and curious onlookers.[89]

Douglas's hike was a masterful stroke of public relations. Throngs of journalists accompanied the trekkers or met them along the way, providing daily updates for newspapers, radio, and television. *Time* and *Life* published articles on the excursion, and newsreels of the event appeared in movie theaters around the country. The attention heightened

opposition to the parkway and stimulated broader debate about the appropriate relationship between roads and parks. Connecticut journalist Warren Gardner maintained that the Potomac bottomlands possessed an intimate beauty that could only be appreciated by the close observation and prolonged immersion available to those on foot. Zahniser added historical imperatives to the wilderness preservation agenda, asserting that one of the canal's principal functions was to transport visitors into America's past. To fully grasp its historic and patriotic significance, one had to experience it at a traditional pace rather than from behind the wheel of a speeding automobile.[90]

Douglas, Barnes, Zahniser, and other key participants prepared an alternative proposal, which they submitted to McKay at the end of March. The key provisions were that the canal property should be preserved as a recreational and historical entity in its own right and that a scenic drive would be provided along a roughly parallel course, primarily by improving existing country roads. Where new roadways were deemed necessary, they would not intrude on the canal reservation, which should receive official national historical park designation. The historic canal and towpath would be restored where practicable. The reservation would be geared toward visitors on foot, bike, boat, or horseback, with camping and sanitary facilities

located at appropriate intervals, but vehicular access would be provided at select locations through short spur roads connected to the parallel parkway system. Douglas emphasized that utilizing existing roadways would afford considerable savings. The *Washington Post* changed its stance, endorsing a modified development plan that closely resembled the canal group's scheme.[91]

Thompson was still wedded to the original proposal, but Wirth began to express reservations. In January 1955 he appointed a committee to reassess the situation. While NPS officials predominated, they represented a wide range of interests. Ben Thompson, chief of the NPS Division of Cooperative Activities, was the committee chair. He was joined by Vint, chief NPS historian Herbert Kahler, chief naturalist John Doerr, and Lloyd Meehean, assistant to the director of the U.S. Fish and Wildlife Service. Vint and Thompson dismissed the idea of cobbling together a parkway out of existing roads and new construction. The roadways lacked the scenic character essential for parkway development, while any attempt to construct a true parkway along the top of the bluffs inland from the canal would be stymied by land acquisition costs. Thompson insisted that the original plan was more practical on technical and legislative grounds and more in keeping with the NPS's mandate to serve a broad cross section of the public. Vint agreed that parkway designation afforded the most politically viable alternative, though personal inspection of the route convinced him that a road-free linear park afforded a more desirable solution. The other three NPS committee members voted against automobile-oriented development, echoing opponents' assertions that the canal's attractions were best experienced through leisurely and intimate enjoyment. Although they dismissed the parallel parkway concept, the committee's other recommendations accorded with the suggestions of Douglas's group. The corridor would be preserved for nonmotorized users, and the canal, towpath, and associated structures would be restored wherever possible. Since this approach precluded using the land acquisition procedures authorized for national parkway development, the committee recommended the property be designated a National Recreation Area. This strategy was cast as a means of appeasing the Maryland natural resources agencies, since recreation areas were managed more flexibly than national parks.[92]

While local and national conservation groups embraced this suggestion, it did not sit well with Beall and his constituents, who had their eyes set on a federally funded roadway servicing the western reaches of the state. Beall and western Maryland congressman Dewitt Hyde pressured Wirth and McKay to reconsider. In March 1956 Wirth announced another compromise. The Chesapeake and Ohio Canal National Historical Park would stretch from Great Falls to Cumberland and be managed for nonmotorized users. A separate parkway located well back from the canal would extend from Hancock to Cumberland. Beall and Hyde introduced legislation to this effect in 1957. Local and national conservation groups rallied around the measure, but Maryland officials renewed their opposition to federal control of the Potomac shoreline. The Army Corps of Engineers also expressed concern that the park would preclude future dam development. These objections delayed authorization of the Chesapeake and Ohio Canal National Historical Park until 1971, though President Eisenhower granted the reservation National Monument status before leaving office in January 1961. The associated parkway proposal fell by the wayside, its recreational value long since rejected and its practical merits minimized by conventional highway construction. Although the historical park designation suggested that the historic preservation constituted the primary impetus, the parkway's rejection constituted a notable victory for wilderness advocates. The significance of this achievement has been obscured by the subsequent emphasis on the canal's historic value and the association of wilderness advocacy with larger and more remote natural areas.[93]

ADDITIONAL PARKWAYS AND PARKWAY PROPOSALS

The NPS considered a range of other parkway possibilities. While some resulted in detailed studies, few progressed beyond the conceptual stage. During the late 1930s a coalition of state planners and private organizations began pressing for the construction of a parkway along both sides of the Mississippi River. The idea was resurrected after World War II as an innovative state, local, and federal collaboration in which most of the route would consist of improved and beautified state highways incorporating existing public land where possible. The NPS and BPR made a detailed study, but with cost projections ranging from $770 million for a parkway along one side of the river to $1.45 trillion for both, the concept was deemed impractical. During the Johnson administration, Secretary of the Interior Stewart Udall expressed support for a National System of Scenic Parkways that included thirty-one proposed parkways totaling 14,394 miles. Most were fairly schematic and likely to be developed along the lines of Mississippi River Parkway, if at all. A few were more conventional, involving intensive studies leading to the possibility of extensive land acquisition and development. The most ambitious and seriously considered of these was the Allegheny Parkway, stretching 632 miles from Harpers Ferry to Cumberland Gap. A 1964 NPS-BPR study recommended its development, but the cost was so high the report was never officially released. A Blue Ridge Parkway extension winding along the southern Appalachians was authorized in 1968 and remained under serious consideration into the 1970s. Several relatively minor parkways were added to the NPS fold. Two of these, Stephen Mather Memorial Parkway, authorized in 1931 to improve access to Mount Rainier National Park, and the 1972 John D. Rockefeller, Jr. Memorial Parkway, connecting Grand Teton and Yellowstone National Parks, ran primarily through public lands and were developed along the lines of conventional park entrance roads. Foothills Parkway, authorized in 1944 as recompense for Tennessee's loss of Blue Ridge Parkway, remains under construction.[94]

Given the low percentage of projects that made it through the approval process and the even smaller number completed as originally envisioned, the national parkway program could be considered a mixed success. As an illustration of the rise and fall of automobile-oriented park development strategies, however, its significance is unmatched. When the program was conceived, parkways appeared to offer the ideal means of uniting the public's enthusiasm for motor tourism with the preservation of natural and cultural landscapes. By eschewing skyline routes for more varied alignments, parkway designers enhanced the motorist's experience while ameliorating the concerns of all but the most extreme wilderness advocates. Satisfying both constituencies became increasingly difficult in the postwar era, as traffic demands and preservation imperatives accelerated both within the park system and the nation as a whole. Economic factors played an equally important role in bringing the parkway development era to a close. The enormous cost of land acquisition and construction slowed existing projects to a crawl and made additional large-scale proposals politically untenable. Federal environmental protection regulations provided the final blow by dramatically increasing costs and curtailing many options. At the same time, existing parkways proved immensely popular. Blue Ridge Parkway was an immediate hit and routinely rates as the most heavily visited unit of the National Park System. Natchez Trace may be less of a national destination, but it is also heavily utilized. Colonial Parkway continues to display the region's natural and historic values. Parkway managers in the National Capital Region have been successful in protecting the natural and cultural resources under their care from repeated threats to sway the balance even more heavily toward transportation. Not only did parkways fulfill Dudley Bayliss's expectations that they would become worthy members of the national park family, but they played a vital role in the agency's ongoing effort to balance the tension between preservation and access. By adapting nineteenth-century precedents to twentieth-century demands, they afforded unmatched opportunities for scenic driving. Parkway drives clearly impacted their immediate surroundings, but the surrounding corridors preserved large tracts of land from more detrimental development. Perhaps even more important given the ever-expanding popularity of recreational motoring, their popularity eased the pressure on other scenic resources.

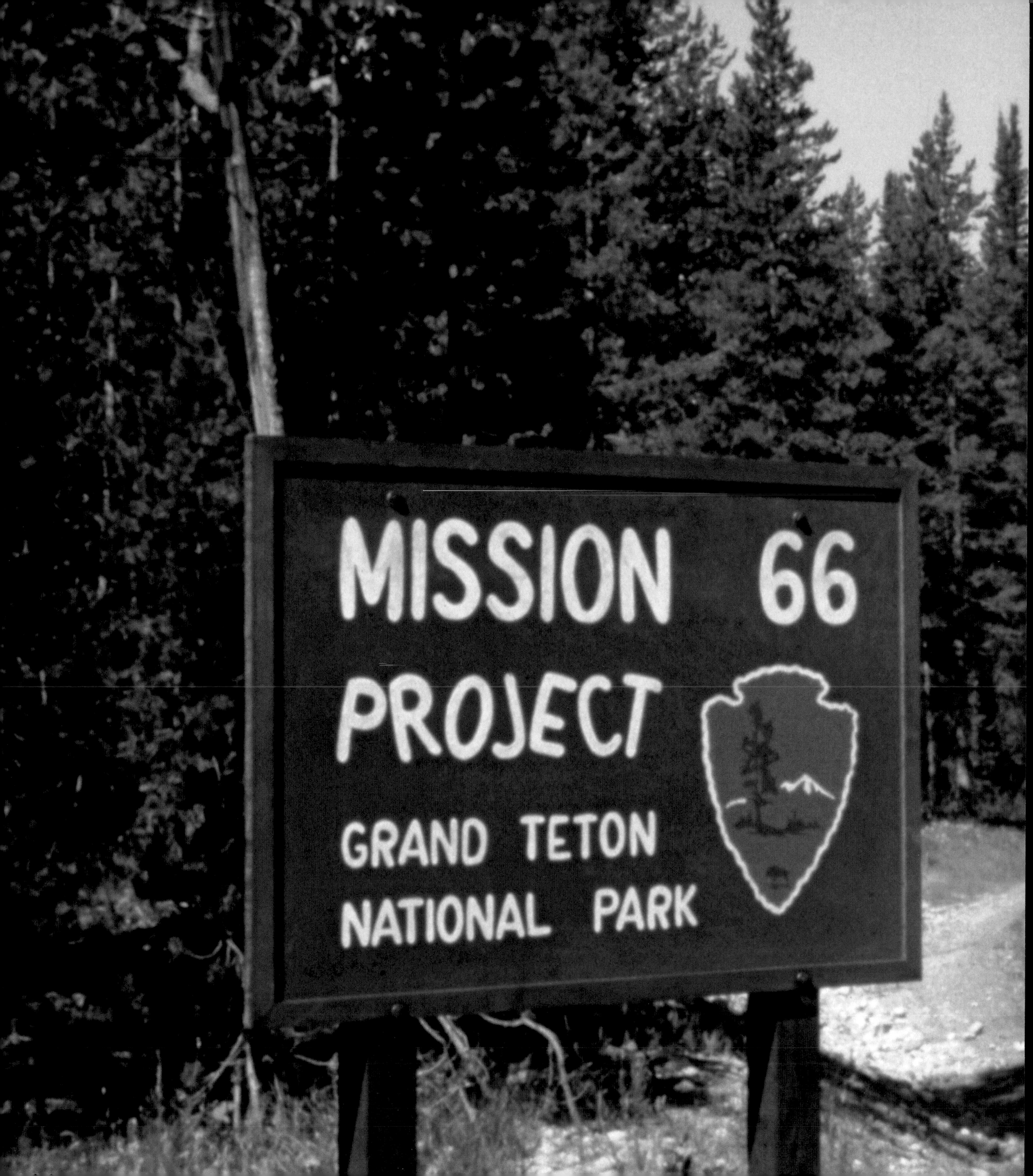
MISSION 66
PROJECT
GRAND TETON
NATIONAL PARK

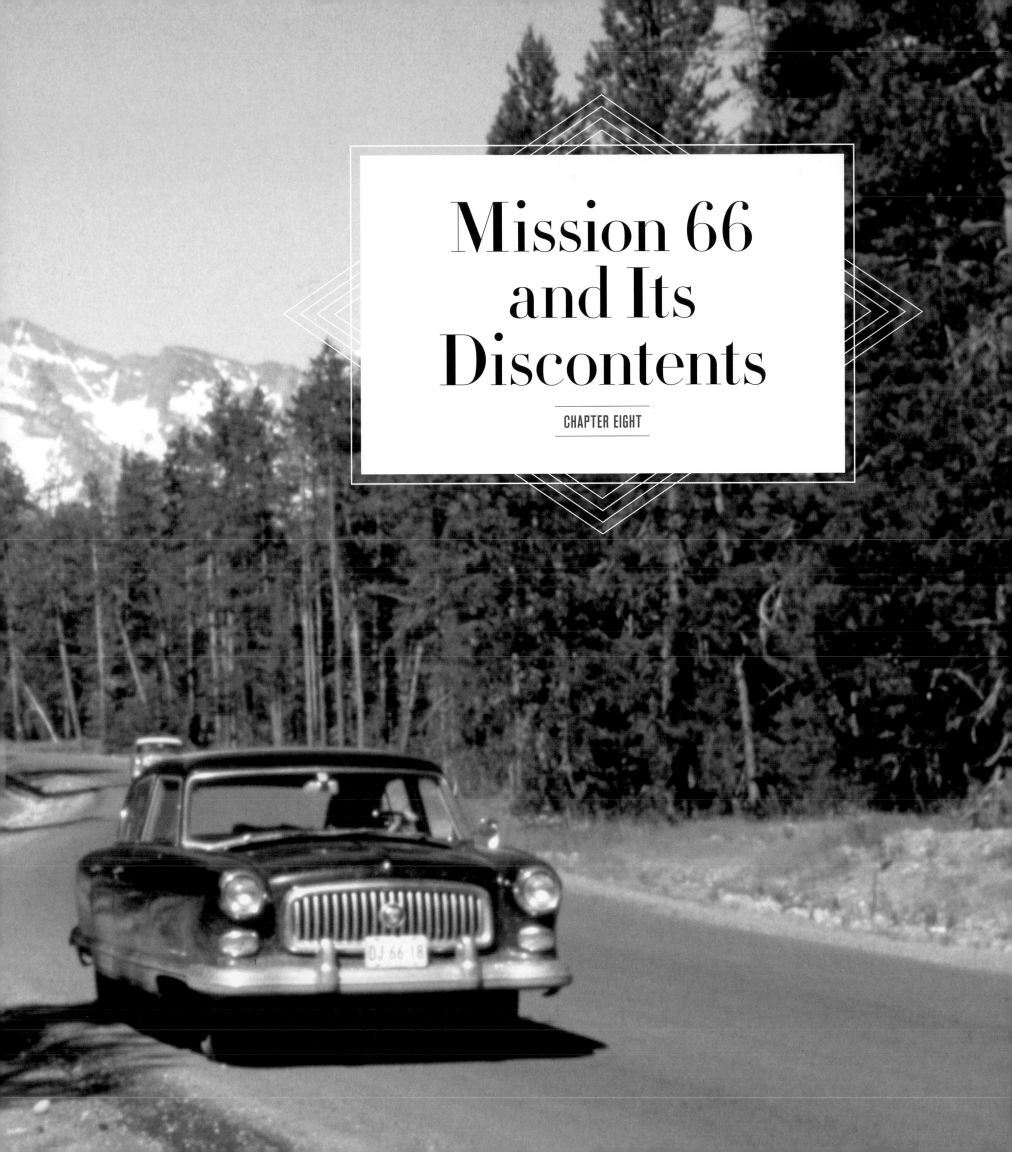

Mission 66 and Its Discontents

CHAPTER EIGHT

but the ongoing attempts demonstrated that threats of traditional impairments were not a thing of the past. The NPS put development plans on hold and strained to keep up with preventive maintenance. Fortunately, gas rationing and other travel restrictions reduced wear and tear. Admissions dropped from 21 million in 1941 to 6 million in 1942 and remained at similar levels through the end of the war.[1]

The end of the war produced a tremendous surge in visitation. Admissions picked up in late 1945 and hit a new record of 21,752,000 in 1946. Yellowstone received 1 million visitors for the first time in 1948 and system-wide visitation approached 30 million. Neither appropriations nor manpower kept pace. The combination of inadequate funding and surging visitation created a national outcry about inadequate conditions. The NPS acknowledged the problem and sought to channel public frustration into congressional action. In a 1949 magazine article titled "The Dilemma of Our Parks," NPS director Newton Drury lamented that visitors encountered deteriorating facilities, crowded and ill-equipped campgrounds, inadequate sanitary measures, and insufficient overnight accommodations. Roads that had been improved before the war required repairs as well as upgrades to handle increased traffic, larger automobiles, and longer trailers. He estimated that $175 million would be needed to accommodate current use and an additional $140 million to prepare for future growth. Completing the parkways begun before the war would take another $181 million. Drury challenged Congress to provide the means for the NPS to fulfill its responsibilities. He also decried the fact that the agency continued to devote excessive energy to beating back attempted incursions by private interests and public agencies. Particularly troubling in the latter regard were the Bureau of Reclamation and the Army Corps of Engineers, who sought to develop dams and reservoirs in western parklands. Drury's resistance to a proposed impoundment in the Echo Park area of Dinosaur National Monument led to his resignation in 1951 at the instigation of Interior Secretary Oscar Chapman, who favored the project. The Echo Park controversy prompted the Sierra Club and Wilderness Society to pursue a more public and contentious form of conservation advocacy, which the organizations would soon employ in response to the NPS's own park improvement plans.[2]

The era of wide-ranging improvements to national park roads and other facilities came to a close with the bombing of Pearl Harbor in December 1941. The United States' entry into World War II brought an end to the New Deal programs that served as the primary source of funding. Regular NPS appropriations were also slashed dramatically. By 1943, the Park Service was scraping by on less than a quarter of its prewar budget. The CCC program also wound down, though a few camps continued to operate with conscientious objectors. The NPS lost nearly two-thirds of its own employees to military service. The central office relocated to Chicago to free office space in Washington for the war effort, making it even harder for the agency to maintain hard-won gains. Logging, mining, and grazing interests took advantage of the situation to insist that wartime shortages demanded access to the parks for essential resources. Most of these requests were defeated,

Drury's successor, Conrad Wirth, would bear the brunt of these criticisms, but his initial challenge was to convince Congress to provide adequate support. Even if Congress had been more sympathetic, the Cold War, the Korean War, and foreign-aid programs such as the Marshall Plan severely limited domestic funding. Not only did conditions continue to deteriorate, but the combination of Baby Boom demographics, increased leisure time, expanding incomes, and rapidly improving highways meant that the agency had to prepare for an era of unprecedented growth.[3]

Wirth's efforts were aided by widespread public dissatisfaction. Articles in conservation magazines and popular publications decried the problem and called for its resolution. Bernard DeVoto's 1953 polemic "Let's Close the National Parks" was particularly forceful. DeVoto was a contributor to *Harper's Magazine*, one of the period's most popular periodicals. He was also a member of the National Parks Advisory Board and had long worked with senior officials to publicize the agency's needs. Combining colorful prose with statistics supplied by NPS leaders, he professed sympathy with the Park Service's plight while painting a grim picture of current conditions. DeVoto laid the blame on Congress, accusing politicians of treating the NPS like an "impoverished stepchild" and forcing it to subsist on "starvation rations." As a consequence, he proclaimed, "much of the priceless heritage which the Service must safeguard for the United States is beginning to go to hell." DeVoto passed on NPS estimates that it would take $250 million to accommodate current demands and significantly more to prepare for future needs. If Congress was unwilling to address the crisis, he asserted, the government should shut down the parks until conditions improved. An even more sensational 1954 *Reader's Digest* diatribe, "The Shocking Truth about Our National Parks," warned readers that a visit to America's most treasured sites was "likely to be fraught with discomfort, disappointment, even danger." The article described bumper-to-bumper traffic, "slum-like" accommodations, and dangerously deteriorated roads. In addition to citing the discrepancy between park use and congressional appropriations, the author chided the Park Service for allowing golfing, dancing, and other inappropriate entertainments, which exacerbated the situation by drawing crowds that should be relegated to less sensitive settings. Reviving another prewar complaint, the author condemned the emphasis on automobile-oriented development, warning that

excessive road construction would turn the parks "into the equivalent of drive-in movies."[4]

Wirth might not have appreciated the suggestion that the NPS had erred in attempting to accommodate automobile owners, but he welcomed the media's efforts to pressure Congress. The director provided pithy quotes and his staff supplied photographs, statistics, and anecdotes to dramatize the situation. Wirth proclaimed that funding shortfalls had forced the Park Service to put "patches on patches." He made it clear that the NPS remained committed to accommodating the American public, but warned that "people are loving the parks to death," coining a phrase that rapidly entered the conservation lexicon. Following DeVoto's lead, most accounts presented the national parks—and, by extension, the American people—as victims of a penurious Congress. Most critics expressed confidence that increased funding would enable the agency's professionals to restore the system to its former glory despite crowds that had doubled prewar records by the early 1950s.[5]

In February 1955, Wirth decided to pursue a strategy that had proven successful for other federal agencies such as the Bureau of Public Roads and Army Corps of Engineers. To avoid yearly haggles over individual projects, administrators proposed comprehensive multiyear programs. Rather than scare supporters away, the jaw-dropping estimates elevated the importance of the agencies' agendas. Congress was also more likely to support programs whose benefits were spread throughout the country. It was no coincidence that Wirth's plan coincided with the final push for the Interstate and Defense Highways Act, which provided an unprecedented commitment of federal funds when it passed with broad support in 1956. With similar boldness, Wirth called for a ten-year program to address current problems and prepare for future needs. If the legislation passed quickly, he noted, the program's culmination would coincide with the National Park System's Golden Anniversary in 1966. Seeking a title that would convey a combination of urgency, ambition, and idealism, Wirth settled on Mission 66.[6]

Wirth assembled a planning team to develop the proposal, along with a more broad-based oversight committee to review the ensuing recommendations. The team was headed by NPS chief landscape architect William Carnes; the steering committee was chaired by Lemuel Garrison, a former park ranger and superintendent. Vint served on the oversight committee along with other NPS division chiefs. Wirth presented a preview at the NPS superintendents' conference in September 1955, which produced favorable reports in the national press. By the end of the year, the team had readied a substantial report. Detailed budgets were developed that called for a doubling of existing appropriations followed by additional increases over the duration of the program, creating a cumulative price tag of $786,545,600. President Eisenhower endorsed the proposal and Congress followed suit. Despite Wirth's encouragement to explore a wide range of options, it quickly became apparent that Mission 66 would follow prewar precedents. Not only did traditional design and visitor-service professionals dominate the committee, but the program was officially launched with a banquet sponsored by the American Automobile Association that featured a specially produced Walt Disney film celebrating national park travel.[7]

The program's goals were detailed in a voluminous report, *Mission 66 for the National Park System*, and summarized in an illustrated booklet, *Our Heritage: A Plan for Its Protection and Use— Mission 66*, which was intended for popular distribution. Both made it clear that the fundamental problem was that a system designed to meet the needs of 25 million visitors was being forced to accommodate more than twice that number. The resultant overcrowding was harming park resources and preventing people from getting the satisfaction they deserved. Given contemporary trends such as expanded leisure time, improved highways, and a growing appreciation for outdoor recreation, the situation would become untenable unless dramatic steps were taken. Rationing park use through entrance quotas was considered, but rejected on the principle that national parks belonged to the people, who had a right to enjoy their benefits at will. Even with annual visitation predicted to reach 80 million by 1966, "modern traffic handling methods and proper development" would enable the NPS to achieve an appropriate balance between preservation and access without slighting either side of the equation.[8]

As Robert Sterling Yard noted during the initial surge in visitation, America's embrace of the automobile presented both the primary challenge and the key to its resolution. The increase in mobility and associated trend toward short-time visits made it both possible and necessary to rethink the distribution of park facilities. Accommodations had to be increased, but they could be located farther from overcrowded attractions. By placing lodgings in less sensitive areas or relying on private parties to build them beyond park borders, the impact

ABOVE Visitor Center, Grand Teton National Park, 1959.

on park resources would be reduced, continuing the process that began with the elimination of horse-drawn transportation. Employee housing and administrative buildings could also be placed at the park periphery or in discreet locations. Given the predilection for automobile travel and trend toward short-term stays, Mission 66 planners concluded that visitors would prefer the convenience of motel-style accommodations, which were cheaper and less formal than traditional hotels and thus better suited to the increasingly broad-based demographics of park users. Another major change was the centralization of visitor services in inviting new buildings surrounded by ample parking lots affording easy access for the motoring masses. Resembling the more elaborate rest areas being developed along modern highways, these visitor centers were Mission 66's signature contribution to the national park landscape. Like the shopping malls springing up across the American landscape, visitor centers afforded one-stop access to everything from maps and permits to restrooms and an increasingly elaborate array of educational offerings. Believing that informed visitors would get more out of their visits and treat park resources with greater respect, Mission 66 put considerable emphasis on enhancing educational opportunities through ranger-led programs, roadside exhibits, popular publications, and audiovisual offerings, which were presented at visitor centers and through other innovative means.[9]

The comprehensive improvement of park roads was a key element of Mission 66. In addition to redressing the problems of deferred maintenance and increased visitation, a smoothly flowing circulation network was essential to the vision of dispersed facilities catering to mobile visitors. Complaints about congested, outdated, and poorly maintained roads were a prominent feature of the criticism leading to the program's development. NPS officials highlighted transportation issues in their pleas for funding. One of the most striking illustrations in *Our Heritage* depicted a narrow roadway with cars careening toward trees and boulders and the aftermath of a collision in the distance. Another showed an entrance station engulfed in bumper-to-bumper traffic, while a third portrayed a car hauling a trailer three times its length. The latter scene was flanked by the Lincoln Memorial and Washington Monument to form a triptych of iconic American landscapes. Automobile clubs and associated industries

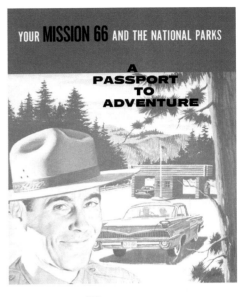

strongly supported Mission 66, as they had earlier road improvement efforts. Shell and Sinclair underwrote publicity efforts and promoted park vacations in their advertising. Seizing on the synergy, the producers of Phillips 66 gasoline produced a pamphlet with a text supplied by the NPS. The cover portrayed a late-model car approaching a modernistic entrance station blissfully unencumbered by traffic. The pamphlet outlined the program's goals and enthused, "Every day, in every part of the land, there is the exciting hum of tires on asphalt and concrete as thousands of Americans take to the road for the high adventure of a visit to our wild places and our priceless national shrines." To ensure visitors made the most of these experiences, Mission 66 called for an expanded program of informational signs and

wayside exhibits, along with additional overlooks, pullouts, and parking areas.[10]

Mindful of the potential for causing alarm, Mission 66 planners underscored that 90 percent of the construction entailed the improvement of existing roads, some of which dated from the stagecoach era. Even roads constructed in the 1920s and 1930s required widening, strengthening, and occasional rerouting to accommodate contemporary use. Approximately 2,000 miles of roadwork was deemed necessary, at a cost of $156.5 million. New construction would be limited to approximately 300 miles, located primarily in newly acquired parks. As in the past, the goal was not to provide access to every part of a park but rather to enable motorists to reach "a fair assortment of interesting or distinguished

Despite its new elements and unprecedented ambitions, the Mission 66 program reflected NPS leaders' conviction that the design and management ethics forged between the two world wars continued to afford the best approach to balancing preservation and access.

BELOW Winning entry in employee contest for new NPS logo, 1949.

OPPOSITE, TOP Ribbon-cutting ceremony for Stevens Canyon Road, Mount Rainier National Park, 1957.

OPPOSITE, BOTTOM Motor nature trail, Great Smoky Mountains National Park, 1966.

features." Mission 66 funding would also further the completion of national parkways and allow for the expansion of campgrounds to accommodate the increasing number and size of camping trailers. The transfer of Baltimore–Washington Parkway and Suitland Parkway to Maryland and the District of Columbia was also cast as a program goal. With these more utilitarian entities excised from the system, the NPS felt confident asserting that the goal of the program was not to construct "speedways" but to accommodate modern traffic demands within the framework of traditional park road development. Echoing Albright's assurances, Mission 66 planners insisted that the developed portion of most parks would comprise a tiny proportion of overall acreage. Publications and official pronouncements emphasized that wilderness preservation was one of the program's top priorities. The Mission 66 prospectus also called for a nationwide survey of recreational opportunities and the development of a national recreation plan designed to spread visitor impact over a wide range of federal, state, and local jurisdictions.[11]

Despite its new elements and unprecedented ambitions, the Mission 66 program reflected NPS leaders' conviction that the design and management ethics forged between the two world wars continued to afford the best approach to balancing preservation and access. Not only did Vint and his staff play a dominant role, but Wirth was a landscape architect by training and had headed NPS outreach to state parks during the Civilian Conservation Corps (CCC) era. Wirth repeatedly emphasized that resource protection for its own sake was not the agency's goal. Like Mather, Albright, and other predecessors, he insisted that national parks fulfilled their purpose only when visitors were provided with the means to experience them. "Without the concept of public use and enjoyment," he declared, "the function of preservation and protection is without meaning." Emphasizing Yellowstone's authorization rather than Olmsted's Yosemite report or the NPS Organic Act, Wirth asserted, "The primary justification for a National Park System lies in its capacity to provide enjoyment in its best sense, now and in the future." At the same time, he emphasized that parks served higher purposes than basic recreation. National parks, the Mission 66 prospectus declared, were "a spiritual necessity, an antidote to the high pressures of modern life, places to regain spiritual balance and to find strength."

Catering to Cold War sentiments while reflecting long-held beliefs, Wirth cast parks as incubators of patriotism where Americans developed "pride in their Government, love of the land, and faith in the American tradition." The ultimate goal of Mission 66, he proclaimed, was to ensure that the national parks continued to yield these benefits to individual visitors and the nation as a whole.[12]

There was no doubt that Mission 66 achieved many of its intended goals. Wirth's funding strategy was a resounding success. Congress exceeded the original request, appropriating slightly more than $1 billion over the life of the program. The increase reflected rising costs, as well as the growth of the National Park System, which added more than sixty areas during the period. Even as the park system was being dramatically enlarged, the NPS alleviated many of the problems that had garnered national attention. Outmoded and deteriorating facilities were refurbished or replaced. More than five hundred campgrounds were added, along with an even greater number of picnic areas and comfort stations. True to the program's goals, the overnight lodging capacity did not increase appreciably, though many facilities were modernized. One hundred visitor centers were constructed along with new entrance stations and more than one thousand informational signs and wayside exhibits. Concessionaire opposition and public pressure presented significant obstacles to the stated goal of moving facilities beyond park boundaries or to less sensitive areas, but there were significant achievements in this regard. At Yosemite, a concession complex was moved from the center of the valley to a less conspicuous location and employee residences along with some service facilities were relocated to El Portal. Mount Rainier's administration center was also repositioned beyond park boundaries. In order to restore a semblance of natural conditions at Yellowstone's Grand Canyon, the cavernous hotel was eliminated and concession facilities relocated to the newly created "Canyon Village" complex, whose shopping mall configuration provided ready access to a visitor center, cafeteria, stores, and five hundred motel units.[13]

Although the modernization of park facilities occupied center stage, Mission 66 funded a wide range of endeavors, including a significant expansion of professional staff, improvements to employee housing, historic preservation initiatives, and museum and interpretation advances. Mission 66 also publicized the NPS's new "arrowhead" logo, which had been adopted in 1951 but rose to prominence through its appearance on publications, new facilities, and ubiquitous signs announcing "This is a MISSION 66 Project." The iconic arrowhead was not the original choice. In 1949, NPS parkways program leader Dudley Bayliss won a contest for employee-generated suggestions with a design featuring a dual-lane roadway curving toward distant peaks. Upon further reflection, NPS officials decided that an arrowhead framing trees, mountains, lakes, and wildlife projected a more desirable image. As Mission 66 unfolded, friends and foes alike may have considered the roadway emphasis to be a more accurate portrayal of the program's priorities.[14]

By conventional measures, Mission 66's road program was a resounding success. More than 2,767 miles were constructed, reconstructed, or authorized for construction. Wirth's assurances that new mileage would constitute just 10 percent of the total proved grossly inaccurate, however. The final tally amounted to 1,570 miles of reconstruction and 1,197 miles of new road. While this raised significant questions, the disparity was arguably not as significant as it seemed. Most of the new construction took place in recently established parks, and a significant amount of the new mileage in older parks was accompanied by the abandonment of bypassed segments or their conversion into low-speed, one-way scenic drives. Service roads for maintenance, administration, and employee housing areas also contributed to the total. Parkway development constituted a significant source of new mileage, though it is unclear whether it was counted toward the general figure. Approximately 150 miles were added to Natchez Trace Parkway. With the addition of 142 miles, the Blue Ridge Parkway was just 17.5 miles short of completion. Mission 66 also produced significant increases in the number and size of parking lots and scenic overlooks. More than 1,500 new parking areas were constructed and hundreds more enlarged. One of the most striking indicators of Mission 66's automotive emphasis was that the number of parking spaces within the park system increased by 50 percent, for a grand total of slightly more than 155,000. Given that nearly all visitors arrived by automobile and overcrowded parking lots spilling cars into roadways and adjacent areas had been a major concern, NPS officials considered the expanded capacity an admirable achievement rather than

a cause for alarm. Other transportation systems were significantly upgraded as well. Nearly 1,000 miles of trails were constructed or rebuilt, along with ninety-three boat docks and fifty marinas, launching ramps, and beach facilities.[15]

For most visitors, road construction and the new centralized service facilities constituted the public face of the program. Primary tour roads were realigned, widened, regraded, and paved to accommodate modern vehicles and traffic loads. Many prominent prewar projects were significantly reconstructed. Acadia's Loop Road was upgraded, as was Great Smoky Mountains' Newfound Gap Road and large portions of Skyline Drive and Yellowstone's Grand Loop. Inadequate and deteriorating bridges were rehabilitated or replaced with wider, more modern structures. Even Yellowstone's iconic Chittenden Bridge was demolished on the grounds that it was dangerously deteriorated and barely wide enough for one modern vehicle, let alone two-way traffic. Narrow unpaved entrance roads to new or increasingly popular parks were widened, straightened, and paved, sometimes with significant shifts in location. In rare instances, entirely new roads were developed to open previously inaccessible regions to the motoring public. Olympic National Park's Hurricane Ridge Road provided sweeping panoramas of the park's interior wilderness. In addition to providing a long-awaited route across the south side of Mount Rainier, the Stevens Canyon Road encouraged visitors to venture beyond overcrowded Paradise Valley. The steepest section of the main road to Paradise was relocated to accommodate the ever-increasing influx of motorists and facilitate winter access. The bypassed section remained in use as a one-way downhill drive. A less-heralded aspect of the Mission 66 road-building program was the creation of "motor nature trails" that posed a striking contrast to the general emphasis on modernization. These low-standard routes often followed old road traces and were generally unpaved single-lane tracks with curves and grades that forced motorists to proceed at a slow pace. Great Smoky Mountains National Park's Roaring Fork Motor Nature Trail afforded a 5.5-mile-long excursion along the course of a historic wagon road. The 10-foot-wide, one-way drive wound around trees, boulders, waterfalls, log cabins, and other historic sites, with a posted speed of 10 mph. In keeping with Mission 66's emphasis on visitor education, numbered posts along the way were keyed

to a guidebook explicating natural and cultural features. Motor nature trails fulfilled Albright's and Kittredge's desire for roads that fostered a more intimate connection between motorists and their surroundings but they upset wilderness advocates by allowing mechanized society to extend its reach. Mission 66 also funded the NPS's first road-related historic preservation project. After heavy flooding severely damaged Yosemite's 1868 Wawona Covered Bridge, the structure was dismantled and restored to serve as a centerpiece of the park's new Pioneer History Center, which opened in 1961.[16]

Few observers equated Mission 66 with covered bridges and primitive dirt roads. While the general public and mainstream press tended to respond favorably, welcoming the new and improved facilities, the conservation community expressed reservations that soon erupted into outright hostility, both to specific projects and the program as a whole. The National Parks Association (NPA) was initially supportive, hailing Mission 66 as a "landmark in sound park planning." Fred Packard, the association's executive secretary, was particularly enthusiastic at the prospect of shifting development beyond park boundaries. The NPA expressed faith in the ability of the agency's professionals to strike an appropriate balance between preservation and access. Pointing to Wirth's assurances that only 300 miles of new roadway would be built, Packard expressed relief that "road construction plans are moderate, geared to actual needs." Packard's primary concern was that publicly available information dealt largely in generalities. The true test would come when the prospectus's grand vision was translated into specific projects. Packard emphasized that the NPA was eager to assist in the process.[17]

The Sierra Club was initially cautiously optimistic, characterizing the program as a "grand conception" that addressed a "desperate need" and applauding the decision to encourage development outside the parks while discouraging inappropriate activities within. Concerns about the road-building component were similarly tempered by Wirth's assurance that new construction would be limited and existing roads would not be inordinately upgraded. The club also expressed concern about the lack of detailed information. Combined with the insular manner in which the proposal was developed, with no input from the major conservation groups, the lack of specificity elicited accusations that the NPS was deliberately shrouding Mission 66 in "the mists of government secrecy." Club leaders called for greater transparency and increased collaboration, along with a more explicit commitment to the preservation of wilderness values.[18]

One of the most prominent strains of criticism centered on the evolving aesthetics of park construction. Many Mission 66 structures were unabashedly modern in design and materials. Although the contrast with traditional NPS rustic style was dramatic, there were practical and philosophical reasons for the change. Mission 66 coincided with the adoption of modernism as the preferred style for public and commercial architecture. NPS architects and private designers hired to assist in the ambitious building program were inclined to work in the idiom of the day, demonstrating that both they and the

NPS were attuned to contemporary trends. In addition to being well-suited for new functions such as expansive visitor centers, modern designs, materials, and technologies were generally more economical than traditional methods. This was vitally important during the lean years leading up to Mission 66, when the trend began, and equally so during the heyday of the program, when a tremendous amount of work had to be accomplished quickly and efficiently. From a practical perspective, the labor-intensive, craft-oriented approach that produced the rustic structures, hand-laid stonework, and subtly sculpted landscapes of the prewar era was no longer a viable option.[19]

The reliance on modern designs and materials became a lightning rod for Mission 66 critics, who contended that conspicuously modern buildings violated long-standing policies about harmonizing park structures with their surroundings. Complaints were particularly severe when modern design replaced existing rustic structures, as when the log-framed observation tower at Clingmans Dome gave way to a futuristic concrete "skypost" accessed by a spiral concrete ramp. The NPA's Devereux Butcher published a series of articles decrying the trend. Butcher assailed the new facilities for their "chicken coop roofs, freak windows, and gaudy colors," accusing them of being "ugly beyond words" and "standing out like a proverbial sore thumb." He characterized Yellowstone's Canyon Village as "colossal in scale and of freak design," compared the skypost to a roller coaster, and characterized Grand Teton's Jackson Lake Lodge as "the ugliest building in the park and monument system," noting that locals had taken to referring to the slab-sided edifice as "Alcatraz." Critics also condemned comfort stations and other utilitarian structures, which, unlike their picturesquely varied prewar predecessors, were usually built according to standardized plans to reduce costs. Visitor centers generated unfavorable comparisons with suburban shopping centers due to their modernist aesthetics and commodious parking. The new Logan Pass visitor center exemplified the transition, replacing a low stone structure that blended with the surrounding outcrops with an assertive modernist edifice replete with Miesian plate-glass expanses and I-beam ornamentation. In many locations visitors had to negotiate expanses of asphalt and seas of parked cars on their way to popular sites and lodgings.[20]

Modern design and technology exerted a

profound influence on road development as well. For casual observers, modernism's impact on the park road experience was most evident in the design of new entrance stations, many of which combined traditional and contemporary attributes. With their massive shingled canopies extending over multiple lanes, Yellowstone's new entrance stations reflected a confluence of traditional park rusticity with the aesthetics and efficiency of drive-in banks and hamburger stands. Along with alleviating traffic jams, the soaring multilane structures were designed to accommodate increasingly large recreational vehicles that could not fit through the portals of prewar entrance stations. The exuberantly angular Saint Mary's Lake visitor center and entrance station complex at Glacier National Park exhibited a similar mating of rustic materials with modern aesthetics. Many parks received more modest tollbooth-like structures sheathed in rustic veneer, evidencing Mission 66's pragmatic approach to utilitarian structures. Park entrance signs tended to display greater standardization and a more minimalist aesthetic. On a more subtle level, at least to most observers, the wider pavements, longer curves, and transition to bituminous concrete, or "asphalt," surfaces embodied modern trends in highway engineering.

A more readily apparent manifestation of modern engineering was the trend toward unadorned concrete and steel bridges, which were both more economical to construct and more in line with the form-follows-function credo of modern architecture. Rustic stone cladding continued to be applied in some situations, but postwar designers fulfilled Goodwin's admonition to explore the aesthetic possibilities of modern materials. In situations where rock outcrops were few and far between, smooth surfaces were also cast as more contextually appropriate than imported stone veneer. The turn toward modern bridge design was not simply a matter of aesthetics. Engineering advances enabled the NPS to build bridges and viaducts that would previously have been impossible, or at least inordinately expensive. This opened up new possibilities in road design and location. In addition to spanning broad gaps relatively economically, prestressed concrete girders and other technologies could be employed to reduce a road's impact on the landscape by carrying it above sensitive terrain on widely spaced supports rather than relying on environmentally disruptive cuts and fills. A variety of prestressed concrete girder, steel

girder, concrete box-beam, and reinforced-concrete rib-arch bridges were employed to carry George Washington Memorial Parkway over the ravines plunging into the Potomac River. A similar mix of technologies was employed on Blue Ridge Parkway, including the 1,028-foot Roanoke River Bridge, the 993-foot Swannanoa River Bridge, and a number of substantial viaducts. At Mount Rainier, the oft-repaired Nisqually Glacier Bridge was replaced by a steel-and-concrete girder span located above the reach of floodwaters.

While the new bridges generated minimal comment, road development emerged as one of the most controversial components of Mission 66. The public embraced the enhanced convenience, but critics revived prewar arguments, complaining about the crowding associated with increased accessibility, the infringement on wilderness values, and the nature of the roads themselves. Not only were the wider, straighter Mission 66 roads more visually intrusive, but they encouraged speeds that many considered incompatible with the park experience. As with concurrent complaints about architectural aesthetics, these criticisms antedated Mission 66, but the program's unprecedented scope brought simmering issues to the fore. Debates about road standards were generally focused on specific projects, but the wilderness issue was of such general concern that the NPS addressed it a separate publication issued a year after the original announcement.

Bob Marshall, Aldo Leopold, and Robert Sterling Yard had long since passed away, but the wilderness movement was on the upswing by the mid-1950s. The highly publicized battle over dam building in Dinosaur National Monument catapulted the concept into prominence, along with its leading proponents, Sierra Club executive director David Brower and Wilderness Society executive secretary Howard Zahniser. This new generation of conservationists honed their advocacy skills while expanding support from a coterie of naturalists, visionaries, and misanthropes to an increasingly broad segment of the American public. The

defeat of the dam proposal emboldened advocates to press for legislation calling for a congressionally mandated wilderness system that would provide greater protection than national park designation by explicitly elevating the preservation motive over all other concerns. Not only would dozens of parks be included in this new category, but the proposal authored by Zahniser and submitted to Congress in June 1956 identified roads and recreational development as primary threats and called on the NPS to make wilderness preservation an integral component of Mission 66. Responding to concerns about the cloistered manner in which Mission 66 plans were being formulated, the bill required the NPS to solicit public comment on proposals that threatened to diminish wilderness areas. It would take years for the wilderness bill to wend its way through Congress, but its introduction signaled a significant transformation in attitudes about the cultural value of primeval landscapes and the role of government in ensuring their preservation.[21]

Critics of Mission 66 contended that the NPS was tipping the balance from preservation to access just when the opposite approach was more necessary than ever. The Sierra Club had historically shared the goal of both preserving and promoting scenic resources, but the accelerating impact of mass mobility prompted a change

in the club's bylaws. The original injunction to "explore, enjoy, and render accessible the mountain regions of the Pacific Coast" was changed from "render accessible" to "preserve." Brower called for a similar revision to the NPS's mandate to unequivocally elevate preservation over access. He highlighted the preservation admonitions of Olmsted's 1865 Yosemite report to bolster this argument, maintaining that the NPS should institute a resource protection-oriented "Mission 65" to honor the centenary of Olmsted's vision and undo the damage caused by Mission 66. Not only did Brower neglect to mention Olmsted's exhortations to improve access, but he was similarly selective in quoting the NPS Organic Act, routinely omitting the instructions to promote parks and provide for their enjoyment. Cautioning against additional upgrades, National Parks Association board member Mark Litton complained the NPS's efforts had already made the valley "too accessible." Other critics complained that agency's policies favored the "motorized millions" and sacrificed park values to accommodate "hordes of amusement-seeking tourists." Beyond the actual damage to park scenery, Brower noted along with fellow Sierra Club board member Harold Bradley, "we must still express concern when those who would enjoy a

national park for itself are crowded out by others who want just another resort."[22]

The elitism of such sentiments was self-evident and, for the most part, unapologetic. Brower complained that if Mission 66 proceeded unchecked, the parks would be "Babbittized" and "reduced to the lowest common denominator." Asserting that "the modern American is no longer able to enjoy nature's handiwork unless viewed from the seat of an automobile," National Wildlife Federation executive director Ernest Swift lamented that the "high standards and values espoused by Aldo Leopold and Bob Marshall" were not shared by the ordinary park visitor." Likening the new breed of tourists to the migrants depicted in John Steinbeck's *Grapes of Wrath*, he protested that the NPS appeared intent on "prostituting the scenic grandeurs of our national parks, monuments and wilderness areas to a destructive mass of human protoplasm." Articles on overcrowded parks decried "the damage done by massed humanity" and derided their lack of interest in traditional pursuits. An oft-repeated anecdote involved a bored tourist imploring, "What are we supposed to do here—look at the scenery?" Benton Mackaye weighed in, defending the right of the wilderness-seeking minority to areas unscathed by the relentless onslaught of "motor and motel." Rallying the opposition with an allusion to patriot orator Patrick Henry's defense of treason in the face of tyranny, he proclaimed, "If this be snobbery, make the most of it!" Brower further irritated agency officials by resurrecting the notion of a national committee on scenic resources management without the NPS at the helm and accusing them of deliberately delaying action on the wilderness bill.[23]

The strength and stridency of the wilderness movement took Wirth by surprise. Like Albright, who leapt to his defense, Wirth was both personally and professionally offended that the NPS's wilderness stewardship was being called into question. In response, he assigned Mission 66 planning committee member Howard Stagner to prepare a publication emphasizing the agency's commitment to wilderness preservation and outlining the ways in which Mission 66 contributed to the effort. Appealingly designed, with striking photographs accompanied by bold quotes in a style that echoed the Sierra Club's advocacy publications, *The National Park Wilderness* proclaimed the agency's devotion to the wilderness ideal while reiterating

Wirth's contention that the Park Service's mission was not preservation for its own sake but to allow the American public to experience outstanding natural and cultural landscapes. The best way to achieve this was to encourage appropriate use through the provision of carefully planned developments that concentrated visitor impact while leaving the majority of most parks untouched. Most visitors would never set foot in true wilderness areas, but Stagner insisted that their existence was important to all. Underscoring the NPS's more expansive perspective, he contended that wilderness could be appreciated in many ways: by hiking or riding deep into the backcountry, by viewing distant landscapes, or in a ten-minute walk from a well-traveled road. Although most wilderness advocates derided such assertions as a diminution of the wilderness concept, *The National Park Wilderness* included views from Blue Ridge Parkway, Going-to-the-Sun Highway, and Trail Ridge Road to illustrate the range of national park wilderness experiences. Stagner maintained that NPS policies had contributed significantly to the growing appreciation for wilderness values by bringing millions of American into closer contact with their natural heritage. He expressed frustration that the more extreme elements of the conservation community sought to channel these sentiments to protest NPS policies. *The National Park Wilderness* reiterated assurances that Mission 66 was focused on reconstructing old roads, not building new ones, and promised there would be no extensions into wilderness areas. Stagner boasted that the NPS was one step ahead of its critics, having already constrained road development where it conflicted with wilderness values in places like Kings Canyon and Olympic National Parks.[24]

Conservationists objected that the NPS viewed such decisions as a discretionary matter rather than a moral and legal imperative. A preliminary version of Stagner's presentation circulated to conservationists had employed Marshall and Leopold's characterization of wilderness as an area without roads. This was deleted from the published version, reflecting the traditional NPS stance that road development did not inherently compromise wilderness values, as well as the agency's unwillingness to have its hands tied by overly specific directives. Similarly troubling to road opponents was the assertion that the bulk of the Mission 66 road program would consist of "rebuilding existing roads to bring them to a

standard required today" and constructing "on a similar scale" in new parks. Given the NPS's own disagreements with BPR engineers, this language was not reassuring. Although he acknowledged that engineering requirements occasionally necessitated compromises with preservation ideals, Stagner insisted the agency's track record afforded sufficient insurance. "Efforts to hold road standards to acceptable limits, to preserve natural conditions along roadsides, to fit park roads to topography while providing scenic and interpretive opportunity, and to achieve the appropriateness in design and location of developments," he proclaimed, "have met with considerable success."[25]

What was new in the case of Mission 66, Stagner maintained, was that greater attention was being paid to the ability of roads to function as "interpretive devices" educating Americans about their natural and cultural heritage. Park roads had always showcased signature features, but traditional design and location strategies would be augmented with markers, signs, and more elaborate roadside exhibits to ensure that "a journey through a park will become a continuous experience in seeing, understanding, and appreciating the natural scene." The same strategy was applied in historical parks. The NPS developed a series of low-speed roads in Colonial National Historic Park. Narrower and more circuitous than the main parkway, these "wilderness loops" allowed visitors to experience the park's landscape at a more leisurely pace and intimate scale. Jamestown's colonial history was portrayed on brightly painted interpretive panels placed along the way. NPS planners maintained that the regenerated woodlands and historical vignettes would fulfill the goal of "leading the most interested visitors deeper into the thoughtful process of understanding the colony." As with the motor nature trails, an integral attraction of this approach was that the benefits could be gained without alighting from the family automobile. Along with embodying the program's educational goals and desire to disperse visitor impact, this strategy was an adroit rebuttal to assertions that automobile tourism was inherently superficial. Thanks to Mission 66 improvements, national park roads would play an active role in educating visitors and instilling proper reverence for park values.[26]

Dudley Bayliss, the head of the NPS parkways program, elaborated on the principles guiding Mission 66 road development in the June 1957

man is a part of the scene—wilderness has little human value without him.

and wilderness reaches outward from the roadside to be experienced fully by those who penetrate it.

issue of *Traffic Quarterly*. In an extended discussion of park road concerns reissued by the NPS as *Planning Our National Park Roads and Our National Parkways*, Bayliss recounted prewar achievements and summarized classic park road design principles. Bayliss illustrated these techniques with photographs taken throughout the National Park System. Examples included native stone guard walls and bridge treatments in Mount Rainier, the preservation of roadside trees in Lassen, roads "laid on the ground" rather than cut through it, and images of the Blue Ridge Parkway winding gracefully through natural and cultural landscapes. Bayliss also included examples of master plans and more detailed design and maintenance diagrams specifying vegetation characteristics, mowing limits, vistas to be kept clear, scenic easements, and the location of stone walls and other features. Parkway-related concerns played a prominent role, with Bayliss summarizing NPS approaches to route selection, land acquisition, design, and construction. This emphasis reflected the considerable amount of work remaining on national parkways as well as the NPS's suggestion that the interstate highway system include wayside camping and recreation areas along with enhanced roadside landscaping. Making interstate highways more parkway-like would render long-distance travel more enjoyable while reducing pressure on parks by affording additional alternatives for those who enjoyed driving through attractive landscapes but were not inclined toward wilderness adventures. Federal highway officials demurred. Not only would recreational features drive up costs and impede efficiency, but with each state retaining authority over its individual components, the logistical challenges would be daunting. Even the more general hope that highway officials would take heed of NPS landscape design policies met with conspicuous failure, at least in the eyes of contemporary observers. The degree to which the NPS's own road-building practice embodied these principles also became a matter of debate.[27]

Mission 66 road building quickly came under attack. One of the earliest Mission 66 road projects, the improvement of Grand Canyon's East Rim Drive, elicited a chorus of complaints. The new road bypassed many curves, eliminated the dips and humps that characterized the old road, and, in the eyes of critics, stood out as a conspicuous intrusion in the landscape. Where the old rim road at Utah's Cedar Breaks National Monument "wound pleasantly through stands of spruce and

fir, and ambled across open, flower-spread parks," its Mission 66 successor was condemned as "a broad new highway" that "pushes through all obstructions, seeming to say: 'Stand back, Nature. Here comes Progress!'" A 1957 visitor to Yellowstone's Gallatin Valley complained that the scenic winding road recalled from previous trips had given way to "a straight, level, new highway dissecting the valley without regard to contours." Contending that the supposed improvement had permanently despoiled the scenery, he declared "a straight speedway like this road has no place in a National Park." The scarring of hillsides associated with the construction of Mount Rainier's Stevens Canyon Road generated considerable controversy, as did the excavations required for Olympic's Hurricane Ridge Road. In addition to suppressing the sense of intimacy with the surrounding landscape and supplanting engaging curves with "uninteresting straightaways," excessively high standards imparted an inducement to speed, whether the motorist was in a hurry or not. As a result, Mission 66 road construction was accompanied by a proliferation of speed-limit signs. The top speed on major park roads was raised to 45 mph in some places, though in mountainous terrain it was generally 35 mph. "If the Park Service seriously intends to hold visitors to this limit," one critic observed, "why provide a road easily capable of sustaining higher speeds? Much better would have been the old roadbed, resurfaced and widened a few feet—and probably much cheaper, too." The prevalence of such sentiments led *National Parks Magazine* to proclaim that "engineering has become more important than preservation" and prompted Devereux Butcher to declare, "Road building under Mission 66 has given rise to greater alarm than perhaps any other phase of the program." Accusing the NPS of emulating the interstate highway bureaucracy, NPA executive secretary Anthony Wayne Smith protested, "The contagion of the big roads program has spread into our national parks and is driving fast highways through the parks in place of leisurely park roads."[28]

Wirth attempted to quell the criticism by meeting with Sierra Club directors and executives of the National Parks Association. Stating from the outset that he would "make no apology for the construction included in Mission 66," Wirth reiterated the rationale behind the service's determination to accommodate the influx

of motorists. "It is the people's right to visit their parks," he declared, "and they do so in large numbers." Given this reality, it was essential to control visitation through carefully conceived development. "There is no surer way to destroy a landscape," he remonstrated, "than to permit undisciplined use by man." Road improvements were an indispensable component of this strategy. Wirth acknowledged that it was natural for visitors to be disturbed by the din of bulldozers, power shovels, and paving machines, as well as to express frustration at associated traffic disruptions, but he counseled patience. While the roar of machines and raw appearance of active construction sites might create the impression that "the entire park is being torn to shreds," road improvements impacted a tiny portion of park landscapes, and constructions scars would be mediated by landscape rehabilitation and the passage of time.[29]

Wirth insisted that the NPS would not be deterred by unfavorable headlines, but the agency was not deaf to criticism. Wirth personally inspected the contentious Grand Canyon project and ordered that the remaining realignment follow the original road more closely. The NPS worked with the Sierra Club to resolve questions surrounding the provision of access to Kings Canyon and sided with conservationists resisting local pressure to upgrade the more primitive of two approaches to Grand Teton National Park. Tourism interests were as eager to see roads improved as conservationists were to maintain the status quo, and just as intent on making their wishes known. State and local chambers of commerce lobbied superintendents, NPS leaders, and the BPR, often bringing additional pressure to bear through their influence with elected officials. The NPS increasingly found itself at odds with the BPR, calling for a less obtrusive approach than the agency's engineers deemed safe and prudent. Tensions between the NPS and BPR grew as the engineers insisted that evolving standards outside the parks necessitated upgrades within. Even the most ardent Mission 66 opponents recognized that the NPS faced enormous challenges in trying to balance the demands of engineers, commercial interests, and mainstream motorists with preservationists' desires to keep improvements to a minimum.[30]

The controversy over park roads came to a head when the NPS announced it was ready to undertake the long-delayed improvement of the central section of Yosemite's Tioga Road. The ensuing debate attracted national attention, provoked widespread recrimination, and produced a profound reassessment of Mission 66 road improvements and NPS development policies in general. Everyone agreed that the narrow, winding, unpaved mountain road needed to be improved, but heated arguments arose about the extent of the improvements, their impact on Yosemite, and their implications for the park system as a whole. The disagreements ranged over all the major elements of park road design: general location, specific alignment, basic engineering standards, the road's impact on its immediate surroundings, and its broader influence on the management and use of the park. As with many Mission 66–related developments, the key issues predated the program's inception.

In 1948, when longtime allies such as William Colby and Duncan McDuffie still dominated the Sierra Club board of directors and Yosemite Advisory Board, both entities approved plans to upgrade the middle section to the standards employed on the end segments during the 1930s. Dissident members led by Brower and Harold Bradley objected, insisting that the wider, straighter roads resulting from the 1932 BPR standards cut conspicuously artificial gashes through the forest, produced excessive scarring, and encouraged speeds of 45 to 70 mph. The sense of intimacy with the surrounding terrain was lost, as was the ability to enjoy park scenery at a leisurely pace, since even motorists who were not inclined to speed were unable to slow down for fear of causing backups or being rear-ended by impatient drivers. The NPS insisted the approach was necessary, noting that existing conditions were "hazardous and extremely disconcerting to the average park visitor." In addition to enhancing safety and eliminating bottlenecks, the upgrades would improve access to Tuolumne Meadows, relieving some of the pressure on Yosemite Valley. Bradley considered this even more problematic since it would destroy the "semi primitive nature" of the region. Colby emphasized that improving access to the High Sierra had been a club objective since the days of John Muir, and McDuffie disparaged Bradley's campaign as an ill-conceived effort to restrict the area's enjoyment to "the hardy few," but the board gave the go-ahead for a bulletin article on alternative approaches to park road development. Colby confided that he hoped this would settle the matter but warned that "the few who entertain sentiments similar to Dr.

ABOVE Upgraded section of Tioga Road, Yosemite National Park, 1938.

Bradley's are unduly tenacious in their opinions."[31]

With Brower fueling the flames and providing editorial assistance, Bradley maintained that earlier NPS improvements had been driven by a legitimate need to improve accessibility, but contended that current conditions called for greater emphasis on preservation. Revising park road policies would both reduce the impact of construction and constrain demands for additional development. Higher standards were fine for roads approaching parks, but within the boundaries the focus should be on preserving scenery and providing a more fulfilling experience. The emphasis should be on "the leisurely enjoyment of unfolding scenes" rather than "the thrill of speed."

Lower-standard roads required more effort on the part of the driver, but their slower speeds and more intimate confines allowed motorists to enjoy their surroundings almost as if they were proceeding along trails, with surprises around every bend and trees meeting like gothic arches overhead. They were also significantly cheaper to build, since they obviated the need for expensive scenery-scarring excavations. Most importantly, in Bradley's estimation, they acted as "filters" to screen out those who were unwilling to make the effort to appreciate parks in the proper manner. The NPS's desire to increase visitation and the BPR's pursuit of technical perfection blinded them to the realization that low road standards could be an effective management tool. By deterring "the merely restless driver," "the trailer tourist," and those seeking "just another recreational resort within easy reach," low-standard roads would protect park landscapes and preserve the traditional park experience, restricting access to "those who know or wish to know the high purpose of the parks." Rangers at park entrances would outline road conditions within, both to discourage mere resort seekers and to help true pilgrims prepare for the "thrilling experiences and dramatic views" to ensue. It would also lessen the chance of motorists arriving at their destinations "fatigued and sometimes almost hysterical," due to the admittedly challenging nature of the Tioga Road passage.[32]

Even Bradley agreed that the "twenty-one tortuous miles of old mine road" created "undue anxiety" and required significant improvement. Rather than adopt the NPS-BPR approach, which embodied the "the ascendancy of engineering standards over national park values," Bradley urged consideration of more modest alternatives. "To provide standards higher than the minimum," he insisted, "is to provide also for the gratuitous sacrifice of the very values which the road is intended to display." The existing road could be selectively improved to eliminate major problem areas, as John White had done in defiance of BPR pressure to radically revise Generals Highway, or a similarly narrow road could be constructed as a parallel one-way route so motorists could enjoy the traditional park road experience with greater security. The latter approach would afford reasonable access and provide "the ideal park road for the functions of display" while retaining the twists, turns, and narrow confines needed to prevent Tuolumne Meadows from turning into a "trailer village." The NPS vetoed both suggestions, along with similar recommendations for the unreconstructed upper section of Big Oak Flat Road. Parallel roads would entail significant additional scarring and still had to be wide enough for faster vehicles to pass. Both Vint and Kittredge dismissed the minor-improvements approach on the same terms levied against the latter's proposal for retaining the old Big Oak Flat Road: while it might suffice in the short term, traffic increases would render it obsolete, necessitating a new alignment and leaving a conspicuous scar in the old location.[33]

Controversy also arose over the road's location. Colby's cohort pointed out that the matter had been discussed at length in the 1930s and the club had strongly supported the planned alignment, but newer board members including Ansel Adams and Richard Leonard called for an alternate route north of the old road that would eliminate impacts on Tenaya Lake and an outstanding example of glacially polished granite known as Pywiack Dome. The new proposal entailed all of the drawbacks of the previously rejected High Line with none of the benefits. Since no one was willing to countenance as dramatic a location as the original, it ran through an area that was not significantly different than other portions of the route. This meant that it would have less impact on sensitive areas, but the corollary was that it would not do as good a job of exposing visitors to the spectacular scenery of the High Sierra. Abandoning the existing road to pursue a radically new course would also bring development into an area of pristine lakes and mountains rather than restricting it to an established transportation corridor. Countering that the existing proposal included a relocated stretch that would also impinge on undeveloped terrain, Leonard maintained that the choice boiled down to invading a primitive area and destroying the character of the Tenaya Lake region or invading a different primitive area and sparing one of the park's most treasured scenic areas. NPS landscape architects and BPR engineers conducted a thorough study of the proposed alternatives in August 1950. Once again, they concluded that the established location was superior on technical, aesthetic, and economic grounds.[34]

Since budget pressures precluded construction, the matter lay dormant until the lead-up to Mission 66, when business interests in the surrounding region began agitating for the road's completion. This prompted a countereffort by the Sierra Club, which had become increasingly critical of NPS policy as Colby's influence waned and a new generation of board members followed Brower's lead. The club decided to prepare a formal policy paper on national park roads, combining Bradley's exhortations with a more explicit enunciation of design attributes. Such specifics were necessary, the board maintained, because the devastation wrought despite previous assurances that park roads would be appropriately scaled and sensitively designed demonstrated that the Sierra Club, NPS officials, and BPR engineers held "wildly divergent interpretations" of suitable engineering standards and landscape treatments. The club's statement acknowledged that NPS officials were being heavily pressured to adopt higher standards but criticized the agency for succumbing too readily. Much of the document echoed NPS statements about the need to minimize disruptions, maximize scenic value, and gear engineering standards to "moderate-speed park traffic." The major points of departure were that the Sierra Club defined maximum-allowable values rather than the engineer's typical minimum values, and that the club's figures represented a return to 1920s specifications. Speeds were limited to 35 mph in flat terrain, 30 mph in rolling terrain, and a maximum of 20 mph in areas "where higher standards would increase the damage to the natural scene," with exceptions permitted on roads with heavy traffic loads. No scenic values could be compromised to accommodate speeds in excess of 35 mph. Grades could range as high as 14 percent, though 7 percent was suggested for heavily traveled roadways. On busy mountain roads, however, grades up to 12 percent should be allowed. Maximum pavement width was capped at 22 feet including shoulders on heavily traveled roads, and 18 feet on more lightly used roadways. Dual single-lane roads were encouraged as a means of reducing impacts even further. There was a prohibition on creating road scars that could be seen from wilderness areas and an admonition to minimize ecological damage. Curvature tables were provided for various combinations of width, speed, and topography. The policy was originally published in the club's March 1953 bulletin, copies of which were sent to California politicians along with requests that they urge the NPS to adopt the club's standards as official policy. A separate pamphlet was disseminated in April 1955 in anticipation of the "tremendous road budgets" forthcoming from Mission 66.[35]

Current president Richard Leonard sent a copy to Wirth along with a cover letter restating the club's opposition to the agency's Tioga Road plans and culminating in the classic "We don't build public thoroughfares through museums, libraries, art exhibits, or cathedrals" adage. Leonard also challenged the Park Service to come up with a similarly detailed and comprehensive road policy of its own. General statements about harmonizing with surroundings and lying lightly on the land were admirable, but without more precise instructions, the results depended not just on bureaucratic perspectives but on the skills and interpretations of the designers. While many national park roads were commendably constructed, Leonard maintained that recent tendencies demonstrated the need for greater specificity, along with increased scrutiny to ensure instructions were properly followed. Not only did different individuals and organizations interpret general maxims differently, but Leonard maintained that Kittredge and other sources had confided that the BPR and its contractors did not always adhere to the Park Service's directives. As a case in point, he asserted that the NPS had assured the club that the end sections of the Tioga Road would have a 20-foot travelway and 3-foot unpaved shoulders, but the Crane Flat section wound up with a 26-foot-wide paved surface conducive to speeds of 50 to 70 mph. If the center section were constructed in the same manner, he maintained, the Tioga Road would become a crowded commercial thoroughfare destroying "the very peace and quiet and departure from civilization that people seek when they go to a National Park instead of to a resort."[36]

Acting NPS director Thomas Allen thanked Leonard for the enclosures, praised the Sierra Club for its concern, reiterated the basic rationale for park road improvement, and maintained there were "no great differences" between the Sierra Club's recommendations and NPS practice. Plans for the final section called for a 20-foot-wide pavement flanked by 3-foot shoulders, which narrowed to 2 feet in cut sections and widened to 4 feet on fills. While this was slightly wider than club preferences, it was narrower than current BPR park road standards. If it were truly a "high speed superhighway," as Leonard had charged, there would be 24 feet of pavement with 10-foot shoulders. Allen also sought to clarify the confusion about the Crane Flat section, explaining that the shoulders were not paved but composed of crushed stone or gravel bound with bitumen. While not as inconspicuous as dirt or turf shoulders, they provided better support for vehicles while helping stabilize the roadbed. Allen insisted that the new construction would be closely supervised and expressed confidence that the final results would be satisfactory to all. In closing, he assured Leonard that the Park Service was "fully aware at all times of its public responsibilities" and committed to preserving scenic areas while at the same time providing for the "enjoyment of these areas by the public for whom they were dedicated." In response, Leonard's successor, Alex Hildebrand, employed the cathedral analogy yet again to underscore that the board of directors was "deeply disturbed" by

the assertion that existing and proposed sections conformed to the club's guidelines. He also expressed concern that upgrading the Tioga Road would play into plans to resurrect an abbreviated version of the utilitarian Trans-Sierra Highway.[37]

The NPS was also receiving pressure from the other end of the spectrum. The BPR agreed that park road requirements should be revised to reflect changes since the plans were drawn up in the 1930s, but in the opposite direction. Insisting that a 22-foot-wide surface with 4-foot shoulders was the minimum for safe and efficient operation, BPR officials informed Wirth that the agency would not proceed unless the specifications were revised upward. Wirth was not pleased with the BPR's refusal to accept what he considered a reasonable compromise. "I have given definite instructions that I do not want a fast road," he declared; "I want a narrow road, because it is the width of the road that controls the speed." Wirth was also concerned that the associated excavation would inflict unacceptable damage in key areas. In an attempt to settle the matter to

the satisfaction of all three parties, Wirth asked Walter Huber to provide his professional opinion. Not only was Huber an accomplished civil engineer with extensive road-building experience, but he was in the unique position of having served as president of both the Sierra Club and the American Society of Civil Engineers. He was also the current chairman of the National Parks Advisory Board and had represented the Sierra Club on park road issues since the 1920s. Huber noted that the idea of turning the Tioga Road into a high-speed trans–Sierra Highway was both inappropriate and unlikely, given the engineering obstacles posed by the eastern approach through Lee Vining Canyon. He also insisted that it was both necessary and desirable to improve the road's ability to "bring an appreciative public to the beauties of the alpine portion of the park." After a thorough inspection, he endorsed the Park Service's plan with the exception of one area where he deemed the BPR's wider shoulder necessary to ensure safety. At the same time, he emphasized that shoulders should be comprised of

ABOVE Tioga Road construction, Yosemite National Park, 1957.

a stabilized base covered with native grass, warning that conventional gravel or aggregate shoulders would soon become indistinguishable from the main travelway, reproducing the conditions the Sierra Club objected to on the Crane Flat section. Wirth forwarded Huber's report to the BPR, along with a statement that if the bureau was unwilling to accept the decision, the NPS would engage a private engineering firm to complete the project. Wirth received what he described as "a very nice reply from the bureau indicating that they would proceed with the job along the lines that Huber and the Park Service wished."[38]

Construction was scheduled to start in the summer of 1956, but severe flooding forced the NPS to focus on repairing damage to more heavily used roads. Work finally began in late 1957, progressing far enough by the end of the season to produce a trickle of complaints that erupted into a flood of outrage as the construction crews made their way past Tenaya Lake. The Sierra Club accused the Park Service of breaking its word by employing standards that were equal to or greater than those used on the much-criticized prewar sections. In January 1958, a report in the club's bulletin provocatively titled "Tioga Turnpike—A New Speedway" declared that the club's fears had been realized "in spite of National Park Service assurance to the contrary." Brower protested that the new road ran roughshod over the countryside, intruded on the lake with a transparently artificial fill, and transformed Tenaya Lake from an object of beauty and veneration to a fleeting attraction that disappeared in the rearview mirror before motorists realized what they were seeing. Bemoaning the loss of the traditional driving experience as well as the damage to the scenery, he lamented, "there will not again be the need, or the opportunity, to feel what we used to feel when, after working our way up and down those old grades and around those tight corners, we saw Tenaya Lake burst upon us." Taking a

National Park Roads

more moderate stance, *National Parks Magazine* noted that the NPS insisted that the roadway only exceeded 20 feet on a few curves where the extra width was necessary for safety. If mistakes were made, the magazine suggested, the BPR was the proper target for road opponents' wrath. Repeating the "Tioga Turnpike" characterization, the magazine observed that the term was favored by those who felt "too much weight has been given to the 'bigger is better' contentions of those like the U.S. Bureau of Public Roads who do the road building, but who have no reason to have park ideals foremost in their minds."[39]

Protests grew louder as construction proceeded past the lake toward Pywiack Dome's celebrated expanse of glacially polished granite. The Sierra Club board of directors met at Tuolumne Meadows in July 1958 to get a firsthand look at the situation. They agreed that the most pressing concern at this point was not the width of the road but its alignment, which was based on the BPR's insis-

tence on low grades and long radius curves. To maintain the desired standards, the road would cut directly across the dome. If those requirements were relaxed, the route could be shifted to a nearby drainage, leaving the scenic and scientifically valuable feature unscathed. The club remained steadfast in its assertion that the proposed route would cause catastrophic damage, while the NPS was equally adamant that the alternative proposal was unsafe and scenically inferior. The steep grade and tight curves of the Sierra Club's route prompted one NPS official to retort, "We might as well build a hospital at the bottom of the hill." Seeking to alleviate the tension, Wirth expressed his willingness to consider modest changes in alignment, though the road would still cross the dome.[40]

The difference of opinion on the scenic implications of the two alignments exposed a less obvious but equally significant source of contention. From the Sierra Club perspective,

carving a road across such a superlative natural feature was inexcusable: sacrificing scenery for the sake of engineering expediency underscored the manner in which Mission 66 made a mockery of the preservation mandate. From the NPS perspective, the preferred routing exemplified the ability of park roads to expose visitors to natural wonders and display scenery to best advantage. Along with providing educational close-ups of the striated granite, the alignment would present eastbound motorists with a stunning panorama of signature Sierra scenery—a more expansive iteration of the dramatic visual "burst" exalted by Brower in his paean to its primitive predecessor. Conservationists countered that the same view could be enjoyed from the scenic pullout the NPS intended with equally dubious logic to hack out of the polished granite. From a park road design perspective, however, it was impossible to imagine a more impressive experience than breaking out of the forest, rounding a curve, and sweeping across the glistening granite while enjoying the breathtaking panorama stretching from Half Dome to Tenaya Lake. While undeniably impressive, a stationary view would afford a less dramatic experience. More importantly, the NPS was unwilling to restrict such pleasures to those who were willing and able to hike from the alternative alignment to a viewpoint located in a less propitious location proposed by critics. Huber again endorsed the NPS's recommendations. Observing that the Sierra Club's route "would not bring out the superb view," he dismissed ascriptions of Pywiack Dome's significance as deliberately misleading. Invoking his lifelong association with the region, he noted that the High Sierra contained "acres, if not square miles" of glacially polished granite, affording ample options for those who sought similar scenery unsullied by human imprint. Colby also supported the NPS alignment and associated parking area. Insisting that the proposed overlook would rival the Wawona Road's celebrated view, he maintained that its impact was "inconsequential compared to the deprivation of public enjoyment that would result if inadequate parking were provided."[41]

A barrage of letters and telegrams to NPS officials and the secretary of the interior persuaded Wirth to halt construction and agree to meet critics at the disputed site to try to put an end to the controversy. In mid-August, Wirth walked the

Unconstrained by the club's preference for discreet consultation, he vowed to do his best to ensure that "the example of Tenaya will be so impressively publicized that such a calamity will never occur again."

ANSEL ADAMS'S REACTION TO
TIOGA ROAD CONSTRUCTION

route with members of his staff, Yosemite National Park officials, and Sierra Club representatives, including Brower, Ansel Adams, and Hildebrand. Wirth decreed that the lower part of the roadway would be constructed as planned but agreed that it was possible to drop the upper portion down a bit, retaining the desired views but reducing unsightly excavations. Having to leave for an official trip to Europe, he left the matter in subordinates' hands. Under pressure to avoid paying exorbitant penalty charges to the idled contractor, Yosemite superintendent John Preston allowed the construction crews to resume work. Preston maintained that Wirth had merely requested additional study, not made a definitive decision, so clearing could continue up to the point where the alternatives diverged. By this time, the Wilderness Society and National Parks Association had joined the Sierra Club's opposition. Executives from all three organizations took their complaints directly to Secretary of the Interior Fred Seaton. Seaton instructed an assistant to visit the scene with conservation leaders and park officials. Brower and his colleagues were incensed when they discovered that work had proceeded past the stipulated stopping point. They were even more upset to see that an NPS-BPR design team had begun to relocate the route at an even higher and more destructive location. This incited another spate of letters and telegrams accusing the NPS of dishonest behavior. In early October Brower reported that crews were hauling boxes of dynamite onto the rock and preparing to blast. Wirth returned from Europe the same day and reconfirmed his commitment to the compromise alignment. The roadway still crossed the dome, but tightening curves and altering the grade dropped it to a slightly less conspicuous location. While the scarring was reduced, Brower acknowledged that it was a Pyrrhic victory. The most concerted opposition to Mission 66 road

development to date had preserved a few hundred feet of precious resources, but the Sierra Club and its allies had been unable to prevent significant scenic damage or limit the increase in traffic through the formerly isolated region. On the bright side, the widely covered controversy focused attention on the perceived excesses of Mission 66 and the impact of NPS road building in general.[42]

Although the NPS felt it was being unduly criticized both in print and in private communications, Ansel Adams was so upset that the Sierra Club had not mounted more effective opposition that he tendered his resignation from the board of directors. Unconstrained by the club's preference for discreet consultation, he vowed to do his best to ensure that "the example of Tenaya will be so impressively publicized that such a calamity will never occur again." Adams followed through with a dramatically illustrated *Sierra Club Bulletin* article in which he contrasted the primitive tranquility of the old route with the broad gash the NPS had "blasted through forest and canyon, blasted through beautiful swells and ridges of granite, blasted through the mood and heart of a priceless treasure of our natural scene." In a parallel *National Parks Magazine* article, Adams portrayed the damage in equally poetic terms. Although the old road "'tip-toed' across the terrain," Adams maintained, the new one "elbows and shoulders its way through the park." Adams agreed that places like Tenaya Lake should be accessible to those who were unable or unwilling to travel long distances on foot as long as the roads were appropriately conceived and sensitively constructed. The problem, as the "Tenaya Tragedy" revealed, was that "this attitude has been lacking in National Park Service developments and must be regained." Adams contended that the former emphasis on fitting roads to the terrain had been subordinated to the engineers' insistence on "artificial standards"

and determination to bend nature to their will. "Good engineering is *appropriate* engineering," Adams remonstrated, "not construction show-off!" He also questioned why the NPS would cede its authority to an organization whose primary responsibility was designing interstate highways. Further misconstruing the chain of events, he maintained that the BPR had vetoed NPS efforts to adopt a less intrusive approach. Although the NPS bore the brunt of the blame, Adams castigated his fellow conservationists for mounting insufficient opposition, noting that their "gentle persuasions" were no match for the "bulldozers of bureaucracy." Invoking the "Tenaya Tragedy" as "an example of what must never happen again in national parks or other wild areas," Adams called for a moratorium on construction projects throughout the National Park System until the agency's mandate was revised to ensure that preservation would never again take a backseat to access.[43]

Adams's remarks were followed by a series of photographs portraying the old and new Tioga Road and emphasizing damages wrought by the new construction. The photos of blasted ledges, machines tearing into hillsides, and expansive roadbeds bulldozed through pristine surroundings were shocking enough, but Brower supplied inflammatory captions that intensified the critique from an indictment of Mission 66 road building to an attack on the NPS's integrity and Wirth's personal credibility. Brower accused Wirth of reneging on promises, pairing the director's quotes with seemingly contradictory photographs and assertions. Passages from Bayliss's park road guide were coupled with photographs that mocked claims that park roads were designed to lie lightly on the land. Brower even implied that the NPS's actions were illegal, juxtaposing proposed legislation on wilderness preservation with scenes of devastation. Bradley,

who was at this point the club's president, sent Wirth an advance copy of the bulletin. This act of courtesy exemplified the coziness to which Adams objected, though the magazine's contents underscored the changing nature of the relationship. In addition to refusing to accept Adams's resignation, the board sought to ease Colby out of the picture, relegating him to the nebulous role of "honorary president."[44]

Wirth expressed few objections to Adams's article, affirming his admiration for the photographer's artistic sensibilities and acknowledging his right to express heartfelt concerns. He did, however, object to Adams's suggestion that the NPS gave insufficient attention to locating the road in the field. If anyone was lax in this area, Wirth suggested, it was the conservationists, who had been given years to evaluate the proposal but waited until construction was under way to raise specific objections. He maintained that Brower's assertions about the park service's changing positions stemmed from miscommunications rooted in the protester's unfamiliarity with location and design documents. When asked to provide evidence that the NPS had agreed to adopt the Sierra Club's standards, Brower acknowledged that the NPS had never formally agreed to the Sierra Club's recommendations but insisted that Wirth had acknowledged their superiority during a conversation between the two men at a Washington reception two years earlier. Wirth also objected to the oft-repeated charges that the NPS was allowing the BPR to dictate terms, relating his rejection of the bureau's recommendations. As for the photographs purporting to document insensitive location and wanton destruction, Wirth dismissed them as intentionally misleading, contending that similar images could be taken on practically any road project—including the Sierra Club's preferred alternative. Wirth also cast the contention that

the NPS was violating its own wilderness policies as another willful mischaracterization, observing that according to the club's own definitions, the old road's presence automatically exempted the area from wilderness consideration. In closing, Wirth lamented that the Tioga Road issue and related controversies had created an atmosphere of bitterness and mistrust that was counterproductive to the broader aims shared by the Park Service and conservation organizations.[45]

Preservation advocates continued to condemn the "Tenaya Tragedy." Additional articles included even more alarming images of bulldozers carving their way across Pywiack Dome. Brower exhibited modest contrition, shifting from attacking Wirth to insisting that the BPR was to blame for ignoring NPS instructions. Pressure continued to be exerted from the opposite extreme as well. The BPR continued to protest that the NPS was forcing it to employ unacceptably low standards, while local politicians and highway officials complained that inadequate roads in Yosemite National Park were stifling economic development and preventing the public from getting full value from their resources. Meanwhile, the construction crews pressed on, albeit through less controversial terrain. The short working season imposed by the high elevation combined with inherent technical

challenges to delay the road's opening until June 1961. Yosemite superintendent Preston suggested naming the controversial scenic pullout "Olmsted Point" to commemorate the contributions of Frederick Law Olmsted Jr., who had passed away in 1957. While conservationists may have considered this a bitter irony and perhaps a deliberate case of adding insult to injury, Olmsted had enthusiastically endorsed the idea of constructing a scenic overlook on the spot as a member of the Yosemite Board of Expert Advisors. From the Park Service's perspective, both the overlook and the road itself embodied the balancing of preservation and access that Olmsted had called for in the agency's founding legislation.[46]

The new Tioga Road was dedicated on June 24, 1961, with the requisite vintage car to express the theme of progress and a ribbon-cutting presided over by NPS, BPR, and DOI officials. William Colby was invited to do the honors but was too ill to attend. He sent a statement recalling his first encounter with the old mine road in 1894, recounting Mather's purchase, and endorsing the new location and design treatment. Asserting that the "rare and inspirational views that it commands" testified to the wisdom of the decision, he also sounded a note of caution: "We all must bear in mind that a tremendous responsibility rests on us all to see that the Tioga Road is not used to destroy or lessen the value of the precious area it penetrates." Wirth steadfastly defended the road's location and function. "We are proud of Tioga Road and of the wonderful opportunity it gives visitors to see and appreciate Yosemite National Park," he declared. Observing that the spectacular view from the ceremony site at Olmsted Point had been accessible only by means of a strenuous hike, Wirth enthused, "Now anyone who can get in a car, no matter how old and feeble, may share this magnificent treasure of the American people." Although Brower claimed that the new secretary of the interior, Stewart Udall, agreed that the NPS had committed an "egregious error," Assistant Secretary of the Interior John Carver Jr. delivered an NPS-prepared speech that was so laudatory that he later expressed concern that certain audiences would consider him to be "an enemy of conservation." Praising the BPR for its cooperation and noting that many in the audience would not have made it to the sublime spot in previous years, he cast the completed roadway as the fulfillment of Mather's vision of sharing the beauties of the High Sierra with the American public. Carver acknowledged that the "marks" of construction were readily apparent but observed that nature was well on its way to healing the disturbance. Applauding the Park Service policy of combining preservation with access, he proclaimed, "To put the wilderness within reach of millions of Americans is to do the work of democracy." Carver called for a return to comity while underscoring the administration's support for conservationists' broader agendas: "Let us unite on the goal of making our park resources match the needs of our society. If you would preserve the right to enjoy wilderness, you must expand wilderness reservations."[47]

Conservationists may have lost the battle for Tioga Road, but it was such a conspicuous defeat that it served as a rallying cry for opponents of Mission 66 and automobile-oriented development in general. The paradigm-shifting impact was analogous to the 1963 demolition of New York City's Pennsylvania Station, which was widely credited with sparking the modern historic preservation movement. The public outcry, political response, and NPS willingness to countenance compromise emboldened conservationists to speak out more strongly and press for concessions on other projects along with broader redefinitions of

NPS priorities. Asserting that "road construction of this kind has no place in the National Parks," National Parks Association executive director Anthony Smith proclaimed, "If this is Mission 66, then the administrative policy of Mission 66 must be changed." Smith called for the formation of external park advisory boards "to make certain that this triple disaster in Yosemite shall never be repeated." Having learned from their failures, Smith declared, "Conservationists intend to have a voice in road location and road standards in the parks from now on."[48]

Wirth was open to informed debate, but he had no intention of letting outside organizations dictate NPS policy on roads or any other matter. During the heat of the controversy, he asked Vint's staff to develop official NPS road standards. There was a succession of road-related directives dating to Mather and Lane that were rooted in principles extending even further back through Chittenden and the senior Olmsted to Repton and Downing, but critics were correct in contending that NPS designers relied on BPR handbooks for precise specifications. NPS officials had always preferred general guidelines, insisting that every project should be designed in light of individual circumstances. A clearly articulated set of official standards would serve multiple purposes. In addition to thwarting efforts on the part of the Sierra Club and BPR to fill the vacuum with their own specifications, it would allow the NPS to choose a path between the two extremes. As it turned out, the standards released in September 1958 were much closer to the Sierra Club's end of the spectrum. Heavily traveled major park roads such as Yellowstone's Grand Loop would have a 22-foot-wide pavement with 3-foot-wide unpaved shoulders and a design speed of 40 mph in rolling terrain or 30 mph mountainous topography. Grades could be as high as 10 percent in the former and 12 percent in the latter. On most park roads, where more moderate traffic was expected, pavement width could be reduced to the 20-foot width used on Tioga Road and grades increased to 15 percent. Wirth's introduction defined park roads as "facilities for presenting and interpreting the inspirational values of a park, monument, or parkway" and insisted they be designed to provide "reasonable and leisurely access." To achieve the desired results, Wirth instructed, "the landscape architect and the engineer shall

exercise imagination, ingenuity, and restraint to conserve park values."[49]

The Sierra Club considered this a positive development, noting the similarities to the organization's recommendations. After further consideration, however, club leaders decided the guidelines did not go far enough, leaving too many factors to the designers' discretion. They called for specified limits on the width of the affected road corridor, the reduction or elimination of shoulders, and explicit directives to employ serpentine curvature, rolling profiles, and other means of avoiding the "freeway effect." In a clear reference to the Tioga Road controversy, the revised policy stipulated that grades and alignments should be adjusted to "eliminate all cuts into natural structures of unusual beauty, interest or occurrence, such as glaciated granite, eroded sedimentary deposits, scenic cliffs, mineral or rock formations, forest groves, meadows, etc." Minimizing shoulders and clear zones would allow natural vegetation to enfold the roadway, while curves and dips afforded "the element of charm, constantly changing vistas, a wide-awake sense of anticipation for what might be disclosed as the turn is rounded, an automatic restraint on speed." The goal should be to "provide leisurely passage through the park, freedom from the sense of hurry or the distraction of 50–60 mph speed, an intimate chance to view park detail, an opportunity to quietly contemplate and absorb the grandeur that presents itself from time to time."[50]

While the Sierra Club maintained that the Park Service's guidelines did not go far enough, others insisted they went too far. In a January 1959 conference titled "Sierra Access" sponsored by the California State Chamber of Commerce, longtime state highway commissioner Chester Warlow assailed the reduced standards, asserting that such outdated "wagon roads" were a waste of the taxpayers' money and an affront to the millions of average citizens who had every right to visit their national parks with a modicum of ease and safety. Turning the classic analogy on its head, he asked, "Of what value is a Cathedral with spiked doors upon which the parish communicants are impaled while seeking to enter?" In another contravention of conservationist logic, he contended that visitors received less benefit from narrow winding roads because they had to focus too much on driving to enjoy the scenery. Warlow criticized the NPS but laid principal blame on the inordinate influence wielded by

self-righteous and self-serving "Apostles of the Wilderness." Not content with the millions of acres of backcountry reserved for their use, this arrogant minority insisted on dictating terms to the 99 percent of visitors who, according to recent statistics, were already confined to 1 percent of park lands. Warlow also attacked the disingenuous tactics employed by road opponents, echoing NPS complaints about the distortions inherent in portraying roads under construction. Warlow's exhortations appealed to a wide variety of local interests, from road-related industries and businessmen in surrounding communities to California residents who feared their access to Yosemite would be curtailed by wilderness enthusiasts. Resolutions calling for higher road standards were adopted by local communities, the state highway commission, and state legislature and forwarded to federal officials.[51]

A month after Warlow's speech, Wirth announced that he was withdrawing the new standards. The official position was that they needed to be restudied to address concerns expressed by both constituencies. Wirth expressed little remorse about the retraction. In fact, he and other officials were secretly collaborating with Warlow, who despite occasional differences was a long-term NPS supporter, having played a key role in wresting Kings Canyon from USFS control. In addition to

providing fodder for Warlow's critiques, Wirth strategized with him about the best means of combating the "confusers" who distorted NPS efforts and threatened its balanced approach. Applauding Warlow's efforts to broaden the debate, Wirth praised his subversion of the cathedral comparison as a masterful maneuver. He also recommended that Warlow contact like-minded advocates, suggesting they might start "a nation-wide group to speak for the millions" who quietly embraced NPS development policies. In another Machiavellian twist, Wirth used Warlow's agitation as leverage to defuse conservationists' demands for greater say in park affairs. The Sierra Club wanted the NPS to agree to the creation of a joint committee to devise new park road standards, while the NPA was lobbying for oversight committees for individual parks. Their intentions were clearly to pack the boards with conservation sympathizers, but Wirth maintained that the proposed panels would have to include representatives of mainstream interests, who outnumbered preservationists by a significant margin. Pointing to the indignation stirred up by Warlow's efforts, Wirth warned, "We may be lucky to hold what we have now." The Sierra Club continued its call for official standards based on its latest recommendations, but Wirth's stratagem quelled the campaign for more authoritative advisory boards. At the same time, the NPS

had no intention of heeding oppositional demands for higher road standards. By playing both sides against each other, Wirth loosened the BPR's grip on NPS road design while circumventing Sierra Club efforts to constrain the agency's options.[52]

Wirth's political guile and personal connections enabled him to beat back both challenges, but balancing the two extremes became increasingly difficult. Not only were conservationists gaining in number and influence, but the BPR continued to angle for greater control of federal road-building activities. The next major battle played out in Mount McKinley (now Denali) National Park. Alaska's first national park was authorized in 1917 to preserve the highest peak in North America along with a vast tract of surrounding mountains, tundra, lakes, and rivers. Its remote location kept visitation to a minimum, even after a railroad was constructed to the park's borders in the 1920s. A primitive road was extended partway into the park in the 1930s. Occasional wealthy tourists shipped their cars to the nearby railway station and ventured out along the narrow graveled track, but most visitors relied on bus service provided by the park concessionaire. This traditional model of park visitation remained the rule throughout the 1940s. Seeing tourism as one of the keys to moving the state's economy beyond mining and other extractive industries, Alaska's business and political

leaders pushed for construction of a highway to the park and improvements within. The NPS was supportive of the idea, both to provide Alaskans with greater access and to encourage motorists to venture north along the Alaska-Canadian Highway. Survey work began in 1947, but funding shortages, routing concerns, and construction challenges delayed completion until 1957. The two-lane gravel "Denali Highway" generated a fivefold increase in visitation during its first year of operation, albeit to a modest total of twenty-six thousand. Alaska's admission to statehood, the growth in leisure travel, and increased publicity created expectations that the number of automobile tourists would continue to rise, producing a demand for improved roads and associated facilities.[53]

The Mission 66 master plan focused on upgrading primitive infrastructure and reorienting the park from the hotel and tour bus system to the contemporary emphasis on independent motorists. This entailed the construction of a visitor center near the park entrance, the provision of motels, cafeterias, and expanded campgrounds, and the improvement of roads accompanied by wayside exhibits and scenic turnouts. A smaller visitor center would be constructed midway along the park road at a scenic overlook where buses normally turned around and headed back to the entrance facilities. Nearly three-quarters of the park's Mission 66 budget was devoted to road construction. The existing road had been built before World War II. Constructed on limited budgets with minimal excavations, the narrow graveled track rode the rolling contours of the tundra, winding in gentle curves around hillocks and crossing streams on simple wooden bridges. In many locations its minimalistic construction allowed it to be concealed by the low tundra vegetation. As usual, NPS officials insisted there were no plans to significantly increase road mileage. The goal was to "make the present park road safe for the increased visitor load, and develop it as one of the park's major tools of interpretation." This involved blacktopping the roadway to the standard 20-foot width with 3-foot shoulders, realigning a few sections to reduce excessive curvature, smoothing out irregular grades, constructing turnouts at points of interest, and replacing primitive wooden bridges with safer modern spans. Although the NPS insisted that the changes were relatively minimal, the contrast between the old and new road proved to be striking, particularly in the open tundra terrain.[54]

Construction got under way in 1958, starting at the main entrance and heading westward across the park. By the end of 1959, approximately 22 miles had been completed. The results raised concerns that the NPS was sacrificing the wilderness quality of the park and the old road's primitive charm to create a modern highway designed more to whisk visitors across the landscape than to encourage them to enjoy the scenery in a more leisurely and meaningful fashion. The noted Alaskan naturalist and wilderness advocate Olaus Murie was one of the first to sound the alarm, broaching his fears that the road was being turned into "another hurry-up speedway" in a *National Parks Magazine* article that elicited an outpouring of letters and a defensive response from NPS regional director Lawrence Merriam. Merriam concurred that a "speedway" was incompatible with park values, insisting that nothing of the sort was under consideration. "If properly handled," Merriam assured, "road building can be constructive rather than destructive, and this is the objective we hope and expect to achieve at Mount McKinley." Improvements were being held to the minimum necessary to meet safety standards while accommodating bus traffic as far as the new visitor center. Since the buses rarely went past this point, Merriam left open the possibility of lowering standards on the remainder of the road.[55]

Conservationists grew increasingly concerned as construction continued. By spring of 1963, 31 miles were paved and another 30 graded. Determined not to sit on the sidelines until the opportunity for intervention had passed, *National Parks Magazine* published a series of articles denouncing the development. Opponents maintained that the nominal 20-foot pavement with 3-foot shoulders was accompanied by ditches extending another 9 feet on either side, creating a disturbed area 44 feet across. Since the road was design to produce standardized grades and curves rather than follow the contours, the number and extent of cuts and fills were markedly increased. Photographs of raw embankments, broad gravel causeways, and unsightly excavations dramatized the damage. Declaring "the speedway-building craze that has come over this continent has begun to penetrate Alaska," Murie protested that park managers' desire to increase visitation led them to embrace "the prevailing enthusiasm for what the bulldozer can do." His brother Adolph ascribed responsibility to the BPR, noting that the NPS had mitigated the engineers' demands and was fighting against even higher standards. Characterizing the new roadway as "official vandalism," Adolph proclaimed that it was "a mistake to permit engineers to impose their values on park developments." Like Adams, Murie claimed that the problem with engineers was that their obsession with displaying their technological prowess made them "unable to comprehend that, for the public, park roads are secondary to park values, and should be made as unobtrusive and simple as possible." Alluding to the Sierra Club's efforts, he suggested that the best way to eliminate the problem was to adopt road standards devised by "non-engineers selected for their appreciation of park ideals and their sensitivity to esthetic values." In an early example of ecologically based criticism, Adolph Murie also complained that the straw used by the contractor to stabilize and reseed excavations was introducing non-native species to the tundra environment. Both Muries maintained that the general public strongly supported their views, along with many NPS employees and even some of the construction workers responsible for the devastation. Letters to NPS officials and *National Parks Magazine* substantiated this claim. Acknowledging that the NPS was under heavy political pressure to improve access to parks in Alaska and elsewhere, one correspondent sought assurance that the agency was not "selling its soul to the public demand for easy comfort and amusement."[56]

Seeking to avoid another Tioga Road controversy, NPS officials proposed a compromise. A. Clark Stratton, the assistant director for design and construction, suggested a program of "telescoping standards." The first 30 miles would be constructed to the full 20-foot paved surface with 3-foot shoulder. The next 40 miles would have a 20-foot pavement, but the shoulders would be narrower, varying in width and not extending beyond the existing roadbed. The final 18 miles beyond the bus turnaround at the new Eielson Visitor Center would not be widened aside from a few parking pullouts and passing areas. The relatively minor concession on the long middle section failed to placate conservationists, who expressed their opposition both in print and in direct complaints to the NPS and the secretary of the interior. The BPR, in turn, asserted that the proposal was unsafe and called for upgrades that would produce significant additional scarring. Worried that the BPR would succeed in imposing

"superhighway standards" on the remaining construction, the Muries and their allies pressured the Park Service to commit to a less destructive approach. In the fall of 1965, NPS officials declared that the higher standard roadway would be constructed for only a few more miles, until the road reached the Teklanika River. Changes to the middle and western portions of the road would be limited to minor repairs and narrowly targeted improvements to allow the buses to negotiate curves more safely. Unbeknownst to the general public, the NPS continued to rebuff BPR efforts to widen the road and defused a scheme by Alaska senator Ernest Gruening to construct a second road to the base of Mount McKinley.[57]

The park's remote location and low visitation eased the decision, but the agreement to curtail a significant program of proposed improvements represented a major victory for those who sought to constrain the impact of park road developments. Congress's long-awaited approval of the Wilderness Act, which was signed into law by President Lyndon Johnson in September 1964, constituted an even more significant milestone. Though Mission 66 would not officially end for another two years, the passage of the Wilderness Act signified an end to the program's underlying ethos in the same way that the 1956 Interstate Highway Act embodied the ideals that informed its inception. Some NPS officials remained skeptical of the act's provisions, but the American public and many agency employees were increasingly inclined to favor the preservation side of the management equation. The growing skepticism about road development was not limited to vast untrammeled wildernesses, moreover. The NPS resisted intense pressure to construct a road along the north shore of Lake Fontana in Great Smoky Mountains National Park that it had committed to in the 1930s. A proposal for a high-altitude loop around the Haleakala Crater was also rejected, despite strong backing from Hawaii's governor. Repeated efforts to construct major highways across the Sierras were rebuffed by the NPS in alliance with the Sierra Club and other conservation groups. The NPS joined forced with the Save-the-Redwoods League, the National Parks Association, and other organizations to combat proposals by highway and timber interests that would have exerted a devastating effect on the redwood forests of northern California. The resulting Redwoods State and National Parks

presented an innovative approach to preserving irreplaceable old-growth groves along with the winding two-lane roads and primitive dirt lanes that afforded leisurely access to the towering forests. Conservationists claimed victory, but Wirth and other NPS leaders could counter that such achievements reflected long-term NPS goals espoused by Mather and Albright and embodied in Mission 66. Despite the controversies over road standards and dramatic expansion of visitor capacity, the program did not result in the large-scale despoliation of pristine backcountry. As Wirth had promised, the proportion of developed to undeveloped acreage remained relatively unchanged from previous decades.[58]

Mission 66 exerted a profound impact on the National Park System. On the one hand, the program produced much of the basic park infrastructure familiar to visitors today. By replacing outdated and inadequate roads, buildings, campgrounds, and other features with modern facilities, Mission 66 not only allowed more people to enjoy the national parks but profoundly shaped the nature of the national park experience, both in terms of the appearance of roads, buildings, signs, and other features and in regard to the underlying assumption that visitors would rely on private automobiles as their primary mode of transportation. On the other hand, Mission 66's perceived excesses created concerns that the traditional model of accommodating an ever-increasing stream of visitors was not sustainable, no matter how well-designed the roads, visitor centers, and associated developments might be. Before the program had run its course, not only ardent conservationists but park professionals and a growing segment of the general public recognized the need to reconsider traditional approaches, both to the relationship between roads and the national park experience and to the fundamental challenge of maintaining an appropriate balance between preservation and access. This process was already in motion as the program drew to a close.

Adjusting the Balance

CHAPTER NINE

The controversies over Mission 66 combined with changes within the conservation community and American society as a whole to reshape the way national parks were conceived, designed, and managed. These adjustments reflected demographic trends, developments within the engineering and design professions, new regulatory frameworks, and evolving attitudes about nature, technology, and society. The boundless faith in progress that led previous generations to believe that good intentions, bureaucratic proficiency, and technological prowess would solve the world's problems gave way to skepticism about the beliefs and institutions that created not just overcrowded campgrounds but urban blight, environmental degradation, and existential threats ranging from global overpopulation to nuclear annihilation. The idea that mass mobility would enable Americans to reconnect with nature lost ground to the perception that automobiles embodied the ills affecting modern society. A new generation of NPS officials shared these sentiments, collaborating with conservationists to promote policies that favored the preservation side of the management equation. Although driving along carefully designed scenic roads remained the primary means through which visitors experienced national parks, both NPS officials and outside critics sought to reduce the impact of automobile traffic. These measures included limiting road development in new parks, revising park road standards, embracing alternative means of transportation, and diversifying recreational opportunities to relieve pressure on popular destinations.

Many of the complaints leveled at Mission 66 were amplified as America became increasingly environmentally conscious in the 1960s. Concern about the automobile's impact on parks became widespread as more people questioned the automobile's influence on American lives and landscapes. It was no coincidence that the Sierra Club's David Brower paired one of his diatribes with a glowing review of John Keats's *The Insolent Chariots*, a scathing indictment of Detroit's impact on American culture. Lest anyone miss the connection, Brower urged readers "to interpolate what will happen to the parks" if current trends continued. Charges that NPS officials focused narrowly on automobile-oriented alternatives and allowed themselves to be bullied by highway engineers echoed accusations by freeway opponents such as Jane Jacobs and Lewis Mumford. Mumford, who complained early and often about the automobile's impact, famously observed that widening roads to solve traffic problems was like combating obesity by buying bigger belts. Like Mission 66 critics, freeway foes contested the process as well as the product, objecting to the lack of public input. The ways in which opponents expressed their discontent were also similar. Following Ansel Adams's argument that genteel collaboration was a formula for failure, activists became more aggressive, staging protests, mounting media campaigns, and engaging in personal attacks that broke traditional bounds of decorum but appealed to a generation that was challenging the status quo on a broad spectrum of issues. While earlier critics complained about visitors attracted by "honky tonk" amusements, they acknowledged the public's right to enjoy the national park experience. From the perspective of the counterculture, it was not just the NPS establishment that was out of step, but the majority of park visitors. Mather's dream that automobiles would make national parks accessible to ordinary people had become a self-fulfilling nightmare in which Middle America imposed its bourgeois banalities on nature's finest spectacles. The not-so-silent majority inundated park roads with rush-hour traffic, transformed primitive campgrounds into suburban cul-de-sacs, and roared around in ever-larger and more luxurious mechanized monstrosities that shattered the stillness, sullied the air, and made a mockery of all that the successors of John Muir and Henry David Thoreau held sacred.[1]

OPPOSITE, LEFT Ribbon-tying ceremony to close portion of Yosemite Valley road system to private automobiles, June 9, 1970.

OPPOSITE, RIGHT National park trailer campers, mid-1960s.

PREVIOUS Classic 1936 sightseeing bus refurbished through partnership with Ford Motor Corporation, Glacier National Park.

The patron saint of this perspective was Edward Abbey. A Pennsylvania native who gravitated to the Southwest in the late 1940s, Abbey spent the summers of 1956 and 1957 as a seasonal ranger in what was then Arches National Monument. At the time, Arches was a little-visited reservation reached by an unpaved road providing access to a few trails and primitive campsites. One evening, while Abbey was relaxing with a cocktail, he was disturbed by the sound of a Jeep approaching from an unexpected direction. Since the area was off-limits to motor vehicles, Abbey prepared to bring the scofflaw to justice. Official duty gave way to personal outrage when the intruders proved to be a BPR survey crew laying out a new entrance road. Exemplifying contemporary concerns about the dangers of technocratic society, Abbey characterized the leader as "a pleasant-mannered, soft-spoken civil engineer with an unquestioning devotion to his work. A very dangerous man." When Abbey questioned the need for such upgrades, the engineer explained that an improved roadway would make it easier for large numbers of visitors to experience the monument. Abbey declined to argue but confided to his readers, "I knew that I was dealing with a madman." Later that night, he set out along the route delineated by the engineers, heaving survey stakes into the sagebrush. While this was not the first time opponents countered engineers' efforts in this manner, Abbey's actions embodied the anti-establishment zeitgeist. His espousals of sabotage, or what he called "monkey-wrenching," as a form of environmental activism popularized the concept and contributed to his legend.[2]

The Jeep episode so perfectly embodied Leo Marx's "trope of the interrupted idyll" that the literary-minded Abbey may have invented or at least embellished the tale in his apostolic autobiography *Desert Solitaire*. Factual or not, the incident provided a pretext for Abbey to rail against the conventional approach to national park management. He bemoaned the hundredfold increase in visitation that followed the road's development and railed against the "indolent millions born on wheels and suckled on gasoline" who expected to find paved roads leading to every corner of the earth. Like earlier critics, he expressed sympathy for the Park Service's plight. Abbey placed primary blame on the forces of "Industrial Tourism": the motel owners, gas station operators, oil and automotive companies, and other business interests that profited from national park vacations. Their principal ally, he noted, was the federal engineering establishment, which capitalized on concerns about overcrowded and unsafe roads to enhance appropriations and bureaucratic power. Unable to withstand the pressure these juggernauts administered through congressional cronies, NPS management was forced to favor access over preservation. The NPS's "Parks Are for People" mantra had merit in principle, but it translated into "Parks Are for People in Automobiles" policies. Echoing earlier critics, Abbey maintained that the emphasis on automobile-oriented development threatened the last remaining pockets of wilderness and impinged on the experiences of the growing number of outdoor enthusiasts who sought to enjoy parks through nonmechanical means. With younger Americans embracing backpacking and other forms active outdoor recreation, this argument carried more weight than in earlier years. The main victims, Abbey asserted, were the motorized masses themselves. Their reluctance to forsake the comforts of their cars prevented them from getting the benefits that parks were meant to provide. According to Abbey, the Park Service's primary challenge was not to build more roads but to "pry the tourists out of their automobiles" so they could experience national parks more fully and through less destructive means.[3]

The best solution, Abbey asserted, was to ban automobiles altogether. "Let the people walk," he

proclaimed. "Or ride horses, bicycles, mules, wild pigs—anything—but keep the automobiles and the motorcycles and all their motorized relatives out." Adding a sexual revolution twist to the classic analogy, he remonstrated, "We have agreed not to drive our automobiles into cathedrals, concert halls, art museums, legislative assemblies, private bedrooms and other sanctums of our culture; we should treat our national parks with the same deference." Abbey had less patience than his predecessors for the argument that eliminating cars catered to the physical and social elite while disenfranchising those unable or unwilling to engage in strenuous activity. Small children could be carried, or wait until they were big enough to go on their own. The elderly had already had their chance; if they had passed on the opportunity, they had no one to blame but themselves. Upon further reflection, Abbey allowed that shuttle buses might be permissible for the mobility-impaired. As a corollary to the ban on automobiles, no new roads should be allowed in the parks. Existing roads would be open only for bicycles, buses, and logistical services. Along with improving the park environment and the health of visitors, the switch to nonmotorized transportation would make the parks seem bigger and reduce the impression of overcrowding, since it would take much longer to cover distances. Without spending a dime, the apparent extent of the National Park System would expand a thousandfold. Money targeted for road improvements could be rechanneled into trail construction. Millions would be saved on road and campground maintenance. Abbey acknowledged that excluding automobiles "would require a revolution in the thinking of Park Service officialdom and in the assumptions of most American tourists," but the only alternative, he declared, was "the gradual destruction of our national park system."[4]

Abbey was intentionally inflammatory, but even for those unwilling to take such radical steps, the seemingly inexorable increase in visitation created daunting concerns. Mission 66's target of 80 million visitors was surpassed in 1960, six years ahead of Wirth's predictions. Actual 1966 visitation exceeded 133 million. The rapid growth coincided with the Baby Boom generation's childhood years. Many parents considered national park vacations to be an essential component of an appropriate upbringing. Renewed prosperity combined with progress on the interstate highway system made such trips substantially easier. As a result, newly upgraded facilities struggled to keep pace with

skyrocketing demand. In another case of park issues mirroring broader trends, complaints about overcrowded parks invoked contemporary anxieties about global overpopulation. Fears that population growth would lead to worldwide crisis had been gaining prominence since the 1950s, fueling worries about the impact of rising birthrates on American society. By the mid-1960s, conservation magazines were again running exposés about national park campgrounds overflowing with tourists. Many blamed excess demand rather than inadequate supply. "The biggest threat to our wilderness areas, national parks, and scenic splendors is not four-lane highways or power projects," *National Parks Magazine* declared in 1966. Those were just symptoms. The real problem was "the pressure of people." Overflowing campgrounds and crowded concessions were juxtaposed with photographs of starving children in Pakistan. What was needed was "a new Manhattan Project"—not to build an atomic weapon but to "defuse the population bomb." Paul Ehrlich's runaway best seller on the topic was published with strong support from Sierra Club executive director David Brower.[5]

More sober minds had begun to address the disparity between population growth and recreational resources in the late 1950s. In a move reminiscent of the 1920s National Conference on Outdoor Recreation, Congress created the Outdoor Recreational Resources Review Commission (ORRRC) in 1958 and charged it with surveying existing resources and forecasting future needs. NPS leaders took this action as an affront. They viewed the ORRRC as a rival rather than an ally. Not only did Congress's action imply that Mission 66 was failing to meet its goals, but no NPS officials were appointed to the committee. This was particularly galling to Wirth, who had overseen the NPS's outreach to state parks during the Civilian Conservation Corps (CCC) era and administered the agency's efforts to conduct a similar assessment under the auspices of the 1936 Park, Parkway and Recreational-Area Study Act. Although little came of that effort, the legislation was still in effect, and reams of associated studies remained on the shelves. Wirth was too savvy to oppose the commission's efforts outright, but his determination to protect bureaucratic turf was evident in a hastily assembled "Parks for America" initiative, which built on earlier efforts to present an NPS-sponsored program for recreational areas. Parks for America was more pragmatically

oriented than the ORRRC's policy deliberations, but it sent a clear signal that the NPS was determined to retain its role as the lead agency for outdoor recreation. In another echo of the 1920s effort, the commission maintained that the NPS's primary function was "not to provide recreation in the usual sense but to preserve unique and exceptional areas." Purely recreational activities should be relegated to national forests and the reservoirs administered by the Army Corps of Engineers and Bureau of Reclamation. Even worse, from Wirth's perspective, the ORRRC established a Bureau of Outdoor Recreation (BOR) within the Department of the Interior. Although the BOR would not actively manage NPS areas, it would issue guidelines and coordinate between federal, state, and local authorities. Along with emphasizing the need to spread recreation among a broader range of resources, the ORRRC noted that most national parks were located far from population centers, reducing their effectiveness in answering America's "crisis of recreation." The emphasis should be on developing facilities in or near major cities, not devoting scarce resources to distant preserves serving a shrinking segment of the American public.[6]

President Kennedy's inauguration was another portent of change. The position of NPS director had been one of the rare high-level appointments that transcended party affiliation. As was the case with the Bureau of Public Roads, whose long-time chief Thomas MacDonald had served six presidents in succession, the agency was regarded as a bastion of apolitical expertise exempt from the staffing turnover associated with presidential transitions. The Kennedy administration, however, was committed to fresh faces and bold new ideas. The new secretary of the interior, Stewart Udall, embodied this outlook. Only forty-one years old when appointed, the former Arizona congressman was a vigorous advocate for the administration's policies on everything from natural resources to civil rights and urban development. Udall outlined the need for a "New Conservation" in his 1963 book *The Quiet Crisis*, which echoed assertions that America's emphasis on technological progress and economic gain had befouled the nation's environment, crippled its cities, desecrated its landscapes, and damaged social relationships. Factories polluted the air and water, the overreliance on automobiles created dysfunctional cities surrounded by suburban sprawl, and the broader landscape was blighted by overblown highways and crass commercial development. The sweeping nature of Udall's critique underscored the sentiment that meeting these challenges would require a comprehensive reevaluation of federal policies, accompanied by a willingness to change and commitment to collaboration between government officials, private citizens, and outside organizations.[7]

A growing number of critics saw the NPS as a prime example of the outdated and insular bureaucracy that was ripe for renewal. Beyond the complaints about Mission 66, the agency's begrudging response to wilderness advocates and ill-concealed resistance to the ORRRC were clear affronts to the administration's agendas. Wirth's insistence on pursuing his own path prompted a search for a replacement who would be open to new ideas and more of a team player. While investigating park possibilities in the Ozarks in 1961, Udall made the acquaintance of George B. Hartzog Jr., who was serving as superintendent of Jefferson National Expansion Memorial. The two men established rapport while boating down the Ozark River. Udall was impressed with Hartzog's people skills and political acumen, both of which were on display in his suggestions for creating what would eventually become a prototype for the National Wild and Scenic Rivers program. This was the sort of innovative thinking Udall was looking for. Hartzog left the NPS the following summer, but Udall enticed him back with the promise of an appointment as associate director in the Washington office, accompanied by assurances that he would be first in line for the directorship. Wirth's retirement soon ensued. Although Wirth gamely insisted he had always planned to retire before the conclusion of Mission 66, the timing appeared to be prompted by the administration's discontent. Even more shocking, given his cordial relations with previous administrations, Wirth's "retirement" was preceded by a scathing public rebuke. Speaking before a gathering of NPS officials in October 1963, Assistant Secretary of the Interior John Carver condemned the agency's resistance to the BOR, accused its leaders of deliberately defying administration mandates, and asserted that the Park Service resembled the Hitler Youth in its overweening arrogance and cultish devotion to self-romanticizing ideals. Leaving the audience, which included Wirth and his closest associates, in stunned silence, Carver returned to

ABOVE Secretary of the Interior Stuart Udall (*on right*) and soon-to-be NPS director George Hartzog, 1962.

Washington and held a press conference that gave the impression that the director had been fired for insubordination. Udall tried to smooth things over, flying out for the last day of the conference to accept Wirth's letter of resignation and offer praise for his exemplary service. Hartzog became the next NPS director when Wirth officially retired in January 1964.[8]

Hartzog made it clear that the NPS would work closely with Udall's office to ensure its policies were in sync with the administration's goals. He embraced the ORRRC's recommendations and evidenced a willingness to accept and solicit outside advice, even from sources critical of agency policies. The key ORRRC findings in Hartzog's opinion were the importance of increasing recreational opportunities for urban residents and the need to expand the amount of land devoted to parks and recreation. Building on the recommendations of the ORRC and BOR along with proposals originating with Mission 66 and other Wirth-era initiatives, Hartzog made tremendous strides in both areas during his eight years as director. Capitalizing on his political skills and strong support from the secretary's office, Hartzog presided over a tremendous expansion of

the number and extent of national parks, recreation areas, historical parks, seashores, wild and scenic rivers, and monuments, many in or near major cities. The goal, Hartzog maintained, was to "complete" the National Park System by 1972, the centennial of Yellowstone's establishment.[9]

In order to manage this vast array of resources, Hartzog divided the National Park System into three categories: natural areas, historical areas, and recreation areas. In addition to creating a more manageable framework, this partition explicitly acknowledged that it had become unrealistic to expect to reconcile the competing demands of recreation and resource protection in every unit of the system. By investing heavily in the acquisition and development of recreational areas such as beaches and reservoirs, which, while attractive, did not possess the natural or historic significance of traditional national parks, the NPS addressed what had been identified as two of the agency's most pressing challenges: redressing the nationwide "crisis in recreation" and reducing pressure on overburdened resources. In "bringing the parks to the people" rather than "bringing people to the parks," San Francisco's Golden Gate National Recreation Area, New York's Gateway National

Recreation Area, and other new offerings near major cities would address the needs of urban residents while reducing demands on traditional parks. Cape Hatteras National Seashore, Lake Mead National Recreation Area, and Glen Canyon National Recreation Area afforded options for those who wanted to engage in boating, swimming, and other activities that were not necessarily compromised by crowds and mechanical conveyances. The NPS also branched out into National Trails, National Wild and Scenic Rivers, and National Lakeshores, further broadening the agency's portfolio in ways that would have been anathema to earlier strict interpretations of national park standards. Demographic trends and the transcendent appeal of the most famous parks ensured that Yellowstone, Yosemite, and other so-called "crown jewels" would continue to experience increased visitation, but the pressure would have been significantly greater had alternatives not been provided.[10]

The nature and purpose of the different types of reservation were outlined in a 1964 memo released over Udall's signature. This self-conscious emulation of the 1918 "Lane Letter" combined a reaffirmation of the principles espoused in the original with prescriptions for contemporary concerns. Wilderness values and ecological principles would play a prominent part in the management of natural areas. Recreational areas would play an expanded role, but there was no pretense that the "staggering demand for outdoor recreation" could be satisfied by the NPS alone. Along with injunctions to provide for the highest-quality use and enjoyment of the park system, expand its holdings, manage wisely and efficiently, and celebrate America's natural and cultural heritage, the NPS was instructed to "participate actively with organizations of this and other Nations in conserving, improving and renewing the total environment." In addition to signaling an end to the practice of developing plans with little or no public involvement, the instruction to think of parks in terms of their broader context reflected the emphasis on the interconnectedness of social and environmental concerns expressed by Udall in *The Quiet Crisis*.[11]

Udall's injunctions bore witness to the rise of environmental awareness fostered by publications such as Rachel Carson's 1962 cri de coeur *Silent Spring*, which awoke Americans to the extent to which man's actions had polluted the nation's land, air, and water. Concomitant with the popular embrace of environmentalism came growing

recognition for the principles of ecology, which called for broad-based scientific analysis of the interrelationships between associated phenomena and fostered the belief that letting natural processes run their course produced better solutions than heavy-handed human intervention. The principal articulation of this ethos in regard to the national parks was developed by an advisory group appointed by Udall to solicit input from the scientific community. Although the panel was ostensibly charged with recommending strategies for wildlife management, the resulting report asserted that ecological principles should provide the basis for all national park policy. The ensuing recommendations were released in March 1963 and universally referred to as the "Leopold Report" in deference to the panel's chairman, A. Starker Leopold, a professor of zoology at the University of California and the son of Aldo Leopold, the pioneering wilderness advocate and apostle of ecological consciousness.[12]

Citing the disruptions posed by overdevelopment and scientifically flawed practices such as predator-eradication programs, which had resulted in catastrophic overpopulations of elk and deer, the report asserted that national parks should be managed by trained biologists to restore the ecological balance presumed to exist before European settlement. The ultimate aim was to remediate past mistakes so that national parks would provide "a vignette of primitive America." Natural processes such as predation and wildfires would be allowed to proceed without intervention, non-native species would be eliminated, and "observable artificiality in any form must be minimized and obscured in every possible way." Since the goal of park management was to "to preserve, or where necessary to recreate, the ecologic scene as viewed by the first European visitors," roads and automobiles were clearly undesirable intrusions. Acknowledging with evident disdain that "the American public demands automotive access to the parks," the report remonstrated that "road systems must be rigidly prescribed as to extent and design." This was exactly what NPS leaders had advocated all along, but the Leopold Report's sympathies lay with those who contended the agency prioritized road building over resource protection. "The most dangerous tool" available to park managers, the ecologists asserted, "is the roadgrader." On the question of balancing preservation and access, the report was unequivocal: "If too many tourists crowd the roadways, then we should ration the tourists rather than expand the roadways." The Leopold Report's conclusions were widely embraced, both by those who believed biological science should play a greater role in shaping national park policies and by more general opponents of automobile-oriented development. For the latter group, the report appeared to afford scientific justification for the more philosophically based arguments of Bob Marshall, Benton Mackaye and their modern-day descendants Abbey and Brower, countering claims that they were elitist and exclusionary intellectual conceits. The Sierra Club published a digest of the report, characterizing it as "one of the most significant statements in the nearly half-century since the National Park Service was established in 1916." An Ansel Adams photograph of a bulldozer cutting across the Tioga Road's granite dome was prominently featured, captioned with the manifesto's pointed denunciation of mechanized interventions.[13]

The Leopold Report did not produce a wholesale effort to turn back the clock of development in national parks, and some of its scientific conclusions were subsequently called into question, but it laid the groundwork for a reorientation of attitudes and policies that increasingly prioritized ecological concerns over the traditional emphasis on recreation and scenic appreciation. This perspective was accorded legislative authority with the passage of the National Environmental Policy Act (NEPA) in 1969. In addition to endorsing the goal of improving environmental quality, NEPA required federal agencies to consider the ecological implications of their actions and seek to eliminate, reduce, or mitigate negative impacts. By mandating that significant construction projects undergo extensive review, NEPA slowed the pace of road development. Associated requirements that agencies seek and respond to public comments reflected complaints about the insular manner in which park plans, highway projects, and urban renewal programs were developed. Echoing earlier responses to the Wilderness Act and ORRRC, some elements within the NPS opposed NEPA, continuing to insist that existing policies afforded sufficient safeguards. No such exemption was forthcoming. NEPA became an integral component of NPS planning, both in terms of road development and resource management in general. The 1966 National Historic Preservation

Act, which was likewise motivated by the excesses of highway development and urban renewal, put further restrictions on decisions affecting NPS roads. The Department of Transportation Act of 1966 further regulated park road building. The key section made it official policy to "preserve the natural beauty of the countryside and public park and recreation lands" and prohibited federal approval of transportation projects that used public parks, historic sites, recreation areas, or wildlife refuges unless there was "no feasible and prudent alternative." In the latter case, officials were instructed to engage in "all possible planning to minimize harm." The definition of harm was expansive enough to include considerations such as noise, smell, and associated pollutants, side effects that had long been decried by wilderness advocates and other road opponents.[14]

The long-anticipated passage of the Wilderness Act in 1964 created additional constraints. By establishing a statutory relationship between roads and wilderness that defined the latter by the absence of the former, the Wilderness Act dismissed NPS contentions that the two could readily coexist. While the NPS was initially resistant to the demands of wilderness advocates, the values embodied in the act increasingly permeated agency policies. The Wilderness Act's primary impact was on the new parks that Hartzog and his successors brought into the system. In sharp contrast to Mather's dictum, it was no longer a given that new parks would be provided with the classic "one good road" to access principal features. Precedents for minimizing road development dated back to Grand Teton, Kings Canyon, and Olympic National Parks, but as shifting attitudes exerted increasing influence, the presumption was that new parks would have limited road development or, in some cases, none at all.

The debate over the creation of a national park in the North Cascades demonstrated both evolving NPS attitudes toward road development and the flexibility afforded by the differentiation of NPS management categories. The challenge in pushing through the long-contested legislation was to reward wilderness advocates who led the campaign while mollifying the opposition by providing recreational opportunities for local residents and the burgeoning population of the Pacific Northwest. The 1968 solution was more of a semantic sleight-of-hand than a dramatic departure from past practice, but it seemed to satisfy

most parties. Rather than grant the entire area national park status and risk criticism for over- or underdevelopment, federal officials established a "national park complex" comprised of a two-part park conjoined with national recreation areas. The recreational areas would absorb the bulk of public use, while the more mountainous portions would be managed as natural parks with an emphasis on wilderness preservation. Unwilling to forsake the idea of public access completely, Hartzog argued for the installation of tramways, monorails, or other devices to transport visitors to selected highlights of the park areas. While this allowed the NPS to proclaim it was moving beyond automobile dependence, the idea of draping the mountains with mechanized conveyances raised objections on aesthetic, environmental, and philosophical grounds. Not only were the groups that labored to preserve the wilderness adamantly opposed, but the prospect of setting a precedent for similar arrangements in other parks caused widespread concern. Environmentalists' objections and bottom-line economics put the tramway plans to rest. The construction of a state highway through the central recreation area provided ample opportunities for motorized diversions while allowing the NPS to maintain that the park itself was unsullied by automobile tourism. Taken as a whole, however, the park complex emulated the conventional development model, with Mather's "one good road" concentrating use along a discrete corridor and the bulk of the reservation devoted to wilderness preservation. As in the past, NPS officials had to contend with local agitation for additional road development. These included calls for major new roadways and proposals to upgrade existing low-standard roads that were intended to function as "motor nature trails" and provide limited access to popular destinations. One of these routes was modestly improved to accommodate the traffic generated by its role as the best automotive access to the region's signature scenery. Preservationists' dreams were at least partially realized in 1988 with the classification of more than 600,000 acres of magnificent backcountry as inviolate wilderness. The aptly named Stephen Mather Wilderness Area afforded an emblematic complement to the nearby Stephen Mather Memorial Parkway, embodying the original NPS director's commitment to balancing preservation and access.[15]

The Leopold Report has been heralded as the period's seminal document, but an equally dramatic manifestation of Hartzog's commitment to seeking new perspectives and soliciting outside opinion focused on the other side of the Organic Act equation. Embracing the Sierra Club initiative stymied by Wirth, Hartzog appointed a committee to reexamine the principles governing park road design and management. The committee's composition and subsequent conclusions underscored the widespread perception that, as committee chairman William C. Everhart phrased it, "park roads are too important to be left in the hands of engineers." While this was a longtime NPS position, Hartzog pushed the concept beyond previous interpretations. Not only were there no federal highway personnel on the panel, but there was only one representative of the design professions that traditionally dominated NPS policy. Everhart's specialty was communications. The presence on the committee of assistant chief scientist Robert Linn exemplified the growing prominence of natural resource concerns. NPS assistant director for design and construction Charles Krueger represented the engineers' and landscape architects' perspectives. The other panelists were Izaak Walton League conservation director Joseph Penfold; Wildlife Management Institute president Ira Gabrielson; and Ansel Adams, whose querulous campaign to give artists a say in park road matters had finally borne fruit. Starker Leopold was invited to join the group but could not make time to participate. Notably absent were the pro-development interests that Wirth had insisted were necessary to provide a balanced assessment. That prospect may have been an empty threat, but with Hartzog in charge, there was no pretense of equanimity.[16]

Hartzog encouraged the committee to think broadly about the ways in which access could be provided without compromising the park experience. Instead of simply revising technical standards, the committee was asked to consider conceptual issues such as what differentiated park roads from ordinary highways and whether or not even the most benign examples afforded appropriate solutions to contemporary management challenges. The specific tasks were to define the purpose of park roads; establish guidelines for speed limits, design, location, and engineering specifications; and explore the possibilities of alternative transportation. Characterizing the ensuing report as "a significant contribution to National Park philosophy," Hartzog proclaimed

that it would have "enormous value to us at a time when road construction decisions constitute one of our most critical management problems." The underlying agenda could be gauged by the background material supplied by Everhart. Along with a collection of previous NPS statements, the packet included a newspaper clipping in which Udall proclaimed, "We shall be honored more for the roads we do not build than for those we do."[17]

It is tempting to interpret the initiative as a concession to environmental activists. Hartzog undoubtedly intended it to be seen that way, and in large part it was. In reality, the guidelines were more an affirmation of shared values than a capitulation to outside influences. Not only had NPS officials been more sympathetic to the Sierra Club's perspective than the Tioga Road furor would suggest, but the new guidelines were geared as much toward combating federal engineers as calming conservationists' concerns. By the 1960s, the tensions between the NPS and BPR—or Federal Highway Administration (FHWA), as it was renamed in 1966—reached the point that both sides were reevaluating the relationship. In 1962 the BPR made another push to assume control of NPS road development by reviving the idea that funding be channeled through federal highway appropriations. The usual arguments about reducing costs and improving efficiency were invoked, but many believed the underlying intent was to ensure that the next time a conflict arose, engineering standards would trump aesthetic and environmental concerns. Tensions were increased by the growing disparity between conventional roads and national park needs. To guide the rapid growth of America's highway network, federal and state engineers developed standard specifications that were released in 1963 under the auspices of the American Association of State Highway Officials (AASHO). Ostensibly intended as guidelines rather than rigid stipulations, the recommendations became de facto national standards. The next time a dispute arose, the NPS would not be questioning the BPR's opinion on park roads but contesting the consensus of the nation's highway engineers. Regardless of the nonbinding "guidelines" characterization, road builders were reluctant to challenge the status quo, especially since doing so could create liability issues for individual engineers and the agencies they worked for. The rising toll of highway fatalities

produced additional pressure. Citing a presidential directive to reduce the carnage, Federal Highway administrator Rex Whitton insisted on the need to be "aggressive in eliminating accident-inducing hazards." The NPS countered that even the more moderate guidelines for rural roads were inappropriate for national parks, where "the integrity of park resources, esthetics of location, harmony with the environment, respect for natural features, and viewing opportunities for passengers" should remain the primary criteria. Strict adherence to conventional standards would force the agency to violate its congressional mandate to protect park resources. Whitton and Hartzog exchanged encomiums about the celebrated relationship between the two agencies, but it was clear their priorities were far apart.[18]

Underscoring their shared interests, NPS officials sought support from the Sierra Club and other allies. Unconstrained by bureaucratic niceties, the Sierra Club's Harold Bradley railed against the BPR's proposal. Proclaiming that "no engineer today belonging to this powerful Bureau has the educational background or the experience to appreciate the reasons why a Park road must be one of very special design and standards," he maintained that it would be a "tragedy" to transfer authority over national park roads to technicians who knew little and cared less about park values or aesthetic concerns in general. Bradley was being characteristically harsh—NPS landscape architects and BPR engineers continued to enjoy a fruitful collaboration on the Blue Ridge Parkway and many other projects—but many observers shared his belief that highway engineers "should not even be employed in Parks except under the direct authority and supervision of Park-trained, experienced and dedicated Park officers." Richard Leonard and even David Brower came to the Park Service's defense, haranguing congressmen and putting the Sierra Club on record as opposing the takeover. The National Parks Association went even further, asserting that regulations be changed to strengthen the NPS's authority to prevent "fast and allegedly safe" design standards from compromising park values.[19]

The end result was a 1964 revised memorandum of agreement that included additional language about efficiency, collaboration, and best practices in engineering but accorded final authority to NPS priorities as expressed in the Organic Act and park master plans. A joint NPS-BPR committee was formed to improve procedures and formulate new standards. Dudley Bayliss was the NPS's senior representative, while the BPR's perspective was strongly influenced by engineers associated with Blue Ridge Parkway development. Given the personal and professional connections between participants, the discussions were congenial and recommendations relatively uncontroversial. A 1966 draft affirmed that park roads should be designed for "safe, easy, leisurely travel," emphasized the importance of harmonizing roads with their surroundings, and addressed technical details, underscoring that published standards should serve as general guidelines rather than inflexible decrees. Broader environmental and cultural concerns were not addressed. Hartzog's personality and the administration's emphasis on bold new initiatives undoubtedly contributed to the decision to pursue an alternative approach. Not only did the technocratic nature of the interagency working group epitomize traditional bureaucratic procedures, but the new director preferred audacious public statements to the informal understandings and cultivation of personal relationships favored by agency officials from Mather through Wirth.[20]

According to Everhart, the immediate trigger for the new committee was a conflict over plans to improve access to archaeological sites in Mesa Verde National Park. The BPR wanted to replace the rugged Jeep trail to Wetherill Mesa with what Everhart described as "a high standard modern highway." The existing road conformed to the terrain, winding up and around a succession of hills. It required low speeds and close attention but afforded a pleasing combination of intimate close-ups and expansive vistas. Insisting that consistently low grades, long curves, and improved sightlines were needed to ensure safety, BPR engineers began clearing the way for a sidehill route entailing extensive cuts and fills. In addition to producing what Everhart characterized as "a devastating impact on the landscape," this approach would eliminate the sensation of surmounting successive hilltops to encounter sweeping views, replacing it with a boring drive with no distinctive features. Hartzog cancelled the contract and called for a new study. When the BPR balked at building a low-standard road, the NPS engaged an independent firm to do the engineering and supervised construction itself. The 1967 redesign largely followed the original route, with minor improvements to ease the most

severe grades and curves. With a gravel surface, a design speed of 25 mph, and a shoulder-to-shoulder width of 20 feet, the Wetherill Mesa Road represented a return to 1920s standards. The goal was to minimize the road's impact on the park landscape, but as Harold Bradley had predicted, the decision also reduced the potential for overcrowding at the delicate site. A high-standard road would have increased traffic by easing the drive, but only those willing to expend additional time and effort ventured as far as Wetherill Mesa, especially since they had to leave their cars at a designated parking area and walk or take a shuttle the rest of the way. Casual tourists could take a quick glance at the principal ruins on the park's main road and continue on their way. Employing flexible design standards rather than one-size-fits-all solutions allowed the NPS to cater to both types of visitors while reducing visual and environmental impacts. Halting the project midcontract created considerable friction with the BPR and local commercial and political interests, however. Citing similar concerns, the NPS also dropped plans to provide automotive access to the signature ruins at Fort

Bowie National Historic Site, even though the alignment was staked and ready for construction. According to Everhart, these conflicts underscored that the NPS had to be more proactive in articulating the form and function of park roads.[21]

Hartzog's park road committee met in October 1967 to develop an initial statement, which was expanded and refined over the next six months. Ansel Adams was the most active participant, providing detailed comments on successive drafts. Most mirrored the committee's consensus, though in some cases he was more extreme and impolitic. Where the published version maintained there was no intent to imply that "those who seek a hurried trip through a park are less desirable visitors and should be excluded," Adams pronounced, "These people are not really important to the park except in a destructive way" and recommended relegating them to recreation areas. He also thought there should be more explicit acknowledgment of previous "errors" such as the Tioga Road and insisted that "Artists (including Photographers)" should be included among the professional disciplines responsible for decision making. Charles Krueger

ABOVE Wetherill Mesa jeep road, Mesa Verde National Park, from 1968 NPS *Park Road Standards*.

was equally upset that there was no reference to the landscape architects' role in the process and contended that the proposed system-wide speed limit of 35 mph was both too rigid and too slow. Other staff members made similar comments, observing that there were many roads where such speeds would create a "frustrating and monotonous" experience. Park planner Robert Bergman objected to the report's accusatory tone, asserting that the NPS had long practiced what the document preached and insisting that the damage ascribed to road construction was overstated. Bergman and others also maintained that it was unrealistic and counterproductive to presume the general public could be convinced to adopt the committee's values. Forcibly separating motorists from their automobiles would not only antagonize the majority of visitors but would bring additional pressures to bear on areas favored by those seeking solitude. Several NPS commentators maintained that the report was so reticent on detailed design matters that it was more of a policy proclamation or public relations piece than a practical document.[22]

Hartzog and the committee undoubtedly agreed with the latter assessment but considered the popular tone to be a virtue rather than a liability. Since the goal was to change the ways in which park transportation was perceived rather than fine-tune construction drawings, presenting park road concerns in accessible language punctuated by pithy pronouncements would be more effective than parsing engineering details in terms unintelligible to the general public. As in the past, the specifics could be addressed on a project-by-project basis. The director did have his say on key parameters, however. Hartzog reduced the standard maximum speed to 25 mph in natural and historical parks and insisted that no road exceed 22 feet in width with a combined 6 feet of shoulder unless specified by preexisting legislation. This was identical to Wirth's Tioga Road compromise but below AASHO standards. Parkways and major roads in recreation areas could go as high as 24 feet of pavement between 4-foot shoulders with top speeds of 45 mph. Minor two-way roads were capped at 20-feet surface width and one-way roads at 12 feet with 2-foot shoulders. The usual prescriptions for minimum curve radius were omitted and grade parameters limited to a single sentence.[23]

With the blessing of Secretary of the Interior Stewart Udall, the report was released in 1968 as the official NPS park road standards. It combined traditional maxims about aesthetically appropriate design with pointed reconsiderations of the relationships between automobiles, roads, and parks. Earlier invocations of civic ideals and the uplifting value of picturesque scenery gave way to the period-appropriate sentiment that "the single abiding purpose of National Parks is to bring man and his environment into closer harmony." The report insisted that the fundamental goal of park transportation was to improve the quality of the national park experience, not to increase the number of visitors. The Organic Act's dual mandate was obliquely invoked, but it was qualified with the assertion that ongoing increases in visitation posed "a profound threat to park values." Citing accelerating attendance figures—61 million visitors in 1965, 103 million in 1966, a projected 300 million in 1977—the document asserted that the only way to accommodate everyone who wanted to drive their own automobiles would be to carry out a continuous construction program with devastating consequences for the park environment. The committee acknowledged the automobile's central role in NPS history but insisted that changing times required reconsideration of the means through which people experienced parks. Just as urban planners were reexamining transportation options, the NPS should explore the potential of tramways, buses, monorails, helicopters, and hydrofoils for providing access without the environmental damage inherent to automobile-oriented solutions. Earlier objections to such technologies were ascribed to a misplaced enthusiasm for motor travel and inability to conceive the extent of future demands. Concerns that visitors would not forsake their automobiles for public transportation were dismissed as outworn shibboleths. Modern visitors, the report proclaimed, understood that new measures were needed to preserve the unique qualities of the national park experience. Given the underutilized potential of alternative transportation and negative impacts of road construction, the report declared, "It is quite possible that, at this point in the history of National Parks, new roads should be considered the last resort in seeking solutions to park access."[24]

Acknowledging that automobiles would play a prominent role in park transportation for the foreseeable future, the report maintained that the pace of travel was more significant than the means of locomotion. "Full enjoyment of a National Park visit is remarkably dependent on its being a leisurely experience, whether by automobile or on foot," the report declared. Reviving earlier arguments that the idiosyncrasies of traditional park roads played a beneficial role by forcing motorists to slow down and pay attention to their surroundings, the committee maintained that many so-called improvements were undesirable on experiential as well as environmental grounds. The message that park roads were intended for leisurely travel was reinforced throughout and highlighted in a handout for park visitors reproduced inside the front cover. "Park roads are designed with extreme care and located with a sensitive concern for the environment," the handout informed. "They are often narrow, winding, and hilly. At times they are little more than trails. But therein lies their appeal." Asserting that "it is almost a truism that the slower you go the more you will see," the handout sought to convince motorists that proceeding at a relaxed pace would provide a richer and more enjoyable experience than blasting through the scenery at highway speeds. Given that park roads were "for leisurely driving only," the card admonished, "If you are in a hurry, you might do well to take another route now, and come back when you have more time." The panel suggested that similar messages should appear on road maps provided by oil companies, in automobile club literature, and on NPS signs and publications.[25]

Not only would the idea of shooing visitors away have been anathema to Mather-era officials, but the panel proposed additional restrictions on the public's right to enjoy the parks as they saw fit. Citing the growing size of recreational vehicles, the report maintained that the NPS was not obligated to expand roads and campgrounds to accommodate the industry's latest products. Roads should be analyzed to determine the sizes and types of vehicles that could be reasonably accommodated. Vehicles that exceeded these standards should be prohibited. Parking areas for oversized vehicles could be provided near or, better yet, beyond park boundaries. Shuttle buses or other forms of alternative transportation would provide access to park destinations.[26]

When road improvements appeared to be the only feasible solution, great care should be exercised to minimize negative impacts and produce an enjoyable, low-speed driving experience. Associated recommendations reiterated long-standing NPS principles. "An esthetically pleasing road," the guidelines instructed, "is one which lies lightly upon the land." Cuts and fills should be minimized, long tangents avoided, and variety of scenery sought out in location, alignment, and roadside treatment. Surfaces should "harmonize with the general character of the landscape" through the use of tinted aggregates and chip seals. Retaining walls, tunnels, and half tunnels should be employed to minimize scenery-scarring excavations. Trestles and half viaducts could be used to similar effect, especially where road location or surrounding vegetation helped conceal artificial structures. Although the guidelines were reticent on the merits of modern design versus traditional rustic treatments, bridges, tunnel portals, retaining walls, and other structures were to be "aesthetically pleasing as well as functional and easily maintained."[27]

Echoes of the Tioga Road controversy reverberated throughout. Hartzog's road-width stipulations were lower than BPR/AASHO standards, but their most striking characteristic was that they employed the Sierra Club's suggestion of stipulating the maximum width consonant with scenic preservation rather than the minimum for safe operation. Special permission from the NPS director was required to exceed these limits. The injunction that "rigidity in laying out horizontal alinement to a uniform design speed should be avoided, by reducing the design speed to fit the terrain" also harkened back to complaints about Tioga Road. Grade specifications were also more in line with Sierra Club suggestions. Seven percent was presented as the preferred maximum, but the guidelines advised that "grades of 8, 9, or even 10 percent should be considered for relatively short distances to avoid excessive cuts and fills." The use of one-way roads was strongly promoted to improve safety without raising engineering standards.

Converting administrative roads and abandoned road or rail beds into Mission 66–style motor nature trails was presented as a low-impact means of accommodating the public's desire for motorized access while ensuring that the "leisurely driving" ethic prevailed. This recommendation embodied the primitive road concept advocated by Bradley and Brower and the motor nature trails of Mission 66. Looking further back, it recalled the reservations that George Goodwin, Horace Albright, and Frank Kittredge expressed about BPR standards. In a similar sense, many of the

ABOVE "Roads are often narrow, winding, and hilly": photograph of Capital Reef National Park, from 1968 NPS *Park Road Standards*.

broader statements reiterated sentiments expressed in the Lane Letter and Mather's exhortations to harmonize improvements with their surroundings and avoid gridironing the parks. The principal departures were the explicit antipathy toward automobiles, the aggressive promotion of alternative transportation, the prominence given to outside counsel, and a stipulation that future projects be reviewed by scientists to evaluate their ecological impact. Albright and Arno Cammerer had asked the NPS chief biologist to review many proposals, but prioritizing ecological analysis over the traditional design professions sent a clear message to NPS staff and the broader conservation community. The new guidelines were distributed widely and enfolded in the administrative policy manuals for all three national park categories.[28]

As Hartzog hoped, most observers focused on the innovative aspects and overall tone rather than the continuity with past practice. The National Parks Association hailed the new guidelines as "a revolutionary change for the better." Taking a pointed swipe at Wirth's management, an article in *National Parks Magazine* noted that the effort embodied "the creative attitude of the present administration in the National

Park Service toward many road problems." The National Parks Association and the Sierra Club expressed reservations about the renewed emphasis on motor nature trails, however, warning that the policy could lead to a proliferation of automobiles in formerly undisturbed areas. Hartzog defended the concept as a means of building support for more preservation-oriented policies. "You can't just order a visitor to get out of his car," he explained to *Christian Science Monitor* reporter Robert Cahn; "you have to entice him out of his car." After experiencing the appeal of more direct and intimate interaction with the park environment, mainstream visitors would be more inclined to take up hiking themselves, set aside areas for others to enjoy the pleasure, or at least appreciate the virtues of roads designed for leisurely enjoyment rather than high-speed travel. In cases such as the North Cascades, moreover, designating existing roads "motor nature trails" could quiet local objections and circumvent pressure to improve them to modern standards.[29]

The NPS was not alone in seeking to develop more broad-based approaches to transportation problems. The excesses of interstate highway development prompted calls to rethink the ways in which freeways were planned, designed, and constructed. Critiques came from a wide range of sources, including landscape architects, planners, citizens' groups, journalists, and eventually, the highway engineering community itself. Yale professors Christopher Tunnard and Boris Pushkarev surveyed the state of highway design and other aspects of modern development in their 1964 volume *Man-Made America: Chaos or Control?* More popularly oriented publications such as Peter Blake's *God's Own Junkyard* and William Whyte's *The Last Landscape* highlighted the consequences of poor planning, bad design, and lax regulations on highways, suburbs, and other American landscapes. The FHWA had established a task force to reevaluate freeway planning and design in 1965. Comprised of engineers, planners, and noted landscape architects such as Michael Rapuano and Lawrence Halprin, the panel similarly emphasized the importance of nonengineering factors. For the FHWA to invite landscape architects to reevaluate freeway development was akin to the NPS asking Ansel Adams advice on park road design. Like the 1968 *Park Road Standards*, such publications helped to raise awareness of the need for more socially, environmentally, and aesthetically sensitive development.[30]

The new park road standards also reflected the ideals expressed in President Johnson's 1965 "Message to the Congress on Natural Beauty." Johnson's statement and an associated high-profile conference addressed a wide range of social and environmental concerns. "The storm of modern change," Johnson declared, "is threatening to blight and diminish in a few decades what has been cherished and protected for generations." In addition to invoking issues such air pollution, water quality, and urban problems, the president expressed his support for the ideals embodied in the Wilderness Act and maintained that many of the most formidable challenges stemmed from the undeniable fact that "more than any other country ours is an automobile society." Johnson proclaimed two particularly relevant goals: "First, to ensure that roads themselves are not destructive of nature and natural beauty. Second, to make our roads ways to recreation and pleasure." The roadside blight afflicting general-purpose highways was his primary concern, but Johnson called attention to the increasing pressure on parks and other scenic areas. "A growing population is swallowing up areas of natural beauty with its demands for living space," he observed, "and is placing increased demand on our overburdened areas of recreation and pleasure."[31]

Concern about park crowding continued to rise as middle-class motorists were joined by the burgeoning population of backpackers and back-to-nature enthusiasts. Mission 66 may have provided the initial impetus, but when Abbey's *Desert Solitaire* appeared in 1968, his anti-establishment attitude captured the contemporary ethos. Even mainstream news outlets questioned whether the NPS had gone too far in accommodating the public's insistence on automotive access. The new park road guidelines came out as reporter Robert Cahn was completing a series of articles on the theme "Will Success Spoil the National Parks?" for the *Christian Science Monitor*. Hartzog afforded full cooperation, both to counter more sensational accounts and to use Cahn as a mouthpiece for expressing the agency's perspective. Cahn hailed the new guidelines and suggested that the NPS and BPR were at odds because the park officials wanted to build "low-speed, narrow, scenic roads instead of straight, wide roads the BPR people say are necessary for safety considerations." Udall was quoted as saying that with parkways affording ample opportunities for scenic driving, "the big national parks should be dedicated to the idea of getting people out of their automobiles." The majority of respondents to a survey conducted at the conclusion of Cahn's series agreed. Three-quarters supported the idea that park roads should be narrow, scenic drives with maximum speeds of 35 mph; half sided with the NPS position that roads within parks should be removed from the national highway system to counter pressure for unwarranted upgrades; one-quarter called for a complete moratorium on road construction. Although *Christian Science Monitor* subscribers could hardly be considered representative of the American populace, Cahn's series was considered sufficiently newsworthy to earn the author a Pulitzer Prize. The authors of a Conservation Foundation analysis of NPS policy made no pretense of journalistic objectivity. Criticizing the NPS for "pandering to the less appreciative and more uncritical section of public taste," the widely publicized report called for more stringent regulations to counter the "traumatic influence" of automobile-oriented development. The ultimate goal should be to reduce and eventually eliminate roads and other facilities catering to the motorized masses.[32]

A small but significant step in this direction took place on July 9, 1970, when a crowd gathered in Yosemite Valley to observe the curious spectacle of a two pieces of ribbon being tied together across a paved roadway, symbolically barring private automobiles from the eastern third of the valley. Visitors unwilling to walk beyond this point could avail themselves of propane-powered shuttle buses. An exception was made for those who had reserved campsites beyond the dividing line. Park Information Officer Larry Quist explained that the closure was needed to reduce traffic congestion along with air and noise pollution. The root of the problem, he declared, was "free and unrestricted automobile access to the valley." Hartzog attended the ceremony, proclaiming that it marked the first time that automobile access had been restricted in a national park and predicting that it would lead to widespread changes. While Hartzog overlooked the original proscriptions on automobile access to Yosemite and other parks, his presence underscored that the ceremony marked a pivotal moment in NPS history. Within a year, Yosemite Valley shuttles transported 1.6 million people, which the NPS equated to four hundred thousand automobile trips. National Park Association executive director Anthony Wayne Smith applauded the NPS for being "in step with the times in recognizing that the automobile is a good servant but an intolerable master." While the Yosemite program represented "an auspicious beginning," Smith insisted that more needed to be done. Road development should be frozen at present levels, future accommodations constructed beyond park borders, and automobile use "substantially curtailed." Implementing such forward-thinking policies would be an imposing task, Smith acknowledged, given the unfortunate reality that "the personal automobile is the Sacred Cow of American society."[33]

Few NPS directors relished taking on sacred cows as much as Hartzog. As recounted in an adulatory 1971 *New Yorker* profile, Hartzog exhorted Yosemite's managers to pursue even stronger measures. "The automobile as a recreational experience is obsolete," he asserted; "We cannot accommodate automobiles in such numbers and still provide a quality environment for a recreational experience." For Hartzog, this meant that the NPS should provide "a park experience, not a parkway experience." Whether in Yosemite or elsewhere, no more roads would be built until all other options were explored. "We've simply got to do something besides build roads in these parks if we're going to have any parks left," he proclaimed. If people could be weaned from their dependence on private automobiles, Hartzog insisted, it would be possible to reduce road mileage within existing parks. Exhibiting his usual flair for the dramatic, he declared, "The beauty is that you can take a dynamite stick and blow up the pavement and then all you have is a hole there and you can fill up the hole." In terms of Yosemite Valley, Hartzog pronounced, "I'm not inflexible on anything except that I'm going to get rid of the damned automobile, and I'm not going to get rid of people in the process." To demonstrate his determination,

Hartzog personally took a jackhammer to a parking lot scheduled for removal, making sure the press was there to record the event.[34]

Even Richard Nixon, whose environmental contributions are often overlooked, gave presidential imprimatur to concerns about overcrowding. "The growing popularity of our parks has created a number of serious problems as millions of Americans have sought the recreation and respite they provide," he declared in 1971. "Traffic congestion and crowded campsites are becoming common. In many places, natural systems are overburdened and damaged by the presence of too many people." Endorsing one of the more

radical approaches advocated by the conservation community, Nixon asserted that carrying capacities should be calculated and quotas enforced to minimize the need for additional development. Capping access in this manner might have seemed a minor matter compared to his contemporary freeze on wages and prices throughout the U.S. economy, but NPS leaders had no intention of taking such a controversial step.[35]

Hartzog and his allies placed great hope in the potential of alternative transportation programs. In 1966 the National Parks Association pointed to Colonial Williamsburg's decision to replace automobile access with a shuttle system as an example of the benefits of such programs. Yosemite instituted its first modern-day shuttle bus program a year later. At first the concessionaire-operated system just offered service between major accommodations on the valley floor. The inconvenience and high fares created calls for free or low-cost shuttles making more frequent stops. This approach was soon adopted, beginning with the program developed to take the place of cars at the east end of the valley. Despite predictions that visitors would object, a shuttle bus driver interviewed in 1972 estimated that most of his riders embraced the service on environmental grounds. Cars were also banned from the historic parking area at Yosemite Village, which was turned into a pedestrian-friendly mall. Specially designed propane-powered "mini-trains" capable of carrying sixty to eighty passengers were introduced in the early 1970s. Turning the valley road system into a one-way loop further reduced congestion and produced a more relaxing experience for motorists and shuttle passengers alike.[36]

In its eagerness to embrace alternative technologies, the NPS considered building tramways, funiculars, light rail systems, and monorails in various parks. Along with the North Cascades proposal, serious thought was given to constructing tramways

National Park Roads

to carry visitors into the Grand Canyon and between Yosemite Valley and Glacier Point. These suggestions were strongly opposed by the Sierra Club, Wilderness Society, and other conservation groups, who protested that the technological intrusions would compromise park values. Critics also contended that experiencing parks from tramways was as contrary to the ideal of bringing visitors into closer harmony with natural environments as viewing them from automobiles. Monorails and light rail systems were opposed on the same grounds. Controversies over these proposals led to strict regulations on the extent to which such options could be considered. NPS management policies were revised to stipulate that "any mode of transportation that requires the construction of surface or elevated trackage, suspended cables, or advanced technologies will not go beyond a conceptual status without approval from the Director."[37]

Despite these reservations, Congress directed the NPS to conduct a study of potential alternative transportation systems as one of the initiatives associated with the 1991 Intermodal Surface Transportation Efficiency Act. As evidenced by the legislation's title, the idea of looking beyond automobile-oriented solutions had gained widespread acceptance by this time. The new law echoed the 1968 *Park Road Standards* in suggesting that planners should consider creative alternatives to building bigger and faster highways. More importantly, the bill made transit systems, trails, and support facilities aimed at separating people from their cars eligible for federal highway funding. The NPS was directed to consider options such as monorails, cog railways, tramways, and the elevated "people movers" that were becoming increasingly popular at airports and theme parks. Associated stipulations evidenced the influence of earlier criticisms. The proposed measures were to "have minimal impact on the natural and cultural environment of the park," "have little impact on visitors who are non-users, including visual effects, noise levels, and air quality," and "be acceptable to the public, environmental groups, and other concerned entities." Yosemite, Yellowstone, and Denali were selected as test cases, and the study was assigned to a consultant with extensive transportation planning experience. With its single main road and established bus system, Denali presented the most straightforward situation. Light rail and monorails were considered, but the grades were deemed too steep for the former, and the latter was rejected

on the grounds that it would constitute "a major visual element that would be incompatible with the surrounding wilderness." A cog railway similar to the system employed at Colorado's Pikes Peak was suggested as a more viable alternative. While the associated illustrations suggested otherwise, the report contended, "Cog railways have a character that could contribute to the mountain ambience of the park." Tramways were also evaluated as means of providing access to scenery along the south slope of the Alaska Range. Acknowledging that both options would require significantly more investment than was currently foreseeable, the report deemed reliance on conventional buses the most realistic alternative.[38]

Devising public transportation for Yellowstone was particularly challenging. The difficulties posed by the park's size and widely varying terrain were compounded by visitors' preferences for entering from one side and exiting on another. A mixture of technologies was proposed to address the situation. A voluntary shuttle bus system could accommodate visitors traveling between West Yellowstone, the primary geyser basins, and the overbuilt and underutilized Grant Village development, a vestige of Mission 66. Private automobiles would be prohibited between the Lake and Canyon visitor complexes to reduce traffic through the environmentally sensitive Hayden Valley. This section might be traversed by one of four means: conventional shuttle buses; longer, high-capacity articulated buses; light rail; or monorail. Although the latter two options would be more visually obtrusive, the consultants suggested that visitors would find the "high technology appearance" of the monorail appealing and that the light rail system could be given a "rustic" character to enhance its appearance. Neither would allow the frequent stopping to view wildlife that constituted a principal attraction of the region, but eliminating this practice would be better for the animals. The monorail would require the highest initial investment, but long-term costs would be lower. If powered by electricity, it could be both silent and nonpolluting. A cog railway was cast as the best means of surmounting the steep grades of Dunraven Pass. While the initial cost would be high, it would afford a long-term solution that, according to the consultants, would "fit into the mountain and alpine environment" and "reduce impacts on the wilderness character of Yellowstone." Visitors would lose their ability to stop and view wildlife, but the captive audience

would benefit from extended lectures by park personnel. As with the Hayden Valley alternatives, the uniqueness of the cog railway experience would afford "extra visitor appeal." In the conventional bus alternative, large motor coaches would service most of the Grand Loop and associated entrance roads, and smaller shuttles would provide short rides in the Canyon and Old Faithful/Geyser Basin areas. The exclusion of private vehicles would require extensive parking areas at entrance points, along with staging facilities for the public transit system. It would also have faced enormous resistance, not just from park visitors but also from commercial interests in gateway communities who believed it would diminish the park's appeal. Concern about potential reactions prompted Yellowstone's superintendent to compose a statement explaining that the study had been conducted at Congress's behest and making it clear that the document was merely a speculative exercise in long-term planning.[39]

The Yosemite component called for expansion of the existing shuttle system augmented by light rail or elevated people movers. Yosemite was lauded for taking the most ambitious approach to reducing the dependence on private automobiles. The park's widely circulated 1978 draft General Management Plan (GMP) identified increasing traffic as "the greatest threat to the natural and scenic qualities of Yosemite" and stated that private automobiles would be "strictly controlled in the most popular and environmentally sensitive areas of the park." Cars would be excluded entirely "when it was economically feasible and when alternative methods of public transportation are acceptable." This highly qualified wording reflected the controversial nature of the proposal. Although the idea of eliminating automobiles from Yosemite Valley was strongly supported by the Sierra Club and other conservation groups, it was adamantly opposed by gateway communities that depended on the lucrative stream of motorized visitors. These interests made their displeasure known through elected representatives at the local, state, and national levels. The proposed automobile ban generated nationwide attention. Many accounts brushed over the alternative transportation proposals, giving the impression that the NPS planned to bar people from the park. By the end of the mandatory public comment period, more than sixty-three thousand correspondents had submitted opinions. The draft GMP included a wide range of recommendations, but the automobile restrictions generated far and away the most comments.[40]

The subsequent document was even more weighted to the preservation end of the spectrum. Combining the Leopold Report's injunction to provide a "vignette of primitive America" with broader criticisms of the contemporary American landscape, the completed 1980 GMP maintained that visitors should be able to "step into Yosemite and find nature uncluttered by piecemeal stumbling blocks of commercialism, machines, and fragments of suburbia." In order for this to happen, the plan declared, "The Valley must be freed from the noise, the smell, the glare, and the environmental degradation caused by thousands of vehicles." To mediate criticism, the process would

be gradual and, for the time being, voluntary. Despite assurances that overall access was not being restricted, the final GMP called for significant reductions in the number of overnight accommodations along with the elimination of approximately 1,300 parking spaces. The shuttle program would be expanded to compensate. Another reason for opting for incremental change was that implementing the plan would be extraordinarily expensive. A 1986 analysis estimated the cost at $70 million. Not only was there little chance of securing this amount, but political considerations mediated against substantial alterations to existing patterns. A few modest steps were taken. In 1991 shuttle bus service was extended to Tuolumne Meadows, where the increased popularity of backpacking created parking problems at trailheads. Two battery-powered buses were tested in 1995 to gauge their potential as alternatives to noisy and polluting diesel conveyances. Seeking to defuse criticism, the NPS helped develop a Yosemite Area Regional Transportation Strategy involving local jurisdictions, the U.S. Forest Service, and the California Department of Transportation in an attempt to extend public transportation solutions beyond the park. Mother Nature also lent a hand. Devastating floods along the Merced River in January 1997 gave an unexpected boost to the GMP's goals by destroying some low-lying campgrounds and overnight cabins and strengthening arguments for the elimination of accommodations in floodplain areas.[41]

During the late 1990s the NPS began to develop a "Valley Implementation Plan" to coordinate, update, and advance the goals articulated in earlier proposals. The key objectives were to "reclaim priceless beauty, reduce cars and congestion," and "allow natural systems to prevail." The plan called for the elimination of an additional thousand parking spaces and another eighty campsites. The associated reduction in traffic would allow the Southside Drive to function as a two-way road so that the North Side Road could be converted to a multi-use trail. The triumph of ecologically infused management philosophies was epitomized by proposals to remove the rustic stone-faced Sugarpine, Stoneman, and Ahwanee Bridges constructed during the Mather and Albright era. Photoshopped before-and-after images dramatized the difference between traditional development philosophies and contemporary ecologically based concerns. From the former perspective, the picturesque structures helped people enjoy the park while complementing the natural beauty of their locations. On a more abstract level, they embodied the harmonious union of nature and technology and transformed raw nature into more aesthetically pleasing and socially beneficial humanized landscapes. From the environmentalist's standpoint, the bridges were unwarranted impositions that disrupted stream flow, enabled the automotive addiction, and impeded the pursuit of primeval purity. Starker Leopold's scientific rationale was conjoined with his father's

Figure 5: Sugarpine Bridge — Existing Conditions

Figure 6: Sugarpine Bridge — Proposed Restoration Simulation

National Park Roads

more mystical musings about nature's needs and desires. According to Acting Superintendent Stanley Albright, eliminating these man-made obstructions would "allow the Merced River to do what the Merced River wants to do." In addition to restoring natural processes, the reduction in noise, congestion, and "visual distractions" would improve the overall visitor experience. Independent auto touring would no longer be an option, but visitors could enjoy signature views from public transport. Other forms of recreation such as walking and cycling would be markedly enhanced. Federal and agency requirements to consider impacts on historical resources were met with the argument that change itself was a prominent characteristic of Yosemite's landscape. Earlier custodians had altered the valley to reflect contemporary priorities. As long as the proposed changes were "governed by design that is intended to be appropriate to place," eliminating structures and behaviors associated with outmoded conceptions of Yosemite Valley as a people's playground or motorist's paradise constituted a continuation of historical patterns. The National Trust for Historic Preservation thought otherwise, condemning the proposed removal and placing Yosemite's bridges on its 2012 list of Most Endangered Places. This action generated widespread media coverage, resulting in a storm of protests calling for the bridges' retention.[42]

The Valley Improvement Plan generated controversy on many fronts. The most ardent conservationists accused the NPS of moving too slowly and not going far enough. Conservative critics cast the proposal as further evidence that the Clinton administration was catering to liberal elites rather than respecting the desires of ordinary Americans. Gateway community leaders accused the NPS of conspiring to "lock people out of the park." California congressman George Radanovich proclaimed, "As long as I represent Yosemite National Park and this beautiful valley, I will not allow it to become an exclusive retreat available only by tour bus, nor a nature preserve which you can get to only on foot." House Subcommittee on National Parks chairman Joel Hefley even contested the assertion that Yosemite Valley was overcrowded. Media coverage inflamed the situation by implying that limits would be set on the number of people allowed in Yosemite Valley rather than on the number of cars. Secretary of the Interior Bruce Babbitt sought to clarify the issue, asserting that the problem was not too many people but too many cars. The subsequent administration was less sympathetic, though many agency professionals remained committed to the plan's ideals. In 2003, NPS director Fran Mainella announced there would be no net loss in parking spaces for the foreseeable future. When a draft management plan mandated by the Merced's designation as a National Wild and Scenic River suggested that the NPS was backing away from its anti-automobile stance, environmentalists filed suit to push the agency toward a more ecologically infused stance.[43]

The courts endorsed some of the charges, but public sentiment and political pressure

According to Acting Superintendent Stanley Albright, eliminating these man-made obstructions would "allow the Merced River to do what the Merced River wants to do."

BELOW Simulation showing proposed removal of park drive, Yosemite Valley, Yosemite National Park, 1997.

OPPOSITE Simulation showing proposed removal of historic Sugarpine Bridge, Yosemite Valley, 1997.

Figure 7: Ahwahnee Meadow — Existing Conditions

Figure 8: Ahwahnee Meadow — Proposed Restoration Simulation

ABOVE Light-rail proposal for Grand Canyon National Park, 1996; due to cost considerations, a more conventional shuttle bus system was implemented instead.

mediated against dramatic alterations. A 2009 survey suggested that despite occasionally crowded conditions, 98 percent of visitors were satisfied with existing arrangements. Scenic driving remained the most popular recreational activity, outpacing hiking, backpacking, and other non-motorized activities. NPS officials engaged in exhaustive public outreach and conducted extensive analysis of factors ranging from hydrologic patterns and bird behavior to scenic viewsheds and crowd dynamics. Released in February 2014, the plan sought to address ecological concerns without alienating mainstream visitors and tourism interests. Approximately 200 acres of meadows and riverbanks would be restored to natural conditions, and some historic visitor facilities would be removed or relocated, but the total number of campsites was slightly increased. The threatened bridges were retained and measures were suggested to mediate their hydrological impact. Yosemite Village lost one hundred parking spaces, but the difference was made up with a new lot on the site of a former employee dormitory. Overflow parking would be provided at El Portal, with a commensurate increase in shuttle service. The regional transportation initiative received additional support. A long-contemplated

and much-resisted quota system for admittance to the valley was authorized. The cap was set at current attendance rates, however, with a generous limit of 18,710 visitors, rising to 20,100 during periods of peak demand. Although the results disappointed ardent environmentalists, the plan reflected a more balanced approach to addressing the tension between preservation and access.[44]

Addressing Grand Canyon's transportation challenges proved to be an equally extended process, with similarly bold visions giving way to more modest but attainable improvements. In November 1997, Babbitt and Transportation Secretary Rodney Slater announced plans for a $14 million light rail system designed to reduce congestion and improve the park experience by restricting automotive access and transporting visitors from a remote parking area to redesigned facilities at the South Rim. A profusely illustrated prospectus presented compelling images of sleek railcars sharing the repurposed roadway with cyclists and pedestrians. Explaining the need for the expensive system, Babbitt pronounced, "The road to [the] South Rim is now jammed with cars, the once fresh and clear air now smells of diesel fumes and asphalt, the stunning view now marred by filling stations and smog, the sound

of breeze-rustled pines now drowned out by the echo of engines and horns." Wilderness Society president Bill Meadows heartily endorsed the proposal, reminding critics that "even in Disney World, cars don't go right to the heart of the park." This may have been an apt analogy, but the fate of the $300 million proposal underscored the difference between privately financed theme parks and cash-strapped public reservations. Funding challenges shelved the proposal in short order. By 2007, the situation had deteriorated to the point that NPS officials characterized the parking and interior circulation systems as "dysfunctional." During peak visitation periods, there were two-hour waits at the main entrance, crippling congestion within, and parked cars strung along shoulders, degrading the environment and creating additional hazards and delays. A comprehensive improvement campaign was completed in 2011. The main entrance and visitor area were redesigned to address parking and circulation concerns while enhancing the overall experience. Roads were rerouted to create an automobile-free zone around the popular Mather Point overlook, parking spaces for six hundred cars and forty tour buses were provided, and an alternative-fuel shuttle bus system was instituted to transport visitors to a range of new and remodeled facilities.[45]

The 1991 Intermodal Surface Transportation Efficiency Act also enabled Zion to develop a less elaborate but more broadly applicable transit system. As many as fifteen thousand people per day jammed the narrow road through scenic Zion Canyon by the 1990s. Many visitors spent fewer than three hours in the park, especially if they were unable to secure parking spots. To remedy the situation, private automobiles were banned from the canyon and replaced with propane-powered shuttle buses. NPS officials worked with representatives from neighboring Springdale, Utah, to develop a new visitor center near the park border with parking dispersed throughout the town. This eliminated the need for a large paved area within the park while encouraging visitors to patronize local businesses. The plan's modest physical requirements combined with successful efforts to garner local support made for relatively uncontroversial implementation. The system went into operation in May 2000. The shuttle carried approximately three thousand visitors per day during the first season, taking the place of an estimated forty-two thousand vehicles. Visitor surveys attested to an

85 percent satisfaction rate. Local officials and business operators also expressed approval. Zion's stature as a relatively low-profile park worked in its favor, as did the configuration of its circulation system. The Canyon Road was a dead-end spur, eliminating problems stemming from travelers wanting to enter and exit at different locations. Motorists in a hurry could drive through the park on the Zion–Mount Carmel Highway and skip the scenic side trip. The Zion arrangement and a similar conventional-technology shuttle system at Acadia afforded compelling models for other locations. Not only was the scale more in line with most parks' needs, but the outreach to local communities provided important lessons about ameliorating potential tensions.[46]

One of the most popular transportation projects forsook futuristic fantasies for an avowedly atavistic approach, retrofitting the vintage motor coaches that had served Glacier National Park since shortly after the opening of Going-to-the-Sun Road. Unveiled in 1936 as the officially approved national park motor coach, the White Motor Company's streamlined fourteen-passenger buses with removable canvas tops assumed iconic status as the motor-age successor to the storied stagecoach. Yellowstone's fleet numbered in the hundreds. Dozens plied Going-to-the-Sun Road decked out in bright-red paint with the Great Northern's mountain-goat logo emblazoned on the side. With improved highways and increased automobile ownership, however, most park transportation companies had fallen on hard times by the 1960s. Glacier's remote location and spectacular but potentially unnerving Going-to-the-Sun Road kept the red buses on the road. For many visitors the opportunity to partake in a unique experience harkening back to an earlier era of national park tourism became an attraction in itself.[47]

Concerns about the safety of sixty-year-old vehicles prompted the NPS to order the buses off the road in 1999. Conventional passenger vans took their place, but the public, park management, concessionaires, and drivers expressed strong sentiment in favor of bringing back the red buses. Technical and financial challenges were formidable, but the Ford Motor Company agreed to attempt a solution. Original body shells were mounted on Ford truck chassis with engines capable of running on propane to reduce emissions. Additional improvements included aerospace-grade honeycombed aluminum floors for lightweight strength, more ergonometric

seats, and updated glass, lighting, and instruments. Heaters were another modern amenity added in the rehabilitation process. The prototype was unveiled in June 2001 with highly publicized ceremonies in Washington, D.C., and Glacier National Park. By 2002, thirty-three of the surviving buses were back on the road. The renovated buses proved equally popular and the NPS touted the project as an illustration of the value of innovative public-private partnerships.[48]

The enthusiasm for alternative transportation did not signal an end to the NPS's road-building activities. Although NPS leaders and the conservation community agreed that new road development should be kept to a minimum, repairs and upgrades were inevitable, and several planned roads remained under construction. There were still three unfinished parkways when the new park road standards were announced, and additional proposals were under consideration. Economic concerns and the prospect of significant environmental objections put the latter ambitions to rest. During the mid-1960s the NPS participated in an elaborate study leading to proposals for thousands of miles of more modestly developed scenic roads managed largely by state highway departments, but the program foundered on political and economic grounds. With the 1969 National Environmental Policy Act imposing additional constraints and mandating expensive and time-consuming review, large-scale parkway development was no longer considered a practicable option.[49]

Projects that had already been approved were allowed to continue. The extent to which the NPS remained committed to minimizing the impacts of park road development was epitomized in the construction of the Linn Cove Viaduct, which enabled the long-delayed completion of Blue Ridge Parkway. NPS officials and landowner Hugh Morton had been deadlocked for decades over plans for the final parkway segment on Grandfather Mountain, a highly scenic peak just north of North Carolina's Pisgah National Forest. When the two sides finally reached agreement in 1968, the NPS faced the challenge of constructing a roadbed over exceptionally steep and ecologically sensitive terrain. Once the general location was determined through extended negotiations and exhaustive field study, NPS landscape architects and FHWA engineers addressed the problem of carrying the roadway across an area of rocky outcrops and unstable boulders known as Linn

Cove. BPR engineer Al Burden recounted that the design team covered every foot of the mountain and laid down so many potential lines that practically every tree in the forest was festooned with flagging. In 1973, FHWA engineer R. B. Cocroft suggested spanning the problem area with an extended viaduct. Scenic road builders had used viaducts to negotiate rugged terrain since the days of Daniel Kingman and Samuel Lancaster. The NPS employed the technique on numerous occasions, including older sections of Blue Ridge Parkway. The Linn Cove Viaduct would be much longer than previous examples, stretching approximately one-quarter of a mile. The extended length combined with the desire to conform as closely as possible with the natural contours required a significantly more complex roadway structure than American engineers had ever attempted. It would also be built in an era of heightened environmental scrutiny, when construction impacts were considered not just scenic impairments but also ecological depredations. To assist in the design work, FHWA engineers engaged in an early attempt at computer-aided simulation. After generating a photomontage of the construction site, the engineers adjusted the curvature and pier locations to account for variations in topography. The technical challenges convinced the NPS to embrace a relatively new construction process employing individually designed precast concrete segments assembled through "progressive" construction. By casting the concrete sections off-site and using the viaduct as a platform from which to extend itself, this technique minimized the structure's physical footprint and eliminated the need for access roads and concrete formwork. Although the Linn Cove Viaduct was not the first precast segmental bridge in North America, the location and geometry made it the most ambitious to date. The curvature required to mimic the mountain's contours required complex calculations and painstaking craftsmanship. None of the 153 segments were alike. Variation occurred in multiple dimensions as the horizontal curvature was compounded by shifting superelevation that transitioned from 10 percent in one direction to 10 percent in the other and back again.[50]

The NPS and FHWA assigned the task to the consulting firm Figg and Muller. Jean Muller was a structural engineer who had pioneered segmental design and construction in France during the 1960s. Muller first employed the progressive placement process in 1972 in the construction of bridges over long stretches of water. The Linn Cove Viaduct was its first application in the United States. Construction began in October 1978. The contract decreed that no tree beyond the path of the viaduct could be cut and that extensive efforts be taken to prevent siltation and water contamination. A complex mating system ensured that the end of each 50-ton segment perfectly matched its neighbor. After being cast nearby in a temporary facility, segments were transported to the end of the structure and lowered into place. Cables were used to posttension the segments and the joints sealed with a special epoxy. In a further effort to minimize environmental impact, only seven piers were used to support the entire superstructure. These were also cast off-site. A combination of concave and convex surfaces reduced their apparent mass. The final segment was placed in December 1982. The contractor completed the rest of the work by the end of 1983, applying a wearing surface to the concrete deck, installing curbs and guard rails, and finishing the abutments on either end. Four more years were required to construct six smaller structures and complete the final 1.3 miles of roadway linking the viaduct to the parkway on either side. The completion ceremony was held on September 11, 1987, exactly fifty-two years after ground was broken on the first stretch of Blue Ridge Parkway. Like Yellowstone's Golden Gate Viaduct, the Linn Cove structure immediately became one of the parkway's iconic elements. With its sinuous curves and striking contrast of nature and technology, the viaduct has been celebrated in federal engineering reports, NPS publications, postcards, calendars, guidebooks, and other souvenirs. Engineering organizations bestowed numerous accolades. The project was one of the first recipients of a newly credited presidential award for federal design efforts. Due to its combination of aesthetic excellence, technological sophistication, and environmental sensitivity, the Linn Cove Viaduct section is considered one of the premier examples of modern park road design.[51]

A similarly striking structure was constructed on Natchez Trace Parkway in the 1990s. The challenge in this case was to cross a picturesque valley with minimal disruption to the scenery. The conventional approach would have been to drop the road into the valley or construct a concrete girder or steel truss bridge. The latter techniques would be efficient but unsightly.

Bringing the road down to the valley floor would require a winding alignment and considerable cuts and fills, along with a grade separation structure to cross a state highway at the bottom. An elegant double-arch configuration was chosen to span the 1,648-foot gap. To minimize visual disruption, conventional vertical supports or spandrels were omitted, and a variation on the Linn Cove Viaduct technique was employed to combine structural strength with minimal construction impact. Precast segments were placed progressively, employing cantilever principles and cables to support the arches until the keystone segments solidified the structures. The superstructure was a variable-depth trapezoidal hollow concrete girder comprised of 196 segments weighing from 36 to 57 tons each. Posttensioned cables and epoxy bonded segments to their neighbors. Masonry facing on the abutments and guard walls matched the color and texture of nearby stonework. A parking overlook was provided at the north end to dissuade motorists from stopping midspan to enjoy the sweeping views. NPS designers conceived the general outlines, and the FHWA and Figg Engineering provided the technical expertise. The project was completed in May 1995. The bridge's sleek profile belied its considerable mass, while the soaring arches echoed the organic forms of the surrounding terrain. Like the Linn Cove Viaduct, the Natchez Trace Parkway Double Arch Bridge garnered numerous honors, including a 1995 Presidential Award for Design Excellence. The parkway itself remained incomplete. Considerable progress had been made under Mission 66, but development was sporadic over the ensuing decades. Funding shortages, land acquisition issues, and routing debates caused considerable delays. By 2001, approximately 22 miles remained unfinished. The final two sections near Jackson and Natchez were finished in 2005, fulfilling the sixty-seven-year quest for the parkway's completion.[52]

Foothills Parkway did not fare as well. The NPS had misgivings about the project since its inception in the 1930s. The 72-mile parkway paralleling Great Smoky Mountains National Park's northwest border would ostensibly afford a compelling scenic drive while relieving pressure on the heavily used park. The underlying motivation was to compensate Tennessee interests for losing out on the routing of Blue Ridge Parkway. The parkway was authorized in 1944,

but construction did not begin until 1951. A short section known as the Gatlinburg spur opened in 1953. Several segments were constructed during the 1950s and 1960s, but funding shortages and technical difficulties hampered progress. The proposed routing entailed significant cuts and fills in geologically unstable terrain. With less than a third of the parkway completed by the 1970s, the NPS considered canceling additional development. Local interests protested strenuously, leading to an agreement in which the State of Tennessee would construct the remainder with a combination of NPS and federal highway funding and FHWA supervision. NPS involvement remained high since it was still a national parkway with the attendant environmental and landscape architectural concerns. Work was halted in 1986 due to landslides and the release of toxic minerals during the excavation process, which poisoned nearby streams. The NPS resumed control when state efforts foundered, focusing on the completion of a 1.65-mile "Missing Link" between the two existing sections. Extensive environmental reviews were undertaken and proposals developed to use viaducts, retaining walls, and extensive fills to minimize additional excavation. The most recent efforts employed Linn Cove–style viaducts to soar above the unstable terrain. The juxtaposition of nature and technology was similarly striking and promised to afford an unforgettable sensation of sweeping around the mountains between the treetops and the sky. Given the technical complexities and funding challenges, the projected completion of the "Missing Link" has been pushed back to 2017, at the earliest. Prospects for realizing the original vision are slim. Even constructing the remaining mileage as a nonmotorized multi-use trail, as some groups have suggested, would be inordinately expensive and environmentally disruptive.[53]

A significant shift in the structure of the NPS-FHWA relationship took place with the passage of the 1982 Surface Transportation Assistance Act. Among its many provisions, the legislation created the Federal Lands Highway Program (FLHP) to oversee FHWA support for federal land management agencies. The principal motivation was to promote consistency between FHWA activities in national parks, national forests, and other federal reservations. A jointly administered Park Roads and Parkways Program was created to conduct the national park component. Washington-based program managers and

ABOVE Double Arch Bridge, Natchez Trace Parkway, completed 1995.

regional coordinators collaborated with FLHP engineers, park staff, and the NPS's Denver Service Center to develop, prioritize, and conduct projects ranging from rehabilitation to new construction, along with a growing number of alternative transportation programs. The primary funding source shifted from annual NPS appropriations bolstered by project-specific "line-item" allocations to the Highway Trust Fund. Every NPS director from Stephen Mather on down had resisted this arrangement on the grounds that maintaining control of the budget gave the NPS final authority if disputes arose about road location or design. With visitation continuing to increase and resources stretched thin by the addition of new parks, shrinking appropriations, and deterioration of aging infrastructure, NPS officials decided that tapping into the Highway Trust Fund afforded the best means of assuring substantial and consistent funding. Some senior design staff objected, but budgetary imperatives prevailed. The revised 1983 Memorandum of Agreement between the two agencies appeared to afford ample assurance that plans and specifications would continue to be

based on objectives outlined in park master plans. Attendant stipulations that roads conform to federal safety standards echoed earlier provisions. While the language was not appreciably different, the underlying budgetary change meant that if conflicts arose, the FHWA could withhold funding and the NPS would not have the option of engaging outside expertise or conducting the work itself. Wirth's solution to the Tioga Road stand-off and Hartzog's Wetherill Mesa response were no longer on the table. With minimal plans for major construction, agency officials may not have been overly concerned. An accompanying Senate report included reassuring statements that lands managed by federal agencies were intended for special purposes so that associated roads did not have to be constructed to conventional highway standards. Each agency was directed to develop guidelines applicable to its needs while adhering to federal safety stipulations.[54]

Signaling a return to the status quo after the experimental ethos of the 1960s, the new park road standards task force was comprised entirely of design professionals. Nevertheless,

the ensuing report heaped praise on its predecessor and was equally adamant about the unique qualities of park roads. Earlier exhortations about leisurely driving and "lying lightly on the land" were repeated verbatim. Anti-automotive sentiments and high-tech transportation fancies were excised, but the 1984 update echoed its antecedent in asserting: "Ideally, perhaps no road would be permitted to violate or despoil the sanctity of park resources." Since national parks existed "in a "world of modern technology," however, "the encroachment of a system of public park roads" was the inevitable result of Congress's mandate to provide for public enjoyment. Reiterating long-standing principles, the 1984 guidelines advised that park roads were intended to provide an "enjoyable and informative experience" rather than simply move visitors from place to place and that they should be "developed with extreme care and sensitivity to the terrain." To fulfill these goals, their design should enforce a relaxed pace, exhibit high aesthetic values, and create a "continuing sense of intimacy" with their natural or historic surroundings.[55]

Like its predecessor, the 1984 publication noted that the dramatic increase in visitation was both "a profound threat to park values" and an opportunity to bring visitors into greater harmony with the natural world. This challenge was complicated by even greater crowding, the escalating size and popularity of recreational vehicles, and the increasing prevalence of tour buses that were too long and heavy for most park roads. The 1984 edition was a much more technical document, directed more toward design professionals than the general public. Poetic exhortations and punchy illustrations gave way to engineering diagrams and tables. The latest engineering standards formed the basis of most calculations, but the need for flexibility was emphasized throughout. Maximum speed was raised to 45 mph, and superintendents were empowered to increase this as they saw fit. Width, curvature, and other values were predicated on the design speed, terrain, and expected use of individual roads. The revision

provided mixed messages on the need to upgrade older roads to meet contemporary expectations. A statement that designs that had been appropriate for earlier conditions "may no longer be adequate" appeared to justify improvements, but the report also maintained that even when they failed to meet current standards, older park roads were "capable in most instances of providing safe, useful service" with minimal alteration. It also noted that reconstruction to modern standards could be "prohibitively expensive and environmentally destructive." As in earlier periods, determining what conditions were unacceptable and how to address them generated controversies that reflected professional biases, institutional agendas, and personal predilections. The potential for disagreement increased as historic preservation concerns compounded aesthetic and ecological agendas.[56]

Unlike its antecedent, the 1984 edition presented the driving experience in a positive light.

Rather than excoriate automobile culture and assail the impact of road development, the new guidelines cast park driving as a constructive activity that was both a means to an end and an end in itself. "It enables one visitor to reach his goal," the report declared. "For another, it is a goal." This was particularly true for celebrated examples such as Skyline Drive and Going-to-the-Sun Highway, where the roads were their park's premier attractions. The general public had long embraced this observation, but as the report proudly proclaimed, roads constructed during the "Golden Age" of NPS development had attained the status of "internationally recognized cultural resources." This bureaucratic formulation reflected a major reconceptualization of the relationship between parks, roads, and American culture. During the agency's early years, equating antiquated roads with hallowed artifacts would have been regarded as the height of folly. Sporadic pleas to save a few

National Park Roads

"old-time" examples were swept aside in the rush to embrace the automobile. The same was true of the postwar era. Neither modernization advocates nor their environmentalist opponents entertained thoughts of historic preservation. Harold Bradley's and David Brower's praise for older roads was based on their experiential qualities and visitor-deflecting functions, not on their stature as icons of American achievement. For antiroad advocates, the addition of ecological concerns in the 1960s compounded their status as embodiments of evil; countering their impact was the equivalent of environmental exorcism. Not only had the ecological fervor begun to abate by the 1980s, but the passage of time afforded enough perspective to understand that national park roads were not simply aesthetic accomplishments, technological feats, or environmental errors but historic artifacts embodying important aspects of American history.

The shift from vitriol to veneration was rooted in academic trends, popular predilections, and bureaucratic agendas. As the twentieth century drew to a close, many Americans grew nostalgic for the halcyon days of automobile culture, romanticizing the period before interstate highways exerted their homogenizing influences and rising gas prices and increased environmental awareness complicated the equation. Initial attention focused on icons such as the Lincoln Highway and Route 66, but interest expanded to encompass virtually every aspect of the automobile-oriented landscape. The growth of fields like environmental history and vernacular architecture, along with the broadening scope of traditional art history, encouraged the study of landscapes that were neither as conspicuously "artistic" nor as technologically complex as the canals and bridges that engaged engineering historians. With landscape architects continuing to play a prominent role in park affairs, considerable attention was focused on the profession's role in shaping the National Park System, including their influence on roads and related features. Beyond their significance to highway engineering and landscape architecture, park roads bore witness to historic events and social trends ranging from the automobile's influence on American culture to the Great Depression, the New Deal, the Baby Boom, and the rising tide of environmental awareness. Although opinions differed about the implications, there was no denying that the automobile-oriented national park vacation played a prominent role in twentieth-century American

life and that the roads created to facilitate this phenomenon were physical embodiments of the nation's cultural heritage.[57]

On the bureaucratic front, the increased emphasis on the historical significance of park roads reflected the National Historic Preservation Act's stipulation that properties more than fifty years old had to be considered for inclusion on the National Register of Historic Places if federal funds were used in their alteration. National Register evaluations proliferated as products of the "Golden Age" of park road development crossed this threshold. In 1983 Going-to-the-Sun Road became one of the first park tour roads to be listed on the National Register. Yellowstone embarked on ambitious study of its road system, which led to multiple National Register listings in the 1990s. The parkways of the national capital region also elicited attention, as did prewar roads throughout the system. In 1997 Going-to-the-Sun Road became the first national park road to achieve National Historic Landmark status. In a related effort with greater emphasis on visual documentation, the National Park Service's Historic American Engineering Record (HAER) surveyed dozens of park roads and parkways between 1988 and 2001, producing more than four thousand photographs, approximately five hundred drawings, and detailed design and construction histories. In addition to creating archival documentation, the program raised awareness of the unique character and historic significance of park roads through a 1997 exhibition at the National Building Museum, brochures distributed at various parks, a portfolio of drawings, and articles in academic and cultural resource management journals. To assist more directly with the rehabilitation of park roads, the NPS Park Historic Structures and Cultural Landscape Program began developing reports combining historical research with specific treatment recommendations.[58]

Another important factor in the rising awareness of historic preservation concerns was that many park roads were showing their age. Pavements and road beds were deteriorating, guard walls crumbling, drainage disintegrating, and bridges undergoing scrutiny for structural stability. Some of the damage could be attributed to inadequate maintenance budgets, but even under the best of circumstances, roads constructed during the classic era of park road development were approaching or exceeding their expected service limits. Many park roads were subject to

ABOVE, TOP Rockslide on Going-to-the-Sun Road, 2013.

ABOVE, MIDDLE Deteriorated guard wall prior to rehabilitation, Going-to-the-Sun Road, Glacier National Park, 2004.

ABOVE, BOTTOM Larger modern vehicles pose problems on historic roads, Glacier Point Road, Yosemite National Park, 2001.

OPPOSITE National Building Museum exhibition, *Lying Lightly on the Land: Building America's National Park Roads and Parkways*, installation photograph, 1997.

harsh conditions, ranging from landslides, floods, and avalanches to temperature extremes, geologic instability, and geothermal activity. Roads in Hawaii Volcanoes National Park were engulfed in lava flows. Heavier vehicles and higher traffic volumes accelerated the damage, especially with the proliferation of commercial bus tours and mammoth RVs. The changing nature of park transportation exacerbated safety concerns, especially in regard to historic guard walls. Not only were older barriers designed to withstand lower impacts, but they were employed more sparingly in the early years, when motorists were expected to exercise greater discretion and liability concerns were less prevalent. Similar questions were raised about pavement width, curvature, intersection arrangements, and the distance between the road's edge and natural or man-made features. New engineering standards required greater separation or "clear zones" between motorists and potentially dangerous obstructions, including the rocky ledges and native vegetation that played important roles in establishing park road character. In some cases, guard walls and bridge abutments themselves were cast as safety hazards. The combination of deteriorating conditions, heavier traffic loads, and changing engineering guidelines created a new round of challenges. From the FHWA's perspective, the obvious solution was to rebuild outdated roads in accordance with contemporary specifications. Preservationists preferred to repair damaged

features or replace them with similar dimensions, designs, and materials. As a result, NPS staff increasingly found itself at odds with FHWA engineers over historic preservation concerns rather than ecological issues.[59]

Both sides expressed eagerness to resolve their differences, but as with the initiation of the NPS-BPR partnership, the integration of historic preservation goals with engineering imperatives did not proceed without significant friction. Solutions that seemed self-evident to engineers could strike preservationists as needlessly destructive, while preservationists' demands often made engineers cringe about safety concerns and cost considerations. Tensions arose over issues such as pavement widths, the architectural treatment of bridges, the height and composition of guard walls, and the extent to which curves, clearances, and sight distances should be increased or retained. As in earlier eras, personal predilections proved as important as professional affiliations, underscoring that road design remained as much an art as a science. Just as 1930s BPR engineers could be as aesthetically attuned as their NPS counterparts, some FHWA officials expressed profound respect for historical values. This was particularly true of senior engineers who had participated in park projects early in their careers. Federal Lands Highway Program administrator Tom Edick and his deputy Allen Burden staunchly supported historic documentation programs and associated initiatives. By the

same token, the NPS was not monolithic in its embrace of preservation principles. Park superintendents might prioritize efficiency and litigation avoidance over preservation values, while some design professionals relished the opportunity to reinterpret park road design in light of contemporary concerns. The decentralization of authority in NPS management structures enhanced the potential for inconsistency. Major variations were generally rooted in master plan directives, but superintendents and staff held considerable sway. This was particularly true in the early years of preservation awareness, when historic character was defined more in terms of engineered structures than broader landscape values. In similar fashion, FHWA regional offices varied considerably in their willingness to depart from standard practices. Preservation-oriented approaches endorsed in one region could be rejected in another depending on engineers' tendencies to view AASHTO standards as rigid specifications or flexible guidelines. The diversity of perspectives created challenges for engineers and preservation advocates alike. When disagreements proved irreconcilable, the NPS could request a "design exception," which documented the underlying considerations in case of subsequent litigation. This approach was often unpopular with NPS staff forced to justify extraordinary measures and could be frowned upon by engineers who considered consistency a fundamental tenet of highway safety. In the most extreme impasses, FHWA engineers reversed the dynamic wielded by Wirth and Hartzog, letting it be known that funding would not be forthcoming for projects entailing preservation measures they believed would compromise safety or engineering standards.

Significant gains were made in resolving tensions between the two perspectives. This progress was due in part to the improved ability of preservationists to understand engineers' concerns and communicate their priorities in technical terms and in part to the engineering establishment's growing willingness to explore creative solutions to meeting broader safety goals. The FWHA 1997 publication *Flexibility in Highway Design* underscored that AASHTO guidelines afforded considerable leeway to adapt general recommendations to individual situations. The emphasis on flexibility accorded with the transportation community's endorsement of Context Sensitive Design, which promoted adaption to site-specific considerations rather than rote applications of engineering criteria. The ensuing embrace of Context Sensitive Solutions provided additional flexibility, since it advocated broadly conceived measures extending beyond the realm of physical design. From a park road perspective, these might include lower speed limits, one-way traffic designations, and vehicle-size restrictions as alternatives to pavement widening or curve easement. Length limits on Going-to-the-Sun Road and proscriptions on commercial tour buses in some locations exemplified this approach. Highway engineers also became more receptive to the argument that roads that did not meet current standards were not inherently unsafe unless their accident history suggested otherwise. Given the rarity of serious accidents on park roads, it made little sense to conduct massive construction campaigns to cure problems that did not exist. Problem areas should be identified and addressed, but wholesale improvements were unwarranted and economically unjustified, especially in an age of shrinking budgets. While couched in the contemporary rubric of risk analysis, this strategy harkened back to the recommendations of Albright, Goodwin, Bradley, and Brower. Another preservation-oriented trend was the transportation profession's acknowledgment of the benefits of "traffic-calming" strategies aimed at inducing motorists to slow down through restrictions on pavement width and other visually prominent

deterrents. This "revolutionary" planning concept had long been a fundamental tenet of park road design, not just for safety purposes but on aesthetic and philosophical grounds.[60]

As with the initial NPS-BPR arrangement, the maturing relationship between engineers and preservationists often produced a strong sense of partnership, with both sides embracing the opportunity to develop creative solutions to complex challenges. Engineers learned that preservationists were not simply impractical obstructionists and preservationists discovered that engineers shared their aesthetic sensibilities and appreciation for the accomplishments of early road builders. The growing spirit of cooperation and search for mutually agreeable alternatives were evident in attempts to resolve the ongoing debate over safety barriers. Given the prominent role that guard walls and guard rails played in establishing the visual character of park roadways, preservationists were reluctant to see them replaced with standardized substitutes such as steel beams or jersey-barrier-style reinforced concrete. Engineers countered that exact replacements would be not only inordinately expensive but also too insubstantial to meet modern needs. The FHWA and NPS collaborated to develop stone-faced concrete-core guard walls and steel-backed timber guard rails that both echoed historical appearances and passed rigorous crash-testing procedures. Since applying stone facing was an expensive process, especially when new safety guidelines called for significant additions, a solid concrete model was also developed. Specially designed forms imprinted masonry patterns and the concrete was tinted in natural stone hues. Sharp-eyed observers might note that the patterns were repetitive, the surfaces suspiciously uniform, and the overall dimensions larger than historic predecessors, but few motorists were likely to discern the difference. Simulated stone was also embraced as an economical substitute in the replacement or rehabilitation of culverts, retaining walls, and bridge abutments. Strict preservationists considered the practice regrettable, but economics, ease of construction, and FHWA endorsement often outweighed the appeal of traditional materials and techniques. Simulated stone was also quicker to construct than conventional masonry. This could be an important factor when dealing with short working seasons or emergency situations like the aftermath of the 1997 Yosemite flood, which destroyed hundreds of yards of guard wall on the

park's busiest approach. Many parks continued to use real stonework at parking areas and other places where visitors might discover the deception. In other efforts to resolve safety barrier tensions, the NPS collaborated with federal highway engineers to conduct a system-wide study of safety barriers and prepare detailed guidance for guard rail replacement on Blue Ridge Parkway. The NPS also began to place greater emphasis on analyzing accident data to document the system's overall safety and pinpoint where improvements were necessary. A 2008 study revealed that the highest accident rate occurred in parking lots of popular destinations, with minimal damage to people or property. Serious accidents and fatalities were generally associated with illegal speeds, vehicles crossing center lines, and other operator errors. Although park road accidents attracted media coverage, the overall incidence was significantly lower than on comparable rural roads.[61]

Fittingly, one of the first national parks to undertake a comprehensive road rehabilitation plan with explicit attention to historic preservation was Yellowstone. Due to its age and popularity, Yellowstone exemplified the challenge of adapting historic roads to modern demands. The park's 1974 General Management Plan highlighted the road system's insufficiencies, and concerns multiplied as conditions continued to deteriorate and traffic pressures increased. By 1988 the FHWA deemed less than a third of the park's roads to be in reasonably good condition. Much of the pavement was severely rutted, potholed, or cracked. FHWA engineers insisted that in many locations complete reconstruction was the only reasonable option. This would allow them to rebuild the road foundation while easing curves and widening the pavement to meet modern standards and accommodate the growing number of oversized vehicles. The rising popularity of bicycle touring created additional pressure since most roads were too narrow for cyclists and large vehicles to pass comfortably. Motorists stopping to view wildlife created additional hazards and congestion. Visitors, park personnel, and FHWA engineers all complained about the poor condition of the park roads and extreme congestion during peak visitation periods.[62]

Although it would have been possible to reconstruct the roads with minor changes in width and alignment, park officials agreed that comprehensive improvements were necessary. At the same time, they acknowledge the importance of

The expensive and technically complex undertaking underscored the degree to which the NPS and FHWA were committed to rehabilitating the landmark roadway in a manner that reconciled safety concerns with historic preservation.

retaining the roads' historic character. In 1992 the NPS, the FHWA, and the Wyoming State Historic Preservation Office agreed on a Parkwide Road Improvement Plan aimed at improving safety and efficiency without compromising historical values. The extensive historical research conducted during the late 1980s and early 1990s was intended to create a documentary record of existing conditions and provide guidelines to ensure that historic qualities were retained. The NPS and FHWA went to great lengths to preserve or reconstruct individual structures such as bridges, guard walls, and culvert headwalls. Simulated stone was often used when the originals were beyond repair or additions mandated by safety requirements or new excavation. Traditional masonry was restricted to areas where visitors came close enough to notice the difference. Park staff developed detailed procedures to address vegetation management and construction impacts. In consultation with FHWA engineers, the NPS decided to adopt a basic road width of 22 feet flanked by 3-foot paved shoulders. Park officials emphasized that the widening was limited to the shoulders and would improve safety by making it easier to pass bicyclists and

wildlife-watchers. Convincing the engineers to go 1 foot narrower than the maximum allotted by the 1984 Park Road Standards was considered a significant achievement. Since the existing shoulders were mostly unimproved gravel, many sections were 6 feet wider than their predecessors. This represented a significant increase when the existing pavement ranged from 20 to 22 feet. The controversial Tioga Road segment had entailed a 20-foot-wide pavement with 2- to 3-foot unpaved shoulders. The 1958 and 1968 standards allowed for 22-foot travel surfaces on high-volume roads but called for unpaved 3-foot shoulders. In many locations the authorized reconstruction entailed the easing of curves and expansion of sight distances and clear zones. These measures often required significant excavation, especially in mountainous country where slopes had to be angled back for stability. The wider, straighter roadways and expanded sightlines made the pavement a more dominant component of the forward view, while the expanded clear zones and broader cuts reduced the sense of intimacy with the surroundings.[63]

Some preservationists, landscape architects, and even engineers believed these changes compromised

ABOVE Going-to-the-Sun Road rehabilitation, Glacier National Park, 2004.

the road's historic character and encouraged speeds that were incompatible with park values. State and national preservation authorities concurred with the park's assessment that the reconstruction achieved the desired results. The difference in opinion reflected divergent views about the defining characteristics of historic roads. The official position was that Yellowstone roads had changed so much throughout the course of history that they should be viewed as evolutionary elements rather than static entities. Kingman had dramatically upgraded Norris's road, Chittenden had widened and straightened Kingman's, and NPS landscape architects and BPR engineers continued the progression in the Mather-Albright era. From this perspective, a well-designed contemporary park road was a more authentic embodiment of Yellowstone's heritage than a continuously evolving design frozen at an arbitrary point in time. Since road width, curvature, pavement composition, and the location and design of safety barriers changed throughout the park's history, it was more important to identify and adhere to general design principles than retain existing configurations. The approved guidelines stipulated that the

reconstructed road lie "gently on the landscape," exhibit "elements of grace in its alignment," and include "architecturally pleasing structures" designed to harmonize with their surroundings. Alterations to accommodate evolving demands were admissible as long as the end product was able to "evoke a feeling that it is a park road and an image that is distinct from those found outside the boundary of the park." The reconstructed roadways were undeniably more attractive than conventional highways, epitomizing the adaptation of traditional park road design principles to modern traffic demands and safety concerns. They wound through the landscape in visually pleasing serpentine curves, afforded compelling views, and were amply protected with sturdy rustic guard walls. While they combined increased efficiency with landscape sensitivity and environmentally conscious attributes earlier designers would not have considered, the expanded dimensions produced a sense of spaciousness and flowing movement that had more in common with modern parkways than with the cramped and crooked configurations that confounded hurried drivers but engendered greater appreciation for the natural environment

and the experiences of mid-twentieth-century motorists. Skeptics continued to express reservations, but numerous segments of the project received FHWA design awards. A succession of superintendents endorsed the approach as essential for accommodating Yellowstone's large automobile-dependent crowds. The question of whether Yellowstone's Parkwide Improvement Plan constituted a skillful synthesis of traditional park road aesthetics and contemporary concerns or an unwarranted sacrifice of historic park road values continued to engender debate among NPS and FHWA professionals. In an adaption of the Yellowstone approach, Grand Canyon's Hermit Road was widened a similarly significant 19 to 24 feet in 2006–8, but limiting the design speed to 30 mph minimized changes to existing curvature and topography.[64]

An equally ambitious project that elicited unambiguous acclaim as an exemplary union of highway engineering and historic preservation was the rehabilitation of Glacier's Going-to-the-Sun Road. The iconic road had been subjected to rockfalls, avalanches, drainage problems, and destructive freezing-and-thawing cycles since its completion in 1932. Hundreds of thousands of vehicles traversing the Continental Divide in a compressed three- to four-month tourist season generated additional wear and tear while making it difficult to conduct repairs without politically untenable road closures. By the late 1980s there were increasing concerns that retaining walls and approximately 43,000 linear feet of guard wall were dangerously compromised. The road itself was in poor condition as were associated features such as the Triple Arch Culvert and the steep slopes above and below the route. These worries were confirmed by geotechnical analysis. In 1990 the FHWA insisted that all historic guard walls would have to be reconstructed to AASHTO standards. An impasse ensued when NPS officials protested that the change would destroy the road's character and compromise historic views. Even the newer stone-clad concrete-core approach was considered inappropriate due to its increased height and bulk. After extensive and often contentious negotiations failed to solve the problem, the FHWA and NPS created a special team to make one more attempt at finding a mutually agreeable solution. They arrived at a strategy that mimicked the historic conformation but gained strength by filling the cavities

ABOVE Rehabilitated Going-to-the-Sun Road, retaining prior width and curvature, Glacier National Park, 2011.

ABOVE Wawona Tunnel view before and after vista clearing, Yosemite National Park.

between hand-laid inner and outer stone surfaces with heavily reinforced concrete. When crash tests proved the design could withstand impacts up to 35 mph, the FHWA granted approval on the condition that the NPS post and reinforce appropriate speed limits. Since widening and straightening the road would have been inordinately expensive and environmentally destructive as well as historically untenable, vehicle size was restricted to eliminate the dangers posed by large buses and RVs. Problems with retaining walls, slope failure, and roadbed deterioration were addressed with a range of visually compatible stabilization techniques. Where additional support was needed, the road and guard walls were constructed on concrete slabs anchored by piles driven into bedrock. Hand-laid stone veneer was applied to exposed concrete surfaces.[65]

The rehabilitation of Going-to-the-Sun Road took longer and was exponentially more expensive than its original construction. The planning process alone extended over a dozen years, from initial historical research to the requisite Environmental Impact Assessment and execution of detailed design drawings. The construction period was prolonged by the short working season and stringent limitations on road closures mandated by the desire to limit the impact on visitors and tourism interests. Estimates prepared in 2002 calculated the ultimate cost in the range of $140 million to $170 million. By 2006, the total was projected to top $200 million. Savings associated with lowered

construction costs during the subsequent recession brought the figures back in line with original estimates and allowed for a revised completion date of 2017. Even considering the rate of inflation, this remained a far cry from Goodwin's $600,000 allotment or the original $2–3 million price tag. The expensive and technically complex undertaking underscored the degree to which the NPS and FHWA were committed to rehabilitating the landmark roadway in a manner that reconciled safety concerns with historic preservation and reinforced a partnership that began the original construction of this iconic roadway.[66]

Park road preservation concerns were not limited to engineered features. Vegetation patterns along park roads changed significantly over time. Planned views were often obscured by unchecked growth, carefully composed contrasts of meadow and forest disappeared, and invasive species overwhelmed native plant communities. Even in cases like Blue Ridge Parkway, where detailed diagrams delineated desired effects, it was difficult to keep undesired growth in check. Overgrown vegetation was generally a product of insufficient maintenance budgets, but in some cases it reflected the transition from a landscape design perspective to an ecological mind-set. Traditional landscape architects had no qualms about manipulating vegetation to enhance scenic enjoyment, but prioritizing ecological processes made selective cutting untenable on scientific and philosophical grounds. The most

conspicuous conflict entailed the celebrated vista from Yosemite's Wawona Tunnel overlook. By the 1990s, large trees that had grown up since the road's completion blocked much of the view. Dispatching native conifers to please sightseeing motorists was a provocative prospect in a park where ecological principles held sway. After considerable discussion, permission was granted to restore the historic vista as part of a comprehensive rehabilitation of the overlook. By the end of 2008, the trees had come down, the vista was restored, and the overlook outfitted with historically compatible walls and walkways to enhance pedestrian safety. Growing appreciation for cultural as well as natural landscape values led the park to develop a scenic vista management plan explicitly acknowledging the "need to restore the vistas that made Yosemite world famous and created memorable experiences for millions of inhabitants and visitors." Despite decades of efforts to deemphasize the automobile's impact, an associated survey revealed that 87 percent of visitors listed scenic driving as their primary activity. All but two dozen of the nearly two hundred vista points identified by a diverse range of respondents were located along historic roads. Underscoring the enduring appeal of traditional park tourism, the report concluded: "Scenic vistas along roadways are perhaps the most significant element for visitors partaking in sightseeing activities."[67]

The proposed rehabilitation of Yosemite's Tioga Road afforded the ultimate illustration of the sentiment that national park roads should be regarded as historically significant resources in their own right. A half million visitors a year were traveling the road by 2010, few of whom paid heed to posted speed limits. The road had some of the highest accident rates in the park, though the figures were not out of line with comparable rural highways. The average road width was essentially unchanged from Mission 66, with a 22-foot-wide travel way flanked by shoulders consisting of 1 foot of pavement supplemented by stabilized earth, narrowing in the controversial stretch above Lake Tenaya. Even the newer sections were showing their age. Pavement degradation, drainage deficiencies, and crumbling curbs were compounded by rampant roadside growth that limited sight distances and exacerbated by undersized and poorly configured parking. When the road first came up for National Register consideration in 1992, lingering sensitivities and failure to meet the

fifty-year threshold combined to prevent official recognition. Not only were historic roads held in higher esteem by 2010, but Mission 66 itself had been embraced as a significant contribution to NPS history. This time, park staff and public comments strongly supported preservation of existing characteristics. In a significant challenge to conventional engineering wisdom, the argument that road-widening inherently improved safety was explicitly rejected. Rehabilitation plans called for reconstructing the road to the same dimensions rather than the 24-foot travelway with 2- to 4-foot shoulders called for by current standards and employed in several other major parks. Drainage would be improved with designs and materials compatible with historical appearances. Roadside vegetation would be selectively thinned within 6 feet of the pavement rather than comprehensively cleared in a 10-foot swath. Reconfiguring the terrain and relocating guard walls and other structures to provide similar

clearance were deemed unacceptable. Parking areas would be improved, along with associated signage and sight distances. Additional efforts would be made to encourage compliance with posted speed limits. Although the technical aspects were not as complex or costly as those of Going-to-the-Sun Road, the short working season was projected to prolong the process until 2018. In the meantime, a reevaluation of the road's National Register eligibility led to formal acknowledgment of the Tioga Road's historic status. However belated, this recognition was well deserved. From its pragmatic nineteenth-century origins to its pivotal role in twentieth-century efforts to embrace and contest the automobile's influence to its apotheosis as an object of veneration in its own right, the Tioga Road epitomized evolving attitudes about the nature and purpose of national park roads.[68]

ABOVE Planned view of Tenaya Lake and surroundings, Tioga Road, Yosemite National Park, 2014.

Looking Down the Road

EPILOGUE

A s the NPS approached its golden anniversary, Interior Secretary Stewart Udall proclaimed that despite ongoing changes within the National Park System and America as a whole, "The accomplishments of the past are not only a source of pride—they are also a source of guidance for the future." American society has continued to evolve, as have the parks themselves, but Udall's remarks continue to resonate. From the earliest attempts to translate eastern tourist practices to the rugged western landscapes through twentieth-century efforts to harness the potential of the automobile age to current social, environmental, and economic challenges, park road builders have adapted historical precedents to evolving conditions. Whether working with picks and shovels, diesel-powered machinery, or digital media, they have showcased signature scenery through minimally intrusive development while leaving the greater part of most parks in undisturbed condition. The commitment to balancing preservation and access remained constant, but ideas about the best means to achieve this goal changed over time.[1]

At the beginning, everyone from Frederick Law Olmsted to railroad tycoons and the traveling public agreed that access was the highest priority. The earliest park roads were crude affairs cobbled together with minuscule budgets and primitive technology, but they played a vital role in transferring ideas about scenic tourism and the social value of public parks to the wonderlands of the American West. By the turn of the twentieth century, sophisticated stagecoach systems sped sightseers along expanded networks displaying natural splendors and engineering achievements such as Yellowstone's Golden Gate Viaduct and Chittenden Bridge. The automobile's ascendency brought this era to a close while introducing new challenges and possibilities. In 1916, the newly formed National Park Service embraced motor tourism as a means of increasing visitation and building support for the enlargement and protection of the National Park System. The agency's engineers and landscape architects adapted traditional design precedents to the motor age, forming a partnership with the Bureau of Public Roads to enhance their capabilities. Signature achievements such as Going-to-the-Sun Road, Skyline Drive, and Blue Ridge Parkway garnered widespread acclaim and expanded both the size and composition of visiting public. The strategy proved so successful that the NPS was accused of neglecting the preservation side of the equation. External criticism and internal concerns prompted renewed emphasis on preservation priorities. Significant projects were curtailed and stringent constraints set in new parks, an increasing number of which were largely auto-free. After World War II, the expansion of leisure time, improvements to cross-country highways, and the expanding rate of automobile ownership produced widespread demands to upgrade roads and other facilities. The Mission 66 program made major strides in this regard, but broadening concerns for wilderness values and rising environmental awareness engendered criticism from an increasingly influential cohort of conservationists and concerned citizens. NPS leaders insisted they were holding development to the minimum consonant with public use, but revised guidelines and ecological agendas bolstered by new federal regulations set additional limits on development. The pendulum swung further toward natural resource protection during the 1970s. Many observers—including a significant portion of NPS personnel—cast park roads as the root of evil rather than the realization of long-held ideals about the social value of public parks. Growing appreciation for the cultural history of national parks softened this stance during the 1980s–1990s, while visitor pushback and tourism industry objections created pressure for moderation. The expansion and diversification of the National Park System helped ease tensions, providing more options at both ends of the spectrum. Throughout these transitions, the automobile-dependent general public never wavered in its enthusiasm.

Motor tourism continues to afford the most popular means of enjoying the National Park System's myriad offerings. Some may interpret this as evidence that the NPS erred in embracing the automobile and developing infrastructure to accommodate it. A cursory review of visitor counts and construction statistics appears to bear this out. The National Park System experienced a record 292,800,082 visitors in 2014, surpassing the previous high set in 1987. This was more than double the number of visitors recorded in 1966 and a far cry from the 326,506 at the agency's founding. Two of the three busiest areas were the automobile-oriented Great Smoky Mountains National Park and Blue Ridge Parkway. Natchez Trace and George Washington Memorial Parkways were also in the top ten, though it is difficult to determine the percentage of visits that were purely recreational. Road mileage exhibited similarly striking growth, multiplying tenfold since the mid-1920s. As of 2012, the National Park System

contained 5,500 miles of paved roads, of which 1,100 miles were parkways. There were also 4,100 miles of unpaved roads. These increases appear astronomical, but the National Park System expanded at an even greater rate. The impact was spread over more than four hundred areas encompassing approximately 80 million acres, more than half of which was officially designated wilderness. The amount of roadless terrain without formal wilderness status experienced similar growth. Not only was Stephen Mather's promise to avoid "gridironing" the parks upheld, but the proportion of roads to untrammeled wilderness actually decreased over the past century. Popular destinations are undeniably overcrowded at peak periods, but the NPS's commitment to reducing the reliance on private automobiles resulted in travel restrictions in many parks and significant investments in alternative transportation. As of 2012, there were 131 transit systems operating in sixty-six parks servicing an annual ridership of approximately 30 million passengers. Options ranged from shuttle services in large western parks to inner-city circulators, the Cuyahoga Valley Scenic Railroad, and ferries in Alaska, Michigan, Florida, and other locations. During the last four decades, the Intermodal Surface Transportation Efficiency Act (ISTEA) legislation and its successors, TEA-21, and SAFETEA-LU, funded significant increases in nonmotorized trail mileage, much of which catered to the renewed interest in recreational cycling. All told, NPS trail mileage is approximately 18,000—more than double the extent of all roads combined.[2]

Many who question NPS road development are unaware of the historical association between

roads and parks or the degree to which driving served as a motivation for park development long before the first steam-powered automobiles lumbered into Yosemite Valley. Earlier critics often held more balanced and historically informed views on the relationships between roads and parks. From Bob Marshall and Aldo Leopold to Benton Mackaye and David Brower, objections centered on the nature and extent of road development, not the essential value of park roads. As both NPS officials and their adversaries understood, improved access played an essential role in the preservation process. By allowing people to enjoy parks with reasonable ease, the combination of improved roads and widespread automobile ownership transformed the national park experience from an esoteric pleasure into a prominent component of the American experience, creating a powerful constituency for their protection. The challenge lay in deciding which areas should remain free from development and the extent to which park roads should incorporate evolving engineering standards or retain the traditional insistence on "lying lightly on the land." Despite several highly publicized debates, decisions about the balance between preservation and access almost always favored the former. Even when they were publicly at odds, NPS officials frequently welcomed conservationists' complaints as counterweights to the demands of highway engineers, commercial interests, and their elected allies. The social and ecological foment of the 1960s reinforced negative perceptions of park road development, but more measured assessments reemerged and predominate today. With environmental theorists questioning the absolutism of earlier distinctions between

nature and culture, moreover, the NPS's contention that properly developed park roads promoted positive experiences of the natural world has gained renewed credibility. Even the long-standing equation of wilderness with roadlessness has lost its aura of infallibility. When the Alaskan National Interest Lands Conservation Act of 1980 designated millions of acres of wilderness, it relaxed strictures on roads and vehicles to accommodate the demands of Native Americans and other Alaskan residents.[3]

The relationship between roads and parks continues to evolve in response to changing social, technological, and environmental factors. Major additions to the NPS road system are likely to be few and far between, but as the agency enters its second century, it faces many of the challenges that Mather and his associates encountered at the outset: financial uncertainties, technological transformations, and the need to attract broader and more diverse audiences. In a reprise of Depression-era developments, the American Recovery and Reinvestment Act of 2009 provided a $318 million boost that assisted road rehabilitation efforts and spurred progress on ongoing projects such as Foothills Parkway, but long-term funding prospects are uncertain. The cost of addressing deferred maintenance was calculated at $6.6 billion in 2012, at which time park road appropriations stood at $240 million a year. Reflecting a nationwide backlash against using transportation funding for broad-based amenities, Congress cut annual funding for park transit systems and related programs

by more than $60 million. With the maintenance backlog compounding, alternative transportation programs strapped for funds, and federal budgets shrinking, the disparity between needs and resources is as dramatic as it was when Mather and his allies pushed through the first major park roads bill and the period preceding Mission 66. As in the past, funding shortfalls reflect broader social and economic factors rather than antipathy toward NPS ideals. Despite widespread concern about the deteriorating condition of America's transportation infrastructure, Congress has been unable to devise a long-term solution to the growing disparity between the Highway Trust Fund's income and outlays. A series of stopgap measures have been implemented, but reduced allocations and the climate of uncertainty place increasing constraints on federal road-building activities. The faith that enfolding park roads into the federal highway budget would solve the agency's funding woes appears to have been misplaced. Earmarks have reemerged as a prominent component of the budget process, with the attendant uncertainties and political tradeoffs.[4]

Park road funding is only a portion of the economic picture. In the most pessimistic assessments, broader infrastructure disinvestment, rising fuel prices, and dwindling middle-class incomes could transform the classic driving vacation into a misty-eyed memory as remote from contemporary experience as nineteenth-century stagecoach travel. On the other hand, technological

National Park Roads

innovations could continue to reconcile traditional desires with evolving circumstances. Despite repeated predictions, the petroleum-based paradigm continues to belie reports of its imminent demise. New extraction technologies and dramatically enhanced fuel efficiency have prolonged the automobile age, for better or, some might say, for worse. The increasing capabilities of electrically powered vehicles are likely to extend the pastime of scenic driving beyond the fossil-fuel era. Given the manner in which the environmental benefits of wind farms and giant solar arrays have ameliorated their status as monumental machines in the garden, even the oft-criticized tramways and monorails may no longer be dismissed as scenery-scarring intrusions. Without changes to the fuel-tax-dependent Highway Trust Fund, however, the rise of more efficient technologies could dramatically reduce maintenance on the interstate highways that facilitated the surge in park visitation and continue to play a vital role today. If deteriorating conditions or rising fuel prices made cross-country motoring untenable, there could be a return to the earlier practice of traveling long distances by public conveyance and touring parks by some form of locally provided transportation. Depending on technological circumstances, environmental sensibilities, and social proclivities, national park visitors might make use of mass-transit systems, alternative-fuel shuttle buses, or independent electrical vehicles. The bike-share programs popping up in cities worldwide

might afford an option in some parks, at least for the physically fit and willing. Given the growing emphasis on sustainability, local sourcing, and artisanal practices, national park tourism might even revert to the formative years of horse-drawn transportation, bolstered, presumably, by advances in dust-laying and methane recovery procedures.

Climate change is another looming concern. Increasingly volatile weather patterns contributed to catastrophic flooding in Mount Rainier National Park in 2006 and Rocky Mountain in 2013 that closed park roads and cost millions of dollars to repair. Wildfires engendered by drought conditions destabilize hillsides, exacerbating erosion and increasing the potential for landslides that close or damage roads. Hurricane Irene's 2011 impact on East Coast parks was a minor prelude to the devastation wrought by Tropical Storm Sandy in 2012. Roads in Gateway National Recreation Area were undercut by roiling waters and buried under tons of sand. Bridges, docks, multiple-use trails, and ferry facilities sustained severe damage. Rising sea levels threaten roads in coastal parks, many of which are already endangered. The main road in Gulf Islands National Seashore clings to a shrinking spit of sand and is submerged by increasingly violent storms. Assateague Island's premier parking lot occupies a similarly precarious position. In both cases, scientifically based recommendations to abandon facilities succumbed to opposition from the visiting public and local businesses. Many challenges stem from decisions predating consideration of environmental impacts. Neither Yosemite's toll road builders, the Army Corps of Engineers, nor the NPS-BPR design teams of the 1930s contemplated such concerns. In Delaware Water Gap National Recreation Area and other low-lying locations, roads dating as far back as colonial times are subject to repeated inundation.

Many environmentally based challenges are of more recent vintage. The NPS is collaborating with the State of Florida to reconfigure the Tamiami Trail, a mid-twentieth-century highway adjacent to Everglades National Park. The existing road was raised above the surrounding wetlands on an earthen berm that acted as a dam, causing a host of ecological issues. The $190 million project is designed to restore the natural water flow by replacing the causeway with a 2.6-mile-long bridge. To reduce the environmental impact of a more traditional park road, the NPS and FHWA relocated the Gibbon Canyon section of

Yellowstone's Grand Loop from its riverside alignment to a new route through woodlands above the canyon rim. Engineers were as eager to eliminate substandard curves and other technical shortcomings as environmentalists were to rescue the river from pollution and mechanized intrusions. The pavement and associated structures were removed, the river bottom rehabilitated, and a scenic overlook and multi-use trail developed in its stead. The new roadway was a paragon of contemporary park road design, with sinuous curves flowing gracefully in harmony with the surrounding landscape. While the Gibbon Canyon project presented a striking alliance of engineering agendas and environmental sensibilities, its historical implications were less sanguine. In a classic illustration of park road design principles, Chittenden had moved the road into the canyon to enliven a long stretch of repetitive scenery and allow visitors to enjoy the sensation of traveling in close proximity to the picturesque river. The relocation eradicated this aesthetic masterstroke and eliminated a significant component of the Grand Loop experience. A similarly well-intentioned effort to restore natural conditions in the Grant Village section of Sequoia National Park resulted in the removal of 282 buildings and more than 1 million square feet of asphalt. Again, the environmental benefits entailed tradeoffs in terms of historical values and long-standing social practices. For families who had enjoyed the accommodations, sometimes for multiple generations, the sense of loss was significant.[5]

In another sign of the times, the NPS has devoted increasing attention to overcoming social barriers to access. Although early NPS officials were justly proud of their achievements in transforming national parks from elite retreats into playgrounds for the motoring masses, twentieth-century visitors were overwhelmingly white and predominantly middle class. As the nation becomes more ethnically diverse, the mandate to provide for public enjoyment has taken on additional connotations. Today's NPS leaders understand that improving access is not just a matter of facilitating physical transportation but of building bridges to underrepresented communities. Numerous initiatives have been developed to provide additional parks, heritage areas, and historic sites catering to a broader range of cultural groups, as well as to enhance the appeal of existing offerings. As in Mather's day, idealism and pragmatism are deeply intertwined. While the emphasis on inclusivity reflects deeply

ABOVE Participants in "Ticket to Ride" program aimed at encouraging young visitors, 2014.   **ABOVE** Google Street View of Wawona Tunnel Overlook, Yosemite National Park, 2014.

held ethical convictions, it is also a matter of institutional survival. With the average age and ethnicity of current visitors departing dramatically from demographic projections, expanding the NPS audience to include younger and more diverse populations is necessary to ensure ongoing political and financial support.[6]

Just as Mather targeted the burgeoning population of automobile owners, current strategies seek to capitalize on contemporary technological trends. Along with increasing the park system's relevance to diverse audiences, the NPS is dramatically expanding its Internet outreach through enhanced website offerings, expanded social media presence, park-related smart-phone applications, and other tricks of the digital trade. Although these activities have become standard practice, especially for institutions seeking to appeal to the coveted Millennial demographic, the enthusiasm for digital technologies has intriguing implications in terms of the relationships between nature and technology, communal versus individual experiences, and the balance between preservation and access. With the explosion of digital technologies, it is now possible to "visit" national parks through stationary web-cams, vast stores of still images, and amateur and professional streaming video. Google Street View allows people to tour park roads from the comforts of their couch or coffee shop. The projected

proliferation of drones opens up even broader realms of possibilities, though current policies prohibit their operation. Would virtual visitors be restricted to existing corridors, or would they be allowed to range free? The former would translate the scripted sequences of traditional park road design into a new medium; the latter would cater to the contemporary emphasis on tailoring options to individual preferences. Just as the invention of the more comfortable carriage influenced the shift from static to dynamic modes of landscape perception that informed park road aesthetics, digital technologies could effect a major transformation in landscape appreciation. Making it possible for individuals to plot their own course through space and time both empowers virtual visitors and deprives them of the assistance of designers conversant with compositional strategies and familiar with the lay of the land. Few armchair explorers are likely to emulate the sophisticated interplay of fortissimo and pianissimo that Stanley Abbott embedded in the Blue Ridge Parkway experience.

With digital culture redefining such seemingly straightforward concepts as "visit," "access," and "preservation," the dual mandate of the National Park Service's Organic Act could take on new connotations. For citizens of the digital age, the information highway might constitute the perfect park road, given its ability to dramatically expand

access with minimal impact on physical resources. Given the increasing prevalence of virtual visits, twentieth-century critiques of the automobile's impact on the national park experience may evolve into debates about the benefits and liabilities of virtual interactions with natural and historic landscapes. Traditionalists might denounce the visual emphasis, fleeting nature, and absence of direct physical contact, but similar charges were leveled against automobile tourism. Virtual visiting would also seem to eliminate the communal bonding experience long touted as a social benefit of public parks, though Internet enthusiasts maintain that community formation is no longer dependent on physical proximity. Digital and conventional park experiences need not be mutually exclusive. Just as twentieth-century park advocates viewed automobile tourism as a means of engendering affections that would lead to more traditional modes of scenic appreciation, virtual visits could be the ideal vehicle for encouraging twenty-first-century Americans to exchange plasma screens for park roads or unpaved paths. For Millennials obsessed with authenticity and the pursuit of highly individualized experiences, digital access could allow them to "curate" more personally fulfilling physical visits. Given the pervasive impact of social media sharing, these ostensibly unique experiences could quickly go viral, triggering swarms of Yosemite-like congestion before giving way to the next Internet sensation.

When Sierra Club leader Harold Bradley declared that park roads determined park history, he was emphasizing the importance of imminent design decisions. Tracing the evolution of national park roads demonstrates the broader implications of Bradley's assertion. Throughout its history, the NPS has tried to strike a balance between the concerns of those who believed it was building too many roads and the demands of those who thought it was building too few. More detailed matters of design and location also generated intense disputes. Each generation built on its predecessor's successes and failures in addressing an expanding array of social, environmental, and technological challenges. Despite occasional setbacks, this process produced a carefully calibrated circulation system that affords access to a compelling collection of scenic and historic landscapes. America's national park roads are internationally renowned as technological marvels and models of aesthetically pleasing and environmentally sensitive resource management. With new challenges under discussion and additional issues sure to arise, questions about the appropriate balance between preservation and access will continue to engender impassioned debate. While there is much to learn from tracing previous developments, the ultimate confirmation of Bradley's wisdom can be found in the parks themselves. Whether motoring through the pastoral landscapes of Blue Ridge Parkway, boarding a shuttle in Denali, Zion, or Yosemite Valley, or hiking through the Wilderness Areas of Kings Canyon or Wrangell–St. Elias, the national park experience embodies evolving ideas about the role of roads in managing our relationships with America's natural and cultural heritage.

ABOVE Going-to-the-Sun Road, Glacier National Park, 2006.

Notes

The primary source of original documents and correspondence related to national park road development is the National Park Service Record Group (RG79) housed in National Archives and Records Administration, College Park, Maryland. Citations have been provided in abbreviated form based on the inventory of records compiled by Edward Hill and revised by Renee Jaussaud in 1997. For example, RG79 E10:2 B1841 refers to Record Group 79, Entry 10, Second Subseries, Box 1841. References to additional record groups and repositories are generally provided in full.

INTRODUCTION

1 Bradley, "Yosemite's Problem Road," 9.

2 The phrase "for public use, resort, and recreation" is from "An Act Authorizing a Grant to the State of California of the 'Yo-semite Valley,' and of the Land Embracing the 'Mariposa Big Tree Grove,' Approved June 30, 1864 (13 Stat. 325)," in Dilsaver, *America's National Park System*, 11; "An Act to Establish the National Park Service and for Other Purposes, Approved August 25, 1916 (39 Stat. 935)," ibid., 46.

3 Chittenden, *The Yellowstone National Park* (1918 ed.), 237.

4 Many general histories of national park development touch on road development, and several relatively recent studies address various aspects of the topic. Linda McClelland's *Building the National Parks* and Ethan Carr's *Wilderness by Design* focus on the period between the formation of the National Park Service in 1916 and the outbreak of World War II. Although both summarize precedents and provide valuable accounts of road building during this period, it is not the central focus of either volume. Carr's *Mission 66* addresses park road issues from the 1940s through the mid-1960s but again as one component of a broader overview. David Louter's *Windshield Wilderness* is more temporally expansive but geographically constrained. Paul Sutter's *Driven Wild* focuses on the relationship between NPS road-building policies and the rise of wilderness advocacy in the 1920s–1930s. *America's National Park Roads & Parkways: Drawings from the Historic American Engineering Record*, edited by Timothy Davis, Todd Croteau, and Christopher Marston, provides a wealth of information about design practices and construction details, along with brief summaries of development in individual parks.

5 Giedion, *Space, Time and Architecture*, 553–54.

I. THE ORIGINS OF NATIONAL PARK ROADS

1 Lasdun, *The English Park*, 5–38, 60–61; Rogers, *Landscape Design*, 257; Garvin, *Public Parks*, 18–19.

2 Lasdun, *The English Park*, 38, 49–50, 62, 119–28; Rogers, *Landscape Design*, 218, 259–60, 275–76; Garvin, *Public Parks*, 16–18; Newton, *Design on the Land*, 233–41; Pückler-Muskau, *Hints on Landscape Gardening*, 114–91.

3 Hunt and Willis, *The Genius of Place*, 1–43; Hunt, *Gardens and the Picturesque*; Hussey, *The Picturesque*; Rogers, *Landscape Design*, 233–66; Cosgrove, *Social Formation and Symbolic Landscape*; Johnson qtd. in Shepard, *Man and the Landscape*, 87.

4 Humphry Repton, "Sketches and Hints on Landscape Gardening" (1795) and "Fragments of a Theory and Practice of Landscape Gardening" (1803) in Repton, *The Art of Landscape Gardening*, 25–27, 49–53, 122. "Heedless travelers" comment is from "Red Book for Stoke Park: Approach from Hereford," qtd. in S. Daniels, "On the Road with Humphry Repton," 179; Hunt, *Gardens and the Picturesque*, 155–63, "windings of a road," 161.

5 Hunt, *Gardens and the Picturesque*, "aged and infirm," 161.

6 Pückler-Muskau, *Hints on Landscape Gardening*, 80–89.

7 Loudon, *An Encyclopedia of Gardening*, 642–43; Loudon, *An Encyclopedia of Agriculture*, 5th ed., 562–612; Loudon, *A Treatise on Forming, Improving, and Managing Country Residences*, 414–16, 590–92.

8 Downing, *A Treatise on the Theory and Practice of Landscape Gardening*; Schuyler, *Apostle of Taste*.

9 A. J. Downing, "Explanatory Notes" to 1851 Mall Plan, excerpted in Reps, *Washington on View*, 126.

10 Sloane, *The Last Great Necessity*, 1–64; Schuyler, *The New Urban Landscape*, 37–56; Sears, *Sacred Places*, 99–117.

11 Schuyler, *The New Urban Landscape*, 55–76, Downing qtd. on 65–66; Newton, *Design on the Land*, 266–70; Rosenzweig and Blackmar, *The Park and the People*, 15–58.

12 The literature on Olmsted and Vaux is extensive. Individual treatments include Roper, *FLO: A Biography of Frederick Law Olmsted*; and Alex, *Calvert Vaux*. For more general assessments, see Schuyler, *The New Urban Landscape*, 59–125; Rogers, *Landscape Design*, 337–71; and Newton, *Design on the Land*, 266–306; for a more critical and socially oriented analysis, see Rosenzweig and Blackmar, *The Park and the People*.

13 Olmsted and Vaux's key writings on the theory and practice of park development are collected in *The Papers of Frederick Law Olmsted*, Supplementary Series, vol. 1, *Writings on Public Parks, Parkways, and Park Systems*: Olmsted, "Mount Royal. Montreal" (1881), "directly remedial," 366; Olmsted, "Public Parks and the Enlargement of Towns" (1870), "all classes," 186.

14 Willis, *The Complete Works*, 604.

15 Richards, "The Central Park"; [Bellows], "Cities and Parks"; New York City Board of Commissioners of Central Park, *Seventh Annual Report*, 31.

16 [New York] Board of Commissioners of the Department of Public Parks, *Third General Report*, 271–74.

17 Rosenzweig and Blackmar also address aspects of the Central Park carriage scene in *The Park and the People*, 211–25.

18 Willis, *The Complete Works*, 604; Olmsted, "Public Parks and the Enlargement of Towns," in *The Papers of Frederick Law Olmsted*, Supplementary Series, quote on 1:200; Olmsted, Vaux & Company, "Report of the Landscape Architects and Superintendents to the Brooklyn Park Commissioners, January 1871," in *The Papers of Frederick Law Olmsted*, vol. 6, *The Years of Olmsted, Vaux & Company, 1865–1874*, 399.

19 Richards, "The Central Park," 296.

20 Examples include Richards, *Guide to Central Park*; and Baxter, *Boston Park Guide*.

21 Olmsted, *Forty Years of Landscape Architecture*, qtd. in Fisher, *Frederick Law Olmsted and the City Planning Movement in the United States*, 64.

22 Olmsted, "Notes on the Plan of Franklin Park and Related Matters" (1886), in *The Papers of Frederick Law Olmsted*, Supplementary Series, 1:493.

23 Olmsted, "Mount Royal. Montreal" (1881), in *The Papers of Frederick Law Olmsted*, Supplementary Series, 1:393.

24 Olmsted, Vaux & Co., "Preliminary Report to the Commissioners for Laying Out a Park in Brooklyn, New York," (1866), in *The Papers of Frederick Law Olmsted*, Supplementary Series, 1:88.

25 Olmsted, Vaux, and Co., "Preliminary Report upon the Proposed Suburban Village at Riverside, Near Chicago," (1868), in *The Papers of Frederick Law Olmsted*, 6:280.

26 Olmsted, "Mount Royal. Montreal" (1881), in *The Papers of Frederick Law Olmsted*, Supplementary Series, 1:372–74, "mere engineering," 1:374.

27 Ibid., 1:372–74, "ultimate development," 1:374

(emphasis in original); Olmsted, "Notes on the Plan of Franklin Park and Related Matters" (1886), in *The Papers of Frederick Law Olmsted*, Supplementary Series, "unnecessary violence," 1:493.

28 For additional information on the origins and evolution of the American parkway, see Schuyler, *The New Urban Landscape*, 126–46, Davis, "The American Motor Parkway"; Davis, "A Pleasing Illusion of Unspoiled Countryside"; and Davis, "Mount Vernon Memorial Highway and the Evolution of the American Parkway."

29 Olmsted, Vaux & Company, "Report of the Landscape Architects and Superintendents to the President of the Board of Commissioners of Prospect Park, Brooklyn, January 1, 1868," in *The Papers of Frederick Law Olmsted*, Supplementary Series, 1:112–46, quote on 130.

30 Olmsted, Vaux and Co., "Preliminary Report to the Commissioners for Laying Out a Park in Brooklyn, New York: Being a Consideration of Circumstances of Site and Other Conditions Affecting the Design of Public Pleasure Grounds," in *The Papers of Frederick Law Olmsted*, Supplementary Series, 1:105–7.

31 Olmsted, Vaux & Co., *Preliminary Report Respecting a Public Park in Buffalo, and a Copy of the Act of Legislature Authorizing Its Establishment*, in *The Papers of Frederick Law Olmsted*, Supplementary Series, 1:166. Additional information on Buffalo's park and parkway system can be found in Schuyler, *The New Urban Landscape*, 128–32; and Kowsky, *The Best Planned City in the World*.

32 For additional discussion of Olmsted's Boston projects, see Zaitzevsky, *Frederick Law Olmsted and the Boston Park System*.

33 [Boston, Massachusetts,] Metropolitan Park Commission, *Report of the Board of the Metropolitan Park Commissioners, January 1893*, 62–67; Senate Committee on the District of Columbia, *Report of the Senate Committee on the District of Columbia on the Improvement of the Park System of the District of Columbia*. For further discussion of these plans, see Schuyler, *The New Urban Landscape*, 126–94; Newton, *Design on the Land*, 318–36, 400–412; Peterson, *The Birth of City Planning in the United States*; and Kohler and Scott, *Designing the Nation's Capital*.

34 The rise of scenic tourism and changing American attitudes toward nature have been recounted in numerous sources, including Nash, *Wilderness and the American Mind*; Huth, *Nature and the American*; Pomeroy, *Tourists in Search of the Golden West*; and Sears, *Sacred Places*.

35 Burke, *A Philosophical Enquiry into the Origin of Our Ideas of the Sublime and Beautiful*. The concepts of the sublime, beautiful, and picturesque are summarized in Huth, *Nature and the American*, 11–12; Nash, *Wilderness and the American Mind*, 45–46; and Conron, *The American Landscape*, 143–45.

36 Gilpin, *Three Essays*; Price, *Essays on the Picturesque*. The classic account is Hussey's *The Picturesque*.

37 Bartram, *Travels through North & South Carolina, Georgia, East & West Florida*; Jefferson, *Notes on the State of Virginia*; Timothy Dwight, *Travels in New-England and New-York*.

38 Alexander Wilson, "The Foresters," in *The Poems and Literary Prose of Alexander Wilson*, 2:111–38.

39 The role of Hudson River landscapes in the rise of American tourism is examined at length in Gassan, *The Birth of American Tourism*; and Schuyler, *Sanctified Landscape*.

40 This is a necessarily brief survey of a well-examined aspect of American cultural history. Classic overviews include Novak, *Nature and Culture*; and Flexner, *That Wilder Image*. More recent studies include R. Bedell, *The Anatomy of Nature*; and A. Miller, *The Empire of the Eye*.

41 Willis, *American Scenery*; Davison, *The Fashionable Tour*. Other popular guides included Theodore Dwight's *The Northern Traveller*; and Appleton's *Northern and Eastern Traveller's Guide*. Thomas Starr King extolled New Hampshire's scenic regions in *The White Hills*. The development of American vacation habits is discussed in Huth, *Nature and the American*, 19–86; Sears, *Sacred Places*; Gassan, *The Birth of American Tourism*; and Aron, *Working at Play*.

42 Davison, *The Fashionable Tour*, 116.

43 Theodore Dwight, *The Northern Traveller*, 25–26.

44 The tedium of canal boat travel is discussed in Davison, *The Fashionable Tour*, 116–17; Willis, *American Scenery*, 135; and Huth, *Nature and the American*, 72–73.

45 Davison, *The Fashionable Tour*, 110.

46 Silliman, *A Gallop among American Scenery*, 109–40, "racehorse swiftness," 140, "rush onward," 134, "Steam Spirit," 131.

47 Paulding, *The New Mirror of Travellers*, "merry motion," 98; Silliman, *A Gallop among American Scenery*, 110; Willis, *The Complete Works*, 410. Panoramas are discussed in Sears, *Sacred Places*, 51–61; and Novak, *Nature and Culture*, 23.

48 Paulding, *The New Mirror of Travellers*, 4–5, 6.

49 Dana, "A Tale of Two Citizens"; T.B.S, "The Unrighteous Bargain."

50 Davison, *The Fashionable Tour*, 41–42; Huth, *Nature and the American*, 77–78; Sears, *Sacred Places*, 66–69.

51 Allan Wallach, "Making a Picture from Mount Holyoke," in D. Miller, *American Iconology*, 81; Davison, *The Fashionable Tour*, 150; Huth, *Nature and the American*, 77. Mount Equinox developments noted in Appleton's *General Guide to the United States and Canada, 1880*, vol. 1; and Taintor, *Saratoga Illustrated*. Kearsarge date given in Harris, "A Sketch of Warner," 427; and Wood, *The Turnpikes of New England*, 241. Mount Moosilauke road described in Kilbourne, *Chronicles of the White Mountains*, 256–57. Mount Mansfield Turnpike information from Wood, *The Turnpikes of New England*, 282; and Aron, *Working at Play*, 52.

52 Silliman, *A Gallop among American Scenery*, 160–65, quote on 162.

53 Milliken, *The Glen House Book*, 33.

54 Winslow Homer, "The Summit of Mount Washington," *Harper's Weekly*, 10 July 1869; Spaulding, *Historical Relics of the White Mountains*, 25–26, 76–77; Kilbourne, *Chronicles of the White Mountains*, 77, 231–43, "eloquent witness," 234; Eastman, *The White Mountain Guide Book*; Milliken, *The Glen House Book*, 98–107; "The White Mountains," *Harper's New Monthly Magazine*, August 1877, 321–32; Bryant, *Picturesque America*, 150.

55 Kilbourne, *Chronicles of the White Mountains*, 227–38. Views appear in many sources, including Sweetser, *Views in the White Mountains*.

II. TOURING AMERICA'S WONDERLANDS

1 The rise of western tourism and the role of western scenery in the American imagination is discussed in numerous sources including Huth, *Nature and the American*; Sears, *Sacred Places*; Runte, *National Parks*; Pomeroy, *In Search of the Golden West*; Novak, *Nature and Culture*; A. Miller, *The Empire of the Eye*; Boime, *The Magisterial Gaze*; and R. Bedell, *The Anatomy of Nature*.

2 Yosemite history is recounted in Runte, *Yosemite*; Demars, *The Tourist in Yosemite*; Sears, *Sacred Places*; Huth, *Nature and the American*, and many other sources. Detailed accounts of the park's physical development include Greene, *Yosemite*; Quin, "Yosemite Roads and Bridges, HAER No. CA-117"; and Johnston, *Yosemite's Yesterdays* (both vols.).

3 Runte, *Yosemite*, 9–14; Sears, *Sacred Places*, 124–27; Johnston, *Yosemite's Yesterdays*, 2:7–29, Hutchings qtd. on 16.

4 "An Act Authorizing a Grant to the State of California of the 'Yo-semite Valley,' and of the Land Embracing the 'Mariposa Big Tree Grove,' Approved June 30, 1864 (13 Stat. 325)," in Dilsaver, *America's National Park System*, quote on 10; Olmsted, "Preliminary Report upon the Yosemite and Big Tree Grove," [August 1865], in *The Papers of Frederick Law Olmsted*, vol. 5, *The California Frontier, 1863–1865*, ed. Victoria Post Ranney, 488–516.

5 Olmsted, "Preliminary Report upon the Yosemite and Big Tree Grove" [August 1865], in *The Papers of Frederick Law Olmsted*, vol. 5, "sublimity," 500, "political duty," 502, "guarded," 506, "pecuniary advantage," 501, "millions," 507.

6 Ibid., 5:506–8.

7 Description of typical Yosemite trip is from Bowles, *Our New West*, 382–83.

8 Olmsted, "Preliminary Report upon the Yosemite and Big Tree Grove," [August 1865], in *The Papers of Frederick Law Olmsted*, 5:508.

9 Olmsted to King, 23 October 1864, in *The Papers of Frederick Law Olmsted*, 5:269–70.

10 Olmsted, "Preliminary Report upon the Yosemite and Big Tree Grove" [August 1865], in *The Papers of Frederick Law Olmsted*, 5:509.

11 Bowles, *Across the Continent*; A. Richardson, *Beyond the Mississippi*.

12 Yosemite visitation statistics for 1868 and 1869 are from Huth, *Nature and the American*, 155; 1870 figure cited in Quin, "Yosemite Roads and Bridges, HAER No. CA-117," 14.

13 Bromley, "The Big Trees and the Yosemite," quote on 269.

14 Muir, *Letters to a Friend*, 55.

15 "The Yosemite," *Appletons' Journal*, 111.

16 Johnston, *Yosemite's Yesterdays*, 2:33; Quin, "Yosemite Roads and Bridges, HAER No. CA-117," 5; Bryant, *Picturesque America*, 487–95.

17 Johnston, *Yosemite's Yesterdays*, 2:34; Quin, "Yosemite Roads and Bridges, HAER No. CA-117," 5–6.

18 Trail mileage reported in Logan, "Does It Pay to Visit Yo Semite?"; J. H. Beadle's characterization of his 1871 descent and Stanton's comment qtd. in Quin, "Yosemite Roads and Bridges, HAER No. CA-117," 12; Johnston, *Yosemite's Yesterdays*, 2:37.

19 Logan, "Does It Pay to Visit Yo Semite?"

20 Harte, "The East at Yosemite," 191.

21 Bryant, *Picturesque America*, 1:475–79, 1:490–91; Buckley, *Two Weeks in the Yosemite and Vicinity*, 1–17, qtd. on 14.

22 Muir, *Letters to a Friend*, 80–81.

23 Qtd. in Pomeroy, *In Search of the Golden West*, 21; Greene, *Yosemite*, 67–68; Quin, "Yosemite Roads and Bridges, HAER No. CA-117," 13–15.

24 Runte, *Yosemite*, 39–40; Greene, *Yosemite*, 91; Johnston, *Yosemite's Yesterdays*, 2:34–35; *Mariposa Gazette* qtd. on 35.

25 "The Yosemite," *Appletons' Journal*, 11.

26 Greene, *Yosemite*, 91–94; Quin, "Yosemite Roads and Bridges, HAER No. CA-117," 17–18; Johnston, *Yosemite's Yesterdays*, 2:35–36.

27 Greene, *Yosemite*, 93–94; Quin, "Yosemite Roads and Bridges, HAER No. CA-117," 18; Johnston, *Yosemite's Yesterdays*, 2:36.

28 Greene, *Yosemite*, 95–97; Quin, "Yosemite Roads and Bridges, HAER No. CA-117," 19–21; Johnston, *Yosemite's Yesterdays*, 2:38–40.

29 Greene, *Yosemite*, 100–101; Quin, "Yosemite Roads and Bridges, HAER No. CA-117," 21–22; Johnston, *Yosemite's Yesterdays*, 2:40–41; Paden and Schlichtmann, *The Big Oak Flat Road*, 247–49.

30 Quin, "Yosemite Roads and Bridges, HAER No. CA-117," 21–22; Conway to the *Mariposa Gazette*, 2 April 1874, qtd. on 22; Johnston, *Yosemite's Yesterdays*, 2:40–41; Greene, *Yosemite*, 100–103; Paden and Schlichtmann, *The Big Oak Flat Road*, 52, 250–53.

31 Johnston, *Yosemite's Yesterdays*, 2:42–43, *Mariposa Gazette* qtd. on 43; Greene, *Yosemite*, 97 (McLean quoted); Quin, "Yosemite Roads and Bridges, HAER No. CA-117," 23.

32 Paden and Schlichtmann, *The Big Oak Flat Road*, 250–55, *Sonora Union Democrat* qtd. on 255; Johnston, *Yosemite's Yesterdays*, 2:42–43; Quin, "Yosemite Roads and Bridges, HAER No. CA-117," 23.

33 Greene, *Yosemite*, 106–7; Johnston, *Yosemite's Yesterdays*, 2:37–38, 45; Quin, "Yosemite Roads and Bridges, HAER No. CA-117," 24–25; Quin, "Wawona Road, Yosemite National Park, HAER No. CA-148," 3–5; "The Yosemite," *Appletons' Journal*, 11.

34 Greene, *Yosemite*, 107–8; Johnston, *Yosemite's Yesterdays*, 2:45–49; Quin, "Yosemite Roads and Bridges, Yosemite National Park, HAER No. CA-117," 25–27; Quin, "Wawona Road, Yosemite National Park, HAER No. CA-148," 5–6.

35 Greene, *Yosemite*, 106; Johnston, *Yosemite's Yesterdays*, 2:47–49.

36 Greene, *Yosemite*, 110–11; Johnston, *Yosemite's Yesterdays*, 2:52.

37 "L.A.," "Impressions of a Careless Traveler," quote on 411; Greene, *Yosemite*, 156–57; Johnston, *Yosemite's Yesterdays*, 2:49.

38 Acting Superintendent S. B. M. Young qtd. in Quin, "Yosemite Roads and Bridges, HAER No. CA-117," 30; Charles A. Bailey, "Unfrequented Paths of Yosemite," *Overland*, 2d ser., 8 (July 1886): 88, qtd. in Pomeroy, *In Search of the Golden West*, 51.

39 Paden and Schlichtmann, *The Big Oak Flat Road*, 255; Greene, *Yosemite*, 157–58.

40 Greene, *Yosemite*, 158–91; Johnston, *Yosemite's Yesterdays*, 1:21–34.

41 Quin, "Yosemite Roads and Bridges, HAER No. CA-117," 13; Clarke qtd. in Greene, *Yosemite*, 272.

42 Greene, *Yosemite*, 252–388; Quin, "Yosemite Roads and Bridges, HAER No. CA-117," 39–50; Senate, *Report of the Commission on Roads in Yosemite*, 56th Cong., 1st sess., 8 February 1900, S. Doc. 155; House, *Free Roads, Yosemite National Park*, 56th Cong., 2d sess., 1 March 1901, H.R. Rep. 2989.

43 Greene, *Yosemite*, 425–30, Acting Superintendent H. C. Benson's 1909 report qtd. on 429; Quin, "All-Year Highway (El Portal Road), Yosemite National Park, HAER No. CA-150," 1–3; Quin, "Yosemite Roads and Bridges, HAER No. CA-117," 39–50.

44 "Memorandum on Tioga Road" prepared by Horace Albright for travel writer Charles Belden, 15 February 1918 (RG79 E9 B312); Quin, "Tioga Road, Yosemite National Park, HAER No. CA-149," 1–8, *Sierra Club Bulletin* qtd. on 8.

45 "An act to Set Apart a Certain Tract of Land Lying near the Headwaters of the Yellowstone River as a Public Park, Approved March 1, 1872 (17 Stat. 32)," in Dilsaver, *America's National Park System*, 28. Key sources on the development of Yellowstone National Park include Chittenden, *The Yellowstone National Park* (1918 ed.); Culpin, *The History of the Construction of the Road System in Yellowstone National Park*; and Haines, *The Yellowstone Story* (both vols.).

46 Haines, *The Yellowstone Story*, 1:85–140; Runte, *National Parks*, 35–39.

47 Haines, *The Yellowstone Story*, 1:140–93; Huth, *Nature and the American*, 152–53; Runte, *National Parks*, 39–47.

48 Haines, *The Yellowstone Story*, 1:155–73, *Helena Herald* qtd. on 170–71; Huth, *Nature and the American*, 152–53.

49 Yellowstone legislation qtd. in Ise, *Our National Park Policy*, 18; "The Yellowstone National Park," *Scribner's Monthly* 4 (1872), 121, qtd. in Nash, *Wilderness and the American Mind*, 113; Langford qtd. in Runte, *National Parks*, 43.

50 Haines, *The Yellowstone Story*, 1:193–96, 265–91; Ise, *Our National Park Policy*, 19–20; Culpin, "Yellowstone National Park Roads and Bridges, HAER No. WY-24," 1–5, "excellent wagon road" and "trail" qtd. on 5.

51 Haines, *The Yellowstone Story*, 1:180–246, 1:449–50, Langford qtd. on 192; Culpin, "Yellowstone National Park Roads and Bridges, HAER No. WY-24," 8–20; Philetus Norris, "Report on the Yellowstone National Park," in U.S. Department of the Interior (hereafter cited as DOI), *Report of the Secretary of the Interior, 1877*, 845.

52 Haines, *The Yellowstone Story*, 1:180–246, 449–50; Culpin, "Yellowstone National Park Roads and Bridges, HAER No. WY-24," 8–20.

53 Hiram Chittenden, "Roads in the Yellowstone National Park," 11–13; Chittenden, *The Yellowstone National Park* (1895 ed.), 130–31; Strahorn, *Fifteen Thousand Miles by Stage*, 1:254–86, quote on 1:268; Hatch qtd. in Culpin, "Yellowstone National Park Roads and Bridges, HAER No. WY-24," 26.

54 Culpin, "Yellowstone National Park Roads and Bridges, HAER No. WY-24," 22–24, Kingman qtd. on 22, 23; Haines, *The Yellowstone Story*, 2:209–13; Bartlett, *Yellowstone: A Wilderness Besieged*, 75–77, Kingman qtd. on 77.

55 Haines, *The Yellowstone Story*, 2:211–15; Bartlett, *Yellowstone*, 77–78; Culpin, "Yellowstone National Park Roads and Bridges, HAER No. WY-24," 24–28.

56 Accounts vary, but Chittenden maintained that Assistant Superintendent G. L. Henderson dissuaded Kingman and christened the location "Golden Gate" (Chittenden, *The Yellowstone National Park* [1918 ed.], 245). Wingate, *Through the Yellowstone Park on Horseback*, quote on 12; Haines, *The Yellowstone Story*, 2:210–15; Bartlett, *Yellowstone*, 77–79; Whittlesey, *Yellowstone Place Names*, 202; Culpin, "Yellowstone National Park Roads and Bridges, HAER No. WY-24," 25.

57 Haines, *The Yellowstone Story*, 2:216–17; Culpin, "Yellowstone National Park Roads and Bridges, HAER No. WY-24," 29–33; "Annual Report of Captain Clinton B. Sears, Corps of Engineers, for the Fiscal Year Ending June 30, 1887," *Report of the Secretary of War, 1887*, Appendix AAA, 3138–39, qtd. ibid., 29–30.

58 Haines, *The Yellowstone Story*, 2:217–20; Culpin, "Yellowstone National Park Roads and Bridges, HAER No. WY-24," 34–35.

59 Culpin, "Yellowstone National Park Roads and Bridges, HAER No. WY-24," 35–38; Haines, *The Yellowstone Story*, 2:220–22.

60 Culpin, "Yellowstone National Park Roads and Bridges, HAER No. WY-24," 35–38, Anderson qtd. on 37, Erwin qtd. on 38; Haines, *The Yellowstone Story*, 2:220–22; Stoddard, *John L. Stoddard's Lectures*, 10:222.

61 Senate, *Roads in the Yellowstone National Park*, 56th Cong., 1st sess., 1899, S. Doc. 226, 7; Culpin, "Yellowstone National Park Roads and Bridges, HAER No. WY-24," 38–39; Culpin, "Golden Gate Viaduct, HAER No. WY-46," "uneasiness and concern," 2; Haines, *The Yellowstone Story*, 2:222–24

62 Kipling, *From Sea to Sea*, 2:78.

63 Chittenden, *The Yellowstone National Park* (1918 ed.), 244–46, "sentimentalism" quote on 246; Culpin, "Golden Gate Viaduct, HAER No. WY-46," 2–3; Haines, *The Yellowstone Story*, 2:224–27.

64 Culpin, "Yellowstone National Park Roads and Bridges, HAER No. WY-24," 43–45; Haines, *The Yellowstone Story*, 2:228–37; Chittenden, *The Yellowstone National Park* (1918 ed.), 243–44.

65 Chittenden, *The Yellowstone National Park* (1918 ed.), 246–48; McClure, "Chittenden Memorial Bridge, HAER No. WY-88," 1–12, Chittenden qtd. on 6; Haines, *The Yellowstone Story*, 2:243–44.

66 Chittenden, *The Yellowstone National Park* (1895 ed.), "defects," 201, "the work itself," 202; Chittenden, "The Government Road System of the Yellowstone National Park," 71–78; other quotes from Chittenden, *The Yellowstone National Park* (1918 ed.), 237.

67 [Chittenden], "Technical Report upon the Improvement of Yellowstone National Park, 1904," 16–34; Chittenden, "Roads in the Yellowstone National Park," "Portland in Maine to Portland in Oregon" quote on 7; Chittenden, *The Yellowstone National Park* (1904 ed.), 264–67, "artistic work," 267; Chittenden, *The Yellowstone National Park* (1918 ed.), 240–67, "good gradients," 245; all other quotes are from Chittenden, *The Yellowstone National Park* (1895 ed.), 202–3.

68 Chittenden, "Roads in the Yellowstone National Park," "free from monotony," 10; Chittenden, *The Yellowstone National Park* (1895 ed.), 264–67; Chittenden, *The Yellowstone National Park* (1918 ed.), 240–67; Chittenden, "The Government Road System of the Yellowstone National Park," "adjusted," 75, "interesting features," 77; [Chittenden] "Technical Report upon the Improvement of Yellowstone National Park, 1904," 16–34, "Army Files," YNP Archives; Culpin, "Yellowstone National Park Roads and Bridges, HAER No. WY-24," 40–67, Hoodoo quote, 54, "view ahead," 50.

69 Chittenden, *The Yellowstone National Park* (1904 ed.), 323–31, "no parallel," 323; Chittenden, *The Yellowstone National Park* (1918 ed.), 247–48, 306–17, "artillery," 248; Culpin, "Grand Loop Road, HAER No. WY-55," "finest road," 35.

70 Chittenden, *The Yellowstone National Park* (1904 ed.), 323–31, "broken and wild" and "road itself," 326, "pick and spade," 330.

71 Chittenden, *The Yellowstone National Park* (1918 ed.), 247–48, 306–17, "kaleidoscopic," 311.

72 McClure, "Addendum to Yellowstone National Park Roads and Bridges, HAER No. WY-24," 187–89, 216–22, 230–32; McClure, "Corkscrew Bridge, HAER No. WY-86," 1–7; Chittenden, *The Yellowstone National Park* (1904 ed.), 287; Haines, *The Yellowstone Story*, 2:244–55.

73 Chittenden, *The Yellowstone National Park* (1904 ed.), 264–67, "future generations," 267; Chittenden, *The Yellowstone National Park* (1918 ed.), 249; Haines, *The Yellowstone Story*, 2:34–41.

74 Chittenden, *The Yellowstone National Park* (1904 ed.), 261–331; Chittenden, *The Yellowstone National Park* (1918 ed.), 271–86; Haynes, *Haynes Official Guide* (1915 ed.), 12–106; Taylor, *Touring Alaska and the Yellowstone*, 296–388, "envelop us," 298; *The Wylie Way Permanent Camping Company*, brochure and guidebook, 1908; Haines, *The Yellowstone Story*, 2:100–140; Barringer, *Selling Yellowstone*, 34–58.

75 Haines, *The Yellowstone Story*, 2:100–140; Chittenden, *The Yellowstone National Park* (1904 ed.), 261–331, "exhilarating," 302; Campbell, *Campbell's New Revised Complete Guide* (1914 ed.), 95–140, "exciting," 115.

76 Stoddard, *John L. Stoddard's Lectures*, 10:230–31; Hubbard and Hubbard, *A Little Journey to the Yellowstone Park*; Muir, *Our National Parks*, 39, 51; *Yellowstone National Park: America's Only Geyser Land*, promotional brochure (Northern Pacific Railway, 1914), 11.

77 Campbell, *Campbell's New Revised Complete Guide*, 95.

78 Thayer, *Marvels of the New West*, 68.

79 Stoddard, *John L. Stoddard's Lectures*, 10:235.

80 Chittenden, "Roads in the Yellowstone National Park," "occasional crank," 13–14.

81 Haines, *The Yellowstone Story*, 2:256–74; Yard, *The Book of the National Parks*, 209.

82 Quin, "Mount Rainier National Park Roads and Bridges, HAER No. WA-35," 2–10; Catton, *Wonderland*, 27–69.

83 Quin, "Mount Rainier National Park Roads and Bridges," 6–8; Catton, *Wonderland*, 46–90; Quin, "Nisqually Road, Mount Rainier National Park, HAER No. WA-119," 2–3.

84 Quin, "Nisqually Road, Mount Rainier National Park, HAER No. WA-119," 5–8; Catton, *Wonderland*, 117–20; Ricksecker's 1904 report qtd. ibid., 119.

85 Quin, "Mount Rainier National Park Roads and Bridges, HAER No. WA-35," 14; Quin, "Nisqually Road, Mount Rainier National Park, HAER No. WA-119," 8–10; Catton, *Wonderland*, 121–22.

86 Quin, "Nisqually Road, Mount Rainier National Park, HAER No. WA-119," 11–15; Quin, "Mount Rainier National Park Roads and Bridges, HAER No. WA-35," 10–14; Catton, *Wonderland*, 122.

III. EMBRACING THE AUTOMOBILE

1 Marx, *The Machine in the Garden*.

2 Oliver Lippincott, "The First Locomobile to Reach Yosemite," *San Francisco Chronicle*, Sunday Supplement, 22 July 1900; Johnston, *Yosemite's Yesterdays*, 1:7; Johnston, *Yosemite's Yesterdays*, 2:59; Zordich, "The First Automobile in Yosemite."

3 W. A. Clarke, "Automobiling in the Yosemite Valley"; Johnston, *Yosemite's Yesterdays*, 1:9–14. The advertisement appeared in the December 1901 issue of *Harper's*.

4 Johnston, *Yosemite's Yesterdays*, 1:14–15; Zordich, "Yosemite's Unwelcome Visitor," 21–22, *Madeira Tribune* qtd. on 22. Benson to Secretary of the Interior James Garfield, 8 July 1907; Paul Morris to Congressman W. F. Englebright, 4 May 1908 (RG79 E10:1 B308). An extensive collection of protests can be found in RG79 E9 B265. Walter Fry to Secretary of the Interior, 23 December 1907 (RG79 E9 B177).

5 O. W. Lehmer, "Transportation and Its Relation to the National Parks," in USDOI, *Proceedings of the National Park Conference Held at the Yellowstone National Park*, 9; Quin, "Yosemite Roads and Bridges, HAER No. CA-117," 52–53; "Report of the Acting Superintendent of the Yosemite National Park," in USDOI, *Annual Reports of the Department of the Interior, 1905–1912*.

6 Quin, "Yosemite Roads and Bridges, HAER No. CA-117," 51–58; "Report of the Acting Superintendent of the Yosemite National Park," in USDOI, *Annual Reports of the Department of the Interior, 1905–1912*, "competent landscape gardener," 1907 report, 562.

7 Robert Marshall, "Park Administration," in USDOI, *Proceedings of the National Park Conference Held at the Yellowstone National Park*, 108–19, quote on 108.

8 Most secondary sources state that Mount Rainier first admitted automobiles in 1908, but the decision to allow them as far as Longmire Springs was announced in August 1907, and the park issued numerous automobile permits that fall (RG79 E9 B115). The 90 percent figure is from Mills, "Touring in Our National Parks," 35. USDOI, *Proceedings of the National Park Conference Held at the Yosemite National Park*, California statistics, 61, "pyrotechnics," 77 (more than five hundred telegrams arrived at Fisher's hotel room on at the beginning of the conference [RG79 E9 B265]); Automobile Club of Southern California to Walter Fry, 12 September 1912, "best class of tourists" (RG79 E9 B177).

9 USDOI, *Proceedings of the National Park Conference Held at the Yosemite National Park*, Fisher, 59; Forsyth, "ideal," 91, "my attitude," 129.

10 Ibid., 61–83, Fisher, 65; Los Angeles Chamber of Commerce, 83.

11 Ibid., 68–76, 109–44.

12 Colby's remarks recorded ibid., 139. Muir expressed these sentiments in a December 1912 letter to American Alpine Club president Howard Palmer, in Muir, *The Life and Letters*, 2:378–79; "most visitors," ibid.; Bryce, "National Parks—The Need of the Future" (1912), 811–16, quote on 813; Bryce, "National Parks—The Need of the Future" (1913), 28–32.

13 Lane's oft-quoted statement supplied in "Memorandum for the Press," 30 April 1913 (RG79 E9 B266).

14 "Automobiles Will Be Admitted to Yosemite Park," *Los Angeles Tribune*, 30 April 1913; Los Angeles Chamber of Commerce President Arthur Kinney to Maj. W. T. Littebrant (RG79 E10:1 B312). "Memorandum for the Secretary, prepared by Colonel Forsyth, in relation to the admission of automobiles to the Yosemite National Park," 4 January 1913 (RG79 E10:1 B308).

15 "Autoists Exult over Victory in Yosemite Fight," *San Francisco Examiner*, 4 May 1913; "Yosemite Decision Delights Local Motorists," *Los Angeles Express*, 1 May 1913; "Report of the Acting Superintendent of the Yosemite National Park," in USDOI, *Annual Report of the Department of the Interior, 1913*, 746–50; "Report of the Acting Superintendent of the Yosemite National Park," in USDOI, *Annual Report of the Department of the Interior, 1914*, 743–65; Johnston, *Yosemite's Yesterdays*, 2:64.

16 "Report of the Acting Superintendent of the Yosemite National Park," in USDOI, *Annual Report of the Department of the Interior, 1913*, 729–30, "Report of the Acting Superintendent of the Yosemite National Park," in USDOI, *Annual Report of the Department of the Interior, 1914*, 728–29; "Report of the Acting Superintendent of the Yosemite National Park," in USDOI, *Annual Report of the Department of the Interior, 1915*, 916–19; Zordich, "Yosemite's Unwelcome Visitor," 23–24; Johnston, *Yosemite Yesterdays*, 1:15–17.

17 Haines, *The Yellowstone Story*, 2:263–67; Bartlett, "Those Infernal Machines in Yellowstone," 20–23.

18 F. J. Haynes, "Transportation in the Yellowstone National Parks," in USDOI, *Proceedings of the National Park Conference Held at the Yellowstone National Park*, 21–29; Senate, *New Roads in Yellowstone National Park*, 62d Cong, 2d sess., 1 July 1912, S. Doc. 871, 17–26, "hazardous to life," 17, "killed or injured," 19.

19 Brett qtd. in Bartlett, "Those Infernal Machines in Yellowstone," 26, Hill's remarks, 30.

20 Senate, *New Roads in Yellowstone National Park*, 1–16; USDOI, *Proceedings of the National Park Conference Held at the Yellowstone National Park*, 28–29.

21 Haines, *The Yellowstone Story*, 2:267–71; Bartlett, "Those Infernal Machines in Yellowstone," 26–29; Bartlett, *Yellowstone: A Wilderness Besieged*, 85, 106.

22 Haines, *The Yellowstone Story*, 2:267–71; Bartlett, "Those Infernal Machines in Yellowstone," 26–29; Yard, *The Book of the National Parks*, 209.

23 Chittenden, *The Yellowstone National Park* (1918 ed.), 121, 250–51; Haines, *The Yellowstone Story*, 2:273–74; "Annual Report of the Director of the National Park

Service," in USDOI, *Annual Report of the Secretary of the Interior, 1917*, 813.

24 Yard, *The Book of the National Parks*, 208–9.

25 The establishment of the National Park Service is related in numerous accounts, including Huth, *Nature and the American*, 182–91; Runte, *National Parks*, 47–54; Ise, *Our National Park Policy*, 185–94; Albright and Cahn, *The Birth of the National Park Service*, 1–53; Sellers, *Preserving Nature in the National Parks*, 28–41; and Carr, *Wilderness by Design*, 55–79.

26 *Century* magazine editor Robert Underwood Johnson was a major proponent of this view (see Johnson to Lane, 3 November 1913; Littebrant to Lane, 18 October 1913; Adolph Miller to Johnson, 7 November 1913 [RG79 E9 B311]).

27 McFarland, "Our National Parks," 148–50; USDOI, *Proceedings of the National Park Conference Held at the Yellowstone National Park*; House Committee on Public Lands, *Establishment of a National Park Service*, 62nd Cong., 2d sess., 24 April 1912; "President Taft's Address" and "For a Bureau of National Parks, Special Message of President Taft to Congress, February 2, 1912," in American Civic Association, *Proceedings of the American Civic Association*, 3–5, quote on 4.

28 "Report of the General Superintendent and Landscape Engineer of the National Parks," in USDOI, *Report of the Secretary of the Interior for the Fiscal Year Ended June 30, 1915*, 843–67, quote on 848; USDOI, *Proceedings of the National Park Conference Held at Berkeley, California*, 6–17.

29 "Report of the General Superintendent and Landscape Engineer of the National Parks," in USDOI, *Report of the Secretary of the Interior for the Fiscal Year Ended June 30, 1915*, 843–46, "least resistance" and "finest scenery", 845; M. Daniels, "Planning to Develop Our National Parks," 21; *Proceedings of the National Park Conference Held at Berkeley, California*, 15–20; Shaffer, *See America First*.

30 Albright and Cahn, *The Birth of the National Park Service*, 9–11, 24, 48–49; Shankland, *Steve Mather*, 83–84, 106–7. Marshall's statements at the 1916 hearings appear in House Committee on Public Lands, *National Park Service*, 64th Cong., 1st sess., 5 and 6 April 1916, 70–86.

31 Albright and Cahn, *The Birth of the National Park Service*, 15–18, Lane qtd. on 16; Shankland, *Steve Mather*, 1–11.

32 Shankland, *Steve Mather*, 7–67, 97–113; Albright and Cahn, *The Birth of the National Park Service*, 18–24.

33 USDOI, *Proceedings of the National Park Conference Held at Berkeley, California*; "Ask Your Congressman to Vote for the National Parks Bill." Mather to Batchelder, 10 January 1917 (RG79 E9 B115).

34 Shankland, *Steve Mather*, 68–113; Albright and Cahn, *The Birth of the National Park Service*, 18–43; Albert and Schenck, *Creating the National Park Service*, 59–84; photograph of the car being towed by mules in NPS Historic Photo Collection; "U.S. Playgrounds Are Valuable and Undeveloped Asset"; Sterling, "The Motorist and the National Parks," quote on 7; "Ask Your Congressman to Vote for the National Parks Bill"; Watrous, "The Proposed National Park Service"; "Resolutions of the Society of American Landscape Architects," *Landscape Architecture*,

April 1916, 111–12; Grosvenor, "The Land of the Best"; preference for a service rather than a bureau expressed in House Committee on Public Lands, *Establishment of a National Park Service*, 62d Cong., 2d sess., 24 April 1912, 19–20; House Committee on Public Lands, *National Park Service*, 64th Cong., 1st sess., 5 and 6 April 1916.

35 Mather, "The National Parks on a Business Basis," quote on 430; USDOI, *Proceedings of the National Parks Conference, Held in the Auditorium of the New National Museum, Washington, D.C.*, Lane, 12; Yard, 275–76; Mills, "Touring in our National Parks"; Mills, *Your National Parks*, 270.

36 USDOI, *Proceedings of the National Parks Conference, Held in the Auditorium of the New National Museum, Washington, D.C.*, Yard, 275–76, Bishop, 293–300, quote on 299, Southern Pacific Railroad executive E. O. McCormick, 344.

37 Mather referred to the automobile as "the open sesame for many thousands" in "The Ideas and Policies of the National Park Service Particularly in Relation to Yosemite National Park," in Hall, *Handbook of Yosemite National Park*, 81.

38 Shankland, *Steve Mather*, 57–59, 62–63; Albright and Cahn, *The Birth of the National Park Service*, 19–21; House Committee on Public Lands, *National Park Service*, 64th Cong., 1st sess., 5 and 6 April 1916, 78–79; Tioga Road transaction documentation in RG79 E9 B311-312.

39 Shankland, *Steve Mather*, 72–73; Albright and Schenck, *Creating the National Park Service*, 82–83.

40 E. E. Newell to Mather, 1 November 1915 (RG79 E9 B312).

41 Shankland, *Steve Mather*, 79–80; Albright and Cahn, *The Birth of the National Park Service*, 27–28, 39; Whitely and Whitely, *The Playground Trail*; "Annual Report of the Director of the National Park Service," in USDOI, *Annual Report of the Secretary of the Interior, 1917*, 802; Dedication of the National Park to Park Highway described in USDOI, National Park Service (hereafter cited as NPS), *Report of the Director of the National Park Service, 1920*, 37–40, quote on 39 (director's annual reports hereafter cited as *AR* followed by the year).

42 M. C. Bedell, *Modern Gypsies*, 148, 221–22; Mather gateway quote, *AR 1919*, 940.

43 USDOI, Office of the Secretary [Stephen Mather], *Progress in the Development of the National Parks*, "gratifying results," 6; Rae, *The Road and the Car in American Life*, 50, 57; nationwide vehicle registration statistics from Bureau of Public Roads tally of "Motor Vehicle Registrations, 1895–1929," available at http:/railsandtrails.com/AutoFacts-1930p15-100-8.jpg.url; visitation statistics from *AR 1917–23* (which differ slightly from figures cited in *Progress in the Development of the National Parks*); Tioga Road increase noted in *AR 1923*, 53.

44 Mather expounded on the civic, patriotic, and economic influence of the national parks in *AR 1918*, 825; *AR 1920*, 13–15; *AR 1921*, 11–13, "refreshed" and "Americanization," 12; *AR 1922*, 14–15; *AR 1923*, 6–7; and Mather, "Progress in the National Parks," 5–13, "thronged," 7.

45 Yard, "The People and the National Parks"; Long, "The Motor's Part in Public Health," quote on 19.

46 The car-camping fad was widely remarked at the time. The classic overview is Warren Belasco's *Americans*

on the Road, which also explicates contemporary beliefs about the automobile's broader role in American society. Contemporary how-to books include Jessup, *The Motor Camping Book*; Brimmer, *Autocamping*; and Long and Long, *Motor Camping*. The distinctions between Dudes and Sagebrushers are elucidated in Albright and Taylor, *Oh, Ranger!*, 26–48, quote on 43; autocamping statistics are from *AR 1917–23*.

47 Mather compared the two approaches in "The Ideas and Policies of the National Park Service Particularly in Relation to Yosemite National Park," in Hall, *Handbook of Yosemite National Park*, 80; *AR 1922*, "roughing it deluxe," 14; Albright and Taylor, *Oh, Ranger!*, "thrilling sight," 43; Shankland, *Steve Mather*, "tin can" quote, 161; Van de Water, *The Family Flivvers to Frisco*, quote on 201.

48 Auto campground issues discussed in *AR 1919*, 960; *AR 1920*, 105, 111; *AR 1921*, 58, 66, 68–69, 74; *AR 1923*, 61, 67–68. The NPS reduced automobile fees in 1917, dropping the rate from $10.00 to $7.50 in Yellowstone; $8.00 to $5.00 in Yosemite; $6.00 to $2.50 in Mount Rainier; $3.00 to $2.50 in Sequoia and Crater Lake; $2.00 to $1.00 in Glacier; and $2.50 to 50 cents in General Grant (*AR 1917*, 805). Manning, "Report of the National Park Committee of the American Society of Landscape Architects, 7 January 1918 (RG79 E9 B404); Platt statement in House Committee on Public Lands, *Construction of Roads*, 68th Cong., 1st sess., 7, 8, 12, and 14 February 1924, 84.

49 Murphy, *On Sunset Highways*, 351–52; Birney, *Roads to Roam*, 129–30.

50 "Extracts from a letter written to a well-known hotel man in the East by a friend for whom he had arranged a trip through the West, including Yosemite National Park," enclosed with letter from Arno Cammerer to Secretary of the Interior John Bartram Payne, 22 September 1920 (RG 48, Records of the Office of the Secretary of the Interior, Central Classified Files [hereafter cited as RG 48 Central Classified Files], 1907-36 B1975).

51 D. L. Reaburn to Superintendent of National Parks, 15 August 1916; Acting Superintendent Joseph Cotter to Rep. William E. Humphrey (n.d.); Maude Morris to Sen. Wesley Jones, 10 September 1917; Jones to Lane, 18 September 1917; E. B. Palmer qtd. in Jones to NPS Acting Director, 10 September 1917 (RG79 E9 B115).

52 *AR 1921*, "wretched," 24, *AR 1920*, "atrocious," 239, *AR 1921*, "tiresome and unpleasant," 79; *AR 1922*, "obnoxious and disagreeable," 5; *AR 1923*, Mather's comments on Yosemite's dangers, 56; *AR 1921*, Yosemite traffic, 69. Reaburn to Superintendent of National Parks, 25 March 1917, "Blow Your Horn Point" (RG79 E9 B136). Birney, *Roads to Roam*, "boilershop," 133; Rinehart, *Through Glacier Park in 1915*, 8.

53 Senate, "A Bill Providing for the Sale of Public Lands for the Purpose of Using the Proceeds Arising Therefrom in the Construction of Roads and Other Permanent Improvements in National Parks," Senate Bill 4472, 65th Cong., 2d sess., 2 May 1918. Salmon to Mather, 13 May 1918; Lane to Henry Moore, Chairman, Senate Committee on Public Lands, 14 May 1918; Raker to Mather, 12 May 1922; Cammerer to Raker, 17 May 1922 (RG79 E9 B395).

54 The Federal-Aid Highway Act of 1916 provided the Forest Service with $1 million per year over the ten-year period beginning in 1917 (Loder, "The Location and Building of Roads in the National Forests"). The AAA's attempt to include a national park road provision is recounted in House Committee on Public Lands, *Construction of Roads*, 68th Cong., 1st sess., 7, 8, 12, and 14 February 1924, 21; disparity discussed in *AR 1919*, 936–37; *AR 1920*, 42–43; *AR 1921*, 23–24; *AR 1922*, 20–21; and *AR 1923*, 10–11.

55 *AR 1919*, 936–37; *AR 1920*, 17–19, 42–43, 91, 171–72; *AR 1921*, 23–24, 54–56, 68–69, 120–21; *AR 1922*, "criticism," 20, "the motorist can not understand," 42, "flood of visitors," 77; *AR 1923*, 10–11, 55–56.

56 *AR 1922*, 20; *AR 1923*, 8; Shankland, *Steve Mather*, 153–56; Sinnott incident recounted in Albright and Cahn, *The Birth of the National Park Service*, 195–96.

57 House Committee on Public Lands, *Construction of Roads*, 68th Cong., 1st sess., 7, 8, 12, and 14 February 1924, Work qtd. on 2, Mather, 3–15.

58 Ibid., 15–109.

59 Ibid., AAA statement, 21–25, quote on 22, Miller, 40–43, Sutherland, 48–51; "To Reconstruct National Park Roads"; "Millions for National Park Roads."

IV. RECONCILING THE MACHINE AND THE GARDEN

1 "An Act to establish the National Park Service and for Other Purposes, Approved August 25, 1916 (39 Stat. 935)," reproduced in Dilsaver, *America's National Park System*, 46.

2 Visitation statistics, *AR 1925*, 1–2, quote on 2; *AR 1926*, 1; Mather's statements on road development policy, *AR 1919*: Yosemite, 938, 980–81, Muir Woods, 1032; *AR 1920*, Yellowstone, 104; Yosemite, 252; *AR 1923*, "against overdevelopment," 10–11; *AR 1924*, 12–14; House Committee on Public Lands, 68th Cong., 1st sess., 7, 8, 12, and 14 February 1924, "sensible road system" and "gridironed,"6. Mather repeated these sentiments in presentations targeted to popular and professional audiences such as "What I Am Trying to Do with the National Parks"; and "Engineering Applied to National Parks." Albright noted the "one good highway" policy in *The Birth of the National Park Service*, 195, as did Shankland in *Steve Mather*, 158.

3 "Superintendents' Resolution on Overdevelopment. Prepared at the National Park Conference, Nov. 13–17, Yosemite Park Calif., With an Explanatory Letter," reproduced in *America's National Park System: The Critical Documents*, 57–61.

4 Albright claimed he wrote a first draft in late 1917, incorporating ideas expressed by Mather and others. He circulated this draft among many of those involved in the creation of the NPS, including McFarland, Yard, Gilbert Grosvenor, and key Sierra Club figures such as William Colby, then submitted it to Mather, who suggested having it issued as formal instructions from the secretary of the interior (Albright and Cahn, *The Birth of the National Park Service*, 68–69). "Lane Letter" reproduced in *AR 1918*, 1074–77; and Dilsaver, *America's National Park System*. Mather's instructions on road building appeared in *AR 1924*, 14.

5 Punchard's reports appeared in *AR 1919* and *AR 1920*; Pray, "Minute on the Life and Service of Charles Pierpont Punchard"; Shankland, *Steve Mather*, 254–55. Mather praised Punchard's contributions in *AR 1919*, 939, quoted; and *AR 1921*, 56. Comprehensive histories of the NPS landscape architecture program are provided in Carr, *Wilderness by Design*; and McClelland, *Building the National Parks*.

6 *AR 1920*, 92–93; *AR 1921*, 56; G. E. Reynolds, "Guardians of Our National Parks: Daniel Ray Hull, Chief Landscape Architect of the U.S. N. P. S.," *Stockton [Calif.] Record*, 29 March 1924; Carol Roland, "Hull, Daniel Ray," in Birnbaum and Karson, *Pioneers of Landscape Design*, 180–84; McClelland, *Presenting Nature*, 93–102.

7 Shankland, *Steve Mather*, 255; McClelland, "Thomas Chalmers Vint," in Birnbaum and Karson, *Pioneers of Landscape Design*, 412–16; McClelland, *Presenting Nature*, 115–228; Carr, *Wilderness by Design*, 189–248; Vint, "National Park Master Plans," reprinted as a pamphlet for broader distribution.

8 Eliot, "The Influence of the Automobile on the Design of Park Roads," quote on 37.

9 Hubbard and Kimball, *An Introduction to the Study of Landscape Design*, 94–95, 148–50, 219–23, 308–11, "lie upon the surface," 219; "necessary evil," "pleasing succession," and "leisurely rate," 309, "hurry and tension," 310.

10 Olmsted, "Notes on Laying Out Roads for Pleasure Travel in Scenic Areas," quote on 282–83.

11 Welch, "State and National Parks"; *AR 1921*, 56; *AR 1922*, 17; "Minutes of the Seventh National Park Conference held in Yellowstone National Park Wyoming, October 22–28, 1923," 43–45 (National Park Service History Collection, NPS Harpers Ferry Center); Abbott, "Ten Years of the Westchester County Park System"; Downer, "Principles of Westchester's Parkway System"; Gilmore Clarke, "The Parkway Idea," in Snow, *The Highway and the Landscape*, 32–35; Davis, "The American Motor Parkway." Vint to Albright, 25 November 1931; Clarke to Vint, 4 November 1931; Kittredge to Downer, 20 June 1932; "Photographs received from Mr. Holleran," Westchester County Park Commission, April 17, 1932 (RG79 E77 B23). McClelland, *Presenting Nature*, 134–35.

12 "Massachusetts' Latest Road Offering"; Lancaster, *The Columbia*; Hill qtd. in Fahl, "S. C. Lancaster and the Columbia River Highway," 114; Davis, Croteau, and Marston, *America's National Park Roads & Parkways*, 362–71. Lancaster's entreaties and associated rebuff in RG79 E9 B368.

13 Albright to Lane, 17 October 1917 (RG48 Central Classified Files, 1907-36 B1975); Lane to Secretary of War, 12 December 1917; Sec. of War to Lane, 13 October 1917 (RG79 E9 B248).

14 U.S. Dept. of Transportation, Federal Highway Administration, *America's Highways 1776–1976*, 46–53, 64–76; W. David Samuelsen, "Bio: T. Warren Allen, New York State," www.usgaarchives.org. Miller to Secretary of Agriculture David Houston, 10 October 1913; Miller to Littebrant, 20 October 1913; Houston to Miller, 8 November 1913 (RG79 E9 B311).

15 Allen to OPR Chief Engineer Vernon Pierce, 2 December 1913 (RG79 E9 B311).

16 Sherfey to Littebrant, 10 February 1914; Littebrant to Sec. of Interior, 11 February 1914 (RG79 E9 B311).

17 Miller to Page, 2 April 1914; Miller to Littebrant, 11 April 1914; Miller to Littebrant, 25 April 1914; Allen to Page, 12 May 1914; Littebrant to Sec. Interior, 3 June 1914; Allen to Page, 10 August 1914 (RG79 E9 B311). Allen to P. St. J Wilson, 14 August 1915 (RG79 E9 B170). U.S. Dept. of Transportation, Federal Highway Administration, *America's Highways 1776–1976*, 75–76.

18 *AR 1918*, 843, 946. Allen's remarks appeared in *Proceedings of the National Park Conference Held at Berkeley, California*, 24–33, "full purpose" and "roads in abundance," 25, "harmonious blending," 32.

19 "George Estyn Goodwin, M. ASCE," *Transactions of the American Society of Civil Engineers* 122 (1947): 1453–55; Albright, *The Birth of the National Park Service*, 103–4; Albright and Schenck, *Creating the National Park Service*, 87–88.

20 Crosby and Goodwin, *Highway Location and Surveying*, 171–87, quote on 171.

21 Ibid., 180–85, "ruthlessly," 181.

22 Ibid., 172, 180–83.

23 Sequoia NP Superintendent John White to Mather, 10 April 1925 (RG79, E9 B195). Cammer to Goodwin, 16 June 1923; Goodwin to Cammerer, 14 July 1923; Goodwin to Cammerer, 14 July 1923; Cammerer to Goodwin, 28 July 1923; Goodwin to Cammerer, 1 August 1923; Mather to Goodwin, 15 September 1923 (RG79 E10 B154).

24 House Committee on Public Lands, *Construction of Roads*, 68th Cong., 1st sess., 7, 8, 12, and 14 February 1924, 60–76, quote on 74.

25 Goodwin to Cammerer, 25 March 1925 (RG79 E9 B195); Cammerer to Mather, 25 March 1925 (RG79 E9 B137); Goodwin to Hull, 28 March 1925 (RG79 E9 B137); Cammerer to Goodwin, 7 April 1925 (RG79 E9 B195); Quin, "Christine Falls Bridge, Mount Rainier National Park, HAER No. WA-48," 4.

26 *AR 1921*, 55–56. Goodwin to Cammerer, 25 March 1925 (RG79 E9 B195); Hull to Mather, 11 June 1921; Mather to Hull, 28 June 1921; Mather to Goodwin, 28 June 1921 (RG79 E9 B136).

27 Mather to Goodwin, 28 June 1921 (RG79 E9 B136). Ben Maddox to Mather, 26 September 1920; Mather to Cammerer, 21 March 1921; Mather to Goodwin, 1 April 1921; Mather to Goodwin, 4 April 1921; Mather to White, 11 April 1921; Cammerer to Albright, 11 April 1921; Albright to Mather, 12 April 1921; Albright to Mather, 26 April 1921; Goodwin to Maddox, 24 July 1921; George Stewart to Mather, 21 September 1921; Cammerer to Stewart, 5 October 1921; Goodwin to Mather, 31 March 1922; Cammerer to Goodwin, 25 April 1922; Cammerer to White, 25 April 1922 (RG79 E9 B194-195).

28 Cammerer to Albright, 23 March 1921 (RG79 E9 B194). White to Mather, 27 October 1922; Mather to John Small, 30 March 1923 (quoted); White to Goodwin, 9 June 1923; Goodwin to White, 29 June 1923 (RG79 E10:1 B429). Mather reiterated his praise in *AR 1923*, 68.

29 Seely, *Building the American Highway System*, 46–99; Lewis, *Divided Highways*, 5–20; U.S. Dept. of Transportation. Federal Highway Administration, *America's Highways, 1776–1976*, 87, 100–114, 176–92.

30 U.S. Dept. of Transportation, Federal Highway

Administration, *America's Highways, 1776–1976*, 103–5, 113; Lewis, *Divided Highways*, 11–18.

31 Cammerer, memorandum for the desk, 10 September 1919; A. E. Demary, Memorandum for Mr. Mather, 23 November 1921; NPS Chief Clerk B. L. Vipond, Memorandum for Mr. Mather, 1 December 1921; William Welch to Mather, 25 January 1922 (RG79 E9 B395).

32 Goodwin to Mather, 21 March 1921; Albright to Mather, 7 April 1922 (RG79 E9 B395).

33 Smither to Mather, 10 June 1924; Cammerer to Goodwin, 16 June 1924: Cammerer to Albright, 16 June 1924 (RG79 E9 B395); problems hiring engineers mentioned in *AR 1923*, 41; and *AR 1925*, 17.

34 Goodwin to Director, 17 June 1924 (RG79 E9 B395).

35 Albright to Director, 17 June 1924 (RG79 E9 B395).

36 G. E. Reynolds, "Needless Slaughter of Calaveras Giant Road Builders"; "A Road Builder's Shame," editorial; Yardley cartoon "What Fools We Mortals Be!," *Stockton (Calif.) Record*, 3 May 1924 (RG79 E70 B4).

37 Demaray to Goodwin, 6 June 1924; Goodwin to BPR District Engineer C. H. Sweetser, 13 June 1924; Goodwin to Mather, 17 June 1924; Goodwin to Mather, 18 June 1924; Goodwin to Elmer Reynolds, Manager Editor, *Stockton (Calif.) Record*, 18 June 1924; Mather to Goodwin, 24 June 1924; Goodwin, "Memorandum to All Principal Engineering Assistants," 2 July 1924 (RG79 E70 B4).

38 Albright and Cammerer to Mather, 2 December 1921; Goodwin to Cammerer [personal], 5 January 1922; Goodwin to Cammerer [personal], 5 January 1922; Albright to Goodwin, 30 January 1922; Mather to Goodwin, 8 February 1922; Cammerer to Goodwin, 11 February 1922; Mather to Goodwin, February 1922 (RG79 E9 B395); Goodwin to Mather, 1 June 1923; Goodwin to Small, 1 June 1923; Cammerer to Albright, 11 June 1923; Albright to Mather, 26 September 1923 (RG79 E9 B195).

39 Hull to Mather, 20 November 1923; Goodwin to Mather, 24 November 1923 (RG79 E9 B40).

40 Thomas Vint, interview by Herbert Evison, 1960 (excerpt in Glacier National Park Archives), quote on 12–13; Shankland, *Steve Mather*, 156–57.

41 Vint interview, quote on 12–13; Shankland, *Steve Mather*, 156–57.

42 Vint interview, 13–14; Shankland, *Steve Mather*, 156–57.

43 Austin to Mather, ca. 14 August 1924 (RG79 E9 B40); Vint interview, 13–14; Shankland, *Steve Mather*, 156–57.

44 Albright to Mather, 18 August 1924; Goodwin to Director, 29 August 1924; Cammerer to Mather, 5 September (RG79, E9, B40); Mather to Cammerer, 5 September 1924; Cammerer to Mather, 5 September 1924 (RG79, E9, B41); Kraebel to Mather, 8 October 1924; Frank A. Kittredge, "Trans-Mountain Highway, Glacier National Park, Report to National Park Service," February 5, 1925 (RG79 E9 B39); F. A. Kittredge, "The Appearance of Highways," paper presented before the Conservation Forum of the Yosemite Wild Flower Festival, Yosemite National Park, 7 June 1935 (RG79 E10:2 B448); Vint interview, 13–14; Shankland, *Steve Mather*, 156–57; "Notes and Correspondence: Frank Alvah Kittredge, 1883–1954," *Sierra Club Bulletin* 40 (1955): 69; Crosby and Goodwin, *Highway Location and Surveying*, 176, 186.

45 Goodwin to Director, 29 August 1924 (RG79 E9 B40); Goodwin to Director, 8 August 1924; Mather to Cammerer, 5 September 1924; Mather to Goodwin, 9 September 1924 (RG79 E9 B41); Kraebel to Mather, 8 October 1924 (RG79 E9 B39); Cammerer to Smither, 9 September 1924; Cammerer to Goodwin, 4 September 1924; Mather to Goodwin, 4 September 1924; Goodwin to Mather, 15 September 1924; Cammerer to Goodwin, 18 September 1924; Goodwin to Mather, 16 October 1924 (RG79 E9 B395).

46 Goodwin to CA State Highway Engineer R. M. Morton, 3 December 1924; Goodwin to Nevada State Highway Engineer Feo. W. Borden, 3 December 1924; Goodwin to Mather, 28 January 1925; Mather to Goodwin, 11 February 1925; Goodwin to Mather, 25 February 1925; Mather to Goodwin, 5 March 1925; Goodwin to Mather, 17 March 1925; Goodwin Memorandum to All Superintendents, 17 March 1925 (RG79 E77 B20). Mather discussed the change in standards in *AR 1925*, 17–18.

47 Mather to Goodwin, 16 February 1925; Mather to White, 16 February 1925; Goodwin to Mather, 19 March 1925; Mather to Cammerer, 2 April 1925 (quoted) (RG79 E10:1 B429).

48 Mather to Hewes, 21 May 1925; Goodwin to Mather, 17 June 1925; Mount Rainier Superintendent Tomlinson to Mather, 20 June 1925; Cammerer to Mather, 5 July 1925; Cammerer to Tomlinson, 27 June 1925; Goodwin to Mather, 5 July 1925; Mather to Goodwin, 5 July 1925; Demaray to Mather, 17 July 1925 (RG79 E9 B137).

49 Mather to Cammerer, 8 July 1925; Cammerer to Mather, 8 July 1925; Mather to Cammerer, 8 July 1925; Cammerer to Mather, 9 July 1925; Mather to Cammerer, 10 July 1925; Cammerer to Albright, 11 July 1925 (RG79 E9 B137); Goodwin's telegram insisting he had not offered to resign qtd. in Cammerer to Secretary Finney, 14 July 1925 (RG 79 E10:1 B112); "George Estyn Goodwin, M. ASCE," 1454–55; Crosby and Goodwin, *Highway Location and Surveying*, 176, 186.

50 Burrell, "Minutes of the Eighth National Park Conference, Held in Mesa Verde National Park, Colorado, October 1 to 5, 1925, Inclusive," 93–95; Demaray to Mather, 12 November 1924 (RG79 E9 B395).

51 "Minutes of the Eighth National Park Conference," 1–8, Mather qtd. on 8; Mather, "Engineering Applied to the National Parks," 1183.

52 "Minutes of the Eighth National Park Conference," 22–28, 94, Hewes qtd. on 26.

53 Ibid., 28–30.

54 "Memorandum of Agreement between the National Park Service and the Bureau of Public Roads relating to the survey, construction, and improvement of roads and trails in the national parks and monuments" (RG79 E9 B310).

55 Toll to Mather, 21 November 1923; Toll, "Instructions Regarding Road Work in the National Parks" (RG79 E9 B171); Albright and Cahn, *Birth of the National Park Service*, 158–63; Albright qtd. in *AR 1926*, 26.

56 Dept. of the Interior, "Memorandum for the Press" (Mount Rainier National Park archives, "Roads General"). Mather to Hull, 16 February 1925 (RG79 E77 B20).

57 Demaray to Albright, 23 December 1927; Albright to Director, 30 December 1927; Demaray to Albright, 17 January 1928; Albright to Hewes, 26 January 1928; Kittredge to Albright, 26 January 1928; Kittredge to Albright, 27 January 1928; Albright to Kittredge, 30 January 1928; Albright to Director, 30 January 1928; Demaray to Albright, 9 February 1928; Albright to Director [confidential memo, n.d.]; Albright to Hewes, 14 March 1928; Vint to Albright, 17 May 1928; Albright to Kittredge, 28 May 1928; Cammerer to Albright, 15 June 1928; Junior Landscape Architect Woskey to Vint, 12 July 1928; Vint to Albright, 30 July 1928 (RG79 E9 B4).

58 Albright to Demaray, 22 October 1927; Mather to MacDonald, 16 August 1928; Mather to Vint, 16 August 1928; Kittredge to Vint, 27 October 1928 (RG79 E77 B21).

59 MacDonald to Mather, 21 August 1928 (RG79 E77 B39); J. A. Elliott, "Memorandum to engineers in charge of park work," 17 October 1928 (RG79 E77 B8).

60 Mather, "Engineering Applied to National Parks," 1183–89, qtd. on 1183; H. K. Bishop, "Discussion of Engineering Applied to the National Parks," *Transactions of the American Society of Civil Engineers*, 1193.

61 U.S. Dept. of the Interior, National Park Service (hereafter cited as USDOI, NPS), "Minutes of the Tenth National Park Conference held in San Francisco, California, February 15 to 21" (National Park Service History Collection, NPS Harpers Ferry Center), Albright, 52–53; Hewes, 53–56, quote on 56, Finch, 69; Kittredge, 73–78, "stampede," 73, "fast standards," 75, "vitally important," 78.

V. THE "GOLDEN AGE" OF PARK ROAD BUILDING

1 The ten-year $50 million program was authorized in 1929. In 1931, the National Park Service received $6 million in regular road construction appropriations, $1.5 million for emergency relief work within the parks, and $1.5 million for the construction of approach roads through national forests ("Memorandum for a Talk by Director Albright," 11 July 1931 [RG79, E10:1 B154]). The Hayden-Cartwright Act (PL No. 393, June 18, 1934) appropriated a total of $200 million to increase public employment through road construction.

2 Sources disagree on the exact amount. According to the acting NPS director A. E. Demaray, the NPS expended $90,199,573 on the construction, reconstruction, and improvement of roads and trails in national parks and monuments between 1916 and 30 June 1941, and $23,649,413 on national parkways (Demaray to Rep. Richard Welch, 27 December 1941 [RG79 E10:2 B449]). A year earlier, Ickes asserted that Congress provided $104,063,507 for roads and trails from 1916 to 1940 and $34,293,896 for parkways, with $119,283,896 allotted from 1925 to 1940 (Ickes to Sen. Joseph O'Mahoney, 10 June 1940 [RG48 Central Classified Files, 1937–53 B3792]). According to the Federal Highway Administration, approximately $90 million was expended to construct 1,781 miles of park roads and 255 miles of approach roads between 1916 and 1941 (*America's Highway's 1776–1976*, 139). Mileage figures are from "Growth of the National Park Service under Director Cammerer" (RG79 E61 B18).

3 For more on the expansion of the National Park Service and the impact of federal relief programs, see Unrau and Willis, *Administrative History*.

4 *AR 1923*, 16. Work to W. A. Welch, 16 February 1924; Temple et al. to Work, 12 December 1924 (RG48 NPS Records, B2011); "Blue Ridge in Virginia Recommended by Committee for Great Eastern Park"; USDOI, Southern Appalachian National Park Commission, *Final Report of the Southern Appalachian National Park Commission*.

5 "Blue Ridge in Virginia Recommended by Committee for Great Eastern Park"; USDOI, Southern Appalachian National Park Commission, *Final Report of the Southern Appalachian National Park Commission*.

6 Albright and Cahn, *The Birth of the National Park Service*, 244–52, 285–97; Mackintosh, *The National Parks* (1991), 18–43; Davis, Croteau, and Marston, *America's National Park Roads and Parkways*, 288–336; Davis, "Rock Creek and Potomac Parkway, Washington, D.C."; Davis, "Rock Creek Park Roads, HAER No. DC-55"; Holmes, "Gettysburg National Military Park Roads, HAER No. PA-485"; Ott, "Shiloh National Military Park Tour Roads, HAER No. TN-37."

7 Mather, "Engineering Applied to National Parks," 1183.

8 Vint made this observation in *AR 1930*, 30.

9 For additional details on NPS roadside design, see McClelland, *Building the National Parks*, 201–378; and Davis, Croteau, and Marston, *America's National Park Roads and Parkways*.

10 Steen, "Going-to-the-Sun Road, HAER No. MT-67," 4–5.

11 Ibid.

12 Ibid., 6–8.

13 Ibid., 8–9.

14 Kalispell Chamber of Commerce to Mark Daniels, 2 October 1915; Kalispell Chamber of Commerce to Sen. T. J. Walsh, 4 October 1915; Sperry to Sec. of Interior Lane, 4 December 1915; Sperry to Mather, 22 September 1916; Sperry to Mather, 14 December 1916, qtd. re: Logan Pass (RG79 E9 B39); Sperry's comments on spectacular engineering qtd. in Steen, "Going-to-the-Sun Road, HAER No. MT-67," 9–10.

15 Goodwin to A. J. Breitenstein, 17 August 1921; J. M. Hyde, "That Fairy Highway through the Glacier National Park," *Cut Bank (Mont.) Pioneer Press*, 29 April 1921 (RG79 E9 B39).

16 Steen, "Going-to-the-Sun Road, HAER No. MT-67," 11–12.

17 Ibid., 16–17. F. A. Kittredge, "The Appearance of Highways," paper presented before the Conservation Forum of the Yosemite Wild Flower Festival, Yosemite National Park, 7 June 1935 (RG79 E10:2 B448).

18 Kittredge, "Trans-Mountain Highway, Glacier National Park, Report to National Park Service," February 5, 1925 (RG79 E9 B39).

19 Ibid., 6–8, "harmonious setting," 6, aeroplane," 8.

20 Ibid., 12–22.

21 Vint, "Memorandum to D. R. Hull . . . re: Report by Highway Engineer Frank A. Kittredge of the 1924 B.P.R. Survey of the Trans-Mountain Road Glacier National Park" (RG79 E9 B39).

22 Steen, "Going-to-the-Sun Road, HAER No. MT-67," 19–20. Vint qtd. on 70.

23 Ibid., 21–27.

24 Ibid., 25–26, Kraebel qtd. on 25.

25 Ibid., 21–27.

26 Ibid., 21–30.

27 Ibid., 627–29.

28 Peters, "Transmountain Highway Construction in Glacier National Park"; Ewen, "Going-to-the-Sun Road Completed," quotes on 435, 437; "The New Highway in Glacier National Park," *Sunset*, March 1933, 11.

29 Steen, "Going-to-the-Sun Road, HAER No. MT-67," 30–31.

30 "Report of the Going-to-the-Sun Highway Dedication, July 15, 1933, Glacier National Park, Montana"; Albright, "Memorandum for Secretary, 17 July 1933 (RG48 Central Classified Files, 1907-36 B1915).

31 Steen, "Going-to-the-Sun Road, HAER No. MT-67," 31–36.

32 Ibid., 37.

33 Quin, "Rocky Mountain National Park Roads, HAER No. CO-78"; Quin, "Fall River Road, Rocky Mountain National Park, HAER No. CO-73"; Quin, "Trail Ridge Road, Rocky Mountain National Park, HAER No. CO-31."

34 Quin, "Rocky Mountain National Park Roads, HAER No. CO-78," 4–7; Musselman, *Rocky Mountain National Park*, 2–15; Buchholtz, *Rocky Mountain National Park: A History*, 1–76, Dunraven qtd. on 72.

35 Quin, "Rocky Mountain National Park Roads, HAER No. CO-78," 7–9; Musselman, *Rocky Mountain National Park*, 7–10.

36 Quin, "Rocky Mountain National Park Roads, HAER No. CO-78," 7–12; Musselman, *Rocky Mountain National Park*, 17–27.

37 Daniels to Secretary of the Interior, 6 July 1915 (RG48 Central Classified Files, 1907-36 B1915).

38 Quin, "Fall River Road, Rocky Mountain National Park, HAER No. CO-73," 4–9.

39 C. R. Trowbridge to Secretary of the Interior, 10 August 1915; R. B. Marshall, "Memo for Mr. Griffith on Fall River Road Plan," 31 August 1917; F. W. Griffith to Albright, 1 September 1917; Way to Mather, 28 August 1917; T. J. Ehrhart to Albright, 25 September 1917; "National Parks," *Rocky Mountain News*, 25 August 1918; Lane to Colorado Governor Julius Gunter, 26 November 1918 (quoted); F. J. Chamberlin to Albright, 4 December 1918; E. E. Sommers to Albright, 20 December 1918; Way to Albright, 7 January 1919 (RG79 E9 B170); *AR 1917*, 26.

40 Lane to Colorado Governor George Carlson, 16 February 1916; Denver Civic and Commercial Association to Mather, 17 May 1916; "Fall River Boulevard Actually Being Built after Tedious Delays," *Denver Post*, 14 October 1917; "Get Busy Messieurs!" and "Motor Club Urges Early Completion of Fall River Road," unidentified clippings ca. January 1919; Cammerer to A. L. Craig, 19 July 1919; "Fall River Road to Grand Lake Most Perfect Drive in America," *Denver Post*, undated clipping (RG79 E9 B170); Quin, "Fall River Road, Rocky Mountain National Park, HAER No. CO-73," 9–10.

41 *AR 1920*, 137; qtd. in Buchholtz, *Rocky Mountain National Park*; Quin, "Fall River Road, Rocky Mountain National Park, HAER No. CO-73," 13–17.

42 Roe Emery to Cammerer, 30 July 1921; Toll to Mather, 31 May 1922; Toll to Goodwin, 3 June 1922; Cammerer to Toll, 12 June 1922; Toll to Mather, 23 June 1923; Emery to Cammerer, 27 July 1923; W. S. Basinger to Cammerer, 3 August 1923; Chicago, Burlington & Quincy Railroad Company Passenger Traffic Manager to Mather, 19 October 1923; Toll to Mather, 18 January 1924; Toll to Chauncey Vivian, 19 July 1924 (RG79 E9 B170); Quin, "Fall River Road, Rocky Mountain National Park, HAER No. CO-73," 17–20.

43 Musselman, *Rocky Mountain National Park*, 29–75, Parkhurst qtd. on 63; Quin, "Rocky Mountain Roads, Rocky Mountain National Park, HAER No. CO-73," 33–35.

44 Roger Toll, "Memorandum Regarding Proposed Road on Trail Ridge," 9 September 1924 (RG79 E9 B171).

45 Quin, "Trail Ridge Road, Rocky Mountain National Park, HAER No. CO-31," 4–10; S. A. Wallace, "Report on Surveys: Rocky Mountain National Park, Colorado," approved, 9 January 1928 (RG79 E77 B40); Albright qtd. in Buchholtz, *Rocky Mountain National Park*, 175.

46 Quin, "Trail Ridge Road, Rocky Mountain National Park, HAER No. CO-31," 4–10; Wallace, "Report on Surveys: Rocky Mountain National Park, Colorado," 4–7.

47 Quin, "Trail Ridge Road, Rocky Mountain National Park, HAER No. CO-31," 9–14, 18.

48 Ibid., 11–27; Buchholtz, *Rocky Mountain National Park*, 174–87.

49 Ibid., 12–27.

50 Ibid., 24–25.

51 Harrington qtd. ibid., 26; *Estes Park Trail* qtd. in Musselman, *Rocky Mountain National Park*, 94.

52 Quin, "Trail Ridge Road, Rocky Mountain National Park, HAER No. CO-31," 12–28, *Estes Park Trail* qtd. on 27; Musselman, *Rocky Mountain National Park*, 89–94.

53 Quin, "Trail Ridge Road, Rocky Mountain National Park, HAER No. CO-31," 40.

54 Anderson, "Addendum to Zion–Mount Carmel Highway, Zion–Mount Carmel Highway Tunnel, Zion National Park, No. UT-39-A," 14–20.

55 Ibid., 21–37; Davis, Croteau, and Marston, *America's National Park Roads and Parkways*, 201–9.

56 Ibid., 22–37.

57 Ibid., 38; Donald T. Garate, *The Zion Tunnel: From Slickrock to Switchback*, quote, n.p. "Ripley's Believe It or Not," *Detroit Evening News*, 14 April 1932.

58 Christina Slattery, "Generals Highway, Sequoia National Park, HAER No. CA-140," 1–11; Dilsaver and Tweed, *Challenge of the Big Trees*, 38–96; "Report of the Acting Superintendent, Sequoia and General Grant National Parks," in *U.S. Department of the Interior, Reports of the Department of the Interior for the Fiscal Year Ended June 30, 1912*, 675–90, qtd. on 680.

59 Goodwin to Mather, 21 July 1919; Mather to Goodwin, 1 April 1921; Goodwin to Endersby, 23 July 1921 (RG79 E9 Box194); Slattery, "Generals Highway, Sequoia National Park, No. CA-140," 12–13.

60 Maddox to Mather, 29 March 1921; Maddox to Gilbert Grosvenor, 29 March 1921; Mather to Cammerer, 31 March 1921; Albright to Mather, 12 April 1921; Stewart to Mather, 21 September 1921 (RG79 E9 B194).

61 Mather to Goodwin, 4 April 1921; Cammerer to Albright, 11 April 1921; Albright to Mather, 26 April 1921;

Goodwin to Maddox, 24 July 1921; Goodwin to Mather, 31 March 1922; Cammerer to Goodwin, 25 April 1922; Cammerer to White, 25 April 1922 (RG79 E9 B194-195).

62 Slattery, "Generals Highway, Sequoia National Park, No. CA-140," 15–19; Mather to Small, 23 March 1923; Mather to Small, 30 March 1923; Mather to Small, 1 June 1923; Goodwin to Mather, 1 June 1923; Cammerer to Albright, 11 June 1923; Goodwin to Mather, 2 March 1925; Mather to Goodwin, 10 March 1925; Goodwin to Mather, 19 March 1925; White to Mather, 10 April 1925 (RG79 E9 B195).

63 Slattery, "Generals Highway, Sequoia National Park, No. CA-140," 19 (Mather quoted); Dilsaver and Tweed, *Challenge of the Big Trees*, 142–44. Mather to Austin, 13 January 1926 (RG79 E9 B427).

64 Albright to Mather, 26 April 1921 (RG79 E9 B194).

65 Some sources credit Tunnel Rock to the CCC, but Mather praised the feature and thanked Austin for providing before-and-after photographs in January 1926 (Mather to Austin, 12 January 1926 [RG79 E10:1 B427]).

66 Slattery, "Generals Highway, Sequoia National Park, No. CA-140," 24–29, quote on 28.

67 Ibid., White, "brown ribbon," 16; Albright to Cammerer, 2 July 1934, quote on 21; Dilsaver and Tweed, *Challenge of the Big Trees*, 127–31. Howard Hayes to Albright, 14 March 1929; Albright to Hayes, 20 March 1929; White to Albright, 3 November 1931, "no matter how good"; White to Albright, 19 May 1932 (RG79 E10:1 B429).

68 Slattery, "Generals Highway, Sequoia National Park, No. CA-140," 27–36; Hewes to MacDonald, 17 April 1930 (RG79 E10:1 B429).

69 Temple et al. to Sec. Work, 12 December 1924 (RG48 Central Classified Files B2011); "Begin Survey of the Hoover Highway," *Luray (Va.) News & Currier*, 3 February 1931 (RG79 E10:1 B44); Albright and Cahn, *The Birth of the National Park Service*, 265–68. For a detailed descriptive and historical account, see USDOI, NPS, National Register of Historic Places, "Skyline Drive Historic District Nomination Form."

70 These complaints extended into the 1940s; Ickes quote is from letter to Virginia Sen. Carter Glass, 2 May 1939 (RG79 E10:2 B1658).

71 Engle, *The Greatest Single Feature*, 17–19.

72 The CCC's involvement is summarized in Engle, *Everything Was Wonderful*.

73 FDR quoted in Engle, *The Greatest Single Feature*, 15.

74 Albright to Ickes, 29 April 1931; DOI press release, 25 March 1931 (RG79 E10:1 B444).

75 Clarke to Demaray, 6 July 1931 (RG79 E10:1 B445).

76 Ibid.; Petersen to Albright, 8 July 1931; Peterson to Demaray, 27 July 1931; Petersen to Albright, 4 August 1931; Petersen to Cammerer, 5 August 1931; MacDonald to Demaray, 29 August 1931; Demaray to Clarke, 3 September 1931; Clarke to Demaray, 14 September 1931 (RG79 E10:1 B445); Peterson to HAER Chief Eric DeLony, 23 May 1996 (HAER office files). Hewes maintained that the BPR employed spiral curvature rather than broken-back curves whenever possible (Hewes, "America's Park Highways," 539).

77 Spelman, "Building Roads in the Shenandoah Park"; USDOI, NPS, National Register of Historic Places, "Skyline Drive Historic District Nomination Form," 18. Ludgate to Austin, 23 June 1932 (RG79 E10:2 B1660).

78 Cammerer to Eakin, 1 December 1931; Cammerer to Kelsey, 1 December 1931; Kelsey to Albright, 20 January 1932; Albright to Bishop, 20 January 1932; Bishop to Demaray, 26 January 1932 (RG79 E10:1 B445).

79 "Memorandum for Director Albright," 13 March 1931; Avery to Demaray, 26 January 1932 (RG79 E10:1 B445); Mackaye, "Flankline vs Skyline."

80 "Colored Laborers' Use on Job Protested," *Washington Star*, 16 November 1931; Peterson to Bishop, 29 January 1932 (RG79 E10:1 B445); Davis, Croteau, and Marston, *America's National Park Roads and Parkways*, 140.

81 William Showalter, "In the Shenandoah Valley of Virginia," *Washington Evening Star*, 10 July 1932; Virginius Dabney, "New Skyline Drive Opened in Virginia," *New York Times*, 13 November 1932, 6; "Skyline Drive Open for Twelve Miles," *American Motorist*, November 1932. Albright to Harlan Kelsey, 17 November 1932; Zerkel to Demaray, 12 December 1932 (RG79 E10:1 B444-445).

82 Harrisonburg Chamber of Commerce to Cammerer, 27 July 1934; Shenandoah Valley, Inc. to Cammerer, 27 July 1934; Winchester Chamber of Commerce, Lions Club, Kiwanis Club, Lions Club, American Legion, Veterans of Foreign Wars, and Women's Civic League to Cammerer, 31 July 1934; Robert Ramsey, Lynchburg Chamber of Commerce to Cammerer, 1 August 1934; Byrd to Cammerer, 15 August 1934; Demaray to Byrd, 17 August 1934; MacDonald to Byrd, 15 August 1934; "President Aids Skyline Drive," *Washington Post*, 16 August 1934; DOI press release, 11 September 1934 (RG79 E10:2 B1660); George Engeman, "Virginia's New Skyline Drive," *Baltimore Sun*, 16 September 1934; "33-Mile Stretch of Skyline Drive Is Opened," *Washington Post*, 16 September 1934; "Skyline Drive Is Inundated," *Washington Post*, 18 September 1934.

83 USDOI, NPS, National Register of Historic Places, "Skyline Drive Historic District Nomination Form," 6, 18–20.

84 Ibid., 18–20; Davis, Croteau, and Marston, *America's National Park Roads and Parkways*, 137–42.

85 Clyde McDuffie to Ickes, 21 October 1938; Phineas Indritz to DOI solicitor Nathan Margold, 12 January 1939; Margold to Ickes, 17 January 1939; Ickes to Margold, 25 January 1939; W. J. Trent, Memorandum for the Secretary, 30 March 1939; Byrd to assistant secretary E. K. Burlew, 9 March 1939; Glass to Burlew 7 March 1939; Burlew to McDuffie, 3 April 1939; Demaray to Ickes, 7 April 1939; Ickes to NAACP secretary Walter White, 11 May 1939 (quoted); Thurgood Marshall to Margold, 8 August 1940; Burlew to Demaray, 7 August 1940; Lassiter to NPS director 3 Sept 1940 (RG 48 Central Classified Files, 1937–53 B3791); USDOI, NPS, National Register of Historic Places, "Skyline Drive Historic District (Boundary Increase)," 82–91; Reed Engle, "Laboratory for Change," *Resource Management Newsletter*, January 1996, www.nps.gov/shen/historyculture/segregation.htm.

86 Earl Godwin, "A Newspaperman Looks at the Shenandoah National Park," in USDOI, NPS, *1941 Yearbook: Park and Recreation Progress*, 15.

87 Quin, "All-Year Highway (El Portal Road), Yosemite National Park, HAER No. CA-150," 2–6.

88 Lewis's statement and related correspondence in RG79 E9 B308.

89 Lane to L. A. Mares, 11 June 1919 (RG79 E9 B308); Lewis to Mather, 1 December 1923; Lewis to Mather, 10 January 1926; Hull to Mather, 30 December 1930; Mather to Palmer, 7 January 1925; Hull to Mather, 12 January 1926 (RG79 E10:1 Box528); Grant, "The Forum of Fantastic Beauty"; Leavitt, "Yosemite—A Motorist's Paradise"; Matthes, *The Geologic History of the Yosemite Valley*, 8; Quin, "All-Year Highway, (El Portal Road), Yosemite National Park, HAER No. CA-150," 6–10.

90 Hull to Mather, 6 February 1926, "Memorandum Covering Road Inspection Yosemite Valley and El Portal Area, Yosemite National Park"; Hull to Mather, 26 March 1926; Mather to Hull, 8 April 1926 (RG79 E10:1 B530).

91 Mather to Lewis, 27 January 1927; Vint to Hull, 5 February 1926; Lewis to Mather, 10 February 1926; Vint to Hull, 5 March 1926 (RG79 E10:1 B530).

92 Quin, "All-Year Highway, (El Portal Road), Yosemite National Park, HAER No. CA-150," 10–12.

93 "Memorandum on Yosemite Road Budget, August 4, 1927" (RG79 E10:1 B530); W. B. Lewis, "Memorandum for the Record," 29 April 1927; LA Chamber of Commerce Traffic Manager H. R. Brashear to Mather, 23 May 1927; Brashear to Demaray, 20 June 1927; Louis Meyer to Albright, 27 October 1931; Albright to Meyer, 2 November 1931; G. G. Thomson to L. V. Peterson, Stockton Record, 13 May 1932 (RG79 E10:1 B527-528).

94 Quin, "Wawona Road, Yosemite National Park, HAER No. CA-148," 11–12. Matthes to Kittredge, 13 April 1929 (RG79 E10:1 B527); Cammerer to Albright, 8 February 1929 (RG79, E10:1 B529).

95 Kittredge to Hewes, 21 November 1928; Kittredge to Matthes, 3 April 1929; Kittredge to Thomson, 3 April 1929; Kittredge to McDuffie, 3 April 1929; BPR District Engineer C. H. Sweetser to Hewes, 13 June 1929; Thomson to Vint, 2 January 1930; "Wawona Tunnel" information sheet, 28 August 1931 (RG79 E10:1 B530-531); Quin, "Wawona Road, Yosemite National Park, HAER No. CA-148," 12.

96 Quin, "Wawona Road, Yosemite National Park, HAER No. CA-148," 12–15; Quin, "Wawona Tunnel, Yosemite National Park, HAER No. CA-105," 4–7; "Wawona Tunnel, Yosemite National Park, California" (RG79 E10:1 B531); "Yosemite Tunnel Approach," 5.

97 Quin, "Wawona Tunnel, Yosemite National Park, HAER No. CA-105," 5–8; "Yosemite Tunnel Approach," 6

98 Quin, "Wawona Tunnel, Yosemite National Park, HAER No. CA-105," 5–8; Quin, "Wawona Road, Yosemite National Park, HAER No. CA-148," 15–16.

99 Quin, "Wawona Tunnel, Yosemite National Park, HAER No. CA-105," 4–7. Thomson to Ickes, 16 June 1933 (RG48 Central Classified Files, 1907–36, Section 12 B1975); Thomson to Albright, 27 January 1933; Albright to Ickes, 16 May 1933 (RG79 E10:1 B531).

100 "Suggestions for Secretary Ickes's Electrical Transcription for Use at the Wawona Dedication" (RG79 E10 B531).

101 Thomson qtd. in Quin, "Wawona Tunnel Yosemite National Park, HAER No. CA-105," 8; "Yosemite Tunnel Approach," 3. Telegram from Louis Johnson, National Commander of the American Legion, forwarded by Thomson, 28 March 1933 (RG79 E10:1 B531).

102 Memorandum on the Yosemite Road Budget, 4 August 1924, 9 (RG79 E10:1 B530); "Big Oak Flat Project, Yosemite National Park: Study of Comparative Locations Full Benched Section vs Balanced Section," Chief Engineer's Office 22 March 1928; Albright to Louis Meyer, 6 October 1931; Kittredge to Thomson, 23 January 1932 (RG79 E10:1 B527); Vint to Thomson, 26 May 1933; Albright to Thomson, 10 August 1933 (RG79 E10:2 B1840).

103 Demaray to Albright, 11 May 1933; W. W. Webber, NPS Engineer, "Big Oak Flat Road Yosemite National Park," 14 January 1934; Kittredge to Albright, 6 June 1933; Kittredge to Albright, 7 June 1933; Vint to Thomson, 26 May 1933; Kittredge to Albright, 5 August 1933; Cammerer to Kittredge, 19 August 1933; Vint to Thomson, 15 September 1933; Cammerer to Thomson, 20 October 1933; Thomson to Cammerer, 30 October 1933; Kittredge to Thomson, 13 November 1933; Kittredge, "Report on Study of the Big Oak Flat Road, 13 November 1933; Yosemite Advisory Board, "Report on Proposed Reconstruction of Big Oak Flat Road," 16 January 1934; Kittredge to Cammerer, 21 August 1934; Vint to Cammerer, 27 September 1934; Kittredge to Cammerer, 6 October 1934; Farquhar to Cammerer, 11 October 1934; Kittredge to Cammerer, 11 October 1934; Kittredge to Cammerer, 8 November, 1934 (RG79 E10:2 B1840).

104 Kittredge to Cammerer, 11 October 1934, quoted; Thomson to Albright, 13 July 1933; Kittredge to Thomson, 13 November 1933: Thomson to Cammerer, 8 January 1934; "Memorandum on Conference Regarding Yosemite Program," 14 February 1934; Thomson to Cammerer, 21 September 1934, quoted; Cammerer, "Memorandum for Assistant Secretary Chapman, 2 November 1934 (RG79 E10:2 B1840).

105 Quin, "Big Oak Flat Road, Yosemite National Park," 14–18.

106 Culpin, *The History of the Road System in Yellowstone National Park*, 129–53, 197; "Yellowstone Park Improves Roads Leading to Its Chain of Geysers," *New York Herald Tribune*, 24 April 1924.

107 Kittredge to Albright, 15 July 1932 (RG79 E10:1 B471); Acting Superintendent Guy Edwards, "Memo for the Files," 25 October 1930; "Report of Kenneth McCarter et al., July 11–17, 1932" (Yellowstone National Park Archives, Box D-3).

108 Kittredge to Albright, 15 July 1932 (RG79 E10:1 B471); Acting Superintendent Guy Edwards, "Memo for the Files," 25 October 1930; "Report of Kenneth C. McCarter et al., July 11–17, 1932" (YNP Archives, Box D-3), additional documentation in RG79 E10:2 B1738.

109 Culpin, *The History of the Construction of the Road System in Yellowstone National Park*, 146–53, 268; Davis, Croteau, and Marston, *America's National Park Roads and Parkways*, 165; Gilmore Clarke, "Report to Accompany Plan of Mammoth Hot Springs Area, Yellowstone National Park, June 1930" (Yellowstone National Park Archives).

110 Horace Albright, "Improved Roads and National Parks," *U.S. Daily*, 22 October 1929; *AR 1937*, 34; *AR 1940*, 164; *AR 1941*, 277–78; *AR 1942*, 163.

111 Albright, "National Parks Open to Motoring; New Roads Increase Tourist Travel," *U.S. Daily*, 14 November 1929; Kittredge, "Preserving a Valuable Heritage"; Thomas MacDonald, "Uncle Sam Considers Roadsides, *American Civic Annual, 1930*, 160–67; Hewes, "America's Park Highways"; Hewes, *American Highway Practice*; Ewen, "Mt. Rainier National Park Highway System Developed through Programmed Construction," 396; Canfield, "Building the Rim Road at Crater Lake"; Cron, "Roads for Vicksburg National Military Park"; Spelman, "Building Roads in the Shenandoah Park."

112 "Yosemite Tunnel Approach," 3–7; Andersen, "Road Building in the Rockies"; Seyffert, "The Going-to-the-Sun Highway"; Houk, "Scenic Highways of the West"; William Ullman, "Roads Improved in National Parks," *New York Times*, 8 February 1931.

113 BPR films included *A Road Out of Rock; New Roads in Mount Rainier; Yosemite's New Road; Tunneling to Yosemite; Roads in Our National Parks; Roads to Wonderland; The Men Who Build the Roads*; and *The Road Goes Through*.

114 *Ford Motor Company Presents . . . Yellowstone National Park*; additional films include *A Visit to Yellowstone National Park, A Visit to Mount Rainier*, and similar films on Yosemite, Grand Canyon, and Rocky Mountain National Parks.

115 Shankland, *Steve Mather*, 284–91; Ise, *The National Park Service*, 321–23; Quin, "Mather Memorial Parkway, HAER No. WA-125," 3–5. The middle section of Mather Memorial Parkway was incorporated within Mount Rainier National Park when Congress expanded the boundaries in 1931.

VI. TROUBLE IN PARADISE

1 Sutter's *Driven Wild* is the most recent account of this phenomenon, which was widely remarked at the time and addressed in HAER reports and other NPS histories.

2 Kittredge, "Big Oak Flat Project, Yosemite National Park: Study of Comparative Locations," 22 March 1928 (RG79 E10:1 B527); Kittredge, "Report on the Study of Big Oak Flat Road," 13 November 1933; Kittredge to Cammerer, 21 August 1934; Kittredge to Cammerer, 6 October 1934 (quoted) (RG79 E10:2 B1840); Kittredge, "Preserving a Valuable Heritage."

3 Thomson to BPR Engineer C. H. Sweetser, 11 May 1933, "pleasant and park-like," "savagely criticized"; Thomson to Cammerer, 21 September 1934 (quoted) (RG79 E10:2 B1840).

4 Vint to Cammerer, 27 September 1934; Vint to Thomson, 28 October 1933; Kittredge to Cammerer, 11 October 1934; Kittredge to Cammerer, 8 November 1934 (quoted); Kittredge to Cammerer, 11 November 1934 (RG79 E10:2 B1840); Kittredge to Cammerer, 29 October 1938 (quoted) (RG79 E10:2 B448).

5 J. Hart Rosdail to Demaray, 12 May 1941; Demaray to Rosdail, 20 May 1941; White to F. B. Williams, 11 April 1940 (RG79 E10:2 B449).

6 Pray, "Danger of Over-Exploitation of Our National Parks," 113; Pray, "The American Society of Landscape Architects and Our National Parks"; Frederick Law Olmsted Jr., "The Distinction between National Parks and National Forests," *Landscape Architecture* 6 (April 1916), 114–15, quote on 114.

7 Olmsted Jr., "Vacation in the National Parks and Forests," 110.

8 Leopold, "The Wilderness and Its Place in Forest Recreational Policy"; Meine, *Aldo Leopold: His Life and Work*; Sutter, *Driven Wild*, 54–99.

9 Leopold, "Wilderness as a Form of Land Use," "virile," 401, "Americanism," 403; Leopold, "Conserving the Covered Wagon," "covered wagon blood," 21.

10 Leopold, "Wilderness as a Form of Land Use"; Leopold, "Conserving the Covered Wagon," "benefaction," "good roads mania," "thrusting," 21, "steam roller," 56.

11 Leopold, "Wilderness as a Form of Land Use," "merry-go-rounds," 402; Leopold, "The Last Stand of Wilderness," "artificial forms," 600; Leopold, "The Wilderness and Its Place in Forest Recreational Policy," "a continuous stretch," 719.

12 Leopold, "The Wilderness and Its Place in Forest Recreational Policy," "networked," 720; Leopold, "The Last Stand of Wilderness," "quiet and harmony," 600; Leopold, "Wilderness as a Form of Land Use," "vanguard," 404; Leopold, "Conserving the Covered Wagon," "steamroller," 56.

13 Greeley, "What Shall We Do with Our Mountains?," "greatest single factor," 14, "penetration," "conquering power," 15, "yellow busses," 81.

14 Hubbard qtd. in Senate, *National Conference on Outdoor Recreation. Proceedings of the National Conference on Outdoor Recreation, May 22, 23, and 24, 1924*, 59–60; Jensen to Mather, 24 December 1924 (RG79 E9 B3); Elwood to Vint, 29 December 1927 (RG 79 E77 B20).

15 Yard, "Standards of Our National Park System," "motorist's invasion," 3; Yard, "The Motor Tourist and the National Parks," pt. 1, 11–12; Yard, "The Motor Tourist and the National Parks," pt. 2; Yard, *Our Federal Lands*, "too dangerous," 349; Miles, *Guardians of the Parks*, 14–94.

16 Yard, "Standards of Our National Park System"; Yard, "The Motor Tourist and the National Parks," pt. 1; Yard, "The Motor Tourist and the National Parks," pt. 2.

17 Yard, "Standards of Our National Park System"; Yard, *Our Federal Lands*, 257–83, 347.

18 Yard, "The Motor Tourist and the National Parks," pt. 1; Yard, "The Motor Tourist and the National Parks," pt. 2, "motorists are motorists" and "modern way," 19; Yard, *Our Federal Lands*, "rushing hordes," 265; Yard, "Standards of Our National Park System," 3.

19 Yard, "Motor-Road vs. Wilderness."

20 Senate, *Proceedings of the National Conference on Outdoor Recreation . . . 1924*, 27–28, 116–18 (RG79 E9 B3); Senate, *Proceedings of the National Conference on Outdoor Recreation . . . 1926*, 61–65, "motorize their souls," 63; National Conference on Outdoor Recreation, *Recreation Resources on Federal Lands*, "unmodified nature," 53.

21 Atwood, "Nature as Created"; Caesar, "National Parks or City Parks?"; Albright, "The Everlasting Wilderness," "not destroy," 28, "those who,"63.

22 Albright, "The Everlasting Wilderness," 28, 63.

23 Ibid., "waterfalls," 63; "wilderness," 66, "adventure enough" and "most beautiful," 68.

24 Albright, "Preserving Wilderness Beauty along Forest Roads." Albright to Yard, 24 May 1938 (RG79 E10:2 B679).

25 Burt, "The Perpetual Wilderness," quote on 137–38.

26 Mather to superintendents, 27 November 1923 (RG 79 E9 B395).

27 Yard to Secretary of the Interior Hubert Work, 11 September 1924 (RG 79 E9 B171).

28 Toll to Yard, 18 September, 1924; Toll, "Memorandum Regarding Proposed Road on Continental Divide," 19 September 1924; Yard to Toll, 29 September 1924; Lane to Yard, 30 September 1924; Cammerer to Mather, 23 September 1924; Cammerer to Demaray, 1 October 1924 (RG79 E9 B171).

29 Steel circular for road proposal, 22 May 1932 ("dainty theory"); "Road to Shore of Lake Envisioned," *Medford (Ore.) Daily News*, 31 July 1931; Steel, "Why Were National Parks Created?," June 1932; Albright to E. C. Solinsky, 22 October 1932; Harry Myers to Albright, 26 May 1932; Albright to Myers, 31 May 1932; Solinsky to Albright, 7 June 1932; Solinksy to Albright, 28 June 1932; Steel, "For Road to Rim," *Medford (Ore.) Mail-Tribune*, 24 May 1932; Steel, "Wants Road to Lake," letter to the editor, *Medford (Ore.) Daily News*, 25 May 1932 (RG79 E10:1 B223).

30 *AR 1920*, 104; *AR 1923*, 49. Albright, "Report on Proposed Road Across the Gallatin Mountains," 2 December 1923 (RG79 E9 B247).

31 Albright to Mather, 20 February 1922; Albright to Wm. Hall, 1 October 1923; Cammerer to Idaho senator William Borah, 17 April 1922; Mather to Borah, 2 February 1924 (RG79 E9 B248); Wm. Davis to Albright, 30 October 1922 (RG79 E10:1 B472). The broader battle with water interests is described in Haines, *The Yellowstone Story*, 2:340–46; Ise, *The National Park Service*, 286–89, 307–17 (Idaho congressman T. Addison Smith qtd. on 308); Lovin, "Fighting over the Cascade Corner of Yellowstone National Park, 1919–35"; Yochim, "Beauty and the Beet."

32 Smith to Mather, 1 May 1923; Albright to Smith, 9 May 1923; Smith to Albright, 17 May 1923; Albright to Moore, 18 September 1923 (RG79 E10:1 B472).

33 Cammerer to Smith, 26 June 1924; Hugh Rankin to Sen. Borah, 12 March 1925; Rankin to Albright, 22 March 1925; Rankin to Albright, 26 March 1925; Albright to Rankin, 4 April 1925; Albright to Mather, 12 May 1925; Mather to Albright, 14 May 1925; Rankin to Borah, 19 May 1925; Cammerer to Borah, 4 June 1925; "Take Your Choice," *Ashton (Idaho) Herald*, 22 April 1926; Albright to W. A. Lansberry, 13 May 1926 (RG79 E10:1 B472).

34 Albright to Mather, 27 July 1925; Albright to Mather, 29 July 1925 (RG79 E10:1 B471).

35 Caparn, "Observations Made during a Visit to Yellowstone Park, September 11–18, 1926"; Albright to Mather, 30 September 1926 (RG79 10:1 B472); Albright, "Everlasting Wilderness," 66.

36 Albright to Walter Sheppard, 1 April 1933; Albright to Franklin Mitchell, 10 April 1933; Asst. Interior Sec. Oscar Chapman to Idaho Sen. James Pope, 13 September 1933; Cammerer to R. N. Packard, 28 September 1933; Toll to

Cammerer, 23 March 1934; Woodring to Cammerer, 30 March 1934; Cammerer to Idaho rep. T. C. Coffin, 30 March 1934 (RG79 E10:2 B1740). The 1931 Leavitt Act increased the NPS road-building budget to $7.5 million for 1932 and 1933, stipulating that $1.5 million per year be spent on approach roads over federal lands (*AR 1932*, 32).

37 Cammerer to Sec. of Interior, 16 March 1938; Demaray to J. W. Emmert, 14 April 1938; E. Hockett to Sec. of Interior, 28 April 1938; Demaray to Montana Sen. Burton Wheeler, 12 May 1938; Albright to Rogers, 14 May 1938; Sec. of Interior to Hockett, 17 May 1938; Demaray to White, 26 May, 1938 (RG79 E10:2 B1738).

38 "Memorandum to Joint Committee, Representing the Seattle Chamber of Commerce, Seattle Commercial Club, Rotary Club of Seattle, Tacoma Commercial Club and Chamber of Commerce, Rotary Club of Seattle," 7 March 1912; Mount Rainier superintendent Ethan Allen to Interior Sec. Lane, 26 June 1913; T. H. Martin to Lane, 11 July 1913 (RG79 E9 B135); Sterling, "The Motorist and the National Parks," 11.

39 Road development in Mount Rainier is discussed at greater length in Quin, "Mount Rainier National Park Roads and Bridges, HAER No. WA-35"; Carr, *Wilderness by Design*, 189–247, Catton, *Wonderland*, 97–104, 219–46; and Louter, *Windshield Wilderness*, 36–67.

40 "Constructed and Proposed Roads in and about the Rainier National Park," received by Sec. Lane, 24 June 1913; Martin to Lane, 11 July 1913; "Plans Finest Road in United States," *Seattle Sun*, 20 September 1913; T. Warren Allen to Logan Page, 28 August 1914; Allen to Page, 28 August 1914; T. H. Martin to Secretary of the Interior, 6 February 1915; Matthes to Clement Ucker, 6 January 1913; Matthes to Mather, 20 February 1915 (RG79 E9 B135); Quin, "Mount Rainier National Park Roads and Bridges, HAER No. WA-35," 16–17; Catton, *Wonderland*, 96–103.

41 Matthes to Clement Ucker, 6 January 1913; Matthes to Mather, 20 February 1915 (RG79 E9 B135).

42 Quin, "Mount Rainier National Park Roads and Bridges, HAER No. WA-35," 22–23. Initially known as the Naches Pass Highway and then the McClellan Pass Highway, the state highway crossed the Cascades at Cayuse Pass. Martin to Mather, 2 June 1919; Mather to Martin, 6 June 1919; Martin to Mather, 17 June 1919; Toll to Mather, 8 September 1919; Toll to G. F. Allen, 26 August 1919; Mather to D. W. Whitcomb, 19 February 1921; Martin to Mather, 2 April 1921; Martin to Albright, 9 May 1919 [personal]; Martin to Albright, 9 May 1919; Mather to Martin, 6 June 1919; Toll to Mather, 28 September 1919; Curtis to Cammerer, 24 November 1920; Goodwin to Mather, 21 October 1924; Tomlinson to Mather, 30 October 1924; Curtis to Mather, 21 November 1924; Albright to Mather, 30 October 1924; John Eddy to Mather, 5 November 1924; Martin to Tomlinson, 12 December 1924, "new dignity,"; D. I. Cornell to Mather, 13 February 1925 (RG79 E9 B136-137).

43 Martin to Tomlinson, 12 December 1924; Martin to Mather, 26 February 1925; Cammerer to Tomlinson, 26 March 1925; "General Policy for Development of Roads in Rainier National Park; Resolutions Adopted by the Joint Committee"; Curtis to Cammerer, 15 April 1925;

Cammerer to Mather, 7 May 1925; "Mount Rainier National Park," *Mountaineer* 17 (April 1925): 4 (RG79 E9 B137); The Mountaineers, "The Administration of the National Parks."

44 Approximately a half million dollars in federal funds were expended on USFS segments and state highway construction (Rainier National Park Advisory Board pamphlet addressed to "Mr. Good Citizen" [RG79, E9 B137]).

45 Curtis to Cramton, 25 February 1927; Curtis to Albright, 25 February 1927; Albright to Curtis, 2 March 1927; Mather to Albright, 3 March 1927; Mather to Tomlinson, 3 March 1927; Tomlinson to Director, 27 May 1930 (RG79, E10:1 B383); Mather qtd. in DOI press release, 27 August 1928 (RG79 E10:2 B250); Quin, "West Side Road, HAER No. WA-122," 3–7, Vint qtd. on 4; Carr, *Wilderness by Design*, 223–24.

46 Curtis to Mather, 17 May 1927; H. A. Rhodes to Mather, 18 May 1927; Tomlinson to Mather, 24 May 1927; Demaray to Tomlinson, 4 June 1927; Albright to Rhodes, 31 June 1927; Sceva to T. H. Martin, 20 July 1928; Martin to Tomlinson, 20 July 1928; Tomlinson to Mather, 20 July 1928; Vint to Mather, 14 August 1928; Mather to Tomlinson, 23 August 1928 (RG79 E10:1 B383); Cammerer to Secretary of the Interior, 20 April 1934; Kittredge "Brief of Essential Correspondence Related to Proposed Tramway," 29 April 1946 (RG79 E10:2 B1462).

47 L. A. Nelson to Tomlinson, [n.d.], with Tomlinson to Albright, 10 January 1931; Vint to Albright, 23 May 1930 (RG79 E10:2 383); Quin, "Stevens Canyon Highway, HAER No. WA-123," 3–5; Carr, *Wilderness by Design*, 226–30; Carl Russell, "Frank Alvah Kittredge, 1883–1954," 70.

48 Caesar, "National Parks or City Parks?"; Tomlinson to Kittredge, 20 December 1927; Tomlinson to Albright accompanying "Development in the National Parks" manuscript, 3 January 1928; Kittredge to Tomlinson, 9 January 1928 (RG79 E10:1 B383); Kittredge to Tomlinson, 9 January 1928 (RG 79 E77 B110).

49 Davidson, "Memorandum for Chief Architect T. C. Vint re: West Side Highway Extension, Mount Rainier Natl. Park, 18 April 1935"; Cammerer, memorandum for Mr. Demaray, 5 July 1935, attached to Davidson's memorandum; Tomlinson to Ickes, 21 September 1938 (RG79 E10:2 B1441); Drury to Edwin Henderson, 7 February 1941 (RG79 E10:2 B1462); Quin, "West Side Road, HAER No. WA-122," 6–10.

50 Many shared ties to the University of California. Both Mather and Albright were graduates and Albright studied law under Colby; Mather's predecessor, Adolph Miller, was a professor of economics (Shankland, *Steve Mather*, 10, 47; Albright and Cahn, *The Birth of the National Park Service*, 1–2, 12, 68–69).

51 Senate, *Report of the Commission on Roads in Yosemite*, 56th Cong., 1st sess., 8 February 1900, S. Doc. 155, 16–17, 21; Manning, "Yosemite Park, July 18, 1917" and "Report of the National Park Committee of the American Society of Landscape Architects," January 7, 1918 (RG79 E9 B404); W. B. Lewis to Mather, 23 November 1923 (RG79 E9 B310; Muir to American Alpine Club Secretary Harold Palmer, 12 December 1912, in *The Life and Letters of John Muir*, 2:379.

52 *AR 1919*, 930, 980–81. Colby to W. B. Lewis, 7 May 1919 (RG79 E9 B310).

53 Colby, "Minutes of the Seventh National Park Conference Held in Yellowstone National Park, Wyoming, October 22–28, 1923," 15–17, 46–48 (quoted) (National Park Service History Collection, NPS Harpers Ferry Center); John Merriam to Mather, 22 July 1923 (RG79 E9 B310).

54 Cammerer to Mather, 21 June 1923, "horde," "black eye" (RG 79 E10:2 B528); Cammerer to Colby, 24 December 1923, "two evils"; Albright to G. E. Reynolds, Managing Editor, *Stockton (Calif.) Record*, 31 October 1923; W. B. Lewis to Mather, 23 November 1923 (RG79 E9 B310).

55 Lewis to Mather, 23 November 1923; Colby to Cammerer, 13 December 1923; Cammerer to Colby, 24 December 1923 (RG79 E9 B310).

56 *AR 1927*, 7; Yard, "Needless Road Project Endangers Yosemite."

57 Merriam to Mather, 22 July 1923; Cammerer to Colby, 24 December 1923 (RG79 E9 B310); "Memorandum on Yosemite Road Budget, 4 August 1927 (RG79 E10:1 B530).

58 Chandler to Albright, 19 March 1930; Don Tresidder to Albright, 9 May 1930; Colby to Albright, 7 November 1930 (RG79 E59 B7); Cammerer to Albright, 19 August 1928 (RG79 E59 B6); Shankland, *Steve Mather*, 207–8; Albright and Cahn, *The Birth of the National Park Service*, 254. Mather enthused about Colby's proposal in *AR 1919*, 978 and "Progress in the National Parks," 8–9.

59 Thomson to Albright 28 October 1930; Tressider to Albright, 4 November 1930; Huber to Albright, 8 November 1930; Kittredge to Albright, 8 November 1930; Albright to Olmsted, 1 December 1930 (RG79 E59 B7).

60 Thomson, "Memorandum for the Director Regarding the Glacier Point Problem," 3 October 1930; Thomson to Albright, 17 November 1930 (RG79 E10:1 B531); Duncan McDuffie, "Memorandum re: Glacier Point Tramway Application," 14 November 1930; Vint to Albright, 21 November 1930; "Report of Committee of Expert Advisors on Yosemite National Park," 12 December 1930 (RG79 E59 B7).

61 Thomson letter, 17 November 1930; Duncan McDuffie, "Memorandum re: Glacier Point Tramway Application," 14 November 1930; Vint to Albright, 21 November 1930; "Report of Committee of Expert Advisors on Yosemite National Park," 12 December 1930 (RG79 E59 B7); Albright to Thomson, 14 December 1931; Albright to Thomson, 19 December 1930 (RG79 E10:1 B531).

62 "Policy of the Sierra Club on Road Construction in the Sierra" and "Report of the Committee on Sierra Roads," *Sierra Club* circular, 25 (May–June 1927), 4–7; *AR 1931*, 77. H. E. Williams, "Report of Proposed Road Up Tenaya Canyon to Lake Tenaya," 20 March, 1930 (RG79 E77 B6).

63 F. A. Kittredge and Walter G. Attwell, "Report of Tenaya Lake Road Reconnaissance, Yosemite National Park, California," 7 September 1932; F. A. Kittredge, "Forward—Analysis of Problem, Tenaya Canyon Study, 9 August 1933," qtd. on 2 (RG79 10:1 B528); Kittredge to Demaray, 26 November 1932 (RG79 E10:1 B531); Kittredge, "Memorandum for the Director" (accompanying draft report), 5 June 1933; Demaray to Thomson, 17 June 1933; Thomson to Albright, 28 June 1933; Chester Warlow to Albright, 28 June 1933; Demaray to Warlow, 8 July 1933; Vint to Albright, 19 July 1933 (RG79 E10:2 B1840).

64 Thomson to C. H. Sweetser, 22 July 1932; Thomson to Albright, 12 August 1931; Demaray to Thomson, 14 August 1931 (RG79 E10:1 B531); Thomson to Albright, 2 June 1933; Carnes to Albright, 14 June 1933; Wosky to Thomson, 18 July 1933 (RG79 E10:2 B1840).

65 C. H. Sweetser to Hewes, 20 August 1931 (RG79 E10:1B531); Kittredge, "Memorandum for Director," 14 August 1933 (RG79 E10:2 B1840).

66 Albright to Demaray, 19 June 1933; Albright to Demaray, 26 June 1933; Thomson to Albright, 13 July 1933; Thomson to Albright, 14 July 1933; Wosky to Thomson, 18 July 1933; Thomson to Albright, 26 July 1933; Colby to Albright, 31 July 1933; Albright to Colby, 2 August 1933 (quoted); Albright to Thomson, 4 August 1933; Albright to Thomson, 5 August 1933; Thomson to Cammerer, 12 August 1933; Thomson to George S. Grant, 14 August, 1933 (RG79 E10:2 B1840).

67 Colby to Albright, 7 July 1933; Demaray to Albright, 17 July 1933; Albright to Thomson, 4 August 1933; Thomson to Cammerer, 19 August 1933; Thomson to Cammerer, 17 January 1934; "Report of the Executive Committee of the Sierra Club on the Proposed Re-Location of the Tioga Road, Yosemite National Park, approved May 1934" (RG79 E10:2 B1840); "Minutes of the Meeting of the Board of Directors," *Sierra Club Bulletin* 18 (December 1933), 161–62.

68 Thomson to Cammerer, 9 January 1935; Thomson's statement praised in H. C. Bryant to Cammerer, 15 January 1935; Ansel Hall to Thomson, 16 January 1935; McDuffie to Thomson, 16 January 1935; Sweetser to Thomson, 17 January 1925; Colby to Thomson, 22 January 1935; Cammerer, "Memorandum for The Secretary," 18 April 1935 (RG79 E10:2 B1840).

69 Dilsaver and Tweed, *Challenge of the Big Trees*, 182–86. "'Sierra Way' Road 800 Miles in Length to Link Park Lands," *U.S. Daily* (Washington, D.C.), 30 April 1932; "California's Sierra Road Due to Surpass Rome's 'Appian Way,'" *Arizona Republic*, 30 August 1932; California State Chamber of Commerce Agriculture and Industry, "The Sierra Way," 1 February 1935 (RG79 E10:2 B450).

70 George Wright to Cammerer, 2 August 1935; "Memorandum for Secretary," 30 November 1935; Cammerer to Colby, 8 January 1936; Cammerer to Yard, 8 January 1936; Cammerer to Frederic Delano, 8 January 1936; Cammerer to William B. Greeley, 8 January 1936; Cammerer to Huber, 21 January 1936, "needless"; Cammerer to Thompson, 27 January 1936, "California people"; Cammerer to Huber, 21 January 1936; White to Cammerer, 4 January 1936; Kittredge to White, 10 January 1936; White to Cammerer, 24 January 1936; White to Cammerer, 16 March 1936; Kittredge, "Memorandum for Director," 19 March 1936 (quoted); Thomas to Cammerer, 24 March 1936 (RG79 E10:2 B450).

71 "Commonwealth Club Warns against Further Road-Building into California's High Mountains," *Sierra Club Bulletin* 21 (June 1936): ix–xii, Commonwealth Club's "Should We Stop Building Roads in California's High Mountains?" report qtd. on ix; Kittredge to Cammerer, 28 April 1926; Kittredge to Cammerer, 4 May 1936; Demaray to Kittredge, 8 May 1936; (RG79 E10:2 B450); Cammerer to Thomson, 22 December 1933; Yosemite Superintendent Lawrence Merriam to Director,

11 June 1940; Demaray to Yosemite Superintendent, n.d. (RG79 E10:2 B140).

72 Quin, "Rockefeller Carriage Roads, Acadia National Park, HAER No. ME-12," 3–26; Maher, "Acadia National Park Motor Roads, HAER No. ME-11," 5–34; Roberts, *Mr. Rockefeller's Roads*, 19–52, 79–33, Pepper's 15 August 1920 letter to Rockefeller qtd. at length, 79; "Hearing on Lafayette National Park Road and Trail Development Held before Secretary of the Interior Work, March 26, 1924," Pepper's statement, 6–9 (RG79 E10:1 B202; an extensive collection of protests and associated correspondence can be found in B202-205).

73 Eliot, *The Future of Mount Desert Island*, 17–19; Hull to Cammerer, 5 July 1927; Cammerer to Hull, 9 July 1927; Mather to Cammerer, 22 July 1927; Cammerer to Hull, 23 July 1927; Hull to Director, 25 July 1927; misc. correspondence (RG79 E10:1 B203-205).

74 Quin, "Rockefeller Carriage Roads, Acadia National Park, HAER No. ME-12," 37–83, 93–95; Maher, "Acadia National Park Motor Roads, HAER No. ME-11," 1–5, "We are here today," 5, 24–43; misc. correspondence (RG79 E10:1 B203-205).

75 Kelleher and Maher, "Great Smoky Mountains National Park Roads and Bridges, HAER No. TN-35," 32–46; Pierce, *The Great Smokies*, 89–153, *Asheville Citizen* qtd. on 102.

76 Kelleher and Maher, "Great Smoky Mountains National Park Roads and Bridges, Newfound Gap Road, HAER No. TN-35-A" (1996), 14–26; Cammerer to C. N. Bass, 10 July 1926; Bass to NPS Director, 20 July 1927; "criticism," Cammerer to Welch, 24 July 1926; Bass to Cammerer, 12 August 1926 (RG79 E10:1 B316).

77 Kelleher and Maher, "Newfound Gap Road," 43–49, Eakin qtd. on 53; Kelleher and Maher, "Great Smoky Mountains National Park Roads and Bridges, HAER No. TN-35," 49–50.

78 Kelleher and Maher, "Newfound Gap Road," 42–70; Kelleher and Maher, "Great Smoky Mountains National Park Roads and Bridges, HAER No. TN-35," 48–63, White qtd. on 59.

79 Edge, *Roads and More Roads in the National Parks and Forests*; Cammerer to Edge, 7 April 1936 (RG79 E10:2 B448).

80 Marshall, "The Wilderness as a Minority Right"; Marshall, "The Problem of Wilderness," quote 148; Glover, *A Wilderness Original*, 1–98.

81 Albright to Marshall, 16 April 1930; Marshall to Albright, 22 April 1930; Marshall to Albright, 23 May 1930; Director's Memorandum for Superintendents and General Field Executives; Ansel Hall to Albright, 18 February 1930; Hall, "Research Reserves in National Parks," 18 February 1930; "Research Reserves," 23 January 1931; "Memorandum for the Press," June 1931; "Wild Areas Set Aside; National Park Research Reserves Will Be Unknown to the Public," *Washington Star*, 14 June 1931 (all in RG79 E10:1 B150). Never thoroughly implemented, the Research Reserve concept did not survive the World War II hiatus (Sellers, *Preserving Nature in the National Parks*, 108–12).

82 "Ickes on the Parks," *New York Times*, 14 May 1933 (quoted); Marshall, *The Forest for Recreation*, 463–87, Marshall, *The People's Forests*, quote on 183; Glover, *A Wilderness Original*, 144–68; Mackintosh, "Harold Ickes

and the National Park Service." Marshall to Ickes, 27 February 1934 (RG79 E10:2 B379).

83 "Launch Asheville-Through-Park Route," *Asheville Advocate*, 19 February 1932; Fred Weede, Asheville Chamber of Commerce to Albright, 12 February 1932; Albright to Weede, 18 February 1932; Cammerer to Albright, 3 February 1932; Eakin to Taylor, 30 January 1932; Eakin to Albright, 16 February 1932, quoted; Weede to Albright, 10 March 1932 (RG79 E10:1 B310); Cammerer to Eakins, 13 February 1939 (RG79 E60 B6).

84 S. B. Locke to Albright, 24 October 1932; Albright to Locke, 31 October 1932; Albright to Robert Lindsay Mason, 8 November 1932 (quoted); Albright to V. E. Shelford, 9 November 1932; Cammerer to Eakin, 10 November 1932; Mason to Albright, 14 November 1932; Locke to Albright, 15 November 1932; Orpheus Shant to Cammerer, 15 November 1932; Cammerer to Albright, 17 November 1932; Shelford to Albright, 21 November 1932; Philip Ayres to Albright, 28 November 1932; Kelsey to Albright, 30 November 1932; Albright to Lorne Barclay, National Parks Association, 28 October 1932; Barclay to Albright, 27 December 1932; E. G. Frizzell, Smoky Mountains Hiking Club to Cammerer, 20 January 1933; Eakin to Albright, 30 July 1932, "extremist"; Eakin to Albright, 9 September 1932; Ludgate to Eakin, 28 November 1932; additional complaints and responses in RG79 E10:1 B310-11; Frizzel to Cammerer, 20 January 1933 (RG79 E10:2 B1135).

85 Marshall, "A Suggested Program for Preservation of Wilderness Areas," report for Ickes, [?] March 1934 (RG79 E10:2 B379); Mackaye, "Flankline vs Skyline" (confidential copy) with Eakin to Cammerer, 2 June 1934 (RG79 E10:2 B1133); a revised version appeared as "Flankline vs Skyline," *Appalachia* 20 (1934): 104–8.

86 Broome, "Origins of the Wilderness Society"; Glover, *A Wilderness Original*, 172–78; Ickes to Demaray, 7 September 1934; Ickes to Cammerer, 21 September 1934 (RG79 E10:2 B448); Marshall qtd. in "Skyline Road Attacked by Marshall," *Knoxville Journal*, 20 October 1934; Cammerer qtd. in "Park Head Says Skyline Road Is 'Necessity,'" *Knoxville News-Sentinel*, 21 October 1934; Ickes to Cammerer, 9 November 1934; Ickes to Marshall, 9 November 1934 (RG 48 Central Classified Files B2010).

87 "A Summons to Save the Wilderness"; "The Wilderness Society Platform"; Ickes, "Wilderness and Skyline Drives."

88 "A Summons to Save the Wilderness"; "The Wilderness Society Platform"; Ickes, "Wilderness and Skyline Drives."

89 Cammerer, "Standards and Policies in National Parks," quote on 19; E. Lowell Sumner Jr., "The Wilderness Problem in the National Parks," October 9, 1936 (RG79 E10:2 B379); Kittredge to Cammerer, 25 October 1938, and 29 October 1938, 1 November 1938 (quoted); Cammerer to Kittredge, 8 November 1938; Cammerer to Kittredge, 21 November (RG79 E10:2 B448); Vint to Albright, 18 March 1932 (RG 79 E10:1 B150); White, "Wilderness Policies"; Thomson, "Public Use Policies"; Nussbaum, "Wilderness Aspects of National Parks," Vint, "Development of National Parks for Conservation."

90 "Isle Royale, Newest National Park"; New York Emergency Conservation Committee, *The Proposed John Muir-Kings Canyon National Park*; "Kings Canyon National Park Established"; Ickes, The Olympic National Park," *American Planning and Civic Annual, 1938*, 11–16; Ickes, "Keep It a Wilderness"; Runte, *National Parks*, 144–68; Miles, *Wilderness in the National Parks*, 68–72, 88–109; Louter, *Windshield Wilderness*, 68–98; E. Richardson, "Olympic National Park."

91 "Kings Canyon National Park Established"; Miles, *Wilderness in the National Parks*, 88–109; Louter, *Windshield Wilderness*, 68–98.

VII. NATIONAL PARKWAYS

1 "Parkways of the Future," Radio Discussion between Mr. MacDonald, Chief of the United States Bureau of Public Roads, and Mr. Demaray, Associate Director of the National Park Service, NBC Radio, April 13, 1935, transcript included in USDOI, NPS, *Parkways: A Manual of Requirements*, 1–12; Demaray qtd. on 5–6; MacDonald qtd. on 12; Bayliss, "Parkway Development under the National Park Service."

2 Davis, "The American Motor Parkway."

3 Ibid.; Newton, *Design on the Land*, 596–606; Gilmore Clarke, "The Parkway Idea," in Snow, *The Highway and the Landscape*, 32–35; James, "Parkway Features of Interest to the Highway Engineer"; G. Clarke, "Is There a Solution for the Through Traffic Problem?"; G. Clarke, "Our Highway Problem"; Nolen and Hubbard, *Parkways and Land Values*, 72–128.

4 G. Clarke, "Westchester Parkways; Downer, "Principles of Westchester's Parkway System"; Abbott, "Ten Years of the Westchester County Park System"; Nolen and Hubbard, *Parkways and Land Values*, 72–128, quote on 113.

5 Evison, "Oral History Interview of Dudley C. Bayliss, 11 February 1971," 6–7; McClelland, *Presenting Nature*, 134–35.

6 Davis, "A Pleasing Illusion of Unspoiled Countryside"; Davis, "The Bronx River Parkway and Photography as an Instrument of Landscape Reform."

7 The automobile's impact on heritage tourism is discussed in Belasco, *Americans on the Road*, 24–30; and Bluestone, *Buildings, Landscapes, and Memory*, 240–55. The cultural tensions of the 1920s and 1930s and their relationship to public history are discussed in Susman, *Culture as History*; Levine, *The Unpredictable Past*; Benson, Brier, and Rosenzweig, *Presenting the Past*; Bodnar, *Remaking America*; and Lindgren, *Preserving the Old Dominion*.

8 Davis, "Mount Vernon Memorial Highway: Changing Conceptions"; G. Clarke, "Mount Vernon Memorial Highway," 179–80; Fairbank, "Modern Design Characterizes Memorial Highway to Mount Vernon"; Simonson, "The Mount Vernon Memorial Highway"; U.S. Dept. of Agriculture, Bureau of Public Roads, *The Mount Vernon Memorial Highway*; U.S. Dept. of Agriculture, *Roadside Improvement*.

9 "Thrill of Americanism," from C. C. Carlin's testimony in House, *Roads. Hearings before the Committee on Roads*, 68th Cong., 1st sess., 25 April 1924, 16–21; "Memorandum of Agreement between the City of Alexandria and the United States of America, represented by the Secretary of Agriculture," dated 20 June 1929 (copy in NPS National Capital Region Land Use Office); Simonson, "The Mt. Vernon Memorial Highway."

10 Albright and Cahn, *The Birth of the National Park Service*, 244–52; Mackintosh, *The National Park Service* (1991), 20–21; Unrau and Willis, *Administrative History*.

11 Bennett, "Colonial National Historical Park Roads and Bridges, HAER No. VA-115," 11–16; Lindgren, *Preserving the Old Dominion*, 75–133, 223–39; Hosmer, *Preservation Comes of Age*, 11–73.

12 Bennett, "Colonial National Historical Park Roads and Bridges, HAER No. VA-115," 16–18 (Carson qtd. on 17; Cramton qtd. on 18); Albright and Cahn, *The Birth of the National Park Service*, 246–47.

13 Bennett, "Colonial National Historical Park Roads and Bridges, HAER No. VA-115," 18–19; USDOI, NPS, Colonial National Monument, "Colonial Parkway Cultural Landscape Report" (1997), 174.

14 USDOI, NPS, Colonial National Monument, "Outline of Development of Colonial National Monument," "visualization," 26, "speedway," 184, "Park Service traditions," "waved and wobbled," and "air of modernity," 193.

15 Peterson's comments and Kittredge's response qtd. in USDOI, NPS, Colonial National Monument, "Colonial Parkway Cultural Landscape Report," 177–78, 259; Kittredge qtd. in Bennett, "Colonial National Historical Park Roads and Bridges, HAER No. VA-115," 37.

16 Bennett, "Colonial National Historical Park Roads and Bridges, HAER No. VA-115," 59–69.

17 Ibid., 28–34, 72; USDOI, NPS, Colonial National Monument, "Colonial Parkway Cultural Landscape Report," 282–97.

18 Bennett, "Colonial National Historical Park Roads and Bridges, HAER No. VA-115," 36–44 Peterson qtd., "dignity," 39.

19 Ibid., 49–56, 76–81.

20 Abbott, "Parkways—Past, Present, and Future," 684–91, "laboratory," 688; Abbott, "Shenandoah–Great Smoky Mountains National Parkway," "national scope," "alluring attraction," 31; Abbuehl, "A Road Built for Pleasure."

21 Quin, "Blue Ridge Parkway, HAER No. NC-42," 24–25, Pratt qtd. on 25; Jolley, *The Blue Ridge Parkway*, 11–19.

22 Quin, "Blue Ridge Parkway, HAER No. NC-42," 26–30, 70; Jolley, *The Blue Ridge Parkway*, 21–32.

23 Quin, "Blue Ridge Parkway, HAER No. NC-42," 40–43; Wirth, "Memorandum for Mr. Cammerer," "The Shenandoah–Smoky Mountain Parkway and Stabilization Project, Proceedings of Meetings Held in Baltimore, Feb. 5–7, 1934"; Vint to Cammerer, 8 June 1934; "Report: Proposed Locations, Shenandoah–Great Smoky Mountains Parkway to Chief Landscape Architect, National Park Service, June 8, 1934"; George Radcliffe, Thomas MacDonald and Arno Cammerer, 13 June 1934 (RG79 E60 B2); Radcliffe, MacDonald, and Cammerer to Ickes, 13 June 1934 (RG48 Central Classified Files B2010).

24 Quin, "Blue Ridge Parkway, HAER No. NC-42," 40–47, Marshall qtd. on 44; Jolley, *The Blue Ridge Parkway*, 57–92; Evison, "Oral History Interview of Dudley C. Bayliss 11–13. "Brief of Hearing in re: Route of Proposed Scenic Parkway . . . ," 24 September 1934; Ickes to North Carolina governor J. C. B. Ehringhaus, 19 November 1934 (RG 48, NPS,

Shenandoah Roads, Park to Park Highway); Evison, "Finding a Route for the Blue Ridge Parkway," 13.

25 Quin, "Blue Ridge Parkway, HAER No. NC-42," 31–38, 50–51; Evison, "Oral History Interview of Dudley C. Bayliss," 5–6; Abbuehl, "A Road Built for Pleasure"; Evison, "Finding a Route for the Blue Ridge Parkway," 11–13; Jolley, *Painting with a Comet's Tail*, 6, 14–15.

26 Quin, "Blue Ridge Parkway, HAER No. NC-42," 37–38; Abbuehl, "A Road Built for Pleasure," 235–37; Jolley, *Painting with a Comet's Tail*, 15–22; Evison, "Oral History Interview of Dudley C. Bayliss," 18–19; Cron information from author's conversation with Federal Lands Highway administrator Thomas Edick and Allen Burden, Federal Lands Highway Program chief, June 1996.

27 Abbott, "The Blue Ridge Parkway," 247.

28 Abbott, "Shenandoah–Great Smoky Mountains National Parkway," "skyline location," 32; Abbott, "The Blue Ridge Parkway," 248–49; Abbott, "Parkways—Past, Present, and Future," 684–85; Abbuehl, "A Road Built for Pleasure," 234; Quin, "Blue Ridge Parkway, HAER No. NC-42," 39, 54–63, Abbott and Austin qtd. on 39.

29 Abbott, "Parkways—Past, Present, and Future," "silks and rayons," 684, "pastoral picture," 686; Abbott, "Historic Preservation," 157. Jolley quoted Abbott's "managed American countryside" characterization in *Painting with a Comet's Tail*, 13. The NPS has long recognized the highly romanticized and culturally biased nature of the Blue Ridge Parkway's presentation of Appalachian history and culture. In addition to the original designers' statements, see Barry M. Buxton, *Mabry Mill Historic Resource Study*; Noblitt, "The Blue Ridge Parkway and the Myths of the Pioneer"; and Davis, "A Pleasing Illusion of Unspoiled Countryside."

30 Quin, "Blue Ridge Parkway, HAER No. NC-42," 36, 57–59; Abbuehl, "A Road Built for Pleasure," 234; Evison, "Oral History Interview of Dudley C. Bayliss," 13–15; Bayliss, "Parkway Development under the National Park Service." 255; USDOI, NPS, *Parkways: A Manual of Requirements*, 3.

31 Abbott, "The Blue Ridge Parkway," "first direct answer," 247, "motor vacation land," 249; Abbott, "Parkways: Past, Present, and Future," "self-sufficient motordom," 684; Abbott, "Shenandoah–Great Smoky Mountains National Parkway," 32; Abbuehl, "A Road Built for Pleasure," 235; Evison, "Oral History Interview of Dudley C. Bayliss," 13–15. For detailed accounts of the planning and development of the parkway recreation areas, see Quin, "Blue Ridge Parkway, HAER No. NC-42," 150–272.

32 Abbott, "Parkways: Past, Present, and Future," 684–88; Abbott, "The Blue Ridge Parkway," 248; Abbuehl, "A Road Built for Pleasure," 233–37; Jolley, *Painting with a Comet's Tail*, 14–28; Quin, "Blue Ridge Parkway, HAER No. NC-42," 104–40, NPS objections to BPR walls, 106–7; Abbott, "Historic Preservation: Perpetuation of Scenes Where History Becomes Real"; Noblitt, "The Blue Ridge Parkway and the Myths of the Pioneer."

33 Quin, "Blue Ridge Parkway, HAER No. NC-42," 65–75.

34 Ibid., 75–82.

35 Ibid., 82–86.

36 Cleven, "Blue Ridge Parkway, Linn Cove Viaduct, HAER No. NC-42-A," 1–15, "Mona Lisa" quote on 14; Evison, "Oral History Interview of Dudley C.

37 Abbott, "Parkways: Past, Present, and Future," 684.

38 Senate, *Natchez Trace Parkway Survey*; 76th Cong., 3d session, 26 February 1940, S. Doc. 148; Phelps, "The Natchez Trace," reprinted from *Tennessee Historical Quarterly* (September 1962): 1–16; Fulton, "Natchez Trace Parkway, HAER No. MS-15," 9–15.

39 Senate, *Natchez Trace Parkway Survey*, 76th Cong., 3d session, 26 February 1940, S. Doc. 148, 2–3; Phelps, "The Natchez Trace"; Fulton, "Natchez Trace Parkway, HAER No. MS-15," 15–16.

40 Fulton, "Natchez Trace Parkway, HAER No. MS-15," 20–26; Phelps, "The Natchez Trace."

41 Fulton, "Natchez Trace Parkway, HAER No. MS-15," 20–26; Phelps, "The Natchez Trace."

42 Senate, *Natchez Trace Parkway Survey*, 76th Cong., 3d session, 26 February 1940, S. Doc. 148, 143–52; Phelps et al., "Administrative History of the Natchez Trace Parkway," V1–V4; Ickes to Demaray, 19 February 1936; Demaray to Ickes, 25 March 1936 (RG79 E10:2 B2776).

43 Senate, *Natchez Trace Parkway Survey*, 76th Cong., 3d session, 26 February 1940, S. Doc. 148, 143–52; Phelps et al., "Administrative History of the Natchez Trace Parkway," V1–V4. Nolen to Vint, 21 March 1934, with informal report and colored schematic; Zimmer to Vint, 6 May 1935 (RG79 E13 B2); Chatelain to Gardner, 1 April 1936; Zimmer to Brownell, 5 October 1936 (RG79 E10:2 B2776).

44 Fulton, "Natchez Trace Parkway, HAER No. MS-15," 33–34, 79–83. Zimmer to Bayliss, 28 August 1936; Spelman to Brownell, 11 September 1936; Nolen to Vint, 2 November 1936; John Nolen, "Alignment of a Section of the Natchez Trace Parkway," 2 November 1936; Demaray to MacDonald, 20 November 1936 (RG79 E10:2 B2776).

45 Fulton, "Natchez Trace Parkway, HAER No. MS-15," 83–89; "Scenic Easements: Your Rights and Ours," *Natchez Trace Parkway Bulletin* 2, no. 11 (December 1941), quoted.

46 Fulton, "Natchez Trace Parkway," HAER No. MS-15," 38–41.

47 Senate, *Natchez Trace Parkway Survey*, 76th Cong., 3d sess., 26 February 1940. S. Doc. 148, v–vi; Fulton, "Natchez Trace Parkway, HAER No. MS-15," 43–49.

48 Fulton, "Natchez Trace Parkway, HAER No. MS-15," 60–62

49 Ibid., 63–72, "our lifetime," 70, Wirth qtd., 71.

50 Ibid., 72–75. Mission 66 mileage figures may include roadwork on associated sites (Phelps et al., "Administrative History of the Natchez Trace Parkway," appendix B, appendix C).

51 Fulton, "Natchez Trace Parkway, HAER No. MS-15," 72–75. Mission 66 mileage figures may include roadwork on associated sites (Phelps et al., "Administrative History of the Natchez Trace Parkway," appendix B, appendix C). U.S. Dept. of Transportation, Federal Highway Administration, Eastern Federal Lands Highway Division, *The Natchez Trace*.

52 Gutheim, *The Potomac*, 252–57; *The Improvement of the Park System of the District of Columbia*, 93–97; Davis, "George Washington Memorial Parkway, HAER No. VA-69," 141–45.

53 Davis, "George Washington Memorial Parkway, HAER No. VA-69," 145–47; Senate, *George Washington Memorial Parkway and Park Development of the National Capital*, 71st Cong., 2d sess., 17 April 1930, S. Rep. 458; Public Law 71-284, May 29, 1930, U.S. *Statutes at Large* 46: 482–85.

54 National Capital Park and Planning Commission, *George Washington Memorial Parkway*, 1930 publicity flyer (George Washington Memorial Parkway vertical file, Washingtoniana Collection, Martin Luther King, Jr. Memorial Library, Washington D.C.; Eliot, "The George Washington Memorial Parkway"; John Frazier, "The Park That Is to Be," *American Motorist* 5 (October 1930), 24–25, 62–63; Dodge, "The George Washington Memorial Parkway." Cammerer, "Push the Washington Parkway," typescript for article to appear in *Review of Reviews* (May 1935); and memo, Cammerer to Wirth, 6 August 1935 (RG79 E10:2 B2774).

55 Davis, "George Washington Memorial Parkway, HAER No. VA-69," 151–53.

56 Ibid., 154–56; Snow, *The Highway and the Landscape*, 114–15; Tunnard and Pushkarev, *Man-Made America*, 203; Halprin, *Freeways*, 37.

57 Davis, "George Washington Memorial Parkway, HAER No. VA-69," 154–56; Mackintosh, "George Washington Memorial Parkway," 38–39; Drury to Devereux Butcher, National Parks Association, 5 May 1950, qtd. on 43; Bayliss, "Parkway Development under the National Park Service," qtd. on 258.

58 Davis, "George Washington Memorial Parkway, HAER No. VA-69," 158–59.

59 Ibid., 156–66; Senate, Committee on Interior and Insular Affairs, *George Washington Memorial Parkway, Hearings before the Committee on Interior and Insular Affairs* (hereafter cited as *George Washington Memorial Parkway Hearings*), Izaak Walton League, 47, Wilderness Society, 46–47, Audubon Society, 49; Seegers qtd. in Mackintosh, "George Washington Memorial Parkway," 90.

60 Davis, "George Washington Memorial Parkway, HAER No. VA-69," 164–65; *George Washington Memorial Parkway Hearings*, Audubon Society, 49.

61 Davis, "George Washington Memorial Parkway, HAER No. VA-69," 166–74.

62 Ibid., 167–70.

63 Duensing, "Baltimore Washington Parkway, HAER No. MD-129," 30–40, Grant qtd. on 39; National Capital Park and Planning Commission, *Work of the National Capital Park and Planning Commission*, 20.

64 Duensing, "Baltimore Washington Parkway, HAER No. MD-129," 43–53.

65 Ibid., 56–61.

66 Ibid., 59–66.

67 Ibid., 66–87.

68 Ibid., 68, 87–97; Tunnard and Pushkarev, *Man-Made America*, 203.

69 Ibid., 113–16.

70 Ibid., 119–23, Wirth and assistant secretary of the Interior Orme Lewis qtd. on 111; Evison, "Oral History Interview of Dudley C. Bayliss."

71 Duensing, "Baltimore Washington Parkway, HAER No. MD-129," 123–28.

72 Evison, "Oral History Interview of Dudley C. Bayliss," 37–38; Krakow, *Historic Resource Study*.

73 A. E. Demaray, "A Discussion of Federal Parkways," presented at January 1936 American Planning and Civic Association," in USDOI, NPS, *Parkways: A Manual of Requirements*; Bayliss, "Discussion of National Parkways." Superintendent's Conference, Jan. 17, 1938 (RG79 E10:2 B2776).

74 "Col. Wilgus Explains Mountain Parkway," *Burlington Free Press*, 3 August 1933; Cummings, "The Green Mountain Parkway Plan"; Bancroft, "Why People Should Favor Green Mountain Parkway"; Cammerer to Dudley Harmon, 3 October 1933; Wirth, Memorandum, 16 October 1933; E. K. Burlew to Cammerer, 23 November 1933; Cammerer to Kelsey, 9 December 1933; Cammerer to Vermont Governor Stanley Wilson, 28 March 1934 (RG79 E10:2 B3050); Goldman, "Vermont's Opportunity," 42–74; 116–23; Hannah Silverstein, "A Road Not Travelled: Vermont's Rejection of the Green Mountain Parkway," 17–22.

75 Cox, "Green Mountain Parkway," quote on 17; Vint to Cammerer, 12 April 1934. E. K. Burlew to Nolen, 19 May 1934; Cammerer to Burlew, 2 July 1934 (RG79 E10:2 B3050).

76 Peach, "Proposed Parkway a Threat to the State's Well Being"; Eaton, "A Little Wilderness in Vermont"; Bryan, *Yankee Politics in Rural Vermont*, 201–33; Goldman, "Vermont's Opportunity," 44–49, 75–92.

77 Cammerer to Olmsted, 23 November 1933; Hubbard to Cammerer, 21 November 1933; Kelsey to Cammerer, 6 December 1933; Kelsey to Cammerer, 7 March 1934; Olmsted to Cammerer, 23 February 1934; Vint, "Report to the Director on the Green Mountain Parkway," 3–9 April 1934; Cammerer to Wilson, 28 April 1934; Kelsey, "Report of Trip of Inspection of Proposed Green Mountain Parkway, Vermont, 21 September 1934" (RG79 E10:2 B3050). AMC President Fay to Ickes, 14 June 1934 (RG48 DOI NPS Files, Roads, Green Mountain Parkway); Bryan, *Yankee Politics in Rural Vermont*, 205, 231; Goldman, "Vermont's Opportunity," 44–49, 92–115; Silverstein, "A Road Not Travelled," 23–29; Cox, "Green Mountain Parkway," 17–18.

78 Peach, "Proposed Parkway a Threat to the State's Well Being," 9–11; Goldman, "Vermont's Opportunity," 47–48, 92–115, GMC president Mortimer Proctor qtd. on 108; Silverstein, "A Road Not Travelled," 23–29; Bryan, *Yankee Politics in Rural Vermont*, 205, 231.

79 Marshall, "Memorandum to the Secretary on the Proposed Green Mountain Parkway," n.d.; Oscar Chapman to Ickes, 19 April 1935; Cox to Demaray, 2 May 1935; Demaray to Ickes, 21 May 1935; Marshall to Ickes, 6 June 1935; Ickes to Demaray, 13 June 1935; Cox to Demaray, 19 June 1935, "amateur" and "no real knowledge" (RG79 E10:2 B3050).

80 "Parkway Is Rejected by Voters of Vermont," *Burlington Free Press*, 4 March 1936; Bryan, *Yankee Politics in Rural Vermont*, 201–33; Goldman, "Vermont's Opportunity," 133–47; Silverstein, "A Road Not Travelled," 11–19, 41–52; Eaton, "A Little Wilderness in Vermont"; Yard, "Green Mountains Saved a Second Time"; Yard, "New and Dangerous Attempt to 'Get' the Green Mountains."

81 Mackintosh, *C & O Canal*, 1–57.

82 Ibid., 55–58; House, *Chesapeake and Ohio Canal Report*.

83 Mackintosh, *C & O Canal*, 59–64; Barnes, "Historic C and O Canal Threatened by Road," 135–37; (Maryland)

Joint Committee on the Chesapeake and Ohio Canal Parkway, *Report of Joint Committee on the Chesapeake and Ohio Canal Parkway*, statement by Board of Natural Resources representative Joseph P. Keller on 50.

84 Anderson, "A Fascinating Restoration."

85 Barnes, "Historic C and O Canal Threatened by Road," 113.

86 Ibid., 135–38.

87 Mackintosh, *C & O Canal*, 66–68, Wirth's response to Olmsted, 20 October 1953, qtd. on 67; Durham, "The C & O Canal Hike," 1–5.

88 Douglas's letter and the *Washington Post*'s response reproduced in Durham, "The C & O Canal Hike," 2–3.

89 Durham, "The C & O Canal Hike," 4–8; Mackintosh, *C & O Canal*, 69–71.

90 Durham, "The C & O Canal Hike," 5–6, 15–17.

91 Ibid., 21–26; Mackintosh, *C & O Canal*, 72–74.

92 Mackintosh, *C & O Canal*, 74–90; Bookman, "Wonderful World of Walking," 1.

93 Mackintosh, *C & O Canal*, 90–102.

94 U.S. Bureau of Public Roads and U.S. National Park Service, *Parkway for the Mississippi*; USDOI, NPS, Division of Design and Construction, Parkways Branch, *National Parkways*; Evison, "Oral History Interview of Dudley C, Bayliss," 58–65.

VIII. MISSION 66 AND ITS DISCONTENTS

1 Ise, *Our National Park Policy*, 447–53. Carr provides a comprehensive overview of the program in *Mission 66*; Sellers takes a dimmer view in *Preserving Nature*, 150–52, 180–91.

2 Drury, "The Dilemma of Our National Parks"; Ise, *Our National Park Policy*, 470–80; Sellers, *Preserving Nature*, 174–79.

3 Wirth, *Parks, Politics, and the People*, 234–36.

4 DeVoto, "Let's Close the National Parks," "stepchild," 49, "heritage," 51, "rations," 52; Drury, "The Dilemma of Our Parks"; Stevenson, "The Shocking Truth about Our National Parks," "danger," 45, "slum-like," 47, "movies," 50. Related examples include Litton, "Yosemite's Beauty Fast Disappearing"; "Yosemite versus Mass Man"; "U.S. Is Outgrowing Its Parks"; and Olsen, "The Challenge of Our National Parks."

5 Wirth, *Parks, Politics, and the People*, 234; Yoder, "Twenty-Four Million Acres of Trouble"; "We've Been Starving Our National Parks"; "U.S. Is Outgrowing Its Parks."

6 Wirth, *Parks, Politics, and the People*, 237–51.

7 Ibid., 238–62; Wirth, "Mission 66"; "Pioneer Dinner Launches Mission 66"; Carr, *Mission 66*, 63–119; Vetter, "Project in the Parks," 41.

8 USDOI, NPS, *Mission 66 for the National Park System*, 1–16; USDOI, NPS, *Our Heritage*, n.p.; Garrison, "Mission 66," 107–8, "modern traffic handling,' 108.

9 USDOI, NPS, *Mission 66 for the National Park System*, 26–38, 92–94; USDOI, NPS, *Our Heritage*, n.p.; Garrison, "Mission 66"; Allaback, *Mission 66 Visitor Centers*.

10 USDOI, NPS, *Mission 66 for the National Park System*, 81–86; USDOI, NPS, *Our Heritage*, n.p.; Moore qtd. in "Pioneer Dinner Launches Mission 66," 59; USDOI,

NPS, *Your Mission 66 and the National Parks*; USDOI, NPS, *Mission 66 Progress Report*, 52–53.

11 USDOI, NPS, *Mission 66 for the National Park System*, 81–103, quoted, 86; USDOI, NPS, *Our Heritage*; Wirth, "Mission 66," 16–17; Garrison, "Mission 66," 107–8.

12 USDOI, NPS, *Mission 66 for the National Park System*, "primary justification," iv, "without meaning," 1, "spiritual necessity," 117, "pride," 120 ; *Our Heritage*, n.p.; "Address by Conrad L. Wirth, Director, National Park Service, at the American Pioneer Dinner, Department of the Interior, February 8, 1956" (copy in Interior Department Library).

13 Wirth, *Parks, Politics, and the People*, 262–84; USDOI, NPS, *Mission 66 Progress Report*; Carr, *Mission 66*, 127–74, 199–254; Haines, *The Yellowstone Story*, 2:375–78.

14 Wirth, *Parks, Politics, and the People*, 262–84; USDOI, NPS, *Mission 66 Progress Report*, 34–54; Carr, *Mission 66*, 175–97. Logo change described on the back cover of Mackintosh, *The National Parks* (2005).

15 Wirth, *Parks, Politics, and the People*, 262–67; USDOI, NPS, *Mission 66 Progress Report*, 23–34. The 1966 progress report provided slightly different figures, reflecting different categorizations or a more complete accounting. Although the 1966 progress report summarized parkway development separately from park roads, Wirth did not; it is unclear whether parkway drives were included in the total road mileage provided in both publications.

16 USDOI, NPS, *Mission 66 Progress Report*, 30–31; Ise, *Our National Park Policy*, 548–49; Haines, *The Yellowstone Story*, 2:374–75; Quin, "Mount Rainier National Park Roads and Bridges, HAER No. WA-35," 111–13; Quin, "Wawona Covered Bridge, Yosemite National Park Roads and Bridges, CA-106"; Kelleher and Maher, "Great Smoky Mountains National Park Roads and Bridges, HAER No. TN-35," 94–100; Bennett, "Colonial National Historical Park Roads and Bridges, HAER No. VA-115," 49–56, "Master Plan for the Preservation and Use of Colonial National Historical Park" [Mission 66 edition] qtd. on 56; Yellowstone park engineer Gerald Rowe to superintendent Lemuel Garrison, "Inspection of Chittenden Bridge," 31 August 1960; Garrison to NPS Region Two director, 2 September 1960 (Yellowstone National Park Archives, Record Group 34).

17 Packard, "An Appraisal of Mission 66," "roads," 91, "landmark," 95.

18 Wayburn and Wayburn, "Mission 66 . . . A Promise for the Parks," "mists," 3; Perlman, "Mission 66: Park's 10-Year Plan," "desperate need" and "conception," 11.

19 These issues are addressed at length in Allaback, *Mission 66 Visitor Centers*; and Carr, *Mission 66*, 127–74.

20 D. Butcher, "For a Return to Harmony in Park Architecture," "beyond words," 151, "Sore thumb," 155; D. Butcher, "More on Park Architecture," "chicken coop," 32; D. Butcher, "Sunshine and Blizzard," "freak design," 28, "ugliest," 29; Smith, "'A Sky-Post' for the Smokies"; Heald, "Urbanization of the National Parks."

21 Zahniser, "The Need for Wilderness Areas," *Living Wilderness*, 21; Humphrey, "The Wilderness Bill"; Brower, "The Sierra Club and the National Scene"; Brower, "Wilderness—Conflict and Conscience"; Kilgore, "Controversy as a Saving Force."

22 Cohen, *History of the Sierra Club*, 89–100, 143–86; Brower, "'Mission 65' Is Proposed by Reviewer of Park Service's New Brochure on Wilderness," 45–47; Litton, "Yosemite's Beauty Fast Disappearing," 164; Gunsky, "Motorized Millions"; Shepard, "Something Amiss in the National Parks," "hordes of amusement-seeking tourists," 150; Bradley and Brower, "Roads in National Parks," caption for photograph between pages 34 and 35.

23 Brower, "'Mission 65' Is Proposed by Reviewer of Park Service's New Brochure on Wilderness," 47; Brower, "Scenic Resources for the Future"; Swift, "Guest Editorial"; Bradley and Brower, "Roads in National Parks," "massed humanity," 35; "The Park Service and Wilderness"; MacKaye, "If This Be Snobbery." Brower to Wirth, 11 September 1957; Ben Thomson to Carnes, "Memorandum on Dave Brower's letter of April 11, 1957" (RG79 E11 B49).

24 USDOI, NPS, *The National Park Wilderness*, 21–25.

25 Ibid., "considerable success," 22; "Preservation of Wilderness Values in the National Park System."

26 USDOI, NPS, *The National Park Wilderness*, 25–27, "journey," 27; Bennett, "Colonial National Historical Park Roads and Bridges, HAER No. VA-115," 49–56; "Master Plan for the Preservation and Use of Colonial National Historical Park" [Mission 66 edition] qtd. on 56.

27 Bayliss, "Planning Our National Park Roads and Our National Parkways"; Bayliss, *Planning Our National Park Roads and Our National Parkways*. Wirth to BPR Commissioner C. D. Curtiss, 8 June 1956; "Meeting with Bureau of Public Roads on Extending Parkway Principles to Federal Aid Highways, Points for Discussion" n.d.; Bayliss to Wirth, 17 October 1956 (RG79 E11 B1034).

28 Butcher, "Resorts or Wilderness?" 51; Heald, "Urbanization of the National Parks," "broad new highway," "uninteresting straightaways," "much better," and "more important," 8; Brower, "Mission 66, Roads, and the Park Idea"; Yellowstone roads critiqued in Levi, "Letter to the Editor," 89; Smith, "Our Unfinished Work."

29 A summary of Wirth's comments to the National Park Association appeared as "Mission 66 in the Headlines."

30 Ibid.; Wirth's Grand Canyon intervention recounted in D. Butcher, "Resorts or Wilderness?," 41; O. Murie, "On Roads and Principles"; "On Park Shrines and Highways," inside front cover.

31 H. C. Bradley, *Tuolumne Meadows Today and Tomorrow*, privately printed pamphlet, ca. 1948, with McDuffie to Drury, 29 November 1948; Colby to Drury, 2 December 1948; Vint, "Statement Concerning Road Development in the High Sierra Section of Yosemite National Park," 1 November 1948; "Tioga Road Construction; from report of the Yosemite Advisory Board" (RG79 E10:2 B1841); Cohen, *The History of the Sierra Club*, 97–100.

32 Bradley and Brower, "Roads in National Parks," "restless driver," 34, "easy reach," 35, "leisurely unfolding," 39, "thrilling," 40, "hysterical," 49, additional comments in captions to photographs between pages 34 and 35. Bradley made similar comments in "Yosemite's Problem Road."

33 Bradley and Brower, "Roads in National Parks," "tortuous," 50, "gratuitous sacrifice," 35–36, "engineering standards," 43; "ideal," 53. Vint, "Statement Concerning Road Development in the High Sierra Region of Yosemite National Park," 1 November 1948; Bradley to Demaray, 18 April, 1949; Kittredge to Bradley, 25 May 1949" (RG79 E10:2 B1841).

34 Leonard, "The Tioga Road and Tenaya Lake."

35 "Roads in National Parks." Sierra Club, *A Policy for Roads in National Parks and Monuments*, April 15, 1955 (RG79 E11 B1034). Richard Leonard to Sen. Thomas Kuchel, 21 September 1954; Brower to Rep. Clair Engle, 21 September 1954; Leonard to Wirth, 5 April 1955 (RG79 E11 B1084).

36 Leonard to Wirth, 5 April 1955 (HAER office files, original in Yosemite National Park Archives).

37 Allen to Leonard, 17 March 1955; Hildebrand to Allen, 10 June 1955; Wirth to BPR Chief Charles Curtiss, 15 March 1956 (RG79 E11 B1084).

38 Wirth, *Parks, Politics, and People*, 358–60, "nice reply," 360. Wirth, "definite instructions," qtd. in Quin, "Tioga Road, Yosemite National Park, HAER No. CA-149," 18; Curtis to Wirth, 19 August 1956; Curtis to Wirth, 7 May 1956; Wirth to Huber, 18 May 1956; Huber to Wirth, 4 June 1946 (RG79 E11 B1084); "Walter Huber Heads Interior Advisers."

39 Graves, "Tioga Turnpike—A New Speedway," 14; Brower, "Mission 66, Roads, and the Park Idea," 15; "Yosemite's Tioga Highway," 123.

40 Brower, "Tioga Protest," 3–4; Wirth, *Parks, Politics, and People*, 359; "hospital" quote in Quin, "Tioga Road, Yosemite National Park, HAER No. CA-149," 20. Lawrence Merriam to Wirth, 19 July 1958; Adams, memorandum on Tioga Road, 11 July 1958; Hildebrand, "Current Tioga Roads Construction," 16 July 1958; Wirth to Hildebrand, 29 July 1958 (RG79 E11 B1084).

41 Brower, "Tioga Protest," 3–4; Wirth, *Parks, Politics, and People*, 359. Huber to Interior Secretary Fred Seaton, 26 September 1958; Colby to Yosemite superintendent John Preston, 17 November 1958 (RG79 E11 B1084).

42 Brower, "Tioga Protest," 5–7; Brower, "Mission 66 Tragedy"; Smith, "The Tioga Road"; Quin, "Tioga Road, Yosemite National Park, HAER No. CA-149," 20. Brower to Seaton, 30 September 1958; Wirth to A. Wayne Smith, 6 October 1958; Wirth to Bestor Robinson, 10 November 1958 (RG79 E11 B1084).

43 Adams, "Tenaya Tragedy," "attitude," 1, "blasted," 2, "gentle persuasions," "bulldozers," and "never," 4; Adams, "Yosemite—1958: Compromise in Action," "tiptoe" and "artificial," 173. Adams to Wirth, 18 July 1958; Adams to Hildebrand, 19 July 1958, "impressively publicized"; Wirth to Hildebrand, 29 July 1958 (RG79 E11 B1084).

44 Brower, "The Tioga Road and Tenaya Lake"; Cohen, *History of the Sierra Club*, 99–104. Bradley to Wirth, 2 December 1958 (HAER Office Files; original in Yosemite National Park Archives).

45 Wirth to Bradley, 9 December 1958 (HAER Office Files; original in Yosemite National Park Archives). Wirth to Bradley, 4 March 1958; Brower to Wirth, 17 March 1958 (RG79 E11 B49).

46 "Mission 66 Tragedy"; Smith, "The Tioga Road"; "Ansel Adams on Yosemite"; demands for higher road standards cited in "On Park Shrines and Highways"; Quin, "Tioga Road, Yosemite National Park, Yosemite National Park, HAER No. CA-149," 21. Huber to Interior Secretary Fred Seaton, 26 September 1958 (RG79 E11 B1084).

47 "Roads and Wilderness," Wirth's statement and "let us unite"; Preston to Colby, 12 May 1961; Colby to Wirth, 18 June 1961; "Statement of William E. Colby"; Carver to Pearl Chase, 19 July 1961; quotes and characterization of Carver's speech based on "Draft or Principal Speech at Tioga Road, for Assistant Secretary John Carver, 29 May 1961: Carver undoubtedly made revisions but related correspondence suggests that he hewed close to the original; Carlos Campbell to Carver, 26 June 1961 (RG79 E11 B1084).

48 Smith, "The Tioga Road," 13. Related statements include Smith, "Our Unfinished Work"; "Roads and Wilderness"; and Gunsky, "Mission 66 Decisions."

49 Vint, "Proposed Park Road Standards," 19 April 1957; Acting Director E. Scoyen, "Standards for Park Roads and Parkways," 23 August 1957; Scoyen to Regional Directors and design offices, 19 November 1957 (RG79 E11 B1034-35); "Handbook of Standards for National Park and Parkway Roads," September 2, 1958, qtd. in Bradley, "Roads in Our National Parks," 6.

50 "Board Acts on Road Standards"; "Sierra Club Policy and Standards for National Park and Other Scenic Roads," "freeway effect," 63, "eliminate all cuts," 68; Bradley, "Roads in Our National Parks," quote on 6.

51 "Talk by Chester H. Warlow, California State Chamber of Commerce Sierra Access Conference, January 7, 1959" (RG79 E11 B1084); Mono County Chamber of Commerce to Wirth, 6 April 1959; Fresno County Chamber of Commerce to Wirth, 9 April 1959; California State Highway Commission to Interior Secretary Seaton, 26 May 1959; J. A. Beek, Sec. of California Senate to Wirth, 18 June 1959 (G79 E11 B1035).

52 Wirth to Warlow, 6 February 1959; Wirth to Huber, 11 February 1959; Wirth to A. Wayne Smith, 11 February 1959; Bestor Robinson to Wirth, December 1958; Wirth to Robinson, 28 January 1959 (RG79 E11 B1084).

53 Norris, *Crown Jewel of the North*, 1:121–33, 157–58.

54 Ibid., 158–62; Tilden and Machler, "The Development of Mount McKinley National Park," 10–12, 1959 McKinley National Park Master Plan qtd. on 11; A. Murie, "Roadbuilding in Mount McKinley National Park," 4.

55 Norris, *Crown Jewel of the North*, "speedway," 170. Merriam to Murie, 14 October 1960, Merriam to Murie, 17 January 1961, "constructive," (RG79 E11 B1065); O. Murie, "Our Farthest North National Park."

56 Tilden and Machler, "The Development of Mount McKinley National Park"; O. Murie, "Mount McKinley," 5; A. Murie, "Roadbuilding in Mount McKinley National Park," "official vandalism," 6, "mistake" and "unobtrusive," 7, "non-engineers," 8; "Some Views Concerning the Development of Mount McKinley National Park," "selling its soul," 18. Murie to Regional Dir. Edward Hummel, 11 January 1965 (RG78 E80 B68).

57 Stratton to Wirth, 17 June 1963; Gruening to Wirth, 7 August 1963; Paul Miller to Gruening, 14 August 1963 (RG79 E11 B1065). Adolph Murie to Wirth, 11 January 1965; NPS assistant director J. Jensen to Murie, 22 January 1965; acting chief of Western Office of Design and

Construction (WODC) P. E. Smith to asst. dir. of design and construction, 21 January 1966; acting NPS asst. dir. Richard Montgomery to Chief of WODC, 1 February 1966; Sierra Club president William Siri to NPS regional director Edward Hummel, 7 June 1965; Mr. & Mrs. W. L. Webb to NPS, 18 July 1965; Myron Means to Stewart Udall, 23 July 1965; John Crawford to Stewart Udall, 7 September 1965; Thomas Braden to NPS Director, 25 September 1965; Bob & Wilma Knox to NPS, 23 October 1965; asst. dir. Charles Krueger to BPR director of engineering and operations G. M. Williams, 16 September 1966 (RG79 E80 B68). Norris, *Crown Jewel of the North*, 170–73; A. Murie, "Roadbuilding in Mount McKinley National Park."

58 Wilson, "Trout Stream Wilderness . . . or Road"; Jasperson, "Is the United States Obligated to Complete the North Shore Road?"; "Haleakala Road Proposal"; R. Butcher, "A Redwood National Park"; R. Butcher, "Freeways versus Redwoods . . . A Legislative Investigation"; R. Butcher, "Freeways versus Redwoods"; Kelleher and Maher, "Great Smoky Mountains National Park Roads and Bridges, North Shore Road, HAER No. TN-35-I"; "The New Redwood National Park"; Leach, "Redwood National and State Parks Roads, HAER No. CA-269."

IX. ADJUSTING THE BALANCE

1 Keats, *The Insolent Chariots*; Brower, "What's Good for Detroit"; Mumford, "The Skyline," pts. 1–3; Mumford, "The Highway and the City"; Jacobs, *The Death and Life of Great American Cities*.
2 Abbey, *Desert Solitaire*, 48–67, quote on 50–51; Abbey, *The Monkey Wrench Gang*.
3 Abbey, *Desert Solitaire*, 51–59, "indolent millions," 56, "pry," 59. *Desert Solitaire* was completed several years after the publication of Marx's well-publicized work. The echo of Marx's phrasings in his characterization of the Jeep's sound as "a discordant note" suggests Abbey may have been aligning himself with literary predecessors.
4 Abbey, *Desert Solitaire*, 60–65, "let the people walk," 60, "sanctums," 60, "revolution," 65.
5 Visitation statistics provided by David Barna, NPS chief of public affairs, 21 October 2011. References to population growth as the primary contributor to overcrowding include Draper, "Parks—Or More People?," "biggest threat," 10, "defuse," 13; Catton, "Letting George Do It Won't Do It"; Bush, "Burdened Acres—The People Question"; Lyon, "An Ecologist's View of the Population Problem"; and Ehrlich, *The Population Bomb*. Brower's influence noted in Ehrlich and Ehrlich, "The Population Bomb Revisited."
6 Foresta, *America's National Parks and Their Keepers*, 62–65, ORRRC report qtd. on 64; Carr, *Mission 66*, 293–306.
7 Ibid., 65–67; Udall, *The Quiet Crisis*.
8 Hartzog, *Battling for the National Parks*, xi–xiii, 72–80; *Oral History Interview with George B. Hartzog, Jr.*, 2; Foresta, *America's National Parks and Their Keepers*, 67–71; Frome, *Regreening the National Parks*, 65–68; Carr, *Mission 66*, 309–14; Wirth, *Parks, Politics, and the People*, 295–314.
9 Mackintosh, *The National Park Service* (1991), 62–63; Hartzog, *Battling for the National Parks*, 86–91.

10 Hartzog, *Battling for the National Parks*, 102–3; *Oral History Interview with George B. Hartzog, Jr.*, 9–10; USDOI, NPS, *Administrative Policies for Natural Areas of the National Park System*; Mackintosh, *The National Park Service* (1991), 63–78; USDOI, NPS, *Administrative Policies for Natural Areas of the National Park System*; USDOI, NPS, *Administrative Policies for Historical Areas of the National Park System*; USDOI, NPS, *Administrative Policies for Recreational Areas of the National Park System*.
11 Udall's letter appeared as a foreword to the three administrative policy documents and is reproduced in Dilsaver, *America's National Park System*, 272–76.
12 Carson, *Silent Spring*; Van Fleet, "Nature Out of Balance"; Sellers, *Preserving Nature*, 214–66.
13 "The Leopold Report Says National Parks Should Be . . . 'A Vignette of Primitive America,'" "vignette," 6, "artificiality," 7, "most dangerous tool," and "ration," 8, "first European visitors," "most significant statement," 4.
14 Sellers, *Preserving Nature*, 214–66. The theory that biological communities achieved a stable "climax" condition was eventually disproved, as was the notion that Native Americans had minimal impact on their environments; the idea that a central function of wilderness was to enable modern Americans to reenact pioneer experiences also fell out of favor. For a more contrarian account of the rising influence of science-based management, see Chase, *Playing God in Yellowstone*. A more detailed presentation of federally mandated environmental compliance policies affecting park roads appears in Davis, *Landscape Line 16*, 35–36, Department of Transportation Act of 1966 quote on 35.
15 USDOI, NPS, North Cascades Study Team, *The North Cascades*; Manning, *The Wild Cascades*; "The North Cascades"; Lauter, *Windshield Wilderness*, 105–63.
16 USDOI, NPS, *Park Road Standards* (1968), n.p.; Everhart, *The National Park Service*, 98. Everhart to Leopold, 11 December 1967 (RG79 E11 B1036).
17 Everhart, *The National Park Service*, 98; USDOI, NPS, *Park Road Standards* (1968), n.p. "Some Background Information on ROADS IN THE NATIONAL PARKS" (RG 79 E62 B7).
18 Smith, "Park Road Planning and Finances"; U.S. Dept. of Transportation, Federal Highway Administration, *America's Highways*, 456–57. Secretary of Commerce Luther Hodges to Udall, 5 September 1962; Bradley to Udall, 9 August 1962; Leonard to Wirth, 10 August 1962; Whitton to Hartzog, 28 October 1964; Hartzog to Whitton, 18 November 1964; NPS rebuttal is from Chief Landscape Architect Merel Sager to Field Design Offices, 5 March 1964 (RG79 E11 B1035). The American Association of State Highway Officials (AASHO) became the American Association of State Highway and Transportation Officials (AASHTO) in 1973.
19 Wirth to Leonard, 22 August 1962 (RG79 E11 B1085); Bradley to Udall, 9 August 1962; Leonard to Wirth, 10 August 1962 (RG79 E11 B1035); Smith, "Park Road Planning and Finances."
20 "Memorandum of Agreement and Regulations Relating to Survey, Construction, and Improvement of Roads," 14 August 1964; Richard Montgomery to Field Design Office Chiefs, 13 September 1965; Robert Hall to G. A. Wilkins,

27 December 1963; J. E. Jensen to Director, 22 January 1965; Hall to Jensen, 29 September 1965; Hall to Wilkins, 31 January 1966; Wilkins to Hall, 17 February 1966 (RG79 E11B1035); Sager to Jensen, 6 February 1964 (RG 79 E62 B7); "3rd Redraft May 1, 1966" and additional information on original committee in resource book prepared by Regional Engineer William Comella for FHWA-NPS Joint Agency Committee Meeting April 4–5, 1972 (NPS Park Roads Program Office Files).
21 Everhart, *The National Park Service*, 97–98, quote on 97. Hartzog to Secretary of the Interior, 8 August 1966; Rep. Wayne Aspinall to Hartzog, 18 August 1966; Hartzog to Aspinall, 23 August 1966; Donald Bressler to Chief, Design and Construction, 6 March 1967; Glen Hendrix to D. C. Harrington, 22 August 1967; Hartzog to F. C. Turner, 26 March 1968 (RG79 E80 B68); Fort Bowie incident described by former NPS deputy director Denis Galvin, conversation with author, 6 May 2014.
22 "Random notes on the first meeting of the National Park Service Road Committee," and "Purpose of Park Roads," undated documents in Park Road Standards File. Adams to Everhart, 14 December 1967; Adams to Udall, 31 December 1967; Ansel Adams telephone conference, 27 March 1968 (quoted); Adams to Everhart, 14 December 1967; Krueger to Asst. Director, Interpretation, 14 December 1967, "frustrating"; Theodore Swem to Asst. Director, Interpretation, 17 February 1968; Bergman to Asst. Director, Cooperative Activities, 11 January 1968; Brown to Swem, 15 January 1968 (RG79 E11 B1036); Adams to Hildebrand, 19 July 1958 (RG79 E11 B1084); USDOI, NPS, *Park Road Standards* (1968), n.p.
23 "Director's Comments on Road Standards," 21 December 1967 (RG79 E11 B1036); USDOI, NPS, *Park Road Standards* (1968), n.p. Former NPS deputy director Dennis Galvin, who served as an NPS civil engineer during this period, recalled widespread dissatisfaction with Hartzog's 25 mph speed limit and expressed doubts that it was implemented in many parks (conversation with author, 6 May 2014).
24 USDOI, NPS, *Park Road Standards* (1968).
25 Ibid.
26 Ibid.
27 Ibid.
28 Ibid.
29 Smith, "A Good Park Road Program"; Alderson, "Instant Roads in National Parks"; *Sierra Club Bulletin* 54 (January 1969): 14, Cahn, *Will Success Spoil the National Parks?*, 18.
30 Tunnard and Pushkarev, *Man-Made America*; Blake, *God's Own Junkyard*; Whyte, *The Last Landscape*; Urban Advisors to the Federal Highway Administration, *The Freeway in the City*.
31 White House Conference on Natural Beauty, *Beauty for America*, "storm" and growing population," 1, "automobile society" and "roads," 6, session on scenic roads and parkways, 213–48.
32 Cahn, *Will Success Spoil the National Parks?*, 13–15, 48–51, quotes on 15; Darling and Eichhorn, "Man and Nature in the National Parks," quote on 24; W. Johnson, "Over-Use of the National Parks"; Lewis, "Back Yards in Paradise."
33 Quin, "Yosemite Roads and Bridges, HAER No.

CA-117," 122–23; "Changing the National Parks to Cope with People—and Cars"; Smith, "The Future & the Parks," "intolerable master"; Smith, "People, Parks, and Traffic," "sacred cows."

34 McPhee, "Profiles: Ranger," quote on 62.

35 Nixon qtd. in National Parks Centennial Commission, *Preserving a Heritage*, 123.

36 "An Olden Tranquility"; "Park Wilderness Planning"; "Progress in Yosemite"; "Yosemite: A Better Way to Run a Park?"; Quin, "Yosemite Roads and Bridges, HAER No. CA-117," 123.

37 Quin, "Yosemite Roads and Bridges, HAER No. CA-117," 123; Lauter, *Windshield Wilderness*, 126–46; alternative transportation policy quoted in USDOI, NPS, Denver Service Center, "Final Draft Alternative Transportation Modes Feasibility Study," vol. 1: 6.

38 USDOI, NPS, Denver Service Center, *Alternative Transportation Modes Feasibility Study*, vol. 1: 15; USDOI, NPS, Denver Service Center, *Alternative Transportation Modes Feasibility Study*, vol. 2, quote on ES-16–ES-17.

39 USDOI, NPS, Denver Service Center, *Alternative Transportation Modes Feasibility Study*, vol. 3, quote on ES-16, ES-19, 79, 97–98; Michael Finley, Superintendent, Yellowstone National Park, memorandum, 24 July 1995 (with copy of report provided to author by park).

40 USDOI, NPS, Denver Service Center, *Alternative Transportation Modes Feasibility Study*, vol. 4; National Park Service, *Yosemite: Summary of the Draft General Management Plan* (1978), quote on 21; NPS, *Yosemite General Management Plan* (1980); Lowry, *Repairing Paradise*, 70–73.

41 *Yosemite General Management Plan* (1980), "uncluttered," 1, "freed," 3; Tim Golden, "In Yosemite, Nature May Have Its Way Yet," *New York Times*, 2 February 1997, 1, 14; "Floods Brought Yosemite the Break of the Century," *Washington Post*, 6 March 1997; Lowry, *Repairing Paradise*, 73–81.

42 DOI, NPS, *Draft Yosemite Valley Implementation Plan Supplemental Environmental Impact Statement*, "reclaim," 30, "appropriate," 173. Albright made this comment at a symposium entitled "Accessing America's National Parks and Public Landscapes: In Search of Balance," National Building Museum, Washington, D.C., 12 November 1997. Account of bridge controversy based on contemporary media accounts and author's professional experiences and conversations with participants.

43 Lowry, *Repairing Paradise*, 81–105, Radanovich qtd. on 98; "Babbitt Announces Plan to Restore Yosemite," *Washington Post*, 15 November 2000.

44 USDOI, NPS, Yosemite National Park, *Merced Wild and Scenic River Final Comprehensive Management Plan and Environmental Impact Statement*, planning process and final recommendations summarized, ES-1-5; preferred alternative detailed, 8–226; 2009 Visitor Survey, 5–132.

45 "Road to the Future: A New Way to Visit," Grand Canyon National Park alternative transportation proposal publicity document, November 1997 (NPS Park Roads Program office files, NPS Facilities Maintenance Division, Washington, D.C.); "The Grand (Canyon) Plan: Automobiles Are Out, Quiet Is In," *Washington Post*, 11 August 1996; "Grand Canyon Plans to Limit Autos,"

Washington Post, 1 February 1997; "Park Plan Limits Cars," *Denver Post*, 16 November 1997; Babbitt and Meadows quoted in "Strict Limits On Cars Set for 3 National Parks," *Washington Post* 26 November 1997; Turnball, "Visitor Transportation at U.S. National Parks," 6; USDOI, NPS, *Grand Canyon National Park 2009/2010 Accomplishment Report*, quote on 1; "Completion of Park Improvements Celebrated," Inside NPS website, 30 June 2011.

46 Wadsworth, "Shuttle to Serenity"; Turnball, "Visitor Transportation at U.S. National Parks," 6–7, USDOI, NPS, Park Roads Program, *Accomplishments in Transportation, 2006–2012*.

47 Vanderbilt, "On the Road Again," 23; Yellowstone National Park Historic Vehicle Collection website.

48 Vanderbilt, "On the Road Again," 23–26.

49 Evison, "Oral History Interview of Dudley C. Bayliss," 44–66; U.S. Dept. of Commerce, *A Proposed Program for Scenic Roads & Parkways*; Whyte, *The Last Landscape*, 332–33.

50 Brian Cleven, "Blue Ridge Parkway, Linn Cove Viaduct, HAER No. NC-42-A," 1–21; author's conversation with Burden, June 1996; Davis, Croteau, and Marston, *America's National Park Roads and Parkways*, 234.

51 Cleven, "Blue Ridge Parkway, Linn Cove Viaduct, HAER No. NC-42-A," 16–35.

52 Fulton, "Natchez Trace Parkway, HAER No. MS-15," 75–77; Davis, Croteau, and Marston, *America's National Park Roads and Parkways*, 280–81; U.S. Dept. of Transportation, Federal Highway Administration, Eastern Federal Lands Highway Division, *The Natchez Trace*.

53 Kelleher and Maher, "Great Smoky Mountains National Park Roads and Bridges, Foothills Parkway, HAER No. TN-5-E"; "Briefing Statement: Completion of the Foothills Parkway," Great Smoky Mountains National Park, May 2009; USDOI, NPS, Park Roads Program, *Accomplishments in Transportation, 2006–2012*; additional update from phone conversation with NPS park transportation program manager Jim Evans, 24 June 2015.

54 USDOI, NPS and U.S. Dept. of Transportation, *Park Roads and Parkways Program Handbook*; "Interagency Agreement between National Park Service and Federal Highway Administration Relating to Park Roads and Parkways, May 1983" (Park Roads Program Office Files); Senate report quoted in USDOI, NPS, *Park Road Standards* (1984), i. Denver Service Center manager Denis Galvin was opposed to the arrangement but gave in to the maintenance division's funding concerns (conversation with author, 6 May 2014).

55 USDOI, NPS, *Park Road Standards* (1984), quote on 1.

56 Ibid., "profound threat," 1, "no longer appropriate," 11, "prohibitively expensive," 34.

57 Key contributions to this trend include the writings of John Brinckerhoff Jackson, collected in *A Sense of Place, a Sense of Time*; Chester Liebs, *Mainstreet to Miracle Mile*; Drake Hokanson, *The Lincoln Highway: Main Street across America*; Michael Wallis, *Route 66: The Mother Road*; John Baeder, *Gas, Food, and Lodging*; and Robert Margolies's myriad offerings such as *The End of the Road* and *Pump and Circumstance*. For an overview of the growing interest in road-related concerns, see Davis, "Looking Down the Road."

58 "Going-to-the-Sun Road nomination form" (1983);

Krakow, *Historic Resource Study*; USDOI, NPS, Register of Historic Places, "Skyline Drive Historic District nomination form"; USDOI, NPS, National Register of Historic Places, "Multiple Property Listing"; Davis, Croteau, and Marston, *America's National Park Roads and Parkways*; Croteau, "Recording NPS Roads and Bridges"; Davis, "Documenting America's Park Roads and Parkways"; Davis, *Landscape Line 16*.

59 The observations in this section are based on the author's experiences and conversations with others involved in national park roads stewardship. These issues are covered in greater depth in Davis, *Landscape Line 16*.

60 U.S. Dept. of Transportation, Federal Highway Administration, *Flexibility in Highway Design*. Under development since the mid-1990s and officially released in 2010, FHWA's "Interactive Highway Safety Design Model (IHSDM)" was a software package designed to analyze multiple risk factors, including accident history along with more conventional metrics. Although it was an improvement over previous methods, recommendations depended on the weight assigned various factors; the authority invested in sophisticated computer modeling could make it harder to challenge the results.

61 National Park Service and Federal Lands Highway Division, "National Park Service Barrier Inventory and Assessment Phase 1 Report, February 11, 2008"; USDOI, NPS, "National Park Service Draft NPS Traffic Safety Overview"; USDOI, NPS, *Blue Ridge Parkway, Guardrail Replacement and Installation Programmatic Environmental Assessment* (September 2009); summary of causes of serious accidents based on 2008 survey and analysis of NPS daily ranger reports.

62 USDOI, NPS, *Parkwide Road Improvement Plan*; "Programmatic Agreement among National Park Service, The Advisory Council on Historic Preservation, Wyoming State Historic Preservation Officer, Montana State Historic Preservation Officer, for Principal Park Road System Improvement, Yellowstone National Park," approved 1992/93 (copy provided to author by park); USDOI, NPS, National Register of Historic Places, "Multiple Property Listing," qtd. on 43.

63 USDOI, NPS, *Parkwide Road Improvement Plan*; "Programmatic Agreement . . . for Principal Park Road System Improvement, Yellowstone National Park."

64 USDOI, NPS, National Register of Historic Places, *"Multiple Property Listing,"* quote on 43. Environmental Assessments for projects associated with the parkwide plan routinely produced "Findings of No Significant Impact." Upchurch, "Preserving a Historic National Park Roadway."

65 Gordon, "Landmark in the Sky"; Vanderbilt and Moler, "Saving a National Treasure."

66 Gordon, "Landmark in the Sky"; Gordon, "The Rehabilitation of the Going-to-the-Sun Road"; Gordon provided updated figures in e-mail to author, 2 February 2014.

67 USDOI, NPS, Yosemite National Park, *Scenic Vista Management Plan for Yosemite National Park*, quoted, superintendent's cover letter and III–132.

68 USDOI, NPS, Yosemite National Park, *Tioga Road Rehabilitation Environmental Assessment*.

EPILOGUE

1 Secretary Udall memorandum to NPS director Hartzog, 10 July 1964, is reproduced in Dilsaver, *America's National Park System*, 272–76, quote on 272.

2 Statistics from NPS IRMA Data System (https://irma.nps. gov/Stats/); NPS press release "National Park Service Draws Record Breaking Crowds," 17 February 2015 (www.nps.gov/ news/release.htm?id=1678); and NPS Park Transportation website (www.nps.gov/transportation/index.html); USDOI, NPS, *Accomplishments in Transportation, 2006–2012*, 4; National Park Service Federal Lands Transportation Program Reauthorization Resource Paper, May 2013 (NPS Park Transportation Program office files). ISTEA is the acronym for Intermodal Surface Transportation and Equity Act of 1991 (Public Law 102-240, 105 Stat. 2038); TEA-21 stands for Transportation Equity Act for the 21st Century (Public Law 105-178, 112 Stat. 107); SAFETEA-LU is the Safe, Accountable, Flexible, Efficient Transportation Equity Act: A Legacy for Users (Public Law 109-59, 119 Stat. 1144).

3 NPS statistics from NPS IRMA Data System and NPS, *Accomplishments in Transportation, 2006–2012*, 4; Miles, *Wilderness in the National Parks*, 305–52.

4 USDOI, NPS, *Accomplishments in Transportation, 2006–2012*, 6–7; Moving Ahead for Progress in the 21st Century Act/MAP-21 (P.L. 112-141, 126 Stat. 405), enacted in 2012; National Park Service Federal Lands Transportation Program Reauthorization Resource Paper, May 2013, provided by NPS park transportation program manager Jim Evans; "Long-Term Transportation Plan for Funding Transportation Remains Far Off," *Washington Post*, 18 June 2015.

5 William Reynolds, "Briefing Statement: Tamiami Trail Modifications: Next Steps," 16 January 2014; Secretary of the Interior Sally Jewell to Secretary of Transportation Anthony Foxx, 29 April 2014 (NPS Park Roads Program Files); USDOI, NPS, *Salute to the Service*, 9.

6 National Parks Second Century Commission, *Advancing the National Park Idea*, 14–25, 42–47.

Bibliography

BOOKS

Abbey, Edward. *Desert Solitaire: A Season in the Wilderness.* New York: Random House, 1968.

———. *The Monkey Wrench Gang.* Philadelphia: Lippincott, 1975.

Albright, Horace, and Robert Cahn. *The Birth of the National Park Service: The Founding Years, 1913–1933.* Salt Lake City, Utah: Howe Brothers, 1985.

Albright, Horace, and Marian Albright Schenk. *Creating the National Park Service: The Missing Years.* Norman: University of Oklahoma Press, 1999.

Albright, Horace, and Frank Taylor. *Oh Ranger! A Book about the National Parks.* New York: Dodd and Mead, 1934.

Alex, William. *Calvert Vaux: Architect and Planner.* Introduction by George Tatum. New York: Ink, 1994.

American Association of State Highway and Transportation Officials. *Roadside Design Guide.* Washington, D.C.: American Association of State Highway and Transportation Officials, 2002.

American Civic Association. *Proceedings of the National Parks Session of the American Civic Association, December 13, 1911.* Washington, D.C.: American Civic Association, n.d. [1912].

Appleton's General Guide to the United States and Canada, 1880. Vol. 1. New York: D. Appleton, 1879.

Appleton's Hand-book of American Travel, Northern and Eastern Tours. New York: D. Appleton, 1873.

Aron, Cindy. *Working at Play: A History of Vacations in America.* New York: Oxford University Press, 1999.

Baeder, John. *Gas, Food, and Lodging: A Postcard Odyssey through the Great American Roadside.* New York: Abbeville Press, 1982.

Barringer, Mark Daniel. *Selling Yellowstone: Capitalism and the Construction of Nature.* Lawrence: University of Kansas Press, 2002.

Bartlett, Richard. *Yellowstone: A Wilderness Besieged.* Tucson: University of Arizona Press, 1985.

Bartram, William. *Travels through North & South Carolina, Georgia, Georgia, East & West Florida, the Cherokee Country, the Extensive Territories of the Muscogulges, or Creek Confederacy, and the Country of the Chactaws.* Philadelphia: James and Johnson, 1791.

Baxter, Sylvester. *Boston Park Guide.* Boston: self-published, 1895.

Bedell, Mary Crehore. *Modern Gypsies: The Story of a Twelve Thousand Mile Motor Camping Trip Encircling the United States.* New York: Brentano's, 1924.

Bedell, Rebecca. *The Anatomy of Nature: Geology and American Landscape Painting, 1825–1875.* Princeton, N.J.: Princeton University Press, 2001.

Belasco, Warren. *Americans on the Road: From Autocamp to Motel, 1910–1945.* Cambridge: MIT Press, 1979.

Benson, Susan Porter, Stephen Brier, and Roy Rosenzweig, eds. *Presenting the Past: Essays on History and the Public.* Philadelphia: Temple University Press, 1986.

Birnbaum, Charles, and Robin Karson, eds. *Pioneers of American Landscape Design.* New York: McGraw-Hill, 2000.

Birney, Hoffman. *Roads to Roam.* Philadelphia: Penn Publishing, 1930.

Blake, Peter. *God's Own Junkyard.* New York: Holt, Rinehart and Winston, 1964.

Bluestone, Daniel. *Buildings, Landscapes, and Memory: Case Studies in Historic Preservation.* New York: Norton, 2011.

Bodnar, John. *Remaking America: Public Memory, Commemoration, and Patriotism in the Twentieth Century.* Princeton, N.J.: Princeton University Press, 1992.

Boime, Albert. *The Magisterial Gaze: Manifest Destiny and American Landscape Painting.* Washington: D.C.: Smithsonian Institution Press, 1991.

Bowles, Samuel. *Across the Continent.* Springfield, Mass.: Samuel Bowles, 1865.

———. *Our New West.* Hartford, Ct.: Hartford Publishing, 1869.

Brimmer, F[rank] E. *Autocamping.* Cincinnati: Stewart Kidd, 1923.

Bryan, Frank. *Yankee Politics in Rural Vermont.* Hanover, N.H.: University Press of New England, 1974.

Bryant, William Cullen, ed. *Picturesque America; or, The Land We Live In.* Vol. 1. New York: D. Appleton, 1872.

Buchholtz, C. W. *Rocky Mountain National Park: A History.* Boulder: Colorado Associated University Press, 1983.

Buckley, J. M. *Two Weeks in the Yosemite Valley and Vicinity.* New York: Phillips and Hunt, 1883.

Burke, Edmund. *A Philosophical Enquiry into the Origin of Our Ideas of the Sublime and Beautiful.* 1757. London: Printed for Robert and James Dodsley, 1787.

Cahn, Robert. *Will Success Spoil the National Parks? A Series Reprinted from the Christian Science Monitor.* Boston: Christian Science Publishing Society, 1968.

Campbell, Reau. *Campbell's New Revised Complete Guide and Descriptive Book of the Yellowstone Park.* Chicago: H. E. Klamar, 1914.

Carr, Ethan. *Mission 66: Modernism and the National Park Dilemma.* Amherst: University of Massachusetts Press, 2007.

———. *Wilderness by Design: Landscape Architecture and the National Park Service.* Lincoln: University of Nebraska Press, 1998.

Carr, Ethan, Shaun Eyring, and Richard Guy Wilson, eds. *Public Nature: Scenery, History, and Park Design.* Charlottesville: University of Virginia Press, 2013.

Carson, Rachel. *Silent Spring.* New York: Fawcett Crest, 1964.

Chase, Alston. *Playing God in Yellowstone: The Destruction of America's First National Park.* Boston: Atlantic Monthly Press, 1986.

Chittenden, Hiram. *The Yellowstone National Park: Historical and Descriptive.* Cincinnati: Robert Clarke, 1895.

———. *The Yellowstone National Park: Historical and Descriptive.* Cincinnati: Robert Clarke, 1904.

———. *The Yellowstone National Park: Historical and Descriptive.* New and enlarged edition. Cincinnati: Stewart and Kidd, 1918.

Cohen, Michael. *The History of the Sierra Club, 1892–1970.* San Francisco: Sierra Club Books, 1988.

Conron, John, ed. *The American Landscape: A Critical Anthology of Prose and Poetry.* New York: Oxford University Press, 1973.

Cosgrove, Denis. *Social Formation and Symbolic Landscape.* London: Croom Helm, 1984.

Crosby, W. W., and George Goodwin. *Highway Location and Surveying.* Chicago: Gillette, 1928.

Darling, F. Fraser, and Noel Eichhorn. *Man & Nature in the National Parks: Reflections on Policy.* Washington, D.C.: Conservation Foundation, 1967.

Davis, Timothy, Todd Croteau, and Christopher Marston. *America's National Park Roads and Parkways: Drawings from the Historic American Engineering Record.* Baltimore: Johns Hopkins University Press, 2004.

Davison, Gideon M. *The Fashionable Tour: An Excursion to the Springs, Niagara, Quebec, and through the New-England States: Interspersed with Geographical and Historical Sketches.* 3rd enlarged ed. Saratoga Springs, N.Y.: G. M. Davison, 1828.

———. *The Fashionable Tour, in 1825: An Excursion to the Springs, Niagara, Quebec, and Boston.* Saratoga Springs, N.Y.: G. M. Davison, 1825.

Demars, Stanford E. *The Tourist in Yosemite, 1855–1985.* Salt Lake City: University of Utah Press, 1991.

Dilsaver, Lary, ed. *America's National Park System: The Critical Documents.* Lanham, Md.: Rowman and Littlefield, 1994.

Dilsaver, Lary, and William Tweed. *Challenge of the Big Trees: A Resource History of Sequoia National Park.* Three Rivers, Calif.: Sequoia Natural History Association, 1990.

Disturnell, John. *The Traveller's Guide through the State of New York, Canada, &c., Embracing a General Description of the City of New-York, the Hudson River Guide, and the Fashionable Tour to the Springs and Niagara Falls; with Steam-boat, Rail-road, and Stage Routes.* New York: J. Disturnell, 1836.

Downing, Andrew Jackson. *A Treatise on the Theory and Practice of Landscape Gardening, Adapted to North America: With a view to the Improvement of Country Residences.* New York: Wiley and Putnam, 1841.

Dwight, Theodore. *The Northern Traveller; Containing the Routes to Niagara, Quebec and the Springs; with Descriptions of the Principal Scenes and Useful Hints to Strangers.* New York: Wilder and Campbell, 1825.

Dwight, Timothy. *Travels in New-England and New-York.* 4 vols. New Haven: T. Dwight, 1821–22.

Eastman, Samuel. *The White Mountain Guide Book.* 6th ed. Boston: Lee and Shepard, 1866.

Edge, Rosalie. *Roads and More Roads in the National Parks and Forests.* Publication No. 54. New York: Emergency Conservation Committee, 1936.

Ehrlich, Paul. *The Population Bomb.* New York: Ballantine, 1968.

Eliot, Charles W., II. *The Future of Mount Desert Island: A Report to the Plan Committee Bar Harbor Village Improvement Society.* N.p.: Bar Harbor Village Improvement Association, 1928.

Engle, Reed. *Everything Was Wonderful: A Pictorial History of the Civilian Conservation Corps in Shenandoah National Park.* Luray, Va.: Shenandoah National Park Association, 1999.

———. *The Greatest Single Feature . . . A Skyline Drive: 75 Years of a Mountaintop Motorway.* Luray, Va.: Shenandoah National Park Association, 2006.

Everhart, William C. *The National Park Service.* New York: Praeger, 1972.

Fisher, Irving. *Frederick Law Olmsted and the City Planning Movement in the United States.* Ann Arbor: University of Michigan Research Press, 1986.

Flexner, James. *That Wilder Image: The Paintings of America's Native School from Thomas Cole to Winslow Homer.* Boston: Little, Brown, 1962.

Foresta, Ronald. *America's National Parks and Their Keepers.* Washington, D.C.: Resources for the Future, 1984.

Garate, Donald. *The Zion Tunnel: From Slickrock to Switchback.* Rev. ed. Springdale, Utah: Zion Natural History Association, 1991.

Garvin, Alexander. *Public Parks: The Key to Livable Communities.* New York: Norton, 2011.

Gassan, Richard. *The Birth of American Tourism: New York, the Hudson Valley, and American Culture, 1790–1830.* Amherst: University of Massachusetts Press, 2008.

Giedion, Sigfried. *Space, Time and Architecture: The Growth of a New Tradition.* Cambridge: Harvard University Press, 1946.

Gilpin, William. *Three Essays: On Picturesque Beauty; On Picturesque Travel; and on Sketching the Landscape.* 2nd ed. London: printed for R. Blamire, 1794.

Glover, James. *A Wilderness Original: The Life of Bob Marshall.* Seattle, Wash.: The Mountaineers, 1986.

Great River Road Association. *The Great River Road: From Pines to Palms.* Jefferson City, Mo.: Great River Road Association, 1967. Copy in the Department of the Interior Library.

Gutheim, Frederick. *The Potomac.* New York: Holt, Rinehart and Winston, 1949.

Haines, Aubrey L. *The Yellowstone Story: A History of Our First National Park.* Vol. 1. Yellowstone National Park, Wyo.: Yellowstone Library and Museum Association, 1977.

———. *The Yellowstone Story: A History of Our First National Park.* Vol. 2. Rev. ed. Niwot: University Press of Colorado, 1996.

Hall, Ansel, ed. *Handbook of Yosemite National Park.* New York: Putnam's Sons, 1921.

Halprin, Lawrence. *Freeways.* New York: Reinhold, 1966.

Hartzog, George B., Jr. *Battling for the National Parks.* Mt. Kisko, N.Y.: Moyer Bell, 1988.

Haynes, Jack E. *Haynes Official Guide: Yellowstone National Park.* 29th ed. Rev. and enlarged. St. Paul, Minn.: F. J. Haynes, 1915.

Hewes, Laurence. *American Highway Practice.* 2 vols. New York: Wiley and Sons, 1942.

Hokanson, Drake. *The Lincoln Highway: Main Street across America.* Iowa City: University of Iowa Press, 1988.

Hosmer, Charles B., Jr. *Preservation Comes of Age: From Williamsburg to the National Historic Trust.* Charlottesville: University Press of Virginia for Preservation Press, 1981.

Hubbard, Elbert, and Alice Hubbard. *A Little Journey to the Yellowstone Park.* East Aurora, N.Y.: Roycrofters, 1915.

Hubbard, Henry, and Theodora Kimball. *An Introduction to the Study of Landscape Architecture.* Rev. ed. New York: Macmillan, 1929.

Hunt, John Dixon. *Gardens and the Picturesque.* Cambridge: MIT Press, 1992.

Hunt, John Dixon, and Peter Willis, eds. *The Genius of Place: The English Landscape Garden 1620–1820.* Cambridge: MIT Press, 1988.

Hussey, Christopher. *The Picturesque: Studies in a Point of View.* London: Putnam's Sons, 1927.

Hutchins, James Mason. *Scenes of Wonder and Curiosity in California.* New York: A. Roman, 1875.

Huth, Hans. *Nature and the American: Three Centuries of Changing Attitudes.* 2nd ed. Introduction by Douglas Strong. Lincoln: University of Nebraska Press, 1990.

Ise, John. *Our National Park Policy: A Critical History.* Baltimore: Johns Hopkins University Press, 1961.

Jackson, John Brinckerhoff. *A Sense of Place, a Sense of Time.* New Haven: Yale University Press, 1994.

Jacobs, Jane. *The Death and Life of Great American Cities.* New York: Random House, 1961.

Jefferson, Thomas. *Notes on the State of Virginia.* London: J. Stockdale, 1787.

Jessup, Elon. *The Motor Camping Book.* New York: Putnam's Sons, 1921.

Johnston, Hank. *Yosemite's Yesterdays.* 2nd ed. 2 vols. Yosemite, Calif.: Flying Spur Press, 1989.

———. *Yosemite's Yesterdays.* Vol. 2. Yosemite, Calif.: Flying Spur Press, 1991.

Jolley, Harley E. *The Blue Ridge Parkway.* Knoxville: University of Tennessee Press, 1969.

———. *Painting with a Comet's Tail.* Boone, N.C.: Appalachian Consortium Press, 1987.

Keats, John. *The Insolent Chariots.* New York: Lippincott, 1958.

Kilbourne, Frederick W. *Chronicles of the White Mountains.* Boston: Houghton Mifflin, 1916.

King, Thomas Starr. *The White Hills: Their Legends, Landscape and Poetry.* Boston: Crosby and Nichols, 1862.

Kipling, Rudyard. *From Sea to Sea: Letters of Travel.* Vol. 2. New York: Doubleday and McClure, 1899.

Kohler, Sue, and Pamela Scott, eds. *Designing the Nation's Capital: The 1901 Plan for Washington, D.C.* Washington, D.C.: U.S. Commission of Fine Arts, 2006.

Lancaster, Samuel. *The Columbia: America's Great Highway from the Cascade Mountains to the Sea.* Portland, Ore.: J. K. Gill, 1926.

Lasdun, Susan. *The English Park: Royal, Private & Public.* London: Andre Deutsch, 1991.

Leavitt, Helen. *Superhighway Superhoax.* Garden City, N.Y.: Doubleday, 1970.

Levine, Lawrence. *The Unpredictable Past: Essays in American Cultural History.* New York: Oxford University Press, 1993.

Lewis, Tom. *Divided Highways: Building the Interstate Highways, Transforming America.* New York: Viking, 1997.

Lindgren, James. *Preserving the Old Dominion: Historic Preservation and Virginia Traditionalism.* Charlottesville: University Press of Virginia, 1992.

Long, J. C., and John D. Long. *Motor Camping.* New York: Dodd, Mead, 1923.

Loudon, John C. *An Encylopedia of Agriculture.* London: Long, Brown, Greene, and Longmans, 1844.

———. *An Encyclopedia of Gardening.* London: Long, Rees, Orme, Browne, Green, and Longman, 1834.

———. *A Treatise on Forming, Improving, and Managing Country Residences.* London: Longman, Hurst, Rees, and Orme, 1806.

Louter, David. *Windshield Wilderness: Cars, Roads, and Nature in Washington's National Parks.* Seattle: University of Washington Press, 2006.

Lowry, William. *Repairing Paradise: The Restoration of Nature in America's National Parks.* Washington, D.C.: Brookings Institution Press, 2009.

Manning, Harvey. *The Wild Cascades: Forgotten Parkland.* Edited by David Brower. San Francisco: Sierra Club, 1969.

Margolies, John. *The End of the Road: Vanishing Highway Architecture in America.* New York: Penguin, 1981.

———. *Pump and Circumstance: Glory Days of the American Gas Station.* Boston: Little, Brown, 1993.

Marshall, Robert. *The People's Forests.* New York: Harrison Smith and Robert Haas, 1933.

Marx, Leo. *The Machine in the Garden: Technology and the Pastoral Ideal in America.* New York: Oxford University Press, 1964.

Mauch, Christof, and Thomas Zeller, eds. *The World beyond the Windshield: Driving and the Experience of Landscape in Twentieth-Century North America and Europe.* Athens: Ohio University Press, 2008.

McClelland, Linda. *Building the National Parks: Historic Landscape Design and Construction.* Baltimore: Johns Hopkins University Press, 1998.

———. *Presenting Nature: The Historic Landscape Design of the National Park Service, 1916–1942.* Washington, D.C.: U.S. Department of the Interior, National Park Service, National Register of Historic Places, 1993.

Meeks, Harold. *On the Road to Yellowstone: The Yellowstone Trail and American Highways 1900–1930.* Missoula, Mont.: Pictorial Histories Publishing, 2000.

Meine, Curt. *Aldo Leopold: His Life and Work.* Madison: University of Wisconsin Press, 1988.

Miles, John C. *Guardians of the Parks: A History of the National Parks and Conservation Association.* Washington, D.C.: Taylor and Francis in Cooperation with National Parks and Conservation Association, 1995.

———. *Wilderness in the National Parks: Playground or Preserve?* Seattle: University of Washington Press, 2009.

Miller, Angela. *The Empire of the Eye: Landscape Representation and American Cultural Politics, 1825–1875.* Syracuse, N.Y.: Cornell University Press, 1993.

Miller, David, ed. *American Iconology: New Approaches to Nineteenth-Century Art and Literature.* New Haven: Yale University Press, 1993.

Milliken, Charles. *The Glen House Book.* Cambridge: John Wilson and Son, 1889.

Mills, Enos. *Your National Parks.* Boston: Houghton Mifflin, 1917.

Mountaineers, The. *The Administration of the National Parks: Report of a Special Committee Adopted by the Board of Trustees of the Mountaineers, November 1922.* Seattle, Wash.: The Mountaineers, 1922.

Muir, John. *Letters to a Friend: Written to Mrs. Ezra S. Carr, 1866–1879.* Boston: Houghton and Mifflin, 1915.

———. *The Life and Letters of John Muir.* Vol. 2. Edited by William Fredric Bade. Boston: Houghton Mifflin, 1924.

———. *Our National Parks.* Boston: Houghton and Mifflin, 1901.

Mumford, Lewis. *From the Ground Up: Observations on Contemporary American Architecture, Housing, Highway Building, and Civic Design.* New York: Harcourt, Brace, 1956.

Murphy, Thomas. *On Sunset Highways: A Book of Motor Rambles in California.* Rev. ed. Boston: Page, 1921.

Nash, Roderick. *Wilderness and the American Mind.* Rev. ed. New Haven: Yale University Press, 1973.

Newton, Norman T. *Design on the Land: The Development of Landscape Architecture.* Cambridge: Harvard University Press, 1971.

Nolen, John, and Henry Hubbard. *Parkways and Land Values.* Harvard City Planning Studies No. 11. Cambridge: Harvard University Press, 1937.

Novak, Barbara. *Nature and Culture: American Landscape and Painting, 1825–1875.* New York: Oxford University Press, 1980.

Olmsted, Frederick Law. *Forty Years of Landscape Architecture: Frederick Law Olmsted, Landscape Architect, 1822–1903.* Edited by Frederick Law Olmsted Jr. and Theodora Kimball. New York: Putnam's Sons, 1922.

———. *Landscape into Cityscape: Frederick Law Olmsted's Plans for a Greater New York.* Edited with an introductory essay and notes by Albert Fein. Ithaca, N.Y.: Cornell University Press, 1967.

———. *The Papers of Frederick Law Olmsted.* Vol. 5, *The California Frontier, 1863–1865,* edited by Victoria Post Ranney. Baltimore: Johns Hopkins University Press, 1990.

———. *The Papers of Frederick Law Olmsted.* Vol. 6, *The Years of Olmsted, Vaux & Company, 1865–1874,* edited by David Schuyler and Jane Turner Censer. Baltimore: Johns Hopkins University Press, 1992.

———. *The Papers of Frederick Law Olmsted.* Supplementary Series. Vol. 1, *Writings on Public Parks, Parkways, and Park Systems,* edited by Charles E. Beveridge and Carolyn F. Hoffman. Baltimore: Johns Hopkins University Press, 1997.

Paden, Irene, and Margaret Schlichtmann. *The Big Oak Flat Road: An Account of Freighting from Stockton to Yosemite Valley.* Yosemite National Park: Yosemite History Association, 1959.

Paulding, James Kirke. *The New Mirror for Travellers: and Guide to the Springs.* New York: G. & C. Carvill, 1828.

Peterson, Jon. *The Birth of City Planning in the United States, 1840–1917.* Baltimore: Johns Hopkins University Press, 2003.

Pierce, Daniel. *The Great Smokies: From Natural Habitat to National Park.* Knoxville: University of Tennessee Press, 2000.

Pomeroy, Earl. *In Search of the Golden West: The Tourist in Western America.* New York: Knopf, 1957.

Price, Uvedale. *Essays on the Picturesque, as Compared to the Sublime and the Beautiful, and, on the Use of Studying Pictures, for the Purpose of Improving Real Landscape.* Vol. 1. 1794. London: printed for J. Mawman, 1810.

Pückler-Muskau, Prince [Hermann Heinrich Ludwig]. *Hints on Landscape Gardening.* Edited by Samuel Parsons. Boston: Riverside Press of Houghton Mifflin, 1917.

Reps, John. *Washington on View: The Nation's Capital since 1790.* Chapel Hill: University of North Carolina Press, 1991.

Repton, Humphry. *The Art of Landscape Gardening.* Edited by John Nolen. Boston: Houghton Mifflin, 1907.

Richards, T. Addison. *Appleton's Illustrated Hand-book of American Travel: The Eastern and Middle States and the British Provinces.* New York: Appleton, 1861.

———. *Guide to Central Park.* New York: James Miller, 1866.

Richardson, Albert B. *Beyond the Mississippi: From the Great River to the Great Ocean.* Hartford, Ct.: American Publishing, 1867.

Rinehart, Mary Roberts. *Through Glacier Park in 1915.* New York: Collier and Son, 1916. Reprint. Boulder, Colo.: R. Rinehart, 1983.

Roberts, Ann Rockefeller. *Mr. Rockefeller's Roads: The Untold Story of Acadia's Carriage Roads and Their Creator.* Camden, Me.: Down East Books, 1990.

Rogers, Elizabeth Barlow. *Landscape Design: A Cultural and Architectural History.* New York: Abrams, 2001.

Roper, Linda Wood. *FLO: A Biography of Frederick Law Olmsted.* Baltimore: Johns Hopkins University Press, 1973.

Rosenzweig, Roy, and Elizabeth Blackmar. *The Park and the People: A History of Central Park.* Ithaca, N.Y.: Cornell University Press, 1992.

Runte, Alfred. *National Parks: The American Experience.* 2nd ed. Lincoln: University of Nebraska Press, 1987.

———. *Yosemite: The Embattled Wilderness.* Lincoln: University of Nebraska Press, 1990.

Schuyler, David. *Apostle of Taste: Andrew Jackson Downing, 1815–1852.* Baltimore: Johns Hopkins University Press, 1996.

———. *The New Urban Landscape: The Redefinition of City Form in Nineteenth-Century America.* Baltimore: Johns Hopkins University Press, 1986.

———. *Sanctified Landscape: Writers, Artists, and the Hudson River Valley, 1820–1909.* Ithaca, N.Y.: Cornell University Press, 2012.

Sears, John. *Sacred Places: American Tourist Attractions in the Nineteenth Century.* New York: Oxford University Press, 1989.

Seely, Bruce. *Building the American Highway System: Engineers as Policy Makers.* Philadelphia: Temple University Press, 1987.

Sellers, Richard. *Preserving Nature in the National Parks: A History.* New Haven: Yale University Press, 1997.

Shaffer, Margaret. *See America First: Tourism and National Identity, 1880–1940.* Washington, D.C.: Smithsonian Institution Press, 2001.

Shankland, Robert. *Steve Mather of the National Parks.* 3rd ed. New York: Knopf, 1970.

Shepard, Paul. *Man and the Landscape: A Historic View of the Aesthetics of Nature.* New York: Knopf, 1967.

Silliman, Augustus Ely. *A Gallop among American Scenery, or Sketches of American Scenes and Military Adventure.* New York: Appleton, 1843.

Sloane, David. *The Last Great Necessity: Cemeteries in American History.* Baltimore: Johns Hopkins University Press, 1991.

Snow, W. Brewster, ed. *The Highway and the Landscape.* New Brunswick, N.J.: Rutgers University Press, 1959.

Spaulding, John H. *Historical Relics of the White Mountains.* Mt. Washington, N.H.: J. R. Hitchcock, 1862.

Stanley, Edwin J. *Rambles in Wonderland: or, Up the Yellowstone, and among the Geysers and Other Curiosities of the National Park.* New York: Appleton, 1878.

Stoddard, John L. *John L. Stoddard's Lectures.* Vol. 10, *Southern California, Grand Canyon of the Colorado River, Yellowstone National Park.* Chicago and Boston: Geo. L. Shuman, 1898.

Strahorn, Carrie Adell. *Fifteen Thousand Miles by Stage.* Vol. 1, *1877–1880.* New York: Knickerbocker Press, 1911. Reprint, Lincoln: University of Nebraska Press, 1988.

Susman, Warren. *Culture as History: The Transformation of American Society in the Twentieth Century.* New York: Pantheon, 1973.

Sutter, Paul. *Driven Wild: How the Fight against Automobiles Launched the Modern Wilderness Movement.* Seattle: University of Washington Press, 2002.

Sweetser, M. F. *Views in the White Mountains, with Descriptions by M. F. Sweetser.* Portland, Me.: Chisolm Brothers, 1879.

Taintor, Charles Newhall. *Saratoga Illustrated: The Visitors Guide to Saratoga Springs.* New York: Taintor Brothers, 1875.

Taylor, Charles, Jr. *Touring Alaska and the Yellowstone.* Philadelphia: George W. Jacobs, 1901.

Thayer, William. *Marvels of the New West.* Norwich, Ct.: Henry Bill, 1892.

Tilden, Freeman. *The National Parks: What They Mean to You and Me.* New York: Knopf, 1955.

Trexler, Keith. *The Tioga Road: A History, 1883–1961.* Yosemite National Park, Calif.: Yosemite Association, 1961. Revised 1975 and 1980.

Tunnard, Christopher, and Boris Pushkarev. *Man-Made America: Chaos or Control?* New Haven: Yale University Press, 1963.

Udall, Stewart. *The Quiet Crisis.* New York: Holt, Rinehart and Winston, 1963.

———. *The Quiet Crisis and the Next Generation.* Salt Lake City, Utah: Gibbs Smith, 1988.

Van de Water, Frederic. *The Family Flivvers to Frisco.* New York: D. Appleton, 1927.

Wallis, Michael. *Route 66: The Mother Road.* New York: St. Martins, 1990.

Whisnant, Anne Mitchell. *Super-Scenic Motorway: A Blue Ridge Parkway History.* Chapel Hill: University of North Carolina Press, 2006.

Whitely, Lee, and Jane Whitely. *The Playground Trail: The National Park-to-Park Highway: To and through the National Parks of the West in 1920.* Boulder, Colo.: Johnson Printing, 2003.

Whittlesey, Lee. *Yellowstone Place Names.* 2nd ed. Gardiner, Mont.: Wonderland, 2006.

Whyte, William. *The Last Landscape.* Garden City, N.Y.: Doubleday, 1968.

Williams, W. *Appleton's Northern and Eastern Traveller's Guide: With New and Authentic Maps Illustrating Those Divisions of the Country.* New York: Appleton, 1850.

Willis, Nathaniel Parker. *American Scenery; or, Land, Lake, and River Illustrations of Transatlantic Nature.* 2 vols. London: George Virtue, 1840.

———. *The Complete Works of N. P. Willis.* New York: J. S. Redfield, 1846.

Wilson, Alexander. *The Poems and Literary Prose of Alexander Wilson, American Ornithologist.* Vol. 2, *Poems,* edited by Alexander B. Grosart. Paisley, Scotland: Alexander Gardner, 1876.

Wingate, George. *Through the Yellowstone Park on Horseback.* New York: O. Judd, 1886.

Wirth, Conrad. *Parks, Politics, and the People.* Norman: University of Oklahoma Press, 1980.

Wood, Frederic. *The Turnpikes of New England.* Boston: Marshall Jones, 1924.

Yard, Robert Sterling. *The Book of the National Parks.* New York: Scribner's Sons, 1921.

———. *Our Federal Lands: A Romance of American Development.* New York: Scribner's Sons, 1928.

Zaitzevsky, Cynthia. *Frederick Law Olmsted and the Boston Park System.* Cambridge: Harvard University Press, 1982.

HISTORIC AMERICAN ENGINEERING RECORD REPORTS

Anderson, Michael. "Addendum to Zion–Mount Carmel Highway, Zion–Mount Carmel Highway Tunnel, Zion National Park, HAER No. UT-39-A." 1993.

Bennett, Michael. "Colonial National Historical Park Roads and Bridges, HAER No. VA-115." 1995.

———. "Jamestown Island Loop Roads, HAER No. VA-116." 1995.

Cleven, Brian. "Blue Ridge Parkway, Linn Cove Viaduct, HAER No. NC-42-A." 1997.

Culpin, Mary Shivers. "Golden Gate Viaduct, HAER No. WY-46." 1989.

———. "Grand Loop Road, HAER No. WY-55." 1989.

———. "Yellowstone National Park Roads and Bridges, HAER No. WY-24." 1989.

Davis, Timothy. "George Washington Memorial Parkway, HAER No. VA-69." 1996.

———. "Rock Creek and Potomac Parkway, HABS No. DC-697." 1992.

———. "Rock Creek Park Roads, HAER No. DC-55." 1998.

Duensing, Dawn. "Baltimore–Washington Parkway, HAER No. MD-129." 2000.

———. "Bronx River Parkway, HAER No. NY-237." 2001.

Fulton, Jean. "Natchez Trace Parkway, HAER No. MS-15." 1998.

Holmes, Amanda. "Gettysburg National Military Park Tour Roads, HAER No. PA-485." 1998.

Kelleher, Michael, and Cornelius Maher. "Great Smoky Mountains National Park Roads and Bridges, HAER No. TN-35." 1996.

———. "Great Smoky Mountains National Park Roads and Bridges, Foothills Parkway, HAER No. TN-35-E." 1996.

———. "Great Smoky Mountains National Park Roads and Bridges, Newfound Gap Road, HAER No. TN-35-A" 1996.

———. Great Smoky Mountains National Park Roads and Bridges, North Shore Road, HAER No. TN-35-I." 1996.

Leach, Sara Amy. "Redwood National and State Parks Roads, HAER No. CA-269." 2003.

Maher, Cornelius. "Acadia National Park Motor Roads, HAER No. ME-11." 1995.

McClure, Nancy. "Addendum to Yellowstone National Park Roads and Bridges, HAER No. WY-24." 1999.

———. "Chittenden Memorial Bridge, HAER No. WY-88." 1999.

———. "Corkscrew Bridge, HAER No. WY-86." 1999.

Ott, Cynthia. "Shiloh National Military Park Tour Roads, HAER No. TN-37." 1998.

Quin, Richard. "All-Year Highway (El Portal Road), Yosemite National Park, HAER No. CA-150." 1991.

———. "Big Oak Flat Road, Yosemite National Park, HAER No. CA-147." 1991.

———. "Blue Ridge Parkway, HAER No. NC-42." 1997.

———. "Carbon River Road, Mount Rainier National Park, HAER No. WA-120." 1992.

———. "Christine Falls Bridge, Mount Rainier National Park, HAER No. WA-48." 1992.

———. "Coulterville Road, Yosemite National Park, HAER No. CA-146." 1991.

———. "East Side Highway, Mount Rainier National Park, HAER No. WA-124." 1992.

———. "Fall River Road, Rocky Mountain National Park, HAER No. CO-73." 1993.

———. "Glacier Point Road, Yosemite National Park, HAER No. CA-157." 1991.

———. "Mather Memorial Parkway, Mount Rainier National Park, HAER No. WA-125." 1992.

———. "Mount Rainier National Park Roads and Bridges, HAER No. WA-35." 1992.

———. "Nisqually Road (Government Road), Mount Rainier National Park, HAER No. WA-119." 1992.

———. "Rockefeller Carriage Roads, Acadia National Park, HAER No. ME-12." 1993.

———. "Rocky Mountain National Park Roads, HAER No. CO-78." 1993.

———. "Stevens Canyon Highway, Mount Rainier National Park, HAER No. WA-123." 1992.

———. "Stevens Canyon Highway, Mount Rainier National Park, HAER No. WA-124." 1992.

———. "Tioga Road, Yosemite National Park, HAER No. CA-149." 1991.

———. "Trail Ridge Road, Rocky Mountain National Park, HAER No. CO-31." 1993.

———. "Wawona Covered Bridge, Yosemite National Park Roads and Bridges, HAER No. CA-106." 1991.

———. "Wawona Road, Yosemite National Park, HAER No. CA-148." 1991.

———. "Wawona Tunnel, Yosemite National Park, HAER No. CA-105." 1991.

———. "West Side Road, Mount Rainier National Park, HAER No. WA-122." 1992.

———. "Yakima Park Highway, Mount Rainier National Park, HAER No. WA-126." 1992.

———. "Yosemite Roads and Bridges, HAER No. CA-117." 1991.

Slattery, Christina. "Generals Highway, Sequoia National Park, HAER No. CA-140." 1993.

Steen, Katherine. "Going-to-the-Sun Road, Glacier National Park HAER No. MT-67." 1990.

ADDITIONAL GOVERNMENT DOCUMENTS

Allaback, Sarah. *Mission 66 Visitor Centers: The History of a Building Type*. Washington, D.C.: U.S. Department of the Interior, National Park Service, Park Historic Structures and Cultural Landscapes Program, 2000.

Bayliss, Dudley. *Planning Our National Park Roads and Our National Parkways*. Washington, D.C.: U.S. Department of the Interior, National Park Service, n.d. [ca. 1958].

[Boston, Massachusetts,] Metropolitan Park Commission. *Report of the Board of Metropolitan Park Commissioners, January 1893*.

Bullock, Alison. *The Flood of 2006 Report, 2007 & 2008 Updates*. U.S. Department of the Interior, National Park Service, Mount Rainier National Park, 2007.

Buxton, Barry. *Mabry Mill Historic Resource Study*. Washington, D.C.: U.S. Department of the Interior, National Park Service, 1987.

Catton, Theodore. *Wonderland: An Administrative History of Mount Rainer*. Seattle, Wash.: U.S. Department of the Interior, National Park Service, Cultural Resources Program, 1996.

Chittenden, Hiram. "The Government Road System of the Yellowstone National Park." In *Proceedings of the International Good Roads Conference held at Buffalo, New York, September 16–21, 1901*. U.S. Department of Agriculture, Office of Public Road Inquiries, Bulletin No. 21. Washington, D.C.: Government Printing Office, 1901.

Culpin, Mary Shivers. *The History of the Construction of the Road System in Yellowstone National Park, 1872–1966*. Historic Resource Study Vol. 1. U.S. Department of the Interior, National Park Service, Rocky Mountain Region, Division of Cultural Resources, 1994.

Davis, Timothy. *Landscape Line 16: Historic Roads*. Washington, D.C.: U.S. Department of the Interior, National Park Service, Park Historic Structures and Cultural Landscapes Program, 2005.

Evison, S. Herbert. "Oral History Interview of Dudley C. Bayliss, 11 February 1971." Copy in Blue Ridge Parkway Library.

Gordon, Jack. "Landmark in the Sky: The History and Preservation of Glacier's Going-to-the-Sun Road." Paper presented at "Preserving the Historic Road in America" conference, Portland, Ore., April 22–25, 2004.

———. "The Rehabilitation of the Going-to-the-Sun Road: An Update." Paper presented at "Preserving the Historic Road" conference, Washington, D.C., September 9–12, 2010.

Greene, Linda. *Yosemite: The Park and Its Resources: A History of the Discovery, Management, and Physical Development of Yosemite National Park, California*. Vol. 1. U.S. Department of the Interior, National Park Service, 1987.

Hammons, Vernon. *A Brief Organizational History of the Office of Design and Construction, National Park Service, 1917–1962*. Washington, D.C.: U.S. Department of the Interior, 1963.

Krakow, Jere. *Historic Resource Study: Rock Creek and Potomac Parkway, George Washington Memorial Parkway, Suitland Parkway, Baltimore-Washington Parkway*. U.S. Department of the Interior, National Park Service, 1990.

Mackintosh, Barry. *C & O Canal: The Making of a Park*. Washington, D.C.: U.S. Department of the Interior, National Park Service, History Division, 1991.

———. "George Washington Memorial Parkway: Administrative History." U.S. Department of the Interior, National Park Service, History Division, March 1996 draft. Author's copy.

———. *The National Parks: Shaping the System*. Produced by the Division of Publications and the Employee Development Division, National Park Service. Washington, D.C.: U.S. Department of the Interior, 1991.

———. *The National Parks: Shaping the System*. Produced by Harpers Ferry Center, National Park Service. Washington, D.C.: U.S. Department of the Interior, 2005.

Marshall, Robert. *The Forest for Recreation*. In Senate, *A National Plan for American Forestry*, vol. 1., 73rd Cong., 1st sess., 30 March 1933, S. Doc 12.

[Maryland] Joint Committee on the Chesapeake and Ohio Canal Parkway. *Report of Joint Committee on the Chesapeake and Ohio Canal Parkway*. December 1952.

Matthes, Francois. *The Geologic History of Yosemite Valley*. U.S. Department of the Interior, Geological Survey. Washington, D.C.: Government Printing Office, 1930.

McClelland, Linda Flint. *Presenting Nature: Historic Landscape Design in the National Park Service 1916–1941*. U.S. Department of the Interior, National Park Service, National Register of Historic Places, 1993.

Musselman, Lloyd K. *Rocky Mountain National Park: Administrative History, 1915–1965*. Washington, D.C.: U.S. Department of the Interior, National Park Service, Office of History and Historic Architecture, 1971.

National Capital Park and Planning Commission. *Work of the National Capital Park and Planning Commission*. Washington, D.C.: Government Printing Office, 1928.

National Conference on Outdoor Recreation. *Recreation Resources on Federal Lands*. Washington, D.C.: National Conference on Outdoor Recreation, 1929.

National Park Service and Federal Lands Highway Division. *National Park Service Barrier Inventory and Assessment Phase 1 Report, February 11, 2008*.

National Parks Centennial Commission. *Preserving a Heritage: Final Report to the President and Congress of the National Parks Centennial Commission*. Washington, D.C., [1973].

National Parks Second Century Commission. *Advancing the National Park Idea: National Parks Second Century Commission Report*. [2009].

[New York] Board of Commissioners of the Department of Public Parks. *Third General Report of the Board of Commissioners of the Department of Public Parks for the Period of Twenty Months, From May 1st, 1872, to December 31st, 1873*. New York: William C. Bryant, 1875.

New York City Board of Commissioners of Central Park. *Seventh Annual Report of the Board of Commissioners of Central Park, for the Year Ending with December 31, 1863*. New York: Wm. C. Bryant, 1864.

Norris, Frank. *Crown Jewel of the North: An Administrative History of Denali National Park and Preserve*. Vol. 1. U.S. Department of the Interior, National Park Service, Alaska Regional Office, 2006.

Olmsted, Frederick Law. *Report of State Park Survey of California*. Sacramento: California State Printing Office, 1929.

Oral History Interview with George B. Hartzog, Jr., Director, National Park Service, 1964–1972. By Janet A. McDonnell. Washington, D.C.: U.S. Department of the Interior, National Park Service, Park History Program, 2007.

Phelps, Dawson, et al. "Administrative History of the Natchez Trace Parkway." Manuscript in Natchez Trace Parkway Headquarters files, Tupelo, Miss. Begun by Phelps in 1965 and subsequently updated by Phelps and others. Accessed electronically, August 2010. www.nps.gov/parkhistory/online_books/natr/adhi.pdf.

Preserving a Landmark in the Sky: Rehabilitation of Going-to-the-Sun Road. Technical Report FHWA-WFL/TD-08-001. Vancouver, Wash.: Western Federal Lands Highway Division, Federal Highway Administration, 2008.

Unrau, Harlan, and G. Frank Williss. *Administrative History: The Expansion of the National Park Service in the 1930s*. U.S. Department of the Interior, National Park Service, Denver Service Center, 1983.

Urban Advisors to the Federal Highway Administration. *The Freeway in the City: Principles of Planning and Design, A Report to the Secretary, Department of Transportation*. Washington, D.C.: Government Printing Office, 1968.

U.S. Bureau of Public Roads and U.S. National Park Service. *Parkway for the Mississippi: A Report to the Congress*. Washington, D.C.: Government Printing Office, 1951.

———. *Parkway for the Mississippi: A Report to Congress. Part II (Technical)*. 1952. Copy in U.S. Department of the Interior Library.

U.S. Congress. House. *Chesapeake and Ohio Canal Report*, 81st Cong., 2d sess., 16 August 1950, H.R. Doc 687.

———. House. *Free Roads, Yosemite National Park*. 56th Cong., 2d sess., 1 March 1901. H. Rep. 2989.

———. House. Committee on Public Lands. *Establishment of a National Park Service: Hearing before the Committee on Public Lands on H.R. 22995*. 62d Cong., 2d sess., 24 April 1912.

———. House. Committee on Public Lands. *Construction of Roads, etc in National Parks and Monuments: Hearings before the Committee of Public Lands . . . on H.R. 524*. 68th Cong., 1st sess., 7, 8, 12, and 14 February 1924.

———. House. Committee on Public Lands. *National Park Service: Hearing before the Committee on Public Lands on H.R. 434 and H.R. 8668*. 64th Cong., 1st sess., 5 and 6 April 1916.

———. House. Committee on Roads. *Roads. Hearings before the Committee on Roads . . . on H.R. 524*. 68th Cong., 1st sess., 25 April 1924.

U.S. Congress. Senate. *A National Plan for American Forestry*. Vol. 1. 73rd Cong., 1st sess., 30 March 1933. S. Doc 12.

———. Senate. *George Washington Memorial Parkway and Park Development of the National Capital.* 71st Cong., 2d sess., 17 April 1930. S. Rep. 458.

———. Senate. *Natchez Trace Parkway Survey.* 76th Cong., 3rd sess., 26 February 1940. S. Doc. 148.

———. Senate. *National Conference on Outdoor Recreation. Proceedings of the National Conference on Outdoor Recreation, 22, 23, and 24 May 1924.* 68th Cong., 1st sess., 6 June 1924. S. Doc. 151.

———. Senate. *National Conference on Outdoor Recreation. Proceedings of the Second National Conference on Outdoor Recreation, January 20 and 21, 1926.* 69th Cong., 1st sess., 14 June 1926. S. Doc. 117.

———. Senate. *New Roads in Yellowstone National Park.* 62d Cong., 2d sess., 1 July 1912. S. Doc. 871.

———. Senate. *Report of the Commission on Roads in Yosemite National Park, California.* 56th Cong., 1st sess., 8 February 1900. S. Doc. 155.

———. Senate. *Roads in the Yellowstone National Park. Letter from the Acting Secretary of War.* 56th Cong., 1st sess., 1899. S. Doc. 226.

———. Senate. *Use of Automobiles in National Parks.* 62d Cong., 2d sess., 15 March 1912. S. Doc. 433.

———. Senate. Committee on the District of Columbia. *Report of the Senate Committee on the District of Columbia on the Improvement of the Park System of the District of Columbia.* Washington, D.C.: Government Printing Office, 1902.

———. Senate. Committee on Interior and Insular Affairs. *Committee Print: The Recreation Imperative: A Draft of the Nationwide Outdoor Recreation Plan Prepared by the Department of the Interior.* Washington, D.C.: Government Printing Office, 1974.

———. Senate. Committee on Interior and Insular Affairs. *George Washington Memorial Parkway. Hearings before the Committee on Interior and Insular Affairs, United States Senate, Eighty-fifth Congress, first session, on George Washington Memorial Parkway, a Review of the Capper-Cramton Act Authorization. July 11 and 12, 1957.* Washington, D.C.: Government Printing Office, 1957.

U.S. Department of Agriculture. *Roadside Improvement.* U.S. Department of Agriculture Miscellaneous Publication No. 191. Washington, D.C.: Government Printing Office, 1934.

———. Bureau of Public Roads. *The Mount Vernon Memorial Highway: History, Design, and Progress in Construction.* Washington, D.C.: Government Printing Office, 1930.

———. Office of Public Road Inquiries. *Bulletin No. 21. Proceedings of the International Good Roads Conference held at Buffalo, New York, September 16–21, 1901.* Washington, D.C.: Government Printing Office, 1901.

U.S. Department of Commerce. *A Proposed Program for Scenic Roads & Parkways.* Washington, D.C.: Government Printing Office, 1966.

U.S. Department of the Interior. *Proceedings of the National Park Conference Held at Berkeley, California, March 11, 12, and 13, 1915.* Washington, D.C.: Government Printing Office, 1915.

———. *Proceedings of the National Park Conference Held at the Yellowstone National Park, September 11 and 12, 1911.* Washington, D.C.: Government Printing Office, 1911.

———. *Proceedings of the National Park Conference Held at the Yosemite National Park, October 14, 15, and 16, 1912.* Washington, D.C.: Government Printing Office, 1912.

———. "Report of the Acting Superintendent, Sequoia and General Grant National Parks." In *U.S. Department of the Interior, Reports of the Department of the Interior for the Fiscal Year Ended June 30, 1912,* 675–90.

———. "Report of the Acting Superintendent of Yosemite National Park, October 3, 1914." In U.S. Congress, House, 63d Cong., 3d sess., 1914–15, H. Doc. 1474, 721–52.

———. "Report of the General Superintendent and Landscape Engineer of the National Parks." In *Report of the Secretary of the Interior for the Fiscal Year Ended June, 30, 1915,* 843–67. Washington, D.C.: Government Printing Office, 1915.

———. *Report of the Superintendent of the National Parks to the Secretary of the Interior for the Fiscal Year Ended June, 30, 1916.* Washington, D.C.: Government Printing Office, 1916.

———. "Report of the Superintendent of the Yellowstone National Park for the Year 1877." In *Annual Report of the Secretary of the Interior for 1877,* 837–54. Washington, D.C.: Government Printing Office, 1877.

U.S. Department of the Interior. National Park Service. *1941 Yearbook: Park and Recreation Progress.* Washington, D.C.: Government Printing Office, 1941.

U.S. Department of the Interior. National Park Service. *Administrative Policies for Historical Areas of the National Park System.* Washington, D.C.: Government Printing Office, 1968.

———. National Park Service. *Administrative Policies for Natural Areas of the National Park System.* Washington, D.C.: Government Printing Office, 1968.

———. National Park Service. *Administrative Policies for Recreation Areas of the National Park System.* Washington, D.C.: Government Printing Office, 1968.

———. National Park Service. *The Alleghany Parkway, West Virginia, Virginia, Kentucky: A Report to the Congress of the United States February 1964.* Washington, D.C.: Government Printing Office, 1964.

———. National Park Service. "Annual Report of the Director of the National Park Service." In *Report of the Secretary of the Interior, 1917–1919.* Washington, D.C.: Government Printing Office, 1917–19.

———. National Park Service. *Annual Report of the Director of the National Park Service.* Washington, D.C.: Government Printing Office, 1920–44.

———. National Park Service. *Blue Ridge Parkway, Guardrail Replacement and Installation Programmatic Environmental Assessment.* September 2009.

———. National Park Service. *Blue Ridge Parkway, Virginia and North Carolina. Draft General Management Plan/Environmental Impact Statement.*

September 2011. Washington, D.C.: Government Printing Office, 2011.

———. National Park Service. *Draft Yosemite Valley Implementation Plan Supplemental Environmental Impact Statement.* U.S. Department of the Interior, National Park Service, 1997.

———. National Park Service. *Grand Canyon National Park 2009/2010 Accomplishment Report.*

———. National Park Service. "Minutes of the Eighth National Park Conference, Held in Mesa Verde National Park, Colorado, October 1 to 5, 1925." NPS History Collection, Harpers Ferry Center.

———. National Park Service. "Minutes of the Seventh National Park Conference, Held in Yellowstone National Park, October 22–28, 1923." NPS History Collection, Harpers Ferry Center.

———. National Park Service. *Mission 66 for the National Park System.* January 1956.

———. National Park Service. *Mission 66 Progress Report.* Washington, D.C.: Government Printing Office, 1966.

———. National Park Service. *Natchez Trace Parkway.* Washington, D.C.: Government Printing Office, 1951

———. National Park Service. "National Park Service Draft NPS Traffic Safety Overview." Prepared by CH2MHILL, April 2008 Author's copy.

———. National Park Service. *The National Park Wilderness.* Washington, D.C.: U.S. Department of the Interior, National Park Service, 1957.

———. National Park Service. *National Parkways Handbook.* Washington, D.C.: Department of the Interior Duplicating Section, June 1964.

———. National Park Service. *Our Heritage, A Plan for Its Protection and Use: "Mission 66."* Washington, D.C.: National Park Service, n.d. [1956].

———. National Park Service. *Park Road Standards.* Washington, D.C.: Government Printing Office, 1968.

———. National Park Service. *Park Road Standards.* Washington, D.C.: Government Printing Office, 1984.

———. National Park Service. *Parkways: A Manual of Requirements, Instructions, and Information for Use in the National Park Service.* Washington, D.C.: U.S. Department of the Interior, National Park Service, 1937.

———. National Park Service. *Parkwide Road Improvement Plan: Yellowstone National Park: Wyoming/Montana/Idaho.* Denver, Colo.: NPS Denver Service Center, 1992.

———. National Park Service. *Proceedings of the National Parks Conference, Held in the Auditorium of the New National Museum, Washington, D.C., January 2, 3, 4, 5, and 6, 1917.* Washington, D.C.: Government Printing Office, 1917.

———. National Park Service. *Salute to the Service: 2007 National Park Service's Director's Report, 2007.*

———. National Park Service. *Yosemite General Management Plan.* Denver, Colo.: NPS Denver Service Center, 1980.

———. National Park Service. *Yosemite: Summary of the*

Draft General Management Plan. Denver, Colo.: NPS Denver Service Center, 1978.

————. National Park Service. *Your Mission 66 and the National Parks: A Passport to Adventure.* Phillips Petroleum Company, n.d.

————. National Park Service. Colonial National Monument. "Colonial Parkway Cultural Landscape Report: History, Existing Conditions, & Analysis." Prepared by Martha McCartney, historian, LANDSCAPES, 1997.

————. National Park Service. Colonial National Monument. "Outline of Development of Colonial National Monument." Typescript report by Superintendent William M. Robinson Jr., 12 July 1933. File 600.03.4, Colonial National Historic Park collection.

————. National Park Service. Denver Service Center. *Alternative Transportation Modes Feasibility Study.* Vol. 2, *Denali.* Denver, Colo.: NPS Denver Service, 1994.

————. National Park Service. Denver Service Center. *Alternative Transportation Modes Feasibility Study.* Vol. 3, *Yellowstone.* Denver, Colo.: NPS Denver Service, 1994.

————. National Park Service. Denver Service Center. *Alternative Transportation Modes Feasibility Study.* Vol. 4, *Yosemite.* Denver, Colo.: NPS Denver Service, 1994.

————. National Park Service. Denver Service Center. "Final Draft Alternative Transportation Modes Feasibility Study." Vol. 1. Prepared by BRW, Inc. Denver, Colo.: NPS Denver Service Center, 1993.

————. National Park Service. Division of Design and Construction. Parkways Branch. *National Parkways: A Report Prepared for the National Park Service Advisory Board, August 15, 1951.* Copy in Department of the Interior Library.

————. National Park Service. Glacier National Park. *Going-to-the-Sun Road Rehabilitation Plan/Final Environmental Impact Statement.* Glacier National Park, 2003.

————. National Park Service. Mount Rainier National Park. *The Flood of 2006 Report and 2007 & 2008 Updates.* Ashford, Wash.: Mount Rainier National Park, 2009.

————. National Park Service. Natchez Trace Parkway. *Final Supplemental Environmental Impact Statement: Old Agency Road Area (Project 3P13) Natchez Trace Parkway, Mississippi/Alabama/Tennessee.* U.S. Department of the Interior, National Park Service, 2001.

————. National Park Service. National Register of Historic Places. "Multiple Property Listing: Historic Resources of Yellowstone National Park." Prepared by Marcie Culpin, 1995.

————. National Park Service. National Register of Historic Places. "Skyline Drive Historic District (Boundary Increase), Shenandoah National Park, Skyland, Lewis Mountain, and Big Meadows." Prepared by Robinson & Associates, Inc., 2002.

————. National Park Service. National Register of Historic Places. "Skyline Drive Historic District Nomination Form." Prepared by Lee Maddex, Kevin McClung, Jeffrey Drobney, and Linda McClelland, 1992.

————. National Park Service. North Cascades Study Team. *The North Cascades: A Report to the Secretary of the Interior and the Secretary of Agriculture.* Washington, D.C.: Government Printing Office, 1965.

————. National Park Service. Park Roads Program. *Accomplishments in Transportation, 2006–2012.* Washington, D.C.: NPS Park Roads Program, 2012.

————. National Park Service. Yosemite National Park. *Merced Wild and Scenic River Final Comprehensive Management Plan and Environmental Impact Statement.* Yosemite National Park, 2014.

————. National Park Service. Yosemite National Park. *Scenic Vista Management Plan for Yosemite National Park: Environmental Assessment.* Yosemite National Park, 2010.

————. National Park Service. Yosemite National Park. *Tioga Road Rehabilitation: Environmental Assessment.* Yosemite National Park, 2011.

————. National Park Service. Yosemite National Park. *Yosemite:* Summary of the Draft General Management Plan, August 1978. Denver, Colo.: NPS Denver Service Center, 1978.

————. National Park Service and U.S. Department of Transportation. *Park Roads and Parkways Program Handbook: Guidelines for Program Implementation.* National Park Service Facilities Management Division, National Park Roads and Parkways Program, 2008.

————. Office of the Secretary. [Stephen Mather]. *Progress in the Development of the National Parks.* Washington, D.C., Government Printing Office, 1916.

————. Southern Appalachian National Park Commission. *Final Report of the Southern Appalachian National Park Commission.* Washington, D.C.: Government Printing Office, 1931.

U.S. Department of Transportation. Federal Highway Administration. *America's Highways 1776–1976: A History of the Federal-Aid Program.* Washington, D.C.: Government Printing Office, 1976.

————. Federal Highway Administration. Eastern Federal Lands Highway Division. *The Natchez Trace: Path to Parkway.* Sterling, Va.: Eastern Federal Lands Highway Division, 2005.

————. Federal Highway Administration. *Federal Lands Highway Program: Activities, Accomplishments, and Trend Analyses for 1991–1996.* 6 vols. 1991–96.

————. Federal Highway Administration. *Flexibility in Highway Design.* Washington, D.C.: U.S. Department of Transportation, Federal Highway Administration, 1997.

White House Conference on National Beauty. *Beauty for America: Proceedings of the White House Conference on National Beauty, Washington, D.C., May 24–25, 1965.* Washington, D.C.: Government Printing Office, 1965.

ARTICLES, THESES, DISSERTATIONS, AND PAMPHLETS

Abbott, Stanley. "The Blue Ridge Parkway." *American Forests,* June 1940, 246–50.

————. "Historic Preservation: Perpetuation of Scenes Where History Becomes Real." *Landscape Architecture* 40 (July 1950): 153–57.

————. "The Mississippi Parkway." *National Parks Magazine,* April–June 1952, 54–58.

————. "Parks and Parkways: A Creative Field Even When the Task Is to Avoid Creation." *Landscape Architecture* 44 (October 1953): 22–24.

————. "Parkways: A New Philosophy." In *American Civic Annual, 1951,* edited by Harlean James, 43–45. Washington, D.C.: American Planning and Civic Association, 1951.

————. "Parkways—Past, Present, and Future." *Parks and Recreation* 31 (December 1948): 681–91.

————. "Shenandoah–Great Smoky Mountains National Parkway." In *American Planning and Civic Annual, 1938,* edited by Harlean James, 31–33. Washington, D.C.: American Planning and Civic Association, 1938.

————. "Ten Years of the Westchester County Park System." *Parks and Recreation* 16 (March 1933): 305–14.

Abbuehl, Edward. "A Road Built for Pleasure." *Landscape Architecture* 51 (July 1961): 233–37.

Adams, Ansel. "Kings River Canyon Qualifies as National Park." In *American Planning and Civic Annual, 1936,* edited by Harlean James, 76–85. Washington, D.C.: American Planning and Civic Association, 1936.

————. "Tenaya Tragedy." *Sierra Club Bulletin* 43 (November 1958): 1–4.

————. "Yosemite—1958: Compromise in Action." *National Parks Magazine,* October–December 1958, 166–75, 190.

Albright, Horace. "The Everlasting Wilderness." *Saturday Evening Post,* 29 September 1928, 28, 63, 66, 68.

————. "Harlan Page Kelsey." *National Parks Magazine,* February 1959, 12–13.

————. "In the Yellowstone Park." *American Motorist,* September 1924, 26–27, 46, 60.

————. "A National Park Platform." In *American Planning and Civic Annual, 1938,* edited by Harlean James, 31–32. Washington, D.C.: American Planning and Civic Association, 1938.

————. "Preserving Wilderness Beauty along Forest Roads." *American Forests and Forest Life* 31 (January 1925): 36–37.

Alderson, George. "Instant Roads in National Parks." *Sierra Club Bulletin* 54 (January 1969): 14.

Andersen, A. E. "Road Building in the Rockies." *Dupont Magazine,* May 1920, 4–5.

Anderson, Harold. "A Fascinating Restoration." *Living Wilderness,* March 1939, 15.

"Annual Meeting Highlights." *National Parks Magazine,* July–Sept 1958, 125–26.

"Ansel Adams on Yosemite." *Living Wilderness,* Autumn 1958, 34–35.

"Ask Your Congressman to Vote for the National Parks Bill." *American Motorist,* July 1916, 15–18.

Atwood, Robert. "Can the National Parks Be Kept Unspoiled?" *Saturday Evening Post,* 16 May 1936, 18–19, 112.

———. "Nature as Created." *Saturday Evening Post*, 28 February 1925, 16–17.

"Auto Club Secures Yosemite Opening." *Touring Topics*, n.d. [ca. April 1913]. Clipping in Yosemite National Park Archives.

Bancroft, Ernest. "Why People Should Favor Green Mountain Parkway." *Vermonter*, January–February 1936, 5–8.

Barber, Alicia. "Local Places, National Spaces: Public Memory, Community Identity, and Landscape at Scott's Bluff National Monument." *American Studies* 45 (Summer 2004): 35–69.

Barnes, Irston. "Historic C and O Canal Threatened by Road." *National Parks Magazine*, July–September 1953, 113–16, 134–38.

Bartlett, Richard A. "Those Infernal Machines in Yellowstone." *Montana: The Magazine of Western History* 20 (July 1970): 16–29.

Bayliss, Dudley. "Parkway Development under the National Park Service." *Parks and Recreation* 20 (February 1937): 255–59.

———. "Planning Our National Park Roads and Our National Parkways." *Traffic Quarterly* 11 (July 1957): 417–40.

[Bellows, Henry]. "Cities and Parks: With Special Reference to the New York Central Park." *Atlantic Monthly*, April 1861, 416–29.

"Blue Ridge in Virginia Recommended by Committee for Great Eastern National Park." *Parks and Recreation* 8 (January–February 1925): 169–80.

"Board Acts on Road Standards." *Sierra Club Bulletin* 44 (September 1959): 6.

Bookman, George. "Wonderful World of Walking: The C & O Canal Hiker's Reunion." *Living Wilderness*, Spring–Summer 1955, 1–4.

Bradley, Harold. "Details on the Tioga Road." *Sierra Club Bulletin* 43 (April 1958): 14.

———. "Guest Editorial: Our Mission for the Parks." *National Parks Magazine*, July–September 1958, 99–100, 136–37.

———. "Roads in Our National Parks." *National Parks Magazine*, February 1959, 3–6.

———. "Yosemite's Problem Road." *Pacific Discovery*, January–February 1950, 3–9.

Bradley, Harold, and David Brower. "Roads in National Parks." *Sierra Club Bulletin* 34 (June 1949): 31–54.

Bromley, Isaac. "The Big Trees and the Yosemite." *Scribner's Monthly*, January 1872, 261–77.

Brooks, Paul. "The Pressure of Numbers." *Atlantic*, February 1961, 54–56.

Broome, Harvey. "Origins of the Wilderness Society." *Living Wilderness*, July 1940, 10–11.

———. "Thirty Years." *Living Wilderness*, Winter 1965–66, 15–26.

Brower, David. "'Mission 65' Is Proposed by Reviewer of Park Service's New Brochure on Wilderness." *National Parks Magazine*, January–March 1958, 3–6, 445–47.

———. "Mission 66, Roads, and the Park Idea." *Sierra Club Bulletin* 43 (January 1958): 14–15.

———. "Mission 66 Tragedy: A Park behind Glass." *Sierra Club Bulletin* 44 (January 1959): 15.

———. "Scenic Resources for the Future." *Sierra Club Bulletin* 41 (January 1956): 1–10.

———. "The Sierra Club and the National Scene." *Sierra Club Bulletin* 41 (January 1956): 3–4.

———. "Tioga Protest: What Happened below Tenaya." *Sierra Club Bulletin* 43 (October 1958): 3–7.

———. "The Tioga Road and Tenaya Lake: Twenty-two Photographs." *Sierra Club Bulletin* 43 (November 1958): between pages 4 and 5.

———. "What's Good for Detroit." *Sierra Club Bulletin* 43 (October 1958): 7.

———. "Wilderness—Conflict and Conscience." *Sierra Club Bulletin* 42 (June 1957): 1–12.

Bryce, James. "National Parks—The Need of the Future." *Outlook*, 14 December 1912, 811–15.

———. "National Parks—The Need of the Future." *Sierra Club Bulletin* 9 (January 1913): 28–32.

Burt, Struthers. "Perpetual Wilderness." *Outdoor America*, November 1923, 136–38.

Bush, Monroe. "Burdened Acres—The People Question." *Living Wilderness*, Spring–Summer 1967, 28–31.

Butcher, Devereux. "For a Return to Harmony in Park Architecture." *National Parks Magazine*, October–December 1952, 150–57.

———. "More on Park Architecture." *National Parks Magazine*, January–March 1954, 31–32.

———. "Resorts or Wilderness?" *Atlantic*, February 1961, 45–51.

———. "Speaking of Park Architecture." *National Parks Magazine*, January–March 1956, 16–17.

———. "Sunshine and Blizzard: Afield with Your Representative." *National Parks Magazine*, January–March 1957, 150–57.

Butcher, Russell. "A Redwood National Park." *National Parks Magazine*, February 1965, 4–9.

———. "Freeways versus Redwoods." *National Parks Magazine*, June 1964, 12–15.

———. "Freeways versus Redwoods . . . A Legislative Investigation." *Sierra Club Bulletin* 49 (September 1964): 4–10.

Caesar, George Vanderbilt. "National Parks or City Parks?" *Saturday Evening Post*, 22 October 1927, 54.

Cammerer, Arno. "Standards and Policies in National Parks." In *American Planning and Civic Annual, 1936*, edited by Harlean James, 13–20. Washington, D.C.: American Planning and Civic Association, 1936.

Canfield, David. "Building the Rim Road at Crater Lake." *Earth Mover*, April 1936, 7–10.

Catton, William. "Letting George Do It Won't Do It." *National Parks Magazine*, March 1964, 4–7.

"Changing the National Parks to Cope with People—and Cars: Interview with George B. Hartzog, Jr., Director, National Park Service." *U.S. News & World Report*, 24 January 1972, 52–55.

Chittenden, Hiram. "Roads in the Yellowstone National Park." *Good Roads*, January 1894, 3–23.

Clarke, Gilmore. "Is There a Solution for the Through Traffic Problem?" *Parks and Recreation* 13 (July–August 1930): 367–75.

———. "Mount Vernon Memorial Highway." *Landscape Architecture* 22 (April 1932): 179–89.

———. "Our Highway Problem." *American Magazine of Art* 25 (November 1932): 287–90.

———. "Westchester Parkways: An American Development in Landscape Architecture." *Landscape Architecture* 28 (October 1937): 318–21.

Clarke, W. A. "Automobiling in the Yosemite Valley." *Overland Monthly*, 2nd ser., August 1902, 104–10.

Cox, Laurie. "Green Mountain Parkway: The Place of Eastern Scenic Areas in the National Park System." *Parks and Recreation* 19 (September 1935): 8–18.

Cramer, Sterling. "Crisis in Yosemite." *National Parks Magazine*, April–June 1950, 43–50.

Cron, F. W. "Roads for Vicksburg National Military Park." *Civil Engineering* 8 (November 1938): 745–48.

Croteau, Todd. "Recording NPS Roads and Bridges." *CRM* 16, no. 3 (1993): 3–4.

Cummings, Chas. R. "The Green Mountain Parkway Plan." *Vermonter*, August 1933, 217–21.

Dana, Ruth. "A Tale of Two Citizens." *Harper's New Monthly Magazine*, June–November 1973, 856–62.

Daniels, Mark. "Planning to Develop Our National Parks." *American Motorist*, January 1915, 21–23.

Daniels, Stephen. "On the Road with Humphry Repton." *Journal of Garden History* 16 (Autumn 1996): 170–91.

Darling, F. Fraser, and Noel Eichhorn. "Man and Nature in the National Parks: Reflections on Policy." *National Parks Magazine*, April 1969, 13–24.

Davis, Timothy. "The American Motor Parkway." *Studies in the History of Gardens and Designed Landscapes* 25 (October–December 2005): 219–49.

———. "The Bronx River Parkway and Photography as an Instrument of Landscape Reform." *Studies in the History of Gardens and Designed Landscapes* 27 (April–June 2007): 113–41.

———. "Documenting America's Park Roads and Park-ways." *Transportation Research Record: Journal of the Transportation Research Board*, no. 1981 (2006): 148–59.

———. "Looking Down the Road: J. B. Jackson and the American Highway Landscape." In *Everyday America: J. B. Jackson and Recent Cultural Landscape Studies*, edited by Paul Groth and Christopher Wilson, 62–80. Berkeley: University of California Press, 2003.

———. "Mount Vernon Memorial Highway and the Evolution of the American Parkway." Ph.D. diss., University of Texas at Austin, 1997.

———. "Mount Vernon Memorial Highway: Changing Conceptions of an American Commemorative Landscape." In *Places of Commemoration, Search for Identity and Landscape Design*, edited by Joachim Wolschke-Bulmahn, 123–77. Washington, D.C.: Dumbarton Oaks, 2001.

———. "'A Pleasing Illusion of Unspoiled Countryside': The American Parkway and the Problematics of an Institutional Vernacular." In *Constructing Image, Identity, and Place: Perspectives in Vernacular Architecture IX*, edited by Kenneth Breisch and Kim Hoagland, 228–46. Knoxville: University of Tennessee Press, 2003.

———. "Rock Creek and Potomac Parkway, Washington, D.C.: The Evolution of a Contested Urban Landscape." *Studies in the History of Gardens and Designed Landscapes* 19 (April–June 1999): 123–237.

DeVoto, Bernard. "Let's Close the National Parks." *Harper's Magazine*, October 1953, 49–52.

"Director Wirth on Park Policy." *National Parks Magazine*, July–September 1952, 101, 134.

Dodge, Clarence. "The George Washington Memorial Parkway." *American Forests*, February 1932, 85–88, 128.

Downer, Jay. "Principles of Westchester's Parkway System." *Civil Engineering* 4 (February 1934): 85–87.

Draper, William, Jr. "Parks—Or More People?" *National Parks Magazine*, April 1966, 10–13.

Drury, Newton. "The Dilemma of Our Parks." *American Forests*, June 1949, 6–11, 38–39.

———. "Planning for National Parks and Parkways." In *American Planning and Civic Annual, 1947–48*, edited by Harlean James, 1–10. Washington, D.C.: American Planning and Civic Association, 1948.

Durham, Jack. "The C & O Canal Hike." *Living Wilderness*, Spring 1954, 1–26.

Eaton, Walter Prescott. "A Little Wilderness in Vermont." *Living Wilderness*, November 1936, 8–9.

Ehrlich, Anne, and Paul Ehrlich. "The Population Bomb Revisited." *Electronic Journal of Sustainable Development* 1, no. 3 (July 2007).

Eliot, Charles, 2d. "George Washington Memorial Parkway." *Landscape Architecture* 22 (April 1932): 190–200.

———. "The Influence of the Automobile on the Design of Park Roads." *Landscape Architecture* 13 (October 1922): 27–37.

Evison, S. Herbert. "Farming on the Blue Ridge Parkway." *National Parks Magazine*, October 1969, 18–20.

———. "Finding a Route for the Blue Ridge Parkway." *National Parks Magazine*, September 1969, 11–13.

Ewen, Jean. "Going-to-the-Sun Highway Completed." *Western Construction News*, September 1934, 433–37.

———. "Mt. Rainier National Park Highway Developed through Programmed Construction." *Western Construction News*, December 1934, 391–96.

Fahl, Robert. "S. C. Lancaster and the Columbia River Highway: Engineer as Conservationist." *Oregon Historical Quarterly* 74 (June 1973): 101–44.

Fairbank, H. S. "Modern Design Characterizes Memorial Highway to Mount Vernon." *American City* 43 (September 1930): 149–50.

Francis, Henry, Jr. "Some Views Concerning the Development of Mount McKinley National Park." Letter to the editor. *National Parks Magazine*, September 1962, 18–19.

Garrison, Lon. "Mission 66." *National Parks Magazine*, July–September 1955, 107–8.

"George Estyn Goodwin, M. ASCE." *Transactions of the American Society of Civil Engineers* 112 (1947): 1454–55.

Goldman, Hal. "'Vermont's Opportunity': Responses to the Green Mountain Parkway." Master's thesis, University of Vermont, 1995.

"Good Road System to Connect National Parks." *American Motorist*, January 1916, 35.

Grant, George S. "The Forum of Fantastic Beauty: California Blasts a New All-Year Road through the Gleaming Barriers of Yosemite." *American Motorist*, August 1926, 15, 34.

Graves, Edward. "Tioga Turnpike—A New Speedway." *Sierra Club Bulletin* 43 (January 1958): 13–14.

Greeley, W. B. "What Shall We Do with Our Mountains?" *Sunset Magazine*, December 1925, 14–15, 81–85.

Grosvenor, Gilbert. "The Land of the Best: A Tribute to the Scenic Grandeur and Unsurpassed Natural Resources of Our Country." *National Geographic*, April 1916, 327–430.

Gunsky, Fred. "Motorized Millions Favored in Parks." *Sierra Club Bulletin* 44 (January 1959): 14.

"Haleakala Road Proposal." *Living Wilderness*, Summer 1959, 31.

Harris, Amanda B. "A Sketch of Warner." *Granite State Monthly*, December 1895, 411–38.

Harte, Bret. "The East at Yosemite." *Overland Monthly*, August 1871, 191–94.

Heald, Weldon. "Urbanization of the National Parks." *National Parks Magazine*, January 1961, 7–9.

Hewes, L. I. "America's Park Highways." *Civil Engineering* 2 (September 1932): 537–40.

"High Wind Blows through the Parks." Editorial. *National Parks Magazine*, December 1963, 2, 15.

Houk, Ivan. "Scenic Highways of the West." *Du Pont Magazine*, April 1933, 7–10, 14.

Humphrey, Hubert. "The Wilderness Bill." *Living Wilderness*, Winter–Spring 1956–57, 13–25.

Ickes, Harold. "'Keep It a Wilderness'—Ickes." *National Parks Bulletin* 14 (December 1938): 9–13, 29.

———. "Mr. Ickes Replies." Letter to the editor. *National Parks Bulletin* 14 (January 1938): 7.

———. "The Olympic National Park." In *American Planning and Civic Annual, 1938*, edited by Harlean James, 11–16. Washington, D.C.: American Planning and Civic Association, 1938.

———. "Wildernesses and Skyline Drives." *Living Wilderness*, September 1935, 12.

James, E. W. "Parkway Features of Interest to the Highway Engineer." *Public Roads* 10 (April 1929): 21–28.

Jasperson, Robert. "Is the United States Obligated to Complete the North Shore Road?" *Living Wilderness*, Spring 1966, 31–35.

Johnson, Paul. "Turn of the Wheel: The Motor Car vs. Yosemite." *California Historical Quarterly* 51 (Fall 1972): 205–12.

Johnson, Warren. "Over-Use of the National Parks." *National Parks Magazine*, October 1967, 4–7.

Kilgore, Bruce. "Controversy as a Saving Force." *Sierra Club Bulletin* 49 (February 1964): 15–18.

"Kings Canyon National Park Established." *National Parks Bulletin* 15 (July 1940): 17–23.

Kittredge, Frank. "Preserving a Valuable Heritage." *Civil Engineering* 2 (September 1932): 533–37.

"L.A." "Impressions of a Careless Traveler: The Yosemite." *Outlook*, 5 October 1904, 411–14.

Lamb, Martha J. "Riverside Park: The Fashionable Drive of the Future." *Manhattan*, July 1884, 57–58.

Leavitt, E. P. "Yosemite—A Motorist's Paradise." *Concrete Highways and Public Improvements Magazine* 11 (April 1927): 99–101.

Leonard, Richard. "The Tioga Road and Tenaya Lake." *Sierra Club Bulletin* 37 (September 1952): 8–9.

Leopold, Aldo. "Conserving the Covered Wagon." *Sunset Magazine*, March 1925, 21, 56.

———. "The Last Stand of Wilderness." *American Forests and Forest Life*, November 1925, 599–604.

———. "The Vanishing Wilderness." *Literary Digest*, 7 August 1926, 54–57.

———. "The Wilderness and Its Place in Forest Recreational Policy." *Journal of Forestry* 19 (November 1921): 718–21.

———. "Wilderness as a Form of Land Use." *Journal of Land and Public Utility Economics* 1 (October 1925): 398–404.

Leopold, A. Starker. "Wilderness and Culture." *Sierra Club Bulletin* 42 (June 1957): 33–37.

"The Leopold Report Says National Parks Should Be . . . 'A Vignette of Primitive America.'" *Sierra Club Bulletin* 48 (March 1963): 4–11.

Levi, Herbert. "Letter to the Editor." *National Parks Magazine* 32 (April–June 1958): 89.

Lewis, Florence. "Back Yards in Paradise." *National Parks Magazine*, November 1968, 16–17.

Litton, Martin. "Yosemite's Beauty Fast Disappearing." *National Parks Magazine*, October–December 1952, 164–68.

Loder, Arthur. "The Location and Building of Roads in the National Forests." *Public Roads* 1 (August 1918): 5–18.

Logan, Olive. "Does It Pay to Visit Yo Semite?" *Galaxy*, October 1870, 489–509.

Long, John C. "The Motor's Part in Public Health." *Annals of the America Academy of Political and Social Science* 116 (November 1924): 19–21.

Lovin, Hugh. "Fighting over the Cascade Corner of Yellowstone National Park, 1919–35." *Annals of Wyoming* 72 (Spring 2000): 14–29.

Lyon, David. "An Ecologist's View of the Population Problem. *Living Wilderness*, Spring–Summer 1967, 31–35.

Mackaye, Benton. "Flankline vs. Skyline." *Appalachia* 20 (1934): 105–8.

———. "If This Be Snobbery." *Living Wilderness*, Summer–Fall 1961, 3–4.

Mackintosh, Barry. "Harold Ickes and the National Park Service." *Journal of Forest History* 29 (April 1985): 78–84.

Marshall, Robert. "The Problem of Wilderness." *Scientific Monthly* 30 (February 1930): 141–48.

———. "The Wilderness as a Minority Right." *Service Bulletin*, 27 August 1928, 5–6.

"Massachusetts Latest Road Offering." *American Motorist*, April 1915, 111–13.

Mather, Stephen. "Engineering Applied to National Parks." *Transactions of the American Society of Civil Engineers* 94 (1930): 1181–93.

———. "The Human Side of the National Parks." *Parks and Recreation* 8 (March–April 1925): 331–39.

———. "The National Parks on a Business Basis." *American Review of Reviews* 51 (April 1915): 429–31.

———. "Progress in the National Parks." *Sierra Club Bulletin* 11 (January 1920): 5–13.

———. "Sixty-Eighth Congress and the National Parks." *National Parks Bulletin* 43 (24 March 1925): n.p.

———. "What I Am Trying to Do with the National Parks." *World's Work*, May 1924, 41–42.

McFarland, J. Horace. "The Defenders of the National Parks." In *American Planning and Civic Annual, 1938*, edited by Harlean James, 7–8. Washington, D.C.: American Planning and Civic Association, 1938.

———. "Our National Parks." *Landscape Architecture* 5 (April 1915): 148–50.

McPhee, John. "Profiles: Ranger." *New Yorker*, 11 September 1971, 45–89.

"Millions for National Park Roads." *National Parks Bulletin* 39 (30 April 1924): n.p.

Mills, Enos. "Touring in our National Parks." *Country Life in America*, January 1913, 33–36.

"Minutes of Meeting of Board of Directors, December 1933." *Sierra Club Bulletin* 28 (December 1933), 1–2.

"The Mt. Vernon Memorial Highway." *American Motorist*, April 1932, 21, 28.

Mumford, Lewis. "The Highway and the City." *Architectural Record* 123 (April 1958): 179–86.

———. "The Skyline: The Roaring Traffic's Boom." Pts. 1–3. *New Yorker*, 19 March 1955, 115–21; 2 April 1955, 97–101; 16 April 1955, 72–81.

Murie, Adolph. "Roadbuilding in Mount McKinley National Park." *National Parks Magazine*, July 1965, 4–8.

Murie, Olaus. "Mount McKinley: Wilderness Park of the North Country." *National Parks Magazine*, April 1963, 4–7.

———. "On Roads and Principles." *Sierra Club Bulletin* 37 (April 1952): 5–7.

———. "Our Farthest North National Park." *National Parks Magazine*, December 1959, 8–10, 12.

"The National Park Conference (1912)." *Sierra Club Bulletin* 9 (January 1913): 67–68.

"New National Park Policy Guidelines." *Living Wilderness*, Summer 1969, 35.

"The New Redwood National Park." *National Parks Magazine* 42 (December 1968): 9.

Noblitt, Phil. "The Blue Ridge Parkway and the Myths of the Pioneer." *Appalachian Journal* 21 (Summer 1994): 394–409.

Nussbaum, Jesse. "Wilderness Aspects of National Parks." In *American Planning and Civic Annual, 1938*, edited by Harlean James, 72–77. Washington, D.C.: American Planning and Civic Association, 1938.

Olmsted, Frederic Law, Jr. "Notes on Laying Out Roads for Pleasure Travel in Scenic Areas." *City Planning* 4 (October 1928): 278–83.

———. "Scenic Highway Development in Mountainous Regions." *Landscape Architecture* 24 (July 1934): 195–98.

———. "Vacation in the National Parks and Forests." *Landscape Architecture* 12 (January 1922): 107–11.

Olsen, Sigurd. "The Challenge of Our National Parks." *National Parks Magazine*, April–June 1954, 51–52, 85.

"On Park Shrines and Highways." *National Parks Magazine*, April 1959, inside front cover, 11.

"On Roads for Proposed Wilderness." *Sierra Club Bulletin* 41 (December 1956): 79–81.

Packard, Fred. "An Appraisal of Mission 66." *National Parks Magazine*, April–June 1956, 61–62, 91, 95.

"The Park Service and Wilderness." Editorial. *National Parks Magazine*, July–September 1957, 104, 129–30.

Peach, Arthur. "Proposed Parkway a Threat to the State's Well Being." *Vermonter*, January–February 1936, 9–13.

Perlman, David. "Mission 66: Park's 10-Year Plan." *Sierra Club Bulletin* 42 (January 1957): 11–12.

Peters, W. W. "Transmountain Highway Construction in Glacier National Park." *Contractors and Engineers Monthly*, May 1928, 321–27.

Phelps, Dawson. "The Natchez Trace: Indian Trail to Parkway." Reprinted from *Tennessee Historical Quarterly* 21 (September 1962).

"Pioneer Dinner Launches Mission 66." *National Parks Magazine*, April–June 1956, 59–60.

"Policy of the Sierra Club on Road Construction in the Sierra." *Sierra Club Circular* 25 (May–June 1927): 46.

Pray, James Sturgis. "Danger of Over-Exploitation of Our National Parks." *Landscape Architecture* 6 (April 1916): 113–14.

———. "The American Society of Landscape Architects and Our National Parks." *Landscape Architecture* 6 (April 1916): 119–23.

———. "Minute on the Life and Service of Charles Pierpont Punchard." *Landscape Architecture* 11 (April 1921): 105–10.

"Preservation of Wilderness Values in the National Park System." *National Parks Magazine*, July–September 1957, 105–36.

Punchard, C. P., Jr. "Landscape Design in the National Park Service." *Landscape Architecture* 10 (April 1920): 142–45.

"Relocation of Tioga Road: Report of the Executive Committee of the Sierra Club on the Proposed Relocation of the Tioga Road, Yosemite National Park." *Sierra Club Bulletin* 29 (June 1934): 85–88.

"Report of Committee on Sierra Roads." *Sierra Club Circular* 25 (May–June 1927): 6–7.

Richards, T. Addison. "The Central Park." *Harper's New Monthly Magazine*, August 1861, 289–306.

Richardson, Elmo. "Olympic National Park: Twenty Years of Controversy." *Forest History* 12 (April 1968): 6–15.

"Roads and Wilderness." *Sierra Club Bulletin* 46 (June 1961): 10.

"Roads in National Parks." *Sierra Club Bulletin* 38 (March 1953): 7.

"Robert Sterling Yard, 1861–1945." *Living Wilderness*, December 1945, 1–4.

Russell, Carl. "Frank Alvah Kittredge, 1883–1954." *Sierra Club Bulletin* 40 (October 1955): 69–70.

Seyffert, W. A. "The Going-to-the-Sun Highway." *Du Pont Magazine*, September–October 1933, 11–14.

Shepard, Paul, Jr. "Something Amiss in the National Parks." *National Parks Magazine*, October–December 1953, 150–51, 187–90.

"Sierra Club Policy and Standards for National Park and Other Scenic Roads." *Sierra Club Bulletin* 45 (December 1960): 57–69.

Silverstein, Hannah. "A Road Not Travelled: Vermont's Rejection of the Green Mountain Parkway." Honors Thesis, Yale College, 1994.

Simonson, Wilbur. "The Mount Vernon Memorial Highway." *American City* 43 (October 1930): 85–88.

Smith, Anthony Wayne. "Clingmans Dome." *National Parks Magazine*, February 1959, n.p.

———. "The Future & the Parks." Editorial. *National Parks Magazine*, October 1970, n.p.

———. "A Good Park Road Program." *National Parks Magazine*, October 1968, n.p.

———. "Mission 66 Reappraised." *National Parks Magazine*, April 1961, n.p.

———. "The North Cascades." National Parks Magazine, April 1966, n.p.

———. "An Olden Tranquility: An Editorial." *National Parks Magazine*, December 1966, n.p.

———. "Our Unfinished Work." *National Parks Magazine*, January 1959, n.p.

———. "Park Road Planning and Finances." Editorial. *National Parks Magazine*, November 1963, n.p.

———. "Park Wilderness Planning." Editorial. *National Parks Magazine*, November 1967, n.p.

———. "People, Parks, and Traffic." Editorial. *National Parks Magazine*, May 1970, n.p.

———. "Progress in Yosemite." Editorial. *National Parks Magazine*, March 1968, n.p.

———. "A 'Sky-Post' for the Smokies." *National Parks Magazine*, February 1959, inside front cover.

———. "Temporary Defeat." *National Parks Magazine*, October–December 1958, 153–54.

———. "The Tioga Road." *National Parks Magazine*, January–March 1958, 10–13.

———. "Wilderness in the Parks: An Editorial." *National Parks Magazine*, October 1965, n.p.

"Some Views Concerning the Development of Mount McKinley National Park." *National Parks Magazine*, September 1963, 18–21.

Spelman, H. J. "Building Roads in the Shenandoah Park." *Civil Engineering* 5 (August 1935): 482–84.

Sterling, Wilbur. "The Motorist and the National Parks." *American Motorist*, July 1916, 7–13.

Stevenson, Charles. "The Shocking Truth about Our National Parks." *Reader's Digest*, January 1955, 45–50.

"A Summons to Save the Wilderness. *Living Wilderness*, September 1935, 1.

Swift, Ernest. "Guest Editorial: Parks or Resorts?" *National Parks Magazine*, October–December 1957, 147–48.

"To Reconstruct National Park Roads," *National Parks Bulletin* 27 (21 January 1924): n.p.

T.B.S. "The Unrighteous Bargain." *Potter's American Magazine*, April 1873, 293–309.

Thomson, C. G. "Public Use Policies." In *American Planning and Civic Annual, 1936*, edited by Harlean James, 25–29. Washington, D.C.: American Planning and Civic Association, 1936.

Tilden, Paul, and Nancy Machler. "The Development of Mount McKinley National Park." *National Parks Magazine*, May 1963, 10–15.

"Tioga Road." *Sierra Club Bulletin* 33 (September–

October 1948): 6–7.

"Tioga Road." *Sierra Club Bulletin* 33 (December 1948): 5.

"The Tioga Road and Tenaya Lake: Twenty-Two Photographs." *Sierra Club Bulletin* 43 (November 1958): n.p.

"To Reconstruct National Park Roads." *National Parks Bulletin* 27 (21 January 1924): n.p.

"Trails and Roads in the High Sierra." *Sierra Club Bulletin* 35 (May 1950): 13.

Turnball, Katherine. "Transportation to Enhance America's Best Idea." *TR News* 267 (March–April 2010): 20–24.

———. "Visitor Transportation at U.S. National Parks: Increasing Accessibility but Preserving the Environment." *TR News* 210 (September–October 2000): 3–8.

Upchurch, John. "Preserving a Historic National Park Roadway." *Transportation Research Record: Journal of the Transportation Research Board*, no. 2123 (2009): 163–71.

"U.S. Is Outgrowing Its Parks." *U.S. News and World Report*, 10 June 1955, 78–80.

"U.S. Playgrounds Are Valuable and Undeveloped Asset." *American Motorist*, January 1916, 37.

Vanderbilt, Amy. "On the Road Again: Glacier National Park's Red Buses." *CRM* 25 (2002): 23–26.

Vanderbilt, Amy, and Steve Moler. "Saving a National Treasure." *Public Roads* 70 (November–December 2006): 22–31.

Van Fleet, Clark. "Nature Out of Balance." *Atlantic Monthly*, February 1961, 52–53.

Vetter, Ernest. "Project in the Parks." *American Forests*, September 1957, 16–18, 40–43.

"A Vignette of Primitive America." *Sierra Club Bulletin* 48 (March 1963): 4–11.

Vint, Thomas. "Development of National Parks for Conservation." In *American Planning and Civic Annual, 1938*, edited by Harlean James, 31–33. Washington, D.C.: *American Planning and Civic Association, 1938*.

———. "National Park Master Plans." *Planning and Civic Comment* (April–June 1946).

———. "National Park Service Branch of Plans and Designs, San Francisco Office of National Parks, Buildings and Reservations." *Landscape Architecture* 24 (October 1933): 31–32.

Wadsworth, Reuben. "Shuttle to Serenity: The History and Impact of Zion National Park's Transportation System." Master's thesis, University of Nevada, Las Vegas, 2009.

"Walter Huber Heads Interior Advisers." *Sierra Club Bulletin* 41 (April 1956): 6.

Watrous, Richard. "The Proposed National Park Service." *Landscape Architecture* 6 (April 1916): 101–5.

Wayburn, Edgar, and Patty Wayburn. "Mission 66 . . . A Promise for the Parks." *Sierra Club Bulletin* 41 (April 1956): 3–4.

———. "Where Should Management Stop?" *Sierra Club Bulletin* 43 (January 1958): 3–6.

Welch, W. A. "State and National Parks." *Parks and Recreation* 6 (September–October 1922): 18–21.

"We've Been Starving Our National Parks." Editorial. *Saturday Evening Post*, 12 February 1955, 10.

White, John. "Wilderness Policies." In *American Planning and Civic Annual, 1936*, edited by Harlean James, 34–38. Washington, D.C.: American Planning and Civic Association, 1936.

"The White Mountains." *Harper's New Monthly Magazine*, August 1877, 321–32.

"The Wilderness Society Platform." *Living Wilderness*, September 1935, 2.

Wilson, Henry, Jr. "Trout Stream Wilderness . . . or Road." *Living Wilderness*, Autumn–Winter 1958, 14–17.

Wirth, Conrad. "Mission 66." *American Forests*, August 1955, 16–17.

———. "Mission 66 in the Headlines." *National Parks Magazine*, January–March 1958, 8–9, 36–38.

Yard, Robert Sterling. "Gift Parks: The Coming National Park Danger." *National Parks Bulletin* 4 (9 October 1923): n.p.

———. "Green Mountains Saved a Second Time." *Wilderness News* 2 (4 July 1936): 3–4.

———. "Making a Business of Scenery." *Nation's Business*, June 1916, 10–11.

———. "Motor-Road vs. Wilderness." *National Parks Bulletin* 8 (November 1927): 4.

———. "The Motor Tourist and the National Parks." Pt. 1. *National Parks Bulletin* 8 (February 1927): 11–12.

———. "The Motor Tourist and the National Parks." Pt. 2. *National Parks Bulletin* 8 (July 1927): 17–19.

———. "Needless Road Project Endangers Yosemite." *National Parks Bulletin* 8 (February 1927): 16.

———. "New and Dangerous Attempt to 'Get' the Green Mountains." *Living Wilderness*, May 1943, 28–29.

———. "The People and the National Parks." *Survey* 48 (1 August 1922): 547–53, 583.

———. "Standards of Our National Park System." *National Parks Bulletin* 8 (December 1926): 1–4.

Yochim, Michael. "Beauty and the Beet: The Dam Battles of Yellowstone." *Montana: The Magazine of Western History* 53 (Spring 2003): 14–27.

Yoder, Robert. "Twenty-Four Million Acres of Trouble." *Saturday Evening Post*, 3 July 1954, 32–33, 78–80.

"The Yosemite." *Appletons' Journal*, 18 January 1873, 111–12.

"Yosemite: A Better Way to Run a Park?" *U.S. News and World Report*, 24 January 1972, 56–57.

"Yosemite Tunnel Approach." *Standard Oil Bulletin* 20 (August 1932): 3–7.

"Yosemite's Tioga Highway." *National Parks Magazine*, July–September 1958, 123–24.

"Yosemite versus Mass Man." *Sierra Club Bulletin* 37 (October 1952): 3–8.

Zahniser, Howard. "The Need for Wilderness Areas." *National Parks Magazine*, October–December 1955, 161–66, 187–88.

———. "The Need for Wilderness Areas." *Living Wilderness*, Winter–Spring 1956–57, 37–43.

Zordich, James. "The First Automobile in Yosemite. *Horseless Carriage Gazette*, September–October 1972, 10–15.

———. "Yosemite's Unwelcome Visitor: The Automobile." *Horseless Carriage Gazette*, January–February 1984, 19–25.

FILMS

U.S. Department of Agriculture. Federal Extension Service. *Building the Mount Vernon Memorial Highway*. 1933. NARA Motion Pictures: ARC 7381.

———. *The Men Who Build the Roads*. 1927. NARA Motion Pictures: ARC 7264.

———. *New Roads in Mount Rainier*. 1927. NARA Motion Pictures: ARC 7268.

———. *The Road Goes Through*. 1925. NARA Motion Pictures: ARC 7228.

———. *A Road Out of Rock*. 1927. NARA Motion Pictures: ARC 7267.

———. *Roads in Our National Parks*. 1927. NARA Motion Pictures: ARC 7265.

———. *Roads to Wonderland*. 1923. NARA Motion Pictures: ARC 7178.

———. *Tunneling to Yosemite*. 1935. NARA Motion Pictures: ARC 7405.

———. *Yosemite's New Road*. 1927. NARA Motion Pictures: ARC 7266.

Ford Motor Company. *A Visit to Yellowstone National Park*. Ca. 1932. Picture Film Documentation of the Diverse Activities of the Department of the Interior, 1916–76. NARA Motion Pictures: ARC 11632.

———. *A Visit to Yellowstone National Park*. 1937. NARA Motion Pictures: ARC: 11369.

———. *Watertown Glacier International Peace Park*. 1937. NARA Motion Pictures: ARC: 11640.

———. *Yellowstone National Park*. Ca. 1940. *Motion Picture Films Relating to the Ford Motor Company . . . and Other Subjects*. NARA Motion Pictures ARC: 91592.

Index

Italicized page numbers refer to illustrations, and NPS and BPR refer to the National Park Service and Bureau of Public Roads, respectively.

roads bill of 1924, 81; of parkways, 189; reducing, 242; Skyline Drive, 138; sweeping, 9, 89, 122, 138, 151; Tioga Road, 126, 234, 237, 254, 271, *271*; Trail Ridge Road, 122; Yellowstone National Park road improvement, 269, 271. *See also* hairpin turns
Cuyahoga Valley Scenic Railroad, 277
cycloramas, 26

D

dams: Bechler River proposal, 163–65; Echo Park controversy, 222; Hetch Hetchy reservoir, 70, 71, 171
Daniels, Mark, 71, 73, 92, 124
Daughters of the American Revolution (DAR), 202, 217
Davidson, Ernest, 87, 121, 169, 170
Davison, Gideon, 24, 27
dedication ceremonies, 29, 39, 40–41, *40*, 42–43, 74, *74*, 75, 122, *122*, 124, 131, 133, 137–38, 142, 145–46, 176, 179, *227*, 239, *239*
deferred maintenance, 200, 222, 223, 225, 278
Delano, Frederic, 213
Delaware Water Gap National Recreation Area, 279
Demaray, Arthur: Colonial Parkway development, 195; Green Mountain Parkway proposal, 215; Natchez Trace Parkway, 202; national parkways radio program, 188; NPS-BPR collaboration, 103; on preservation of traditional park road experience, 156; on proposed Tenaya Road, 174; and Yard's proposed road along Continental Divide in Rocky Mountain National Park, 162
Denali Highway, 242
Denali National Park. *See* Mount McKinley National Park
Denver (CO), 123, 126
Denver Mountain Parks: as attraction for motorists, 124; Engineer's Lariat, 93, *94*
Department of Transportation Act (1966), 251
Desert Solitaire (Abbey), 247, 256
DeSilets, Eugene, 194
DeVoto, Bernard, 223
digital technologies, 4, 280–81
Dinosaur National Monument, 222, 229, 230
diversity, 70, 140–41, 279–80
Division of National Park and Forest Roads (Office of Public Roads), 92
Doctor Syntax Sketching the Lake (Rowlandson), *22*
Doerr, John, 218
"Does It Pay to Visit Yo Semite?" (Logan), 37
Dorn, George, 131
Double Arch Bridge (Natchez Trace Parkway), 264, *265*
Doughty, Thomas, 23
Douglas, William O., 217–18, *218*
Downer, Jay, 90, 138, 190, 191, 195, 197–98
Downing, Andrew Jackson, 15–16, 17, 20, 34, 53, 240
drainage: Central Park, 19; deterioration, 267; Going-to-the-Sun Road, 119, 271; Mount Rainier National Park, 59, *278*; Sequoia National Park, 132; Tioga Road, 273; Yellowstone National Park, 48
drinking (water) fountains, 87, 115, 135, 139, 140

drones, 280
Drury, Newton: against additional road development in Mount Rainier National Park, 170; on George Washington Memorial Parkway's status as urban parkway, 207–8; Natchez Trace Parkway, 205; opposition to Dinosaur National Monument dam proposal leads to resignation, 222; outlines need for post–World War Two improvement program, 222; succeeds Cammerer as NPS director, 141
Dunraven, Earl of (Thomas Windham), 123
Dunraven Pass Road (Yellowstone National Park), 54, *54*, 55, *268*
Durand, Asher, 23
Dwight, Theodore, 24
Dwight, Timothy, 22

E

Eakin, J. R., 121, 179, 181, 183
earmarks, 278
East Entrance (Sylvan Pass Road; Yellowstone National Park), 55, 77; station, *229*
Echo Park controversy, 222
Ecological Society of America, 182
ecology, 267; growing influence on park management, 3, 8, 12, 45, 243, 250, 251, 255, 260, 262, 267, 272, 277, 279; and historic preservation concerns, 266, 268; Leopold Report, 250–51, 260; and relocation of Gibbon Canyon section of Yellowstone's Grand Loop, 267, *274–75*, 279, *279*; *Silent Spring* popularizes, 250; and Yosemite master plans, 260–62. *See also* environmentalism
Edge, Rosalie, 180
Edick, Tom, 268
editorial cartoons. *See* cartoons
Ehrlich, Paul, 248
Eisenhower, Dwight D., 208, 219, 224
Eliot, Charles (1859–1897), 21
Eliot, Charles W., 2d (1899–1993), 87, 88, 177–78, 206
elitism: of European parks, 12–13, 34, 38; in objections to park road development, 68, 79, 88, 154, 159, 160, 165, 172, 180, 182, 214, 217, 230, 233–34, 246–48, 253, 257
Elliott, J. A., 120
El Portal Road (Yosemite National Park), 81, 102, 143, 144, 147
Elwood, P[hillip]. H., 159
Emerald Necklace (Boston), 21
Emergency Conservation Committee, 180
Emergency Conservation Works, 110, 137
Emerson, Ralph Waldo, 29
engineering: American Society of Civil Engineers, 106, 235; as attraction, 29, 44, 54, 55, 57, 93–94, 95, 101, 103, 117, 119, 131, 135, 259, 264; increased flexibility beginning in 1990s, 269; and landscape architecture united in park roads, 4, 19–20, 27, 33, 53, 84–85, *85*, 89–91, 92–95, 97–107, 110, 113–15, 126–27, 131, 146, 150, 188, 208, 209, 211, 228–29, 240, 263–64, 269–72,

276, 279, 281; mentality as not appropriate for park work, 238, 243, 247, 252; national park roads as welcome challenge for, 53, 55, 107, 121, 150; needed to improve access to parks, 70, 91–92, 103; Olmsted on relationship between engineering and aesthetics, 18–20; rigid and rising standards criticized, 18–20, 96, 97, 98, 107, 147–49, 154–56, 166, 202–3, 231–39, 242–43, 252–53; seen as conflicting with park values, 18–20, 96, 97, 98, 147–49, 154–56, 166, 202–3, 231, 232, 234, 239, 242–43, 246, 252–53, 268–69; standards, 3, 19, 94, 101, 154, 156, 161, 184, 233, 234, 243, 252, 255, 268, 269, 277. *See also* Bureau of Public Roads (BPR); Civil Engineering Division (National Park Service); U.S. Army Corps of Engineers
Englischer Garten (Munich), 13
English gardens and parks, 12, 13–14, 15
entrance roads, 227
entrance stations, 9, 92, 115, 139, 225, 226, 228, 259
entrance stickers, 75–76, *76*
entranceways, 76
environmental impact studies, 6, 272
environmentalism: climate change, 279; versus historical values, 279; Johnson on, 256; Leopold Report, 250–51, 260; and Linn Cove Viaduct, 263; National Environmental Policy Act, 251, 263; opposition to tramways, 251, 254, 259; rising influence of, 248–51, 277; Tamiami Trail, 279; and vista management, 271; and Yellowstone National Park road improvement plan, 271; and Yosemite master plans, 259–62. *See also* ecology; preservation; wilderness
environmental protection regulations, 219, 251, 263
Erie Canal, 24, *24*
erosion, 19, 139, 166, 279
Erwin, James B., 50
Essays on the Picturesque (Price), 22
Estes Park (CO), 123, 124, 129, 162
European precedents, 12–16, 20, 21–22, 34, 38, 50, 52, 71, 72, 74, 90, 93
Everglades, 185, 188, 279
Everhart, William C., 252, 253
"Everlasting Wilderness, The" (Albright), 161, 168, 169, 180
Ewen, Jean, 121, 150
excavation: Baltimore–Washington Parkway, 210, 211; Foothills Parkway, 264; Generals Highway, 133; Going-to-the-Sun Road, 119, 120, 121; Hurricane Ridge Road, Olympic National Park, 232; Mount McKinley National Park, 242; National Park Service guidelines, 105, 114; parkways, 189; recovering from, 99; and Tioga Road modernization, 235; Trail Ridge Road, 128; Wawona Road reconstruction, 145; Yellowstone National Park road reconstruction, 149; Zion–Mount Carmel Highway tunnel, 130

F

Fall, Albert, 80
Fall River Road (Rocky Mountain National Park), 122–26; call for retaining, 156; convict labor on, 124;

Hull, Daniel (*continued*)
  Goodwin, 95; criticism of BPR work on El Portal
  Road, 143; as Division of Landscape Engineering
  head, 86–87; on Goodwin's Carbon River Road,
  95, 102; on Goodwin's work on Going-to-the-Sun
  Road, 99–100; at National Park Conference of 1925,
  103; newspaper depiction of, *86*; with Mather and
  Goodwin, *93*; returns to private practice, 177
hunting parks, 12–13
Hutchings, James, 33, 38
Hyde, Dewitt, 219
Hyde Park (London), 13

I

Ickes, Harold, *137*; on Blue Ridge Parkway, 197, 198;
  Going-to-the-Sun Road praised by, 122; on Green
  Mountain Parkway proposal, 215; and Bob Marshall,
  181, 182, 183, 185, 197, 215; on Natchez Trace
  Parkway, 202–3; on racial segregation in Shenandoah
  National Park, 141; relationship with NPS officials,
  141, 181, 183, 185, 215; reservations about road
  development, 137, 146, 181, 183, 184, 185, 215;
  with Roosevelt at Shenandoah National Park, *137*;
  Wawona Tunnel dedication, 146
Intermodal Surface Transportation Efficiency Act
  (ISTEA) (1991), 259, 262, 277
Internet outreach, *280*, 280–81
Interstate and Defense Highways Act (1956), 224, 243
interstate highways, 224, 232, 243, 255–56, 267, 279
Introduction to Landscape Design, An (Hubbard and
  Kimball), 89
Inyo Good Roads Club, 74
irrigation interests, 159, 163–64, 165
Irving, Washington, 23
Isle Royale National Park, 185
Izaak Walton League, 181–82, 208, 217, 252

J

Jackson, William Henry, 32, 47, 123
Jackson Hole (WY), 50, 158, 162
Jacobs, Jane, 246
Jamestown (VA), 191, 192, 194, 195, 231
Jeffers, Thomas, 210
Jefferson, Thomas, 22, 180
Jensen, Jens, 159
Johnson, Junius, 127
Johnson, Lyndon B., 209, 219, 243, 256
Johnson, Samuel, 14

K

Kahler, Herbert, 205, 218

Keats, John, 246
Kelsey, Harlan, 111, 138, 214
Kennedy, John F., 209, 248
Kent, William, 13
Kimball, Theodora, 89
King, Clarence, 35, 123
King, Thomas Starr, 33
Kingman, Daniel C., 48–49, 50, 52, 59, 263, 271
Kings Canyon National Park: national park status sought,
  96, 159, 176, 184, 241; road construction minimized
  in, 6, 134, 159, 251; as wilderness-oriented park, 185; in
  wilderness policy debates, 159, 176, 184, 185, 231, 251
Kipling, Rudyard, 50, 66
Kittredge, Frank, *106*; background, 118; becomes
  NPS chief engineer, 105–6; Big Oak Flat Road
  reconstruction, 147, 148, 155, 156; Colonial Parkway
  development, 194; in debate over Tioga Road High
  Line proposal, 174, 175, 176; Generals Highway,
  135; Going-to-the-Sun Road, *100*, 101, 118–20, *119*,
  121, 174; Lancaster, studied with, 118; and Mission
  66 Tioga Road controversy, 234; Mount Rainier
  National Park road development, 102, 168, 169;
  on NPS-BPR collaboration, 107, 121, 156, 235; as
  NPS western regional director, 156; on preserving
  traditional park road experience, 147, 155, 156, 227;
  and scenic preservation, 107, 147–48, 168, 174, 175;
  on Sierra Club board, 168; and Sierra Way proposal,
  176; and standards for national park roads, 107,
  118, 147, 148, 155, 156, 227; at Superintendents'
  Conference of 1929, *106*; Trail Ridge Road, 127; and
  Vint, 105, 119, 147, 156, 168, 174, 175; on Wawona
  Road reconstruction, 144, 145; on wilderness areas
  for Yosemite National Park, 184, *184*; on wilderness
  preservation, 156, 169, 175, 176, 184; and Yellowstone
  Golden Gate tunnel proposal, 149
Knight, C. H., 68–69
Korean War, 210
Kraebel, Charles, 100, 101, 103, 120, 121
Krueger, Charles, 252, 253–54

L

Lafayette National Park. *See* Acadia National Park
Lake Mead National Recreation Area, 250
Lancaster, Samuel, 90, 91, 93, 118, 263
landscape architecture: American Society of Landscape
  Architects, 70, 73, 156, 171, 198; early writings
  on automobile roads, 88–89; as essential to NPS
  success, 71, 86; European precedents, 12–14; in
  freeway planning task force, 256; and municipal park
  precedents, 15–21; National Park Service landscape
  treatment guidelines, 104–5; and 1968 *Park Road
  Standards*, 254; tension with engineers, 19–20, 95, 97,
  99–101, 105–7, 121, 141, 143, 147–48, 149, 156, 168,
  174–75, 198; in Washington, D.C., parks, 112; Yosemite
  National Park's request for landscape architect, 91
Landscape Engineering Division (National Park Service):
  and Civil Engineering Division consolidated, 105;

collaboration with Civil Engineering Division,
  92, 93–95, 103, 105, 118–20, 127, 145; concerns
  about BPR methods, 105, 106, 121, 143, 147, 181,
  203; establishment of, 86–88; general role in park
  development, 86–89, 95, 105; master planning
  process, 87, 104; in NPS-BPR, 97, 103, 104, 105,
  113–15, 143, 198, 210, 213, 219; responsibilities per
  NPS-BPR agreement, 104; technical assistance to
  state parks, 111; tensions with NPS engineers, 95,
  99–101, 105, 121, 147–48, 149, 156, 168, 174–75.
  See also Hull, Daniel; Punchard, Charles, Jr.;
  Vint, Thomas
landscape painting, 23, 24
Lane, Franklin, 66, 69, 71, 72–73, 80, 86, 124
"Lane Letter," 86, 170, 250, 255
Langford, Nathaniel P., 46, 47–48
Lassen Volcanic National Park, 81, 94–95, 176, 232
Lassiter, James, 138
Laurel Hill Cemetery (Philadelphia), 16
leases, agricultural, 203–4
LeConte, Joe, 171
Lee, W. I., 198
Leonard, Richard, 234–35, 252
Leopold, A. Starker, 250–51, 252, 260
Leopold, Aldo: advocates wilderness preservation, 157–59,
  161; casts roads as primary threat to wilderness, 157–
  58, 165, 277; and debate over Mission 66 program,
  229, 230, 231; Bob Marshall compared with, 180; at
  National Conference on Outdoor Recreation of 1924,
  161; son Starker, 250, 260; wilderness defined by, 158,
  231; wilderness values articulated by, 157, 214
Leopold Report, 250–51, 260
"Let's Close the National Parks" (DeVoto), 223
Lewis, W. B., 142
light-rail systems, 258, 259, 262, *262*
Lincoln, Abraham, 34
Lincoln Highway, 74, 75, 124, 267
Linn, Robert, 252
Linn Cove Viaduct (Blue Ridge Parkway), *ii*, 263–64
Lippincott, Oliver, 62–63, 142
Littebrant, William, 91
litter, 38, 77
Litton, Mark, 230
"local experienced men" (LEMs), 110
Logan, Olive, 37
Logan, William, 117
logging, 72, 73, 124, 159, 176, 243
log structures, 115
London, 13
Long, John C., 77
Longmire, James, 58, 59
Long Trail, 213, 214
Lorrain, Claude, 13, 22
Loudon, John Claudius, 15
Ludgate, Roswell, 138, 182
lunch stations, 68, 70, 140

M

MacDonald, Thomas: Baltimore–Washington Parkway, 210; Blue Ridge Parkway, 196, 197; Going-to-the-Sun Road, 101, 102, 106, 121, 122; helps Albright defeat Bechler River Road proposal in Yellowstone National Park, 165; managerial style as Bureau of Public Roads "Chief," 96–97, 248; Mount Vernon Memorial Highway, 191; and NPS-BPR collaboration, 96–98, 103, 104, 106, 121, 122, 150, 165; pressures NPS to accept BPR assistance, 97–98, 101; radio program on national parkways, 188; Zion–Mount Carmel Highway dedication, 131

Mackaye, Benton, 139–40, 182, 183, 198, 214, 230, 251, 277

Maddox, Ben, 132, 133

Mainella, Fran, 261

Mammoth Cave (KY), 112, 196

Man-Made America: Chaos or Control? (Tunnard and Pushkarev), 256

Mann Brothers, 36, 37

Manning, Warren, 78, 171

Mariposa Big Tree Grove (Yosemite National Park): as attraction of Mann Brothers' Trail and Wawona Road, 36, 43, 67, 144; in debate over automobiles in Yosemite National Park, 67; "Fallen Giant," 43, 63, 78; incorporated into national park, 44, 63; Olmsted on improving access to, 35; park personnel discuss road development in, 84; and Wawona Road reconstruction, 144; Wawona Tunnel Tree, *41*, 43, 63; in Yosemite park authorization, 33–34

Mariposa Road. *See* Wawona Road (Yosemite National Park))

Marshall, Bob (Robert), 180–81; and Albright, 180, 181; on Blue Ridge Parkway routing, 197; conflict with Cammerer, 183; and debate over Mission 66 program, 229, 230, 231; Green Mountain Parkway proposal opposed by, 212, 214, 215; helps found Wilderness Society, 183; and Ickes, 181, 182, 183, 185, 197, 215; and Leopold Report, 251; National Park Service officials resent, 185; opposes proposed road development in Great Smoky Mountains National Park, 182–83; and wilderness preservation, 180–81, 182, 183, 185, 277

Marshall, Robert B.: assesses suitability of Yosemite roads for automobile travel, 67; brusque manner of, 72; on committee on admission of automobiles to Yellowstone National Park, 69; and Mather, 73; on need to improve access to national parks, 64; plan for Glacier National Park, 117; and proposed road out east end of Yosemite Valley, 171; as superintendent of national parks, 71–72

Marx, Leo, 62, 88, 247

master plans: Blue Ridge Parkway, 232; Eliot's Acadia report as, 178; of Mission 66, 242; Natchez Trace Parkway, 205; of National Park Service, 86, 87, 104, 115, 177, 252, 265, 268; Olympic National Park, 185; on wilderness zones, 184

Mather, Stephen, 72, *93*, *104*; and additional roads proposed for Yosemite National Park, 171, 172, 173; on Ahwahnee Hotel, Yosemite National Park, 143–

44; All-Year Highway, 142, 143; at American Society of Civil Engineers meeting of 1928, 106–7; on auto camping, 77; on automobile's importance to national parks, 74, 76, 85, 156, 184, 246, 280; on balancing preservation and access, 85; becomes National Park Service director, 70, 72–73; camping trip to Sequoia National Park, 73; Civil Engineering Division established by, 92; on dangerous road conditions, 79; Division of Landscape Engineering set up by, 86; entranceways promoted by, 76, 134; on extending Yellowstone National Park southern boundary, 159; on Federal-Aid Highway Act of 1916, 80; funding sought for national park roads, 79–81; Generals Highway, 132, 133, 134, 135; Going-to-the-Sun Road, 99, 100, 101, 115, 118, 122; and Goodwin, 92, 94, 96, 98–99, 100, 101, 102, 132, 133, 135, 148; with Goodwin and Hull, *93*; against "gridironing" parks with roads, 85, 111, 132, 179, 277; helps establish National Parks Association, 159; with Hewes, *104*; illness and death of, 151; on importance of Mount Rainier National Park's Carbon River Road, 102; and Lancaster, 91; and "Lane Letter" policy statement, 86; and MacDonald, 96, 97, 103, 106; Memorial Parkway, 151, 219, 251; on minimizing impact of road construction, 84, 86, 101, 103, 105, 106, 143, 148; and Mission 66 program, 243; as motorist, 72, 74; Mount Rainier National Park road development, 165, 167, 168, 169; National Conference on Outdoor Recreation of 1924, 161; at National Park Conference of 1925, 103; and National Park Service wilderness preservation, 85, 168, 185; National Park-to-Park Highway supported by, 75, 111; and NPS-BPR collaboration, 96–98, 101, 102, 103, 104, 105, 106, 110, 113, 118, 143; on need to increase park visitation, 73, 76–77; and 1924 park roads bill, 80–81, 84, 95, 99, 101, 102, 164, 278; and 1968 *Park Road Standards*, 255; "one good road" development strategy, 85, 251; overdevelopment of park roads opposed by, 85–86; personality of, 72, 74, 95, 96, 97, 100, 142; and pressure for additional roads in Yellowstone National Park, 163, 164; promotional flair, 72, 73, 74, 75, 76, 81, 98, 103, 133, 142; realizing vision of, 149–51; on removal of Army Corps of Engineers from parks, 91; seeks Kings Canyon National Park, 96, 185; and Sierra Club, 72, 74, 170; on social and economic value of parks, 73, 76, 77, 85, 142, 160; on standards for national park roads, 99, 100, 101, 102, 154, 240; third National Park Conference organized by, 73; and Tioga Road, 74–75, 170, 174, 239; views motor tourism as best means of protecting and expanding national park system, 76, 84, 163–64, 184; Wawona Road reconstruction, 144–45; Welch advises, 89; Wilderness Area, 251; Yellowstone National Park road reconstruction, 148

Matthes, Francois, 143, 144, 166

Mazamas, The, 165

McAdam, John, 15, 18, 59, 114

McCarter, Kenneth, 87, 191

McCormick, E. O., 74

McDuffie, Duncan, 145, 172, 175, 233

McFarland, J. Horace, 70–71

McKay, Douglas, 218, 219

McLean, John, 39–40, 43

Means, Howard, 129–30

Medicine Bow Forest Reserve, 123, 124

Meehean, Lloyd, 218

Melan, Joseph, 52

Merced Grove of Big Trees (Yosemite National Park), 39, 40

Merriam, John C., 172

Merriam, Lawrence, 242

Mesa Verde National Park: as catalyst for 1968 *Park Road Standards*, 253, *253*; conflict with BPR over road standards in, 253; Daniels on need to improve road in, 71; and evolution of NPS historical parks, 192; National Park Conference of 1925 at, 103

Millennials, 280

Miller, Adolph, 71, 72, 73, 91, 92

Miller, John, 81

Mills, Enos, 123–24, 126

Mineral King Toll Road, 132

Minton, Henry, 68

Mission 66 for the National Park System (report), 224

Mission 66 program, 221–43; accomplishments, 226–27, 243, 276; accused of emphasizing access over preservation, 229–30, 246; architectural criticism of, 228; arrowhead logo publicized by, 226–27; automotive emphasis of, 225, *225*, 227, 230, 240, 242, 246; Blue Ridge Parkway construction, 200, 201; criticism of, 227–43, 246, 249, 276; embraced as significant part of National Park Service history, 273; as extension of prewar policies, 224, 226; funding, 224, 225, 226; goals, 223–26, 227, 230–32; on informational signs and wayside exhibits, 225, 231; Interstate and Defense Highways Act (1956) and, 224, 243; modernist aesthetics of, 205, *224*, 228, *229*; motor nature trails, 227, 255; Mount McKinley road controversy, 241–43, *241*; parallels to broader developments, 225; Natchez Trace Parkway construction, 206; park roads in, 225–43; Phillips 66 brochure on, 225, *225*; planning methods criticized, 228, 231, 240, 243; project sign at Grand Teton National Park, *220–21*; prospectus, 225, *225*; road design criticized as excessive, 232–43; road design criticized as insufficient, 240–41; Tioga Road controversy, 233–40; visitation projections, 224, 248; visitor centers, *224*, 225, 226; visitor education emphasis, 225, 227, 231, 240; Wilderness Act of 1964 and, 243; and wilderness preservation, 229–31

Mississippi River Parkway proposal, 219

modernist aesthetic, 95, 205, 211, 225, 228

Mohawk Trail (MA), 93

Monida and Yellowstone Stage Company, 69

monorails, 251, 254, 258, 259, *259*, 279

Moran, Thomas, 32, 47, 50

Morristown National Historical Park, 192, 196

Morton, Hugh, 200–201, 263

Moses, Robert, 189

motor clubs. *See* automobile clubs

motor coaches, *244–45*, 263

N

Skyline Drive (Shenandoah National Park), 136–41, *141*; accolades, 140, 141; Appalachian Trail and, 139; and Blue Ridge Parkway, 197, 198, 200; CCC crews at, *111*, 137, *137*, 139; Chesapeake and Ohio Canal Parkway proposal compared with, 217; conservation, recreation, and employment relief combined in, 196–97; criticism of, 138, 160, 182; design of, 138, 139, 140; FDR and, 137–38, *138*, 140; Great Smoky Mountains National Park Skyway proposal compared to, 181; Hoover and, 137; as main attraction of park, 7, 136, 266; in Mission 66 program, 227; National Industrial Recovery Act and, 111, 137; scenic overlooks, 139, *139*; segregation and, 140–41; skyline drives, 162, 181, 182, 183, 198, 214

Skyway proposal (Great Smoky Mountains National Park), 181–84, *182*, *183*

Slater, Rodney, 262

Smith, Anthony Wayne, 232, 240, 256

Smith, Charles, 215

Smith, Glenn, 111

Smith, John Rubens, *Catskill Mountain House*, *26*, 27

snow removal, 125, 163

social media, 280

Southern Appalachian National Park Committee, 111–12

Southern Pacific Railroad, 74

Southwest Circle Tour, 129

souvenirs: Great Smoky Mountains National Park, 179, *181*; Mount Washington Cog Railway, 27, 29; proliferation of, 38; Rocky Mountain National Park, 128; Yellowstone National Park, 52, 55, 56, *56*, 57; Yosemite National Park, 43, 44, 144, 146

"spectacularity," 92, 131, 135

speed limits: Blue Ridge Parkway, 200; Colonial Parkway, 193; in Context Sensitive Design, 269; Going-to-the-Sun Road, 272; Grand Loop, 69; Hartzog on, 252; Krueger on Hartzog's, 254; Mesa Verde National Park, 253; Mission 66 program and, 232; 1984 *Park Road Standards* on, 266; in park road preservation, 272; Skyline Drive, 138; Tioga Road, 234, 240, 273

Spelman, Harold J., 194, 198, 203, 210

Sperry, Lyman, 117

spirals and spiral transitions, 55, 90, 130, 138, 179, 189, 200, 210, 228

stagecoach travel: automobile access to Yellowstone National Park opposed by stage companies, 68, 69–70; automobile tourism contrasted with, 77, 154; Muir on, 160; rail and canal travel compared with, 24; robberies, 42, 56; White Mountains, 27; Yellowstone National Park, 45, 48, 53, 55, *55*, 56, 57, *57*; Yosemite National Park, 33, 37, *39*, 42, 43, 44, 71

Stagner, Howard, 230–31

Standard Oil Company, 146, 150, 242

Stanley, Edwin, illustration from his *Rambles in Wonderland*, *47*

Stanley, F. O., 123

Stanton, Elizabeth Cady, 37

state parks, 89, 111, 160, 226, 248

steamboat travel, 24–26, *27*, 93

Steel, William, 162–63

stereopticon views, 29, 38, 57

Stevens Canyon Road (Mount Rainier National Park), 168, 227, *227*, 232

Stewart, George, 132

Stoddard, John, 50, 57

Storm King Highway, *82–83*, 89, 93, 100

Strahorn, Carrie Adell, 48

straightaways, 18, 114

Stratton, A. Clark, 243

Strauss, Theodore, 196, 197

sublime, the: Burke on, 21–22; in Catskill Mountains, 27; Goodwin's "spectacularity" and, 92; in Mount Washburn Road, 55; in Mount Washington Carriage Road, 29; and national parks, 32; painters seek scenes of, 22; in steamboat travel, 25; technological, 29, 44, 93, 146; in Yosemite National Park, 33, 146

Suitland Parkway, 212; George Washington Memorial Parkway compared with, 208; military measure, 209; seen as not true parkway, 211, 212; on transferring ownership, 226; as weighted toward utilitarian access, 209

Sumner, Lowell, 184

superelevation, 189, 199, 210

superintendents' conferences, 86, *106*, 171, 224

Surface Transportation Assistance Act (1982), 264–65

Sutherland, Dan, 81

Swift, Ernest, 230

switchbacks: as attractions, 93, 101, 117, 131, 132, 135; Big Oak Flat Road, *42*, 66, 147; Broadmoor–Cheyenne Mountain Highway, 93; Columbia River Highway, 90; as defacement of landscape, 100, 101, 145; early national park roads, 33; Engineer's Lariat, Denver Mountain Parks, 93, *94*; Fall River Road, 125, *125*, 126; Generals Highway, 132, *134*, 135; Going-to-the-Sun Road, 100, 101, 117, 118; Mount Rainier National Park, 59; Olmsted Jr. on, 89; Pike's Peak as unsuited for auto traffic, 101, 124–25; Sequoia National Park, 95; Trail Ridge Road, 127; Wawona Road reconstruction, 145; Yosemite National Park, 36, 42, 66; Zion–Mount Carmel Highway, 130, 131

T

Tacoma (WA), 58, 160, 166

Taft, William Howard, 71

Tamiami Trail, 279

Taylor, James, 213

Taylor, Oliver, 181, 192–93

Temple, Henry, 111

Tenaya Road (Yosemite National Park), 171–74, *173*

Tennessee Valley Authority, 197

"Thanatopsis" (Bryant), 22

Thayer, William, 57

Thompson, Ben, 218

Thompson, Harry, 217, 218

Thomson, C[harles] G[off]: on balancing preservation and access, 147, 148, 155–57, 184; in Big Oak Flat Road reconstruction, 147, 148, 155–57; on NPS-BPR collaboration, 147; on preservation of traditional park road experience, 147, 155–57; on proposed tramway to Yosemite's Glacier Point, 172–73; on relationship between parks and roads, 173, 175; Tenaya Road proposal opposed by, 174; and Tioga Road High Line proposal, 172, 173, 174, 175, 176; in Wawona Road reconstruction, 145, 146, 155–56; on wilderness preservation, 184

Thoreau, Henry David, 29, 77, 180, 246

Tioga Road (Yosemite National Park): Adams on, 234, 238, 239, 253; construction as Great Sierra Wagon Road, 45; dedication ceremonies, *74*, *239*, 239; Generals Highway, compared with, 134; High Line proposal of 1930s, *174*, 174–75, 176, 234; Mather in acquisition of, 74–75, 170, 174, 239; Mission 66 controversy, 6, 233–40, *233*, *235*, *239*, 255, 270; New York City's Pennsylvania Station, compared with, 240; 1968 *Park Road Standards* and, 253, 254, 255; rehabilitation in 2010s, 272–73, *273*; Sierra Club support for acquisition and improvement, 45, 74, 233

Toll, Roger, 86, 104–5, *106*, 126, 162

toll roads: in Massachusetts, 27; Mineral King Toll Road, 132; modern highways replace, 143, 144; at Yellowstone National Park, 47; at Yosemite National Park, 33, *39*, 43, 44, 63, 66, 67

Tomlinson, Owen, 165, 168, 169–70

tour buses, 242, 261, 262, 266, *267*, 268, 269

tourism: Abbey on "industrial," 247; Alaskans seek, 241–42; Blue Ridge Parkway and, 197; bureaus, 86, 146; depression of mid-1870s impact on, 43; disparagement of, 22, *22*, 26, 37, 38, 43, 68, 76, 79, 159, 160, 172, 180, 182, 214, 230, 233–34, 246–48, 253, 257; eastern, 32, 276; European versus American infrastructure, 71; future prospects for, 279; heritage, 191, 192, 212; industry, 33, 173, 191, 197, 214, 277; interests, 75, 124, 166, 196, 232; lobby, 157, 196; and Mission 66 program, 232; motor (automobile), 59, 67, 69, 70, 88, 103, 111, 115, 133, 150, 154, 157, 160, 163, 166, 171, 179, 184, 219, 242, 276, 277; *National Geographic* magazine promotes domestic, 73; See America First movement, 71, 81, 116, 150; in Swiss mountains, 34. *See also* scenic tourism

traffic-calming strategies, 269

Trail Ridge Road (Rocky Mountain National Park), 126–29; as attraction in itself, 7; construction of, *128–29*; elevation of, 123, 129; Fall River Road, compared with, 126, *127*, 129; Far View Curve, 127; funding, 81, 122, 126, 129; Going-to-the-Sun Road, compared with, 126, 127, 128; landscape protection during construction, 128; Long's Peak from, *113*; *National Park Wilderness* invokes, 230; in 1924 park roads bill, 81, 126; NPS-BPR collaboration in, 122, 126–27; The Rock Cut, 128, *129*; Tundra Curves, *3*, 126, *128*; Yard's proposed road along Continental Divide compared with, 162

tramways, 130, 168, 170, 172, 173, 251, 254, 258–59, 279

Transmountain Road (Glacier National Park). *See* Going-to-the-Sun Road (Transmountain Road; Glacier National Park)

Tressider, Donald, 172, 173

Truett, Randle, 202

Illustration Credits

Illustrations not otherwise credited are from the author's collection. Photographers and drawing or photograph numbers are noted parenthetically where identified.

Bibliothèque nationale, Paris (The Bridgeman Art Library): *page 12*

California Historical Society Collections at the Autry/ Gift of Albert M. Bender (The Bridgeman Art Library): *page 38*

From *A Contribution to the Heritage of Every American: The Conservation Activities of John D. Rockefeller, Jr.* by Nancy Newhall (New York: Alfred Knopf, 1957): *page 178 (left and right)*

Josiah William Bailey Papers, David M. Rubenstein Rare Book and Manuscript Library, Duke University: *page 196*

Copyright © Dumbarton Oaks Research Library and Collection: *page 15*

Denver Public Library Western History Collection: *page 75*

Eastern National Park & Monument Association: *pages vi (detail), 242 (top)*

Federal Highway Administration Eastern Federal Lands Highway Division (EFLHD): *pages 276, 278 (left)*

Federal Highway Administration Federal Lands Highway Program: *page 265*

Getty Images: *page 218 (Robert Phillips, The LIFE Images Collection)*

Google: *page 280 (right)*

Historic American Engineering Record (HAER), Prints and Photographs Division, Library of Congress: *pages ii, 2, 5, 227 (bottom) (David Haas, photographer); pages 3, 6, 9, 177, 266 (Jet Lowe, photographer); pages 4, 8 (right and left) (Brian Grogan, photographer); page 58 (Office Collection); pages 62, 133 (top) (copies of photographs in Sequoia National Park collection); pages 110, 188 (copies of photographs in Blue Ridge Parkway collection); page 111 (copy of photograph in Shenandoah National Park collection); page 130 (copy of photograph in Zion National Park collection); pages 154, 169 (copies of photographs in Mount Rainier National Park collection); page 190 (NY-327-7); page 211 (copy of photograph in National Capital Region collection); page 230 (Jack Boucher, photographer)*

Historic American Engineering Record (HAER) drawings, Prints and Photographs Division, Library of Congress, adapted/revised by Todd Croteau: *pages 39 (CA-117-3), 100 (MT-67-3), 131 (UT-39A-3), 144 (CA-117-8), 147 (CA-117-6), 167 (WA-35-2)*

Historic American Engineering Record (HAER) drawings, Prints and Photographs Division, Library of Congress, adapted by Christopher Marston: *pages 88 (TN-35-5), 127 (CO-78-4&5)*

Scott Lambert: *page 273*

Library of Congress: *page 25*

Kevin McCardle: *page 272 (right)*

Museum of the City of New York: *page 17*

National Archives and Records Administration (NARA): *pages 65 (RG79 E9 B265), 77 (center right) (RG79 E9 B368), 87 (RG79 NPS Photography Collection), 104 (RG79 NPS Photographs, Stephen Mather Collection), 119 (RG79 E9 B39), 149 (RG79 E10:2 B1738), 150 (bottom) (RG79 E9 B531), 155 (RG79 E9 B530), 173 (RG79 E10:1 B528), 174 (RG79 E10:2 B1840), 184 (RG79 E10:2 B450), 204 (RG79 E13 B2), 208 (RG30-N, National Parkways), 227 (top) (RG79 NPS Photography Collection), 233 (RG79 NPS Photography Collection), 236 (RG79 E10:2 B1841)*

Reproduced courtesy of the National Parks Conservation Association: *page 241 (left and right)*

National Park Service, *Alternative Transportation Modes Feasibility Study Volume III* (1994): *page 259*

National Park Service, *Draft Yosemite Valley Implementation Plan Supplemental Environmental Impact Statement* (1997): *pages 260 (left and right), 261 (left and right)*

National Park Service, Frederick Law Olmsted National Historic Site: *pages 16, 20–21*

National Park Service, Glacier National Park: *pages 114 (right), 120, 244–45 (David Restivo, photographer), 267 (top and middle), 270 (left and right), 271, 277 (right), 281 (David Restivo, photographer)*

National Park Service, Great Smoky Mountains National Park: *page 182*

National Park Service Historic Photo Collection (NPSHPC), Harpers Ferry: *pages xii–1, 40, 67 (bottom), 72, 76 (all), 78 (top left and top right), 81 (top and bottom), 86, 93, 98, 99, 106, 107, 108–9, 114 (left), 122, 128 (right), 135, 137, 142, 143, 163, 185, 199 (bottom left), 201, 205, 220–21, 222, 224, 225 (top right), 226, 229 (top right and bottom), 247 (left and right), 249, 257, 258*

National Park Service, History Program Library: *page 203*

National Park Service, Mount Rainier National Park: *page 278 (right)*

National Park Service, National Park Foundation: *page 280 (left)*

National Park Service, Park Roads Program: *page 262*

National Park Service, Rocky Mountain National Park: *page 126*

National Park Service, Shenandoah National Park: *pages 136, 139, 141 (left)*

National Park Service, Yellowstone National Park (NPS-YNP): *pages 47, 49 (YELL#7625), 50 (YELL#22600), 52, 53, 54 (top left) (YELL#22106), 55 (YELL#43533), 56 (YELL#127062/YELL#119420-01/YELL#182082), 67 (top) (YELL#1928), 68 (YELL#89783), 78 (bottom right) (YELL#39992-1), 274–75 (Jim Peaco, photographer), 279 (Jim Peaco, photographer)*

National Park Service, Yosemite Museum: *page 74*

National Park Service, Yosemite Research Library (NPS-YRL): *pages 42 (YRL 14-890), 64 (YRL 979-447), 66, 77 (far left and far right), 78 (bottom left), 80, 85, 146 (left and right), 151, 152–53, 159, 223, 235, 239*

© Collection of the New-York Historical Society (The Bridgeman Art Library): *pages 23, 30–31 (#1897.2)*

Print Collection, Miriam and Ira D. Wallach Division of Art, Prints and Photographs, The New York Public Library, Astor, Lenox and Tilden Foundations: *pages 10–11, 26*

© 2014 Olde America Antiques/Jack and Susan Davis: *pages 45, 46, 54 (bottom right), 57, 77 (center left)*

Private Collection/© Arthur Ackermann Ltd., London (The Bridgeman Art Library): *page 13*

Sierra Club Colby Library and Marion Patterson: *page 242 (bottom)*

Collection Center for Creative Photography, The University of Arizona, © The Ansel Adams Publishing Rights Trust: *page 237*

Memorial Art Gallery of the University of Rochester, Gift of the Margaret M. McDonald Memorial Fund: *page 24*

University of Washington Libraries, Special Collections: *page 158 (UW#18772)*

U.S. Commission of Fine Arts: *page 207*

U.S. Department of the Interior Library: *pages 216, 231 (top and bottom), 253, 255*

U.S. Department of Transportation Library: *page 191*

Victoria & Albert Museum, London (The Bridgeman Art Library): *pages 14, 22*